5+

CHINA (PRC)

Population: 1,130,000,000
Area (Sq. Miles): 9,705,360

THE WORLD

INDIA (RI)

Population: 850,000,000
Area (Sq. Miles): 1,266,595

GOVERNMENTS AND POLITICS

In a Changing World

GOVERNMENTS AND POLITICS

In a Changing World

Robert E. Gamer

University of Missouri-Kansas City

WCB Brown & Benchmark
PUBLISHERS

Madison, Wisconsin • Dubuque, Iowa

Book Team

Executive Editor *Michael Lange*
Developmental Editor *Roger Wolkoff*
Production Editor *Ann Fuerste*
Designer *Kristyn A. Kalnes*
Art Editor *Jodi Wagner*
Photo Editor *Shirley Lanners*
Visuals/Design Developmental Consultant *Marilyn A. Phelps*
Visuals/Design Freelance Specialist *Mary L. Christianson*
Marketing Manager *Elizabeth Haefele*
Advertising Coordinator *Colleen Howes*

WCB Brown & Benchmark

A Division of Wm. C. Brown Communications, Inc.

Executive Vice President/General Manager *Thomas E. Doran*
Vice President/Editor in Chief *Edgar J. Laube*
Vice President/Sales and Marketing *Eric Ziegler*
Director of Production *Vickie Putman Caughron*
Director of Custom and Electronic Publishing *Chris Rogers*

 Wm. C. Brown Communications, Inc.

President and Chief Executive Officer *G. Franklin Lewis*
Corporate Senior Vice President and Chief Financial Officer *Robert Chesterman*
Corporate Senior Vice President and President of Manufacturing *Roger Meyer*

Cover photos © Bob Gamer

Copyedited by Anne Caylor Cody

A Times Mirror Company

Library of Congress Catalog Card Number: 92–71556

ISBN 0–697–14730–4

Printed in the United States of America by Wm. C. Brown Communications, Inc.,
2460 Kerper Boulevard, Dubuque, IA 52001

10 9 8 7 6 5 4 3 2 1

To my Aunt,

HELENA M. GAMER,

A pioneer in medieval studies who helped keep the University of Chicago a haven of research-driven learning.

"It's reSEARCH, not REsearch," she told me many times. "When students and teachers combine their energies and insights, they can find new treasures in old chests. Neither can do it alone."

Brief Contents

part 4   INFLUENCE AND PEOPLE'S LIVES

part 5   SYSTEMS, INFLUENCE, AND CHANGE

EXPANDED CONTENTS

PREFACE

Welcome to the study of comparative politics. Regardless of your prior coursework, this field is not entirely new to you, because much of it concerns how you and others think and act.

You probably exert some influence at home, and perhaps at school and elsewhere. If you vote, belong to a group, express opinions about government or policies, or attend meetings, you may have deliberately or accidentally influenced government leaders. You have views and attitudes, perhaps even some strong ones, about politics in this and other countries; so you have probably done some thinking about the topics we will be discussing here. But unless you have taken another course on the subject, you probably have not thought very methodically about why politics is an essential part of life. Why do people behave as they do when they engage in politics? What factors cause politics to operate differently in different countries? Why are some people more successful than others at getting what they want? And you may not have thought much about why you think and act as you do with regard to politics, and how your political behavior (or lack of it) might affect your life for ill or good.

The fact that you come into the course with opinions about the subject can be both an advantage and a drawback. Opinions may induce curiosity, or make us rigid about how we approach information. If you allow your opinions to arouse your curiosity, this course will help you examine the validity of your own opinions and see how politics may affect your life.

Throughout this book, we shall be discussing nine political systems. Two of these systems underwent dramatic changes in the late 1980s and early 1990s. One, Germany, became a single nation-state in 1871, but was separated into East and West from the end of World War II until 1990; therefore, when appropriate, we shall discuss it as two separate nation-states which recently reunified. The other system, Russia, has been a single political unit for many centuries, gradually conquering other peoples. In 1921, it was organized into fifteen separate republics as the Soviet Union; in 1991, those fifteen republics all declared themselves independent and the USSR dissolved. However, the republics remain bound by strong economic ties and share remnants of a formerly unified military. Some of them created a loose organization called the Commonwealth of Independent States in an effort to sort these ties out.

As we summarize discussions at the end of chapters, you will see these nine systems grouped like this:

United States (USA)
West Germany (FRG)
United Kingdom (UK)

Commonwealth of Independent States (CIS)
East Germany (GDR)
China (PRC)

India (RI)
Peru (RP)
Nigeria (FRN)

Those in the first group are commonly called industrialized democracies, and those in the third, developing nations. Those in the center group are (or have been until recently) communist systems. The book notes many common characteristics within these groupings, but does not generally label them in this manner.

Systems in one group share characteristics with systems in the others. Yet each is to some extent unique in its history and culture, with attributes not shared by the others. Many citizens and a variety of leaders in all these systems exert influence, and affect the ways rewards and punishments are distributed; many other citizens do not. The pattern of who exerts influence, and who does not, varies from system to system.

Some of these systems distribute material rewards more equally, and allow more freedoms, among their citizens than others. All are undergoing changes which could make those distributions different in the future. Who receives what rewards and freedoms depends on powerful, impersonal forces, and subtle interactions among political, military, social, technological, and economic institutions. But it also depends, in a very personal way, on the attitudes of people, and the influence they are capable of exerting—on how you and I and others think and act.

For example, Americans are becoming aware that it is vitally important to maintain our manufacturing base if our standard of living is to remain high. Yet, the factors that affect our manufacturing base are complex and uncertain. Consider this: The former Soviet Union became a military superpower, rivalling the United States in its output of weapons and giving most of its populace education and access to media. The USSR and another communist system, China, surpass India in distributing goods among their own people.

Yet China and India are more successful than the former Soviet Union at manufacturing goods which sell on world markets. They have access to the sea, long traditions of buying and selling, fertile agriculture, and other traits that help create that success. The former Soviet Union (like China) has a road system far more primitive than India's, and, unlike China and India, its people have little experience manufacturing, buying, and selling on free markets. Now that the Soviet superpower has collapsed, can the nation-states formed from it compete with China and India, not to mention Western Europe and the United States? Will the post-Soviet republics develop modern economies, or will they prefer to isolate themselves from the political and economic freedoms offered by the outside world?

The answers to these questions depend on how their attitudes evolve, and how they use their growing influence. If the CIS nation-states return to isolation, the Cold War could resume, bringing with it the high cost of massive arms production and maintenance of bases and troops around the world. Meanwhile, China may increasingly take jobs from American workers as its production capacities increase, while remaining a communist state. Personal attitudes and attributes, as well as broad, impersonal forces, interact to determine the economic and political futures of all these systems.

Consider also the movement toward democratization around the globe. In Latin America, Peru (which has known many decades of military rule) took the lead in attempting to establish democratic government. Yet Peru exports 60 percent of the world's cocaine, and the U.S. Drug Enforcement Agency has discovered that its political system blocks all efforts to control this trade. The military government of Nigeria, Africa's largest and most populous country, has led the way in attempting to establish democratic government there. The system they are trying to create is slow in coming; its success or failure will have a strong impact on the success of democracy elsewhere in Africa and the Middle East. That, in turn, can affect the political stability of this region, where the United States has maintained a long military presence. Once again, the attitudes of people in those countries, and the influence they learn to exert, will determine whether the democratic institutions created there can work. Our attitudes toward their democratization (or our lack of knowledge about it) will also play a role; it is generally easier and more effective to use subtle aid and pressure while positive events are taking place than to send troops in after crises emerge.

We know something about our own country and some of the countries of Europe. Often, the rest of the world remains a bit of a void. This book will introduce you better to our own country, as well as to several countries in various parts of the world. And it will let you see how the lives of others around the globe relate to ours.

The book proceeds in a logical progression. Part 1 quickly introduces basic concepts and themes of the course. Part 2 examines *why* people think and act as they do in politics. Part 3 looks at *how* people think and act; it suggests that when more people are involved in politics, view their leaders and national policies as legitimate, trust one another, and feel effective and willing to compromise, the result may be greater equality, freedom, protection for the environment, and public order. Part 4 examines whether this premise proves true in the real world. And part 5 looks at how technology, economics, and social forces effect political change.

You can follow one country through the book by using the index and the chart at the end of this preface, which indicates where longer discussions about each country appear. Because an understanding of the future requires understanding of the past, these longer discussions will familiarize you with some of the history of these lands.

After you learn some basic vocabulary in chapter 1, and gain an understanding of how political systems are organized in chapters 2–4, chapter 5 introduces the main themes of the book. The book is divided into 33 separate chapters, rather than a few long ones, so that you can think through each of these themes one step at a time. Each chapter opens and closes with a summary of the chapter. In addition, the beginning of each chapter features a phrase or question **in boldface** to highlight the chapter's central theme. Make a habit of thinking about these highlighted themes before you read a chapter, and perhaps reviewing both the introduction and the end-of-chapter summary before you delve into the chapter itself.

At the end of each chapter are Exercises designed to help you understand the chapter. The section that instructs you to "think about the book thus far" at the beginning of the exercises asks you to take a couple of minutes to relate the chapter you have just read to those that came before it. Your ability to do this is a good measure of whether you are grasping the themes of each chapter and putting them in context. Answering the questions and defining the words and phrases will also help you focus on the main ideas and alert you to important terms that will appear throughout the text. Notice that these terms are **highlighted in boldface** in each chapter. They appear in the exercise in the same order they appear in the chapter, and they are also listed in the index.

In the Thinking it Through exercise at the end of each section of exercises, you will have a chance to integrate the chapter concepts and relate them to the main question discussed in the chapter. By filling in the charts and answering the questions in this section, you will single out the significant elements in the narrative and better understand how the book ties together.

If the summary at the end of the chapter is not completely clear to you, work on the exercises. If it remains unclear, ask your instructor about the parts you do not understand. If you understand the summaries, you understand the book; if not, you are not grasping the main themes.

This book talks about places, events, and people—past and present—that you may or may not be familiar with. It usually defines and discusses them briefly. But if you want to know a bit more about the Protestant Revolution or the Renaissance; or if you find differences between communist and capitalist marketing systems confusing, or are confronted with information that is not familiar and not adequately explained, ask about it. Learning begins with asking questions, and it blossoms when you think these questions through. The exercises and your instructor will give you questions to stimulate your thoughts; ask your own as well, focusing on what you know, do not know, and are interested in.

The footnotes, gathered at the end of each chapter, contain a lot of human interest stories, statistics, recommended reading, and explanations of points that may not be clear.

As a science, political science is concerned with how and why things happen. That requires analysis—a somewhat imposing word that simply means you must think through how separate parts relate to a whole. Especially in the beginning, you will need to memorize some words, details about how authority is distributed and elections are held, and the like. But starting in chapter 2, the text emphasizes comparison. As you approach a chart, table, or paragraph discussing more than one country, ask yourself: "Which has more, and which has less? How does this compare with what we discussed in the last chapter?" Finding the patterns in the answers to these questions can move you beyond memorization to analysis. You will also find that what you are learning here will profoundly impact the way you live your life.

ACKNOWLEDGMENTS

First and foremost, I want to thank May and Keith for their patience while this dragon tiptoed through, nibbling away big chunks of my time, and sometimes even roaming from my office to sprawl on the dining room table or the living room rug with the grin of a beast that had just swallowed the house.

Writing a successful text means obtaining the input and advice of many people. Whitney T. Perkins of Brown University, Bill Hunt of William Jewell College, and Angela Burger of the University of Wisconsin, Wausau, gave me invaluable insight from their careful reading of the early manuscript. Large numbers of my students helped me focus my perspective as I used increasing portions of the manuscript in various classes. I would like to thank the following reviewers for their helpful criticisms and suggestions: David Atkinson, University of Missouri–Kansas City; Paul Barton-Kriese, Indiana University East; John Bendix, Lewis & Clark College; Robert Evanson, University of Missouri–Kansas City; Trond Gilberg, Penn State University; the late Charles Gillespie, University of Wisconsin, Madison; Jack Heysinger, University of Missouri–Kansas City; Victor LeVine, Washington University; James Lutz, Purdue University; Steve Mazurana, University of Northern Colorado; Peter Merkle, University of California, Santa Barbara; Joseph Ripple, Missouri Western State University; Sanford Silverburg, Catawba College; and Kathleen Staud, University of Texas, El Paso.

Oleg I. Gubin of Moscow State University, David Guillet of Catholic University of America, my colleagues, Dale Neuman and Ross Stephens, and one of my students, Charlie Dell, provided me with useful information. I am grateful for a lot of help from the staff of the UMKC library, and to the staff at the Library of Congress for use of the private research room and their help in tracking down material. Henry Mitchell, the UMKC Associates, Max Skidmore, Nona Bolling, and Dave Finestead gave needed practical assistance and moral support at various stages along the way. Randy Bush of Gustavus Adolphus College provided beneficial suggestions when he used the manuscript in class. Though it doesn't show enough, Jack Reak and James McKinley helped simplify and clarify my writing. Kip May, Henry Mitchell, Peggy Mitchell, Roy Gridley, Rodney Wilson, Gordon Seyffert, World Wide Photos, Mike Gamer, Nona Bolling, Gary Widmar, and Dolores Potts let me use some fine photos. Keith Buchanan created initial designs for illustrations, as well as some of the final renditions. Anne Caylor Cody did a superb job of copy editing.

Our hosts abroad are so numerous I fear that an attempt to list people or institutions would lead to too many omissions; I have learned much from you, and have benefited from many a good deed. But Professor Bian and Yu Xunda, our hosts at Hangzhou University during the spring and summer of 1989 and again in 1993, have a special place in our hearts and must be mentioned. And, Harry and Hilda, this book is for Elsa, too.

More Detailed Discussions about Individual Systems[1]

Chapter	Topic	USA	USSR, CIS	FRG	GDR	UK	PRC	RI	RP	FRN
4	Access of candidates to media and money	*		*		*				*
9	Employment			*	*		*			
11 14	National identity and political efficacy		*							
15	Attitudes about equality	*	*	*	*	*	*	*	*	
16	Attitudes about power and authority	*	*							
17	Beliefs about law	*	*	*	*	*		*		
19	Political party systems									*
20	Interest groups	*	*	*	*	*		*	*	*
21	Consensual parties and change						*	*	*	*
23	Totalitarianism			*	*	*				
	Bureaucracy		*					*	*	*
	Military rule								*	*
25	Incomes							*	*	*
26	Opportunity for women and minorities	*	*	*	*	*	*	*	*	*
27	Freedoms	*	*	*	*	*	*	*	*	*
28	Protection for the environment	*	*	*	*	*	*	*		
31	Innovation and change	*	*	*	*	*	*			
32	Innovation and change							*	*	*
33	Productivity						*			

[1]See explanation of abbreviations, page 39.

part 1

BASICS

The first six chapters introduce basic concepts and ideas. The exercises at the end of each chapter are important. By familiarizing yourself with the definitions and rearranging ideas in the section called ''Thinking It Through,'' you will quickly (though not without some effort) see the book's major themes and develop the capability to follow them through.

Chapter 1 introduces twenty-two of the most basic words and phrases used in the study of comparative politics. Chapters 2 and 3 will familiarize you with the most common ways political systems organize themselves. Chapter 4 expands on what you learn in chapter 3 and blends it into the central themes of the book. Chapter 5 lays out those themes, and chapter 6 explores them in more depth and detail.

chapter 1

ACQUIRING A VOCABULARY:
HOW TWENTY-TWO WORDS AND PHRASES RELATE TO YOU AND EACH OTHER

This book explores eight political systems. One, Germany, was divided into two parts until its reunification in 1990. Another—the Soviet Union—split into fifteen separate republics in 1991 and formed a loose confederation called the Commonwealth of Independent States. Each system has unique strengths and problems; yet we shall try to compare the systems. To do so, we must acquire a vocabulary that allows us to describe the workings of political systems.

Political scientists commonly use certain words and phrases when they compare the way politics is practiced in different countries. This chapter will familiarize you with twenty-two of those words and phrases and help you understand how the activities they describe affect the way we live. The five chapters which follow this one use these terms to teach basic facts about the eight systems and to introduce questions we need to ask in comparing them. Once you have digested the basic information, you will be ready to start looking at people, events, and places with a sense of how to fit them into a larger tapestry.

When you study physics, astronomy, or engineering, you expect to learn new words, or more precise definitions of familiar ones. The same holds true when you study comparative politics. You need to know essential terms, and you need to know how these terms relate to one another.

Like biologists, sociologists, anthropologists, archaeologists, economists, philosophers, and theologians, political scientists study human beings and how they think and behave. What is a human being? You and I are a collection of parts—arms, legs, head, shoulders. But these parts are not just stuck together at random. They fit together in an interrelated manner, around a common principle or form; they cohere. The common form is that of a human being, an integral whole which consists of some essential parts, some incidental (though useful) parts, and is more than the sum of these parts. Someone may describe you in terms of incidental parts—as having red hair and long arms and legs. But if you lost those parts, you would still be a whole human being. Someone else might come closer to describ-

ing what makes you a human being if they note that you are a living organism with a potential for emotion, reasoning, and manipulating your surroundings. Those qualities, taken together, are essential to defining what a human being is; without them, one is not fully human. And in the same way, we can define and combine some of the essential qualities of a political system to understand what such a system is.

A biologist, a theologian, a psychologist, and a philosopher defining a human being might each go into more detail describing one or another of the essential human traits. For example, a biologist might emphasize that the *organism* is a mammal, with certain parts interacting in certain ways to survive; a psychologist or theologian might describe the *emotional* realm in terms of psyche, soul, and spirit; a philosopher might emphasize that *reasoning* and *manipulation* involve judgment, inference, and invention surpassing the capabilities of other animals. But unless they are like the six blind men of Industan, who each described the elephant only on the basis of the body part they had touched and thus entirely failed to comprehend what it was,[1] each of those specialists are likely to include *all* these traits in their description of a human being. All of these aspects go into the common principle which we share as human beings, which unites the parts we are composed of, and yet makes us more than just the sum of those parts.

The same holds true of the country in which you live; it is not just a collection of people and paraphernalia stuck together at random. It, too, has a common form or principle (political scientists are more apt to say "system") which unites essential parts into a coherent whole. The dominant systems in today's world are nation-states, which in turn contain political systems. A number of parts cohere to form the political system of our nation-state; the political systems of other nation-states consist of similar parts. We need to know how those parts are defined and how they relate to one another. So, to begin, we shall examine **the parts of a nation-state's political system** and explore **how those parts relate to one another, to you, and to me.** This chapter introduces you to twenty-two words and phrases which together describe the political system of a nation-state. Examine these words and phrases, and work through the exercise at the end of the chapter, and you should begin to sense how these concepts relate to one another and how you personally fit into your political system.

NATION-STATES AND THEIR GOVERNMENT INSTITUTIONS

As you read this section, ask yourself: Which of these words and phrases describe institutions? Which of those institutions have sovereignty?

We live within a **nation**—territory inhabited by people who desire to live together. All three aspects of this definition are essential to the concept of nationhood. A nation must have territory—habitable land, set off from other parts of the world by boundaries. That territory must contain people. And these people must desire to live together. Territory without people, or people without a desire to live together, cannot form a nation (see figure 1.1).

Figure 1.1   Nation.

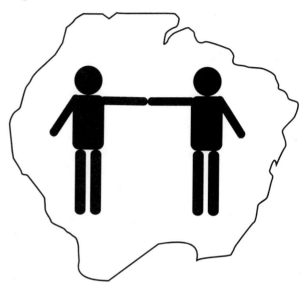

Our nation is governed by institutions. **Institutions** are groups of people who regularly cooperate with one another in a structured effort to achieve common goals. This means that each individual within an institution does the same sort of task repeatedly. His or her efforts complement the efforts of coworkers, so that together they can achieve common goals.

The Greek philosopher Aristotle, who lived from 384 to 322 B.C., is sometimes called the first political scientist. Aristotle said that "a state, in its simplest terms, is a body of officeholders adequate in number for achieving self-sufficient existence." In describing this self-sufficiency, Aristotle used the word autarky, which means that which by and of itself makes life desirable and lacking in nothing. Thus, in Aristotle's view, a state need not turn to any association outside of or above itself for all the resources necessary for full and complete human development.*

*Ernest Barker, The Politics of Aristotle (New York: Oxford University Press, 1958), pp. 7–8, 95.

F*igure 1.2*   Exercising sovereignty.

F*igure 1.3*   Conferring authority.

Governing, directing and controlling the people of a nation, is a goal, a valued objective. A **government** is the complex of institutions formed to accomplish that goal, the interacting institutions of state (of high status) through which the people of a nation are governed. A nation's government is likely to comprise a number of separate institutions, each with a particular set of tasks to accomplish. If all these institutions share an interest in controlling the people of the nation and keeping the nation intact, and if they interact to do so, these various state institutions form one government. A government with the ability to direct and control the people of a nation, without effective interference from inside or outside the national boundaries, is **sovereign; it exercises sovereignty.** (The word *sovereign* derives from the Latin word *super,* meaning *above,* which later became *soverain* in old French—supreme, chief, superior to or above all others). A government directs and controls (exercises sovereignty) by making and enforcing **laws,**

which are the prescribed rules of behavior in the nation. A sovereign government has the *ability* to make and enforce laws (figure 1.2).

Although government institutions may have the ability to direct and control the nation and to make and enforce its laws, some citizens of the nation may not believe this government has the right to exercise sovereignty and will not authorize it to do so. If the citizens of a nation give their government the right to make laws and to determine how they are enforced, that government has **authority**—it is authorized by its citizens to direct and control. Authority is the *right* to make and enforce laws, a right conferred by citizens on government (figure 1.3).

The question of whether a government has authority is subjective; people may declare allegiance to a government out of fear rather than out of conviction that this government has the right to direct and control them. Especially when the rules of government have not been in place for a long time, we often must judge authority on the basis of people's declared allegiance, rather than on what they may inwardly feel. Thus, government may have sovereignty, or the ability to direct and control people, but not the authority that stems from the people's willing acceptance of that control.

In their desire to live together, the people of a nation are likely to wish to declare their allegiance to only one government. The United States, for example, has one central government the nation's people declare allegiance to. The vast majority of those in our nation probably believe that the government has the *right* to make and enforce the laws; hence, it has authority to govern. It also has sovereignty—the *ability* to make and enforce laws within the territory that contains all the people of our nation. However, the people of another nation may desire one government with the ability to make and enforce laws, but wish it were a government different from the one which currently has that ability; in this case, the government would have sovereignty, but not authority. Still another possibility: the nation's people might authorize only one government, yet reside in a territory divided between two separate sovereign governments; this would create one nation with two states. One nation with one sovereign government is a **nation-state.** The United States is an example of a nation-state.

Aristotle defined the state in its most complete sense as the *polis,* a "stock" of people who have reached full self-sufficiency in supplying all that they need "for the sake of a good life." The polis includes everyone from the lowliest member of a village to the highest office-holder in the state; a good life might include an adequate water supply, a harbor, and other amenities; military fortification; and sufficient territory to hold the stock of people and their offspring.*

*Ernest Barker, The Politics of Aristotle *(New York: Oxford University Press, 1958), pp. 4–5, 98–99, 294–295, 306–309.*

Thus, our government has sovereignty, the ability to make and enforce laws within our territory. And (for most Americans) it has authority, the right to make and enforce those laws. It is composed of institutions—people interacting to help achieve the goal of making and enforcing laws. Each institution has its own role to play in that concerted effort. Let's look at those government institutions, and then at other types of institutions that affect government.

Governmental institutions called **legislatures** have the right and the ability to decide what the laws will be (in Latin, *legis* means *law*). The members of a legislature are usually elected by voters or other legislative bodies, or composed of certain segments of the populace (for example, those with titles of nobility).

Aristotle did not call the law-making body of government a "legislature," but referred to it as the first of the three sovereign powers in government, the "deliberative" element. This element may be composed of all the citizens deciding all issues, some of the citizens deciding all the issues, or some of the citizens deciding some issues and all citizens deciding others.* Today, legislatures are usually composed of some citizens, while all adult, nonfelon citizens are at times allowed to vote on some issues. Citizens choose legislatures and sometimes the chief executive; in other cases, the legislatures choose the executive.

*Ernest Barker, The Politics of Aristotle *(New York: Oxford University Press, 1958), p. 189.*

Other government institutions have the right and ability to force people to obey laws; these are executive institutions (in Latin, *executus* means to follow to the end). The **chief executive** is the individual who regularly has the final word on the government's actions and the ability to enforce decisions when they are not willingly obeyed. In some systems, an individual who is not formally part of the government's executive institutions may play this role. He or she may lead a centralized political party, or command the public's allegiance for some other reason.

> **A**ristotle calls the second of the three elements or powers in the government of a state the "executive," or system of magistracies. Sometimes members of the executive element were chosen by election, and sometimes by drawing lots.

A government's judicial institutions have the right and ability to decide (judge) whether the behavior of particular individuals and institutions conforms to laws or customs and to punish those whose behavior does not. The judges who preside over the courts where these decisions are made may be appointed by legislatures and executives or elected by citizens.

> **A**ristotle called the third element of government the "judicial," or the law courts.* He wrote about electing judges and choosing citizens by lot to judge particular trials; we still choose judges and citizen juries in this way today.
>
> *Ernest Barker, The Politics of Aristotle (New York: Oxford University Press, 1958), pp. 201–2.

Together, these decision makers—members of legislatures, persons holding executive positions, and judges—are **public officeholders.** They occupy public offices, meaning that they hold positions of trust or authority pertaining to governing the people of the nation. These offices are conferred by acts of government for certain terms of time with specified duties relating to the exercise of sovereignty.

Bureaucratic institutions, or government offices or bureaus, regularly assist the officeholders responsible for making legislative, executive, and judicial decisions. The people who work in and manage government bureaus often are referred to collectively as the civil service, because they are servants of the citizens (*civis* in Latin). Civil service workers are hired, not elected. In England, a *bureau* is a writing desk with drawers; the suffix *cracy* comes from the Greek *kratos*, meaning strength or combining form. In a bureaucracy, workers and their desks (or bureaus) are clustered together, with one person supervising or exercising strength to organize their efforts.

Sovereign states usually contain all these types of institutions—legislative, executive, judicial, and bureaucratic. But nations may sometimes fall under the jurisdiction of more than one sovereign state, and a sovereign state may contain portions of more than one nation. Among laws passed by the governmental institutions of a nation-state are those defining who formally belongs to the nation-state—who

> **A**ristotle defined a citizen as an officeholder. "He who enjoys the right of sharing in deliberative or judicial office attains thereby the status of a citizen of his state." Since many had the right to serve on popular courts and assemblies in democracies, citizens could include large numbers of people; in what Aristotle called an oligarchy, where "inequality in the distribution of office is considered to be just" and only those with property hold office, far fewer had that right. Aristotle believed that sons and daughters of original inhabitants of states should not have the right to hold office, but slaves, freed slaves, resident aliens, and perhaps artisans and laborers should not serve in such capacities and hence should be excluded from citizenship. He said that "a citizen proper is not one by virtue of residence in a given place." (Today, most citizenship is defined by residence—where one is born, how long one has lived in a given place—so as to include greater portions of the populace.) Ultimately, Aristotle recognized that a citizen is whatever the government says it is, though that is not always just; "those who have received . . . office after a change in the constitution must, in practice, be called citizens."*
>
> *Ernest Barker, The Politics of Aristotle (New York: Oxford University Press, 1958), pp. 95, 97, 107–110, 117, 302.

its **citizens** are. Some residing within a nation-state's boundaries may not be citizens, and some citizens may reside in other nation-states.

Finally, a **constitution** (*politeia* in Greek) is a document that lays out the most fundamental laws under which the political system operates. By stipulating the duties of various officials and the rights of citizens, such a document attempts to place limits on the exercise of sovereignty. A constitution only works effectively when citizens give it authority by insisting it be adhered to. When they do, government leaders and institutions have authority to take only those actions or make only those laws that agree with the constitution.

Aristotle considered a constitution the principle of officeholding for the common interest of all members of the polis. He said that "though [citizens] differ [in the capacities in which they act], the end which they all serve is safety in the working of their association; and this association consists in the constitution." Aristotle also asserted that when a group of people overthrow a government and establish a new one with a new constitution, that constitution rests on force unless the personal "moral excellence" of the citizens, and their definitions of the good life on which their association rests, changes to accord with it. In that case, the old polis changes into a new one. "Those constitutions which consider the common interest are *right* constitutions, judged by the standard of absolute justice. Those constitutions which consider only the personal interest of the rulers are all *wrong* constitutions, or *perversions* of the right forms."*

Ernest Barker, The Politics of Aristotle *(New York: Oxford University Press, 1958), pp. 98–99, 101–102, 112.*

OTHER INSTITUTIONS

As you read this section, ask yourself: Are any of the following institutions a part of government?

The institutions within a nation-state extend beyond government; in fact, many institutions exist outside of government. You and I have an institution we perceive to be our most basic unit for social interaction: the **family.** In a family, we cooperate with one another to achieve common personal goals, such as providing ourselves with food, clothing, shelter, emotional and motivational support, and daily companionship. It is within the family that we learn many of the values that become our goals. For most people, the family consists of near relatives. It might come to include lovers, close friends, adopted children, and others who are not related; and people may choose to exclude certain relatives or former spouses from those with whom they interact as family.

In addition to our families, all of us identify with certain types of people because we like the food they eat, the way they speak, the subjects they talk about, their habits of dress and furnishing their homes, their attitudes about how we were created and should conduct our lives, and other attributes. **Cultural or religious institutions** promote and foster such attitudes and goals; individuals may support these institutions by formally joining them, or by behaving and thinking in accordance with the norms of those institutions.

Furthermore, we all need *goods* and *services* to provide us with food, clothing, and shelter; to educate our young, move ourselves around, defend the nation-state, and perform many other activities. Institutions that engage in the production, distribution, or consumption of such goods and services are **economic institutions.** Insofar as the family is involved in such activities, the family itself is an economic institution; the same holds true for cultural and religious institutions.

When government makes laws, and directs and controls people, it often affects these nongovernmental institutions by telling them they cannot interact as they do or that they cannot pursue certain goals. Officials in a sovereign government can settle many disputes that affect the goods and services people within these institutions receive, the cultural traditions they practice, the ideas they express, and other matters of importance to them. This body of laws, rules, and official behavior intended to distribute goods and services or affect attitudes and behavior is called **governmental policy.** Citizens

Economic institutions: Stores along Bond Street, London, England.
Bob Gamer

affected by governmental policy may wish, in turn, to persuade government leaders to make policy decisions favorable to themselves. The primary way they can do so is to create interest groups and political parties.

An **interest group** is an institution that unites people with common interests as they try to persuade people in government to uphold those interests when making policy decisions. If a government official already agrees with my institution's goals, it is in our interest to reinforce his or her attitude. If the government official disagrees, it is in our interest to change that attitude, or replace him or her with someone who agrees. It matters whether we have the ability to do so, because government officials may settle disputes affecting the goods and services we receive, the cultural traditions we may practice, the ideas we may express, and much else of importance to our group. That is why individuals and institutions form interest groups.

Interest groups may play a role in removing people from government institutions or recruiting new officials to those institutions, but their primary function is to influence people already in government. Institutions that choose individuals to seek public office, and that keep those public officeholders cooperating on a variety of shared objectives, are called **political parties.**

All nation-states contain families, and religious, cultural, and business institutions which may occasionally act as interest groups. Sometimes such institutions may create new, separate institutions to serve as their interest groups. Most nation-states also have one or more political parties to help recruit people into public office and keep them cooperating on a variety of shared objectives. So interest groups and political parties, institutions that are not part of government, participate in politics along with government institutions.

POLITICS AND THE POLITICAL SYSTEM

As you read this section, ask yourself: How do each of these words or phrases relate to government? How do each relate to those who are not in government?

You and I make demands on other people, asking them to change their attitudes and behavior. **Politics** is the conflicting demands people make on one another, and how those demands are resolved; to resolve demands, one or more participants in the conflict must change their attitudes or behavior. A father and daughter arguing about what time she will return home from a date, or whether she can use the car, are engaging in politics. They are making conflicting demands on one another; the father is asking the daughter to change her behavior, and she is asking him to change his attitude. The resolution to this conflict depends on many factors: the relationship between father and daughter, their relationships with the rest of the family, the details of the proposed date, the condition of the car.

Conflicts pertain to *values*. One person wants another to behave or think in a certain way. The other person does not wish to behave or think in this way. They value different attitudes and behaviors.

Conflicts that can be resolved within a family, or among immediate friends, constitute politics but do not necessarily involve governmental institutions. Governmental institutions become involved in conflict when people break laws or demand changes in government policies, or when government creates conflict by initiating new policy. As we have seen, government institutions direct and control the people of a nation. A **sovereign** government has the ability to direct and control by making laws; hence, it is able to allocate certain values, to make the ultimate decisions about how people may behave, or how rewards and punishments are distributed. It determines whether people do, and get, what they want—what they value. If the people of the nation believe the government should have this ability, it also has **authority;** authority itself is a value shared by people. When you and I

approve or disapprove of the government, or of the way it makes decisions about what we get or don't get, we are making a value judgment.

People usually place importance—or value—on the home they live in, food, clothing, and shelter, jobs, health care, and education. They are interested in quantity—how much of these things they have access to, and whether the amount they have of one is proportionate to the amount they have of another. They are also interested in quality. Their sense of quality derives in part from culture, what they and those they identify with have been taught about the right way to behave and to acquire material goods and services; one person may cherish a house or job which another despises. Most people also place importance on knowing that others are able to acquire food, clothing, shelter, jobs, education, and agreeable cultural surroundings. Conflicts emerge when there is not enough to go around; some can have these assets in the way they want, and others cannot.

If such conflicts come to involve enough people, interest groups and political parties are likely to try to persuade government to resolve them—in their favor, of course. It is government's job to decide who may do what, when, and how. If the government actually has authority and sovereignty (the right and ability) to make such decisions, it can resolve these demands and diminish political conflict. Once government has decided, people generally obey, though the losers may try to convince government leaders to retract or modify the decision.

Because they help decide who will be involved in government institutions, and because they try to affect the attitudes and behaviors of those within government institutions, political parties and interest groups are part of a nation-state's politics. As we stated earlier, a number of parts cohere to form the political system of a nation-state. Those parts, we now see, include political parties, interest groups, and government institutions. Together, these three develop a regular pattern of human relationships through which conflicts may be resolved—competition over goods and services as well as over cultural traditions, ideas, and other values. This pattern of interaction to resolve conflict is the **political**

system of the nation-state (in Late Latin, *systema* means ''to place together''). You and I are part of a political system which has the ultimate control over whether we attain what we want. If you do the exercise at the end of this chapter, you will see how the other twenty-one words and phrases we have just discussed relate to this one; the exercise centers around what you and I want and how that relates to what the political system lets us get.

LOOKING AHEAD: THREE TYPES OF POLITICAL SYSTEMS IN NATION-STATES

Our planet contains over 170 nation-states. In one textbook, we could make random comments about many or all of them as we discuss the various parts of a system. We could describe many subtle differences in the way these parts function. We could learn a little bit about a lot of places.

Instead, we will take a ''three-of-three'' approach, examining three types of political systems, and three examples of each type. One type of system is a nation-state which has absorbed much of its populace into an advanced industrialized economy and which allows competing political parties and interest groups. Our three examples of such a system are the United States, the United Kingdom, and the Federal Republic of Germany. A second type of system is a nation-state which has absorbed much of its populace into a less advanced industrialized economy and which does not allow political parties, interest groups, or economic institutions to compete. Our three examples of this type of system are the former East Germany, the former Soviet Union, and China. Finally, a third type of system is a nation-state which absorbs low percentages of its populace into modern economic institutions, which are free to compete with one another. Our three examples of this type of system are India, Peru, and Nigeria.

This book, then, introduces you to a few entire political systems. Because we will have a sense of how the parts of these nine systems cohere—and do not cohere—we will be in a position to see how and why the systems are changing, and how they will

change in the future. We will learn a lot about relatively few systems—nine systems that in some ways represent many others.

Throughout the book, we will emphasize how the nation-states in each of these groupings share common characteristics, but also exhibit a number of variations. No two nation-states, of course, are exactly alike. We will look at systems with and without extensive natural resources. One is an island, and the others are on the mainland. Our sample includes nation-states with populations large and small, ethnically diverse and culturally homogeneous; nation-states where various religious groups have learned to get along with one another and where they have not: older nation-states and those formed more recently. We will examine one nation-state that is in the process of disintegrating into several new ones, as well as one that is being absorbed into another. We'll explore both parliamentary and presidential systems, with and without individual states; with only civilian rule, and alternating with military rule; able and unable to transfer power via elections. None of these systems, however, are governed by other nation-states, or by monarchs or self-styled autocrats who monopolize sovereignty in their own families. None have parliamentary rules that frequently allow governments to fall. The many gradations in systems and cultures keep this subject lively, and remind us that what applies in one country does not always apply in another.

One of the industrialized, democratic systems we shall examine is our own, the United States, a nation-state which has furnished a home for people of many nationalities. You will thus be able to compare what you learn about other countries with what you know about your own. We shall look also at the political systems of Germany and the United Kingdom. Germany might be compared to a two-yolked egg; from 1945 to 1990, this nation had two sovereign states that created very different national experiences. The United Kingdom is an amalgam of four areas with differing national histories (England, Wales, Scotland, and Northern Ireland) that came together under one sovereign state. Today, these three industrialized democracies—the United States, the

United Kingdom, and Germany—face serious economic and political challenges. Will they continue to keep the groups they are composed of prosperous and harmonious?

Three of the systems we will study—the former Soviet Union, China, and the former East Germany—are or have been communist. With varying speed, and in differing ways, they are shedding or changing traditional communist government. East Germany had a relatively small population of 17 million people when it reunited with the Federal Republic of Germany, while a fifth of the earth's population resides in China. China and the former Soviet Union both contain numerous nationalities; China, even with 1.2 billion people, has a far deeper historical tradition of holding diverse ethnic groups together under one sovereign state. In 1991, the Soviet Union dissolved and restructured itself into a Commonwealth of Independent States, giving each state sovereignty. If the United States were to divide into fifty sovereign states, they would still find themselves highly interdependent economically and politically, because they have long functioned as part of a single unit; that is the case with the fifteen republics of the former Soviet Union as well. Will these systems develop more open political and economic competition and independence from one another?

The remaining three nation-states—India, Nigeria, and Peru—are commonly referred to as "developing nations." India (with 850 million people) is the most populous developing nation, and Nigeria (with 88 million) is Africa's most populous nation-state; with 22 million people, Peru is among the less populous developing nations. All three have diverse ethnic groups and short, unstable histories of holding these groups together under one state. Democratic institutions have taken firmer root in India

than in the other two. The International Monetary Fund and other nation-states are putting pressure on all three of these nation-states to develop competition among political parties. Will that happen? Will it help these three integrate more of their people into their economies as well?

SUMMARY

The study of comparative politics involves looking at political systems. Political systems are composed of three types of institutions which make and resolve demands on each other—government institutions, interest groups, and political parties. But demands—and the conflicts that grow from them, as well as cooperation to resolve those conflicts—start within other institutions to which people belong. Unless you are a hermit, you belong to and behave and think in accordance with various institutions, starting with your family. Anytime you make a demand on another person, you engage in politics. In a nation-state with sovereignty, government institutions have the ability to make ultimate decisions about who gets what they demand; citizens decide whether or not to confer on government the right, or authority, to make those ultimate decisions. So a government may have sovereignty without authority, or authority without sovereignty, or both. Institutions outside government interact with these government institutions in a regular pattern to establish who gets what. As we examine nine particular nation-states, we will see whose demands receive attention from government, and how. The twenty-two words and phrases you are learning in this chapter all relate to the political system, and thus to those demands and to the way government responds to them.

NOTES

1. "The first approached the animal and, happening to take the squirming trunk within his hand, thus boldly up and spake. 'I see,' quoth he, 'the elephant is very

like a snake.' The second, feeling of a limb, said 'surely you'll agree, the elephant is very like a tree.' John Godfrey Saxe, *The Blind Men and the Elephant.*

EXERCISES

Think about the book thus far:

1. According to the chapter introduction, what is the main purpose of this chapter?
2. What, in brief, do the words and phrases in the following list have in common?
3. Relate the definition of *demands* to three of the definitions in the list of Key Words and Phrases.

KEY WORDS AND PHRASES

Define the following terms:

nation	chief executive	economic institution
institution	judicial institution	governmental policy
government	officeholder	interest group
law	bureaucratic institution	political party
sovereignty	citizen	politics
authority	constitution	political system
nation-state	family	
legislature	cultural or religious institution	

THINKING IT THROUGH

Political scientists sometimes think of a political system as having inputs and outputs. People in society, you and I, bring needs, demands, and requests to the government, which then processes them to produce rules, services, and resources in response to those demands. The competition over goods, services, cultural traditions, ideas, and other values—and the people and institutions involved in that competition—are the inputs. The people and institutions which resolve those conflicts, and the processes by which they do so, are the outputs. Think about each of the twenty-two terms in the list to define: Is it an input, an output, or involved with both?

Now place each of the terms into one of these four columns.

Inputs	Outputs	Both Input and Output	Sometimes Input, Sometimes Output

Now, ask yourself:

1. Why did you place each term in a certain column?
2. Which of these terms belong to the nation, and which to the state?
3. How can a father and daughter arguing over a car become part of a political system?
4. What gives a leader authority to rule?
5. Can government have sovereignty without authority?
6. Would you want to live under a government with sovereignty but without authority?

chapter 2

GOVERNMENT INSTITUTIONS

Americans believe government's sovereignty should be limited, to protect citizens' freedoms. But a government that is too limited may not be able to hold the nation-state together or carry out actions needed to protect the health, security, and general welfare of its citizens. This chapter and the next discuss limits on the chief executives of the political systems we are examining. When sovereignty is divided among officeholders chosen independently of one another, the top officeholder—the chief executive's—ability to make and enforce laws is limited. Which chief executive has the least limits on sovereignty, the greatest ability to do whatever he or she wants: the military ruler, the democratically elected president or prime minister, or the leader of a one-party state? The answer may surprise you.

Now that communism has fallen in the Soviet Union and Eastern Europe, we hear a lot of talk about the prospects and potentials for "democracy." But often people are not very sure what these terms mean. This chapter will discuss how government organizes itself to make policy—in "communist" systems and in our own "democratic" one, as well as in four other types of systems. Comparative politics requires the use of a particular vocabulary (which we focused on in the first chapter), but it is not about vocabulary. Nor is it only about how systems are organized to create public policy, and how they choose the officeholders who do so. But understanding the basic vocabulary and the nuts and bolts of government organization will allow you to grasp much more about the specific systems later. This chapter and the next will thus introduce you to six types of government organization and discuss how each type chooses its officeholders. Then you will be ready to approach the ideas in the rest of the book with clarity.

You will notice that chapters 2 and 3 contain a large number of figures and charts. To discuss government organization, we must look at a number of details about who does what, in what order, for how long. These charts provide the necessary detail to guide you through our discussion. Although you need not memorize them, you may wish to refer to them later in the course to clear up some question on why particular officeholders, political parties, or interest groups behaved as they did.

This chapter will help you understand how our government, and five other types of governments, work. Chapter 3 examines the selection of government officeholders in different systems. Once you absorb these basics, we will be ready to begin using that knowledge to discuss how politics affects people's lives.

Think about this: The political system of a nation-state, as we learned in chapter 1, is continuously involved in resolving competition among its citizens. You and I want the same thing, and only one of us can have it. Whoever has the ability to make and enforce laws that determine who gets what is sovereign within that system; they will determine whether you, or I, obtain what we want. If those engaged in conflict accept these laws, or can be forced to accept them, the conflict is resolved; one of us gets what we want, and the other goes along with the decision. But if the citizenry cannot be made to accept these laws, the government is not sovereign, and the nation-state is on shaky ground. In short, government requires sovereignty—the ability to make and enforce laws.

Each institution of government has its own role to play in the effort to resolve conflict. But there must always be one, or a few, institutions with the final word on how laws are made and enforced. Sovereignty may be divided among several institutions. But ultimately, one officeholder—the chief executive—usually has the final word.

How much sovereignty does the chief executive hold, and how much is spread among other government institutions? This is the question we will explore in this chapter.

When you are finished reading this chapter, you should be able to distinguish six ways chief executives and legislatures can share sovereignty, and to recognize how cabinets, other chief executives, and state and local governments may share in sovereignty as well. The end-of-chapter exercise will help you sort out which countries have which characteristics, and thus which chief executives face the most competition in exercising sovereignty. How much control does our president have over your life as a citizen, and how does that compare with the control chief executives in other lands exercise over their citizens? This is what we will begin to explore here.

Read this chapter through to get the broad picture of the six ways governments may organize and allocate sovereignty. One caution: Don't try to memorize all the details about the individual countries. Use the figures, tables, and footnotes to fill in the chart in the exercise section at the end of the chapter; the chart will help you integrate what you've learned. One detail you will want to memorize: the abbreviations for the nine political systems we are discussing. (You can find a list of these abbreviations at the end of this chapter, as well as on the maps inside the covers of the book.) They are: USA (United States), USSR (Soviet Union) and CIS (Commonwealth of Independent States), FRG (Federal Republic of Germany, or West Germany), GDR (German Democratic Republic, or East Germany), UK (United Kingdom, or Great Britain),

PRC (People's Republic of China), RI (Republic of India), RP (Republic of Peru), and FRN (Federal Republic of Nigeria).

SIX ARRANGEMENTS OF SOVEREIGNTY

We learned in chapter 1 that a sovereign government has the ability to direct and control by making laws. In this chapter, we will examine six of the most common institutional arrangements for determining who has sovereignty—in other words, who has the last word in making and enforcing laws, and what limits this person or institution faces in making and enforcing those laws. The six arrangements of sovereignty we will discuss are:

1. presidential systems
2. parliamentary systems
3. military rule
4. monarchies
5. theocratic states
6. one-party political systems

A **legislature** is a body of citizens with the right and ability to create laws. Three of these systems—presidential, parliamentary, and one-party—regularly have legislatures. As table 2.1 indicates, all the governments we examine in this book have used at least one of those three systems, so all have had legislatures. Two have also, at one time or another, been under military rule, a system which generally operates without a legislature.

Legislatures may be **unicameral,** or composed of one body (literally, one private room or chamber), or **bicameral**, composed of two separate chambers. In a bicameral legislature, the lower chamber or house includes members representing smaller territorial units or districts. These lower house members are usually directly elected by the populace. The members of the upper house in a bicameral legislature are generally elected within larger districts, and in some cases, these members are not directly elected by voters. Table 2.2 lists the legislative bodies of our nine systems.

T*able 2.1*

Type of System

Presidential	Parliamentary	One-party	Military Rule
USA	FRG	USSR (1917–90)	RP (1968–80)
USSR (1990–91)	UK	GDR (1949–90)	FRN1 (1966–79,
CIS republics (1992–)	RI	PRC	1983–)
RP	FRN (1960–66)		
FRN2 (1979–83, after 1993?)			

T*able 2.2*

National Legislative Bodies

	Lower House	Upper House	Combined
USA	House of Representatives	Senate	Congress
USSR (1990–91)	Congress of People's Deputies	Supreme Soviet Soviet of the Union Soviet of Nationalities	
CIS republics (1992–)			
FRG	Bundestag (Federal Diet)	Bundesrat (Federal Council)	Parliament
GDR	Volkskammer (People's Chamber)		
UK	House of Commons	House of Lords	Parliament
PRC	People's Congress		
RI	Lok Sabha (House of the People)	Rajya Sabha (Council of States)	Parliament
RP (1980–92)	Chamber of Deputies	Senate	Congress
RP (1992–)	Constituent Congress		
FRN1	No legislature		
FRN2	House of Representatives	Senate	National Assembly

Figure 2.1   Inequalities in upper house representation.

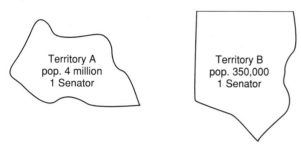

Territory A
pop. 4 million
1 Senator

Territory B
pop. 350,000
1 Senator

Figure 2.2   Passing a bill into law. Bills go to the lower and upper houses of the legislature, which can pass or reject them. If the chief executive signs the bill, it becomes law (path 5a); if the chief executive vetoes the bill, it may return to the legislature for an override vote in each house.

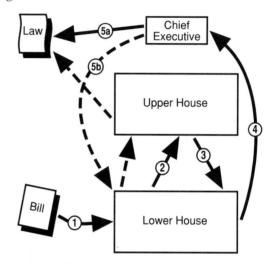

Who gives legislatures the right to decide what the laws will be? Certain groups of people do so; these groups choose legislators and authorize them to make the laws on their behalf, to **represent** them. Voters directly elect the lower houses in eight of these nine systems—all except China. Because lower houses are intended to directly represent individual voters, each lower house member comes from a geographic territory containing approximately the same number of people.

Unlike lower houses, upper houses are meant to represent different states, regions, and cultures, so the emphasis is on representing all geographic regions or cultural groups equally rather than on representing equal numbers of people. A territory with a large urban population may thus have the same number of upper house representatives as another territory with only a fraction of that population; this may give rural people more representation per person than urban people.[1] (See figure 2.1.)

When the upper house is not directly elected, people of high social standing tend to occupy its seats. In the United Kingdom, for example, the upper house is composed *entirely* of people who are part of the old landed nobility, church prelates, other officials who have traditionally held prominence in the countryside, and people given special recognition by the king or queen. Table 2.3 indicates how each of the nine systems chooses the members of the upper and lower chambers of the legislature.

A **bill** is a written draft of a proposed law formally presented to a legislature for its consideration. For a bill to become law in these systems with leg-

islatures, the bill usually must pass the lower house. In some systems, a bill must also pass the upper house; for example, in the presidential systems, if the upper house votes down a bill, it simply does not become law. The same holds true for about two-thirds of legislation in the parliamentary systems of West Germany and India.[2] Thus, the chief executive must share sovereignty with the lower legislative chamber in all of these systems, and with the upper chamber in the presidential systems and some parliamentary systems. In the other systems, upper houses cannot block legislation.[3] (See table 2.4.) Figure 2.2 summarizes passing a bill into law.

Although bills do not always need to pass upper houses to become law, upper houses are generally free to act independently of chief executives. In presidential systems, lower houses are freer to refuse to pass, or to amend, bills than in parliamentary or one-party systems. Let's take a closer look at how each of the six types of government passes bills into law, and at how each chooses its law makers and chief executive.

Table 2.3

Who Chooses National Legislatures

	Lower House	*Upper House*
USA	voters	voters
USSR (1990–91)	voters	lower house
CIS*	voters	lower house
FRG	voters	state legislatures
GDR	voters	
UK	voters	nobility and certain officeholders
PRC	state legislatures	
RI	voters	state legislatures
RP (1990–92)	voters	voters
RP (1992–)	voters	
FRN1		
FRN2	voters	voters

*Legislatures of the fifteen independent states; there is no legislature for the CIS as a whole.

Table 2.4

Majority Vote in Upper House of Legislature Needed

	To Pass All Legislation	*To Pass Most Legislation*
USA	yes	
USSR (1990–91)		yes
CIS*		yes
FRG		yes
GDR		
UK	no	no
PRC		
RI		yes
RP (1980–92)	yes	
RP (1992–)		
FRN1		
FRN2	yes	

* In the fifteen independent states

Presidential Systems

To understand why the lower house is independent of the chief executive in a presidential system, we must discuss how such a system chooses the chief executive and members of the legislature. In a **presidential system,** the members of both chambers of the legislature are chosen independently of the president, who is chief executive (see figure 2.3). This means that voters vote separately for the president and for members of the legislature; although the elections are held at regularly specified intervals (table 2.5), voters need not vote for both the chief executive and legislators on the same day, or even during the same year. In addition, a voter may cast a vote for one party's candidate for president, and for candidates from other parties to sit in the lower and upper houses. Legislators are free to vote down bills proposed by the president, who is not a member of the legislature, and to introduce and pass bills of their own. Thus, lower houses in presidential systems are more independent of the chief executive and therefore hold a greater share of sovereignty in the system.

Figure 2.3 Voting in a presidential system.

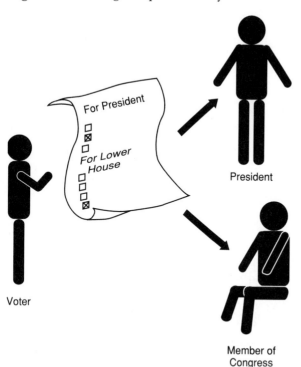

Voter

President

Member of
Congress

Table 2.5

Lengths of Terms in Presidential Systems

	Lower House	*Upper House*	*President*
USA	2 years	6 years	4 years†
USSR (1990–91)	5 years	5 years	5 years
CIS*			
RP (1980–91)	5 years	5 years	5 years‡
FRN2	4 years	4 years	6 years

* Term lengths vary in the fifteen independent states; the CIS as a whole has no president or legislature.

†No President may serve more than ten years.

‡From 1980 to 1992, presidents could serve only one term. In 1992, President Fujimori ordered the Constitution to be rewritten; the one-term limit will probably be revised.

To become law, a bill must pass both houses of the legislature and be signed by the president. If the president **vetoes,** or formally refuses to approve, the bill, it can still become law if both houses of the legislature **override** the presidential veto by voting a second time to pass the bill. Usually, as table 2.6 shows, rules require that two-thirds of those voting approve an override to pass the bill into law.[4]

Nigeria experimented with a presidential system from 1979 to 1983 and, in 1993, anticipated returning to a presidential system. In 1990, the Soviet Union introduced a modified presidential system in which its president, who was chief executive, presided over the lower house of the legislature, the Congress of the People's Deputies. The Soviet Union created the Congress in 1989 as the "highest organ of state power." (In a more typical presidential system, such as the United States, the legislature would choose its own chief officer—rather than the chief executive—to run its meetings.) Initially, the Congress of People's Deputies chose Mikhail Gorbachev (who was not an elected member of the legislature) to be the first president, with the provision that after five years the next president would be elected.

After the aborted coup of 1991, the Congress of People's Deputies and the Supreme Soviet voted to disband and replace themselves with one Supreme Soviet; this body met only once.[5] Later in the year, the individual republics declared their sovereignty and formed a new Commonwealth of Independent States[6] whose only governing body would be a council composed of the presidents of each republic. Each of the new sovereign republics began using modified presidential systems along the lines of that created for the Soviet Union in 1989 and 1990, electing their own presidents and legislatures. There is no chief executive or legislature for the Commonwealth of Independent States as a whole.

In presidential systems, legislatures have the right to make laws without the chief executive's approval. The chief executive has the ultimate authority to enforce the laws.

T*able 2.6*

Presidential Veto

	Over Lower House	*Over Upper House*	*Required to Override*
USA	yes	yes	two-thirds of both houses
USSR (1990–91)	no	yes	two-thirds of both parts of Supreme Soviet
CIS* (1992–)	yes	yes	half of either house
RP (1980–92)	no	no	
FRN2	yes	yes	two-thirds of both houses

* In Russia and some of the other fourteen now-independent states; the CIS as a whole has no president or legislature.

P resident Lyndon B. Johnson signs the 1964 Civil Rights Act, with Martin Luther King, Jr. and Congressional leaders present.

AP/Wide World Photos

Parliamentary Systems

Under a **parliamentary system,** the chief executive (usually entitled ''prime minister'') is elected not by the voters, independent of the legislature, but by the lower house of the legislature (see figure 2.4). Voters elect the lower chamber of the legislature, which then selects the chief executive from among its own members; he or she, in turn, selects other members of the lower chamber to head the major ministries of the bureaucracy.[7] Although parliamentary systems

Figure 2.4   Voting in a parliamentary system.

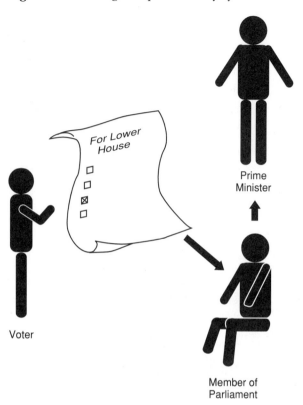

For Lower House

Voter

Prime Minister

Member of Parliament

sometimes also designate a president, this person fulfills largely ceremonial roles, while the prime minister acts as chief executive.

In a parliamentary system, bills are proposed by the chief executive in consultation with the heads of the major ministries; since the chief executive is chosen by a majority of members of the lower house, these members are prone to cooperate by passing those bills into law. The legislature does not draw up major legislation on its own.

Elections for parliament are not held at regular intervals; rather, the legislature's resistance to passing the chief executive's bills may trigger new elections. The tendency for the lower house to cooperate with the chief executive is increased by their knowledge that a vote against a bill could result in an im-

mediate new election, and that the prime minister might keep them from seeking reelection (we will discuss this in more detail in the next chapter). In any given parliamentary system, custom dictates how much resistance to passing proposed legislation is tolerable before a new legislative election must be held. In the United Kingdom, the House of Commons seldom even amends the prime minister's legislation (and nearly always receives the prime minister's consent before doing so).[8] Failure to pass any bill introduced by the chief executive[9] is interpreted as a **vote of no confidence** in the prime minister and may cause the king or queen to call for a new parliamentary election. In India's lower house, the Lok Sabha, fifty or more members may call for a formal vote to censure the prime minister; should the censure vote pass, or should the prime minister lose any vote in Parliament on a major bill, he or she will resign. The president will then ascertain whether a new government can be formed around some other member of the Lok Sabha. If this is not possible, the president announces new elections. In West Germany, the Bundestag theoretically has the right to vote down legislation proposed by the chancellor, but seldom does. A German chancellor who loses the ability to secure a majority of votes asks the federal president to determine whether a majority can be formed around some other member of the legislature. If so, this member becomes the new chancellor; if not, the president will call a new legislative election.[10] Figure 2.5 summarizes the election of the chief executive in presidential and parliamentary systems.

These parliamentary systems, then, all have additional heads of state to perform some functions and to represent the nation-state at ceremonial occasions. The United Kingdom's kings and queens, of course, hold hereditary positions. Germany's federal president is chosen every five years by a Federal Assembly of all Bundestag members meeting with an equal number of deputies from state parliaments. India's president, who also serves a five-year term, is chosen by a vote of all members of national and state legislatures, with a complicated formula to determine how much each of their votes count.

Figure 2.5 Presidents are elected for fixed terms; terms of prime ministers may vary.

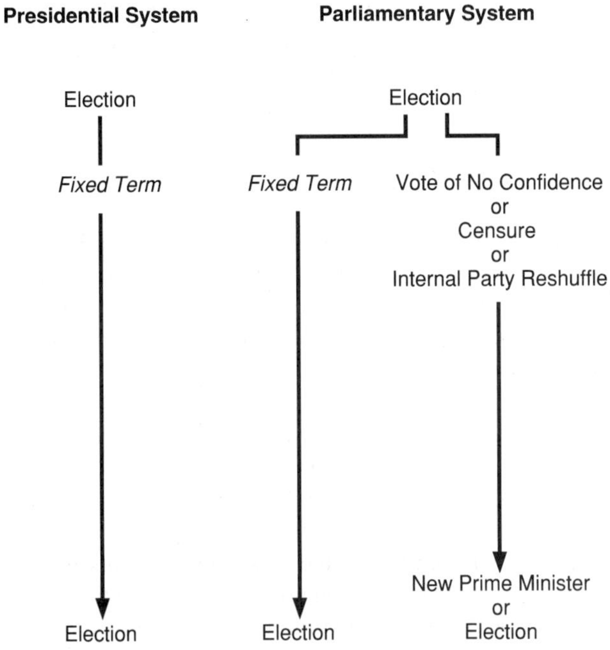

Presidential System	Parliamentary System

Election — Fixed Term — Election

Election — Fixed Term — Election

Election — Vote of No Confidence or Censure or Internal Party Reshuffle — New Prime Minister or Election

Table 2.7

Lengths of Legislative Terms

	Lower House	*Upper House*
FRG	4 years maximum	varies
UK	5 years maximum	life
RI	5 years maximum	6 years

If one political party can elect enough of its candidates to constitute a majority of members in the lower house, they will select the chief executive from among their own ranks, who in turn is likely to choose all heads of ministry from that party. As long as the members of the majority party maintain the discipline of **party responsibility** by voting for all the bills proposed by the prime minister or chancellor, their party will maintain control over the legislature. If no party gains a majority in the lower house, two or more parties must band together to support someone as chief executive; that person will choose heads of ministry from both parties. Should a majority of the Members of Parliament from the ruling party (or parties) decide at any time to withdraw their support from their leader as chief executive, they must select a new prime minister,[11] or new elections will be called.

Should an election for the lower house not be called within a certain time limit—five years in the United Kingdom and India, four in Germany—the ceremonial head of state is mandated by law to call a new election. For this reason, a prime minister is wise to call for a new election, or "engineer" a vote of no confidence, at a time when the party is doing well in the public opinion polls, rather than wait for the last possible date.

Members of a minority party in the lower house choose a "shadow" prime minister from among their own ranks. That person then serves as a spokesperson for the party in legislative debates. When elections are called, voters know that the shadow prime minister will serve as prime minister or chancellor if that party gains a majority of seats in the lower house.

As long as the parliamentary chief executive retains the confidence of a majority of lower house members, he or she can make policy with little interference from that body. The chief executive and the lower house share in sovereignty, but they work in unison.

As we saw earlier in the chapter, the upper houses of these legislatures are independent of the chief executive; those in India and West Germany can keep most bills from becoming law and thus force amendments in exchange for cooperation in passing them.

Military Rule

Under **military rule,** a military leader acts as chief executive. Sometimes sitting legislatures ask the highest ranking person in the military to become chief executive. At other times, armed forces units physically seize the buildings housing the chief executive and legislature, and force their officeholders to step down; whoever leads the coup (usually a colonel or general) keeps or takes control of the armed forces and becomes chief executive. Military personnel then work with the civilian bureaucracy to operate all levels of government. If the military government retains a legislature, with or without opposing political parties, the legislature is inclined to cooperate with the military leader for fear of being dissolved. The military ruler may found a new party and use it to obtain a majority in the legislature, which allows him or her to convert the system to parliamentary rule. If not, resistance from within the armed forces, the bureaucracy, the legislature (if there is one), and the public eventually tends to force a return to civilian rule.

Fifty-two of Peru's eighty presidents have been military leaders; Peru was under military rule for 100 of the 159 years from 1821 to 1980. Some of these leaders seized power by force, while others attained power by elections or at the request of the legislature. Nigeria, independent since 1960, has been under military rule from 1966 to 1979, and since 1983.

To rule, military leaders need considerable help from military and civilian bureaucracy. Those are the principal groups they share sovereignty with.

Monarchies and Theocratic States

In a **monarchy,** a chief executive may bequeath the chief executive post to one of his or her offspring. That individual may rule with the assistance of relatives who serve as governors and advisors. He or she may also allow an elected legislature, placing limits on who may vote, or threatening imprisonment or loss of privileges to assure the cooperation of legislators.

Britain used to be led by its kings and queens with assistance from the Parliament; by the eighteenth century, the chief executive's powers were shifting to the prime minister as the government evolved from a monarchy into a parliamentary system. In some nation-states, a military ruler may pass his or her office to a son or daughter and establish a monarchy. Successive dynasties in China were led by the offspring of those who overthrew the prior dynasty. Monarchies were once very common.

Sometimes a monarch is also the head of a religion, or the nation-state is ruled by the head of a religion who passes rule to his or her successor. Such a system is called a **theocratic state.** If a legislature exists in a theocracy, it is usually dominated by religious leaders. Monarchs and heads of theocracies share sovereignty with relatives, nobility, religious leaders, and other associates.

One Party Rule

Until 1990, the Constitution of the Soviet Union declared the Communist Party "the leading and guiding force of Soviet society and the nucleus of its political system, of all state organizations and public organizations." When a single political party exercises such sovereignty, a nation-state is under **one-party rule.** In the Soviet Union, only members or close associates of the Communist Party could run for the legislature or be appointed to public offices or the bureaucracy. The chairman of the Communist Party decided what the laws would be and how they would be executed; he thus served as chief executive. Sometimes the party chairman took official titles within government, and sometimes not; in either case, he and the Secretariat of the Central Committee of the Communist Party exercised sovereignty.

Until 1990, East Germany also had a one-party system. China still does; to complicate matters further, when a senior Chinese party leader formally retires as party chairman, the new, younger party chairman and the public will still defer to the retired chairman's wishes, leaving him with ultimate sovereignty.

Table 2.8 summarizes the way each of the nine systems chooses its chief executive. Chief executives are chosen by voters in presidential systems, by the lower house of the legislature in parliamentary systems, by the military under military rule, by heredity in monarchies, by religious bodies in theocracies, and by the ruling political party under one-party rule. In both presidential and parliamentary systems, upper houses, chosen independently from the chief executive, may be able to block legislation

T*able 2.8*

Who Chooses the National Chief Executive

USA	voters
USSR (1917–90)	ruling party
USSR (1990–91)	lower house of legislature
CIS*	
FRG	lower house of legislature, from among its members
GDR	ruling party
UK	lower house of legislature, from among its members
PRC	ruling party
RI	lower house of legislature, from among its members
RP	voters
FRN1	military
FRN2	voters

* Varies among the fifteen independent states; in most, the voters choose the chief executive.

proposed by the chief executive. In presidential systems, both the lower and upper houses have that ability, and they can initiate bills themselves. Under military or one-party rule, monarchies, and theocracies, the chief executive may make laws with little interference from legislatures.

OTHER COMPETITORS IN EXERCISING SOVEREIGNTY

As we just discussed, chief executives under presidential systems face considerably greater competition from legislatures in creating laws than chief executives in the other five types of systems. But that is only part of the story. Chief executives cannot enforce laws alone. To do so, they must control armed forces, police, and a civilian bureaucracy. Quite obviously, if the military and police refuse to be controlled by a civilian chief executive, military rule will ensue. But even under presidential, parlia-

mentary, and one-party rule, the extent to which the chief executive shares control of the police, the military, and the civilian bureaucracy varies from system to system. All chief executives must share the enforcement of laws—and hence part of their sovereignty—with other individuals and institutions, to varying degrees.

It is also clear that chief executives and national legislatures are not the only ones who propose and pass laws; they work with others in formulating laws at the national level. Lower levels of government also make laws, and chief executives and national legislatures generally do not have complete control over these lower levels.

Cabinets

Cabinets are institutions composed of the heads of the most important bureaucratic institutions (which assist in implementing and enforcing laws in such areas as foreign affairs, agriculture, trade, banking, energy, the environment, social services, and defense). Cabinet members meet with the chief executive to help formulate policy and propose laws.

In parliamentary systems, as we have seen, the prime minister or chancellor chooses other members of the legislature to head bureaucratic institutions and meets with those heading the most important ones as a cabinet.[12] The cabinet must meet to formulate policy and propose bills; the prime minister or chancellor always has the last word in deciding what these policies and bills will be, but they are formally presented to the public and legislature as the cabinet's recommendations. The prime minister or chancellor cannot bypass the cabinet.

In a presidential system, the president chooses a cabinet from among individuals who are not members of the legislature (figure 2.6). Cabinet members head bureaucratic agencies and meet with the president to assist with policy formation or hear reports on the president's plans. In the United States, Peru until 1992, and Nigeria, the upper house of the legislature must approve appointments of these heads of bureaus.

Chief executives in most presidential and parliamentary systems can select and fire members of

Figure 2.6   Routes to cabinet membership.

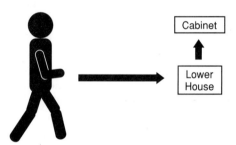

Presidential System

Cabinet

Legislature

President chooses cabinet from outside the legislature; upper house must confirm the appointment.

Parliamentary System

Cabinet

Lower House

Prime minister chooses cabinet members from within the lower house of the legislature.

their cabinet.[13] As a result, cabinet members are apt to be cautious about opposing the chief executive. In both types of systems, firing a cabinet member can cause momentary political embarrassment to a chief executive. In a parliamentary system, dismissal of a cabinet member could even lead to a loss of confidence within the legislature; under most circumstances, however, that is unlikely.

Under one-party rule in communist systems, the General or First Secretary (chairman) is among a handful of people who constitute the Secretariat of the Central Committee of the Party. The Central Committee contains several hundred people and sel-

dom meets. The Secretariat, by contrast, meets regularly to formulate policy.[14] Since they contain the top leaders of the single ruling party, these party groups are in a position to remove the First Secretary from control of both the party and the nation-state; unlike the chief executive of a parliamentary system, whose popularity with voters might save him or her from removal by detractors within the parliament, the one-party chief executive can be removed and replaced without voter approval. That may make him especially sensitive to the wishes of the top party leaders and thus give them a significant role in formulating policy. In addition, a State Council, or Council of Ministers, composed of the heads of the major bureaucratic units, meets (often without the chief executive present) to coordinate the enforcement of these policies.[15] Figure 2.7 summarizes the relationship between a communist chief executive and cabinets.

Until its dissolution in 1991, the Soviet Union retained a Council of Ministers, which took on roles of a fully functioning cabinet.[16] Then all bureaucracy was transferred to the control of the individual republics, which have their own councils of ministers.

Monarchs meet with the heads of their main bureaucratic agencies (many of whom may be princes from their own families) and may refer to these leaders as their cabinets. In addition to meeting with heads of bureaucratic agencies, military rulers confer regularly with the military high command, and theocratic rulers consult with other religious leaders; since those bodies are in a position to remove the chief executive,[17] their views are likely to be taken seriously.

Cabinets generally serve at the pleasure of the chief executive, who can dismiss individual members and (in consultation with members of their political party, extended family, religious hierarchy, military high command, and/or legislature) replace them with others. But, depending on the type of system, the chief executive must stay on good terms with at least one of these groups; they may remove him or her from office if they lose confidence. Such groups usually include individuals whose views differ.

Figure 2.7   Communist chief executive and cabinets.

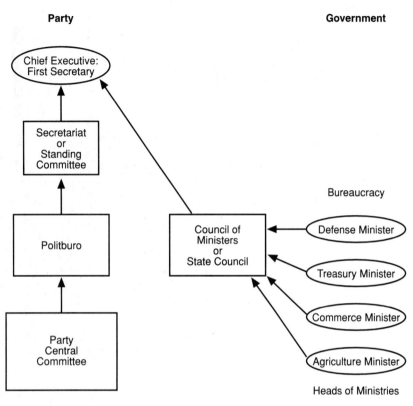

Hence, the chief executive is likely to choose cabinet members who represent different strands of opinion and to pay some attention to opinions expressed by cabinet members.

Other Top Executives

We have already mentioned that parliamentary systems have formal ceremonial heads of state. Immediately after an election in which no party wins a majority in the lower house, or after the legislature expresses no confidence in the chief executive, the ceremonial leader may have some choice as to who will form a new government, or whether to hold new elections. Ceremonial heads of state perform other roles as well.[18]

All these ceremonial heads of state may at times affect the thinking and behavior of a chief

executive, but, except when selecting a new chief executive, a ceremonial head of state plays little role in making policy. Still, if the chief executive (and others they deal with) trust them, ceremonial leaders may offer advice that is likely to be heeded. Also, because the ceremonial heads in the United Kingdom, India, and Germany are not chosen by the chief executive (see table 2.10), they can very discreetly mobilize some public support when the chief executive contemplates acts they or those who chose them disapprove.

Other Levels of Government

Other levels of government also compete with the chief executive and the national legislature for sovereignty. In all nine of the political systems we are examining, elected executives and legislative

Table 2.9

Cabinets

	Functional Cabinet	Government Cabinet (if different)
USA	Cabinet	
USSR (1991)	Federation Council Council of Ministers Security Council	
CIS*	Council of Presidents	
FRG	Cabinet	
GDR	Secretariat of Central Committee	State Council†
UK	Cabinet	
PRC	Secretariat of Central Committee Standing Committee	State Council†
RI	Cabinet	
RP	Cabinet	
FRN1	Military Government	ministers
FRN2	Vice president and ministers	

† Composed of ministry heads who are also party Central Committee members; headed by Premier (China) or Chairman (East Germany).

* Presidents of independent republics meet to coordinate the Commonwealth of Independent States; individual republics have their own councils of ministers.

Table 2.10

Government Leaders

	Chief Executive	Ceremonial Head of State
USA	President	
USSR (1991)	President	Prime Minister†
CIS*	President	Prime Minister/Vice President†
FRG	Chancellor	Federal President
GDR	party leader	Chairman of State Council†
UK	Prime Minister	King or Queen
PRC	party leader	Premier†
RI	Prime Minister	President
RP	President	
FRN1	President	
FRN2	President	

* Within the fifteen independent republics; there is no chief executive or ceremonial head for the CIS as a whole.

† Chosen by the chief executive.

councils govern cities, counties, and some other regions; except in China, the former communist systems, and Nigeria and Peru under military rule, these lower levels are often controlled by political parties other than that of the national chief executive. These lower-level officials make some laws and policy decisions. But their ability to formulate and enforce those decisions independently of the national government is heavily influenced by their ability to raise money and control bureaucracy.

When state, county, and local executives have their own bureaucracies and tax revenues, their ability to act with some independence from the national executive increases. In the United States and the United Kingdom, local, regional, and county governments have both these resources.[19,20] That is *not* the case in any of the other systems. German cities have staffs and taxing powers of their own, but derive most of their revenues from the state and national governments. German states do have extensive bureaucracies and revenues they collect themselves.[21]

Local and district governments in India are almost entirely staffed and financed by the state and national governments and civil service; states derive most of their revenues from the national government.[22] Most bureaucracy and police working for China's cities and towns are hired in conjunction with the national government, and until recent years the national government provided most of their revenue as well. Economic liberalization has shifted that dramatically; now the national government depends heavily on local and regional governments' investments and tax collections for most of its tax revenues.

In Peru and Nigeria, and formerly in the Soviet Union and East Germany, local, county, and regional units obtain most of their revenues and bureaucracy from the national government; while counties and municipalities in China are becoming increasingly independent about raising revenues, the bureaucracy is still subject to extensive control by the national government. In 1991, the Soviet Union's taxing powers and bureaucracy switched into the hands of the independent republics of the Commonwealth. Local, county, and regional (oblast) governments still have little formal power to tax

Figure 2.8 Differences in local, county, and regional governments. Arrows pointing up indicate features that strengthen local, county, and regional governments. Arrows pointing down indicate features that weaken local, county, and regional governments.

Local, County, and Regional Governments

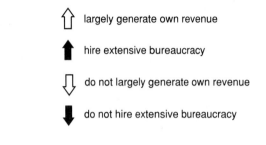

(see figure 2.8), but increasingly find new sources of revenue and fail to pass along revenues owed to central government.

Chief executives in all these systems need local governments to carry out many basic functions and must share both revenues and bureaucracy with them. This gives local governments some power to affect policy implementation, as well as some control over who gets local jobs and services. Military rulers depend especially heavily on good relations with bureaucracy at all levels to retain power since they do not have a party organization of their own.

All these systems except the United Kingdom, East Germany, and the individual republics of the Commonwealth of Independent States are divided into states (also called republics, regions, or provinces; see table 2.11).[23] Part of the territory of the CIS republics is divided into autonomous republics. The states hold elections to choose legislatures, as table 2.12 indicates. In the United States, Germany, Peru, Nigeria, and the autonomous republics of the CIS, voters choose the state legislatures in elections the national chief executive has little control over.

Table 2.11

State-Level Units of Government

USA	states
USSR	republics and autonomous republics
CIS*	autonomous republics
FRG	Land (pl. Laender)
GDR	
UK	
PRC	provinces
RI	states
RP	regions
FRN	states

* The fifteen independent republics (once state-level units of the USSR) contain the autonomous republics; the rest of their territory is not divided into states.

China's provincial legislatures are composed of delegates from county Congresses, which both provincial and national Communist Party leaders help select.

As table 2.13 indicates, United States and (since 1990) Nigerian voters directly choose state governors, who serve as chief executives of their states. Germany's, Peru's, and India's chief executives are chosen by their state legislatures. National authorities, in consultation with provincial State Councils, appoint China's provincial governors.

Thus, all these systems except the United Kingdom, East Germany, and Nigeria under military rule, have state-level chief executives and legislatures which can make some laws independently of the national chief executive. Through his control of the national Communist Party apparatus, and his role in appointing both provincial chief executives and party leaders, China's national chief executive can considerably dampen that independence. But as we shall see later, China's provincial party does not entirely take orders from the national leadership;[24] even in communist systems, state-level leadership has some independence.

Table 2.12

Who Chooses State-Level Legislatures

	Lower House	Upper House
USA	voters	voters*
USSR† (1990–91)	voters	lower chamber
CIS††		
FRG	voters	**
GDR		
UK		
PRC	county Congresses	
RI	voters	voters, lower chamber
RP	voters	
FRN1		
FRN2	voters	

* All except one state-level legislature are bicameral.
** All except one state-level legislature are unicameral.
†Legislatures of the fifteen republics, now independent.
††The CIS republics, the states of the USSR, are not fully divided into states. Autonomous republics have their own legislatures.

In India, different political parties often control the state and national governments. But the national government can pose some threats to keep the states from being too independent: The national president appoints governors, who play many of the same roles at the state level as the president performs at the national level. At the request of a governor, the president may take (and frequently has taken) control of all executive functions in a state and shift lawmaking from the state legislature to the national parliament.[25] After winning a national election, the prime minister sometimes asks the president to dismiss governments in states controlled by opposition parties and calls for new elections in those states.[26] The national prime minister (as we shall see in the next chapter) chooses his or her party's nominees to

Table 2.13

State-Level Chief Executives

	Title	Chosen By
USA	Governor	voters
USSR* (1990–91)	President	legislature of republic, or voters
CIS**		
FRG	Minister-President	legislature of Land
GDR		
UK		
PRC	Governor	national authorities and State Council
RI	Chief Minister	state parliament
RP	Governor	regional assembly
FRN1	Governor	military ruler
FRN2	Governor	voters

* Refers to the fifteen republics, now independent, formerly the states of the Soviet Union.

**The CIS republics, the states of the USSR, are not fully divided into states. Autonomous republics have their own chief executives.

Table 2.14

State-Level Ceremonial Heads

	Title	Chosen By
USA		
USSR* (1990–91)	Prime Minister	President
CIS		
FRG		
GDR		
UK		
PRC	Chairman of State Council	party and state legislature
RI	Governor	President
RP		
FRN1		
FRN2		

* Refers to the fifteen republics, now independent, and formerly the states of the Soviet Union.

run in state legislative elections and thus also chooses the chief minister in states where the party wins control of the legislature. In addition, all national revenues distributed to the states must pass through an independent Finance Commission appointed by the president.

State-level legislatures and executives, like local governments, may be more independent of the national government if they raise their own revenues and hire their own bureaucracies (figure 2.9). In the United States and Germany (notes 19 and 21), states have extensive powers to tax, and hire sizable percentages of their nation-states' bureaucrats. They are often controlled by political parties other than that of the national chief executive. China's municipalities and provinces collect most of the central government's taxes and keep a portion for themselves; the percentage of total revenues they control is rising rapidly.[27] In India,[28] Peru, and Nigeria, national laws heavily restrict the power of state-level units of government to raise money by taxation. Nigeria's states hire about half the bureaucrats in that country

Figure 2.9 Differences in state governments. Arrows pointing up indicate features that strengthen state governments. Arrows pointing down indicate features that weaken state governments.

State Governments

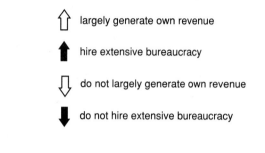

⇧ largely generate own revenue

⬆ hire extensive bureaucracy

⇩ do not largely generate own revenue

⬇ do not hire extensive bureaucracy

CIS**
USA (USSR*) FRG GDR   UK PRC RI RP FRN

* Refers to the fifteen republics that were states of the Soviet Union.
** The now independent republics have no states, but some territories are designated "autonomous republics," with extensive powers to generate revenue.

but derive most of their revenue from the national government.[29] India's states, largely using revenue furnished directly or indirectly by the national government, hire extensive numbers of police and civil servants; states in China and Peru do not. The republics of the Soviet Union had little power to tax or hire bureaucracy; under the Commonwealth, they control most taxes and bureaucracy and have no states of their own to share them with.[30] However, autonomous republics increasingly refuse to pass along revenues to the republics.

In India, Peru,[31] Nigeria, the CIS republics, and formerly in East Germany and the Soviet Union, the power to tax largely resides at the national level. In China, Peru, the CIS republics, and formerly in East Germany and the Soviet Union, the central government hires most of the nation-state's bureaucracy—including police forces. This strengthens the power

of the national chief executive. However, under one-party rule in the Soviet Union and East Germany, political party bureaucrats at all levels competed with the government bureaucrats, complicating control from the top. This is still true in China (see chapter 3).

The 1992 Constitution in Nigeria provides for separate state and local government bureaucracies, but a national bureaucracy performs at all levels and a unified police force is controlled by the national chief executive. If elected governors try to use their bureaucracies to enforce state laws against the wishes of the national chief executive, or if they choose not to help enforce national laws, they may meet resistance from the national bureaucracy.[32]

To recap, in the Soviet Union before 1991, the CIS republics (though to a constantly decreasing extent), the former East Germany, Peru, and Nigeria, the chief executive controls the bureaucracy and most of the revenues at all levels of government. Governments at the state level or below have more direct control over revenues and bureaucracy in the United States, the United Kingdom, and the Federal Republic of Germany. While state and local governments in India depend on the national government for most revenues, states control extensive bureaucracies; that situation is reversed in China, where the national government has more control over bureaucracy than revenue.[33]

In addition, all these chief executives must share responsibilities with a national legislature or military council, an inner circle of civilian leaders, and other officials. Thus no chief executive has sovereignty entirely in his or her own hands. Other decision-makers retain some capacity to block or modify the chief executive's directives.

SUMMARY

The six most common ways for a nation-state to arrange the sharing of sovereignty within government are presidential systems, parliamentary systems, military rule, monarchies, theocratic states, and one-party rule. Within each of these systems, a chief executive may share sovereignty with legislatures, other officials, and lower levels of government.

The presidential system gives the legislature a greater share of sovereignty (and the chief executive less sovereignty) than the others. But even under parliamentary rule, the upper house of a legislature may retain considerable discretion. Party Secretariats in one-party states and military high commands under military rule can also challenge the chief executive.

When they have the ability to raise extensive revenues and bureaucracies, state, regional, and local governments are able to resist central government policies; if their legislatures and chief executives belong to opposition political parties, they may be especially prone to do so. All chief executives also meet with a cabinet, and some share authority with a ceremonial head of state. Finally, chief executives need bureaucracies at all levels to carry out policy. Any of these groups—cabinets, bureaucracies, lower levels of government, and legislatures—may work with the others to resist or transform government policy. No chief executive exercises sovereignty alone.

Notes

1. Voters directly elect upper houses in the United States (two senators per state), Peru before 1992, and the forthcoming civilian government of Nigeria, which are all presidential systems. In West Germany and India, the state legislatures choose upper house members; all West German states have at least three members, but they may get as many as six if their population is larger.

   The upper house in the Soviet Union, from 1990 to 1991, was divided into two parts. The Congress of People's Deputies chose representatives for both parts from among its own members. The Soviet of the Union represented the fifteen republics, and the Soviet of the Nationalities the autonomous regions set aside within the republics to protect the rights of minority nationalities. Up to a fifth of the members in each of the two Soviets (which had a total of 542 members) were replaced each year, so theoretically each of the 2,250 members of the Congress of People's Deputies could serve. Within the Congress of People's Deputies, a third of the members came from districts designed to have equal population, and a third from districts designed to represent minorities and autonomous republics, regions, and areas.

   The Commonwealth which replaced the Soviet Union in 1991 did not form a legislature. Each of the nation-states created out of the Soviet Union has a legislature.

   In Peru prior to 1992, candidates for senator had to come from different parts of the country. But they ran nationwide for their seats, so all voters voted for all Senate seats. In 1992, President Fujimori created a unicameral legislature without a senate.

2. In the Federal Republic of Germany, all bills pertaining to taxation, administrative, or territorial rights of individual states must be approved by the upper house; all other bills can become law even if the upper house rejects them, by a two-thirds revote in the lower house. In India, bills pertaining to taxing, spending, and money can become law simply by a revote in the lower house, but most other bills require the approval of the upper house.

3. Chief executives in East Germany, China, and now Peru have had no upper house to contend with. In the Soviet Union's modified version of a presidential system, in effect from 1990 to 1991, some bills became laws after being passed by only the lower house, or only the upper house; in these cases, they were not even presented to the other house for approval. In other cases, bills went through both. Similar systems were adopted by the individual republics of the CIS. The United Kingdom's House of Lords can delay a bill for a month to a year by forcing it to be resubmitted for a vote in the House of Commons. The House of Lords can also veto "statutory instruments," as well as legislation which lengthens the period between parliamentary elections to more than five years. In 1968, they rejected sanctions against Rhodesia as a statutory instrument. More recently, they rejected legislation allowing trials of Nazi war criminals. In response, Prime Minister John Major used a power invoked only three times since the Parliament Act of 1911 removed the ability of the House of Lords to reject bills, forcing this instrument into law without the House of Lords' approval.

4. Before 1992, the President of Peru did not have the right to veto legislation passed by both houses. Within the now independent Russian state, the Russian president can veto legislation passed by the legislature, which can then override that veto by a simple majority vote. In both these systems (as with the present Constituent Congress in Peru), the president initially proposes most major legislation, or reviews bills proposed by members of the legislature, so the president has at least some part in formulating them.

The 1990–91 Supreme Soviet met for six to eight months during the year, and the Congress of People's Deputies less frequently. Some legislation could become law if both parts of the Supreme Soviet approved it. The president could veto such legislation, but it could still become law if repassed by two-thirds of the members of each part of the Supreme Soviet. The Congress of People's Deputies (whose decisions the president could not veto) could also pass certain legislation into law without submitting it to the Supreme Soviet.

In the United States, many bills are proposed by a member of the legislature without the endorsement of the President, who must then decide whether to veto them.

5. Gorbachev referred to it as a "constituent assembly," not unlike the one Lenin closed in 1918.

6. Initially, all but Lithuania, Latvia, and Estonia joined the CIS. In 1993, Russia, Kazakhstan, Belarus, Uzbekistan, Tajikistan, Kyrgyzstan, and Armenia signed a new charter for the organization. At that time, the Ukraine and the remaining seven republics were reluctant to participate.

7. In India, the heads of ministries may be from either the Lok Sabha (lower house) or the Rajya Sabha (upper house). Indira Gandi was first called to be prime minister when she was a member of the Rajya Sabha; she subsequently won a seat in the Lok Sabha, and that precedent has not been repeated. On rare occasions, heads of major ministries in the Federal Republic of Germany are drawn from outside the Bundestag (lower house).

8. A study of bills from 1967–71 found that 907 amendments were introduced by cabinet ministers, of which 906 passed. Other Members of Parliament introduced 3,510 amendments; most of the 171

which passed were not opposed by the Government. J. A. G. Griffith, *Parliamentary Scrutiny of Government Bills* (London: Allen & Unwin, 1974).

9. Occasionally, bills may be presented with a stipulation that members are free to "vote their conscience." In that case, a vote against the bill would not qualify as a vote of no confidence.

10. A "positive vote of no confidence" requires members of parliament to propose that the chancellor be replaced by the leader of another party, or another member of parliament from the chancellor's own party, and ask for a secret ballot of members of the Bundestag. It was through such a maneuver that Helmut Kohl replaced Helmut Schmidt as chancellor in 1982. Both men were from the same party, which was returned to office by the voters the following year.

11. In 1990, the members of the majority party in the British House of Commons, the Conservative Party, held a series of private meetings in which they removed Margaret Thatcher as party leader and replaced her with John Major. The Queen then asked Major to replace Thatcher as prime minister, without calling a new election, even though there had been no "vote of no confidence" within the House of Commons. This rare procedure allowed for a party with a majority in the Commons to change prime ministers without triggering elections. It is more common for that to happen when no party has a majority, and two parties in a coalition government maneuver to change leaders without an election.

12. These members of the legislature often share control over their units of bureaucracy with professional civil servants who serve as permanent heads of these agencies.

13. Until 1992, Peru's Congress could ask for the resignation of cabinet officers, a formal power the legislatures in the other systems do not have. In most systems, this power belongs to the chief executive alone.

14. China's Communist Party has a Standing Committee with six members, and a Secretariat with eleven; these are the top decision-making bodies.

15. In China, about twenty-five to thirty-five top leaders direct policy through the Standing Committee of the State Council, the Party Secretariat, the Military

Affairs Commission, and the Politburo of the Party—a larger body which meets less frequently. Kenneth Lieberthal and Michel Oksenberg, *Policy Making In China: Leaders, Structures, and Processes* (Princeton: Princeton University Press, 1988), pp. 40–41.

16. Before the 1991 coup, the chief executive (by then the President, instead of the Party's General Secretary) also met on a daily basis with a nine-member Security Council. The members of this Council were chosen by President Gorbachev and approved by the Supreme Soviet. After the coup, Gorbachev met with a Federation Council (composed of high officials of the republics and autonomous ethnic territories and regions which wished to participate). Since the members of this latter Council were not chosen by the president, they were more likely to challenge his views, finally discarding both him and the Soviet Union. The Commonwealth which replaced the Soviet Union has a Council of Presidents composed of the chief executives of the republics and chaired by the President of the Russian Republic.

17. In some situations, they may fear assassination, imprisonment, or other punishment if they attempt to do so.

18. The president of India is commander in chief of the armed forces and appoints governors, judges, and many major national officials. He or she can also veto acts of parliament (other than money bills), though a simple majority of both chambers can overturn a veto. Since the president acts as the agent of the prime minister, this veto power extends the Prime Minister's sovereignty, weakening the parliament and the states. But the president also pledges to uphold the constitution; if a prime minister's proposed actions in any way appear to conflict with the constitution, the president may cite advice of legal counsel and pressure the prime minister to back off from carrying them out.

　　Germany's federal president signs all laws and appoints judges and civil servants. He or she cannot do any of this without the approval of the chancellor, but the president can offer advice and recommendations to the chancellor before carrying out these actions.

　　In the Soviet Union, China, and East Germany, ceremonial leaders chair (or chaired) the councils of ministers who head the bureaucracy. This enables these leaders to consult regularly with the chief executive and to affect the way laws and government decisions are carried out.

19. In the United States, 13.3 percent of state and local revenues come from the national government. Governments Division, Census Bureau, U.S. Department of Commerce, *Government Finances in 1987–1988,* GF–88–5; *Public Employment in 1988,* GE–88–1; *Statistical Abstract of the United States, 1989.* Local governments collect 66.9 percent of the money they spend, but use their own bureaucracies to deliver half again as many services as they pay for (which are largely funded by states).

20. In Northern Ireland, the number of city bureaucrats who draw their pay from the city government outnumber those who draw their pay from the central government two to one; in England, Wales, and Scotland, the ratio is four to one. Contrary to practice in the United States, many of these city employees (especially in education and social services) may be directly supervised by employees of the central government, because national and local programs are often heavily intertwined. In Northern Ireland, about a fifth (and elsewhere about half) of local revenues come from central government grants. Cf. Ian Budge and David McKay, *The New British Political System* (London: Longman, 1985), pp. 122, 128. Legislation by the Thatcher Government in 1987 did away with the rates, the property taxes set by local councils that provided 56 percent of local revenues, and replaced them with a poll tax, paid by everyone (with up to an 80 percent rebate to those on state benefits). Under this system, the national government determined about three-fourths of local expenditure. The rest came from the poll tax. The poll tax had to be raised if local government was to increase services in ways not determined by the national government; the legislation placed limits on how high poll taxes may go. Joe Rogaly, "A Tighter Grip on the People's Choice," *Financial Times,* August 17, 1987. A storm of public protest followed enactment of this law; Mrs. Thatcher was forced to resign as prime minister, and the law was revised.

21. The national government generates about 55 percent of all tax revenue and relieves both states and cities of deficits by sharing part of this revenue with them. States derive about a fourth of their income from the

national government. David P. Conradt, *The German Polity*, 5th ed. (New York: Longman, 1993), p. 198.

22. A third of the national government's revenues goes to the states. The states spend as much as the national government—using loans, taxes, and overdrafts to cover the other part of their budgets. K. P. Joseph, *Indian Express*, November 10, 1992.

23. The fifteen republics which constituted the states of the former Soviet Union are now independent, but they have no states within them except for twenty autonomous republics created by the Soviet Union to accommodate various minority nationalities (which have their own parliaments). The states of the United States were initially created as British colonies; new states were added as citizens of existing states moved into new territories.

    When Germany was unified in 1871, its many smaller territories were consolidated into twenty-five states. The ten states created by the Allies after defeating Germany in World War II and restructuring its government included three of the original twenty-five—Bavaria, Hamburg, and Bremen. At that point, the Soviet occupying forces in East Germany abolished the states and did not replace them. When Germany reunified in 1990, East Germany was divided into five states, to join the ten redrawn in West Germany after World War II.

    In 1987, Peru abolished its twenty-five departments and replaced them with twelve regions, with their own elected assemblies, and additional elected mayors and councils in municipalities, districts, and provinces within the regions. In 1956, India created fourteen states, attempting to combine areas with linguistic similarities; this number has expanded to twenty-one states and five union territories. Nigeria began its independence simply divided into four regions; in 1967, the military government divided the nation into twelve states, which it has further broken into thirty (including

nine created in August, 1990, on the eve of elections for new state legislatures).

24. Also, the provincial legislature and Party choose a Chairman of the State Council, who performs some of the same roles as the Premier at the national level.

25. The constitution also allows the national legislature to create, alter the boundaries of, and even abolish states through ordinary legislation. A bill to abolish a state might be expected to meet strong resistance among members of the Rajya Sabha, who are chosen by state legislatures. But a bill to alter or to declare an emergency in a state dominated by a minority party might have a chance to pass if that body is dominated by other parties. Emergency suspensions of rights must be declared by the president, but also pass both houses of parliament.

26. The Supreme Court declared this constitutional in 1977.

27. Some coastal provinces like Guangdong (surrounding Hong Kong) receive ten times more than they pass on to the national government, while most keep a fourth or less. Shanghai keeps 25 percent. On average, in 1989, provinces kept 4 percent of total central government revenues. Tai Ming Cheung, "Centrifugal Forces," *Far Eastern Economic Review* 151, 14 (April 4, 1991). The share of revenues retained and earned by provinces continues to rise.

28. However, while the constitution forbids the states to levy income tax, it gives them the exclusive right to levy property taxes. At times they resist national pressures to tax large landholders.

29. *Federal Civil Service Manpower Statistics*, 1979. See Anthony Kirk-Greene and Douglas Rimmer, *Nigeria Since 1970: A Political and Economic Outline* (London: Hodder & Stoughton, 1981), pp. 75, 123ff.

30. During the months prior to the formation of the Commonwealth, the legislatures of some republics defied the national government by refusing to pass along revenues they had collected for it. Normally,

bureaucrats collected the taxes from state businesses, and the presidents of the republics deposited these funds in banks for transmission to Moscow. The central government used these revenues to pay for defense and other national programs and apportioned a percentage to return to the republics as operating budgets. After the August 1991 coup, republics passed along only as much money as they chose. By the end of 1991, the central government had run out of money and was disbanded by the republics as they formed the new Commonwealth.

In 1992, 56 percent of Russia's revenues were raised by its national government. Of the 44 percent raised locally or by autonomous republics, a portion was to be passed along to the central government. Local governments and autonomous republics bargain over what that portion will be.

31. President Alan Garcia, who served from 1985 to 1990, strongly advocated decentralizing the government. But even he did not attempt to give lower units of government greater taxing powers.

32. Under the 1992 Constitution, state governments no longer have liaison ministries with local governments; this further reduces the states' ability to interfere with activities of the national bureaucracy working at the local level and gives greater control to the national president.

33. Daniel Elazar, "State Constitutional Design in the United States and Other Federal Systems," *Publius: The Journal of Federalism* 12 (Winter 1982): 8, asserted that in 1982, only eighteen countries had federal forms of government in which states and central government share powers. He classified the United States, West Germany, India, and Nigeria—but not Peru or China—as federal systems. The other systems he characterized as federal are Argentina, Australia, Austria, Brazil, Canada, Czechoslovakia, Malaysia, Mexico, Pakistan, Switzerland, the United Arab Emirates, Venezuela, and Yugoslavia. Nigeria, and several other of these governments, share little power with states. Some systems not on the list share more power with states than these do.

EXERCISES

Think about the book thus far:

Choose three of the Key Words and Phrases and explain how each relates to the term *sovereignty.*

KEY WORDS AND PHRASES

Define the following terms:

legislature	presidential veto	military rule
unicameral	override (of a presidential veto)	monarchy
bicameral	parliamentary system	theocratic state
representation	vote of no confidence	one-party rule
bill	party responsibility	cabinet
presidential system		

1. Place the following legislative bodies in the appropriate boxes:

Congress of People's Deputies   Volkskammer   House of Commons
Bundestag   House of Representatives (2)   Chamber of Deputies
House of Lords   People's Congress   Lok Sabha
Rajya Sabha   Supreme Soviet   Constituent Congress
Senate (3)   Bundesrat

	Lower Houses	*Upper Houses*
USA		
USSR		
FRG		
GDR		
UK		
PRC		
RI		
RP		
FRN		

2. Place the following words and phrases in the appropriate boxes:

President   Land, Laender   states (3)   provinces
Governor (4)   republics   Chief Minister   Minister-President
Chairman of the State Council   regions

	State-Level Units	*State-Level Chief Executive*
USA		
USSR		
FRG		
GDR		
UK		
PRC		
RI		
RP		
FRN		

3. How is the chief executive chosen in

   a. a parliamentary system?
   b. a presidential system?
   c. a one-party system?

THINKING IT THROUGH

This chapter centers around one question:

Which chief executive faces the most competition in exercising sovereignty?

Fill out the following chart to compare the amount of sovereignty each chief executive exercises. At the top of the chart are the names of the nation-states; on the left is a list of potential competitors for sovereignty in each of these nation-states. If, in a given nation-state, the competitor provides the chief executive with significant competition on a regular basis, place a numeral 3 in the box. If the competitor provides important but relatively minor competition for the chief executive, place a numeral 1 in the box. (You may assign a value of 2 if you are undecided.) Leave the box blank if the competitor doesn't exist in that nation-state, or if it provides no significant competition in exercising sovereignty.

Use the figures and tables in the chapter for quick reference as you decide what value to assign in each case. Then total the scores for each nation-state. A higher score indicates that the chief executive has relatively greater competition from other individuals and institutions in exercising sovereignty. In chapter 3, we will continue this exercise, examining some additional factors that affect the extent to which a chief executive exercises sovereignty. The numbers you total on the charts do not have "scientific" meaning, but they do give you a simple way to pull together the information in these two chapters and to get some sense of what types and degrees of competition each chief executive faces.

Keep in mind that the CIS has no chief executive. But the individual sovereign republics have chief executives, whose systems operate along the lines of the reforms instituted throughout the Soviet Union in 1989. Think of those chief executives and the restraints on them as you answer these questions.

Nation-State	Abbreviation
United States of America	USA
Union of Soviet Socialist Republics, 1922–91	USSR
Commonwealth of Independent States (formed from USSR in 1991)	CIS
Federal Republic of (West) Germany	FRG
(East) German Democratic Republic (absorbed into Federal Republic of Germany in 1990)	GDR
Great Britain (England, Wales, Scotland)	GB
United Kingdom (England, Wales, Scotland, Northern Ireland)	UK
People's Republic of China	PRC
Republic of India	RI
Republic of Peru	RP
Federal Republic of Nigeria (under military rule, 1966–79, 1983–) (presidential system, after 1993?)	FRN1 FRN2

	USA	USSR 1922–89	USSR 1990–91	CIS 1992–	FRG	GDR	UK	PRC	RI	RP	FRN1	FRN2
1. national legislature, lower house												
2. national legislature, upper house												
3. ceremonial head of state												
4. government Cabinet												
5. single-party Secretariat/ military high command												
6. local and regional governments												
7. state-level governments												
Total of lines 1–7												

Now, ask yourself:

1. In each of the seven horizontal columns, what differentiates a 1 from a 3 in your mind? For example, what makes one legislature a stronger competitor in exercising sovereignty than another?

2. The United States, Peru, and perhaps Nigeria after 1993 all have presidential systems; in which does the chief executive have the most competition from these seven sets of institutions?

3. Do chief executives in systems with one-party or military rule have less competition from these sources than those in presidential and parliamentary systems?

chapter 3

POLITICAL PARTIES AND ELECTIONS

We saw in the last chapter that chief executives in parliamentary and presidential systems need cooperation from legislatures. In both systems, the chief executive must work behind the scenes through a political party to secure that cooperation during and after elections. The chief executive in a one-party system is also head of a political party. In which of these three systems—presidential, parliamentary, or one-party—is it easier for the chief executive to gain cooperation from other members of his or her political party? And is it beneficial to you and me if our chief executive has that ability?

What role do elections and political parties play in determining the amount of sovereignty that ends up in the hands of the chief executive? As we continue our discussion from the last chapter, we will address that question here. How much effect can you and I have on who obtains sovereignty and thus has ultimate control over what we do? How can our involvement in politics affect the way that control is distributed and exerted? How should that control be distributed and exerted? In this chapter, we will explore all these issues.

FACILITATING COOPERATION AMID COMPETITION

Elections are the ultimate device by which you and I can choose those who exercise sovereignty and affect the way they behave. Elections have long been an important part of the political picture in the United States, but voter participation in elections is declining. One reason may be that many Americans do not understand how political parties and elections work, and therefore do not fathom the degree of influence individual citizens can exert through them; this is a subject we will address in the second section of this chapter. Voters may also become confused by some of the technicalities surrounding elections; the last section of this chapter helps you understand three of the most confusing of those technicalities (registration, gerrymandering, and multi- or single-member districts with plurality or majority win).

But first, many citizens do not comprehend the role elections play in determining whether their government can act to address problems or remains paralyzed. Elections may or may not help induce cooperation among those who share sovereignty as they seek to address problems.

We begin by examining how elections can most effectively facilitate cooperation. As you read the next eight paragraphs, see whether you think cooperation among elected officials is easier to obtain when general elections are open to all sorts of candidates, or when they are not.

A **general election** is a government-sponsored event, usually lasting an entire day, in which all citizens legally defined as eligible voters may register their choices for who will hold particular public offices. To do so, voters go to public buildings designated for the day as polling places and record the candidate of their preference for each open public office (or ''seat'') within the executive, legislative, or judiciary branches of government. Each voter

Congress party voter assistance booth, Calcutta, India, election day, 1967.
Bob Gamer

records his or her choices by drawing an X on a printed ballot, writing in a name, or using some sort of voting machine.

A **candidate** in a general election is anyone seeking an office or seat. Candidates who win occupy the public offices for which the elections are held. If voters were simply to write down names at random, it would be hard for anyone to amass many votes, and people who did not seek or desire the offices might receive many votes. Therefore individuals are usually nominated, or chosen, ahead of time by political parties. These parties then formally register their choices for each office with government election officials.

The individuals parties select to submit to the voters in general elections are the parties' **nominees,** or people who seek office with the endorsement of the political party. Many individuals may indicate their desire to be nominated by their party, but once the party makes its choices, those not selected usu-ally withdraw as candidates and shift their support to the party's nominees. If the rules allow it, individuals not affiliated with a political party may also solicit enough signatures from registered voters to get their names on the general election ballot; such individuals are **independent candidates** seeking public office without the endorsement of a political party. Finally, while party nominees and independent candidates may appear on the ballot, some voters may also write in other names on their ballots—names which may or may not be counted. Figure 3.1 sums up the process of selecting candidates for a general election.

Citizens who vote in the general election make the final choice as to who will occupy the public offices at stake; those candidates who win the general election become **elected officeholders**. Elected officeholders have the authority to exercise sovereignty because the people confer this authority through the act of voting. They have the right to

Figure 3.1   Narrowing the field: Choosing candidates for a general election.

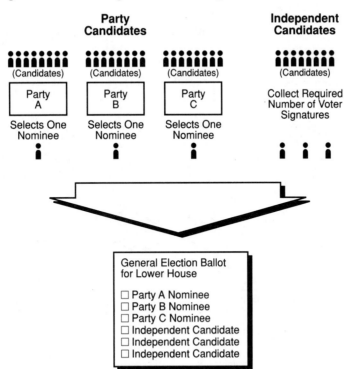

perform specified duties for a certain length of time because government confers this right through law.

As we learned in chapter 1, political parties choose individuals as their nominees to run in general elections for public offices, and they try to keep the nominees who become elected officeholders cooperating on a variety of shared objectives. If one political party excludes other parties from submitting nominees, and does not allow individuals unaffiliated with parties to seek or occupy elected offices, voters at general elections have a "choice" of only one candidate, or perhaps two from the same party. Such a one-party election is not competitive. By contrast, a **competitive general election** as shown in figure 3.2, offers voters a choice of independent candidates and nominees from different political parties, with the same rules applying to all candidates and a fair, secret, voting process.[1] The two main objectives of a political party—

electing officeholders, and getting them to cooperate after they are elected—are not easy to accomplish in a nation-state with competitive elections. To be elected, nominees must attract enough votes to win; that usually means trying to appeal to a lot of voters with diverse points of view. To govern, those who share sovereignty must cooperate; if officeholders come from different parties which are antagonistic to one another, or from one party which contains people with many different viewpoints, that cooperation may be hard to achieve.

Cooperation may be induced by limiting the extent to which officeholders other than the chief executive share in sovereignty. We learned in the last chapter that under parliamentary systems, lower houses must cooperate with the chief executive or risk triggering new elections. In presidential systems, the threat of a presidential veto may induce legislative cooperation. Some upper houses of the

Figure 3.2   An open or competitive election: Nominees from each party may appear on each ballot.

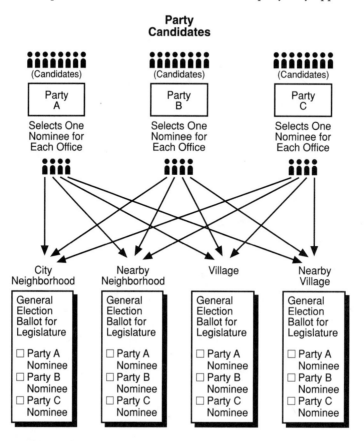

legislature cannot prevent legislation from passing. Some systems have no states to compete in exercising sovereignty, or states with few revenues or bureaucrats. Even when state and local governments have their own bureaucracies, national laws may give the chief executive the right to direct their activities. All these arrangements foster cooperation by limiting the sovereignty of officeholders other than the chief executive; officeholders with little power are less likely to oppose the chief executive's proposals. Still, as we also saw in the last chapter, it is difficult for any chief executive to entirely eliminate competition in sharing sovereignty. If nothing else, he or she must rely on various levels of bureaucracy to carry out policy. Even if bureaucrats hired by

national officials operate at the state and local levels, officials and private citizens in those localities may share in directing the bureaucrats' behavior.

Another way to create cooperation among government officials is to place limits on which parties may run in elections. As the "nucleus" party in the Soviet Union, the Communist Party simply outlawed all other parties. The Communist Party in China, like the communist party in the former East Germany, strictly defines which parties may and may not run in elections; this largely excludes other parties from sharing in sovereignty. It is generally arranged that the few approved parties will not compete directly against one another; in some areas, one fields a nominee, and in another area, another does

Figure 3.3   A closed election: Only one party's nominee appears on each ballot.

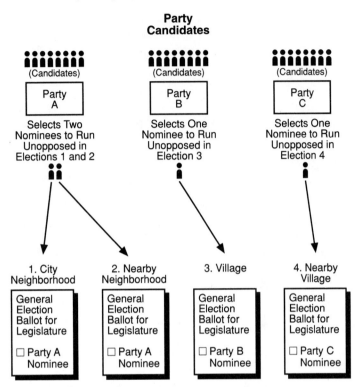

so (figure 3.3). All the winners thus come from parties which cooperate with one another in selecting nominees, and these officeholders can be expected to continue cooperating after their assured elections (assured because they run unopposed).

In 1990, East Germany merged with West Germany; the Communist Party in the Soviet Union ceased being defined as the "nuclear" party in 1990, and was outlawed in 1991. Under military rule in Nigeria, no parties were allowed to organize or run for office; the 1992 constitution allows the existence of only two parties, set up by the military government. Yet even when other parties are outlawed, ruling parties or coalitions try to include leaders from various regions, ethnic and cultural groups, social classes, and professions; the rulers act on the premise that it is better to have such groups inside, where they can be watched, than outside, where they may grow angry and rebellious. Bringing them into the party or ruling coalition introduces the potential for conflict and competition, but the party can control these conflicts from within. Figure 3.4 shows whether each system we are studying allows freely competing political parties.

Let's review what we have discussed thus far. Chief executives have strengthened ability to induce cooperation from other officials

- if they lead a parliamentary system under which they write and pass all major legislation (or, at least, are authorized to veto legislation under a presidential system),

- if they have no state governments to compete with,

Figure 3.4   National variations in parties' freedom to compete.

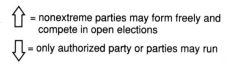

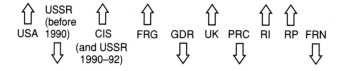

Figure 3.5   Controlling competition: Ways in which a chief executive can control competition.

Chief Executive

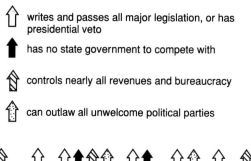

- if other levels of government control little bureaucracy or revenues, and/or
- if they can outlaw any unwelcome political parties.

As we have discovered, and as figure 3.5 shows, it is rare to find a chief executive with all these attributes; even with them, a chief executive may find it hard to gain cooperation within his or her own political party. Chief executives need cooperation from a great variety of groups (figure 3.6). In modern nation-states, it is difficult to build this cooperation without organizing a political party at the grassroots to thrash up support. A chief executive without a political party (for example, a military ruler) must either create one or ally with other institutions which can assist in obtaining cooperation from government officials and private citizens.

Is cooperation easier to obtain when a system allows for only one party, or when parties can compete freely? If the latter, are parties better able to induce cooperation under a presidential or a parliamentary system? Those questions engage political scientists who study how political systems handle conflict. We shall return to them in the third

Figure 3.6   Even strong chief executives need help and support from other officials and various groups.

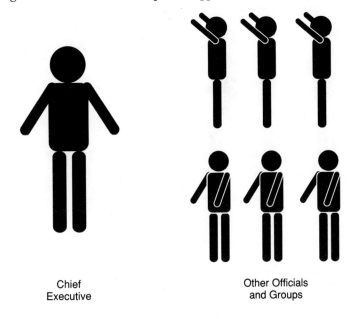

Chief
Executive

Other Officials
and Groups

section of this chapter. But first, let's focus more closely on how political parties choose their nominees and on how that can affect cooperation among officeholders.

PARTY RULES AFFECTING COOPERATION

A chief executive's ability to induce his or her party's members to work together is affected by three aspects of party organization. Rules which make it easier for the chief executive to induce cooperation may also make it harder for individual citizens to affect the choice, and the behaviors, of officeholders. Three such rules involve membership, permanent staff, and the way a party chooses its leaders and nominees.

Membership

Except for in the United States, political parties in all these systems have formal membership. The tightest membership rules apply in the communist parties and Peru's Alianza Popular Revolucionaria

Americana (APRA). In these parties, local party officials choose the party members; to join, one must wait for a period of time and be judged as a candidate for membership. The party may also expel those who dissent from its policies (see figure 3.7). The new political parties forming in the CIS generally indicate that membership is open to anyone over sixteen years of age willing to pay dues; but the parties reserve the right to refuse membership to, or take it from, those who do not conform to party guidelines. As with communist parties, national party officials reserve the final decisions about who can be a party member. All these parties also charge dues (required annual membership fees) and hold regular meetings for members. Voting on important issues, such as choosing officers, is reserved for a smaller group of members chosen to serve on branch committees; higher levels of the party must also approve candidates for membership on those committees.

National leaders of parties with such strict membership rules may exclude or expel groups and individuals who might wish to challenge the party's

Figure 3.7 Choosing party members in Peru, USSR, CIS, East Germany, and China.

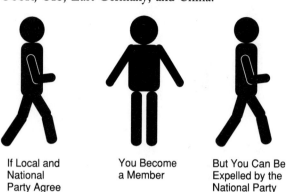

If Local and National Party Agree

You Become a Member

But You Can Be Expelled by the National Party

Figure 3.8 Differences in party membership rules. Arrows indicate features that strengthen political parties' ability to control membership.

Major Political Parties

⇧ choose members

⬆ charge dues

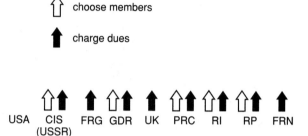

USA   CIS (USSR)   FRG   GDR   UK   PRC   RI   RP   FRN

national policies.[2] At the same time, a party wishing to retain support throughout the nation-state must be responsive to issues and groups important in each region. That makes it necessary to admit individuals from groups, and with ideas, different from those which dominate at the national level. Primary party organizations of communist parties operate in neighborhoods, collective farms, industries, the military, unions, schools, professional organizations, and other institutions throughout great, culturally diverse regions; such groups inevitably disagree on many matters.

In the United Kingdom, West Germany, and India, anyone willing to pay dues may join one of the major political parties. Members of labor unions in the United Kingdom are automatically enrolled in the Labour Party.[3] While these parties do not choose their members, they have some idea of who will attend party meetings. While India's Congress party officially has 10 million paying members, who are free to join, party participation is limited to 250,000 "active" members chosen by the party. Nigerian political coalitions have largely been loose affiliations of ethnic associations, trade unions, youth groups, and political parties; their membership lists have probably not been carefully kept. Political parties in the United States have no formal membership lists or dues;[4] that makes it difficult for either local or national leaders to know who might participate in party activities.

Figure 3.8 highlights differences in political parties' membership and dues policies in the nine systems under study. Systems that allow political parties to choose members and charge dues may give the chief executive greater opportunity to gain the cooperation of party members. But they also make it harder for outsiders to challenge party and government policies.

Permanent Staff

Another rule that affects a chief executive's ability to secure party cooperation involves the party's ability to hire and pay a permanent staff. The Communist Party of the Soviet Union had 150,000 to 200,000 full-time paid staff, the **apparatchiki,** who were sent throughout the country to work with local and regional party organizations.[5] These workers were not part of the government, but they closely monitored the activities of government officials to see that they accorded with the wishes of the party. Even when the Communist Party was outlawed in 1991, many *apparatchiki* stayed on the payrolls; in republics where the Communist Party simply renamed itself, they often continue to function as before. The East German Socialist Unity Party (the communist party in East Germany) had similar *apparatchiki,* as does the Communist Party of China, which calls them **cadres.** Orders can be handed

Figure 3.9 In communist systems, party employees monitor government officials.

Party Employees

⇑ monitor government officials

| USA | USSR | FRG | GDR | UK | PRC | RI | RP | FRN |

down through, but also resisted and restyled by, such workers. They may strengthen the hand of the national leadership by reporting on local party or government officials' efforts to resist national directives; they may also choose to join in that resistance, quietly or overtly, by developing ties with local officials. Political parties in the other six political systems hire few full-time paid workers (figure 3.9).

Choosing Party Leaders and Nominees

Formal membership and permanent staff can make it easier for chief executives to control officeholders. In addition, a chief executive who personally selects his or her party's officers and nominees for general elections has the ability to control the legislature and keep the party unified; all party officials and legislators know they will not be nominated to serve again if they fail to cooperate with this party leader. A chief executive with no control over nominations cannot expect cooperation from officeholders, since they can obtain and keep their offices even without the support of the chief executive or their party's leader. Let's look at how nominees are chosen in the nine systems, noticing how the control chief executives exert over the process varies.

The chief executive in the United States has little direct control over the selection of party nominees. In fact, you as a citizen may have a more direct effect than the president on picking a party's nominees and, ultimately, the officeholders.

In some states, government-sponsored elections called **primary elections** take place at public polling places prior to the general election. Both the major political parties, the Republican and Democratic parties, use primary elections to choose their officials and nominees. Anyone who presents election officials with a prescribed number of signatures from eligible voters endorsing his or her candidacy may appear on one of the ballots at these elections—even someone who has never been a party official, officeholder, or even active in the party's activities. To save money on operating the polls,[6] both the Republican and the Democratic primaries are usually held on the same day. Anyone registered to vote may participate; they simply go to their normal polling place, anytime during the day of the primary, and ask for the Republican or Democratic ballot (each voter can vote in only one party's primary).[7] Public and party officials in each state decide whether and when to hold such elections and what candidates will be chosen through them.

In some states, parties choose their nominees for the House of Representatives, the Senate, the presidency,[8] and state party officers in primaries. Other states rely entirely on another process, called a caucus, to choose all nominees, or hold caucuses to choose nominees for certain offices and primaries to choose nominees for others. Primary elections for presidential candidates actually elect delegates to the national presidential nominating conventions; at the convention, these delegates will choose the party's nominee to run for president in the general election.[9] Primary winners for offices within the state simply become the party's nominee in the general election. Figure 3.10 shows the process by which states with primaries choose their nominees for the House of Representatives for a general election.

In states which choose to hold them, any registered voter may attend a party **caucus,** a meeting held in a church, school, or private home to choose party officers and delegates for party conventions (see figure 3.11). Party officers often prefer not to widely publicize these meetings. Participants must take the trouble to find out where the meeting in their ward, township, or county will be held and

Figure 3.10   Choosing nominees for the U.S. House of Representatives: States with primaries.

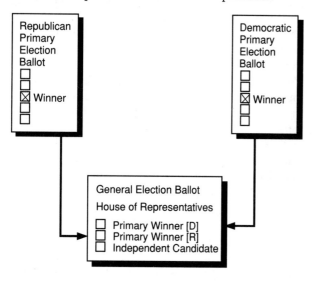

Figure 3.11   Choosing nominees for the U.S. House of Representatives: States with caucuses.

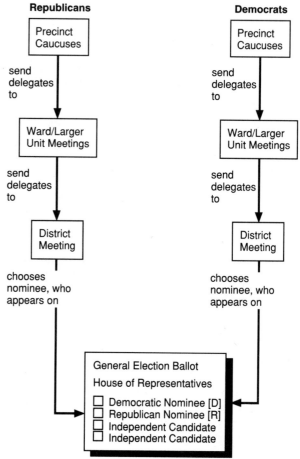

must devote an entire evening to attending it; the rules of procedure at these meetings are intricate. This keeps down the number of participants and makes it easier for party officials and their closest friends to control the proceedings. Usually certain individuals announce they are candidates seeking certain offices (and visit with local party officials to make promises and deals) before the caucus; the names of those individuals are likely to be proposed from the floor, perhaps along with names of individuals who have not previously announced they are seeking office. Sometimes a candidate deliberately running as an outsider works to pack the rooms with supporters who do not normally attend such meetings. Those attending indicate their selection by dividing into separate parts of the room and raising their hands or filling out slips of paper.[10] They then choose delegates to regional and/or state meetings,[11] which in turn choose state-level nominees and state delegations to the national presidential nominating conventions.[12] Some states choose their delegates to the presidential nominating conventions by caucuses, and others by primaries (figure 3.12).

Under the U.S. system, it is hard for anyone to control a political party. Parties can make rules that help party leaders gain some control—rules specifying that elected officials be entitled to participate in state and national presidential nominating conventions, or that primaries and caucuses be held at times when turnout will be limited; rules making it easier for those already holding office to control who runs for state party offices in the primaries and caucuses, or assuring that more delegates come from

Figure 3.12 Choosing U.S. presidential nominees: How parties choose their candidates in states with primaries and states with caucuses.

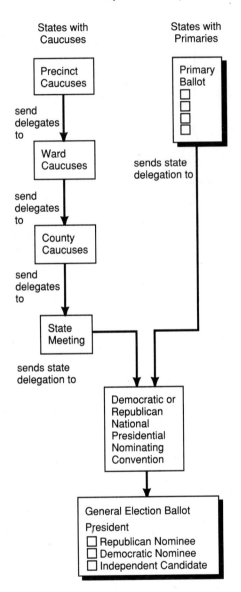

wards and precincts where officeholders have clout. The individual party organizations of each state decide on some of these details, so rules vary from state to state in both major parties. But because many people are involved even in making choice-limiting rules like these, no one person has a definitive last word on nominees.

The system in the United Kingdom gives more control to party leaders. The Members of Parliament from the Conservative and Liberal parties choose the national leaders of their parties (and thus the shadow or sitting prime minister) from among their own ranks. Since 1981, the Labour Party has chosen its leader and its final list of nominees for Parliament by first allowing local party organizations to shorten the list, then making final selections in a conference of delegates, with the Members of Parliament from that party holding 30 percent of the vote (figure 3.13).[13] When an election is called, even sitting Members of Parliament must be chosen by this conference to run again for their own seats. In contrast, the leaders of the Conservative and Liberal parties—rather than a conference of delegates—decide whether sitting Members of Parliament can run for office when an election is called. These parties do have committees to interview prospective nominees,[14] and they allow local party organizations to make the final nominating selections for districts in which they do not have a Member of Parliament, or in which the current Member will not seek reelection. But because party leaders decide whether sitting Members may run again, Members of Parliament who vote against bills presented by a prime minister from their party[15] run a risk; they may not be allowed to seek reelection as a nominee of their party. Obviously, this makes them inclined to cooperate with their party's prime minister.

India's Congress party gives party leaders still more power. In addition to choosing nominees for the Lok Sabha, the leader of the Congress party (chosen by a caucus of members of the Lok Sabha) also chooses nominees for the state assemblies, in close consultation with state and provincial party leaders. This often results in a tug of war, with no

Figure 3.13   Selecting party leaders and nominees for Parliament in the United Kingdom.

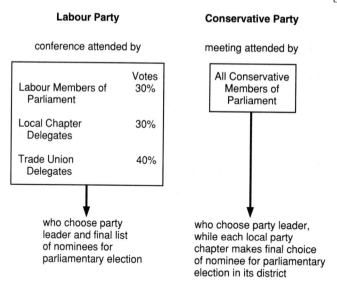

clarity as to who makes the final choices. The Congress party leader has frequently faced strong challenges from portions of the party which resist this control; parts of the party have even split away to form or join other parties. Leaders of rival parties also attempt to exert control from the top.

Peru's system is equally straightforward. Most political parties center around one individual, who has a strong voice in selecting all party officers and candidates. The most organized party, APRA, is led by a central committee which chooses party officers and candidates in both national and regional elections. Nigerian political parties have also centered around individual leaders. A military ruler, General Babangida, tried to end this individual control in 1989 by outlawing all but two newly created parties, and by introducing legislative primaries open to all voters.[16]

The Chancellor of the Federal Republic of Germany has less control over his or her party's nominations than prime ministers in India and the United Kingdom. As figure 3.14 shows, delegates chosen by local party chapters attend state party conventions, which approve state party lists of nominees

for Bundestag seats; since both national and state party leaders are likely to command support at these gatherings, these leaders have considerable say over who is nominated. However, German voters cast two votes in their parliamentary elections; one for a candidate from the state party lists, and another for an individual candidate. The individual candidates are nominated by a secret primary ballot of all party members in the district or by a selection committee chosen by all district party members.

In China, and formerly in East Germany and the Soviet Union, the national leaders of the communist party appoint all party officials and approve all nominations for legislative elections.[17] *Apparatchiki* or *cadres* appointed by the central party are always part of that process. Once people have entrenched themselves in local and provincial[18] party offices, where they can choose local party members and exchange favors such as jobs or money, it becomes hard for national party leaders to remove them from office; they usually have many friends in important local positions, because they themselves assured that those individuals gained their positions! Local party officials who entrench themselves in this way can

Figure 3.14 Selecting new nominees for parliamentary elections in the Federal Republic of Germany. Voters cast two votes: one for the party list, one for an individual nominee.

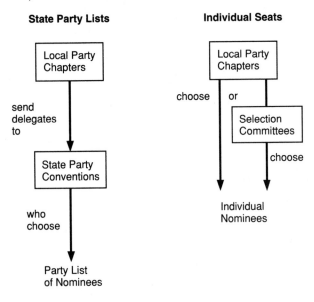

often resist the national party leader and may have incentive to do so if people in their region disagree with national party policies. Thus, the national leaders are disposed to closely consult local officials when making nominations.

The system in the former Soviet Union is changing rapidly. Before the 1989 elections, under **glasnost** (Gorbachev's political reform program), public meetings were held where additional nominees were selected; they then had to pass a screening by an election commission dominated by the Communist Party. Thus, for the first time, nominees could emerge, both within and outside the party, who were not the first choices of local party leaders and *apparatchiki;* however, they still had to run as nominees of the Communist Party. In 1990, the constitution was amended to allow groups to select nominees who were not affiliated with the Communist Party. As long as they did not foment social unrest, and as long as they obeyed the law, they could even form political parties, and these parties could submit their candidates to election commissions for approval. However, those commissions sometimes rejected nominees on technicalities, or declared others to be the rightful nominees, or allowed dozens of candidates to run for a seat in the general election, hoping to split the opposition vote so their favorites had a better chance.

Even after the Communist Party was outlawed, these election commissions remain within the individual republics; they retain the same powers, and they are often controlled by the same people. The Communist Party simply renamed itself in each CIS republic and continues to function and win some elections. Since the election commissions control who eventually appears on the ballots, this system falls short of being a full **multiparty system,** where any group of citizens is free to form its own political party and (if not deemed by the government as too extreme) submit nominees to voters in competitive general elections. It does allow the legislatures in the republics to include deputies from a variety of political parties, and it allows differing political parties to control the legislatures and executives of individual republics.

In India and Peru, the national leaders of each party, in consultation with regional party leaders they selected,[19] choose their party's nominees for the lower house of the legislature. In China (and the former East Germany), the chief executive has final say on nominations for the national party Congresses and legislatures but must negotiate with local leaders. In the United Kingdom, the CIS, the United States, Nigeria, and West Germany, the chief executive's control over these nominations is less direct—in the United States, considerably less. But in the United Kingdom and West Germany, the chief executive can play a strong role in preventing a sitting Member of Parliament from running again. Figure 3.15 compares the way each system chooses nominees for the lower house of the legislature. The less the chief executive controls these nominations, the less he or she controls officials elected to legislatures. That makes it harder to induce cooperation from them.

Figure 3.15   Differences in selecting nominees for the lower house of the national legislature. Arrows pointing up indicate features that weaken a chief executive's or party's control over nominations; arrows pointing down indicate features that strengthen a chief executive's or party's control over nominations and ability to secure cooperation.

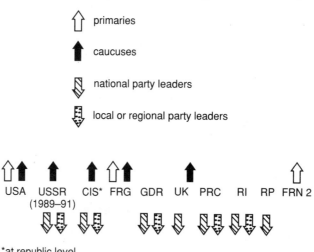

*at republic level

Consensual Parties, Splinter Parties, and Cooperation

We have learned that the rules under which they operate give some chief executives a freer hand than others to induce cooperation from elected officials. But *should* other elected officials (for example, the United States Congress) cooperate with the chief executive? The answer to that can be very personal: If you or I like what the chief executive is doing, we will welcome such cooperation, so that these actions can succeed. If we do not like what he or she is doing, we may prefer that other officeholders or bureaucrats refuse to cooperate.

In the latter case, one way to make our legislature independent of our chief executive is to keep the nominating process loose, with considerable input from rank-and-file party participants. Doing so allows a great variety of groups to enter the party and increases the chances that the party will occa-

sionally nominate candidates who agree with our views. However, an open nominating process may also decrease the party's chances to arrive at a consensus once it obtains power. If a nominee did not need to cooperate with other party members to attain office, he or she may have less incentive to cooperate once in office.

Even a party whose nominations are controlled from the top may gain diversity if other parties effectively oppose it. Parties which seek to appeal to (or to obtain votes from) high percentages of the populace from varying regions and groups are called **consensual parties.** A chief executive recognizes that opposition from another consensual party must be taken seriously if the party is popular enough to elect its party leader to the post of chief executive in a forthcoming election. The opposition party, in turn, seeks support from many individuals who voted for the ruling party. This gives them an incentive to appear reasonable and to avoid making

Figure 3.16 Consensual parties seek the support of many diverse groups; splinter parties appeal to narrow groups of voters.

Target Audience

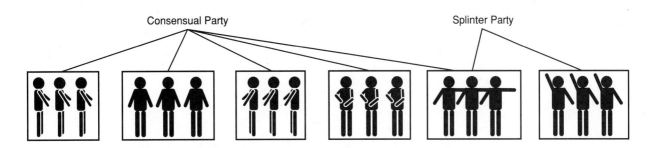

statements or taking actions that might offend potential voters. In other words, if opposition parties are capable of taking over the chief executive's position, they may restrain their opposition somewhat to avoid offending anyone who might help elect their nominee. Consensual parties thus promote diversity, but in an atmosphere conducive to cooperation.

The United States, the United Kingdom, and West Germany each have two consensual parties; rule usually alternates between them. India's only consensual party, the Congress party, has held the prime minister's post during most of its history as an independent nation-state, but it faces coalitions of parties that can unseat it. Nigeria's military created two consensual parties in 1989, anticipating a return to civilian rule.

Even if a nation-state contains only one party with a rigid ideology, it still has incentive to seek supporters within all institutions it needs to run the economy and government and to control the populace of various regions; that support can make it a consensual party. Without opposition, though, such a ruling party is likely to become careless about appealing to high percentages of the rank-and-file members of all those groups. As we shall see later, East Germany's communist party carefully cultivated allied splinter parties among all segments of the populace. But as soon as citizens had the chance to vote for competing parties, few continued to vote for the communist party and its allies. Once the Soviet Union let voters select nominees from opposition parties, many did so as well. When the Communist Party was outlawed later in the year, it left the individual republics, and eventually the CIS, without a consensual party, although many continue to vote for nominees of the Communist Party's successor parties. The Communist Party sought support among all ethnic groups. So does China's Communist Party, which retains one-party rule.

Parties whose members are rigid in their support of a certain ideology, or in their support of a few special policies or interests, appeal to only narrow segments of the populace; such parties are called **splinter parties** (figure 3.16). Since they lack broad support and have little chance of filling the chief executive's position, splinter parties may be tough and tenacious in their opposition. They can at least remain a permanent irritant to the chief executive, reminding him or her of views that might otherwise be muffled in the quest for cooperation.

Splinter party members have a greater chance of winning seats in a legislature than as chief executive, especially if those who support them can vote, live together in the same district, and need not constitute a majority in that district to win. Some ruling communist parties (like those in East Germany and

Figure 3.17 Existence of consensual parties and/or splinter parties in each system. Arrows pointing up indicate features that strengthen ruling consensual parties; arrows pointing down indicate features that strengthen the opposition parties.

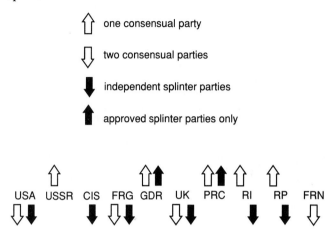

China) reserve seats for the splinter parties they approve of, while outlawing all other parties (figure 3.17). After opposition parties were authorized in the Soviet Union in 1990, many splinter parties began winning votes in central and republic elections. In the past, civilian rule in Nigeria has always been secured through coalitions of splinter parties; the 1992 constitution, however, bans splinter parties. Peru's APRA is a consensual party, but has only held the presidency for one five-year term; Peru is usually governed during civilian rule by short-term coalitions of temporarily formed splinter parties. India's Congress party is opposed by coalitions of splinter parties.

All nine of these political systems have **universal suffrage**, meaning that all adult citizens have the right to vote unless they have serious criminal records. All have come to this gradually. When the United States was founded, voting was confined to white males with property and education. In the United Kingdom, Germany, and the United States,[20] voting rights gradually expanded during the nineteenth century; women did not receive the franchise (vote) until this century.[21] After their respective revolutions in 1917 and 1949, the Soviet Union and China initiated suffrage for all adults. India and Nigeria adopted it after they won their independence (in 1947 for India and 1963 for Nigeria); in northern Nigeria, women only achieved suffrage in 1976. Until 1979, Peruvians illiterate in Spanish could not vote.

When suffrage is very limited, splinter parties that appeal only to voters can win national elections. If the groups they appeal to have few differences, government officeholders from the different parties can easily cooperate and work together. Expansion of suffrage can result in a proliferation of splinter parties battling one another in legislatures, or in the creation of consensual parties to temper that conflict. The more universal the vote, the greater the chance that a variety of views will emerge and clash. Since splinter parties must form coalitions to take control of a chief executive's office, and since they are often not willing to compromise, it is difficult for them to induce cooperation between chief executives and legislatures. If one party in the coalition disagrees with the others on a particular issue, that party is liable to withhold cooperation from the chief executive.

ELECTION RULES AND CONSENSUAL PARTIES

Three sets of rules about election procedures can make it easier, or harder, for consensual parties to form and sustain themselves. These rules involve registration, gerrymandering, and whether a district is single- or multi-member with a majority or plurality win.

Registration

Even with universal suffrage, not everyone may be entitled to vote in any given election. In the United States, citizens must formally **register** to vote before they can vote in an election; many adults, especially among those with less education, fail to do so.[22] This means that on election day, suffrage is not actually universal, because not everyone is registered (and therefore entitled) to vote. In most states, people have had to register in a public place, making it inconvenient to do so. Some states have passed "motor-voter" laws which let people register when renewing their driver's licenses, at welfare and unemployment offices, or by postcard. In 1993, Congress passed, and President Clinton signed, a national "motor-voter" law.

In the other eight political systems, registration is far easier. In the United Kingdom, election authorities mail postcards to voters, which the voters must return; only 5 to 10 percent fail to do so. In Germany, the Soviet Union, the CIS, and China, election authorities keep track of eligible voters through other records, and individuals need merely appear at a polling place to vote. In India, Peru, and Nigeria, the government keeps less accurate records of residents, and election officials go to villages and neighborhoods to draw up lists of voters (who need not themselves make the effort to register). India manages to keep rather accurate records in this fashion. In Nigeria, the records are so inaccurate that people may find the election lists do not contain their names when they arrive at the polls. Since the unregistered come disproportionately from among the less educated portions of the populace, registration requirements handicap parties which cater to such voters. This hampers the formation of splinter parties appealing to the less educated and narrows the range of voters consensual parties must appeal to.

Gerrymandering

Sometimes voting rules call for all eligible voters in the entire nation, state, county, or city to cast their votes for candidates to a particular office. At other times, the rules call for one of those permanent political units to divide into two or more parts, each with an equal number of people,[23] so that the unit contains more than one **district.** Officials (usually a chief executive or legislators) must then draw temporary **district lines** to group together areas containing equal numbers of people; as the population grows, declines, or moves over the years, they must redraw those lines. At times, officials may be tempted to group together the neighborhoods and rural areas where their party receives more votes and to divide neighborhoods where opposing parties are stronger. Redrawing the lines to benefit one party or group is called **gerrymandering.**

Gerrymandering was named after a politician named Elbridge Gerry, who drew district lines that looked like long, wiggly salamanders to suit his purposes. To better understand gerrymandering, imagine that one ethnic group lives in a certain area and you do not want them represented as a group. You can split their territory between three larger districts, where they will constitute a smaller percentage of the total votes cast (figure 3.18); in this way, gerrymandering can help consensual parties. Similarly, if your ethnic group members are scattered and you want to combine them to give them a stronger influence, you can draw a long salamander to include them all in one district where they constitute a majority of voters. In this scenario, gerrymandering can help splinter parties with limited appeals. No nation-state is immune from gerrymandering.

Multi- or Single-Member Districts with Plurality or Majority Win

Along with registration and gerrymandering, complicated rules about who wins a district may help or hurt a political party. Election rules (whether in a

Figure 3.18   Two ways to divide three legislative districts. Gerrymandering combines certain voting groups to give them more power.

Dividing Legislative Districts

With Rectangular Boundaries

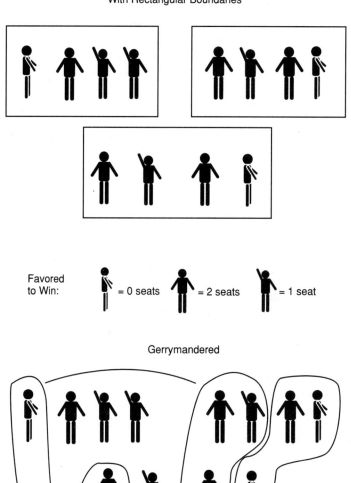

Favored to Win:
👤 = 0 seats   👤 = 2 seats   👤 = 1 seat

Gerrymandered

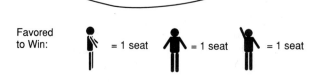

Favored to Win:
👤 = 1 seat   👤 = 1 seat   👤 = 1 seat

Figure 3.19 Election in a single-member district with majority rule. This rule helps consensual parties, who appeal to high numbers of voters, win seats.

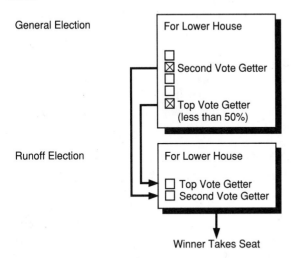

Figure 3.20 Election in a single-member district with plurality rule. This rule still favors consensual parties, though splinter parties may have slightly better chances of winning the seat.

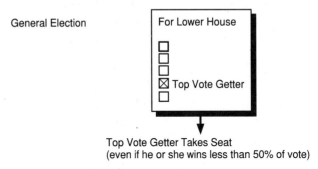

primary or a general election) may specify that a candidate must receive a majority (more than half) of the votes to win a seat. This would mean the district would be represented by only one individual. If more than two candidates ran for office in such a single-member, majority-win district, and if no one candidate received a majority of the votes, it would be necessary to allow for a **run-off election,** perhaps the following week, to let voters choose between the two candidates with the highest votes on the first round. These rules help consensual parties, which are geared to attracting high percentages of voters (figure 3.19).

On the other hand, election rules may specify that a candidate in a single-member district can win with only a **plurality** of votes, which means at least one more vote than any other candidate. This rule allows a candidate with less than 50 percent of the votes to win, but still makes it hard for splinter parties to win elections; splinter parties usually find it difficult to amass more votes in a district than the better-known consensual parties (figure 3.20).

Finally, the rules may specify that the two or three candidates with the most votes in a district all take seats, making it a **multimember district.** A candidate from a splinter party can win a seat, even with a small percentage of the vote in such a district, as long as he or she comes in second or third (figure 3.21). Sometimes the voters within a multimember district may be allowed to vote for more than one candidate to represent their district. This assures an even greater diversity of views in the legislature and allows splinter parties a greater chance to win seats.

Dividing larger districts into smaller ones with one representative each can have the same effect if the districts are drawn up to include minorities with similar voting patterns; in this case, even people who constitute a minority within a district, city, county, or state can hope to elect an officeholder sympathetic to their views. The representatives from those districts may still come from consensual parties, but multimember (or physically smaller) districts give splinter parties a better chance to compete nationwide and add more sharply critical voices to the legislature.

National legislatures in the United States,[24] the United Kingdom,[25] the former East Germany, and India all have (or had) single-member districts;

Figure 3.21 Election in a multimember district. This allows splinter parties a better chance to win seats and results in a more diverse legislature.

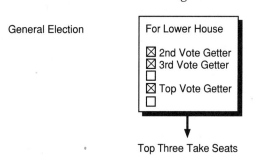

candidates can win these districts with a plurality of votes. The rules in Nigeria, China, the Federal Republic of Germany, Peru, and Russia require a bit more explanation. In Nigeria,[26] legislative districts are single-member with a plurality win. But the president must receive a majority of the vote, with a run-off election should that fail to happen on the first round. To further assure that the president represents all regions, he or she must win a third of the vote in two-thirds of the states, and political parties contesting presidential elections must hold offices in all local governments. Such arrangements encourage candidates to broaden their appeal, so they can win support from a variety of voters. So far, the Nigerian rules have only succeeded in creating temporary alliances of splinter parties and have encouraged mass fraud in election returns so that parties can artificially reach these goals. To prevent such abuses, Nigeria banned splinter parties in its 1992 constitution.

In China, units (for example, villages, neighborhoods, state factories, and military or cultural organizations) voting for delegates to party and peoples' congresses usually may select more than one candidate out of a larger list, which means they have multimember districts. This helps the "democratic parties" (splinter parties long allied with the Communist Party) to win seats; they are unlikely to use their positions to oppose government policies. Villages often contain several factions; different factions within the national and provincial party may work with factions at the village level to gain support for their candidates. As a result, the competition in the election campaign can become intense.

In the Federal Republic of Germany, as we saw earlier in the chapter, voters cast two votes in the Bundestag elections—one for a candidate on the general list drawn up by a state convention of one of the parties, and the other for a particular candidate running for a single-member seat in their district (who can win with a plurality of votes). If a party receives 5 percent of the total vote on the state lists, or wins majorities or pluralities in at least three districts, but does not receive as high a percentage of the single-member seats as its percentage of the total vote, a commensurate number of the candidates on its state lists will be chosen to serve. This gives each eligible party the same percentage of seats as their percentage of the vote, or **proportional representation.** This especially helps the splinter Free Democratic Party, which has been able to be part of coalition governments when the two major consensual parties—the Christian and Social Democrats—come close to a tie and need the Free Democrats to produce a majority and form a new Government.[27]

Peru had proportional representation in both houses of its legislature. For the Senate (which was abolished by President Fujimori in 1992), each party drew up one list of about a hundred nominees. Each voter cast one vote for a political party in the Senate race; the percentage of votes each party received determined how many of those on the list became senators. For the lower house, now called the Constituent Congress, formerly the Chamber of Deputies, the process is similar. Each region is allotted a certain number of seats (that is, each region is a multimember district), depending on its population. The parties create lists of nominees within each region; voters cast one vote for a political party to represent them in the Constituent Congress, and

Figure 3.22   Differences in elections for members of the lower house.

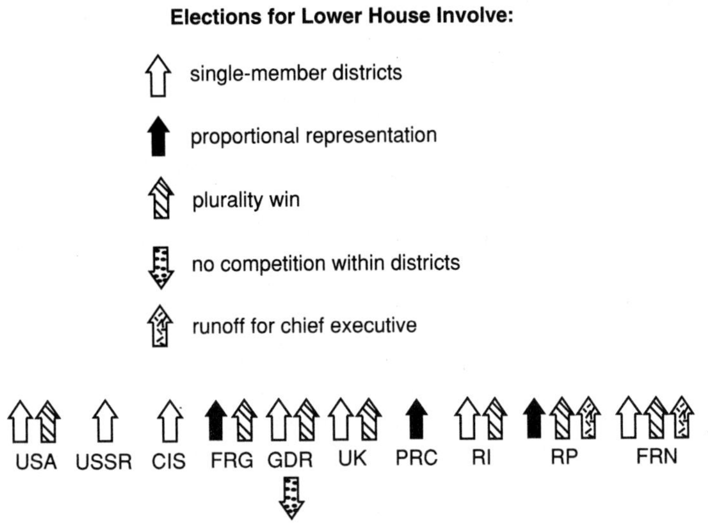

Elections for Lower House Involve:

⇧ single-member districts

⬆ proportional representation

⇪ plurality win

⬇ no competition within districts

⬆ runoff for chief executive

⇧⇧ ⇧ ⇧ ⬆⇪ ⇧⇧ ⇧⇧ ⬆ ⇧⇧ ⬆⇪ ⇧⇪⇧
USA USSR CIS FRG GDR UK PRC RI RP FRN
⬇

each party receives the same percentage of the region's seats as its percentage of the vote. Again, this is proportional representation. In the Peruvian presidential election, a run-off results if no candidate receives at least 36 percent of the votes on the first round.[28]

The Chinese, West German, and Peruvian proportional representation arrangements help small splinter parties win legislative seats with a low percentage of the total vote.[29] Citizens need not feel their vote is wasted if they vote for a party which will receive few votes; such a party still has a chance of winning seats. The single-member seats in the United States, the United Kingdom, East Germany, India, and Nigeria aid consensual parties; people know that parties that appeal to only a minority of voters in a district have no chance to gain a seat, so they tend to vote for those that do have a chance. That might help reduce the ferocity of competition within the legislature. However, in a nation-state with great ethnic diversity such as India,[30] Nigeria, or the Soviet Union, radical parties who happen to be popular in one region, but not nation-

wide, may still win legislative seats; that is why Nigeria banned splinter parties. The Soviet Union, trying to reduce that risk, used a single-member majority system; they required that each district of the Congress of People's Deputies elect only one deputy by a majority of votes. This system required run-off elections. Similar systems are still used in the individual republics.[31]

Figure 3.22 sums up the means by which each system elects representatives to the lower house of the legislature.

All these systems except Nigeria have contained both splinter and consensual political parties. Chief executives from consensual parties have led all these political systems except Nigeria; chief executives from splinter parties have led Peru, Nigeria, India, and the United Kingdom. In China, consensual parties other than the Communist Party are outlawed; that used to be the case in the Soviet Union and East Germany as well. No consensual parties have emerged in the CIS republics, while Peru and India each contain only one. The United States and the United Kingdom (with single-member, plurality-win districts), and Germany (with proportional representation) have more than one consensual party. There is no clear correlation between election rules and the presence of consensual parties.

CONCLUSION

No chief executive holds sovereignty alone. He or she needs cooperation from others within the government and political parties. Even Nigeria's and Peru's military rulers found it necessary to work with leaders of the parties they outlawed to control the civilian bureaucracy. Presidential, parliamentary, and one-party civilian systems are usually headed by leaders of consensual political parties with members from diverse backgrounds, or by leaders of splinter parties in coalition with leaders of other parties representing diverse backgrounds.

All these chief executives must contend to some extent with other elected officials they do not personally nominate. All must operate through bureaucracies they do not completely control. The inevitable diversity in these institutions makes cooperation more difficult to achieve.

One way to create cooperation is to place few limits on the chief executive, who can then pass legislation and administer laws with little interference. The peace created in this manner, though, can be deceptive. Ultimately, a chief executive who does not enjoy the support of the populace, and hence lacks authority, may appear to be strong but in fact be weak. He or she may give orders bureaucrats or the populace will not willingly obey. Military rulers, as well as leaders of consensual parties that ban other consensual parties, suffer from this danger. When the Berlin Wall fell, and East Germany's Socialist Unity Party suddenly faced competition from the consensual parties of the West, it suddenly became a small splinter party with little electoral support. Once Mikhail Gorbachev, who was not elected, faced competition from elected presidents of republics, those elected officials, who had the support of

voters, were able to take command of the direction of the nation-state. A fresh win by a substantial majority in a competitive general election can confer authority.

SUMMARY

To govern, those sharing sovereignty must cooperate with one another. If these officials are from opposing political parties, or from one party containing people with many different views, that cooperation may be hard to achieve.

It is easy for those with sovereignty to cooperate in governing, but harder for them to gain cooperation among all segments of society, when the chief executive can (1) outlaw other political parties, (2) control the admission of members into his or her own political party, (3) command a permanent full-time party staff, and (4) personally select party leaders and nominees for public office.

It is harder for those with sovereignty to cooperate in governing, but easier for them to gain cooperation among all segments of society when the system provides (1) nonmember access to party decision making, (2) primaries and caucuses to select nominees for office, (3) universal suffrage, and (4) plurality-win, multimember districts freely contested by both splinter and consensual parties.

To settle conflicts between groups within the nation, those with sovereignty also need authority, which derives from the respect and willing cooperation of the public. Ruling parties or coalitions, seeking that cooperation, generally try to include members and leaders from various regions, ethnic and cultural groups, social classes, and professions in their ranks. But when a chief executive maintains tight control over a political party, the wishes of portions of the populace may be ignored. At that point, such a chief executive, though appearing to exercise tremendous sovereignty, sacrifices some authority to rule and may be in danger of losing sovereignty.

NOTES

1. Unfair applications of voting rules include rounding up potential opposition candidates for police questioning during periods when they must personally appear at the election board to have their names certified for the ballot; excluding candidates from the ballot because they have a police record as a result of being rounded up for such questioning; preventing opposition candidates from holding campaign rallies or reaching voters through the media; killing opposition candidates during elections; keeping voters away from the polls with guns; allowing individuals to vote more than once; cheating on counting the votes; marking ballots so one's vote is not secret; and failing to allow properly elected candidates to occupy the offices for which they were chosen. In Nigeria, voters stand in line in front of the booth or candidate of their choice to cast their vote, meaning their votes are not secret.

2. In October 1990, the Politburo of the Communist Party of the Soviet Union threatened to expel Mikhail Gorbachev. To avert this, he quickly turned away from the reforms he had been trying to implement. Two months later, Foreign Minister Eduard Shevardnadze resigned, warning that a "shadow government," consisting of members of the military and the KGB, ruled from behind the scenes. Shevardnadze announced that he was helping create a new nationwide opposition party, the Democratic Reform Movement. When the Central Control Commission of the Communist Party called him before a disciplinary tribunal, he resigned from the party, saying that the party had agreed it would no longer expel members who dissent. The new parties in the CIS retain provisions in their charters allowing them to expel dissenters.

3. The October 1983 Conference Report of the Labour Party indicated that in 1982 the party had 273,803 individual members, 57,131 members through socialist societies, and 6,185,063 members affiliated with member trade unions.

4. American political parties keep large computer data banks of potential contributors, from whom they solicit financial contributions. One need not contribute financially to participate in party activities.

5. The party had apprenticeships; 2 percent of apprentices became full-time *apparatchiki*.

6. The government pays those who allow their buildings to be used for, and who operate, the polling places.

7. Some states have closed primaries; voters must ask for the same party's ballot for at least two elections in a row. This prevents them from switching from one party's primary to the other's in each consecutive election.

8. Thirty-six states held presidential primaries in 1988; in 1968, few did. By 1992, some states switched back from primaries to caucuses.

9. In most Republican and some Democratic primaries, the candidate receiving a plurality of votes (that is, more than any other candidate) on his or her party's ballots receives all the state's delegates. In the remaining states, the parties distribute delegates according to the percentage of the vote a candidate receives; the rules for that distribution can be complex.

10. If fewer than a specified percentage (for example, 15 percent) of those attending support a particular candidate and this percentage is insufficient to support a delegate, supporters of other candidates may try to persuade them to change their votes. Once everyone has settled on a candidate, the caucus will decide how to divide the group's delegates to the regional and/or state conventions. Each state party makes up detailed rules on this, using the guidelines of the national party; those rules may still be vague enough to allow caucus attenders to challenge the method used to divide delegates.

11. Nominees for county offices or legislative districts are chosen by meetings at those levels. Some delegates to the national presidential nominating conventions may be selected at regional meetings (for example, at a meeting attended by locally chosen delegates from all wards within a district served by a member of the U.S. House of Representatives). Other delegates to the national conventions may be selected at a state convention. Delegates to the state conventions are chosen at regional meetings attended by delegates from caucuses. Some delegates to the presidential nominating conventions are also selected directly by state party officers. All this varies between the parties, and from state to state.

12. In the general election, voters are actually voting for delegates to another convention, an electoral college. Each state is assigned a certain number of electoral votes, based on population. Before the general election, each nominee chooses individuals to serve as his or her "electors" for that state. A nominee receiving a plurality of votes in any state receives all that state's electoral votes to be cast by his or her chosen electors. On a given day (after the general election), the electors cast their votes—a custom which has been dubbed the "electoral college." To become president, a candidate must receive a majority of votes in the electoral college. If no one receives a majority, the House of Representatives picks the president from among the top three electoral college vote recipients (with each state delegation casting one vote).

13. Forty percent of the vote goes to the trade union delegation, and 30 percent to delegates from constituency parties. Party leaders have suggested changes in this system to make the final selection of nominees by mailing ballots to all party members, who would return them by mail (much as the constituency nominees are chosen in Germany). Sitting Members of Parliament would be allowed to stand again without balloting, unless a certain number of party members request a ballot in their district. Trade unions strongly resist those changes.

14. These committees include members close to the party leaders; such committees can prevent prospective candidates from proceeding further toward seeking their party's nomination.

15. The prime minister may then mandate that the "whip be withdrawn" from the Member. The whip is a Member of Parliament responsible for enforcing party discipline. If the whip is asked by the prime minister to withdraw from contact with a Member, it is a sign of radical displeasure with that Member.

16. When parties were allowed to organize in 1989, thirty groups formed; thirteen of them applied for recognition from the National Electoral Commission. General Babangida, the military leader, refused to recognize any of them and instead set up two parties, for which the electoral commission "synthesized" manifestos from those of the disbanded thirteen parties. The government also provided cars and offices for the parties, and the primaries were marked by massive fraud. This is discussed further in chapter 19.

17. East Germany and the Soviet Union held elections for legislatures. China's legislatures are each chosen by the next lowest legislature; local legislatures are chosen by local party leaders, consulting with cadres from the national party.

18. For an account of the important role played by provincial first secretaries as political go-betweens, see David S. G. Goodman, "Provincial Party First Secretaries in National Politics: A Categoric or a Political Group?" in David S. G. Goodman, ed., *Groups and Politics in the People's Republic of China* (Cardiff, England: University of Cardiff Press, 1984), pp. 68–82.

19. Before 1972, India's Congress party members who lived within a block elected their own committee members, who then elected some city or district committee members, who then elected state committees. In 1972, those elections were suspended to cut down on the independence of the state committees. In 1992, they were reintroduced.

20. In 1916, women could vote in only sixteen states, with 10 percent of the population. A constitutional amendment gave them nationwide suffrage in 1920. Cf. Alan P. Grimes, *The Puritan Ethic and Woman Suffrage* (New York: Oxford University Press, 1967). See also J. Morgan Kousser, *The Shaping of Southern Politics: Suffrage Restriction and the Establishment of the One-Party South, 1880–1910* (New Haven, Conn.: Yale University Press, 1974).

21. Women finally received the vote in Swiss national elections during the 1970s. The last Swiss canton excluding women from voting was ordered by the courts to allow women to vote in 1990.

22. Each state enacted its own registration laws, often with the intention of limiting suffrage among certain groups political leaders hoped would vote in smaller numbers. For discussion of the pros and cons of registration, see Walter Dean Burnham, "The Changing Shape of the American Political Universe," *American Political Science Review* 59 (March 1965): 7–28; Philip E. Converse, "Change in the American Electorate," in Angus Campbell and Philip E. Converse, eds., *The Human Meaning of Social Change* (New York: Russell Sage, 1972), pp. 266–301; Walter Dean Burnham, "Theory and Voting Research: Some Reflections on Converse's 'Change in the American Electorate.'" *American Political Science Review* 68 (September 1974): 1002–23; and Frances Fox Piven

and Richard A. Cloward, *Why Americans Don't Vote* (New York: Pantheon, 1988), pp. 26–95.

23. For example, a state may be entitled to more than one member in the lower house of the national legislature and will certainly have a number of separate members in the lower house of the state legislature. If each county, or city, were to get a certain number of seats, an area with very small population might be entitled to one officeholder, and another with a much larger population would also get only one officeholder. For the sake of fairness, each officeholder should represent the same number of people. That requires periodically redrawing lines to group together units containing the same number of people; those lines may cross over county, city, or other permanent lines on the map. Ten years later, the lines for the voting district may be redrawn to reflect shifts in where people live; the county and city lines will remain permanent (unless they have been redrawn for other reasons).

24. The U.S. president also wins on a plurality basis. Each state holds a certain number of electoral votes for the presidential race. The candidate with a plurality of votes in a given state wins all the electoral votes of that state. A candidate must win a majority of electoral votes, but may do so without winning a majority of popular votes. During this century, Presidents Wilson, Truman, Nixon, and Clinton have all won presidential elections without winning a majority of the popular vote.

25. In 1987, the Labour Party received 33 percent of the vote to the Alliance's 24 percent, but came away with 229 seats in the House of Commons (35 percent of the total), while the Alliance won only 22 seats (3 percent). In a system where a plurality wins the only seat in a single-member district, a close second is not good enough. In the same election, with 43 percent of the vote, the Conservatives took 373 seats (57 percent). At that point, some members of the Labour Party called for changes in the electoral system to provide for proportional representation. In 1992, the Conservatives received 43 percent of the vote and 52 percent of seats, Labour 35 percent and 42 percent, and the Liberal Democrats 18 percent and 3 percent. Not surprisingly, the Liberal Democrats advocate proportional representation. Were proportional representation in effect in 1987 and 1992, the Alliance and Liberal Democrats would

have received many more seats and become part of a coalition Government.

26. From 1979 to 1983, and again after 1993 if the government returns to civilian rule.

27. The Free Democrats usually get 6 to 10 percent of the total votes, giving them that portion of seats in the Bundestag. Even if their individual nominees do not win in any single district, as long as they have over 5 percent of the total vote, they receive the same portion of seats in the Bundestag (from their general list) as their percentage of the vote; without this system, they would receive no seats. Since neither the Christian Democrats nor the Social Democrats have gained a majority of seats in an election since 1949, they have often needed the Free Democrats' deputies to form a majority; hence, they include them in the Cabinet. Without this system, it would often be possible for one of these two major consensual parties to win a majority and rule on their own (see also footnote 25).

28. In the 1990 presidential election, Vargas Llosa received 33.9 percent and Alberto Fujimori 29 percent of the vote on the first round. Under a straight plurality-win rule, Llosa would have become president. As it was, Fujimori defeated him on the second round of votes.

29. In the first election for the Constituent Congress, held in 1992, the two parties backed by President Fujimori won 38 percent of the vote—five times more than any other single party. That gave these two parties an advantage in passing legislation, even though they are splinter parties.

30. To further assure diversity in India, the Scheduled (untouchable) Castes receive 79 seats, and the Scheduled Tribes 40 seats, in the Lok Sabha. Scheduled Castes seldom constitute more than a third of the voters in their districts, but Scheduled Tribes often constitute a majority in theirs. If no Anglo-Europeans have been elected, the president can also appoint two Anglo-Europeans, along with twelve other individuals who have distinguished themselves in the arts and professions, to the Lok Sabha.

31. Voters cross out the names of everyone on the ballot except the person they are voting for. If all names are crossed out, no one receives a vote, so even an unopposed candidate could receive less than half the votes. Under the system in place before 1989, one

could cross out the name on the ballot and write in a new name, but only by going into a special voting booth reserved for write-ins—another interference with a secret ballot. In 1989, a third of the seats were apportioned not on the basis of equal population, but to include various autonomous regions. Since Russians outnumber the regional nationalities in most of the autonomous republics (Jonathan Steele, "Decolonizing the Complex Soviet Mind," *Manchester Guardian Weekly,* October 20, 1991), the majority rule helped cut down on the chances that these nationalities would gain office; no candidate could hope to win if he or she offended the Russian majority.

EXERCISES

Think about the book thus far:

Choose five of the Key Words and Phrases and explain how each relates to the word *authority*.

KEY WORDS AND PHRASES
Define the following terms:

general election	primary election	registration (to vote)
candidate	caucus	district lines
nominee	glasnost	gerrymandering
independent candidate	multiparty system	run-off election
elected officeholder	consensual party	plurality
competitive general election	splinter party	multimember district
apparatchiki	universal suffrage	proportional representation
cadre		

THINKING IT THROUGH

This chapter has centered around one question:

What role do political parties and elections play in determining the amount of sovereignty that ends up in the hands of the chief executive?

We have found that the rules by which parties and elections operate may help other elected officeholders to be somewhat independent of the chief executive. Or, on the other hand, they may strengthen the chief executive's control over those individuals.

Fill in the following charts by marking each box with a Y for "yes" and an N for "no." Some may require you to make a judgment call. As you review, pay special attention to the chapter Summary and take another look at the figures within the chapter that pertain to the points enumerated in the Summary. Once again, think of the CIS chief executives as those of the individual republics.

Rules Which Give Other Elected Officeholders Some Independence from the Chief Executive

	USA	USSR 1922–89	USSR 1990–91	CIS	FRG	GDR	UK	PRC	RI	RP	FRN1	FRN2
officials who share sovereignty may come from rival political parties												
chief executive from consensual party or coalition of parties												
primaries and caucuses used to select some party nominees for legislative seats												
competitive general elections												
universal suffrage												
freely contested plurality-win multimember districts												
Total Number of Ys												

Rules Which Strengthen the Chief Executive's Control over Other Elected Officeholders

	USA	USSR 1922–89	USSR 1990–91	CIS	FRG	GDR	UK	PRC	RI	RP	FRN1	FRN2
one-party system												
party leaders can remove or keep out members												
large, centrally directed, full-time party staff												
chief executive chooses his or her party's nominees for lower house of legislature												
Total Number of Ys												

Now, as in the last chapter, try quantifying to get some sense of where the restraints on a chief executive's sovereignty are greatest. Count the total number of Ys in each column, and combine them with the scores in the Thinking It Through section of chapter 2, in the following chart:

	USA	USSR 1922–89	USSR 1990–91	CIS	FRG	GDR	UK	PRC	RI	RP	FRN1	FRN2
1. Score from prior chapter												
2. Total Ys from first chart												
3. **Add** lines 1 and 2												
4. Total Ys from second chart												
5. **Subtract** line 4 from line 3 to determine final total												

A low score indicates fewer restraints on the chief executive's sovereignty than in a system with a higher score. As in the prior chapter, these numbers have no scientific meaning. They do not, for example, take into consideration that some of these factors may be more powerful restraints than others, and that other factors may play a part as well. But they do provide a simple way to pull together the information in chapters 2 and 3. Use your chart to answer the following questions about the information we have discussed thus far.

1. Which of these systems place the fewest restraints on the chief executive?
2. Which systems place the most restraints on the chief executive?
3. Do prime ministers, military rulers, and leaders of one-party systems appear to face more or fewer restraints than presidents?
4. How might it help you as a citizen if other elected officials share sovereignty with the chief executive? How might it harm you?
5. Compare your totals for the USSR and the CIS. Do the CIS republics appear to place more or fewer restraints on their chief executives than the USSR placed on its chief executive?
6. Can any of these chief executives avoid sharing sovereignty with the bureaucracy?

chapter 4

CITIZEN PARTICIPATION

The last two chapters examined how rules surrounding government institutions, and elections and political parties, affect who shares in sovereignty. Now we will look at how citizens themselves can participate in politics under these rules. Bureaucrats, officeholders, and those in the top ranks of the ruling political party have the best access to those with sovereignty when there are few restraints on the chief executive; even then, government-organized interest groups, and efforts by the ruling party to include many types of people within itself, may give some other citizens access as well. Systems with more restraints on their chief executive give additional portions of the populace access to those with sovereignty. In both cases, citizens participate, but the groups in the best position to participate may differ. Can ordinary citizens affect the behavior of government leaders if no competitive elections take place in a given system? Do competitive elections improve the chances for ordinary citizens to participate in politics?

In chapter 3, we continued to explore how sovereignty is shared within governments, and how it is affected by political parties and elections. Now we shall examine how political parties, elections, and interest groups may affect the willingness of those with sovereignty to seek cooperation from all segments of society. Citizens may sway the decisions of government leaders by voting in elections, expressing ideas, behaving (or threatening to behave) in ways government leaders dislike, and withholding from government things it needs. Groups of citizens may unite to form political parties and interest groups, or individuals may attempt to influence government on their own. All the nine systems offer opportunities for citizen participation, but one person's opportunity may be another's obstacle. Freer voting and expression of ideas will clearly help increase opportunities for some to participate; perhaps surprisingly, it could also reduce those opportunities for others. **Can citizens better sway government decisions when elections are competitive?** Does it matter whether you take advantage of the opportunity to participate in politics?

CITIZEN LINKS WITH GOVERNMENT

Political systems, as we have seen, are the regular pattern of human interactions that resolve competition over goods and services and conflicts over cultural traditions, ideas, and other values. We endow governments with the final authority to resolve these conflicts. Thus, governments are obviously part of the regular pattern of human relationships through which conflicts are resolved, and the citizens who act as officeholders and bureaucrats in the government obviously participate in the political system. But most citizens of a nation-state are not elected officeholders or bureaucrats, and many of the conflicts government attempts to resolve begin with

Student demonstration at Hangzhou, China in 1989.
Bob Gamer

people outside government. When citizens outside of government select officeholders and inform them about their demands, they, too, take part in the political system.

The Roman forum and the Greek agora were open campuses in the centers of cities, amid principal government buildings, where citizens could partake in government.

In these forums and agoras, bureaucrats, military officers, elected officeholders, chief executives, and judges could interact with people who held no position in government. These individual citizens made (or cheered or jeered or quietly listened to) speeches, exchanged gossip, and celebrated cultural events together. Those who lived close to these centers could participate (take part) in events that shaped the thinking of government. Although we tend to think of political parties and interest groups as recent innovations, formal political parties vied for votes, and various groups with common interests organized to persuade government decision makers,

even in ancient Greece and Rome. Citizens could also speak directly to their leaders in the agoras and forums.

Today, the sheer size of nation-states and populations reduces opportunities for government decision makers to hear directly from random individuals. A constituent who catches the ear of a legislator in a store or at a public meeting, or who is interviewed by a television reporter on a street, may happen to change the mind of a government leader. But much of our participation today takes place within or in association with interest groups and political parties.

There are many ways to participate in a political system (figure 4.1). One way is to withhold cooperation from government, or behave in ways which make it more difficult for government leaders to resolve conflict until they meet demands. For example, citizens may refuse to pay taxes, object to serving in wars, leave ballots blank in elections with compulsory attendance, or destroy grain rather than

Figure 4.1 Different ways to participate in the political system.

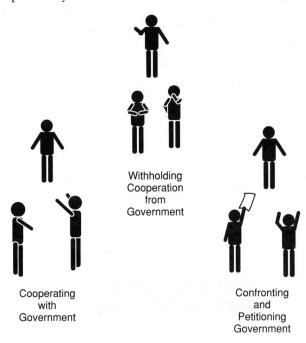

Withholding
Cooperation
from
Government

Cooperating
with
Government

Confronting
and
Petitioning
Government

freely. Many citizens will prefer to use these channels for participation without resorting to direct confrontation; others may use their freedom to organize groups which deliberately cause a nuisance. Such nuisances (like Rosa Park's refusal to sit at the back of an Alabama bus and Martin Luther King's peaceful sit-ins at lunch counters that refused to serve blacks) can draw attention to the plights of forgotten people and result in popular support for relieving these plights. People who create such nuisances may cause leaders to give in to their demands just to restore peace. That, in turn, may induce other citizens to counteract their actions, sometimes producing violent confrontations, or to vote for leaders who promise not to give in to such demands. All this can cause government to seek compromise solutions to the conflicting demands, or it can cause government to fragment in disarray.

While some citizens participate by confronting government in such ways, many citizens participate in the political system by communicating with government officials—by talking with them, writing letters and telegrams, presenting research results, attending meetings, and otherwise making government leaders aware of what citizens want them to do. Some of these activities can be carried on by individuals acting alone to persuade government officials; most, however, involve people acting in concert as interest groups, or in response to pleas from interest groups and political leaders. Such activities take place in every political system. Citizens of one-party, parliamentary, and presidential systems organize in political parties to promote ideas and candidates for public office and to vote in elections. When the constitution guarantees free speech and the right to organize groups and participate freely in elections, people participate in more ways through such groups, because it is harder for government to stop them from doing so.

Individuals and groups outside of government, then, participate by cooperating with, withholding cooperation from, informing or confronting government officials. Individuals within government also communicate with others in government; that, too, is a form of participation. Someone within a bureaucracy or the Cabinet may converse with another

sell it to government to persuade government officials to change or give up on certain policies. Such individuals often set up networks to communicate and cooperate with one another, and so develop formal interest groups. The same is true of people who march, strike, picket, or occupy buildings to advocate their ideas, or people who detonate bombs, burn buildings, or abduct government leaders to call attention to their causes.

Leaders of the Soviet Union and Eastern Europe firmly cracked down on dissent like this for many decades. Once Mikhail Gorbachev eased restrictions in the late 1980s and early 1990s, dissent quickly grew to such proportions that the old regulations could not easily be reimposed; hundreds of thousands of citizens poured into the streets to defy government actions they did not like, and even military conscripts practiced such disobedience.[1] When people choose their own chief executive and legislatures in competitive elections, courts can restrain the chief executive's behavior, and interest groups form bureaucrat; a member of the legislature may talk to a member of the bureaucracy; a bureaucrat may ask a legislator for help, or military and civilian bureaucrats may exchange views. In all these situations, government officials may ask other members of government to resolve a conflict in a particular way. They may speak strictly for themselves. Often, they may make requests for organizations they belong to or represent. In the latter case, these officials are acting as part of an interest group—trying to persuade someone in government to consider and reward the interests of their group. Interest groups that include government leaders are well-placed to affect decisions in any kind of political system; members of the group may actually help make some of those decisions themselves, have regular contact with those who make them, or be needed to help execute the decisions after they have been made.

It is harder for those outside government or the top ranks of political parties to affect decisions. Sometimes the government itself creates interest groups just to give outsiders a chance to affect decisions. Those interest groups seek members among people who otherwise have little contact with government. Individuals from such groups may later rise to government leadership and promote improvements to benefit their members. And, as we saw in chapter 3, even ruling parties in one-party systems often attempt to include a wide variety of groups within their own party.

Unless competing groups can organize, however, such benefits may be limited. Once the ruling party or government has provided benefits to the groups it created, it will ask them to restrain their demands. Unless other groups are permitted to make additional demands, increasing the pressure on the government, the government is in a position to decide what it will and will not give, and members of the interest group will have nowhere else to turn to press their cause.

By contrast, if more than one interest group may be formed to represent, say, manual laborers, a manual laborer who is dissatisfied with the way one interest group is representing him or her can join another. Freely competing interest groups, however, can cause another kind of problem. To keep tight control at all levels of society, communist parties organized themselves down into work units. They recruited even manual laborers into their organizations, and gave some of them offices at local and higher levels. Once these parties were removed from control in East Germany and the Soviet Union, new interest groups were free to organize if they wished. They were not obliged, as the communist party was, to organize among all these ranks of workers. If no group turns out to speak effectively for manual laborers in their nation-states, the laborers may have less effect on policy than when they were represented by one government-created interest group. Thus, while it *allows* more types of individuals and groups to participate in politics, free party and interest group competition does not ensure their participation—in fact, it can present obstacles to that participation.

In the remainder of this chapter, we shall examine why some groups may have advantages participating in three realms of activity, even when interest groups and parties can organize freely:

1. Some groups may play special roles in choosing those with sovereignty, and thus are in a position to ask for special favors.
2. Members of some groups may be better positioned to become officeholders, and thus to share in sovereignty themselves.
3. Some groups may be needed to carry out decisions those with sovereignty make, and thus may reap benefits from those decisions.

CHOOSING OFFICEHOLDERS

In systems with military or one-party rule—such as China, Peru and Nigeria under military rule, and East Germany and the Soviet Union before 1990—chief executives are chosen by senior military officers or party officials, without elections. In the one-party states, the chief executive and party officials choose who will rise in the party organization or run for legislative offices. Often, those nominations come from among themselves, their friends, and their associates. Even when others are able to run for local elected bodies (as in China), election commissions review the candidates and disqualify any they deem unacceptable. These are also systems in which the chief executive has few restraints. Military officers and top party officials thus have considerable effect on who will be chief executive, who will serve in important offices, and who will collect favors from government. When government leaders discuss important policy issues, they will consider the views of these officials. As we just noted, party and military leaders are likely to advance some ordinary workers who support them within party organizations. Since people who disagree with these leaders cannot organize outside the ruling party, they are reduced to withholding cooperation in the ways we discussed. If they try to coordinate their dissenting activities with others, their efforts may be brutally put down. Thus, in one-party and military systems, government bureaucrats and party leaders at all levels can participate; others are tightly restricted in their efforts to do so.

Presidential and parliamentary systems with competitive elections move far beyond this closed process; they let many additional groups participate in nominating and electing officeholders. Primaries and caucuses (which select some legislative candidates in the United States, the former Soviet Union and CIS, the Federal Republic of Germany, and Nigeria) may seem to broaden those opportunities even more. However, to do so, both primary and general elections must give candidates the opportunity to tell voters what they would like to do upon achieving office. If voters cannot hear such messages from all, or at least two or three of, the candidates running for an office, they do not really have a choice. A candidate or party which is free to run but cannot make itself known to the voters has little chance of winning an election. If certain groups make it possible for some candidates, but not others, to spread their message widely, those groups are likely to gain the ear of the officeholders they help elect.

In the Federal Republic of Germany, radio and television are controlled by state-run corporations but representatives from various political parties and interest groups serve on the boards of these corporations to minimize bias. Some private television

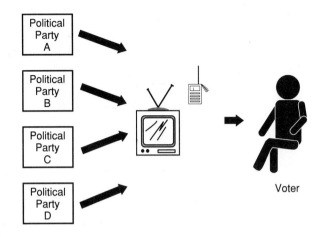

Figure 4.2 In Germany and the United Kingdom, parties have inexpensive access to radio and television.

broadcasting is also allowed, and newspapers are privately owned. The United Kingdom has both government-owned and private radio and television channels. Newspapers are private. All media are free to report on government scandals and other sensitive news, though chief executives in both countries have on occasion forbidden the media to report on sensitive subjects. Public television allots considerable free time for forums including candidates from all parties, and even for free television spots advertising the various parties;[2] this means that voters have an opportunity to hear the views of all major candidates without requiring the candidates to spend large amounts of money for radio and television coverage. This type of system makes it difficult for any one group to use media access to their advantage. Even small parties and interest groups can communicate their message to broad segments of the populace and mobilize support for and against certain candidates (figure 4.2).

In the other seven systems, it is more difficult for candidates from opposition parties to gain access to the media. China and the former East Germany forbid unauthorized opposition parties; the ruling party controls radio, television, and newspapers (figure 4.3). All radio and television stations in the United States are privately owned (though licensed

Figure 4.3 Differences in governments' ability to control radio, television, newspapers, and businesses.

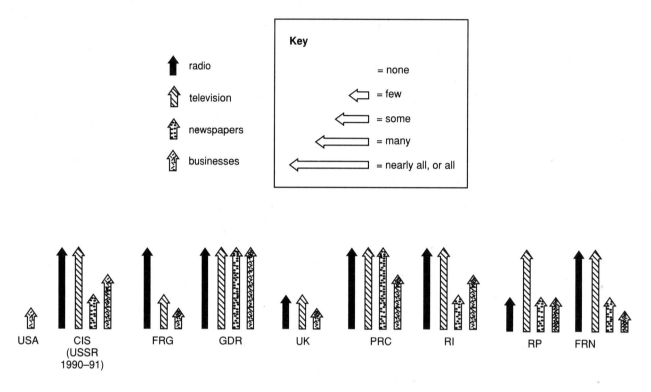

Government Bureaucrats or Affiliated Agencies Control:

by government), as are newspapers. These media are free to report on what they want. Many newspapers devote considerable space to explaining the positions of various candidates and of the two major parties; independent candidates and small parties generally receive little coverage. Television networks present two or three forums with presidential nominees and interview them on talk shows. Otherwise, candidates (unless they are independently wealthy) depend on extensive contributions from private contributors to pay for television commercials; this creates obligations to those contributors and prevents small parties from gaining much access to television and radio time. In Peru, where the government runs all television and some radio stations, and many private radio stations and newspapers are free to say what they wish (with some limits), the media give political parties a number of hours of free air time; but, to reach large numbers of people, nominees usually must invest in extensive radio and television advertising,[3] paid for by private contributors to whom they subsequently owe favors.

Indian opposition parties find it even harder to get on radio or television. Television is government-controlled at the national level, and radio at the state level; newspapers are privately owned (each political party owns at least one) and are often critical of government, but they reach only a small audience. Since differing parties often control the state and national governments, one party may dominate national television and another state radio. Though other parties have received air time during campaigns since 1977, they get much less time on the air than the sitting officials from the ruling party, and even a party which dominates one state cannot get coverage in another state. Central control of television is useful for a consensual party like the Congress party, which has ruled India most of the time since independence.[4]

In Nigeria, individual state and local governments control the twenty-nine radio and thirty-two television stations, as well as 75 percent of newspapers, and they use these media to the advantage of the political parties which control their regions; other parties cannot easily access either radio or television. Private newspapers are generally free to print what they like but reach a small audience. In most of the post-Soviet republics, the media are much freer than in the past, with some small independent newspapers and magazines making a debut; television and radio remain a government monopoly.[5] Parties that do not control the governments of the CIS republics have little access to the media. This means that controlling parties do not need to depend on large contributions to reach voters through radio and television, but opposition parties have little access to these media except through televised parliamentary debates. The bureaucracy surrounding the media plays an important role in determining access.

Campaigns, of course, involve other expenses besides paid television and radio advertising. In India, Nigeria, and to a lesser extent in Peru, they also involve expensive bribes. One of the biggest expenses for Indian parties is paying people in local factions to help run campaigns. Voters are often given money as well; some accept a few rupees from each candidate, while some only accept money from the candidate they intend to support. In Nigeria during the last period of civilian rule, campaigns were very expensive. Over a million people were needed to distribute lanterns (for light in areas without electricity), ballot boxes, and election rolls; watch the polls; and count and report the returns. The last election before the military takeover of 1983 cost the government over $1.5 billion; government officials spending this money could aid supporters by paying them to do these tasks. In addition, factions with money from development

corporations or other groups might bribe election workers to bend the results.[6] In Peru, too, election rallies must sometimes include refreshments and small gifts for those who attend.

Obviously, even when a system includes competitive elections it does not assure that all groups can participate equally in presenting their views to voters. Without government intervention to assure fair media access, groups (including government groups) which control the media, or which provide the money to buy access to the media, can determine whose voice voters hear. Government bureaucrats can use their positions to bend the results of elections in exchange for later favors. Private contributors to campaigns can expect rewards for their gifts.

If parties and candidates can raise money without depending on extensive private contributions, they will owe fewer obligations to particular groups. But that is difficult to achieve. In all of these countries except the United States, most campaign bills are paid by the party organization. In the Federal Republic of Germany, even small, radical parties (whose advertising costs for posters and literature can be high, despite the public radio and television forums) receive large government subsidies to help with these expenses. Private donations make up the remainder of campaign warchests (up to 40 percent),[7] along with membership dues and investments. Each recent election has cost all parties a collective total of around $100 million, half of which the government paid.[8] Government subsidies, membership dues, investments, and donations help free the political parties from extensive financial dependence on interest groups—but not entirely. In the Soviet Union during 1990 and 1991, the government provided campaign funding for candidates approved by electoral commissions; still, some candidates endorsed by well-off (and often well-connected with the Communist Party) organizations received more funds than their opponents, who turned to private sources for the modest cost of their campaigns. The future will tell whether that pattern continues in the individual republics.

Campaigning is not expensive in the United Kingdom,[9] and parties receive substantial revenues from investments and individual party memberships. But most Conservative (about three-fifths)[10] and Liberal party income comes from private individual business donations, and the Labour Party depends heavily on the affiliation (membership) fees paid by unions; these arrangements create obligations to particular groups. In Peru, where costs for television advertising are rising but campaigns (like President Fujimori's) can still be successfully run with little money, parties depend almost entirely on private contributions, also creating obligations.

Political parties in Nigeria and India depend heavily on private contributions. As we just saw, parties in power use government funds to support their own campaigns; other parties must rely heavily on wealthy donors. In India, money is also raised from wealthy donors through special party dues and contributions; members of legislatures make monthly contributions, and businesspeople give to avoid harassment when they need licenses and services.[11] In the United States, most campaign funds are raised from large contributors by individual candidates rather than parties; these contributions are extensive.[12] Government subsidies to presidential candidates pay only a third of campaign expenses.

Figure 4.4 summarizes how difficult or easy it is for opposition parties to raise funds and gain access to the media in each nation-state. In all the one-party systems, bureaucrats and party officials determine who can seek office, who has access to media, and who can participate in party and interest group activity. In Nigeria, India, and Peru, parties not in control of the national or state governments can seek office, but they have little access to media; they need large private campaign contributions to get their message out to voters. In the United Kingdom and Germany, opposition parties can access media but still must rely on large contributions from labor unions, businesses, and other groups. In the United States, all parties need extensive contributions to access media.

That makes it hard for new groups to form and become politically active, especially if they lack money. If a smaller party cannot get on television and radio, or organize as well as existing parties and interest groups and the bureaucracy which permanently surrounds government, they may have little chance to elect officeholders or communicate with those in power. In a system with free competition, bureaucrats may even be able to link up with private groups by offering them services, strengthening both the bureaucracy and the interest group. Political parties can organize to counter that, but they can only compete if they can get their message to voters who are willing to work and vote for them.

When funding passes through political parties, party leaders can at least attempt to develop compromises among the interests of various contributors; individual officeholders will usually go along with those compromises because they need the party to finance future campaigns. When contributions go directly to individual officeholders, they may find it difficult to cooperate with their own party leaders because their first concern is not to offend their contributors. In all of these countries except the United States, most campaign bills are paid by the party organization. In the United States, candidates raise and spend most of their campaign funds personally; campaign "reform" laws even limit the amounts that parties can contribute to individual campaigns.

BECOMING OFFICEHOLDERS

We have seen, then, that in one-party systems without free elections, officeholders owe obligations to party and government bureaucrats, or businesses with government contracts. The same holds true in India, Nigeria, the CIS, and Peru, where parties owe favors to private donors too. In the Federal Republic of Germany and the United Kingdom, parties can gain office with little support from bureaucracy, and without depending heavily on special contributors

Figure 4.4 Differences in opposition parties' access to the media and to fundraising resources. Arrows pointing up indicate features that strengthen opposition parties; arrows pointing down indicate features that weaken them. The longer the arrow, the greater the access to or dependence on resources, or the higher the costs.

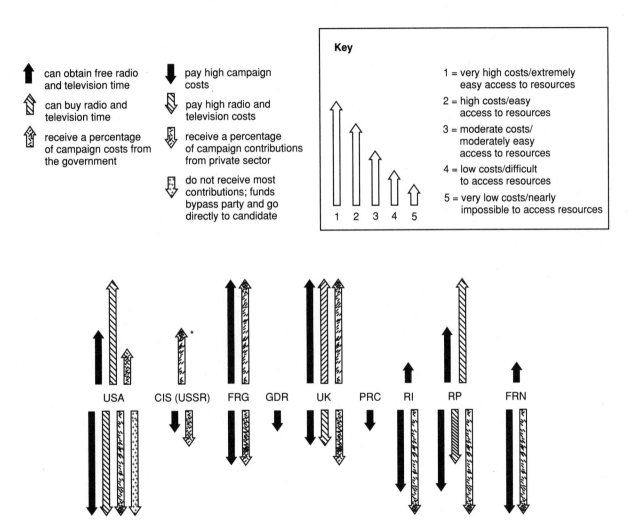

Opposition Parties

can obtain free radio and television time

pay high campaign costs

can buy radio and television time

pay high radio and television costs

receive a percentage of campaign costs from the government

receive a percentage of campaign contributions from private sector

do not receive most contributions; funds bypass party and go directly to candidate

Key

1 = very high costs/extremely easy access to resources

2 = high costs/easy access to resources

3 = moderate costs/moderately easy access to resources

4 = low costs/difficult to access resources

5 = very low costs/nearly impossible to access resources

1 2 3 4 5

USA CIS (USSR) FRG GDR UK PRC RI RP FRN

*not available to all parties

T*able 4.1*

Interest Groups

L = formally represented in legislature
A = formally affiliated with political parties

	USA	CIS (USSR)	FRG	GDR	UK	PRC	RI	RP	FRN
Writers		AL		AL	A	AL	A	A	
Intellectuals		AL		AL	A	AL	A		A
Scientists		AL		AL		AL	A		
Economists		AL		AL		AL	A		
Farmers		AL	L	AL		AL	A		
Women		AL		AL	A	AL	A		
Youth	A	AL		AL	A	AL			
Trade unions		AL	L	AL	A	AL	A	A	A
Nationalized businesses		AL		AL		AL			
Businesses			L				A	A	A
Consumer cooperatives		AL		AL		AL			
Religious groups				AL	L				
Bureaucrats		AL	L	AL		AL	A	A	A
Environmentalists			AL		AL				
Armed forces		AL				AL			
Nobility					L				
Regional interest groups			AL		A		A	A	A

for financial backing—but they still need some. In the United States, candidates need large individual contributions from private donors, which leaves them owing more to their contributors than to their party.

The involvement of particular interest groups inside political parties, and among their nominees for public office, can also benefit certain groups disproportionately. As we have noted, in systems where opposition consensual parties are outlawed, the dominant political party may find it useful to create interest groups that allow individuals from various walks of life to affiliate with the ruling party. In systems with competing consensual parties, some interest groups may choose to affiliate with a particular political party. Both circumstances offer certain groups of citizens special access to political leaders.

In China, representatives from the bureaucracy, the army, the Communist Youth League, the Federation of Labor Unions, the Women's Federation, the Federation of Commerce and Industry, eleven other scientific and professional organizations, and eight splinter ''democratic'' parties are chosen to run for legislative offices (table 4.1). The Communist Party sets up basic units in factories, mines, stores, schools, neighborhoods, and army units. Many enterprises elect their own directors and other personnel. Villages often contain several factions, who work with factions in the party to support their candidates for local offices and delegations to party conferences and legislatures. Competition for such positions can be fierce.

The Soviet Union had the same system. A third of the members of the Congress of People's Deputies were chosen directly because of their affiliation with such interest groups or local party chapters.[13]

East Germany was ruled by the Socialist Unity Party, a merger between the former Communist and Social Democratic parties. The Socialist Unity Party united with a number of splinter parties and groups to form the National Front. In elections for local, county, district, and the national legislature, the parties did not run against one another in the same district, but issued a joint program on which they all campaigned; in this way, these splinter parties were able to win a percentage of seats. National Front groups represented writers, intellectuals, scientists, economists, farmers, women, youth, trade unions, national enterprises, religious organizations, and consumer cooperatives.

In the Federal Republic of Germany, bureaucrats, trade union leaders, and leaders of industry, business, agriculture, and environmentalist groups run as candidates of both the consensual Christian Democratic Union and Social Democratic parties and of splinter parties to become members of the Bundestag and the legislatures of the Laender, from which they can affect selection of the Bundesrat. About 60 percent of the Bundestag is composed of such individuals; bureaucrats are given six-week leaves of absence to run for office. A number of regional parties contest Laender elections, and some splinter parties have strong ideological slants.

The United Kingdom, too, has regional splinter parties, strongly ideological parties, and an ecology party; because the U.K. has single-member districts and no state legislatures, candidates from these parties have less chance of attaining seats than splinter parties in the Federal Republic of Germany. The consensual Conservative and Labour parties hold most seats. The upper house of Parliament, the House of Lords, is composed of members of the nobility (from families with titles, or personally awarded a title for life by the king or queen to honor distinguished careers), and a few judges and church officials, all of whom thus have an opportunity to push for some amendments to legislation. The Research Department of the Conservative Party, together with its neighborhood associations and affiliates such as the Scottish Party and the Ulster Unionists' Council, present policy proposals. The Labour Party has both neighborhood and trade union members: those who join on their own, and those who are enrolled (whether they like it or not) when they pay their union dues. The party also incorporates groups like the Womens' Conference, the Labour Party Young Socialists, and the Militant Tendency, though it is moving away from those affiliates.

In Peru, many of the forty or so splinter parties formed around individuals who lead or are prominent in interest groups of civil servants and professional people, government workers' unions, development corporations, and bureaucratic units with pet projects. The same holds true in Nigeria, where parties also form around tribal organizations; the 1990 ban on parties formed this way attempted to force these groups to cooperate in forming larger consensual parties. India's Congress party solicits into active membership prominent members of local and national interest groups. Active members have the right to vote at party meetings.

As we have seen, interest groups in the United States do not formally affiliate with political parties; instead, they ally closely with individual legislators. As we shall see in chapter 10, the United States, like all these other systems, tends to fill its legislatures with educated professional people. In the one-party systems, at least some of these legislators are assigned to speak for groups of people with less education and in other professions. When these representatives have no such formal ties to interest groups, they have more freedom to act on behalf of groups of their own choosing. High percentages of legislators in the parliamentary and presidential systems come from business, commercial agriculture, law, other professions, and sometimes trade unions. In addition, it is common practice in presidential and parliamentary systems to consult major interest groups when formulating legislation which might pertain to them; since officials traditionally consulted these major groups, it is often difficult for new groups to form and become prominent enough to be consulted in the same fashion.

In all nine systems, interest groups representing a variety of regions, occupations, and concerns have access to legislatures and the governing political parties. Even in the one-party systems, the representatives of lower-paid workers often do not come from among the ranks of those workers, and often they serve in legislatures which play only a small role in setting policy. In the parliamentary and presidential systems, few representatives come from or represent those with lower pay and education.[14]

CARRYING OUT DECISIONS

Bureaucrats have an additional way to affect governmental decisions; government and party leaders need a bureaucracy to carry out policy. Bureaucrats have some freedom to interpret how policy will be enforced and implemented. Bureau chiefs have contact with government leaders, and bureaucrats handle money and other resources and exercise some discretion over how these resources will be used.

Political parties and interest groups also need bureaucrats to help carry out their functions. We mentioned the bribes in India and Nigeria that go to the petty bureaucrats occasionally needed to run elections. Those with more permanent and responsible jobs can demand bigger bribes and make important decisions.

In the Soviet Union and CIS, China, and India, many major industries and businesses are government-run. That was true in the former East Germany and, until the 1980s, in the United Kingdom as well. The directors of these businesses wear three hats: government worker, party officer, and business representative. This gives them ample opportunity to influence government decisions.

Any young citizen can strive to land such a job, or at least to make friends with those who have them. Obviously, some are more likely than others to obtain a good job in the bureaucracy or make friends with well-placed bureaucrats.

When ample opportunities exist for citizens to participate in the political system, and many citizens believe that government officials should abide by the laws, it is easier for elected officeholders to control bureaucracy. The elected officials know that if they do not enforce the law they are in danger of being voted out of office. If a bureaucrat fails to obey the instructions of an elected official, his or her actions may be publicized in the media and brought into line. That weakens their influence. When public participation in elections and constitutional guarantees of free speech and organization are weak, bureaucrats are likely to participate actively and are less restricted by public opinion.

CONCLUSION

In all nine of the political systems we are studying, citizens can join interest groups and political parties. They can seek bureaucratic jobs or make friends with bureaucrats. They may communicate ideas to people in such groups. And they vote on who will occupy some official positions. In these ways, citizens affect the decisions of those with sovereignty. In all nine systems, a variety of leaders are involved in making decisions; that increases the chance for interest groups to make contact with those who make the decisions. As we shall see in later chapters, the former East Germany and Soviet Union, China, India, Peru, and Nigeria restrict the formation of interest groups (figure 4.5); none of them, however, denies all interest groups access to political leaders. Thus, all these systems allow citizens to compete as they seek to affect the decisions of government leaders about issues which concern them.

A system which forces you to join a particular interest group or a restricted-membership party (such as the noncompetitive communist parties in China, and formerly in East Germany and the Soviet Union; or the Congress party, which has dominated

Figure 4.5 Differences in government control over interest group formation.

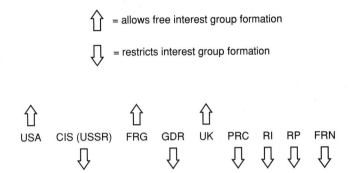

India during most of its independence) in order to compete for desirable jobs inherently excludes many people from participation. One that allows citizens to vote in competitive elections for chief executives and legislatures, that supports unrestricted speech and press, and that permits anyone to form an interest group broadens participation. Yet, because office-seekers need some groups to gain their positions or to carry out policy, or because office seekers come from certain groups, those groups may have more chance than others to affect policy. The systems without free competition tend to make some attempt to organize people of low income and give them at least a degree of access to those who make decisions; in the systems with free elections, the less educated, lower-income groups are unlikely to gain much access unless they organize.

Even systems like the United Kingdom, the United States, or the Federal Republic of Germany, which allow you to form or join virtually any interest group you like[15] and vote for chief executives through competing consensual as well as independent splinter parties, do not guarantee that you will be able to affect the decisions of government leaders. To do so, you must learn the rules and determine what you must do to compete effectively. Individuals who cannot, or refuse to, learn and play by the rules will not be effective. You will soon see that even though the rules vary, the characteristics of those who learn them and are willing to abide by them are often similar.

SUMMARY

All nation-states have some degree of citizen participation. When groups play special roles in choosing those with sovereignty, supplying government or party officeholders, and carrying out decisions, their chances to benefit from government policies increase. In one-party systems, various bureaucrats are able to monopolize all three roles; to counterbalance that, these systems formally bring other types of groups into political parties and legislatures. Parliamentary and presidential systems with competitive elections allow many more interest groups to form and seek access to those with sovereignty. However, some groups may have better chances to gain such access because they are needed by those who seek elected office, or because they include officeholders among their ranks; some, often among segments of the populace with lower income, tend to remain unorganized, play neither of these roles, and thus exert less influence over government. In every system, government leaders need bureaucrats to carry out policy. This gives the members of the bureaucracy some influence over government, though the degree of influence varies, depending on the system.

NOTES

1. In 1990, 21 percent of youths called up for conscription in the Soviet Union refused to report. Others deserted after reporting. This lack of willingness to serve was probably reflected among those who did report, and helped keep the armed forces indecisive during the 1991 coup attempt. Stephen Foye, "Crack-down Ordered to Enforce Military Draft," Radio Liberty *Report on the USSR* 3 (January 18, 1991): 7–9.

2. German parties may not purchase additional television advertising. The parties and stations negotiate to determine the number of spots allocated to each. Smaller parties get fewer spots than major ones. Each spot is two and a half minutes long and begins airing a month before the election. In the 1990 election, spots were aired a total of sixty-seven times, usually after the evening news, with eight each for the major parties. Christina Holtz-Bacha and Lynda Lee Kaid, "The Impact of Television Advertising on Perceptions of Political Leaders in Germany," paper presented to the American Political Science Association, August 1991.

3. President Fujimori had the advantage of having hosted a popular television program before his candidacy, affording him extensive free exposure on television. The front runner in the 1990 presidential campaign, Vargas Llosa, offended many voters with slick television advertisements featuring only Caucasian performers in expensive settings.

4. India's Prime Minister, V. P. Singh, fulfilling a campaign promise, limited news about him on government television after the lavish daily coverage of his predecessor Rajiv Gandhi; Singh's government toppled after only a few months in office.

5. After the aborted 1991 coup, the new head of broadcasting found that a third of his employees were with the KGB. *Kansas City Star*, August 29, 1991.

6. Daniel C. Bach, "Managing a Plural Society: the Boomerang Effects of Nigerian Federalism," *Journal of Commonwealth and Comparative Politics* 27, 2 (July 1989): 218–45. With 161,000 polling places, mostly in inaccessible places, the job of supervising elections is difficult. It is hard to find many who are literate in English, honest, and willing to work. On the other hand, it is easy for factions—especially those with money from development corporations—to find people who might use their positions to bend the rules.

7. The Free Democrats get 40 percent, the Christian Democrats 25 percent, the Christian Social Union 20 percent, and the Social Democrats 10 percent from business contributors. Gordon Smith, "Federal Republic of Germany," *World Encyclopedia of Political Systems and Parties,* 2nd ed., vol. II (1987): 396–405. But the Social Democrats receive more donations from trade unions than the other parties do.

8. Ibid.

9. The 1979 election which brought Margaret Thatcher to the prime ministership cost all parties, collectively, about $39 million, $16 million of which the government provided. William G. Andrews, "The United Kingdom of Great Britain and Northern Ireland," *World Encyclopedia of Political Systems and Parties,* 2nd ed., vol. II (1987): 1090.

10. Ibid.

11. *India Today,* June 16–30, 1981, reported that the winning candidate in one by-election (an election to fill a vacant seat) for the Lok Sabha spent $2.5 million (in U.S. dollars). That was not a record amount.

12. The 1980 U.S. presidential election campaign cost the candidates $309 million. The total spent on all campaigns that year was $1.2 billion. Herbert Alexander, *Financing Politics: Money, Elections, and Political Reform,* 3rd ed. (Washington, D.C.: CQ Press, 1984), p. 9. Campaign expenditures in 1988 for local, state, and national elections (including presidential) amounted to $2.7 billion—over twice the amount in 1980. The 1988 presidential race cost $500 million, with $178 million supplied by the government. Herbert Alexander and Monica Bauer, *Financing the 1988 Elections.* In 1990, nominees for Senate races each spent an average of $1.87 per voter. Senator David Boren, quoted in David S. Broder, "Bogus Campaign Finance Reform," *Washington Post,* June 2, 1991. In 1989–90, Political Action Committees contributed $150 million to members of Congress. Harold W. Stanley and Richard G. Niemi, *Vital Statistics on American Politics* (Washington, D.C.: CQ Press, 1992), p. 178. According to the Federal

Election Commission, House and Senate candidates raised $125 million in 1980, and $369 million in 1992. The government funds for presidential campaigns come from a one-dollar checkoff box on tax forms, allowing voters to designate a dollar (raised to three dollars in 1993) of their tax payment for this purpose. In 1980, 28 percent of taxpayers did so; in 1992, 19 percent.

13. That was to end with the 1994 election, which was called off when the Congress of People's Deputies disbanded in 1991.

14. Samuel P. Huntington and Joan M. Nelson, *No Easy Choice: Political Participation in the Developing Countries* (Cambridge, Mass.: Harvard University Press, 1976), pp. 130–60, argue that increasing chances for participation benefit the middle class more than the poor, though the economic development which accompanies the increase may benefit both.

15. As we shall see presently, even these systems place some restrictions on who can organize.

EXERCISES

Think about the book thus far:

1. Explain the relationship between the topic of chapter 3 and the topic of this chapter.

2. Look back at chapter 2 or 3 and point out a rule that limits the sovereignty of government leaders. How might this rule affect the ability of a citizen to inform a government leader about his or her demands?

THINKING IT THROUGH

1. Why is the type of citizen participation that took place in the Greek agora difficult to achieve in today's world?

2. What are some ways citizens can participate in all nine of these political systems?

3. How do opportunities for participation extend to a greater portion of the populace when

   a. chief executives and legislatures are chosen in competitive elections?
   b. speech and media access are unrestricted and available without cost to a wide range of candidates?
   c. anyone can form an interest group?
   d. bureaucracy obeys the publicly proclaimed instructions of elected officials?

4. Which of the systems provide opposition parties

   a. the most access to radio and television?
   b. the least access to radio and television?
   c. substantial government funding?

5. The communist systems all have (or had) many interest groups affiliated with the party and directly represented in the legislature, including low-income earners and the less educated. Do you think that gives these types of citizens more voice than when parties and interest groups can enter politics freely but without the support of the ruling party?

chapter 5

INFLUENCE

This chapter lays out the main themes of the book, which revolve around one idea: that people differ in the amount of influence they exert.

Regardless of the opportunities citizens may have to participate (which, as we have seen, vary from system to system), not everyone takes advantage of those opportunities. Even if the rules by which government institutions, parties, and interest groups operate allow widespread participation, many people fail to participate. Their ability to do so also depends on personal traits. Changing the rules to allow wider participation does not expand participation unless additional people are prepared to acquire the ability to participate.

This chapter—and ultimately, this book—centers around two questions: **Who has influence on those with sovereignty? Does it matter who has influence on them?**

As we have seen, politics is the conflicting demands people make on one another and how those demands are resolved. Demands are resolved when some or all parties to the conflict change their attitudes or behavior. **Influence** is the capability to change or reinforce the attitudes and behaviors of others. All of us exert influence on someone—even a baby rousing parents in the middle of the night by crying. But not everyone exerts influence on government leaders who wield sovereignty. If you and I decided to vote or communicate with political leaders, could we change their attitudes or behavior, or reinforce their intent not to change their attitudes or behavior? If so, we have potential influence on them.

Which of our fellow citizens (and citizens in other nation-states) have influence on political leaders, and why? Does it help their well-being if they do have such influence, and harm it if they do not?

That, more precisely, is what we will explore in this chapter and in the chapters to follow.

As we proceed through the book, we shall divide the first question (who has influence?) into two parts. First (in part 2) we shall ask how people acquire influence. Then (in part 3) we shall ask how they use it. After this, in part 4, we shall examine whether those who are effective at using influence better achieve what they desire than those who are not effective. And finally (in part 5), we shall explore how these patterns of influence and achievement develop and change. The sections of this chapter will mirror the parts of the book, introducing the framework for the remainder of the text.

PART 2: HOW PEOPLE ACQUIRE INFLUENCE

In the last, two chapters, we learned that people affect the decisions of those with sovereignty by voting, participating in parties and interest groups, and becoming members of government. Not every-

Figure 5.1   Five characteristics of influential people.

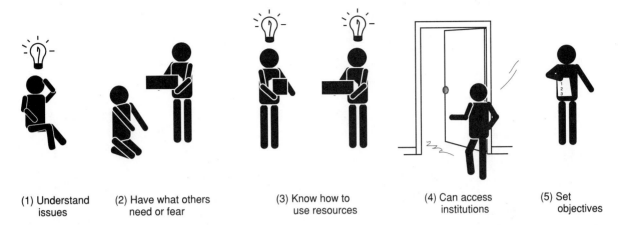

(1) Understand
issues

(2) Have what others
need or fear

(3) Know how to
use resources

(4) Can access
institutions

(5) Set
objectives

one engaged in these activities acquires the ability to share in sovereignty, or to affect the decisions of those with sovereignty—that is, to assert influence over those decisions. Why are some people more likely to engage in such activities and to be successful when they do so?

Five qualities characterize such influential individuals. First, they have some understanding of public issues. Second, they have things other people need, fear, defer to, or desire. Third, they understand how to use the things other people need, fear, defer to, or desire, in order to achieve their own objectives. Fourth, they have access to institutions. And finally, fifth, they have clear objectives for how they want issues resolved (figure 5.1).

Understanding Public Issues

The decisions of those with sovereignty constitute policy about public issues. To affect these decisions, one must first know something about the issues, or at least be capable of learning about them (figure 5.2). If a citizen knows nothing about an issue, and is likely to know nothing in the future, those with sovereignty are not likely to be concerned about that person's opinion when they make a decision regarding the issue. Some issues affect me directly; I may

directly feel the results of policies. To translate that feeling into influence, I must at least be capable of concluding that what has happened to me (for example, the economy is bad and my income is down) is somehow related to decisions made by political leaders. I must also understand that I can vote against those leaders or withhold my support in some other way if their decisions do not please me. If I just act on hunches or impressions and do not really keep track of the decisions those with sovereignty make, they can make their decisions with the knowledge that I probably never will realize what they decided about this or anything else (especially policies that affect me in less noticeable ways). Those with sovereignty also know they can deal with me later without discussing their decisions by blaming someone else or diverting my attention to their charming personality or to some other issue. Meanwhile, they will have to face people who do know what they are deciding, and who have the other four characteristics mentioned here; those people are in a better position than I am to change their attitudes and cause them to make different decisions.

To find out about issues that do not directly affect us (as well as those that do), we may turn to friends, speeches, books, pamphlets, magazines,

Figure 5.2 The first characteristic of influential people: They understand issues.

Figure 5.3 The second characteristic of influential people: They possess or control what others need, fear, defer to, and desire.

newspapers, radio, or television. For many people in today's world, television is a primary source of news; a more informed understanding of the issues requires some reading as well. People without information—those who do not even know the names of their political leaders—may still affect the decisions political leaders make, to some degree, because their economic transactions or social interactions necessitate a response from the government, or because leaders fear they could become informed later about a government action they would object to. However, people with some knowledge about what is going on in their community or nation-state have a better basis for knowing what to ask political leaders to do. Even when government decision makers recognize that a certain policy is required to deal with a broad economic or social problem, their political instincts will lead them to shape the policy so it

pleases those with knowledge—especially if the knowledgeable individuals share the four other characteristics of influential people as well.

Commanding Political Resources—What Others Need, Fear, Defer To, or Desire

Political scientist Robert Dahl says that "a **political resource** is a means by which one person can influence the behavior of other persons; political resources therefore include money, information, food, the threat of force, jobs, friendship, social standing, the right to make laws, votes, as well as a great variety of other things."[1] As figure 5.3 indicates, people who need, want, are afraid of, or respect the political resources you have may, as a result, change their attitudes or behavior. And, in turn, their resources may change your attitudes or behavior. A political system may provide you with political resources like the right to vote or

Figure 5.4 Degrees of influence: (a) Equal influence: Both have similar resources. (b) Unequal influence: One has more resources.

(a)   (b)

make laws. An economic system may provide you with a political resource by making you part of a national economy which political leaders want to preserve. Your parents may provide resources in the form of an inheritance of money or social standing; and you may develop those or some other resources with your own effort and skill. The other four characteristics of influence—knowledge, understanding of how to use resources, access to institutions, and objects—are themselves political resources which each individual must personally nurture. A person who has personally nurtured those four characteristics may benefit markedly from an expansion of political resources like voting, while a person who has not nurtured them may not. Two people who both acquire such characteristics may stand and bargain with one another (figure 5.4); when one acquires them and the other doesn't their relationship is more unequal (see figure 5.3).

Understanding How to Use Need, Fear, Deference, and Desire

To exert influence, you not only must have some political resources, you must notice that you have them and understand how to use them to gain what

you want (figure 5.5). The right to vote, or money or good looks, are not political resources until you comprehend that you can use them to induce fear, or to flatter, or to satisfy the needs of others in exchange for doing what you want them to do. A person may have things others want, need, fear, or respect yet not understand how to use that advantage to achieve his or her objectives; though such an individual has political resources, he or she does not know how to translate them into influence upon another person. A politician fears your right to vote only if you might use your right to retaliate against his or her decisions or actions.

Accessing Institutions

To exert influence, one must be able to affect who enters the institutions that exercise sovereignty, be able to join them oneself, and have some means to communicate with those who occupy them (figure 5.6). We have seen that the institutions which exercise sovereignty vary from country to country. So do the means by which people may be recruited into public offices, the bureaucracy, political parties, and interest groups. A person may be well-informed,

Denver, Colorado. What political resources do you see here; what might people need, want, fear, or respect? How may each person in the picture be responding to a political resource?
© *Mike Gamer*.

F*igure 5.5*   The third characteristic of influential people: They know how to use their resources. If, as in (b) one person's resources are fewer or weaker, superior understanding of how to use them can strengthen their effectiveness.

(a)   (b)

F*igure 5.6*   The fourth characteristic of influential people: They have access to institutions.

possess a variety of political resources, and know how to use them, yet be isolated from the institutions that exert influence over government leaders. Individuals who are successful at wielding influence in one nation-state might be less so had they been born into another because of differences in institutions. Some social groups may find it easier to access institutions than others; chance and skill both play a part.

Setting Objectives

A person with all of the other characteristics is still at a disadvantage in exerting influence over government if that person does not know what he or she wants the government to do, or if he or she has objectives that markedly differ from those of government leaders. Which government policies is one interested in? How does one want government to resolve those issues? To affect government policy,

Figure 5.7 The fifth characteristic of influential people: They set objectives.

people must ask and answer those questions. To get others to do what you want them to do, you must first know what you want them to do.

In each of these political systems, only a minority of the populace has all these characteristics: knowledge of the issues, political resources and an understanding of how to use them, access to institutions, and specific objectives. That minority tends to be better educated and to come from better-educated parents. The percentage of the populace with only some of these characteristics varies markedly among the nine systems. We shall sort out these differences in part 2 of the book, as we explore who acquires these characteristics and why.

PART 3: HOW PEOPLE USE INFLUENCE

We live in a period when political systems are rapidly changing. Soviet dominance over Eastern Europe disintegrated in the early 1990s, and the Soviet Union split apart. China is embracing market reforms. Popularly elected rulers are becoming the norm in Latin America, and African governments are experimenting with new ways to hold competitive elections. People in the United States and Western Europe think that "democracy" and "liberal" economies are spreading to other parts of the world.

As we shall see (beginning in chapter 6), it will be hard for these systems to ignore the social and economic realities which require shifts in old habits. But habits do not change easily. When a nation-state has no competitive news organizations committed to informing the citizenry, independent of government or party control, it is not easy to form them. That hampers discussion of political issues and the ability of citizens to formulate clear objectives for what they would like government to do. Similarly, the distribution of political resources among various members of the populace is not necessarily expanded by disbanding the Communist party and declaring independence, or altering political institutions. Those who receive new political resources, such as voting for additional offices and parties, still may not understand how to use these resources effectively. Moreover, those who already exert influence have more experience doing so than newcomers to the process; they may use their influence to assure that new institutions operate in familiar ways so that their experience continues to give them an advantage. Hence, a nation-state with no background in representative government, or in forming independent interest groups, may find it hard to rapidly acquire those traits. This means that the people who exert influence, and the way they exert it, may not change easily. A system can change rules and rename institutions. Those changes do not change long-standing habits.

However, social and economic changes do affect the extent to which youth are educated, what people own and how they work, who they know, their access to the media, and other aspects of life. Because social and economic changes redistribute political resources and foster people's understanding of how to use them, such changes can shift people's potential to exert influence.

To understand how people exert influence in a given nation-state, one must further examine how the institutions through which they exert influence

Figure 5.8 Institutional arrangements vary. Which institutional arrangement will give these two individuals the most equal access?

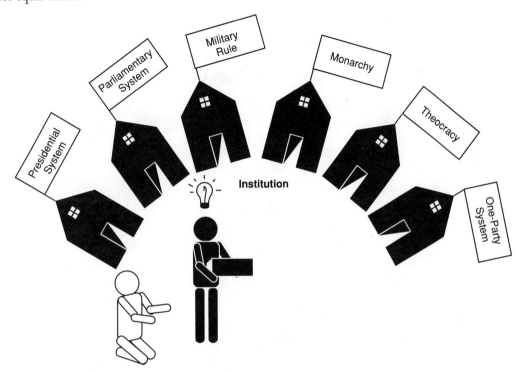

function—the subject we introduced in the last three chapters. It is also necessary to see what sorts of people exert influence within those institutions, and what habits they have acquired in doing so. In addition, we need to ask how social, economic, and institutional changes affect who exerts influence and their habits as they do so. Part 3 of the book examines all these issues as it explores how people use influence in different types of systems (figure 5.8).

PART 4: THE RESULTS OF INFLUENCE

Some people, then, may wield little influence within a political system, while others wield a great deal. Can those who are effective at using influence better achieve what they desire than those who are not?

We suggested in chapter 1 that people usually place importance on the homes in which they and

their families live, their clothing and shelter, their jobs, education, and health care. They are interested in quantity—how much of these resources they have access to. They are also interested in quality— whether the resources they have adequately meet their needs. Their sense of quality pertains to culture, what they and those they identify with have been taught is the right way to behave and acquire material goods and services. Most people also place importance on making sure others can also acquire goods and services.

In part 4 of the book, we shall examine who has satisfying food, clothing, shelter, jobs, education, health care, and cultural surroundings. Are those with influence more apt to find these aspects of their lives agreeable (figure 5.9)? One important aspect of cultural surroundings is the amount of freedom people have to buy and sell, continue and change traditions, and express themselves. We

F*igure* 5.9   Will both these people receive the same rewards under different institutional arrangements?

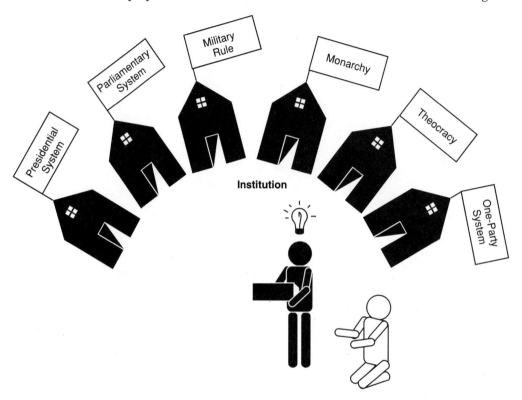

shall also examine how these freedoms affect our ability to exert influence.

Along with freedom, ecology and public order affect and are affected by influence. Sometimes people consider the physical environment when they exert influence, and sometimes they ignore it. In either case, the decisions they make affect the planet they live on. And because exerting influence can cause conflict, it can also affect public order. Declines in the environment and public order may, in turn, affect the distribution of influence. We shall examine both of these aspects as well in our study of the results of influence.

PART 5: CHANGING SYSTEMS

We live in an age of rapid technological innovation. The way people exercise influence affects those shifts in technology, and technological changes, in turn, may change the way people exert influence. Political institutions, and the portions of a nation-state's populace who can exert influence within them, may not remain the same tomorrow as they are today (figure 5.10). Part 5 examines how changes in the use of technology could transform current political systems and the lives of their citizens.

Figure 5.10   When institutions transform (for example, from one-party to parliamentary), do individual resources transform as well?

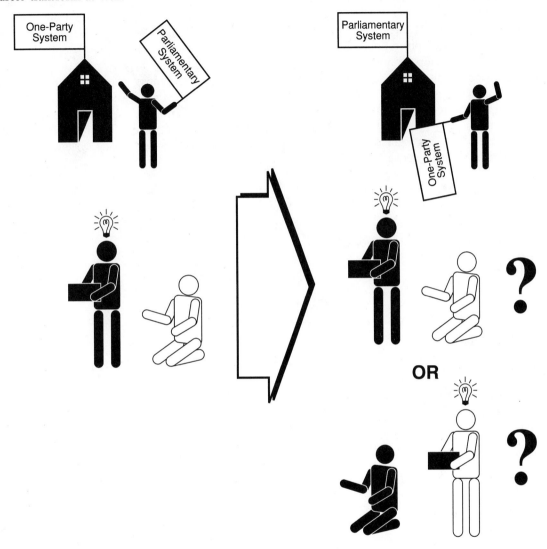

SUMMARY

Everyone exerts influence on someone. The amount of influence individuals may exert over government leaders varies with (1) their understanding of issues, (2) the amount of other political resources they amass, (3) their understanding of how to use the political resources they have, (4) their access to the institutions which exercise sovereignty, and (5) the extent to which they have clear objectives compatible with those of government leaders. Not everyone capable of exerting influence actually does so to the full extent of their ability, and rule changes for government institutions rarely are sufficient to remedy this if social and economic institutions remain the same. Habits and institutions affect who will acquire and use influence, as well as the sorts of food, clothing, shelter, jobs, education, health care, and cultural surroundings people find agreeable. A relationship may exist between those who use influence and those who are satisfied with these aspects of their lives. And the future may bring shifts in the distribution of influence which are profound enough to change the overall character of some or all of today's political systems.

NOTES

1. *Modern Political Analysis,* 4th ed. (Englewood Cliffs, N.J.: Prentice Hall, 1984), p. 31.

EXERCISES

Think about the book thus far:

How does influence relate to politics?

KEY WORDS AND PHRASES

Define these terms:

influence
political resource

How do parts 2, 3, 4, and 5 of this book pertain to influence?

THINKING IT THROUGH

From the nine systems we have been studying, select one that restricts political participation (System A on the chart), and one that lets citizens participate freely (System B on the chart). Then consider three individuals:

a. A woman whose family earns a small income working in agriculture

b. A government bureaucrat

c. A middle manager in a large private business

Now, think about the potential each of these three individuals has to acquire (1) an understanding of public issues, (2) other political resources, (3) the ability to use these resources, (4) access to institutions, and (5) political objectives in each system. Fill in each column with an H (high), M (moderate), or L (low) potential for acquiring these characteristics under each of the two systems. Follow your instincts; this exercise is intended to stretch your thinking about influence rather than to produce "correct" answers.

Systems You Are Comparing A _____ B _____	System A Restricted Participation Characteristic					System B Free Participation Characteristic				
	1	2	3	4	5	1	2	3	4	5
a. The agricultural worker										
b. The bureaucrat										
c. The middle manager										

Now, ask yourself:

1. Is it harder for any of these three people to acquire influence in one of these systems as opposed to the other system? Why?

2. Is it harder in general for any of these three people to acquire and exert influence? Why?

chapter 6

POLITICAL RECRUITMENT, SOCIALIZATION, AND CULTURE

Whether a person acquires traits which make it possible to exert influence depends to a great extent on how they are raised. Some families, schools, religious institutions, neighborhoods, television programs, and governments offer individuals more incentives to acquire those traits than do others. Thus, in any given nation-state, certain individuals are offered more incentives to acquire influence. Individuals living in similar circumstances in a neighboring nation-state may be offered fewer (or more) incentives to acquire influence. The objectives of those who have these traits will also affect how well a political system responds to the needs of its citizens; objectives must be in line with the government's ability to respond.

Political recruitment refers to the way people come to play influential roles within the institutions of a political system.[1] In chapter 5, we discussed the characteristics people must acquire to become influential. Those who actively participate in government, political parties, and interest groups, and exert influence through these institutions, have been recruited into the regular pattern of human relationships through which competition over goods and services and conflicts over cultural traditions, ideas, and other values are conducted and may be resolved; they are thus part of their political system. Some may move beyond this to be recruited directly into government institutions which share in exercising sovereignty.

Political socialization is the process by which people come to decide how they will participate in politics—whom they will support to rule them, what they want from government, what they will learn about government and political issues, and how they will acquire other skills and resources needed to wield influence. **Political culture**—people's knowl-

edge of, feelings toward, and judgments about their political system—is an outcome of this socialization process, which in turn contributes it to the next generation. Political socialization and culture both help determine who will be recruited into influential roles and how those roles will be performed. They thus have a bearing on the way government officials distribute goods and services and affect attitudes and behavior—they influence governmental policy. What you and I have been taught affects the way we—and officeholders—behave in politics, so it matters how that teaching takes place.

Stated more succinctly, **socialization is how people acquire their values and habits, while culture is the values and habits they acquire. Those habits affect who the system recruits into political roles, and the way those with sovereignty behave in response to political conflicts.**

In chapter 5, we indicated that part 2 of this book examines how people acquire influence. Socialization and recruitment—how people develop habits and how they are recruited into political

The Kremlin, Moscow, May Day 1968. Impressive public buildings and national celebrations help reinforce identification with the nation-state.

Bob Gamer

roles—pertain to the acquisition of influence. Part 3 examines how people use influence. Culture and policy—the political habits people have acquired and the behavior of those resolving conflicts—bear on the use of influence.

POLITICAL SOCIALIZATION AND RECRUITMENT

How do people come to decide whom they will support to rule them, what they want from government, what they will learn about government and political issues, and how they will acquire other skills and resources needed to wield influence? We are all part of institutions composed of people who regularly cooperate with one another, structuring their interaction to achieve common goals. We are born into families. As young people we become parts of our neighborhoods or communities, schools, and perhaps religious institutions. When these groups teach us about their goals and values, and we decide to accept or reject those goals and values as our own,

socialization takes place. When families, communities, and educational and religious groups instill attitudes about who should rule, what government should do, and what individuals should learn and do in regard to government and politics, political socialization takes place.

Young people who have the opportunity often spend a lot of time watching television. This is another example of structured interaction with an institution which teaches goals and values. Books, magazines, and newspapers offer another such interaction. A bit later in life some young people join the military, and most take jobs. These situations provide intense interaction with two additional institutions which teach goals and values. Most of our political socialization takes place through this combination of institutions—family, education, religious institutions, community, career, and the media.

If the institutions we most closely identify with teach us loyalty to the nation-state and its leaders, and civic responsibility, that socialization may stick. If we rebel against these institutions, we may also rebel against the socialization. This sequence is not inevitable, however; we might rebel against an institution but accept its values. In any case, to study political socialization, we must learn about what these institutions teach and how well the lessons seem to stick.

In the previous chapter, we discussed five characteristics which might enhance a person's ability to wield influence. Whether a person has some of those characteristics—for example, political resources such as good looks, a sparkling personality, a family farm, a lot of money, and certain ethnic origins—is partly a matter of luck, but also sometimes a matter of motivation. Whether a person understands public issues and how to influence them, seeks access to the institutions where they are resolved, develops clear objectives for resolving issues, or seeks to attain various skills and resources depends to a large extent on how that person is socialized. Even a person with all these attributes may prefer to occupy his or her time in other ways and not bother to exert influence.

In any political system, certain types of people can never achieve influence no matter what they do, because they have some characteristic that those with influence deem unacceptable, or because they lack characteristics the same people deem necessary. Even this is a matter of socialization; the desirable characteristics stem from people's attitudes. Some individuals may be born with resources others must work years to obtain; that gives them a built-in advantage. Beyond this, motivation becomes important. A person who does not bother to learn about public issues and how to influence them, or to seek skills and resources needed to achieve influence, is not likely to be recruited into a position of influence even if he or she was born with or has already acquired some useful political resources.

Political recruitment also depends on the nation-state's political and governmental institutions. By changing political party systems, rules about interest group involvement, the role of legislatures, the institutional position of the chief executive, and the like, nation-states can affect who they recruit into influential positions (figure 6.1). Those who benefit most

Figure 6.1   New rules may open the door.

from such changes are individuals who had acquired the characteristics needed to exert influence but were formerly excluded from the system by those who held sovereignty. When homes, schools, neighbors, and religious institutions have been socializing values different from those espoused by government, there might be many such individuals. If the new system allows some of those individuals to achieve sovereignty, they may then seek to include others like themselves, resulting in a great expansion of participation in politics. Those new participants (as in Eastern Europe) may choose to include, or exclude, those who formerly excluded them.

On the other hand, changing rules to allow expanded participation may result in few new participants if people have not been socialized to participate, or if they have been socialized to allow only small portions of the populace to participate. At that stage, the expansion of political participation depends on whether families, schools, neighbors, religious institutions, the media, the military, and places of work change their values to better acquire the traits they need to encourage their members to participate. Often, expanded participation also depends on whether these socialization agents broaden their definitions of who (women? Jews?

Figure 6.2   People learn to open or block the door.

ethnic minorities? manual workers? ideological opponents?) should be permitted to hold influential positions (figure 6.2). If such attitudes do not change, the same few people may continue to wield most of the influence.

POLITICAL CULTURE,
GOVERNMENT POLICY,
AND CORRUPTION

Political culture is everything people know, feel, and judge about their political system. It determines whether citizens give their government authority, the right to exercise sovereignty. When citizens feel that their government fits their traditions, is legally entitled to rule, and gives them choices about who will occupy key positions, and when those with sovereignty are personally appealing and have compatible attitudes, citizens are likely to give the government the right to exercise sovereignty. Citizens of two nation-states may have very different ideas about what makes a government legally entitled to rule, or what makes a leader personally appealing; their political cultures are not the same. Both may think their government has the right to rule, but for very different reasons.

Whether a particular citizen thinks his or her government has authority is a personal matter. One may conclude that in some respects the government has the right to rule, but in other respects it does not; an individual may even be undecided about whether the government has authority and may not tell anyone else what he or she really thinks about this. Thus, even within a given nation-state, political culture is not entirely uniform. However, various institutions do attempt to teach people how they are expected to behave when engaging in politics.

Those expectations matter. For example, Richard Dawson and Kenneth Prewitt[2] assert that "children learn, early and fervently, that there are significant political groupings in society and that some groups are friends and others are enemies." They may, at the same time, learn that government should help their friends and harm their enemies. Gabriel Almond and Sidney Verba explore an alternative attitude toward friends and enemies—an alternative political culture. They call it a **"civic culture"** which features

1. a substantial consensus on the legitimacy of political institutions and the direction and content of public policy,

2. a widespread tolerance of a plurality of interests and belief in their reconcilability, and

3. a widely distributed sense of political competence and mutual trust in the citizenry.[3]

This means more than simply a willingness to compromise with other citizens or government leaders. It also implies that people will develop tolerance for a variety of groups and viewpoints and that they will even welcome and respect diversity. It implies that they will try to resolve issues with both their own objectives and those of others in mind. It implies not only a willingness to hear opposing viewpoints, but to change one's own viewpoint and objectives, if necessary, to accommodate the interests and needs of other groups.

Any country is likely to contain both types of people—those who would harm and those who would accommodate their political "enemies." Any young person will be exposed to both types of people, and must choose which set of values to accept. If people with accommodating attitudes attain positions of sovereignty in a nation-state where most politically influential people have the other attitude, they may have little opportunity to create public policy which assists a diversity of groups. A civic culture, or a political culture in which most politically influential people have an accommodating attitude, is more conducive to resolving political conflict in a manner which benefits a great variety of groups.

Some of the political systems we are studying come closer to having civic cultures than others. This will become especially evident in chapters 14 through 18, when we examine attitudes toward national identity, equality, power, and authority, as well as about who the system should recruit into politics. A civic culture is ultimately associated with political rules that allow greater participation, though some leaders of single-party or military systems may also encourage some of these attitudes. However, a sudden expansion in political participation may be accompanied by a decline in the ability of political leaders to promote consensus, tolerance, and mutual trust, especially if a majority of citizens do not trust one another. A parliamentary or presidential system with competitive elections in a nation-state whose leaders and citizenry do not share a civic culture may function much differently from one in which the leaders and citizens have created such a culture.

Historically, civic culture attitudes are associated with the Renaissance, the Reformation, and the Enlightenment. The kings and princes of feudal Europe, and the Roman Catholic Church of that time, controlled commerce tightly and demanded absolute obedience from their subjects. Few people could read, much less discuss ideas freely. Government and church leaders taught one set of beliefs, and people were often suspicious of those with other beliefs. Then, in the fourteenth to seventeenth centuries, **Renaissance**[4] thinkers and artists began to advocate individual expression, trade in worldly goods, independent city-states, and rediscovery of the ideas of ancient Greece and Rome. The invention of the printing press and the subsequent spread of education allowed these ideas to flourish. During

the **Reformation**[5] of the fifteenth and sixteenth centuries, individuals rebelled against the authority of the Pope and founded protestant denominations which emphasized personal reading of the Bible and direct communication with God. In the eighteenth century, **Enlightenment**[6] thinkers attacked intolerance, censorship, and restraints on economic and personal activity and argued that human reason (whether used by individual readers or "enlightened despots") could bring social progress. The Renaissance began in Italy and spread to northern Europe, while the Reformation began in Germany; these movements had little impact upon Russia, China, or Peru. The Enlightenment, which began at a time when British influence was growing in India and Nigeria, had strong advocates in England, Germany, the United States, and among some of Russia's tsars. All three movements (which arose soon after the introduction of the printing press created widespread dissemination of knowledge) encouraged public involvement in commerce, government, and policy formulation, as well as exposure to and tolerance for a variety of beliefs and interests. Even in countries where these movements spread, not everyone was equally affected by the values they espoused. And countries not touched by these movements contain many people who have had little contact with these ideas.

Political leaders today must be sensitive to how policies affect various groups of people if they want—in keeping with the Reformation, Renaissance, Enlightenment, and civic culture—to distribute goods and services equitably and to encourage a diversity of values to flourish. It is not enough to simply pass laws which accommodate the needs of diverse groups; political leaders must also implement the laws in a manner which accommodates those needs. When laws claim to benefit one group but are implemented in such a way that they benefit another group, the system becomes **politically corrupted.** For example, if those enforcing the laws secretly divert goods and services to groups not entitled to them by law, or if they fail to protect someone the law requires them to protect, that corrupts the law. If the political culture does not make people sensitive to such corruption and provide means to enforce the laws under such circumstances, the best intentions of citizens and leaders become nullified. Do members of the populace support limits on government when authorities step out of line? We will discover that political cultures differ markedly in this regard. But without such limits, corruption is likely to persist.

Today all parts of the globe are experiencing economic change. Not only are new products becoming available, but institutions are changing as well. Small workshops and stores are giving way to larger establishments. Families are moving from small communities into metropolitan areas. People receive news from network television rather than from a hometown newspaper. They may spend less time in religious institutions and more time associating with people of different backgrounds. Changes are occurring in social and economic values, attitudes toward work, relationships, consumption, savings, and much else. With these changes come changes in political culture.

Every nation-state contains people who have become a part of the more modern institutions and absorbed the ideas associated with them. Others continue to live in smaller communities, buy simpler goods, watch less television, and spend more time with people much like themselves. Such individuals are less likely to accept a civic culture; they also differ in other ways from those with more access to modern institutions. To complicate matters, even those who have absorbed a "civic culture" are often intolerant of those who have not. This creates an instability that does not bode well for working out compromises which reduce conflict. It also opens the door to corruption in public policy implementation.

East Germany contained few people who lacked access to modern institutions, but the rest of eastern Europe has many. So do the CIS, China, India, Peru, and Nigeria—all systems that had little exposure to the Renaissance, Reformation, and Enlightenment. This aspect of political culture, which tends to make political systems unstable, has an especially important bearing as the forces of change sweep across the political institutions in some of these nation-states.

We will now proceed to part 2 of the book, which examines how people acquire influence. We will discuss how people are socialized and recruited as we examine this subject. In part 3, we will explore how people use influence, focusing especially on the habits people acquire as a result of political culture, the behaviors of those who resolve conflicts by making and implementing policy, and the institutions through which these people function. In part 4, we examine whether the use of influence has any bearing on how people live and on how satisfied they feel with how they live. Do those with more influence also have more reason to be satisfied? Do the political systems whose political cultures have attributes of civic culture, and whose political institutions allow greater citizen participation, provide their citizens with more reason to be satisfied? If the answer is "yes" to these questions, is there reason to believe that the improved well-being results from having influence, or from a particular kind of culture? These are the questions we will tackle in the chapters ahead.

SUMMARY

Some individuals come to play influential roles in their political system, while others do not. Whether they do is determined to some extent by how such individuals learn to participate in politics, and to what ends. Prevailing attitudes about these matters affect the way new generations learn about participation, and the behavior of government decision makers is also affected by participation. When participants have (1) a substantial consensus on the legitimacy of political institutions and the direction and content of public policy, (2) a widespread tolerance toward a plurality of interests and a belief in their reconcilability, and (3) a widely distributed sense of political competence and mutual trust, government can respond more effectively to the needs of broad portions of the populace. Or can't it?

NOTES

1. Jack C. Plano and Robert E. Riggs, *Dictionary of Political Analysis* (Hinsdale, Ill.: Dryden, 1973), p. 80. It is through such roles that people come to exert more influence than others on the allocation of values. Samuel P. Huntington, "The Change to Change: Modernization, Development, and Politics," *Comparative Politics* 3 (April 1971) defines political leaders as "the individuals in political institutions and groups who exercise more influence than others on the allocation of values." According to Plano and Riggs, "political recruitment refers to the filling of formal, legal positions, such as President, legislator, or civil servant, as well as less formal roles, such as lobbyist, party activist, or propagandist."

2. *Political Socialization: An Analytic Study* (Boston: Little, Brown, 1968).

3. *The Civic Culture* (Boston: Little, Brown, 1965); *The Civic Culture Revisited* (Boston: Little, Brown, 1980).

4. Renaissance means renewal of life, the rediscovery of ancient art and literature after Europe's Dark Ages. Leonardo da Vinci, Raphael, Michelangelo, Albrecht Dürer, Hans Holbein, Boccaccio, Rabelais, Shakespeare, Cervantes, Machiavelli, Sir Thomas More, Descartes, Erasmus, Copernicus, and Galileo helped shape this era.

5. Some chose to reform from within the Church, while others formed new denominations. John Wycliff, who translated the Bible in England, John Hus of Bohemia, and Renaissance thinkers such as Erasmus and Zwingli, who attacked Church abuses, were forerunners. The Reformation began in earnest in 1517 when theology professor Martin Luther, in alliance with urban merchants and with German princes who wanted independence from the Pope and the Holy Roman Empire, nailed his ninety-five theses to the door of the castle church at Wittenberg, attacking the Church's domination over matters of faith, commerce, and political authority. Anabaptists soon advocated an even stronger break from religious and political authorities. John Calvin of Geneva, the Huguenots in France, and John Knox of Scotland all encouraged economic advance among their followers. In England, Henry VIII broke with the Pope to found the Church of England, Anglicans.

6. The eighteenth century is also sometimes called the Age of Reason. In that century, earlier writings of John Locke, Francis Bacon, Sir Isaac Newton, Descartes, and Spinoza helped shape the thinking and writings of Diderot, Voltaire, Baron de Montesque, Jean Jacques Rousseau, Jeremy Bentham, David Hume, Jonathan Swift, Adam Smith, Edward Gibbon, Immanuel Kant, Thomas Paine, Thomas Jefferson, Benjamin Franklin, and many others.

EXERCISES

Think about the book thus far:

What are the five characteristics shared by individuals with influence, introduced in chapter 5?

KEY WORDS AND PHRASES
Define the following terms:

political recruitment	civic culture	Enlightenment
political socialization	Renaissance	political corruption
political culture	Reformation	

1. Describe how one of the five characteristics shared by individuals with influence over government leaders relate to each of the terms on the definition list.

2. How do the Renaissance, Reformation, and Enlightenment relate to civic culture and corruption?

Thinking It Through

Answer the following questions:

a. Do you give authority to our political institutions?

b. Do you agree with the direction and content of our nation-state's public policy?

c. Are you tolerant of the views of your fellow citizens? Do you trust them?

d. Do you think we can find compromises for the most controversial issues that divide our nation (for example, race, abortion, sex, crime, poverty)?

e. Do you feel that you have the ability to effectively participate in politics?

Now, ask yourself:

1. If you hesitated on any of the previous answers, explain why.

2. Do your answers show that you believe in a civic culture? Why or why not?

3. Think of someone who might be less inclined than you are to answer "yes" to the previous set of questions. Think of someone who might be more inclined to do so.

   a. Can you think of any socialization differences that might account for these variations in response?

   b. How might these attitudes affect the government's ability to appeal to a great variety of groups and to resolve conflict? Can government do these things if most citizens answer "no" to these questions?

4. Can military rule, a monarchy, a theocratic state, or one-party rule be maintained in a nation-state where a civic culture prevails? Can these types of systems end without developing a civic culture?

part 2

ACQUIRING INFLUENCE

In part 2 we will examine the characteristics which make it possible for individuals to be recruited into politics. We will also explore aspects of political socialization that affect who can acquire influence and who cannot and how those who acquire it use it.

As we have seen, a nation-state may have laws and political institutions which allow everyone to exert influence. However, people who lack motivation or personal ability may still be unable to do so. So before we look further at laws and institutions in part 3, we shall first examine who has the capability to acquire influence. That will give us a basis for examining whether laws and institutions can provide influence to those who do not have it, or restrain those who do, and whether those with influence receive better treatment than those without it.

chapter 7

POLITICAL RECRUITMENT

UNDERSTANDING PUBLIC ISSUES

In chapters 7–10 we examine the five characteristics that help a person to be recruited into a position of political influence. This chapter explores the first of those characteristics—understanding public issues. To understand public issues, a person must first learn about them. Without some basic ability to read, count, and calculate numbers, and without access to information, it is difficult to learn about the issues. Not everyone has the opportunity to acquire those political resources; those who do have the opportunity do not always take advantage of it. That affects their chance to be recruited into an influential role in their political system.

An old saying tells us that the squeaky hinge gets the oil. To squeak in politics, it is necessary to acquire influence. That means learning to participate in the institutions through which influence is exerted—and then actually doing so. Some people accomplish this better than others.

Who acquires influence? In chapter 5, we suggested there are five characteristics which can enhance a person's influence and enable that person to be recruited into influential roles in the political system. In this chapter, we shall examine the first of these, the ability to understand public issues. Those with access to news and education are obviously in a better position to do this. **In these nine nation-states, who has access to news and education?**

ACCESS TO NEWS

As you look at figure 7.1, it is immediately apparent that individuals in China, India, Peru, and Nigeria might have less ready access to newspapers, television sets, and radios than in the other six systems. How does this affect an individual's opportunity to acquire influence?

In China, people post newspapers on public bulletin boards in most villages and neighborhoods, public loudspeakers broadcast the morning and evening news, and television sets are occasionally placed outdoors so that whole neighborhoods may watch them. Growing numbers of town and city dwellers own television sets. Most villages have electricity, and a radio or television set in at least one home. Despite that, many villagers hear little news beyond simple themes[1] repeated enough times to catch their attention on the way to or from work; they have little chance to hear about anything in detail. In the cities, those with the best access to news are those with short-wave radios, which are inexpensive and run on batteries. They can listen to BBC and the Voice of America. A German student who took a random bicycle trip through the countryside of Zhejiang province found a short-wave radio in every village where he spent the night. The radios belonged to individuals who purchased them on occasional visits to towns and cities; these individuals listened to foreign broadcasts and discussed them with friends in the village. Villages without access to even the mud roads that the cyclist traversed are less likely to have access to such electronics or to newspapers; most of these people are in the extreme inland region, which has a sparser population.

About a fourth of India's villages have a radio in a public place. About 5 million people in several hundred of India's 600,000 villages have access to

Figure 7.1   Per capita (a) newspapers, (b) televisions, and (c) radios in each of the nine nation-states. *(a) and (c)* UNESCO Statistical Yearbook 1990. *1988 figures. (b)* UNESCO Statistical Yearbook 1990. *1988 figures.* PRC, RI, FRN Television and Video Almanac 1993.

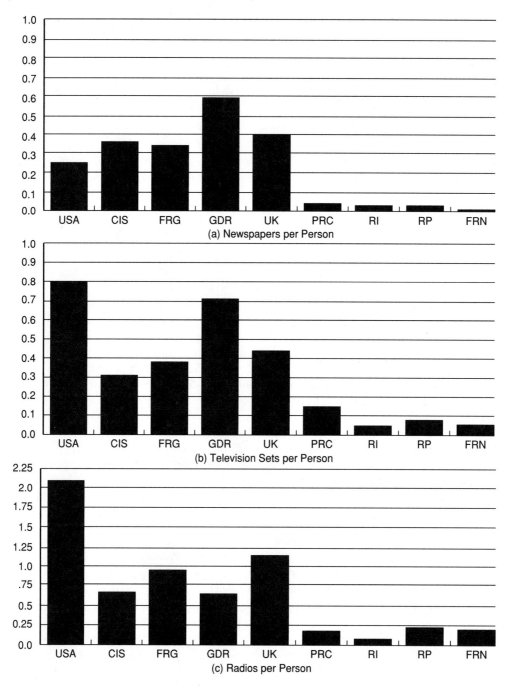

a television set serviced by a satellite in a public place. India has far fewer radios *per capita* (per person) than China, and many villagers can reach a town only by traveling on foot; such villagers are likely to have little access to news. Those living in the poor squatter colonies, which house about half of the 28 percent of the populace living in cities, along with those who live in villages accessible to town, are likely to see occasional programs or listen periodically to the radio and to at least hear about newspaper reports from neighbors. More established urban dwellers have a much greater chance to gain direct access to one or more of these media.

Many of Peru's people live in remote mountain areas without access to any of these sources of news. Most of the radios, television sets, and newspapers are around Lima (the capital city)[2] and Arequipa. The 5 million citizens of those cities thus have a better chance to access these media. So do inhabitants of regional towns, where many of the people with higher educations live.

Rural dwellers of Nigeria have little access to radio, television, or newspapers.

In the nation-states where radios, television sets, and newspapers are readily available to much of the populace, not everyone uses them to learn about the news. A 1976 study in the United States found that 28 percent of Americans read stories about national politics regularly in the newspaper, and 54 percent (including most of the 28 percent) watched national evening news on television regularly; a 1991 survey found that 54 percent got their news exclusively from television.[3] A 1979 study in the Soviet Union found that about two-thirds of Soviet citizens watched television news regularly.[4] A 1977 study in the United Kingdom found that 54 percent of respondents said they watched television news every day, while 36 percent listened to it on radio.[5] In 1973, 31 percent of West German respondents told pollsters they read about politics in a daily paper and watched news on television, while 45 percent watched news on TV but did not read it in newspapers.[6] With a similar ratio of radios and television sets to people, and access for many to West German

broadcasts as well as to their own prior to reunification, similar ratios in East Germany would not be surprising.

So, even with ready access to the media, at least a third of the populace in the United States, the Soviet Union, the United Kingdom, and Germany do not use the media to learn about news. Still, higher percentages of the populace at least have the opportunity to read and hear differing viewpoints on the news than in China, India, Peru, and Nigeria.

More people obtain news from television than from newspapers. Newspapers can generally discuss the complexities behind the issues more thoroughly than television news programs can. With this in mind, it seems safe to conclude that fewer than half of the people in any of these nation-states systematically follow issues in the news; in China, India, Peru, and Nigeria, those percentages must be much smaller.

ACCESS TO EDUCATION

Education is also a factor in one's ability to understand public issues. There are significant differences in levels of education. Statistics show high percentages of the population to be literate in the United States, the CIS republics, the United Kingdom, and Germany; primary education is compulsory and universally available in all these systems. The United Nations ranks the United States 49th among 158 member countries in literacy levels; studies find between 13 and 30 percent of American adults to be functionally illiterate.[7] One in seven students leaving the United Kingdom's primary schools are functionally illiterate.[8] In all of these countries at least 10 percent of the adult populace cannot read or write.

Many older Chinese are uneducated, though primary education (often of poor quality) is now universally available; some 15 to 35 percent of the Chinese populace is illiterate.[9] Since the introduction of the responsibility system, which permits a return to family farming, Chinese peasants in poor areas have increasingly been keeping their children away from school to work on their plots.[10] In India,

60 percent of adult men and 80 percent of women are illiterate;[11] many school children study in their regional languages in schools with mud floors and very low levels of instruction. Among highland peasants, who constitute half of Peru's population, a third of pupils drop out of primary school during the first three years,[12] and many of their parents are illiterate.[13] In Nigeria, at least a third of males and two-thirds of females are illiterate.[14]

As figure 7.2 shows, in all but Nigeria, a third or more of those in the relevant age group attended high school in 1988; in the United States,[15] the Soviet Union, Germany, and the United Kingdom[16] well over 75 percent attended in 1986, 1987, or 1988. Nigeria's statistics are skewed even more by the fact that over 60 percent of secondary school enrollment was around Lagos and Port Harcourt, meaning that less than 6 percent of rural youths are enrolled in high school.[17] Mass education through the secondary level is far better established in the United States, the CIS republics, the United Kingdom, and Germany than in the others. Interestingly, nearly twice the percentage of East German teenagers graduated from secondary school as West German teens.

All but Nigeria, India, and China count 20 percent or more of those aged twenty to twenty-four in higher education; only the United States surpasses 35 percent. University education also has the longest history in Germany, the United Kingdom, and the United States; far more Americans receive education beyond the secondary level than in the others. As of 1978, all but 9,000 of East Germany's 127,473 higher education students were enrolled in technical fields;[18] less than 4 percent of the adult populace in the United Kingdom, and East and West Germany,[19] have university educations. About 10 percent of Peruvians have attended university.[20]

In all these nation-states, only a few attend the oldest and most prestigious universities. In the United States we have Harvard, Yale, and Princeton. The United Kingdom has Oxford and Cambridge (founded before 1200). With eighteen universities founded before our own oldest university, Harvard (founded 1636),[21] Germany has several universities of considerable prestige. In Russia, the place to go for children of the **nomenklatura,** the high-status officials and professionals, is Moscow University; in China, Beijing University; in Peru, San Marcos, and in Nigeria, the University of Ibadan. Higher education also has a long, and complex, tradition in India; it is useful to attend the leading university in one's region, or to go to England to attend Oxford or Cambridge. Many who attend these institutions first attend prestigious preparatory grammar and secondary schools (called **public schools** in England and **academies** in communist countries); the public schools are private, while the academies are run by the state.

In all these cases, parents with better educations, money, information, and other attributes that enhance influence, aspiring to send the children to such schools, enroll them in the prep schools these institutions regularly recruit from. The students themselves must be bright and do well in school. But this process helps assure that a high percentage of these student bodies come from well-educated parents.

The capacity for such individuals to understand complex political issues should normally increase. In fact, because admission standards for such schools are very tight, just mastering what to emphasize in talking to admissions officers requires one to learn something about exerting influence! But it may be the parent, and not the student, who steers the son or daughter through the admissions process. The curricula of these schools often do not force students to pay attention to the news. One can pass tests in introductory courses without much grasp of how details relate to the big picture. A student may be far more interested in the theater, art, literature, medicine, business, or rock music than in practicing the skills of reading, listening, and thinking needed to understand complex issues. Studies, however, show that those with more education are more inclined to read newspapers than those with less education. And graduates of prestigious prep schools often gain access to institutions through which influence can be exerted, and where such reading, thinking, and discussing do take place.

Figure 7.2   Percentage of youths still in school, by age and sex. (a) Female and (b) male primary students; (c) female and (d) male secondary students; and (e) female and (f) male students aged twenty to twenty-four years.

UNESCO Statistical Yearbook 1990, *Table 3.2.*

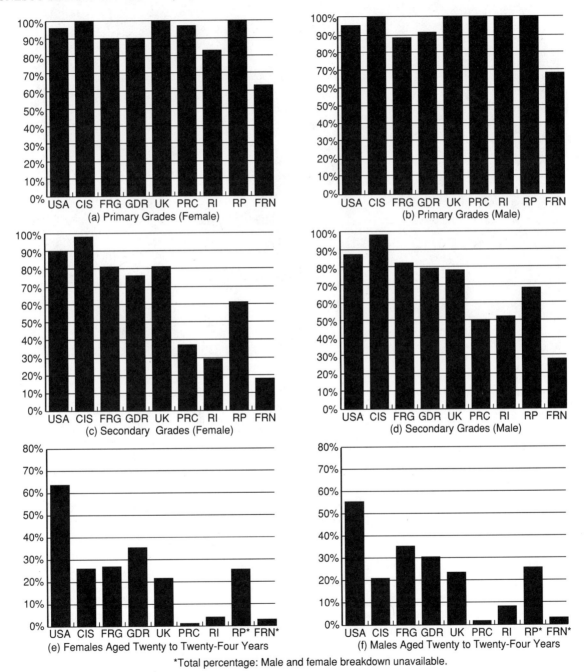

(a) Primary Grades (Female)

(b) Primary Grades (Male)

(c) Secondary Grades (Female)

(d) Secondary Grades (Male)

(e) Females Aged Twenty to Twenty-Four Years

(f) Males Aged Twenty to Twenty-Four Years

*Total percentage: Male and female breakdown unavailable.

Wells Theological College students play cricket in Cathedral courtyard, Somerset, England.
Bob Gamer

The chance that a young person will attend any institution of higher education increases if his or her parents earned a higher education. A 1980 to 1983 nationwide survey of college graduates in the United States found 46 percent had a father who attended college, while only 27 percent had a father with less than a high school education.[22] A 1980 study in the Soviet Union found that children of blue collar workers were half as likely as those of professionals to advance from eighth to ninth grade, and a third as likely to obtain a higher education.[23]

A 1981 government survey in the United Kingdom found that only 3 percent of children from manual workers' families stay in school from ages twenty to twenty-four, while 29 percent of children of professionals attend school at the same ages.[24]

In West Germany during the 1970s, 60 percent of university and professional school students were the offspring of white-collar employees; only 13 percent were the children of industrial workers.[25] A 1973 report showed that 67 percent of children from West German middle-class homes reach the university-preparatory secondary school, the **Gymnasium,**[26] compared to only 8 percent of the children of manual workers; only 12 percent of working-class children who reach that level go on to university, while 50 percent of middle-class children do.[27] An East German study found that 55 percent of polytechnic and university students were the offspring of middle-class families; an additional portion of those described as ''workers'' were probably members of the intelligentsia.

In China, less than 2 percent of the populace aged twenty to twenty-four is in school; a significant percentage of these are sons and daughters of officials, cadres, and intellectuals. In India, some 4 percent of women and 8 percent of men in the relevant age group are enrolled in English-language junior colleges, colleges, and universities; nearly all are from relatively affluent families and have attended private schools.

Peru has established numerous universities in recent years; in contrast to all these other nation-states, the majority of graduates in Peru are offspring of peasants without education. Nigeria's fourteen universities draw their 80,000 students from among the tenth or less of the populace who speak fluent English.[28] About 30,000 others study abroad, and often do not return; as of 1984, fewer than 3 percent of those aged twenty to twenty-four were in school. Two-thirds of university entrants are from the nine southern states; a higher percentage of Ibos and Yorubas (from those regions) have higher education than other tribal groups.

There are parallels between the statistics on education and the statistics on access to news. The nation-states where more people receive an education also can count a higher percentage of people hearing or reading news. Not all those with education pay attention to news, though there are indications that they may have more tendency to do so than those with less education. Furthermore, not all those who pay attention to news pay close attention to it.

People with primary or secondary school educations—or no formal education at all—are in a position to understand some complexities, especially about local matters. Any advanced education (regardless of the prestige of the university) can add to that capacity. But those with no education, or barely a grade school education, and with poor access to newspapers, radio, and television often do not have the capacity to understand complex issues. And there is some evidence that one's motivation to understand such matters increases with increasing education. Among the nine nation-states, the United States, the CIS, East and West Germany, the United Kingdom, and Peru have the highest percentages of people with at least secondary education and easy access to media.

At this point in the discussion, then, the United States, the post-Soviet republics, Germany, the United Kingdom, and Peru would seem to have the highest percentages of people available for political recruitment. Even there, less than half of the populace would seem to be able and motivated to comprehend public issues. As we look at four other factors which have a bearing on political recruitment, however, we will see those percentages shrink.

SUMMARY

Some people are cut off from access to radio, television, newspapers, books, magazines, and other means by which news and information are disseminated. Some have no formal education, or little education. This makes it difficult for them to understand public issues. Individuals with higher education and access to news and other information may still not understand public issues; but they have a better chance of doing so.

NOTES

1. In the United States, political parties and government leaders hire media consultants to put a "spin" on the day's news—they highlight basic facts, interpretations, or topics they want to see in the headlines. The press may or may not report on these themes. With government-controlled radio and television, as in China, those themes simply become the "news."

2. Of 200 private and public radio stations, 37 are in Lima. There are fourteen daily newspapers, mostly circulated in Lima.

3. Center for Political Studies, University of Michigan, *1976 American National Election Study* (ICPSR). Roper national poll between December 1990 and February 1991. "Americans Turning to TV for Most News, Poll Says," *Kansas City Star,* May 3, 1991. About a fifth get their news exclusively from newspapers, while another fifth get it from a mixture of newspapers and television.

4. Ellen Propper Mickiewicz, *Media and the Russian Public* (New York: Praeger, 1981), p. 120. Mickiewicz found news about domestic politics to be the least popular feature in periodicals, except among Communist Party activists and those with at least a high school education or more. News analysis programs were viewed largely by better-educated people.

5. David Watt, "Education for Democracy," *Financial Times,* April 1, 1977.

6. E. Noelle-Neumann and E. P. Neumann, *Jahrbuch der Offentlichen Meinung 1968–1973* (Allensbach: Verlag fur Demoskopie, 1974), pp. 180–181.

7. A 1982 study by the United States Census Bureau found 13 percent of adults illiterate in English. A 1975 University of Texas study found 20 percent of adults functionally illiterate to the point of not being able to read a newspaper want ad or write a grocery list. *New York Times,* April 21, 1986. Jonathan Kozol, *Illiterate America* (New York: Anchor-Doubleday, 1985), estimates that a third of America's 174 million adults cannot read a newspaper and 25 million adults (44 percent of whom are black) cannot read or write at all. He says a third of mothers receiving welfare, and two thirds of unemployed adults, are functionally illiterate.

8. Sarah Bosley, "Prince Hits Out At School 'Illiteracy'," *Manchester Guardian Weekly,* April 28, 1991.

9. Official Chinese government figures show illiteracy dropping from 22.8 percent in 1982 to 15.8 percent in 1991. James L. Tyson, "Han Writing Seen on Ethnic Wall," *Christian Science Monitor,* January 7, 1991. *UNESCO Statistical Yearbook 1990,* Table 1.3, estimates 34 percent illiterate in 1982 (20 percent of males and 50 percent of females). *World Development Report 1990, World Development Indicators,* Table 1, p. 178, estimates 31 percent of the total population and 45 percent of females to be illiterate in 1985.

Europa World Yearbook 1990 estimates 34.5 percent (20.8 percent of males and 48.9 percent of females) illiterate in 1982.

10. In 1982, the percentage of children in the appropriate age group enrolled in secondary school may have been as high as 46 percent; by 1986, it may have been as low as 30 percent. Nicholas Lardy, seminar, University of Missouri–Kansas City, March 25, 1986.

11. These figures are according to the World Bank *World Development Report 1990,* Table 1. *UNESCO Statistical Yearbook 1990,* Table 1.3 estimates that in 1981, 45 percent of all males and 74 percent of all females were illiterate. In remote areas of Rajasthan, fewer than 2 percent of females are literate, and the figure seldom reaches 10 percent in remote rural areas. Barbara Crossette, "India's Decline," *New York Times Magazine,* May 19, 1991.

12. Thomas G. Sanders, "Peru's Population in the 1980s," *University Field Staff International Reports* 27 (1984): 8. This does not show up in official statistics.

13. World Bank *World Development Report 1990* estimates 15 percent of adults and 22 percent of females illiterate in 1985, while *Europa World Yearbook 1990* estimates 8.5 percent for males and 15.2 percent for females. These are conservative estimates.

14. World Bank *World Development Report 1990* estimates 58 percent of adults and 69 percent of females to be illiterate in 1985. *UNESCO Statistical Yearbook 1990,* Table 1.3, estimates 49 percent of adults, with 38 percent of males and 61 percent of females, to be illiterate. *Europa World Yearbook 1990* estimates that 65 percent of the populace was illiterate in 1984.

15. But about 25 percent of students in the United States quit before finishing high school. In 1988, about 85 percent of eighteen-year-olds were still in school, according to OECD statistics. See "Bottom of the Class," *The Economist,* October 29, 1992.

16. But only 40 percent finish their O- or A-level "graduation" qualifications. Bosley, "Illiteracy." In 1988, only 35 percent of eighteen-year-olds were still in school. OECD.

17. Anthony Kirk-Greene and Douglas Rimmer, *Nigeria Since 1970: A Political and Economic Outline* (London: Hodder and Stoughton, 1981), pp. 115–116.

18. Jonathan Steele, *Socialism with a German Face* (London: Jonathan Cape, 1977), p. 171 reports that in 1972, 17 of every 1,000 people between ages eighteen and forty-five in East Germany were attending a polytechnic college or university, versus fourteen in West Germany.

19. Jaroslav Krejci, *Social Structure in Divided Germany: A Contribution to the Comparative Analysis of Social Systems* (New York: St. Martins, 1976), p. 86.

20. This was true as of 1981. Sanders, *op. cit.* At the same time, 31 percent had attended secondary school.

21. By then Scotland had four universities—St. Andrews (1411), University of Glasgow (1453), University of Aberdeen (1494), and College of Edinburgh (1582)—while England still had only Oxford and Cambridge. Germany had Heidelberg (1386), Cologne (founded 1388; closed 1798), Erfurt (founded 1392; closed 1816), Leipzig (1409), Rostock (1419), Freiburg (1457), Tübingen (1477), Ingolstadt (1472; moved to Munich by 1826), Trier (1473), Mainz (1477; closed 1816), Wittenberg (1502; closed 1815), Marburg (1527), Jena (1558), Helmstedt (1575 to 1809); Altdorf (1526 to 1807), Strasbourg (1566), Giessen (1607), and Rinteln (1607 to 1809).

22. Everett Carll Ladd, *The American Polity* (New York: Norton, 1985), p. 52.

23. Alex Pravda, "Is There a Soviet Working Class?" *Problems of Communism* 31 (November-December 1982): 19.

24. *General Household Survey,* London, HMSO, 1981.

25. Lewis Edinger, *Politics in West Germany,* 2nd ed. (Boston: Little, Brown, 1977), p. 54.

26. All children attend *Grundschule* (grammar school) for four years. After another five to six years of *Hauptschule* (higher school), about 70 percent take a job combined with three-and-a-half years of part-time vocational school; the government pays for the schooling, and the business for the job training. The rest proceed either to *Realschule* for six years, followed by work, or to *Gesamptschulen* (comprehensive schools) and *Gymnasium* for nine years, which could lead to university. Only 1 percent of students drop out of school before completing the stream they are in. Donna McGuire, "Low Dropout Rate Makes Germany a Model," *Kansas City Star,* May 11, 1991. In 1988, 81 percent of eighteen-year-olds were still in school. OECD.

27. Hans J. Weiler, "The Politics of Education Innovation: Recent Developments in West German School Reform." (Report to the National Academy of Education, October 1973).

28. The percentage of the populace speaking fluent English may decline if the 1990 policy allowing schools to conduct primary education entirely in regional languages continues.

EXERCISES

Think about the book thus far:

1. How do the topics discussed in this chapter—access to news and to education—relate to influence?

2. Why does part 2 of the book begin with this topic?

3. Which of the five characteristics of influential people (see chapter 5) are we discussing here?

KEY WORDS AND PHRASES

Define the following terms:

nomenklatura
public school
academy
gymnasium

THINKING IT THROUGH

Answer each of the following questions by placing an X in the appropriate boxes on the chart.

1. Which of these nation-states has the lowest percentage of television sets in comparison to the total population?
2. In which of these nation-states is it safe to say that half the populace see and hear news programs?
3. Which of these nation-states has the lowest portion of the relevant age group in high school?
4. Which of these nation-states grants the lowest percentage of the populace access to higher education?
5. Which of these nation-states has the highest percentage of university students whose parents are not middle-class?
6. Which of these nation-states has the lowest percentage of people who are both literate and have access to news?

	USA	CIS (USSR)	FRG	GDR	UK	PRC	RI	RP	FRN
1. Television sets									
2. News									
3. High school									
4. Higher education									
5. University students									
6. Literacy and news access									

Now, ask yourself:

7. Why might individuals with higher education have an advantage in acquiring influence? Will you be influential?
8. Does higher education ensure that a person will understand public issues? Why or why not?
9. Do those whose parents have secondary or higher education often have better access to education and news? Why or why not?

chapter 8

POLITICAL RECRUITMENT
RESOURCES: FOOD, CLOTHING, AND SHELTER

We turn now to the second characteristic which helps a person to be recruited into a position of political influence: political resources beyond those needed to understand public issues. As we saw in chapter 5, many resources can enhance one's influence. Here we look at three such resources which are often overlooked, but are vital to human life: food, clothing, and shelter. They are useful political resources because they are so vital.

We learned in chapter 5 that people who need, want, are afraid of, or respect what you have may, as a result, change their attitudes or behavior. If this is the case, what you have is a political resource. Robert Dahl indicated that money, information, food, the threat of force, jobs, friendship, social standing, the right to make laws, votes, and a great variety of other things can be political resources. These are factors which help people acquire influence.

We have already looked at one of these factors—information and the ability to understand it. Chapter 7 discussed that political resource in depth; we learned that in China, Peru, India, and Nigeria, only small percentages of the populace have easy access to information, and in the other nation-states, less than half of the people are both able and motivated to understand public issues. In this chapter, we shall focus especially on another resource on Dahl's list: food. Food and other basic necessities can be a valuable political resource along with information. **In some systems, food is a more widely distributed political resource than information;** by looking at it next, we can restore some balance to our analysis.

A political resource is a means by which one person can influence the behavior of other persons. Food is among the most fundamental human needs. If people grow their own, they need not adjust their behavior to obtain it from someone else. When people grow surplus food, they have something other people need, and hence might be able to influence the behavior of others in exchange for food; this is why Dahl refers to food as a political resource. In similar ways, people who produce clothing and shelter possess a political resource. Producers have a political resource; consumers need that resource. Let's look at each group in turn.

PRODUCERS

In four of the systems we are studying, the ability to understand public issues is not a widely distributed political resource—those systems are China, Nigeria, India, and Peru. Are these nation-states also places where food, clothing, and shelter are not widely distributed political resources?

Seventy to seventy-five percent of the Chinese population lives in the countryside.[1] Nearly all of these rural dwellers personally till fertile, well-watered land leased to their families and grow food for themselves; high percentages of them supply surpluses to the urban populace and have sufficient amounts left for seed. They also have animals and human excrement for fertilizer. Hence, these peasants have a political resource: they produce food for their own use, and for others.

About 80 percent of Nigerians live outside cities; two-thirds of the work force earn a living through agriculture.[2] Unlike the Chinese, however, few Nigerians grow surpluses and many need supplementary food sources; drought and poor land make crops uncertain, and road access to urban areas is often unreliable. Nigerians have little income to buy seed and fertilizer. Most food for urban areas is imported through large firms or comes from farms in areas immediately surrounding the cities. Much of the populace that does not grow food, or grows insufficient food, depends on these few importers and growers; that confines food as a political resource into fewer hands.

A third to half of Indian[3] and 15 percent of Peruvian[4] families own land; many are not served by roads suitable for transporting agricultural produce, and many have little access to irrigation, seed, or fertilizer. With rainfall uncertain and their plots small, most barely grow enough food for themselves and must either purchase it from private dealers or trade labor for it. In India, about a fifth of landowners supply food to markets outside their own villages.[5] In Peru, those without land in much of the highlands area work for neighbors or absentee landlords; residents of towns and cities buy food from a small percentage of farmers and from import firms. Few have surplus food as a political resource.

Thus, while high percentages of Chinese may have little chance to understand public issues, they do have a political resource in the form of surplus food needed by others. Much lower percentages of Nigerians have that resource, and even lower percentages of Peruvians and Indians.

The other five systems offer higher percentages of their populace the chance to understand public issues; the percentage of their populace who can add to (or make up for the lack of) that capacity by producing food varies. Most agricultural production in the former Soviet Union was run by the state; the CIS republics continue this system. **State farms** are run by bureaucrats and hired workers, who are guaranteed jobs. Bureaucrats run **collective farms** as well, but their profits are theoretically distributed among those who work on them. Fifteen million collective farm families, and 17 to 18 million workers and office employees, are allotted private plots amounting to 3 or 4 percent of the nation-state's total arable land, on which they grow food; these plots produce a third of the milk, meat, eggs, and vegetables, two-thirds of the potatoes, and half the fruit, accounting for a quarter of the total food supply. The collective farm workers (on 29,600 collective farms) and the workers on 18,000 state farms (together, 13 percent of the total work force) supply most of the rest of the food.[6] Some ethnic groups in southern and eastern parts of the CIS still live in more traditional rural villages, where they grow their own food (though some are officially classified in other occupations); they constitute about 8 percent of wage earners. In total, nearly a third of wage earners are involved with growing food for themselves, and for the urban population; they have a political resource.

In West Germany, about 5 percent of the populace works in agriculture; the majority of those owning land supplement their income with other jobs.[7] In addition, seven million West German families live in rural houses with space for substantial gardens. About 14 percent of East Germany's work force was employed on 5,000 collective and state farms.[8] Most of them went bankrupt after reunification allowed suppliers in the West to stock stores, though some farms continue to produce raw materials now processed in more modern plants. Each family working on an East German collective farm was allotted a one-acre private plot. So now, a portion of families supply part of their own food; most food comes from a fourth or less of West Germany's one million farms and from some of the former state and collective farms.

In the United Kingdom and the United States, very few people have access to food-producing land beyond backyard vegetable gardens. Less than 2 percent of the work forces in the United Kingdom and the United States are involved in farming; many of those do not own their own land. In the United States, most surplus food for the market comes from the 300,000 private farms which control two-thirds of the farmland;[9] a substantial amount of food is

F*igure 8.1* Percent of labor force employed in agriculture, forestry, or fishing.
Europa World Yearbook, *1990*.

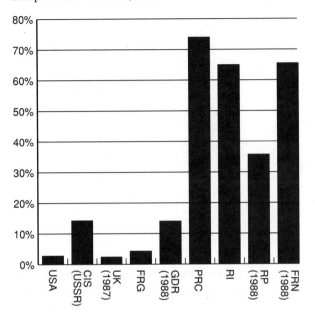

F*igure 8.2* Some people depend on others for food or other commodities.

imported, mostly through the largest processing and distributing firms. In the United Kingdom, the surplus food comes from a declining portion of some 200,000 farms and from imports.[10] The great majority of the large populations in these two countries thus rely on relatively few farms and marketing firms for their food (figure 8.1).

Though over half of Nigerians grow their own food, most do not grow all they need and cannot count food as much of a political resource. In China, high percentages of the populace grow surplus food, and thus have food as a potential resource to influence the behavior of others. In India, Nigeria, and Peru, some of those with little access to information at least have some access to land and food as a resource. Except for in China, high percentages of all nine of these populations rely on small numbers of producers and distributors for at least part of their food supply.

Hence, in all these nation-states except China, small percentages of the populace can use food as a political resource. High percentages of the populace need to obtain food from others (figure 8.2).

Growers are not the only ones who control food surpluses. Those lending capital or supplying equipment to farms have a hand in that control; sometimes these are government agencies, sometimes private banks and firms. Marketers also exert control over this political resource. In some of these nation-states, food is marketed by government agencies;[11] otherwise, marketing is handled by the farmers themselves, processors,[12] or trading firms.

In the United States, Germany, and the United Kingdom, farmers growing surplus food often have good educations and access to information; so do those in Peru, Nigeria, and India. The people who lend them capital, supply equipment, and purchase and market their output have good educations and information as well. In the post-Soviet republics, where much food comes from private plots, food producers may have less education; but those individuals market part of their output through government agencies, and they work for managers with education and information who run the collective and state farms. The managers, who sometimes diverted food into the black market under communism, now barter with bureaucrats from various urban areas to obtain various manufactured goods. In all these systems, then, surplus food growers, suppliers, and distributors have the combined political resources of food, education, and information.

In China, where food growers constitute a much higher portion of the populace, they nonetheless often lack education and information. Some of these growers market a portion of their output themselves. Government bureaucrats purchase a lot of their output, supply seed and fertilizer, help with irrigation, and otherwise assist them. Some of those bureaucrats are well educated and informed. They bargain with peasants and strike deals with other bureaucrats to sell commodities like grain and cotton, or trade these goods for favors.

How do suppliers of surplus food use food as a political resource? Food helps give them the basis to resist changes they do not desire, and to pressure government to make changes they do desire, such as subsidies, loans, educational extension, electrification, and regulation of market prices. We shall examine shortly whether food producers have other attributes of influence as well.

CONSUMERS

Those who must purchase food may also exert influence over the government. As consumers, they may want to pressure government to assist them if their food supplies run short, cost too much, or are poorly distributed, or if choice is limited, or quality is not satisfactory. In the United States, the post-Soviet republics, East and West Germany, and the United Kingdom, a sizeable percentage of those who must purchase food have enough access to information and education to give them some ability to influence government. In India, Peru, and Nigeria, lower percentages of those who must purchase food have such access.

People who produce their own food possess a political resource in the negative sense—they need not submit to others to obtain this essential commodity because they both produce and consume it themselves. If they produce surplus food, their influence is enhanced; because others depend on them for a basic commodity, they possess a political resource to influence the behavior of others. To take full advantage of this resource, they need other traits that give them influence, such as education and information, so they know how to make the best use of what they have. Their influence also increases if government needs their food; government policy makers who need their food to feed bureaucrats, soldiers, and political supporters, are more inclined to pay attention to them.

People who do not produce food must eat. They depend on surplus food controlled by other people. Because they lack food as a political resource, they must use other political resources to affect government policy on food production or distribution. However, neither they, nor the government, are likely to push for changes which threaten their only source of food. Unless alternative food suppliers are available, the people who supply foods can argue that the proposed changes indeed threaten the food supply. In fact, they can themselves propose changes they feel are necessary to protect the food supply. Non-farming food consumers reject these suggestions at their own risk; unless they thoroughly understand the food business, they may find it difficult to persuade government leaders that they can reject the suppliers' suggestions without endangering food supplies. Consumers cannot afford to be without food. That gives an advantage to those who control food surpluses.

In the United States, the post-Soviet republics, the United Kingdom, and Germany, substantial percentages of those who do not produce their own food are able to obtain education and information useful for exerting influence on government and producers. But the food suppliers in those systems also have education and information. In all these nation-states, both the government and substantial

F*igure 8.3* Each person may know he or she has something the other wants.

majorities of the populace procure food from these producers; that gives the government and the majority a common interest in protecting and regulating the same food supply. When the government protects its own food supply, it also protects that of large segments of the populace on whom it depends for political support. As we shall see in chapter 9, these governments also have an interest in protecting a large work force, which they rely on for other goods as well, and for maintaining a vigorous economy; that requires a steady food supply for most of the populace. The producers of food surpluses, meanwhile, depend on government, which must be responsive to consumers as well as producers, for subsidies and income. They constitute only a small portion of voters and depend on the good will of the majority. All this interdependence keeps influence dispersed (figure 8.3). When food producers are dissatisfied with their conditions, or consumers with their food supplies, government has reasons to respond.

All nine of these systems also rely on small numbers of managers and distributors for substantial portions of their food supplies. Prices for grains and produce are set by government agencies, commodity exchanges where investors bid to purchase future crops, or foreign suppliers. Whether buying raw grains and produce or preprocessed foods, consumers usually must choose among a handful of large distributors for the food they purchase. If they were to boycott those suppliers, they would have no food. But if their dissatisfaction over supplies or prices becomes intense enough, those with the right to vote in competitive elections can pressure government to regulate and withdraw payments from growers and distributors. United States, United Kingdom, and German voters have that capacity. In the CIS, voters are beginning to gain that leverage as well.

Food producers in all these systems have persuaded government and consumers that a steady and secure food supply requires heavy subsidies and import quotas. On top of every dollar they earn, American farmers receive nearly fifty cents from the government in the form of subsidies. United Kingdom and German farmers receive an additional dollar. Most of this goes to the largest producers. Producers argue that cuts in these taxpayer-funded subsidies will raise food costs and endanger food supplies, but studies about this are inconclusive. Uncertainty about what might happen if they were removed helps keep subsidies in place.[13]

In China, producers of surplus food make up a much larger portion of the populace; high percentages of families produce their own food and some food surpluses. They have poor access to education and information. Since they are both the principal food consumers and the principal suppliers, neither group has access to education and information. That distributes influence equally between producer and consumer because they are one and the same. Government in China relies on all these same peasants (not just a small portion of them) for its own food supply and authority and hence retains an interest in their welfare and productive capacity. Moreover, government relies on the suspicion created among peasants when urbanites demonstrate to expand their political rights; as long as food producers support the government, it can squelch such demonstrations. And peasants sometimes demonstrate. This, too,

F*igure 8.4*   The person who needs food may have more information than the person producing it.

F*igure 8.5*   The person producing surplus food may also have more information.

gives food producers some influence over government. Still, many urban dwellers have better educations and information than their rural compatriots. That gives them some political resources as consumers (figure 8.4) even though they do not produce food.

India, Peru, and Nigeria provide a stark contrast to this. Substantial portions of the populace do not produce their own food, nor are they in a position to obtain education, information, or other characteristics needed to acquire influence. High percentages of those who do grow their own food can supply only part of their own needs and have little access to education or information. But those who produce and control surplus food often are well educated and informed (figure 8.5). Since the government and urban dwellers obtain food from small numbers of such firms, they need not be concerned with the welfare and productivity of the rest of the uneducated, uninformed populace. In addition, the

government does not need this uninformed populace to produce other goods, to pay taxes, or to consume goods that keep the economy sound. If these people starve, it does not hurt the government politically or economically. This leaves high percentages of families with little ability to influence the economic institutions which produce food.

Because everyone eats, all those who do not produce food must obtain it from those who do. That gives food producers an advantage which nonproducing consumers must redress by amassing other political resources such as education and information. In the United States, the post-Soviet republics, the United Kingdom, and Germany, most of the populace does not produce food but has good access to education and information. Food producers, too, have good access to education and information. In China, most of the populace produces enough food to feed itself, and also produces surplus food; but they have limited access to education and information. Urban dwellers who do not produce food have better access to education and information than the rural food producers. In all those systems, government acquires food from the same producers that supply it to a majority of the populace; government thus has political incentive to keep much of the populace eating. In contrast, small percentages of the populace produce food surpluses in India, Peru, and Nigeria; most of those without food have inadequate money to buy it and also have little education, information, or other means to influence government. The governments in these countries have little interest in whether these nonproducers get enough to eat.

We seldom think about how much food affects political behavior. As long as we produce food ourselves, or can influence institutions that do, and are surrounded by vast surpluses of food, we may ignore the role of food as a political resource. Beggars in Calcutta or famine victims who must live entirely on begged, donated, or scavenged food are certain food affects their behavior; they know food is an important political resource. So do many who fall short of that extreme, but find that they must spend much of their time working to purchase food. Often, they face limited choices, unpredictable quality, high prices, and uncertain supplies, and there is little they can do to rectify any of this. These are problems for many people in India, Peru, and Nigeria. To varying degrees, they are problems for individuals in the rest of these systems as well.

OTHER NECESSITIES

In addition to food, people also need clothing, housing, and other consumer goods. These basic goods, too, are political resources if one controls them.

In the United States, 65 percent of houses are owner-occupied.[14] Savings and loan firms often hold the mortgages on these houses, and large firms own

or hold the mortgages on much rental housing. Many CIS citizens in villages, towns, and collectives also own their own houses; two-thirds of CIS citizens are provided flats by their work units or government agencies. In the former East Germany, many live in aging houses they own or, more commonly, rent from government, work units, or small owners; about a fifth live in newer public housing flats. In West Germany and the United Kingdom, about 60 percent of families buy their homes, while most of the rest rent housing from a number of building and real estate firms; the buyers finance through banks. Some rent public housing, though in the United Kingdom most of this has been sold. In China, over 90 percent of urban dwellers live in public housing supplied by government or their employers. Most of the rural populace own their own homes; many have built new houses or modernized old ones, using extruded concrete, brick, and other components supplied by government-run factories. So in all these systems, substantial portions of the populace acquire or occupy their housing with the assistance of government or large private firms.

In the United States, the United Kingdom, and the Federal Republic of Germany, most people purchase most of their clothing, and cloth for sewing, supplied by large private manufacturers; this is true of many other consumer goods as well. The government owns stock in many of West Germany's corporations. In East Germany before reunification, most goods were manufactured by government-run firms. Soviet citizens purchased goods from government factories and stores and from millionaire black marketers. These black marketers produced goods illegally, after hours, in government firms by bribing supervisors and officials. About half of the goods in China are produced by government-run firms; the other half, however, come from collective enterprises owned and operated by workers and townships or jointly owned by urban or provincial governments and private foreign firms.

Just as the food agencies and suppliers have potential leverage over issues related to food, so these agencies and firms have some leverage over

Figure 8.6   Interdependence: Each needs the other.

issues related to housing and consumer goods; but they also depend on the public to purchase their goods. This demonstrates **interdependence,** when people with one set of political resources adapt their behavior to the needs of those with other political resources, and vice-versa (figure 8.6). The manufacturing firms' political resource is the goods and services they supply. The government's and public's political resource is their ability to purchase or reject the goods; they can work together to place pressure on the suppliers.

In China, the CIS, and the former East Germany, government and consumer influence is weakened because the government heavily subsidizes unprofitable businesses, so producers do not need to worry whether consumers will buy. However, the subsidies themselves constitute a form of interdependence. In this case, government is providing needed funds to companies it needs to produce goods. Also, government needs profits from some plants to subsidize others. The suppliers produce large quantities of goods even if the quality and selection lag. One reason for the decline of the Soviet Union and East Germany was their inattention to that problem; people stopped buying goods made by government firms, leaving too many in need of subsidies.

In systems where private firms compete freely to attract consumer purchases, government and con-

sumers have some direct leverage over those firms; they can buy their housing, supplies, clothing, and other consumer goods from competing producers, so producers and consumers are somewhat interdependent. Even in China, where many joint ventures and cooperatives now compete to sell many types of goods, consumer leverage is growing rapidly. But in the former Soviet Union and East Germany, and with urban housing and some other basic items in China, this leverage fails. The government subsidizes firms that do not sell their goods to guarantee the employees jobs. The company thus has no incentive to make a profit.[15] Managers and distributors may also connive to withhold goods from the market. The consumers' only alternative is to purchase at much higher prices on the black (illegal) market, which has ties to those same managers and distributors, or to buy expensive produce from the private plots of collective farmers. Because there are no competitive elections to remove chief executives who perpetuate this economic system, consumers' leverage is further weakened. They must resort to competitive legislative elections, consumer boycotts, demonstrations, strikes, violence, or other civil disobedience to change the system.

Consumers in Peru, Nigeria, and India often have even less leverage over consumer goods. Many purchase virtually everything they have from the black market: in Peru, Nigeria, and India, the firms which sell to government are often different from those which sell to the general populace. Most villagers build their own housing from locally obtained materials. Most urban dwellers live in squatter colonies, in shacks they build themselves.

Between 1960 and 1984, while the government spent $173.6 million on housing, Peruvians spent $8 billion on houses built without permits.[16] Many rural dwellers do buy cloth or ready-made clothing from manufacturing firms; many others produce their own yarn and cloth, together with other household wares. Of the 8,000 clothing factories and 2,000 shoemaking establishments in Lima, Peru, over 90 percent are not registered with the government. They produce 85 percent of clothing and 74 percent of shoes. Some 65 percent of construction, 95 percent of transportation, and 78 percent of furniture manufacturing also takes place within this so-called informal sector, and about 300,000 peddlers sell their products in this way.[17] The informal economy is quite separate from the manufacturing firms that sell or rent housing and provide consumer goods to established urban dwellers and to the Peruvian government. Participants in the informal economy are not needed as workers or customers in the economy run by established wage earners, whose firms also supply goods and taxes to government. If people do not like the quantity or quality of goods they buy in the unregulated **informal sector,** which produces and sells without permits from or contributions to government, there is little they can do to influence the system to improve. Even food producers within the formal economy sell part of their output in less regulated street or weekly village markets where they blend with the informal sector.

In Nigeria, as well, most of the populace buys much of what they consume (other than food) from the informal sector; some villagers can even sell or barter food within the informal sector. In India, about a third of the populace lives outside villages; well over half of these town and city dwellers work and buy in the informal sector. As we saw earlier in this chapter, perhaps 20 percent of rural Indian landowners, whose families constitute about an eighth of the rural populace, buy modern equipment for their farms and sell on the regular market as well as in local informal street markets. Most of the rest produce and purchase largely in the informal sector; yet they may produce half the national income.[18]

In cities of India, Peru, and Nigeria, participants in the informal sector occupy public and private land illegally to build rough housing. They barter labor or scavenged goods from streets or garbage dumps in exchange for materials to build this housing. These areas often have no running water or sewerage except for occasional public water pumps. Children may be kept from school to work long hours at hauling, picking, peddling, and building, or to work in these shacks or other makeshift buildings

Early in the morning on a warm October day in 1992, we arrived at the international airport in Bombay, India. To get downtown, our taxi driver chose a route lined by the squatter shacks which house half of Bombay's ten million inhabitants. The shacks are like small tents constructed of scrap wood, cardboard, plastic sheeting, mud, and other scavenged materials. Many are jammed into vacant lots and fields. Many others are built along the entrances to shops and dwellings; the doorway of each building on a city block may be flanked by six or eight of these makeshift dwellings on each side. Great numbers of men and women, rousing in the morning light, were squatting to defecate in the storm drain along the road. At intersections, they walked through the mud to gather water, brush their teeth, and bathe at the public water pumps. The roadway contained only taxis, trucks, and buses speeding to other destinations. This scene continued over the ten miles of our ride.

On December 5, we returned to the airport at the end of our stay in India. This time the taxi driver drove along the coast on Marine Drive and Lala Lajpatrai Marg, lined with beautiful hotels, apartments, and shops. Ladies in bright saris were buying groceries, clothes, and flowers. Billboards aimed at the commuters in their new Suzuki Marutis advertised the latest offerings on the booming stock market. Occasionally, we glimpsed a few squatter shacks, and at each stoplight beggars solicited outside the taxi window. A few hours later, rioting (discussed in chapter 17) broke out in the neighborhoods we had passed through on our first taxi ride; some of the rioters killed people and burned buildings along the route of our second ride.

manufacturing goods. The government does not regulate health, safety, or working hours. Health care is often unavailable. In the other systems, far fewer people live exclusively within the informal sector for consumption beyond food. Suppliers are interdependent with government and most of the populace.

Girls selling a bottle, a flashlight battery, a chrome rim, a plastic measuring spoon, a strainer, a pot, an eraser, and a baby bottle nipple along the main road of a Peruvian village. Such items are often scavenged from garbage dumps.

© *Kip May.*

CAPITALISM, COMMUNISM, AND SOCIALISM

In the modern world, two principal economic systems have arisen to distribute food, clothing, shelter, and other consumer goods: capitalism and communism.

By law, 1789 France contained three orders—the clergy, the nobility, and the Third Estate, which consisted of everyone else. Only members of the clergy and nobility could serve in legislatures and courts, and in most positions in the bureaucracy and other high offices; they exempted themselves from many taxes, created monopolies which gave them the exclusive right to sell salt and other necessities, and strictly regulated the sale of grain. The growing middle class, benefitting from increased European trade and the introduction of new technology, had rising income subject to heavy taxation. As members of the Third Estate, they resented the tax exemptions the other two orders gave themselves and the monopolies which stopped the middle class from investing in major parts of the economy, sending their offspring to universities and into high bureaucratic positions, or having a voice in government.

Because he needed to raise taxes, the French monarch Louis XVI let his finance minister call for an assembly in 1789 to pass tax legislation. For the first time, this assembly was to be elected by all three orders.[19] They endorsed a revolutionary concept: Prior to this, it was assumed that sovereignty lay with the monarch, who received his authority to rule from (depending on the political theory to which you subscribed) ancient law, God,[20] or the first two orders. Now the delegates elected by the Third Estate declared that government authority stemmed from the Third Estate—the ordinary people, with or without title, who constitute the nation.[21] They wrote and passed a Declaration of the Rights of Man, which stated that ''men are born and remain free and equal in rights,'' that ''all citizens . . . are equally admissible to all public dignities, offices, and employments,'' that ''taxation . . . should be apportioned equally among all citizens,'' and that ''no one may be deprived of property'' without ''just compensation.''

That document, and the United States Constitution, which had taken effect the prior year, opened the door all over Europe in subsequent decades to legislatures elected by ever-increasing portions of the population. These legislatures ended old monopolies, tore down many tariff barriers between nation-states, established uniform weights and measures, wrote laws to protect contracts, and formed new bureaucracies to regulate commerce and banking. They created a **free enterprise system** by freeing anyone

Figure 8.7 Three relationships between investors and production. In a free enterprise system, investors can invest directly in production; in a capitalist system, investors pool their funds in institutions that invest directly in production; and in a communist system, only the state can invest in production.

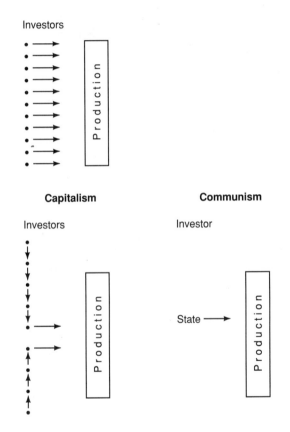

Free Enterprise

Investors

Capitalism

Investors

Communism

Investor

nies allowed smaller, middle-class investors to buy shares in corporations. Some who began with the largest investments, or started with little but were adept investors, accumulated even larger amounts of capital from profits. Land, businesses, labor, and production increasingly fell into fewer hands, as investors gained the ability to buy and sell whatever they needed to produce. This is known as a **capitalist system.** The United States, the United Kingdom, the Federal Republic of Germany, India, Nigeria, and Peru have capitalist systems.

As a result of the rise of capitalism and industrialization, many people moved from rural areas to cities to work in large firms. In 1848, Karl Marx and Friedrich Engels published the *Communist Manifesto,* which suggested that these new working classes should unite (form communes) to control the new industrialization themselves. In 1917, Vladimir Ilyich Lenin led a revolution against the tsars in Russia to establish the Soviet Union as the first communist nation-state. After World War II, Mao Zedong led a similar revolution in China, and the Soviet Union set up communist governments in Eastern Europe. Cuba and Yugoslavia founded similar systems. These **communist systems,** designed to give workers control over the production and distribution of goods, in fact transferred control to government and political party bureaucracies; government and party leaders seized land, houses, manufacturing facilities, and wholesale and retail establishments from their former owners without compensation, and the state took over these establishments in the name of the workers. In communist systems, the government assigns workers to jobs at these various places of business, and assigns them housing for which they pay low rent. Everyone is guaranteed a job and access to inexpensive social services provided by government-controlled work units, or by the government. Rural dwellers are guaranteed access to land and income from it, either by working for a large work unit or by being apportioned a plot of land for their own use. Centralized bureaucrats decide what can be manufactured or grown, and how products are to be distributed. In communist systems, political parties independent of the communist party are outlawed.

with capital—money or other assets—to invest in enterprises creating and selling any products for which there might be a demand (figure 8.7).

While free enterprise spurred intense competition, the development of new metals, chemical, and cloth making technologies allowed factories to become large, which in turn required great amounts of capital. Commercial banks were formed to lend these large sums of money, and joint stock compa-

China is a communist system. East Germany was one before its merger with West Germany. Under *glasnost,* the Soviet Union moved away from one-party rule. Since the Soviet Union dissolved in 1991, individual republics are determining whether they will retain a communist economic system, or adopt features of socialist and capitalist systems.

The word **socialist** is commonly applied to any government ownership of the means of production and distribution of goods. Sometimes officeholders use government to create jobs, provide housing or social services, stimulate production, and assure wider distribution of consumer goods while retaining a capitalist system and competitive political parties. They may combine some socialist ownership with a capitalist system in a **mixed economy.** The government of India operates many basic industries, including steel, fertilizer, and petroleum production. The government of the Federal Republic of Germany owns stock in many large enterprises, while the United States government provides the main support for many private firms through defense contracts. During recent decades, the British government owned and operated many industries. Peru experimented with government ownership of farms and industries, and Nigeria with marketing basic commodities through government marketing boards. China, as we shall see in the next chapter, is increasingly blending capitalist elements into its communist system of ownership.

Much higher percentages of Chinese citizens (as opposed to citizens of the CIS or the former East Germany) control production of surplus food, clothing, and shelter; though all are communist systems, the distribution of political resources varies from one system to another in this regard. High percentages of Indians, Peruvians, and Nigerians produce no food, clothing, or shelter needed by government or urban dwellers, have little information or education, and are not needed as consumers within the formal sector of the economy. They obviously have few political resources. By contrast, the high percentages of Americans, Britons, and West Germans who do not control production of food, clothing, or shelter have more access to information and education; as we shall see in the next chapter, they are also needed as both producers and consumers. Thus, the distribution of political resources varies greatly among capitalist systems as well.

SUMMARY

People who produce and distribute surplus food have something everyone needs. That gives them a political resource to influence the behavior of government or other citizens, who need this resource to survive. In some nation-states, high percentages of the populace possess this political resource; in others, low percentages do. But those who lack surplus food as a political resource may have other resources, such as information and education, sovereignty, or the ability to produce other necessities like housing and clothing. These resources give them ability to influence the behavior of food suppliers and producers.

In some nation-states, high percentages of the populace have none of these political resources. They may depend on others for these necessities, but others do not depend on them. This has a tremendous negative impact on their ability to exert influence in their political systems.

NOTES

1. L. J. Peel, *The Agriculture of China* (New York: Oxford University Press, 1991).

2. *World Tables 1991, A World Bank Publication,* says 68 percent earn a living through agriculture. Most own some land.

3. In 1980, 69.7 percent of India's work force was in agriculture, according to *World Tables 1991;* the *Europa World Yearbook 1990* gives a figure of 65 percent. In 1988, 27 percent of India's population lived in cities, according to *World Development Report 1990, World Development Indicators,* Table 31,

pp. 238–39. So about two-thirds of Indian families are employed in agriculture. Previn Visaria and S. K. Sanyal, "Trends in Rural Unemployment in India: Two Comments," *Economic and Political Weekly,* January 29, 1977, pt. 2, table 3, pp. 245–48, estimates that in 1971 and 1972, 27.4 percent of rural households had no land, 32.9 percent controlled less than 2.5 acres each; 29.3 percent, 2.5 to 10 acres each; and 10.4 percent, over 10 acres per household. The term *control* in these statistics simply means living on and cultivating land, so these figures may include tenants, or relatives acting as fronts for larger landowners trying to get around laws limiting the amount of acreage one person can own. Thus, there were fewer owners than these figures might indicate; certainly no more than half of India's households own some land. If a quarter of land "controllers" are tenants (see chapter 21), and others are simply disguising portions of larger landholdings, less than a third of India's households own land. Those that do must often borrow money at high interest rates to obtain seeds, fertilizers, water, and other necessities.

4. Robert E. Gamer, *The Developing Nations: A Comparative Perspective,* 2d ed. (Boston: Allyn & Bacon, 1982), pp. 300–304.

5. During the 1960s, most of the surplus food for domestic consumption came from the 7 percent of cultivable land (and 65 percent of irrigated land) producing improved strains of wheat and rice. B. L. Sukhwal, *India: A Political Geography* (Bombay: Allied Publishers, 1971), p. 35. Since then, more farming families are producing these improved strains, using irrigation, but only 23 percent of agricultural land is irrigated. According to Sanyal, *op. cit.,* 45 percent of farming families controlled less than 2.5 acres each, which means these farms are generally too small to make use of advanced technology or produce surpluses. The 14 percent of landowners with over 10 acres of land (controlling 53.2 percent of total farmland) could be expected to contribute food to urban areas. Their 195 million acres of land include many of India's 92 million irrigated acres. Only a portion of the 18 percent of farming families whose plots are between 5 and 10 acres have adequate irrigation to produce sufficient surpluses to sell outside their villages; even a lower portion of the 22 percent with plots between 2.5 and 5 acres can do so. In 1970, India had about 80 million agricultural

households. Indira Gandhi's programs to help those with dry, unirrigated farms of under 7.5 acres found over 50 million eligible. Since there were only 60 million landowners or tenant-operators at the time, that means only a sixth of farmers had irrigated or naturally watered fields; the amount of area under irrigation has grown modestly since then.

The percentages in the prior paragraph do not include landless people, except for the 80 million agricultural households, 20 million of which were landless.

6. The 1992 agricultural reforms discussed in chapters 31 and 33 still leave food production largely in the same hands.

7. In 1972, there were a million farms of over 1 1/4 acres in West Germany; nearly 700,000 of them depended on outside income. Two percent of them were over 125 acres, averaging about 200 acres; that percentage is growing. M. Schnitzer, *East and West Germany: A Comparative Economic Analysis* (New York: Praeger, 1972), p. 72.

8. With half a million acres (1,000 square miles), religious organizations were East Germany's largest nongovernment landholders. East Germany measured 41,825 square miles.

9. Between 1900 and 1990, the number of United States farms dropped from 5,737,000 to 2,100,000. By 1974, the number of Americans living on farms had dropped below 10 million and was steadily declining. The *Kansas City Star,* March 24, 1987, reports that between 1980 and 1987 some 170,000 farm families left their land. The *Kansas City Star,* January 27, 1986, reports that by 1986, there were 634,000 commercial farms. In 1900, farms over 500 acres occupied 266 million acres of America's 838 million acres of farmland; by 1954, 663 million acres of 1,160 million acres of farmland. By 1991, nearly a third of America's farmers were approaching sixty-five years of age, with sons and daughters who had entered other lines of work; many of these were selling their family farms to agribusinesses. ABC Nightly News, October 3, 1991. In 1989, two-thirds of American farms had sales below $40,000 a year, with only 0.7 percent of that income derived from farming. By 1992, only 1.6 percent of America's work force were farmers. "What Makes Farming Different?" *The Economist,* December 12, 1992.

10. As of 1976, 2.7 percent of the U.K. work force was working in agriculture on 275,310 farms. Some 19 percent of this land was owned by governments and 42 percent by aristocracy; about half of all land was used for farming. Of 41,879,000 acres in Great Britain, 18 million acres (mostly in Scotland) belonged to some 200 titled families. "The trend on the big estates is for more and more land to go out of productive use." Diamond Commission Report (Royal Commission on the Distribution of Income and Wealth, Background Paper, 1978). Between 1975 and 1985, the size of the average farm in England and Wales grew from 350 to 500 acres. A 1992 survey found that a third of farmers had purchased land during the previous five years. "What Makes Farming Different?" *The Economist*, December 12, 1992.

11. Until 1987, Nigerian producers of export commodities such as peanuts had to sell to government marketing boards at low prices; the marketing boards then sold the commodities abroad for higher prices and kept the profits for the central government or themselves.

12. For example, half the meat in the United States in 1982 was processed by five companies (Iowa Beef Processors, MBPXL, Spencer, Swift, and Dubuque). Swift estimated that Iowa Beef Processors (a division of Occidental Oil Company) alone processed 24.2 percent of all the meat sold. MBPXL belonged to Cargill, the world's largest grain company. Lynn O'Shaughnessy, "Big Packing Plants are Only Sure Winners in Food Revolution," *Kansas City Times*, May 13, 1982.

13. See "Grotesque: A Survey of Agriculture," *The Economist*, December 12, 1992. Two Australian economists, Kym Anderson and Rod Tyers, say the subsidies cost each taxpayer an average of $1,400 a year. An OECD study asserts that removing the protections and subsidies would add $500 billion a year to the world economy.

14. *Statistical Abstract of the United States*, 108th ed., 1988.

15. According to Gorbachev's speech to the Central Committee in June 1987, in which he first proposed doing away with the bureaucratic pricing structure and allowing individual production units to set prices, the Soviet economy spent $115 billion U.S. dollars a year on such subsidies, two-thirds of which went to agriculture. (In contrast, imported jeans were marked up to seven times cost.) Production units could make up for inefficiency and rising costs simply by taking government subsidies; subsidies to agriculture rose from 4 billion rubles in 1966 to over 50 billion in 1986. *Kansas City Times*, June 29, 1987.

16. Mark Falcoff, "The Only Hope for Latin America," *Commentary* 87, 4 (April 1989): 36.

17. Thomas G. Sanders, "Peru's Economy: Underemployment and the Informal Sector," *University Field Staff International Reports* 4 (1984): 4. Hernando de Soto, *El Otro Sendero* (Lima: Instituto Libertad y Democracia, 1986). Geof Barnes, "Inca Cola," PBS "Latin American Journey" series.

18. Lloyd I. Rudolph and Susanne Hoeber Rudolph, *In Pursuit of Lakshmi: The Political Economy of the Indian State* (Chicago: University of Chicago Press, 1987), p. 397.

19. Georges Lefebvre, *The Coming of the French Revolution* (New York: Vintage Books, 1960) provides a classic, concise, and readable introduction to this subject.

20. Mesopotamian kings claimed that the law was handed to them by gods. Those traditions were frequently repeated in history.

21. The Declaration of the Rights of Man stated: "The principle of all sovereignty rests essentially in the nation. No body and no individual may exercise authority which does not emanate from the nation expressly." Sieyes, in his pamphlet *What is the Third Estate?* answered: "The Third Estate has within itself all that is necessary to constitute a nation. . . . Take away the privileged orders, and the nation is not smaller, but greater." Lefebvre, *op. cit.*, p. 53.

EXERCISES

Think about the book thus far:

1. How does the subject of chapter 8 relate to that of chapter 7?
2. Which of the five characteristics of influence introduced in chapter 5 are we discussing in this chapter?

KEY WORDS AND PHRASES

Define the following terms:

state farm	informal sector	communist system
collective farm	free enterprise system	socialist
interdependence	capitalist system	mixed economy

THINKING IT THROUGH

Answer each of the following questions by placing an "X" in the appropriate boxes on the chart.

1. Which of these nation-states has the highest percentage of population with access to land?
2. Which has the lowest percentage?
3. In which of these nation-states do most urban dwellers depend on more than 10 percent of the total work force for most of their food?
4. In which of these nation-states are those who control surplus food likely to have education and be well informed?
5. In which are those who control surplus food unlikely to have education or be well informed?
6. Which of these systems have high percentages of consumers who obtain most of their clothing and shelter from informal sectors of the economy and who lack access to education and information?
7. Which have high percentages of consumers who grow their own food or buy it from the formal sector of the economy and who have access to education and information?

	USA	CIS (USSR)	FRG	GDR	UK	PRC	RI	RP	FRN
1. Access to land									
2. Lack of access to land									
3. Dependent for food									
4. Educated food suppliers									
5. Uneducated food suppliers									
6. Informal economy, no education									
7. Formal economy, education									

Now, ask yourself:

8. Why is food a political resource?

9. Who can use food as a political resource?

10. What can result when food is a widely distributed political resource among producers who have little information? In which system(s) is that the case?

11. When consumers depend on a few well-informed producers for food, how can they balance that dependence? In which system(s) does that take place? In which system(s) does it not take place?

12. Do the communist systems distribute food as a political resource to wider portions of the populace than the capitalist systems? Why or why not?

13. In which of these countries do high portions of the populace lack both food and information as political resources?

chapter 9

POLITICAL RECRUITMENT

RESOURCES: JOBS AND SKILLS

In this chapter, we will continue to discuss the second characteristic that can enhance a person's influence by looking at two more political resources vital to human life—jobs and skills. Whether these resources are available to any given person depends partly on that person's talents and motivation; it also depends on the nature of political and the economic institutions the person interacts with. Your job and your skills not only affect your ability to provide for yourself and your family; they also affect your ability to exert influence.

In the past two chapters, we have been discussing political resources—things or attributes a person may possess which others need, want, fear, or respect enough to cause them to change their attitudes or behavior. **People need jobs** to produce or provide their own food, clothing, and shelter. **Employers need skills** to produce goods and services. **Jobs and skills can be political resources.**

Jobs are a political resource for employers; if employees need their jobs, they are more likely to defer to employers' wishes. Skills are a resource for employees; when employers need people with certain skills, they may make concessions to obtain them. Consumers able to choose their purchases can use this choice as a political resource when dealing with those who need them as customers—they exert influence by buying or failing to buy. Employers who take jobs away from employees they need as customers do so at the risk of losing sales.

Government is involved in this triad of jobs, skills, and consumption. Government requires goods, services, and taxes to operate; it therefore depends on those with skills to furnish these goods and services, and on taxes from job income and the sale of goods. Those with skills and jobs, in turn, need help from government to stimulate sales and purchasing power and to create and

maintain jobs. If government does not respond to those needs, it loses essential goods and services, tax revenues, and perhaps political support; at the same time, those with skills and jobs lose sales and income.

GETTING GOVERNMENT'S ATTENTION

A high proportion of the population in the United States, the post-Soviet republics, Germany, and the United Kingdom depend for their jobs on firms which supply basic goods and services *to both government and much of the public.*

In the United States, nearly half the populace is in the labor force (see figure 9.1). A third to a half of that force work for large corporate enterprises as white collar workers, an additional fourth work for some level of government, and another fifth work for industries.[1] All these workers—a large proportion of the total work force—are tied in to the national economy. If the economy falters, the government loses goods and services, tax revenues, and political support.

Likewise, nearly half the populace of the post-Soviet republics is in the labor force; about half that force is in industry and mining, a fourth do white collar work for government and government

133

Figure 9.1   Percent of labor force employed in manufacturing. (a) Percent of population in labor force; (b) percent of labor force in manufacturing; and (c) percent of population in manufacturing.

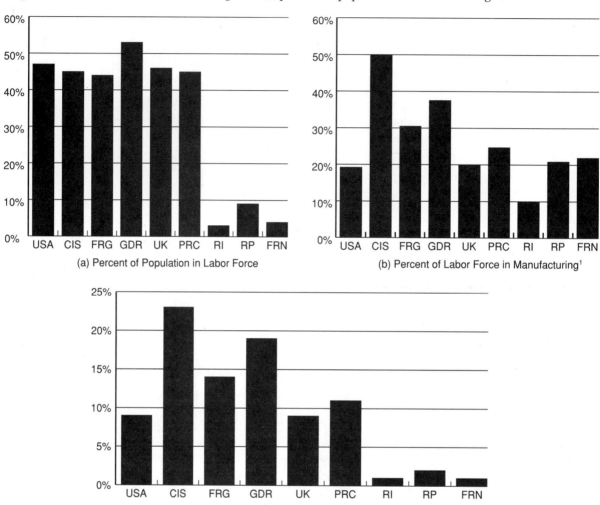

(a) Percent of Population in Labor Force

(b) Percent of Labor Force in Manufacturing[1]

(c) Percent of Population in Manufacturing

[1] ILO *Yearbook of Labour Statistics* 1989–90. Figure on China (which includes commerce) from CIA, *The World Factbook 1990*; it does not include workers in cooperatively-owned manufacturing enterprises. Figure on India from *The Europa World Yearbook 1990*. Figure for Soviet Union is *OECD Economic Surveys,* including mining.

service-sector enterprises, and 13 percent work on collective or state farms. They, too, are tied in to the national economy that the government, along with nearly everybody else, depends on.

Over half of East Germany's populace was in the labor force just before reunification in 1990; a third worked in state-run industry, a fourth for government agencies, 10 percent on collective and state farms, and another fourth with smaller government-run and private service-sector firms. Nearly half of West Germany's populace is in the labor force; about a third are employed in industrial corporations, an eighth work for government, and many of the rest are employed in white collar capacities by large corporations.

In the United Kingdom, too, nearly half the populace is in the labor force; a fifth are in industry[2] and 5 percent work for government, while many of the rest work in retail and other service jobs. As in Germany, few U.K. workers are self-employed. In these three systems, most families are again tied to the national economy on which the government depends.

In all these countries, most workers are employed by firms in the formal sector of the economy. Those firms export a great deal, but *most of their output is for consumption at home.*

When firms rely on domestic consumption for much of their income, employers needing customers have an interest in avoiding high unemployment and excessively low wages; unemployed or poorly paid workers cannot buy much. Similarly, workers often want to keep their current jobs, and they thus have an interest in the continuing welfare of their employers. If the employers cease producing, or produce poor goods people do not want to buy, the public and government who buy from them, and their employees, will be without goods or income. Tax revenues will fall off, and voters will be angry. Thus, the government has an interest in the welfare of these employers. All three groups—employers, employees, and government—benefit when the economy is strong, when production and consumption are at high levels.

Because government depends on employers to provide the goods, services, and revenues it needs to operate, these groups have leverage when it comes to public issues relating to the economy. When the government aids employers, it may indirectly aid much of the populace, who work for them. Failure to act may cost jobs, income, and consumption, and make the public angry with government. Once government takes on the responsibility of providing compensation to the unemployed, it also creates problems for itself when unemployment rises. Government thus has an interest in making sure employers and their employees prosper.

Communism confuses these relationships. With the state subsidizing businesses that lose money and forbidding employers to fire employees, neither employers nor employees need be concerned about whether workers buy the business's output. Government tries to assure that basic food, clothing, and shelter are available at controlled, affordable prices. People may have little choice as to what they buy, and manufacturers have little incentive to improve quality. Skills are needed to keep production going, and everyone is expected to contribute in some way, but harder work or greater skill may have little relationship to higher rewards. Neither workers nor government have an incentive to keep individual firms productive. But eventually government may go broke from the subsidies, and the public may tire of shoddy goods.

The reunification of Germany in 1990 destroyed many East German businesses. Their former employees are educated, informed, and politically active. They have extensive personal savings. If they can earn new income, they are receptive to replacing their old consumer goods with state-of-the-art merchandise. They are skilled. They have been exposed to years of television advertising from West Germany, and want many consumer goods. This gives government and employers incentive to create new jobs for them, to incorporate as many as possible into the work force.

By contrast, in India, Peru, and Nigeria, the institutions which supply basic goods to government and the salaried urban population can get by with low percentages of the populace acting as workers or customers. In India, less than 3 percent of the populace is part of the formal labor force[3] (with about 60 percent of that small group working for public sector industries, 5 percent for the government, and the rest working for private industries and businesses).[4] Only 10 percent of Peru's total populace is occasionally employed in the formal sector of the economy[5] (a third in industry, construction, or mining, and the rest in the service sector). Only about 4 percent of Nigerians (3.5 million out of 88 million) have salaried jobs; of those, a third work in manufacturing, mining, and construction, a third are in the civil service or the armed forces, and a tenth raise export crops.[6] Although the governments of these three nation-states may show an interest in the welfare of these institutions, they are interested in the welfare of institutions which employ few people. Protecting those institutions protects few jobs.

The rest of the population (over 90 percent in Nigeria and Peru, and at least 85 percent in India) work in the informal sector— a part of the economy which is untaxed and unregulated by government and which sells goods and services largely to poor peasants and those without regular income.[7] Citizens who provide services often do so as individuals working for other individuals. Many have no regular employment. The few basic goods they produce are not used by government. They buy little from the regulated, taxed firms which sell to government and to regularly employed citizens, and they supply little tax revenue. Government has little reason to be interested in them, even though they comprise huge majorities in each nation-state. In turn, such workers have no interest in the continuing welfare of the economic institutions which supply basic goods and services for government and the rest of the public.

In Nigeria, India, and Peru, then, high percentages of the populace obtain their jobs, goods, and services from economic institutions other than those which produce basic goods and services for government. In the other six systems, majorities tend to obtain jobs, and basic goods and services, from the same economic institutions as government does.

In India, Nigeria, and Peru, the government can give great attention to the needs of economic institutions which supply it with basic goods and services and still not assist large portions of the populace. The skills of that large portion of the populace are thus not effective political resources for influencing government. When the governments of the other six systems assist those institutions, they may at the same time assist much of the population, whose skills are used by those institutions. Because government needs these skills, the skills of these citizens are effective political resources that allow them to get government attention and to influence government actions.

BASIC, GENERIC, AND SPECIALIZED SKILLS AS POLITICAL RESOURCES

Civilization was built on skills. Before *homo sapiens* learned to farm, they had to hunt; before that, they had to forage for plants. Foraging, hunting and farming involve **basic skills**—skills that directly provide the goods and services all of us need to obtain food, clothing, and shelter. Basic skills include activities such as planting fields, tending livestock, understanding the seasonal cycles of plant life, carpentry, thatching, weaving, sewing, tanning hides, and making and using other tools and weapons. Basic skills must be learned. Some groups learned such skills before others, giving them a head start on the road to civilization. These basic skills do not require reading, writing, or arithmetic.

Basic skills tended to be evenly dispersed within such groups. In a farming society, virtually every family had all the skills needed to farm. The only important role differences were between men and women—the women concentrated on some aspects of farming and the men on others. Since family units were composed of both men and women, most families had adequate skills to survive, and few had markedly greater access to basic skills than others. Members of one family were not constantly dependent on members of other families to supply them with skills.

Eventually, small portions of the populace in different places acquired **specialized skills**—skills requiring special resources and training to perform specific tasks. The emergence of specialized skills created unequal access to skills. Specialized skills generally require literacy in language and mathematics, as well as months or years of training and apprenticeship. As history progressed, certain individuals developed specialized skills pertaining to metallurgy or to organizing bureaucracies and armies. These skills allowed them, or those they worked for, to force farming communities to hand over a portion of their yield as taxes. The taxes allowed the organizers to survive without knowing how to forage, hunt, or farm. They simply had to know how to organize to collect taxes, or defend themselves against others. They survived and thrived without acquiring basic skills because they had mastered specialized skills.

These role differences still might leave farmers able to provide their own food, clothing, and shelter. Controllers of armies needed the basic skills of farmers to provide their armies with food; farmers needed the specialized skills of armies to protect them against other armies. Thus, skills can create a **mutual dependency;** those with one set of skills may have to adapt their behavior to meet the needs of those with other skills. When one group's skills cause another group to modify their behavior, those skills become a political resource. Obviously, the basic skills involved in supplying the goods and services we all need can be a political resource. Providing some of those goods and services may also require specialized skills. And specialized skills are needed to organize states.

Pre-Civil War America was principally composed of people able to grow their own food, spin and weave their own fabrics, build their own houses, and protect themselves from assault. Nearly everyone had some of these basic skills, and most had immediate neighbors they could call on to supply the rest. The same holds true for Russia and Germany up to that time, and for Britain until earlier in the nineteenth century. People with specialized skills in organizing armies, transportation, land acquisition, and manufacturing pursuits already lived in several towns and cities. The public needed these organizers to protect them against outside enemies and to supply some goods. The organizers, in turn, needed the public to provide surplus food and fibers. Without food and fibers to consume and sell, these organizers would have been helpless. Nearly everyone possessed a needed skill. At that time, this political resource—the skills involved in providing basic goods and services—remained widely dispersed.

Late in the nineteenth century, the picture began to change. The rise in population pushed people off the farms, and advances in technology pulled people into cities. For the first time since the dawn of civilization, large numbers and percentages of people grew up who did not know how to forage, hunt, or farm. They depended for food, clothing, and shelter on those with specialized skills for organizing transportation, commercial agriculture, and mass-production manufacturing, as well as educational institutions, foundations, interest groups, government agencies, law firms, and other such organizations needed to keep economic institutions running. The organizers, in turn, largely needed only simple **manpower** (and **woman** and **childpower**), or people with **generic skills**—interchangeable workers who could easily learn to run machinery, work on a factory assembly line, sort paper, enter data, wait on customers, or perform other simple and frequently repeated tasks. Employers often didn't need to adapt their behavior to such easily replaced employees. Employees were especially vulnerable, since they no longer had the basic skills to supply their own needs and could no longer easily learn these skills from other members of the family and community. Nor did they have the land or materials to perform such skills, even if they did know how. Only a small percentage of workers needed slow-to-master, specialized skills, so these skills could only be marketed to certain types of employers. The basic skills involved in producing goods and services were no longer so widely dispersed as a political resource.

Even the nature of skills as a political resource changed at this juncture. One must be careful not to confuse skills and education. Unlike basic skills, specialized and generic skills are hard to acquire without mastering some reading, writing, and arithmetic. But often, those with even the best educations do not have the basic skills needed to supply themselves with food, clothing, and shelter. Those basic skills are seldom learned in school; many specialized skills are not learned in school, either. An educated populace is not necessarily a populace with either basic or specialized skills. Modern technology and organizational structures call for specialized skills that are a step removed from actually extracting or creating food, clothing, and shelter, but also a step removed from intellectual discourse. We must run organizations, make machines that produce parts for machines, handle vast quantities of numbers and information, operate machines, and convey information. Every product or service may require the input of many people, each applying different specialized skills. A technical proficiency, such as an automotive mechanic may have, may take months to learn; skills such as practicing law, medicine, or nuclear physics may take many years. These skills are partly learned in school, and partly in practice; some specialized skills are entirely learned in the work place, after the worker completes a formal education. All leave one heavily dependent on strangers. A modern community needs a huge variety of specialized and generic skills, and interactions with other communities, to survive. A community which contains the entire complex of basic skills needed to supply food, clothing, and shelter does not. That makes the modern community vulnerable; though it may contain many educated people, it may not be able to supply its members' basic needs if interactions go awry. It is true that those with education are easier to train for generic or specialized jobs. But there may not be enough jobs to go around, or the jobs available may not match the specialties people are trained for.

Aristotle observed that basic skills are best learned by growing up within a family which is supplying itself with food, clothing, and shelter. He wrote of the "art of acquisition" (providing oneself with goods) and "household management" (using them well) and suggested that experience is often the best teacher.*

*Ernest Barker, The Politics of Aristotle (New York: Oxford University Press, 1958), pp. 18–38.

Germany and the United Kingdom softened this vulnerability by retaining a need for many workers with basic skills, along with workers supplying simple manpower and specialized skills. As pioneers of the Industrial Revolution, Britain and later Germany experienced an early migration of population to the city. Germany was the leader in developing joint stock companies which spawned vast industrial complexes; Britain, to a lesser extent, also followed this

trend. Yet the school systems in both countries emphasized acquiring both basic and specialized skills. Many students were taught how to use tools, the fundamentals about how machinery and electricity operate, woodworking, information about plant and animal life, and how to exercise frugality and care in handling material objects. They became apprentices in specialized crafts or industries, or aimed for specialized careers in law, bureaucracy, medicine, or other fields.

In the United Kingdom, that emphasis has declined, and now many students leave school early; less than half the nation-state's work force has specialized skills, versus 85 percent in West Germany. Many Germans and some Britons still learn basic crafts, so they may repair and make goods for individuals without being part of large organizations. In many industries, including textiles, food processing, brewing, optics, watchmaking, carpetmaking, hat making, automobile production, and engineering, substantial numbers of Germans are still employed in skilled capacities within small plants using methods not far removed from those of a hundred years ago. Many such plants are located in small towns and villages, and sons and daughters of workers often take up their parents' professions. In East Germany, each school was linked to a nearby agricultural cooperative or factory; for example, 80 percent of the research at the University of Jena was done for the nearby Carl Zeiss optical firm.[8] Pupils thirteen and older spent part of one day a week learning on the premises of the manufacturing facility, and their school curriculum was heavily weighted toward science and mathematics. In West Germany, the Siemens electric equipment company has similar arrangements with universities near some of its plants. German industries have many formal apprenticeships to train those who recently left secondary school, giving them pay and benefits while they learn to do jobs they often keep permanently. In both East and West Germany, industries often provided clinics, holidays, housing, special pension plans, and other services for their employees; this helped tie workers to the firm for life.[9] The firms needed the specialized skills of the workers, who could not simply be replaced by workers with generic skills that can be learned in a few hours. These firms continue to have good reason to keep their workers by providing generous benefits.

Workers in such settings have some reciprocity, or mutual dependence, in their relations with employers. If they live in small towns close to grandparents and other relatives, they can often help one another with repairs around the home or with services which would otherwise need to be purchased. They also cannot easily be replaced in their jobs by outsiders, who might not be welcome in a small community. These smaller businesses often do not need giant intervening organizations to sell their products, and so they do not need to listen to such organizations in relations with their employees. In East Germany, many people moonlighted after working their regular jobs by building homes, summer cottages, and other private projects. Because such workers had outside income and were often not willing or able to move, the industries could pay them less. But the workers also had an advantage; they could bargain directly with their employers and could supply some of their own basic needs. Though, like West Germans, they seldom went on strike, their independence allowed them to withstand long strikes if necessary. That made the employers more prone to keep them satisfied, so they would not strike. All these circumstances made the workers more self-sufficient and harder to replace, thus enhancing the value of their skills as political resources.

Today this is changing in the United Kingdom and in Germany; unemployment is rising, firms are consolidating ownership, jobs requiring less skill or simple generic skills are on the increase. Employees are moved around more. Some 200,000 West German firms merged with larger competitors between 1955 and 1975; in 1968, 1 percent of industrial firms employed 40 percent of the labor force.[10] With around a thousand mergers taking place each year, the concentration of many workers in a few firms grows greater, and the ties to home regions loosen. The grandfather of a technician with specialized skills working on an East German collective farm might have worked a piece of private land, or worked for an individual, rather than for an impersonal business. When reunification destroyed their jobs, people like this technician could not start back into farming because they lacked the basic skills of their grandparents. They also might not be able to adapt to the more rigorous routine demanded by Western industry because their particular specialized skills might not be suitable.

West Germany's industries were extensively destroyed during World War II, and an additional number were dismantled after the war by France and the other Allies. The West Germans rebuilt them after the war using the latest automation, and their output requires extensive labor with specialized skills. This provides jobs for much of the population. Southern Europeans and Turks, who receive little education or social services, provide these industries with unskilled manpower. The introduction of comprehensive schools in the United Kingdom and West Germany, which no longer separate students into university preparation and vocational tracks, is cutting back further on training specialized technical skills for those not planning to attend university. As a result, West German industry apprenticeships find applicants for only half the positions available.[11] Prior to reunification, Germany, while still short of workers with specific specialized skills, was beginning to experience some unemployment among unskilled workers. Unskilled workers face much competition for jobs requiring only generic skills. Workers with some specialized skills are finding job shortages or facing early retirement as well.

East Germany's industries suffered less damage from bombing, but much of their sophisticated machinery was shipped to Russia after the war. Many skilled workers also fled. With its smaller population and (until recently) closed borders, East Germany was short both of workers with specialized skills and of people to perform generic labor. It absorbed more women into the labor force, giving pay and benefits incentives to workers in unpleasant occupations. Therefore most of its labor force was employed in its industries and cooperatives and received extensive benefits from employers. Because these firms have modernized little since World War II, many jobs performed in the West by robotics were still done by hand, leaving some workers with specialized skills which may now be outmoded. These workers, whose skills were formerly in demand, now find their skills of little value as plants are being rebuilt with the latest technology. Many must either take the time and effort to master new specialized skills or settle for lower-paying, generic jobs, for which competition is heavy.

The West German government and trade unions own stock in many West German firms. When they open branches abroad, many Germans go along to form an extensive portion of their employees; principal manufacturing facilities remain at home. The great majority of manufacturing in eastern Germany will be German-owned. Manufacturing capacity continues to expand within Germany. That helps keep alive the mutual dependency between German industry and its workers.

The United Kingdom, meanwhile, retained nineteenth century industrial plants and mines at the end of the war; many have since closed. Those rebuilt in the 1980's have often been designed to operate using a reduced work force requiring largely generic skills. Few apprenticeships are available to help students enter industry while they are still in school. Increasingly, products once manufactured within the United Kingdom are imported from the continent or Japan. British businesses investing abroad use few British workers in their foreign plants. Thus, unemployment rose rapidly during the 1980s, leaving many skilled laborers without work they are trained for. In addition, many in the United Kingdom do not have skills and have not experienced the benefits enjoyed by German workers.

In the United States, demand both for generic manpower and skilled workers has remained high; those without basic literacy are far less in demand.[12] Those without specialized skills cannot command high wages, are vulnerable to periodic unemployment, and often do not receive health and pension benefits. Even those with specialized skills sometimes find a decline in demand for their particular specialties; they must often work for themselves, or as contract labor, reducing their job security. Increasingly, manufacturing plants have closed and relocated abroad, hiring foreign workers.

In the Soviet Union, workers with and without specialized skills were tied to jobs by an artificial constraint: the government would not allow them to be fired. Organizations were required to retain workers whether or not their skills were needed. As we shall see in part 5, this has led to many problems, including low pay even for specialized skills due to lack of competition. High percentages of the populace in the United States and the CIS have jobs which do not require long and specialized training. Jobs requiring only generic skills are on the increase, along with the number of applicants seeking them. In the United States, engineers, accountants, and others face diminished demand for their specialized skills. On the other hand, not enough applicants are available to fill jobs in computer programming and operation, and in other new technical areas that require people with specialized skills, so pay increases in these fields (figure 9.2). Most people in the U.S. work force can find some kind of employment if they are literate.

Many Indians, Peruvians, and Nigerians, like their counterparts in the more industrialized nation-states, have quit the land and left behind skills and resources needed to supply their own basic needs. Few have acquired specialized skills to replace their former skills; government and the formal business sector have little need for such skills, *or for raw generic manpower.* People scarcely have the potential to look after their own basic needs, and few can purchase more than the barest necessities from formal economic institutions. Many people may be able to provide generic manpower and specialized skills. But they cannot use them as political resources because there are few jobs requiring such skills. Skills are only a political resource when they are needed, desired, feared, or respected by others. Many people have developed basic skills to feed, clothe, and shelter themselves; deprived of access to land, money, and other resources, it is hard to use those skills effectively even in the informal sector.

Figure 9.2 If there are fewer people with characteristics fitting ❑ than ○, which person (❑ or ○) might have the better chance of getting a job? Which has the better chance of receiving higher pay?

These people are waiting for job interviews

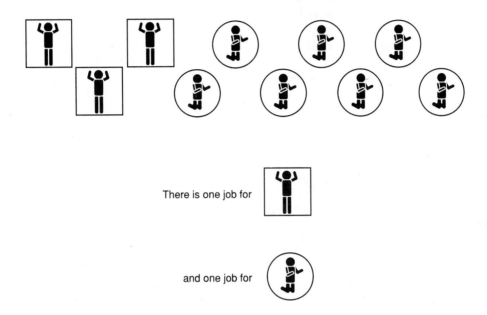

There is one job for

and one job for

One exception to this is Peru's most lucrative export business, the cocaine trade. This industry requires the skills of many peasants who own and work on small plots of land to grow the cocaine. Peasants whose other crops are not needed in markets outside their own impoverished regions can grow and market this export crop. Because cartels control the marketing, there is no price competition. But the cartels need the cooperation of the peasants for protection against drug enforcement agents, and they need the coca leaves they raise. Unlike many of their neighbors, peasants who grow cocaine have skills that constitute a political resource.

In India, Peru, and Nigeria, many people are not needed as employees, consumers, or taxpayers. In the United States, CIS, the United Kingdom, and Germany, employers and government have developed mutual dependencies. In China, a special situation exists.

CHINA'S SPECIAL MUTUAL DEPENDENCIES

China provides still a different scenario of mutual dependency. There (unlike any of the other eight systems), basic skills that provide basic goods and services are widely dispersed, and nearly everyone is involved in either agricultural or industrial production within the formal sector of the economy. The distinction between those who control basic goods and services and those who use them is far less clear than in the other systems.

High percentages of Chinese grow their own food, as well as food for government and urbanites. Many of these same people make industrial goods, also used widely both by the government and the general populace for revenue and consumption. So, in a sense, the institutions providing basic goods and services are the same as those using them. Yet these people are not working only for themselves; nor are they purchasing only from themselves. The government has a strong influence on their welfare. They, in turn, have an interest in the health of the general economy.

After communists took command of China in 1949, they gradually took control of private land in the countryside. During the 1950s, they consolidated land into large communes. All families living in surrounding villages were combined into production teams, which in turn were divided into brigades. All peasants worked for brigades and received a portion of the brigade's profit on the basis of work points they accrued for their labor. Before 1982, communes were responsible for local government, schools, health care, tax collection, public information, supervising land improvement and construction projects and light industries within the villages, and planning for production; they set aside some 20 percent of income for these purposes. The communes and brigades were managed by salaried administrators. Output was marketed through government channels, with the production teams receiving the sale price. All members had their own private plots, and they could sell these privately produced crops at urban markets for personal profit.

The **household responsibility system**[13] instituted in 1978 permits communes to divide all or part of their land and lease parcels to members. All families in the commune are eligible to receive land, which stays with the peasant until the end of his or her lease. Many initial leases ran for two to five years, but now leases often extend for thirty years. If the family moves to town to start a small business, it may be required to yield the lease, presumably after being compensated for improvements made; in practice, people often turn the land over to relatives. They cannot sell it. A family saving and borrowing money to buy a small tractor, or who owns a hand-pulled cart, can purchase crops and take them to nearby towns or cities to sell. The system varies in each province. In some regions, the government issues contracts to individuals or work teams for specified quotas (below record yields) of crops; they are paid for what they produce under the contracts, and anything beyond this belongs to them

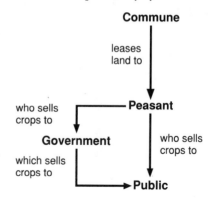

Figure 9.3   The responsibility system.

to eat, sell, or use for seed. Peasants are often assigned permanent use of draft animals and farm implements; officials are supposed to take care to see that all families have similar amounts of land, but in practice some get better land than others. Peasants prominent in the local party or government are able to borrow money from government lending institutions to improve their fields; peasants also have substantial savings of their own to invest. The government distributes seed and fertilizer at subsidized prices and hands them out through these local authorities.

The grain, soybean, meat, and vegetable quotas are purchased by government marketing boards, which in turn sell them in the cities (figure 9.3). These boards used to sell these commodities at substantially reduced prices, costing the government considerable money. Those subsidies are now lower, meaning that food prices in the cities are higher; they may be eliminated entirely in coming years. The peasant is paid a relatively high price for the produce, and the urban worker buys it for a lower price; the government pays the difference.

In 1982, education, health, welfare, and other public functions formerly assumed by communes were turned over to township governments. These townships do not have the direct income which communes received from agricultural production, and must therefore resort to taxation—for example, charging tolls for traffic on roads. It is difficult to

New peasant houses, Dali, Yunnan, China, 1989.

Bob Gamer

Figure 9.4 In China, manufacturing is owned by three different groups: government, joint ventures between government and foreign companies, and employees.

Manufacturing Ownership in China

tax peasants or production teams directly, since their income can easily be disguised and there are few educated or experienced people to supervise taxation. So townships, cities, and provincial governments have joined with foreign corporations to open factories and other businesses as **joint ventures,** investments jointly owned by both the Chinese and foreign partner. They, as well as urban and rural workers, have started **cooperative businesses**—factories and other firms whose workers share in their proceeds (figure 9.4). For many, work in their cooperative is a second job. By 1992, 19 million rural cooperatives employed 96 million people and produced over a quarter of industrial output and exports. In 1993, that output rose a phenomenal 65 percent.[14] A third of urban and a fourth of rural workers were part of manufacturing cooperatives. Some 20,000 joint ventures with foreign firms produced a fourth of the industrial output. Unlike many state enterprises (which produce the rest of the industrial output), these collectively and jointly owned firms care about making a profit. They can make use of basic skills such as sewing and carpentry which are not so widely disseminated in other work forces.

Although a tenth of its populace has become at least partly unemployed amid all this growth, the vast majority of China's people can look after at least some of their own basic needs. They have both the skills needed to produce basic goods and services and the organizations to use them. China's land and grain are largely in the hands of individual peasants who produce for themselves and for the market. Much of the grain for the cities is controlled by administrators charged with purchasing it from these peasants and selling it to consumers. Most of the vegetables, eggs, meat, fowl, and fish are raised or caught, and sold, by individual peasants and cooperative businesses; nearly all peasants produce some of these food items. Government controls the transportation of raw materials for heavy industry, as well as the products of heavy industry. Small peasant and worker cooperatives provide most of the transportation of food; farm products seldom move long distances. So peasants supply much of their own food, and are in extensive demand to help with transportation and marketing and to provide markets for goods.

The administrators, and the Communist Party leaders to whom they turn for policy guidance, do not firmly control what will be grown on the land, food transportation and marketing, or the proceeds that come from sales. Since the peasants do not rely heavily on sophisticated farm implements or heavy infusions of investment capital, the influence of bankers is dampened. Since grain is not transported and marketed nationally, decisions about price, and the profit percentages to be retained by the peasants who produce the grain, take place largely at a regional level and involve several interacting layers of state and party organizations, along with the producers themselves.

Increasingly, cooperatives are competing with joint ventures and state firms to produce cloth, ready-made clothing, and building materials for houses. Most Chinese purchase some consumer goods, such as bicycles, refrigerators, stereos, television sets, and washing machines, produced by large factories. Within these factories, whether state-owned or joint ventures, most employees engage directly in production, rather than management or marketing; smaller cooperatives often construct individual components and transport them to factories. These workers depend on some moderately large organizations for part of their food, clothing, and shelter; part comes from small organizations or private individuals, and, especially among the peasant majority, part they provide for themselves. *This is a nation-state of producers who largely produce for their own consumption. Most of these producers work within small organizations.*

Unlike the other eight systems, China has never fully moved into the stage requiring specialized skills and generic manpower. Most people retain the potential to look after most of their own basic needs. Government institutions rely on domestic economic institutions. The economic institutions, in turn, rely primarily on the basic skills needed to produce food, clothing, and shelter (rather than specialized skills); those skills are scattered among millions of people. A political resource is a means by which one person can influence the behavior of other persons. A person with the skills and assets to look after his or her own basic needs, and whose skills are needed by those in authority, possesses an important political resource. High percentages of the Chinese population possess this resource; it is rarer elsewhere.

In China, basic and specialized skills are potentially a political resource for a greater percentage of the populace than in the other eight systems. Specialized skills are both widely dispersed and needed (hence, usable as a political resource) in Germany, the United Kingdom, the United States, and the CIS. Those systems also have a considerable need for workers with generic skills. In India, Peru, and Nigeria, far more people have all three types of skills than there are jobs available; these skills are weak political resources in these three systems.

CONCLUSION ON RESOURCES

We have reviewed a variety of resources which might contribute to one's influence: information; education; the ability to supply food, clothing, shelter, and other necessities; the ability to buy food, clothing, shelter, and other necessities; jobs; and skills. This by no means exhausts the list of political resources. It does introduce some of the more obvious ones, and some less commonly explored.

These resources are much less widely dispersed among the populations of India, Peru, and Nigeria than in the other six systems. In these nation-states, few people have access to land, tools, or jobs to provide themselves with food, clothing, and shelter. Nor are most people needed as customers by the larger firms supplying these basic goods. Huge portions of the populace lack the political resources that accrue from education, watching the news, having savings, owning or renting land, or possessing needed skills.

In the other six nation-states, smaller percentages of the populace fall into this extreme category. Those who do have the same problems.

High percentages of Chinese are able to supply and purchase food, clothing, and shelter. But those who do often lack education and information. The suppliers of basic goods and services in the other eight nation-states are often educated and informed, and constitute smaller portions of the total populace.

Substantial percentages of citizens in the United States, the CIS republics, Germany, the United Kingdom, and China have at least one of the political resources we have been discussing. Substantial percentages of the populace in India, Nigeria, and Peru have none of them.

In the next chapter, we turn to the other three items on our list of characteristics needed by those who would exert influence in public affairs: knowing how to use resources, having access to institutions, and setting objectives.

SUMMARY

Once, small communities had all the resources and basic skills they needed to feed, clothe, and shelter all their members most of the time; today, families generally do not have these basic skills or the land, tools, and other assets they need to provide for their own consumption. In China, large numbers of families do have those basic skills and assets and can still largely provide for their own consumption. Elsewhere, families generally need money from jobs to obtain adequate food, clothing, and shelter. There are growing numbers of generic "manpower" jobs—jobs that a literate person can learn in only a few hours—in many nation-states, but the pay is low and the competition to obtain them great. Jobs requiring specialized skills that take a long time to learn generally pay more—if employers have job openings for people with these skills. To produce, employers need skills; to consume, employees need jobs. So both skills and jobs are political resources; those who have them can bargain with those who need them.

If employers need their workers as customers, and government needs the products those jobs and skills produce, the taxes derived from them, or the good will of people who seek jobs, the value of jobs and skills as political resources rises. People who are not needed for jobs are often short on other political resources as well; in some systems, their numbers are great. In a formal economy which requires few people with basic, specialized, or generic (manpower) skills, and which separates large portions of its populace from land and raw materials, those skills are degraded as a political resource. If skills are to be useful as either an economic or a political resource, the system must provide opportunities for jobs that require these skills.

NOTES

1. For all these percentages on industry and agriculture, see *Europa Statistical Yearbook 1990* and *OECD Economic Surveys*. In 1965, over a fourth of the U.S. labor force worked for industries.

2. In 1965, 35 percent of the United Kingdom's labor force were working for industries.

3. As chapter 8 indicated, about an eighth of the rural populace in India might be involved in mechanized agriculture supplying markets outside villages; this 3 percent figure (based on enterprises subject to social and economic legislation) does not include family-owned businesses. If all these businesses were included, the formal sector would contain 15 percent (rather than 3 percent) of the total national work force. In addition, many of these farms employ relatives, and also give occasional jobs to neighboring landowners who are unemployed or seeking extra work. So they may provide some jobs to those in the informal sector as well.

4. Ministry of Finance, *Economic Survey 1983–84,* pp. 121–22.

5. In the 1981 census, out of Peru's total population of 17.7 million, 10.4 million were counted as being in the work force. Of these, 5.7 million (or 56 percent) were defined as economically active; by that criterion, 44 percent of those over age fifteen did not hold a job and had no plans to hold one. The International Labour Organization (ILO), using different figures and criteria, reported that the work force contained 5.6 million people in 1989, with 2.2 million economically active. One researcher, taking into account the cost of living in a country where inflation often exceeds 1,000 percent a year, estimated that only 17 percent of families in Lima were adequately employed in 1984 (versus the official estimate of 60 percent, based on the minimum wage in 1967). Thomas G. Sanders, "Peru's Economy: Under-employment and the Informal Sector," *University Field Staff International Reports* 39 (1984): 1–3.

A 1991 estimate found only 5.3 percent of Lima's economically active populace adequately employed. Sally Bowen, "Peru's Fujimori Weighs In on Behalf of Street Sellers," *Christian Science Monitor*, March 4, 1991.

6. ILO, *Yearbook of Labour Statistics 1989–90.* Paul Collier, "Oil Shocks and Food Security in Nigeria," *International Labour Review* 127, 6 (December 1988): 714.

7. About 12 percent of Nigerians work in unregulated cottage industries; most of the rest are in agriculture. About 23 percent of Indians in the informal sector work in cottage industries or petty trades, or provide services; the remainder are in agriculture. For information on Peru's informal sector, see chapter 8.

8. Jonathan Steele, *Socialism With a German Face* (London: Jonathan Cape, 1977), p. 178.

9. See Christopher S. Allen, "Germany: Competing Communitarianisms," in George C. Lodge & Ezra Vogel, eds., *Ideology and National Competitiveness* (Boston: Harvard Business School Press, 1987); Alexander Gershenkron, *Bread and Democracy in Germany*, 2d. ed. (Ithaca: Cornell University Press, 1989); Geoffrey Ingham, *Capitalism Divided? The City and Industry in British Social Development* (London: Macmillan, 1984); Samuel H. Beer, *Britain Against Itself: The Political Contradictions of Collectivism* (New York: W. W. Norton, 1982); and Andrew Shonfield, *Modern Capitalism: The Changing Balance of Public and Private Power* (Oxford: Oxford University Press, 1978).

10. In 1975, 600 persons controlled the 130 largest industries, banks, insurance companies, wholesalers, and retail chains. Eight of these industries (Volkswagen, Siemens, BASF, Hoechst, Daimler-Benz, Bayer, Verba, and AEG Telefunken) accounted for 25 percent of exports. J. Dornberg, *The New Germans: 30 Years After* (New York: Macmillan, 1975), pp. 175–77.

11. The number of apprenticeships dropped from 1.8 million to 1.5 million between 1988 and 1991. Many German young people prefer to work in banks or insurance companies. Joel Kotkin, "They Order These Things Worse in Europe," *Manchester Guardian Weekly*, October 13, 1991.

12. A 1989–93 Congressional study—the most comprehensive government literacy study to date—found that half (90 million) of American adults lack simple reading and math skills needed for most entry-level (generic) jobs. Many cannot write a simple business letter, read a bus schedule, or figure the difference between a sale price and a regular price on a calculator. More than half of high school graduates are in this category. *Washington Post*, September 9, 1993.

13. See Jean Oi, *State and Peasant in Contemporary Society: The Political Economy of Village Government* (Berkeley: University of California Press, 1989).

14. "China Records 27 Percent Industrial Growth in First Five Months," *The Straits Times*, June 11, 1993. Output in state enterprises had risen 16 percent, and in urban cooperatives 46 percent, while output of joint ventures was up 73 percent over the first five months of 1992.

EXERCISES

Think about the book thus far:

1. How do jobs and skills—the topics of this chapter—relate to understanding public issues (the topic of chapter 7) and food, clothing, and shelter (the subject of chapter 8)?

2. Which of the five characteristics of influence are we discussing when we focus on jobs and skills?

KEY WORDS AND PHRASES

Define the following terms:

basic skills	man/woman/child power	joint venture
specialized skills	generic skills	cooperative business
mutual dependency	household responsibility system	

THINKING IT THROUGH

1. Think about yourself. Under which of the following circumstances do you have the most political clout on a job—the ability to change the attitudes or behaviors of your employer:

   a. when you have specialized skills?
   b. when you provide generic skills (manpower)?

2. Which of the following countries have the most use for specialized skills?

   a. Germany
   b. the United Kingdom
   c. China

3. In which of those countries are specialized skills most useful as a political resource, and why?

4. How does the relationship between employers and employees differ in China from that in the other eight systems? Why might skills constitute more of a political resource for Chinese peasants than for peasants in India, Peru, and Nigeria?

5. In the United States, more service jobs are being created. How will that affect your ability to use specialized skills as a political resource?

chapter 10

POLITICAL RECRUITMENT
INTO INSTITUTIONS

We turn now to the last three of the five characteristics which give an individual influence, or the ability to be recruited into the institutions political competition is conducted in: knowing how to use resources, gaining access into institutions, and setting objectives. Political systems are selective about who may be recruited into such institutions; criteria differ widely from system to system. Regardless of the criteria, however, those who have acquired appropriate resources and have the motivation to use them to achieve their own objectives have a greater chance of actually playing an influential role in these institutions.

Up to now, we have been discussing passive attributes people acquire, but may or may not actually use to exert influence. In this chapter, we will examine the last three of the characteristics of influence discussed in chapter 5. When a person possesses these three traits simultaneously, he or she is influential. **These characteristics—knowing how to use resources, gaining access to institutions, and setting objectives—constitute active participation in the political system.**

UNDERSTANDING HOW TO USE RESOURCES TO INFLUENCE THE OUTCOMES OF ISSUES

A person with political resources may induce cooperation from other people simply because they fear that he or she will use those resources to exert influence in retaliation if they don't cooperate. Thus, it is sometimes politically useful to have political resources even when one does not actively use them. But a person wishing to exert influence over people who have no such fears must do more than simply possess political resources; he or she must actually use them. And using political resources requires one to understand how to use those resources to influence the outcome of issues.

An obvious way to influence the outcome of issues is to vote. Voting is a political resource universally available in all nine nation-states, for offices at one level or another. The number of political parties and elected offices, and other factors that affect how voting takes place, make the usefulness of that resource vary from system to system. Moreover, within any nation-state, some exert more influence through voting than others. Voting is more influential when it is deliberate. Individuals who always vote for or against a particular candidate or party regardless of what happens are likely to exert little influence over officeholders from their own party, or over opposition party candidates, who know their votes are unlikely to change. By contrast, when candidates fear that certain actions they take may cause some of their supporters to withhold support or to vote against them, they may avoid taking those actions.

In a one-party state with mandatory voting, voters may deliberately withhold their votes by leaving their ballots blank, or refusing to go to the polls. In elections with more than one candidate, voters can withhold their votes by voting for another candidate, or again, by not going to the polls. But people cannot withhold their votes deliberately if they do not ordinarily vote, or if they do not know what actions officeholders are taking. Therefore, candidates are interested in the information intake of the public.

People who do not learn about public affairs directly through newspapers, magazines, books, radio and television news, or public affairs programs may still learn about them through conversations and by going to political rallies. Those who do not participate in any of these activities are unlikely to be informed about the behavior of candidates; they can be swayed by simple messages in television commercials or even by rumors. Informed voters may be found in all these nation-states; their numbers and sophistication are hard to assess.

People who can be counted on to influence the votes of others compound their influence. Candidates will be especially interested in gaining their support or avoiding their opposition. Often, such people are active in political parties or interest groups; those who understand how to influence the outcomes of issues recognize the importance of joining such groups, because such groups can combine the political resources of large numbers of people. This compounded influence can affect the outcomes of elections or the execution of policies, and thus help gain the ear of officeholders with sovereignty.

Clearly, only a portion of those joining such groups use them to influence public issues. If a person votes and joins interest group activities, it does not mean he or she knows how to use resources to influence issues; but those who do know how are likely to be among the participants in groups like these. They also are likely to take advantage of the fact that most of the membership is not actively engaged in exerting influence. An individual joining such a group and using its money, membership, access to media, prestige, relationships with officeholders and bureaucracy, and other political resources to affect public policy greatly enhances his or her political influence, if that individual knows how to persuade the group to take actions. An individual who is not part of such a group, and cannot pull together such resources, is at a decided disadvantage in exerting influence over officeholders.

In China, and formerly in East Germany and the Soviet Union, where voting is (or was) compulsory,

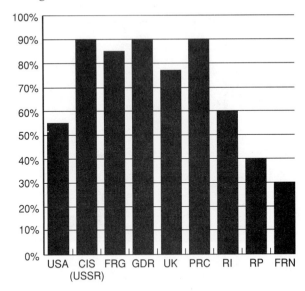

Figure 10.1 Percentage of voting age population voting in national elections.

over 90 percent of adults vote in national elections (see figure 10.1). Over 85 percent consistently vote in West Germany,[1] 77 percent in the United Kingdom,[2] 60 percent in India,[3] 50 percent in the United States,[4] and 40 percent in Peru (where voting also is mandatory, but Sendero Luminoso terrorists threaten voters in some regions). In Nigeria, less than a third of the eligible voters voted in the most recent national election (although ballot-box stuffing makes actual turnouts hard to estimate).[5]

Only a minority of adults in any of these nation-states belong to interest groups. About 4 percent of Americans,[6] 3 percent of Britons, 8 percent of West Germans, and 2 percent of Indians belong to political parties or organizations. About 9 percent of Soviet adults[7] and 20 percent of East Germans,[8] belonged to the Communist Party; 5 percent of Chinese[9] still do. Those leaving the party in Germany and the CIS may join other parties, but many may stay away from further party activity.

One study found 32 percent of Americans involved in some kind of cultural or social organization such as a trade union, scouting, or the PTA;[10] another found 13 percent belonging to groups that

Figure 10.2   Percent of adults belonging to trade unions.

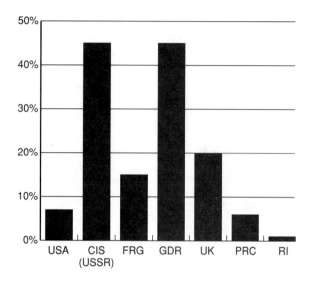

Table 10.1

Political Participation:
Response to Survey Questions

	USA	UK	FRG
"I follow accounts of political and governmental affairs regularly"	27%	23%	34%
"I have attempted to influence local government"	28%	15%	14%

Inter-University Consortium for Political Research Codebook, *The Five Nation Study* (Ann Arbor, Mich.: ICPR, 1968), pp. 29, 83.

take a stand on national issues.[11] A British study found 19 percent of Britons involved in political interest groups, but three-fourths were not politically active beyond voting;[12] West Germany probably has a similar percentage.

About 7 percent of Americans,[13] 15 percent of West Germans,[14] 45 percent of East Germans and CIS citizens,[15] 20 percent of Britons,[16] 6 percent of Chinese,[17] 1 percent of Indians,[18] and 4 percent of Nigerians belong to trade unions (figure 10.2).

Smaller percentages actively participate in the political activities of these groups. Without committing to memory the statistics in the next four paragraphs, consider whether any of them indicate high participation in interest group activities (and whether political participation is as high in the United States as in the other systems).

In a study of the 1976 United States presidential election,[19] only 5 percent of adults reported working for a candidate or party, and 10 percent giving money to a candidate or party, though 38 percent said they followed governmental affairs and talked to others about the election. Education was clearly a factor in participation. Only 7 percent of those with

incomes below $3,000 did *four or more* of the activities on the pollsters' list (which also included attending meetings, writing letters, and wearing buttons);[20] 35 percent with college educations and over $20,000 annual income did so. Yet, even among the 19 percent of the total sample reporting participation in four or more activities, less than a third knew which party controlled the House of Representatives. One might therefore surmise that less than 10 percent of adults were well-informed, active participants in the election. It would also appear that very few of this 10 percent came from the lowest income and educational strata.

A similar survey in the United Kingdom found only 7 percent engaging in five of ten political activities. Studies of voting patterns find that in West Germany and the United Kingdom, the less educated populace is almost as inclined to vote as the better educated portion of the populace, while in the United States they are far less inclined to do so.[21] However, United States citizens may be more likely to attempt to influence government at the local level (table 10.1).

Another study found that 11 percent of Americans in the lowest educational categories had contacted a politically powerful person or government official on behalf of a social group they were associated with, while 51 percent in the highest educational category had done so; only small percentages of the total populace are in the highest educational

Antiapartheid march near the state capitol building, 1980s, Denver, Colorado.

© *Mike Gamer*

category. Comparable figures on the same survey were 0 percent and 16 percent, respectively, in India.[22]

A 1971 study in the Soviet Union found 7 percent of adults working on committees to organize elections for the Supreme Soviets.[23] A 1974 study found 8 percent volunteering to help with elections for local and regional government; the Soviet Union at that time elected 2.25 million deputies to 50,000 soviets—all in noncompetitive elections.[24] Others estimate that 15 percent of the general populace were involved with street and house committees, parent committees in schools, councils of clubs and libraries, women's councils, pensioners' councils, volunteer fire brigades, volunteer militia, comradely courts, shop and restaurant commissions, and factory brigades; 85 percent of Communist Party members were involved in such groups.[25] Similarly, only a third of all newspaper readers read all the articles on politics and ideology; 56 percent of party readers

did so.[26] At any given time, about 2 percent of West Germans and 1 percent of East Germans[27] serve(d) on local and district councils.

Substantial percentages of citizens in the United States, the CIS republics, East and West Germany, the United Kingdom, and China have at least one of the political resources we have previously discussed; it would appear that only a portion of these citizens are politically active beyond voting. Substantial percentages of the populace in India, Nigeria, and Peru have none of the political resources we discussed; some of this latter group do at least vote or have access to an interest group. Election rallies in those three countries draw large crowds; in India, most who attend are men. In the United States, the United Kingdom, and West Germany, men are also more likely than women to engage in all these modes of participation.[28]

DEVELOPING ACCESS TO THE INSTITUTIONS WHERE ISSUES ARE RESOLVED

As we just learned, it is hard to determine the information and education levels of those who join and are active in political parties and interest groups, though there is some indication that they come disproportionately from among those with better incomes and educations. There is clearer evidence that those who achieve top positions in such institutions, and become officeholders in government institutions where issues are resolved, tend to be drawn from the ranks of the better educated and better informed. Few people in these systems attain top political posts without higher educations and at least middle class status (though their parents may come from other social classes). This is true despite some marked differences in recruitment processes.

In the United States, most post-Soviet republics, and in Peru and Nigeria under civilian rule, the voters elect the chief executive into office. In the United Kingdom, West Germany, and India, the elected legislature chooses the chief executive. Formerly in the Soviet Union and East Germany, and currently in China, the top leaders of the only ruling party choose the chief executive, and the public has no choice as to whom those top leaders are. In all nine of these systems voters vote directly for members of legislatures, ranging from local to national bodies, which vary in the decision-making powers they possess. All nine nation-states have policy makers other than chief executives who are appointed to their posts rather than elected. And all contain people who, from behind the scenes, strongly influence these formal leaders even though they themselves hold no formal titles.

These positions, both formal and unofficial, generally go to people with higher education. In all these nation-states, children whose parents had little education may obtain higher educations and rise to powerful positions, though it is difficult to do so. And some high posts go to people who do not have higher educations. Revolutionary governments, when they recruit leaders, sometimes even give preference to members of classes which have been previously excluded from educational opportunities. Free elections with universal suffrage can also increase the chances for people with less education to seek elective office. Yet people with higher educations continue to rise to the top. This does not mean that those with education and other attributes enhancing influence all have an equal chance of being recruited; members of certain ethnic, religious, and cultural groups often have greater chances than others. Women always have to battle prejudices against recruitment. Without trying to commit to memory the statistics in the next nine paragraphs, consider whether they indicate that top posts are dominated by those with higher education and who generally come from among families with higher social status.

In 1982, 65 percent of the 435 members of the United States House of Representatives came from business and professional families, while 1 percent came from laboring families.[29] A 1970s study of leaders of law firms, foundations, corporations, educational institutions, media, civic groups, government, and military organizations found that 80 to 94 percent had upper-middle to upper class origins. A 1980–81 study of such leaders found that 56 percent were graduates of Ivy League universities (figure 10.3); only 5.7 percent had not completed

Figure 10.3 Percent of leaders in various U.S. institutions who attended Ivy League Universities (1980–81).

Thomas R. Dye, Who's Running America: The Reagan Years, *3rd ed. (Englewood Cliffs, N.J. Prentice-Hall, 1983), p. 196.*

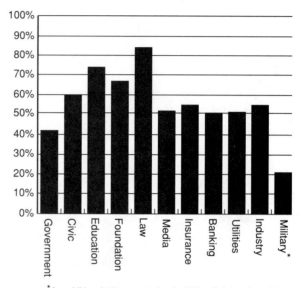

*An additional 49 percent attended West Point or Annapolis.

college.[30] More than a fourth of "high federal officials" (including the Supreme Court and Cabinet) from 1789 to 1980 attended Harvard, Yale, or Princeton.[31] There are, however, numerous prominent positions in the civil service and in legislative assemblies at lower levels of government for those with less educational attainment.

In contrast to the longstanding tradition in the United States, Mikhail Gorbachev was the first top Soviet leader with a formal earned university degree; in 1981, he was the only Politburo member from Moscow University. Still, even in 1967 a higher percentage of the Communist Party membership than of the Soviet population as a whole had secondary and higher education; those percentages grew even higher in later years (see figure 10.4).[32] In 1981, 57.4 percent of the secretaries of primary party groups, 70 percent of the candidates of republic central committees and members of regional and

Figure 10.4   Percent of manual workers, peasants, and professionals in (a) general population,
(b) Communist Party, and (c) Politburo in USSR in 1983.
David Lane, State and Politics in the Soviet Union *(London: Basil S. Blackwell, 1985), pp. 151, 169; David Lane,*
The End of Social Inequality *(London: George Allen & Unwin, 1982), pp. 119–200.*

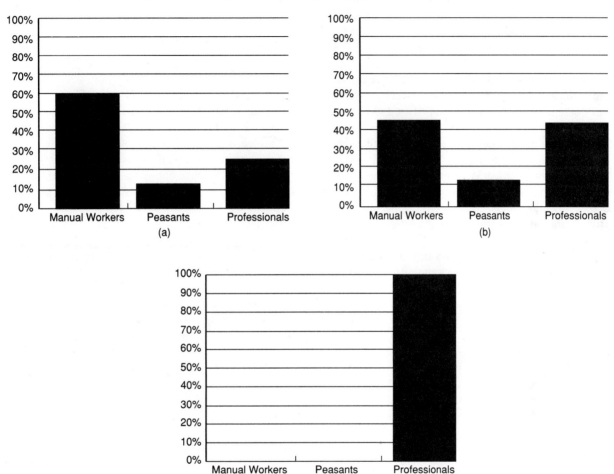

district committees, 99.9 percent of the secretaries of republic party central committees and of district and regional committees, 90 percent of the Central Committee of the Communist Party, and 100 percent of the Politburo had higher educations.[33] *Glasnost* speeded the inclusion of people with higher educations in high positions; while 46 percent of the members of the 1984 Supreme Soviet were classed as workers, collective farmers, or nonprofessional office employees, only 22 percent of the 1989 Congress of People's Deputies members fit that category.[34]

A similar shift occurred in East Germany. During the 1950s, high percentages of those in top political posts lacked higher education, partly because of the exodus of educated people to the West. By the time of reunification in 1990, higher education was the norm at that level.[35] As of 1975, over half the East's military high command were under age fifty-seven, with many from working-class or middle-class backgrounds; that year in West Germany, only 5 percent were under age fifty-seven, with 16 percent aristocrats and 37 percent sons of high ranking officers.[36] Since the East joined the political system of the West, many former top civil servants from East Germany have lost their jobs and been replaced by West German civil servants.

About 8 percent of the members of the West German Bundestag were manual or lower-level white collar workers when Germany reunified in 1990; around 60 percent were administrators or leaders of interest groups.[37] By 1987, some 30 percent of members had doctorate degrees; 95 percent had secondary education or more.[38] In 1975, half of all judges came from the top 5 percent of the population in terms of socioeconomic status, while only 6 percent came from working class families. Leading civil servants also have high educational attainment, but state governments help in their recruitment and thus keep them regionally diverse in background.

Very few business or union leaders have ever achieved Cabinet positions in the United Kingdom if they were not graduates of Oxford or Cambridge; John Major, the son of a circus performer, who became prime minister in 1990, is the first in that position lacking a university education.[39] Between 1945 and 1970, 46 percent of all Members of Parliament were educated at prestigious public (in the United States, we would refer to them as private) schools, while about 4 percent were workers.[40] That percentage of manual workers is rising. In 1984, 37 percent of the Labour Party Members of Parliament were former manual workers; still, most Labour MP's were university educated, with 14 percent from prestigious public schools (private grade and high schools).[41] Even higher percentages of Conservative Members of Parliament come from prestigious public schools and professional occupations, though a third who were entering for the first time in 1987 did not have university degrees.[42] Thus, offspring of working families are making some inroads into the House of Commons. Other institutions offer them a greater challenge. Fifty-one percent of those

Table 10.2

Worker Recruitment

U.S. House of Representatives	1%
German Bundestag	8%
UK Labour Party MPs (1984)	37%
China Communist Party Cadres (1982)	40%

who entered the bureaucracy via the Civil Service Selection Board in 1978 came from public schools; 52 percent of that percentage were from Oxford or Cambridge.[43] A 1971 study of people of highest rank in various sectors of government, industry, the military, the church, commerce, banking, insurance, education, the media, and industry found 70 percent had attended public schools, 27 percent the six most prestigious.[44]

Peasants and workers with little education have a greater chance to achieve a prominent political position in China than in any of the other systems (table 10.2). Some 2 percent of Chinese adults become cadres, the permanent party officials who enforce the party's dominance. When the People's Republic of China was founded in 1949, after the peasant-based revolution brought one-party communist rule to China,[45] the Communist Party recruited 80 percent of its cadres from among largely illiterate peasants. Before 1980, preference was given to offspring of workers and peasants when selecting cadres; since then, efforts have been made to bring in cadres with specialized training. Because about a third of the 52 million members of the Communist Party were recruited during the period of the Great Proletarian Cultural Revolution,[46] many cadres still have little education. Between 1979 and 1981, about half of the 400,000 leading cadres had graduated from a Central Party School established to indoctrinate them in Marxist-Leninist-Mao Zedong thought and give them the equivalent of a high school education. A 1982 study found that more than 40 percent of cadres—especially in the middle ranks of regional and provincial organizations—still had less than a junior-high level of education. Those entrenched officials are often reluctant to promote lower-level, younger cadres with higher educations.[47]

In contrast to cadres, the National People's Congress, the Central Committee of the Communist Party, and the national civil service are dominated by people with university educations.[48] The Chinese notion of **guanxi,** or bonds of mutual obligation, causes them to promote individuals they have family ties with, or people from their own region, that they went to school with, or who have personally served the same person as themselves. That means new recruits to positions may share common experiences and connections with the occupants of the next higher positions. Since 1978, increasing numbers of peasants and workers have entered higher education; without the right connections, they may still find it hard to rise in either the middle or higher echelons of the cadre system, which continues to draw from the cadres' friends and families.

India, Nigeria, and Peru, in contrast, offer little chance for people from working families to be recruited into leadership positions at any level. In India, those who belong to interest groups, plan elections, and run for public office are usually administrators, large landowners, businesspeople, and professional people. Although the Congress party has 10 million paying members who are free to join, its local branches are operated by 250,000 "active" members. The active members, who are chosen by the party, consist largely of professional people[49] and landowners with over thirty acres, and (increasingly) other landowners in mechanized agriculture. Villagers (who rarely attend university) tend to vote for those with education, land, and political influence; so the village, neighborhood, and district councils are dominated by large landowners and businessmen. The same holds true for higher political office and the civil service.

In Peru, where illiterates did not even have the right to vote until 1979, top political and bureaucratic posts have been dominated by those with university (generally San Marcos, or a school abroad)[50] or military academy educations. Town leaders come from leading families; the military offers the best chance of career advancement for boys from peasant or working families in the regional towns and villages. The same holds true in Nigeria, where political recruitment to such positions is reserved for the less than 20 percent of the populace who speak English; graduates of the University of Ibadan and English universities and military academies are viewed favorably in political recruiting.[51]

There are also occupational differences in the backgrounds of those recruited to comparable institutions. Britain's House of Commons counts almost no commercial farmers among its members. Currently serving civil servants may not run for the legislature in the United Kingdom or the United States. Military leaders have less opportunity to hold top political posts in the United States, the United Kingdom, East and West Germany, and India than in the other four systems. This does not mean that farmers, civil servants, and the military are without influence in these nation-states; they have the bases for influence discussed in chapters 8 and 9, and they can exert influence from other institutional positions. But those with access to the institutions where issues are resolved generally have more than the average educational attainment, and they constitute low percentages of the populace.

Thus, in all these political systems, only a low percentage of the populace have all the attributes we have discussed in chapters 7, 8, 9, and 10. Yet, of that small percentage, few have the attribute we will discuss next. People who have only a portion of these attributes, but who acquire the attribute discussed next, still may become highly influential.

SETTING CLEAR OBJECTIVES FOR RESOLVING ISSUES

The traits we have discussed thus far give a person the potential to exert political influence. But only when voters or leaders acquire an interest in issues and the processes by which they are resolved, and only when they develop strategies for achieving these objectives by working within these processes, are they well on their way toward achieving political influence.

As we have seen, all these systems allow people from various walks of life to achieve positions of influence if they acquire education and follow the procedures laid out by the system. People from certain racial groups, regions, social classes, and other demographic segments find this easier to achieve than others—if for no other reason, because it is easier for them to obtain a good education.

Modern nation-states did not reach this stage without struggle. Each has, in its history, experienced periods when only people from certain social classes, races, or regions could achieve political influence at the highest levels; it is still easier for some groups to achieve influence in any of these systems. We will discuss more about that in the next chapter.

Each of these nation-states has developed different procedures for an individual to achieve exceptional influence. The potential effectiveness of voting varies widely. But no set of rules will hand influence over to those without clear objectives for resolving issues. People without objectives are almost certain to be surpassed in politics by those who do have objectives and who carry them out. A person with objectives—accompanied by some understanding of the complexities behind the issues, an understanding of how to use resources to influence issues, and access to the institutions where the issues will be resolved—has an opportunity to wield influence. That opportunity is enhanced if the individual becomes associated with an institution that government and much of the populace depends on for basic goods and services.

CONCLUSION ON RECRUITMENT

In all these nation-states, people who exercise influence have the five traits we discussed in chapter 5; they

(a) understand public issues,

(b) have resources to influence the outcome of issues,

(c) understand how to use resources to influence the outcome of issues,

(d) have access to the institutions where issues are resolved, and

(e) set clear objectives for resolving the issues.

The individuals who have these characteristics, and who thus have the capability to exert influence, tend to come from among the better educated portions of the population. That pool, as a percentage of total population, is especially large in the United States and West Germany. Only a portion of the individuals from this group will actually be recruited into leadership positions.

In Peru, Nigeria, and India, much of the populace does not have the potential influence that derives from purchasing necessities and working for institutions that service the government. In addition, they have little chance to serve in the various branches of government. In Nigeria and Peru, many firms that service the government are foreign. All this makes it especially difficult for the high percentages of the citizenry who have meager educations and poor access to information to exert influence. In India and Peru, at least, such people may vote in competitive elections.

In the United States, the United Kingdom, Germany, and the former Soviet Union, high percentages of the populace purchase necessities from and are employed by institutions which service the government. People from a variety of backgrounds also acquire influence by serving in the various branches of government. Education and information is widespread. In addition, in the United States, the United Kingdom, and Germany, high percentages of the populace vote for a variety of offices in competitive elections, have access to a free press, and can freely form interest groups. This makes it easier for those with moderate educational attainment to exert influence.

In China, high percentages of families are the institutions the government and urban people acquire food and many other basic necessities from. Many that produce other goods and services are employed by economic institutions which service the government. This enhances the potential influence of the large rural populace. However, their influence is diminished by low levels of education and information in the countryside and the lack of competitive elections and freedom to form independent interest groups. But many cadres with prominent party positions come from among the ranks of peasants.

In all these systems, only small percentages of the populace have all the attributes of influence—information, education, the ability to produce basic goods and services, jobs or skills, voting habits, participation in political institutions, and the ability to formulate clear objectives. That small percentage which does have all the attributes has a high potential to exert influence. They have been recruited into public politics, and perhaps into influential roles in the institutions of the political system.

SUMMARY

To exert influence in a political system, one must develop access to the officeholders and bureaucrats who devise public policy. Access can be gained by participating in elections and interest groups, or by becoming a leader in government and political organizations. Those who do so tend to have more education and information, and more of the other resources discussed in three previous chapters. Simply participating in these groups is not enough to impart influence, however. It is necessary to participate with clear objectives in mind.

NOTES

1. Under West Germany's proportional representation, a few votes can make the difference between whether a party has a representative in the legislature; that encourages people to vote.

2. In ten national elections since 1950, an average of 77 percent of the electorate in the United Kingdom voted; similar percentages continued into the 1990s. Less than half vote in local elections. See G. Bingham Powell, Jr., "Voting Turnout in Thirty Democracies," *Electoral Participation: A Comparative Analysis,* ed. Richard Rose (London and Beverly Hills: Sage Publications, 1980); G. Bingham Powell, Jr., "American Voter Turnout in Comparative Perspective," *American Political Science Review* 80 (March 1986): 17–43.

3. The 53 percent turnout in the 1991 election following the assassination of Rajiv Gandhi was the lowest in Indian history. *Kansas City Star,* June 17, 1991.

4. From 1920 to 1992, the percentage of adults voting in presidential elections has ranged from 43 percent to 63 percent, and from 30 percent to 40 percent in Congressional elections. Until the 55 percent turnout in 1992, those figures were steadily declining, and, as we saw in chapter 3, registration requirements drive the percentage of adults eligible to vote lower in the United States than in any of the other systems. The national "motor voter" law passed in 1993 may raise those numbers. U.S. Bureau of the Census, *Historical Statistics of the United States: Colonial Times to 1970,* part 2, pp. 1073, 1084. Idem., *Statistical Abstract of the United States,* 1984, p. 262. Paul R. Abramson, John H. Aldrich, and David W. Rohde, *Change and Continuity in the 1988 Elections* (Washington, D.C.: CQ Press, 1990), pp. 90–95; Paul Kleppner, *Who Voted? The Dynamics of Electoral Turnout, 1870–1980* (New York: Praeger, 1982); Walter Dean Burnham, "The Turnout Problem," *Elections American Style,* ed. A. James Reichley (Washington, D.C.: Brookings Institution, 1987).

5. Some 90 percent voted in Nigeria's first parliamentary election in 1965; by 1979, that figure had dropped to 35 percent. Martin Dent, "Conflict and Reconciliation in Nigeria: The Approach to the Elections," *Conflict Studies,* Institute of Conflict Studies, London, 1983. In the Peruvian congressional election called after President Fujimori arbitrarily dissolved the former Congress in 1992, 23 percent of eligible voters refused to show up, and 20 percent more cast blank ballots.

6. Sidney Verba and Norman H. Nie, *Participation in America* (New York: Harper & Row, 1972), pp. 31, 354.

7. David Lane, *State and Politics in the Soviet Union* (London: Basil Blackwell, 1985), p. 151. In mid-1991, Gorbachev disclosed that the Communist Party had lost 4.2 million members during the prior eighteen months; membership fell to 15 million, its 1973 level, by the time it was outlawed. David Remnick, "Overhaul Aimed At Regaining Lost Confidence," *Washington Post,* July 26, 1991.

8. During 1989 and 1990 the East German communist party lost nearly all of its 2.4 million members.

9. Tony Saich, "Workers in the Workers' State: Urban Workers in the PRC," in *Groups and Politics in the People's Republic of China,* ed. David S. G. Goodman (Cardiff, England: University of Cardiff Press, 1984), p. 160. After the Tiananmen Square repression of 1989, the Chinese Communist Party gained 2.4 million new members. Michael Kenney, "Chinese March to the Stock Exchange," *Kansas City Star,* September 8, 1991. In 1993, it has 52 million members.

10. Verba and Nie, *Participation in America.*

11. *The Gallup Poll, Public Opinion 1981* (Wilmington, Del.: Scholarly Resources, Inc., 1982), pp. 177–78. Twenty-one percent of college graduates, and only 2 percent of those with only grade school educations, belonged to such groups. Twenty-two percent of those making more than $25,000, and 7 percent of those making less than $15,000, belonged to such groups.

12. M. Horton, *The Local Government Elector* (London: HMSO, 1967), pp. 113ff. Russell J. Dalton, *Citizen Politics in Western Democracies* (Chatham, N.J.: Chatham House, 1988), pp. 47–48, cites statistics which show that 23 percent of Americans vote as well as participate in both campaign activities and organized groups; only 8 percent in Britain and 14 percent in West Germany do all three. While 22 percent in West Germany and 19 percent in the United States reported that they tried to convince others how to vote and attended political rallies, only 9 percent of British respondents reported doing either of these.

13. Those U.S. trade union membership figures were much higher in the 1950s and steadily declined until the 1990s, when they began to level off. See Thomas Byrne Edsall, *The New Politics of Inequality* (New York: W. W. Norton, 1984), p. 170. Membership dropped from 22 million in 1979 to 17 million in 1989. Harold W. Stanley and Richard G. Niemi, *Vital Statistics on American Politics,* 3rd ed. (Washington, D.C.: CQ Press, 1992), p. 190.

14. During the 1950s, 45 percent of German workers belonged to labor unions; since then, the percentage has leveled off at about 33 percent (9.3 million in 1986). David P. Conradt, *The German Polity* (New York: Longman, 1978), p. 96.

15. *The Soviet Union Today* (Moscow: Progress Publishers, 1975), p. 73. CIA, *The World Factbook 1990* estimates that 98 percent of the Soviet and 87.7 percent of the East German work force belonged to trade unions.

16. While British industries have been declining, white collar unions have been growing. Max Beloff and Gillian Peele, *The Government of the UK: Political Authority in a Changing Society,* 2nd ed. (New York & London: Norton, 1985), pp. 274–79.

17. Saich, "Workers in the Worker's State," pp. 162, 167.

18. Lloyd I. Rudolph and Susanne Hoeber Rudolph, *In Pursuit of Lakshmi: The Political Economy of the Indian State* (Chicago: University of Chicago Press, 1987), p. 22.

19. Center for Political Studies, University of Michigan, *1976 American National Election Study* (ICPSR).

20. Other polls show similar percentages of the populace participating in these activities in different presidential elections (though there seems to be a general decline between 1956 and 1984 in those wearing political buttons or displaying bumper stickers). Dalton, *Citizen Politics,* p. 42.

21. Dalton, *Citizen Politics,* p. 54. In Europe, trade unions and working class parties can bring out the vote. In the 1988 United States presidential election, 63 percent of white (versus 40 percent of black) adults voted; 45 percent of whites with family incomes under $10,000 voted, while 78 percent with family incomes over $75,000 did, with a steady rise in all categories between. The same difference occurs when looking at occupation, class, or level of education (47 percent with eighth-grade educations or less versus 83 percent of college graduates voted); the higher the level, the higher the percentage voting. Abramson, Aldrich, and Rohde, *Change and Continuity,* pp. 98–99. Raymond E. Wolfinger and Steven J. Rosenstone, *Who Votes?* (New Haven: Yale University Press, 1980), pp. 13–36, argue that education is the most important variable to explain who turns out to vote in America.

22. Allan S. Zuckerman and Darrell M. West, "The Political Bases of Citizen Contacting: Cross-National Analysis," *American Political Science Review*, 79, 1 (March 1985): 123–25.

23. *Soviet Union Today*, p. 51.

24. See Jan S. Adams, "Citizen Participation in Community Decisions in the USSR," in *Politics and Participation under Communist Rule*, eds. Peter J. Potichnyj and Jane Shapiro Zacek (New York: Praeger, 1983); Everett M. Jacobs, ed., *Soviet Local Politics and Government* (London: Allen & Unwin, 1983); William Taubman, *Governing Soviet Cities* (New York: Praeger, 1973).

25. In 1983, a fourth of engineers, technicians, and teachers; half of all writers and scholars with advanced degrees; and three-fourths of journalists were members of the Communist Party. CDSP 35, 39 (October 26, 1983): 6.

26. Lane, *State and Politics*, p. 223; Ellen Propper Mickiewicz, *Handbook of Soviet Social Science Data* (New York: Macmillan, 1973), p. 120.

27. In 1983, 204,742 East Germans belonged to local elected assemblies, 384,638 were on standing committees chosen by local assemblies, 51,177 were lay magistrates of county and district courts, 54,290 on arbitration commissions, and 249,414 on the Workers' and Farmers' Inspectorate. Also in 1983, 2,319,543 served as elected union officials, and 233,365 served on grievance committees. *GDR Facts and Figures '83* (East Berlin: Zeit im Bild, 1983), p. 20.

28. Margaret Inglehart, "Political Interest in West European Women," *Comparative Political Studies* 13: 299–326. However, employed women participate at almost the same rate as men. Keigh T. Poole and L. Harmon Ziegler, *Women, Public Opinion, and Politics* (New York: Longman, 1985), pp. 121–27. Since 1980, higher percentages of American women have been voting than men. Abramson, Aldrich, and Rohde, *Change and Continuity*, p. 97. In the United Kingdom and West Germany, there is little difference between the percentages of men and women voting: while women lag behind men in talking about politics, belonging to groups, and showing interest in politics, the gap is closing. Nancy J. Walker, "What We Know About Women Voters in Britain, France, and West Germany," *Public Opinion* (May/June 1988): 49–52.

29. Forty-four percent of the Representatives were lawyers, 31 percent from business and banking backgrounds, 1 percent labor leaders, 6 percent from agriculture, and 14 percent educators. A 1976 survey of a sample of 2,762 business, intellectual, media, party, feminist, black, farm, and labor leaders found that except for the black, farm, and labor leaders, over 60 percent in each category had fathers in professional, technical, or management positions. Of the remaining three groups, 24 percent (black), 21 percent (farm), and 24 percent (labor) had fathers with such positions. Seventy-three to 94 percent of the leaders in all groups were college graduates, and most had done graduate work. Thirty-six percent of business, 48 percent of intellectual, 16 percent of black, and 26 percent of media leaders were graduates of Ivy League universities. Sidney Verba and Gary R. Orren, *Equality in America: The View from The Top* (Cambridge, Mass.: Harvard University Press, 1985), pp. 81–82.

30. Thomas R. Dye, *Who's Running America: The Reagan Years*, 3rd ed. (Englewood Cliffs, N.J.: Prentice-Hall, 1983), p. 196.

31. Philip Henry Burch, Jr., quoted in Richard Reeves, "So Long, Harvard, Yale, and Princeton," *Kansas City Times*, December 21, 1984.

32. In 1961, 85 percent of the members of the Central Committee of the Communist Party came from families of workers or peasants; people labeled as workers and peasants accounted for 33 percent of the delegates to the Party Congress that year. Still, in 1967, 19 percent of Communist Party members had some higher education, compared to 5.7 percent of the population; 31.8 percent had secondary (versus 16.5 percent) and 49.2 percent primary (versus 77.8 percent) educations. Ninety-five percent of Russian Republic *obkom* first secretaries born after 1914 had university degrees; 44 percent of those born prior to 1914 did. By 1973, 22 percent of men and 6 percent of women aged thirty to sixty were party members; of citizens with completed higher educations, 30 percent (and 50 percent of men) were party members. In 1983, manual workers constituted 60 percent of the populace and 44.1 percent of the Communist Party membership; peasants, 13.3 percent and 12.4 percent, respectively; employees (professional people) 25.8 percent and 43.5 percent. Thus, the percentage of professional people in the Party had at least doubled.

In 1983, about 9 percent of the total populace belonged to the Communist Party. M. Matthews, *Class and Society in Soviet Russia* (New York: Walker, 1972), pp. 223–24. Lane, *State and Politics,* pp. 155, 169. Jerry Hough, *The Soviet Union and Social Science Theory* (Cambridge, Mass.: Harvard University Press, 1977), pp. 7, 73–74, 123, 125–39.

33. Lane, *State and Politics,* p. 169; David Lane, *The End of Social Inequality* (London: George Allen & Unwin, 1982), pp. 119, 120. In the early 1980s 10 percent of new recruits for Party membership were peasants, while 30 percent were white collar. John H. Miller, "The Communist Party: Trends and Problems," in *Soviet Policy for the 1980s,* eds. Archie Brown and Michael Chaser (Bloomington: Indiana University Press, 1982), p. 15; Lane, *State and Politics,* p. 151.

34. The 1989 Supreme Soviet contained 18 percent. Dawn Mann, Robert Monyak, and Elizabeth Teague, Center for International and Strategic Studies and Radio Free Europe/Radio Liberty, *The Supreme Soviet: A Biographical Dictionary* (Washington, D.C.: Radio Free Europe, 1989), p. 31.

35. Some 5 percent of the members of the Central Committee of the Socialist Unity (Communist) Party were workers. Jaroslav Krejci, *Social Structure in Divided Germany: A Contribution to the Comparative Analysis of Social Systems* (New York: St. Martin's, 1976), p. 105. However, in 1985 the Volkskammer (People's Chamber) membership was 23 percent "intellectual" and 18 percent "office worker," while 48 percent were "workers" and 11 percent "cooperative farmers." Albert P. Blaustein and Gisbert H. Flanz, eds., *Constitutions of the Countries of the World,* German Democratic Republic (Dobbs Ferry, New York: Oceana Publications, March 1986), p. 23.

36. Jonathan Steele, *Socialism with a German Face* (London: Jonathan Cape, 1977), p. 217.

37. In 1949, manual or lower-level white collar workers occupied half the seats in the Bundestag. Krejci, *Social Structure,* p. 104.

38. David P. Conradt, *The German Polity,* 5th ed. (New York: Longman, 1993), pp. 137–38.

39. He passed six 0-level subjects by correspondence course (not the higher A levels, entailing additional study, required for university admission) and then became an Associate of the Institute of Bankers, which entails some study and job experience after secondary school. James Lewis, "0-level of Concern Over Qualifications," *Manchester Guardian Weekly,* April 28, 1991.

40. Anthony Sampson, *The New Anatomy of Britain* (London: Hodder and Stoughton, 1971), pp. 11, 241. Sampson is probably not counting those with university educations as workers.

41. Sixteen percent were white collar workers, and 47 percent professionals. Max Beloff and Gillian Peele, *The Government of the UK,* pp. 221, 230–232. The percentage of Labour MP's who are manual workers without higher education has declined during recent decades.

42. Only thirty-three of the fifty-three new members responded to the *Times* questionnaire. Seventeen of the twenty-three who attended university had been to Oxford, Cambridge, or London Universities. Over half the thirty-three were executives, directors, or self-employed businesspeople. One was a farmer. The others were all in professions. Robin Oakley, "Tough, Expert: Thatcher's New Followers," *The Times,* August 15, 1987.

43. Trevor Noble, *Structure and Change in Modern Britain* (London: Batsford Academic and Educational Ltd., 1981), pp. 306–7. As of 1968, 59 percent of senior civil servants were from Oxford or Cambridge. Sampson, *New Anatomy.*

44. Noble, *Structure and Change.*

45. See chapter 21.

46. This is also discussed in chapter 21. The Communist Party had a membership of 39 million people in 1984—3 percent of the population. Some 16 million of the 39 million came into the party during the Cultural Revolution; new members are constantly added, so as to diminish their influence. Intellectuals and workers make up about 10 percent of membership. Saich, "Workers in the Workers' State," p. 160. In 1993, the party contained 52 million members.

47. Alan P. L. Liu, *How China Is Ruled* (Englewood Cliffs, N.J.: Prentice-Hall, 1986), pp. 162–70.

48. In 1982, 2.7 percent (or nine) of the members of the Communist Party's Central Committee were workers' representatives; two were actual workers. Twenty percent of the delegates to the 1983 National People's Congress were "peasants." Virtually all the rest were educated professional people. One member of the

Politburo of the Communist Party in 1984 was a trade union representative; 40 percent were from the military and 40 percent were administrators, mostly with higher educations. Qi Wen, *China: A General Survey,* 3rd ed. (Beijing: Foreign Language Press, 1984), p. 41; James C. F. Wang, *Contemporary Chinese Politics,* 2nd ed. (Englewood Cliffs, N.J.: Prentice-Hall, 1985), p. 128; Saich, "Workers in the Workers' State," pp. 160–61.

49. Dilip Hiro, *Inside India Today* (London: Routledge & Kegan Paul, 1976), p. 99.

50. Though increasing numbers of peasant children are able to attend the regional universities (see chapter 7), their diplomas often do not lead to a job of any stature in the bureaucracy.

51. Though a new national program allows schools to teach in the regional dialects rather than English, the 1992 constitution says that government proceedings shall take place in English and, when practical, in Yoruba, Hausa, and Ibo.

EXERCISES

Think about the book thus far:

1. Which of the five characteristics of influence introduced in chapter 5 are we discussing in this chapter?

2. How do these characteristics relate to the topic of part 2—acquiring influence?

3. What portion of part 2 have we now completed?

KEY WORDS AND PHRASES

Define:

guanxi

THINKING IT THROUGH

Give *three* statistics from surveys which indicate that:

1. Participation in interest groups increases with level of education

    a.

    b.

    c.

2. Those with more education have more contact with officials

    a.

    b.

    c.

3. High office and higher education go together

    a.

    b.

    c.

4. Those without higher education may hold political office

    a.

    b.

    c.

Now, ask yourself:

5. Which of these systems offers the greatest chance for an uneducated worker or peasant to achieve an important political position?

6. In which political activities do more than 20 percent of the adult populace in all these nation-states sometimes participate?

7. In which of the systems would influence seem to be most (and least) widespread?

chapter 11

POLITICAL SOCIALIZATION
WHO CAN RULE?

We move now from recruitment to socialization. We have already examined the five characteristics which can enhance a person's influence. We turn now—in this and the next two chapters—to examining why some people acquire the characteristics of influence and why they develop particular objectives. This chapter explores how a person develops loyalties to various groups and the nation, and how developing loyalty to the nation is affected by one's sense of effectiveness in inducing others to change their thoughts and behaviors.

We have discussed a variety of political resources which can contribute to influence. Whether a person has such resources is partly a matter of luck—being born with good looks, a sparkling personality, a family farm, or a lot of money may be up to chance. But acquiring political resources may also depend on motivation. Whether a person understands public issues and how to influence them, seeks access to the institutions where they are resolved, or develops clear objectives for resolving issues depends to a large extent on how that person is socialized.

Political socialization, as we defined it in chapter 6, is the process by which people come to decide how they will participate in politics. For most people in today's world, the socialization process occurs through the home, community, religious institutions, school, printed and electronic media, and involvement in military and civilian jobs. The ways in which each of these institutions affects socialization varies with the individual.

Socialization helps determine the decisions a person makes about

(1) whom they will support to rule them,

(2) what they want from government, and

(3) what they will learn about government and political issues.

These three factors, in turn, help determine

(4) whether and how people will acquire and use influence.

These are the four topics we shall discuss next. In this chapter, we shall discuss the first, how people decide **whom they will support to rule them. Do they support the existing nation-state and political system, or do they desire a new one? Under what circumstances will they refuse to obey an order?** To find the answers to these questions, we shall discuss how long the nine systems have been nation-states and which cultural groups comprise their populations. We will also explore whether loyalty to one's cultural group ever conflicts with loyalty to the nation-state, the circumstances which might cause loyalty to lag, and how a citizen's feeling of effectiveness affects his or her willingness to support those with authority.

HISTORICAL EXPERIENCE AS A NATION-STATE

The Chinese, English, Germans, and Great Russians have each thought of themselves as a people for centuries. As we shall see shortly, none of these groups comprise the entire populations of their nation-states, but each does represent a large core group. China, Britain, and Russia have been single political units for many centuries, though Germany was never united until 1871. When the United States Constitution was ratified in 1788, settlers of the thirteen colonies were mostly from the British Isles and had nearly two centuries of common experiences under British rule. So China, England, Germany, Russia, and the United States have some long traditions to unite them.

During the eighteenth and early nineteenth centuries, the notions that sovereignty stems from the citizens rather than a monarch, and that government is chosen by and works for the citizens, came to the fore in Britain. The United States was founded on those principles in 1787. Peru became an independent nation-state in 1821. China, Germany, and Russia did not overthrow their monarchies until the twentieth century. India and Nigeria did not become independent nation-states until after World War II.

In 1500 B.C., Shang kings of Anyang, in what is now Henan province in China, used written language, art, conceptions of authority, and customs which have gradually evolved into the present Chinese culture. Confucius and the founders of Daoism lived during the succeeding Zhou dynasty. In 221 B.C., the ruler of the state of Qin (which the name *China* comes from) further up the Yellow River conquered the several warring feudal Zhou rulers and briefly united much of the territory that constitutes today's China. While their rule over the territory has subsequently waxed and waned, and at times several dynasties have competed in controlling it, rulers have continued to use the language, culture, and concepts of authority which sprang from the Shang, Zhou, and Qin dynasties and the dynasty which immediately followed them—the Han Dynasty. The people who speak the Chinese language and order their social interactions in accordance with this culture are referred to as **Han,** regardless of their racial origins. Except for Tibet, China's present provinces have largely been under Chinese control and cultural dominance since the thirteenth century A.D. The Manchus, Mongolians, Islamic peoples living in the northwest, and Tibetans have largely failed to assimilate the Han culture, but many other groups

Grand Canal, Souzhou, China. Begun in the sixth century B.C., this thousand-mile canal is the world's longest, and is jammed with traffic night and day. It ties Beijing to the most populated regions along the coast. *Bob Gamer*

have. After coming to power, the Communist Party formally recognized the existence of fifty-six nationalities; by their definitions, the Han nationality constitutes 94 percent of the current population of China. China has only .16 miles of largely unpaved road per square mile of territory; about a fourth of its villages (including a high portion in the non-Han regions) are not connected to roads. That makes national consciousness especially difficult to achieve among the 6 percent of minority nationalities; among the Han, this sense of identity as a people has had thousands of years to develop.

The United Kingdom of Great Britain and Northern Ireland comprises England, Wales, Scotland, and Northern Ireland. England was conquered by the Normans in 1066, and in turn conquered Scotland, Wales, and Ireland. Wales was finally subdued in 1282. Scotland was a separate kingdom (though it sometimes shared the same king as England) until it united with England in 1707 and gave up its parliament. After continuing civil war since

England first attempted to conquer Ireland in the twelfth century, Great Britain granted Ireland, which is largely Catholic, independence in 1922. However, the northernmost area of **Ulster,** mostly settled by Protestants from Scotland, resisted this; they were eventually allowed to form a separate political entity, attached to the United Kingdom, now called Northern Ireland. Wales, Scotland, and Ireland were settled and culturally influenced by tribal groups from eastern France and southern Germany, whose art, architecture, languages, literature, and social customs are referred to as **Celtic.** During the fifth century A.D., Germanic peoples, Angles and Saxons, migrated to the British Isles and formed kingdoms in what is now northern, central, and southeastern England; these **Anglo-Saxon** people developed the cultural traditions of England. Most of the earliest settlers of the English colonies in America were Anglo-Saxon; those colonies confederated in 1781. The English constitute 82 percent of the current population of the United Kingdom and Northern Ireland. The language and many customs in the United States originated in England.

Germanic tribes already dominated northern Europe at the time of the Roman invasion during the first century before Christ. Though they came to speak common languages, Germany was not united as a nation-state until 1871, when the King of Prussia, William I, became emperor of a united Germany. Nearly all Germans come from families which have spoken German for many generations.

The Slavic portions of the Commonwealth of Independent States also have a long history. Other regions have been added in recent centuries. By the ninth century A.D., Slavic peoples occupied the area from Novgorod (near present-day St. Petersburg) down to the Volga River. During that century, Scandinavian warriors united some of them from a capital in Kiev. Under siege from Mongols and Lithuanians, their successors retreated to other capitals; during the fourteenth century the grand dukes of Moscow began to consolidate power. Tsars in the seventeenth century (contrasting their subjects from the ''Little Russians'' of the Ukraine) began referring to the Slavic peoples of that general area as **Great Russians**; they constitute about half the present population of the Commonwealth of Independent States.[1]

In 1552, Ivan the Terrible, crowned tsar, extended his rule to the former Muslim khanates of the lower Volga and began to annex Siberia. The Romanov Dynasty, which ruled from 1614 to 1917, soon extended rule into part of the Ukraine. During the eighteenth century, Peter the Great and later Catherine the Great extended rule to the Baltic Sea, parts of Poland, the Crimea, Belarus, the rest of the Ukraine, and the shores of the Black Sea. Peter the Great established the tsar's control over the Russian Orthodox Church, whose chief patriarchs had been closely associated with the central rulers from the time of the Kiev capital. Hence, Russia has a long history as a political entity. However, its empire contained over a hundred very diverse nationalities, often brought together against their will. Communication remains difficult, with only .12 miles of mostly unpaved road per square mile of territory, and 90,000 miles of railroad connecting 8.6 million square miles of territory (see figure 11.1).

Many of the main features of the political systems in the United Kingdom, the United States, Russia, Germany, and China evolved over long periods of time. The United Kingdom and the United States operate under the common law system established after the Normans conquered England. Germany's traditions of regional, bureaucratized, civilian-controlled government extend far back in time. Most Americans, Germans, English, and Scots regularly speak the same language. Russia long experienced centralized, hierarchical, absolute control by the tsars; this continued after the communists took control in 1917. China's traditions (continued after the communists took power in 1949) of giving power both to the central ruler and to a balanced mixture of administrative and military elites, extend back at least to the Han Dynasty in the second century B.C. and ultimately to the Shang dynasty in the thirteenth century B.C.

In contrast, Nigeria was drawn on a map late in the nineteenth century, grouping together tribes who never thought of themselves as being part of the

F*igure 11.1* Miles of (a) roads, (b) railroads, and (c) waterways per square mile of territory. (Note that the scale is different on the three graphs.)

CIA, *The World Factbook, 1990.*

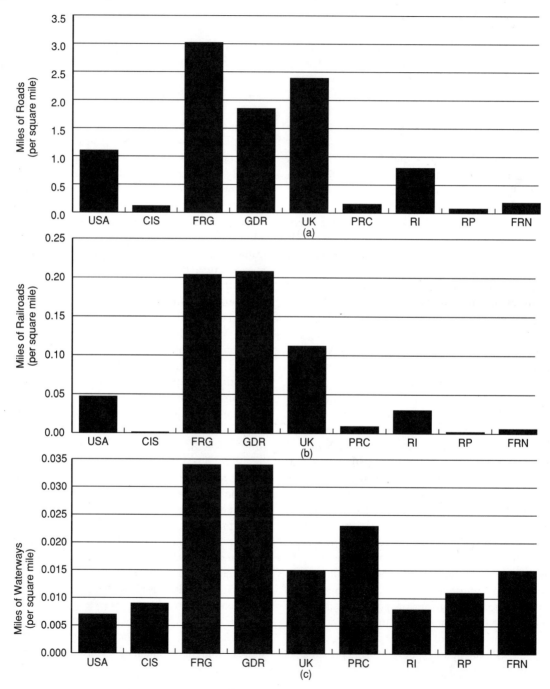

same people, and who had never before been associated through any central authority or on an interregional basis; some, perhaps many, of these tribal people still fail to perceive themselves as Nigerians. With over 250 different ethnic groups speaking many languages, and spread over 357,000 square miles, Nigeria contains under 35,000 miles of paved or tarred and 33,000 miles of dirt roads (.19 miles of road per square mile), only 5,300 miles of navigable rivers and creeks, and less than 2,200 miles of railroad. As we saw earlier, few have radios or television. Thus, many villagers are cut off from the outside world.

The highland peasants in the mountain portion of Peru had large political systems of their own prior to Spanish conquest in the sixteenth century, but those who did not learn Spanish—about half of Peru's population—were not even granted a vote in the new system prior to 1979 (though some of their former leaders intermarried with the Spanish). With 496,000 square miles (almost the size of Alaska), Peru contains 3,800 miles of paved and 17,000 miles of unpaved road (plus 20,000 miles of jeep trails), totaling .081 miles of road per square mile running through some of the most rugged mountain terrain on the planet. Peru also has only 1,200 miles of railroad. Many villages are completely cut off from the outside world, and many others virtually so.

India's political system has more continuity than the systems in either Nigeria or Peru. Since 300 B.C., empires ruled over parts of India with the help of regional states. The empires taxed the smaller states with the help of bureaucracies and their own armies, but allowed the states to administer the governance of their own people. Though these empires were often from Muslim or other cultures, they developed palace ceremonies based on Hindu concepts of rulership to induce loyalty to themselves while allowing individual cultures to flourish within the states; Hindu traditions emphasize loyalty to tribe, family, and caste, all of which the emperor was supposed to protect. Still, members of those cultures often resented the empires imposed on them by military conquest. When the British con-

quered and took control of India during the nineteenth century, they continued these ceremonies and methods of indirect rule, with one important difference: the British began to attack some tribal and caste customs.

India's people speak some 800 languages and dialects,[2] many of which do not relate to one another, and practice at least eight major religious traditions (Hindu, Muslim, Buddhist, Jain, Parsi, Sikh, Jewish, and Christian). At the time it gained its independence, India was still divided into 860 different political entities; princes presided over 562 of them. While these disparate states traditionally support the rule of any emperor who could conquer them, they have no tradition of thinking of themselves as one nation. With 1.3 million square miles of territory, India has 38,000 miles of railroad, and 320,000 miles of paved and tarred roads. But nearly 80 percent of its people live in at least 590,000 villages.[3] One in three is over five miles from an improved road; only one in nine has an all-weather road running through it. Most villages do not have radio or television reception. Moreover, India contains twenty-two states, each of which owns its own radio station; 70 percent of broadcasts are in local languages, and there are no private stations. This allows broadcasters to highlight regional rivalries. All these factors throw obstacles to achieving a sense of national unity in India.

As you can see, Indians, Peruvians, and Nigerians have far less historical experience as members of a nation than the inhabitants of the other six systems. They also face formidable obstacles to creating a sense of nationhood.

TRADITIONAL OBEDIENCE TO AUTHORITY

The problems of establishing support for the political systems in India, Peru, and Nigeria extend beyond cultural diversity and isolation. These nation-states also lag behind the others in teaching their children loyalty to the nation-state.

Among the groups we just discussed in the United States, the post-Soviet republics, the United

Kingdom, Germany, and China, home and community usually reinforce schools, media, the work place, and military training in instilling loyalty to the nation-state. Schools teach children to obey their teachers.[4] Teachers promote appreciation for the nation-state.[5] Schools, communities, and the popular media give exposure to national symbols such as flags, maps, and anthems, and teachers lead children in patriotic songs and rituals. Employers and the military teach deference to supervisors and officers and often provide exposure to national symbols. Families, in turn, tend to teach respect for authority.

Religious institutions often closely identify both with the family and the nation-state. In the United States, the Anglicans who settled Virginia, the Catholics in Maryland and Louisiana, the Congregationalists in Massachusetts, and the Quakers in Pennsylvania each temporarily established their own religion as the only church in their colony, making them highly supportive of the established order; those seeking religious freedom appreciated the freedom to worship as they wished in Rhode Island and elsewhere.[6] The Russian peasant was closely affiliated with the Russian Orthodox Church,[7] and England established its own Church of England. The Confucian philosophy, which has dominated China for two thousand years, teaches that filial piety (reverence for family members in authority) is the cornerstone of moral rectitude; children must obey their parents, wives their husbands, younger brothers their older brothers, families their community leaders and the Confucian scholars who served as local magistrates, and everyone the emperor. Under communism, cadres, civil servants, and the top party leader command that same obedience.

In East Germany, the desire to unite Germans was balanced against separate institutional ties. East and West had different economic institutions and school systems; a person qualified for a job in one system might not always be qualified for a similar position in the other. As Germany reunified, many former East Germans lost their jobs and had no training for new ones; some of them, regretting the loss of their former job security, felt uncertain about giving support to the new unified economic and political system that caused this disruption.

To further complicate matters, Germany's religious history is complex. Princes and smaller aristocrats rallied around Martin Luther to free them from the grip of the Pope, the Holy Roman Emperor, and various kings. Huguenots, the Reformed Church, and other protestant dissidents also arose in protest. They were resisted by Catholics to the south, who are still the dominant group in Bavaria.[8] This religious division contributed to the fragmentation of Germany. After intense religious wars, the Treaty of Westphalia in 1648 brought religious peace. Each of the separate feudal kingdoms and chartered towns established its own religion. People had to move to places where their religion was established or which declared religious freedom. The religions then encouraged loyalty to the princes and town leaders who supported them. As Germany unified in 1871, the Prussian Kings created established **Volkskirche** (literally, the people's churches) for the Catholics, Lutherans, Reformed, and Protestant United Churches: If your parents were born into one of these churches, you are expected to pay church tax to it. At the same time, one was permitted to join the Church of the Brethren, Mennonites, Huguenot, and other such churches who had no connection to the state but whose freedom was protected by law. Both East and West Germany continued this system, which encourages the churches to support those in power (but allows individual clerics to lead some opposition). When Germany merged again in 1990, the Volkskirche system merged with it; those running it are likely to support whoever is in power so as to keep it intact. While institutional differences will persist, economic unification may create a similar merging of loyalties.

In outlying republics and oblasts of the Soviet Union, and in non-Han (that is, non-Chinese) regions of China, families, religious institutions, and communities do not always reinforce loyalty to the nation-state. The loyalty of many Great Russians was often more to Russia than to any greater empire. Nearly half the population of the Soviet Union was not Great Russian. The post-Soviet republics contain ninety-one ethnic groups with over 10,000 members each, and many more with fewer members, who speak dozens of languages from at least seven major (and very different) language groups.[9] Much of this populace lives in regions Great Russians conquered over recent centuries or decades.

A survey of Latvian adolescents during the 1970s found that 23 percent described themselves as religious believers (largely Lutheran, partly Catholic); only a tenth of the populace shows signs of practicing their religion.[10] About a third of Estonians may be practicing Lutherans, while about half of Lithuanians are officially described as practicing Catholics. The Catholic church, especially, was a rallying point for nationalist sentiments against Moscow's rule; the central government responded with severe limits on the number entering Catholic seminaries and convents.

Along the southern borderlands, over 50 million people of Muslim origin still adhere in varying degrees to the customs and practices of that religion. Only two hundred mosques were officially open during the last days of Soviet rule, but many informal religious teachers and leaders still led groups of practicing Muslims; those numbers are mushrooming since religious freedom was declared. The formally approved leaders attempt to unite Islam with modern life and government ideology; many informal leaders resist modern customs and government authority. Many Muslim communities, like Buddhist communities farther east, remain tightly knit and adhere to traditional customs even when civil authorities frown upon these customs.

There are some 2.5 million Jews in the post-Soviet republics; outside of Lithuania, few can still speak Yiddish. Most are urban, taking jobs in the modern sector, and not practicing religious observances; many marry non-Jews. Anti-Semitism lingers, however, often barring Jews from top jobs, and many resent the loss of their cultural heritage.

The many religious traditions in the post-Soviet republics cause divisions between groups and hamper the development of a national identity. Many Christian Armenians continue to fear their Muslim neighbors. Many Georgians, Moldovans, Ukrainians, and members of other ethnic groups have long considered themselves separate nations. The communist regime reinforced such attitudes by issuing identity cards containing one's ethnic origin and creating *nomenklatura* (high-status officials and professionals) among all ethnic groups who could use their influence within the party to benefit their groups.[11]

In China, various cultural and religious traditions also impede the non-Han people from developing a sense of unity. Mongol, Tibetan, Manchu, Uygar, Muslim, and Korean regions of China contain nomadic groups that have never absorbed the Chinese traditions based on settled valley farming. Han traditionally referred to these people as "barbarians," or "natives" who lived on horses or moved their fields from place to place strip farming. These nomadic peoples remain outside the Confucian tradition. Religious leaders in these regions have never endowed a Chinese emperor, or nuclear families, with the legitimacy they receive among Han Chinese. They prefer deference to extended families and religious leaders independent of central political authorities. The communists counted these among the fifty-five "non-Han" nationalities they defined as living in China; they also included some groups which had absorbed Chinese culture, but which party leaders thought of as being outside it. As a result, people who formerly thought of themselves as Chinese increasingly view themselves as being outside that culture.[12] The "non-Han" nationalities constitute 60 million people, or 6 percent of the total population, but they occupy 60 percent of the land mass. This does not reinforce loyalty to the nation-state.

Some marginal groups thus have reduced commitment to the nation-state in many of these systems. Many Tibetans and others from western and southern portions of China do not consider themselves a part of China; the same may be true of sizable numbers of Muslims and other non-Russian groups in the post-Soviet republics. A sizable minority of Scots, Welsh, and Northern Irish do not feel assimilated into the British system.

In India, Peru, and Nigeria, the disunity which can result from ethnic diversity is compounded by still other factors. The majority of Indians spend substantial amounts of time simply staying alive; malnutrition is widespread. The majority of urban inhabitants live in squatter colonies and remain unemployed or underemployed. About half of the

Scotland established Presbyterianism. Ireland remained Catholic. Unitarians, Quakers, Puritans, and Methodists sprang up among townspeople and gentry throughout Great Britain. Centuries of bloody warfare were required to settle the question of whether England would be ruled by Presbyterian or Catholic kings and queens, or by Anglicans from the Church of England. From 1649 to 1660, after a bloody civil war, the British crown was overthrown and the country was ruled by Puritans. By the nineteenth century, religious toleration was only gradually becoming government policy. There are still members of various faiths who resent being tied to a crown which is formally Anglican; notable among them are Northern Irish Catholics, who are opposed by Ulsterites whose ancestors came from Scotland and remain adamantly protestant and unwilling to become a part of Catholic Ireland.

population has an income below 150 U.S. dollars a year and inadequate land to support themselves. All of this weakens the family and community and their tendency to espouse social cooperation. Those controlling the bulk of the land often have little social contact with village dwellers, which also weakens community solidarity. School teachers are often local, poorly trained, and lax about their responsibilities. Official business is conducted in English or Hindi, rather than the languages most Indians speak; this does not allow many to even talk with public officials who have power to distribute money and resources.[13] The government has outlawed the Hindu caste system. It has ceased to enforce obligations owed by higher castes to lower castes or to deal exclusively with the highest caste members of communities; many high caste people have been reduced to menial occupations. Muslims are allowed to slaughter cows and affront other Hindu religious practices, to the chagrin of Hindu leaders. The 60 million non-Hindu, non-Muslim people in India are often concerned about losing the solidarity of their communities in a nation-state dominated by cultures and languages they do not participate in. And the

100 million Muslims frequently resent actions of the Hindu-dominated government (though Hindus constitute 83 percent of the populace).

As we have seen, only about a tenth of Peru's work force is active in the modern (formal) sector of the economy; a portion of them are unionized and frequently challenge government through strikes. Rural communities commonly find private property owners encroaching on their land without providing them alternative means of support. Even the extensive land reforms of the 1970s (discussed in chapter 21) removed more land from traditional communities than it gave to them; the privately owned, great landed estates, **latifundia** and **haciendas,** became the property of their workers, who often then suspended the rights of surrounding communities to graze animals on them. Those receiving land under the reforms have found it hard to sustain adequate technology, to obtain and repay loans, and to cope with inflation sometimes surpassing 3,000 percent a year. Increases in government bureaucracy often mean a decline in functions controlled by village leaders, who therefore mistrust government officials. Church leaders wish to avoid such disputes. While some priests support the government, others preach liberation theology and the need to right social wrongs. School teachers are often graduates of the regional universities who resent returning to such menial jobs; they face little supervision as to what they teach and often do not stress support for the government. Unemployment in the countryside causes young people to migrate to the cities, where they find themselves living in squatter colonies, cut off from their families and the daily support of their former communities. Those gaining influence in such neighborhoods may keep money and other resources for themselves, further contributing to the breakdown of family, community, and national cohesion.

The many Nigerian tribal groups have a long history of conflict with one another. To further complicate matters, about a third of the traditionally Muslim north (dominated by the **Hausa,** who constitute 30 percent of Nigeria's populace) has become

Christian, while half the **Yoruba** (who dominate the southwest and make up 20 percent of the populace) have become Muslim. Yoruba, Ibo, and a few others to the south have attended British universities since the nineteenth century; most of Nigeria's universities were founded in 1975 and 1976 and accept few Hausa (whose primary pupils still largely learn the Muslim Koran, because of local control of the curriculum). Yet most of the population is in the north. In 1967, the **Ibo** to the southeast (17 percent of the populace) broke away to form the **Republic of Biafra**; they were subdued in a bloody civil war and returned to Nigerian control.

Most of the nation-state's business is conducted by part of the 2 percent of the populace who speak fluent English. During the past twenty years, the central government has greatly intensified efforts begun years earlier at the village level to frontally attack the political power of community and religious leaders. Those leaders turn to their towns, villages, and mosques for support against the central government. The central government has few socializing mechanisms to fight back with; few people have access to roads, radios, or television sets.

Thus, in India, Peru, and Nigeria, the government cannot count on family, religion, and community to strongly support obedience to authority, and schools, the work place, the military, and the media do not effectively reach large numbers of people to advocate adherence to authority. Similarly, in the post-Soviet republics, as well as in China, obedience to authority does not necessarily mean obedience to the central authorities. The percentage of those with questionable loyalty is lower in China.

ECONOMIC HARDSHIP AND DISOBEDIENCE

People who face economic hardships and uncertainties are more likely to reject a political system, especially if it is not well established, or if relations between the individual's cultural group and the system are shaky. This destabilization is aggravated when people who have achieved economic success experience setbacks.[14] In Germany after World War I, many small farmers, bureaucrats, small shopkeepers, craftspeople, small investors, and white collar workers were displeased that the economy was declining under the Weimar Republic, and they helped Hitler remove it. Similar uncertainty prevailed among many officials, intellectuals, and businesspeople in China after World War II. And such attitudes among southern planters helped bring about the American Civil War.

In recent decades, the possibility of such radical uncertainty among prominent and successful people has receded in West Germany, China, and the United States, and is not notably present in the United Kingdom or India either. In eastern Germany, some former communists fell from high positions into unemployment or positions of lowered influence where they do face such uncertainty; in the post-Soviet republics, the officials that remain in high positions have used their influence to disrupt the economy and sour people on reforms. Frequent economic displacements and downturns pose similar problems for many elites in Peru and Nigeria. All nine systems contain people who are unhappy because of economic setbacks and uncertainty. All contain people who are not socialized to support the central government and who have grievances against their political system.

One might think, then, that eastern Germany, the post-Soviet republics, Nigeria, and Peru (with many people perhaps not socialized to support the government, and radical economic uncertainty) would be candidates for revolution, and that the other nation-states might be candidates for civil unrest. But lack of support does not inevitably imply a desire for a new government. Nor does it necessarily indicate a proclivity to disobey the present government. Loosely affiliated people may understand so little about government that they do not support measures for placing limits on its authority and cannot sufficiently unite to break away.

Efficacy, Obedience, and Limits

Young people sometimes reject the values of their parents. Sometimes they rebel because they accept the values their parents taught them, but do not believe their parents are living up to those values. Rejection of parental values, however, does not always entail rejection of the total political system. People who do not support the political system, who are affected by economic distress, or who reject parental values might seem more inclined than others to be disobedient. They might also be inclined toward submissiveness and conformity to those around them. This can be especially true if their parents or other institutions taught them to be submissive,[15] or if their family lives are unstable and they do not feel they can control their own lives. They may fall in with a peer group which chooses to disobey the government and go along with these peers. It is more common, however, for such individuals to find themselves surrounded by those who are supportive of or indifferent to government and to go along with them. Furthermore, a person's verbal or emotional rejection of the political system does not necessarily mean that person will actively reject the system; it may actually signify that they like the system and want it to improve, or that in practice they are indifferent toward it.

Government is a fact of life; it is there. It will not go away unless people act against it. For this reason, political leaders welcome (and usually find) a high degree of **political latency**—unused potential for exerting political influence—among the populace. Latency may be a sign that people are satisfied. Or it may be a sign that they are dissatisfied, but submissive. It is often hard to tell the two apart. But latency is, at the least, a clear sign that people do not care enough about changing government to attempt to do so.

For people to feel they can have a personal effect on politics—that they have **political efficacy**—usually requires that they be socialized in a manner which shows them they can have an effect, their personal actions can influence the behavior of government officials and thus place limits on government authority. Before people can feel efficacious in such wide-scale matters, they need some self-confidence in their ability to control their own immediate environment—a sense that they can affect the behavior of family, friends, teachers, or prospective employers. One way to create this self-confidence is to include children in family decision making. Another is to teach them in school how they can influence government,[16] or to give them responsibilities for making decisions in the work place or in civic organizations.[17] Among women, efficacy is greater among those who work outside the home than among women whose primary careers are as homemakers; sense of efficacy increases with education levels in both groups.[18]

Socialization that teaches personal efficacy may be more the exception than the rule. Those exposed to opportunities for controlling their social environments are often children whose parents have more education, and who send their children to better schools, which gives them access to better jobs; therefore, they have higher socioeconomic status. There are far fewer children in this category in Nigeria, Peru, India, China, the post-Soviet republics, and East Germany than in West Germany or the United Kingdom. The portion of United States citizens exposed to these socialization agents for experiencing efficacy probably far surpasses all the others; even there, however, the percentage may not be high. If chapter 3 bored you when it explained how you personally can help choose nominees and induce cooperation among officeholders, the chances are great that you yourself have low efficacy.

Some cultural settings may be more conducive to creating efficacy than others. In the United States, businesses are increasingly set up so that teams, task forces, and employee groups make decisions on a cooperative basis, rather than establishing strict hierarchies where orders come down from the top. As early as the nineteenth century, Alexis DeTocqueville noted that American children are raised to respond to persuasion rather than punishment and to consider themselves on a par with adults. American children learn to express pride in their own accom-

Table 11.1

Political Efficacy: Responses to Survey Questions[1]

Percent That Agreed with the Statement:	1959–60			1974[2]		
	USA	UK	FRG	USA	UK	FRG
"I can do something about an unjust national regulation."	75%	62%	38%	78%	57%	56%
"I would likely have success if I tried to change a harmful national regulation."	41	25	13			
"I can do something about an unjust local regulation."	77	78	62	71%	64%	67%
"I would likely have success if I tried to change a harmful local regulation."	52	36	32			
"I regularly or occasionally discuss politics."	76	70	60			

[1]Gabriel A. Almond and Sidney Verba, *The Civic Culture* (Boston: Little, Brown, 1965), pp. 116, 169, 185.

[2]Samuel H. Barnes and Max Kaase, *Political Action: Mass Participation in Five Western Democracies* (Beverly Hills and London: Sage, 1979), p. 141.

plishments,[19] ask for what they need, address strangers informally, demand privacy, question what they hear from authorities, and band together with peers to resist conforming to adult demands. German children, in contrast, were traditionally raised in a stricter, more hierarchical manner; those habits are loosening among younger Germans (see table 11.1).[20] Chinese children, in the Confucian tradition, are taught to obey their fathers, older brothers, husbands, and government officials without question; leaders have found that they can often stop unwanted political activities by reminding participants of this obligation. East Germany, the Soviet Union, China, India, and Peru have encouraged workers and villagers to involve themselves in councils that push for better labor and housing conditions, day care facilities, and other matters that affect them; however, because these demands are often ignored, such activities could actually even discourage a sense of efficacy among participants. People in these latter systems may believe that those at the top of the social system are different from those below and that they should defer to them and keep their distance.

People need a sense of efficacy to actively oppose government. In developing that sense, and experiencing success at resisting or changing government initiatives, one may at the same time become less inclined to distrust the entire system.[21] Gabriel Almond's definition of civic culture involves "a widely distributed sense of political competence [efficacy] and mutual trust," combined with enough latency to let government carry on its business. The leaders must know that if they err, people may resist, but that in the interim people trust what they are doing.

If people who do not trust the system are also socialized to be submissive, they do not pose a danger until people they relate to as peers begin to actively oppose the system.[22] In most times and places, few choose to lead such active opposition;

those who do are often easy to jail, kill, or bribe, and thus remove as a threat. Unless a government offends many participants and nonparticipants at the same time, it is likely to retain general allegiance.

Nigeria, Peru, and India may have fewer people who are socialized to support the political system, and more people dissatisfied with it, than the other political systems. At the same time, they may have more people who are socialized to be submissive and do not have a sense of efficacy. This reduces the chance that the people in these nation-states would actively seek a new political system or fail to obey the present one. It also reduces the possibility they would seek to place limits on the authority of public officials.

The economy of the Soviet Union dissatisfied many prominent participants in the system. In regions where support for centralized rule was never strong, they triggered demands for breaking away from the system, even among some who are normally politically latent. Many prominent participants took advantage of reform to secure control of economic assets for themselves and become prominent in new parties. They joined with "outsider" dissidents who had formerly opposed the communist power structure to split the Soviet Union apart. Those who already felt efficacious and were active in politics became immediately active in new institutions, as they were in the old; many presidents and legislators in the new CIS republics are former communists. Once in power, both former communists and dissenters are tempted to use military force and to jail opponents—from both their own nationality groups and from others—to gain their ends. And some former leaders of rebellion may remain predis-

posed to operate outside the system, not easily adjusting to conventional politics, even when they have the chance.[23] Widening the circle of those who share sovereignty, and who participate in politics and interest groups, is therefore not easy.

People who do not feel efficacious and do not support the system have little incentive to understand the complexities behind issues and how to use resources to influence them. They are seldom motivated to seek access to institutions where issues are resolved or to develop clear objectives for resolving them. This leaves them unable to use influence against the system.

SUMMARY

The nine systems we are studying vary in the length of time their citizens have thought of themselves as one people, and in the length of time they have been together as nation-states with authority to rule coming from their citizens. Some of their citizens are socialized by family, religious institutions, community leaders and peers, school, media, the work place, and military training to obey those in authority. Other citizens do not experience all those socializing forces and may even undergo some socialization which advocates disobeying those in authority. Similarly, some are taught that they can be efficacious in exerting influence to change the behavior of those in authority, while others learn to remain submissive. A submissive populace helps those who rule continue to hold power. And efficacious people often learn to support the system or mold it to their own wishes.

NOTES

1. The Slavic population is 146 million out of 290 million total citizens. Ten million Belarussians, called "White Russians," closely affiliate themselves with the Great Russians; Belarus lies between Moscow and Poland.

2. Some estimate 1,600 languages and dialects in India; there are many subtle regional variations.

3. Estimates sometimes go as high as 700,000 different villages in India.

4. Robert Hess and Judith Torney, *The Development of Political Attitudes in Children* (Chicago: Aldine, 1967),

p. 126, argue that "compliance to rules and authority is the major focus of education in elementary schools."

5. A 1960s study found American schools spending more time on "political education" than those in the Soviet Union. George Z. F. Bereday and Bonny B. Stretch, "Political Education in the USA and USSR," *Comparative Education Review* 7 (June 1963): 9–16. When Eastern Europe ended communism and the Soviet Union split up, teachers suddenly switched to support of freer markets and new national loyalties.

6. Most of the earliest colleges and universities were founded by religious bodies, who were thus able to influence the educated elite. Primary and secondary education, as it gradually shifted into the hands of government, was controlled at the local level, where religious leaders had close liaison with politicians. All this gave strong incentive for religious leaders to preach support for the established authorities.

7. Even when Cossacks found it convenient to ally with Poland, their religious affiliation lay with a church closely allied with the tsar of Russia. Peasant revolts were directed against princes and landowners, but not against the tsar.

8. That resistance continued during the nineteenth century when the Lutheran Prussians joined with other protestant groups along the Rhine River to begin industrialization; this was resisted by Catholic Bavaria.

9. S. V. Kalesnik and V. F. Pavlenko, eds., *Soviet Union: A Geographical Survey* (Moscow: Progress Publishers, 1976), pp. 165–73.

10. Helene Carrere d'Encausse, *Decline of an Empire: The Soviet Socialist Republics in Revolt* (New York: Newsweek Books, 1979), pp. 221, 223.

11. See Gerhard Simon, *Nationalism and Policy Toward the Nationalities in the Soviet Union: From Totalitarian Dictatorship to Post-Stalinist Society* (Boulder: Westview, 1991), pp. 265–90.

12. For example, the second largest minority in China (with 1.2 million members) is called the Bai. Prior to 1958, that term was not used as an ethnic label. Their forebears include members of several Southeast Asian groups (in the region now inside the Province of Yunnan) who began to assimilate with conquering Chinese groups in the eighth century A.D. More than half the words of the dialect they speak are Chinese. Those living in cities are hard to distinguish from Chinese on the basis of cultural habits. In rural areas, some older women wear distinctive garb, but their social customs are similar to those of Chinese. During the 1940s, the people later defined as Bai told researchers they were Chinese. But since being defined as a separate nationality, many are embracing separate ethnic status. David Yen-ho Wu, "The Construction of Chinese and Non-Chinese Identities," *Daedalus* 120, 7 (Spring 1991): 167–70.

13. Hindi, spoken by 42 percent of the Indian population, has no linguistic connection with the languages of the south.

14. See Lypard P. Edwards, *The Natural History of Revolution* (Chicago: University of Chicago Press, 1927) for an earlier discussion of this thesis and Ted Robert Gurr, *Why Men Rebel* (Princeton: Princeton University Press, 1970) for a more recent view.

15. Some researchers, such as Robert Lane, see submissiveness as one possible adaptation to an upbringing which discourages children from participating in family decisions. Some think submissive children can grow into "autoplastic" personalities more interested in changing themselves (for example, in artistic directions) than changing the world. See Talcott Parsons, *The Social System* (Glencoe, Ill.: Free Press, 1951), chapter 7; Robert Merton, *Social Theory and Social Structure* (Glencoe, Ill.: Free Press, 1957).

16. It may not be enough to merely teach about good citizenship. A child who is taught that he or she could theoretically be effective, but must meanwhile submit without question to teachers and other authorities, may develop submissive habits. Just telling the child that the system allows individual participation may not be enough. And to develop a true sense of efficacy, the child must know something about how the system works.

Evidence on the role of education in influencing efficacy is inconclusive. Paul R. Abramson, *Political Attitudes in America: Formation and Change* (San Francisco: Freeman, 1983), pp. 154–57, states: "There is very little evidence of differences in the implicit values taught in American schools or of differences in 'educational climates' within schools. . . . Impressive data document the assumption that persons with restricted opportunity develop low feelings of self-confidence . . . there is considerable support [that] . . . persons deprived of opportunity and denied respect have low levels of self-confidence and . . . feel that they cannot control their social environment . . . there is some support [that] . . . black children (and children from other disadvantaged subcultural groups) with high feelings of self-confidence . . . feel more politically efficacious (and more trusting) than those with low feelings of self-confidence." Richard Merelman, "Democratic Politics and the Culture of American Education," *American Political Science Review* 74 (June 1980): 319–32, argues that lessons about political efficacy in civics classes are counteracted by the hierarchical approach of the school in keeping order and discipline by obeying orders, and teachers' tendency to avoid discussing controversial subjects. Two books give interesting insight on this subject: Maurice Stein, *The Eclipse of Community: An Interpretation of American Studies* (New York: Harpers, 1964); Alice Miller, *Thou Shalt Not Be Aware: Society's Betrayal of the Child* (New York: Farrar, Straus, and Giroux, 1984).

17. In many rural areas of Central Asia and the Caucuses in the former Soviet Union, non-Russian men find it demeaning to be seen outdoors with their wives. Women's councils have been set up to organize family nights with dancing, drawing the men into public with the women. This helps give women self-confidence to enter the work force. These committees have also become active in pressuring management for better labor conditions, day care facilities, regulation of alcohol sales, and other matters. Susan Bridger, *Women in the Soviet Countryside* (Cambridge, England: Cambridge University Press, 1987), pp. 190–95.

18. Keigh T. Poole and L. Harmon Ziegler, *Women, Public Opinion, and Politics* (New York: Longman, 1985), pp. 136–40.

19. A 1991 Times-Mirror poll found 63 percent of Americans, but only 46 percent of Britons and 38 percent of Germans, disagreeing with the statement that "hard work offers little guarantee of success." The respective figures for disagreement with the statement that "success in life is pretty much determined by forces outside our control" are 57 percent, 42 percent and 33 percent. *Christian Science Monitor*, November 22, 1991.

20. For example, see Maya Pines, "Unlearning Blind Obedience in German Schools," *Psychology Today* (May 1981). When asked in a public opinion poll whether one is free to state his or her political opinion, only 55 percent of West Germans said "yes" in 1959, while 73 percent replied in the positive in 1976. In 1952, 40 percent of poll respondents said they never or hardly ever express their political views; by 1975, only 21 percent responded this way. In 1951, when asked what they stressed in raising children, 41 percent said "love of order and industriousness," 25 percent "obedience and deference," and 28 percent "independence and free will;" by 1976, those figures were 41 percent, 10 percent, and 51 percent, respectively. Gabriel A. Almond and Sidney Verba, *The Civic Culture Revisited* (Boston: Little, Brown, 1980), p. 252.

The vicar of one of East Berlin's city churches commented: "In the factories people criticized a lot. The older generation may be afraid to open their mouths, but not the younger ones. They realize they have a part to play." Jonathan Steele, *Socialism with a German Face* (London: Jonathan Cape, 1977), p. 149. In 1989, brave young people defied authorities in the streets of Leipzig and other cities to bring about the fall of the communist government.

21. There is some evidence that distrust does diminish. See Martin B. Abravanel and Ronald J. Busch, "Political Competence and Political Trust, and the Action Orientation of University Students," *Journal of Politics* (February 1975), p. 73; Joel Aberbach and Jack L. Walker, "Political Trust and Racial Ideology," *American Political Science Review* 63 (December 1970).

22. Richard D. Shingles, "Black Consciousness and Political Participation: The Missing Link," *American Political Science Review* 75 (March 1981), pp. 76–91, found that black activists had high efficacy and low trust. Russell J. Dalton, *Citizen Politics in Western Democracies* (Chatham, N.J.: Chatham House, 1988), pp. 50–57, 68–69, found that those engaging in unconventional protest such as demonstrations, strikes, and boycotts had higher political efficacy than those engaging in conventional political activities.

23. See Abravenel and Busch, "Political Competence;" Edward N. Muller, "A Test of a Partial Theory of Potential for Political Violence," *American Political Science Review* 66 (September 1972): 928–59; David Schwartz, *Political Alienation and Political Behavior* (Chicago: Aldine, 1973).

EXERCISES

Think about the book thus far:

1. What main topic is discussed in chapters 7–10? in chapters 11–13?

2. How do the topics discussed in this chapter affect the five characteristics examined in chapters 7–10?

3. How do the matters discussed in this chapter affect the ability of political leaders to exercise sovereignty?

KEY WORDS AND PHRASES:

Define the following terms:

Han	Volkskirche	Ibo
Ulster	latifundia	Republic of Biafra
Celtic	haciendas	political latency
Anglo-Saxon	Hausa	political efficacy
Great Russians	Yoruba	

THINKING IT THROUGH

Answer each of these questions by placing Xs in the appropriate boxes below:

1. Which of these political systems has been a single political entity with nearly the same boundaries for over four centuries?

2. Which of these political systems has been ruled as a single entity for over four centuries, but with gradually expanding boundaries?

3. In which of these political systems do over two-thirds of the populace come from an ethnic group which shares the same language and cultural traditions?

4. Which of these political systems have existed as a single unit for over two centuries?

	USA	USSR	FRG	GDR	UK	PRC	RI	RP	FRN
1.									
2.									
3.									
4.									

Now, answer each of the following questions in a sentence or two.

5. Do Xs in the boxes increase or decrease the chances that large portions of the populace will be loyal to their nation-state?

6. Mention some groups in which the main socializing institutions may fail to instill loyalty to the nation-state. Why?

7. If I am not socialized to obey central government, am I likely to be socialized to change its behavior or place limits on its authority? Why or why not?

8. What might cause loyalty to lag among people who have been socialized to support their nation-state?

9. Why do governments generally have little fear that dissatisfied people will revolt?

10. What kinds of experiences make people feel efficacious? Do you feel efficacious?

11. Why are efficacious people usually not a threat to governments?

Now, ask yourself:

12. Why can't government count on the family, religion, and community in much of India, Peru, and Nigeria, and in many parts of the CIS and China, to support obedience to authority?

chapter 12

POLITICAL SOCIALIZATION

WHAT DO I SEEK FROM RULERS?

In chapters 11 through 13, we are focusing on why some people acquire characteristics which let them exert influence and why they develop particular political objectives. In this chapter, we examine how individuals come to identify with certain groups, and how they perceive they should help these groups. We will also discuss how that, in turn, affects the system's ability to forge compromises which benefit wide portions of its citizenry.

In chapter 11, we discussed how people decide how much support or opposition they will give to those who rule them. In this chapter, we will discuss **whom they want the government to help, how much they feel they must learn about their political system, and how this affects the ability of their political system to benefit wide portions of their populations.**

WHAT PEOPLE WANT FROM GOVERNMENT

What do people want government to do? What do they want it to avoid doing? The mere fact that people tend to accept the existence of government and fail to openly disobey it does not necessarily imply that they do not have opinions about what it should or should not do.

All of us identify emotionally and intellectually with regional, tribal, ethnic, cultural, religious, class, or other groups; we develop **group identification.** As we discussed in chapter 6, Richard Dawson and Kenneth Prewitt assert that ''children learn, early and fervently, that there are significant *political groupings* in society and that some groups are friends and others are enemies.'' [emphasis added] If the child grows up in a tight-knit family he or she closely identifies with, this lesson will probably be taught within the family. Otherwise, the child's

exposure to the combined values of family members and peers will probably teach the child who are ''friends'' and ''enemies.'' In simplest terms, the child learns that government should help favored political groupings—whether they be regional, tribal, ethnic, religious, cultural, occupational, or class-related. Early learning helps us choose groupings we will identify with, and this identification is likely to endure throughout life.

Still, we encounter many other socialization agents as we move through life, including schools, the military, and jobs. All of these may either expose us to or isolate us from various groups. The nation itself is a group one may or may not identify with. Other groups one identifies with may lie entirely within the nation or include members outside the nation. In either case, one's loyalty to one's nation and to other groups may at times conflict. Some people have trouble sorting out such conflicts, while others seek to reconcile them. And some people view certain groups as mortal enemies with whom there can be no compromise, while others would never adopt such a rigid stance toward accommodating any group.

Schools are capable of teaching children and adolescents about group identification in a variety of ways. Children meet peers to imitate and identify with. They listen to teachers who may try not to offend any group, but often slant their orientation

People like these Nigerian girls, who spend hours each day carrying water home from a public tap, have little contact with people beyond their village.
© Rodney Wilson

toward the particular groups they themselves identify with. In a nation-state whose members speak many languages, schools can broaden or limit access to other groups through the languages in which they teach. The classroom may contain several classes and races, or only one. And students may learn that they should or should not pursue jobs that expose them to other groups.

Military service also may or may not expose an individual to people from a variety of groups and backgrounds. The behavior of officers and peers sends messages about the relative value of different groups and of cooperating with them. In the Soviet Union, Muslim, Baltic, Ukrainian, and other recruits were often segregated in separate military units and experienced negative treatment at the hands of some Great Russians; that helped create powerful perceptions about who were friends and foes. Integrated units with good relations among members of different races can help break down prejudices.

A job often requires deference to supervisors, fellow employees, customers, suppliers, and others; those individuals may come from a variety of groups. Certain behaviors toward other groups may help you get ahead, while other behaviors may impede your advancement. Jobs may teach an individual to change old habits to benefit others. They teach values about acceptable and unacceptable behaviors when dealing with other groups.

Few people in Peru, India, and Nigeria have any exposure to such socializing experiences which might help broaden their identification with different groups. The one contact they might make with institutions such as schools, the military, and the work place is in primary schools; these schools often contain only children from the same village or urban

Figure 12.1 Some people constantly meet other people who have values and attributes different from their own; others rarely do.

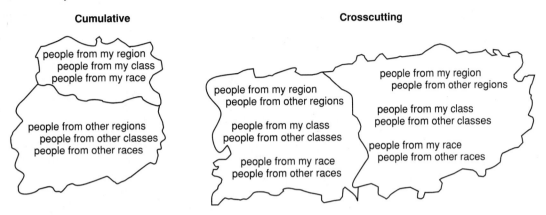

squatter colony and offer little intellectual exposure to other groups. Primary education textbooks in the other nation-states give varying coverage to other groups. In all nine systems, children often receive little exposure to other racial, socioeconomic, regional, and religious groups at school. The same may also be true in their place of employment as adults.

Some people constantly meet other people who have values and attributes different from their own; others rarely do. One can think of these people as being in enclosed areas; some areas contain a variety of people who cross over from one area to another, while others contain only people who are very much alike in many ways and never leave their own area. Some people stay in their own area and accumulate contacts with others much like themselves because they are physically isolated from other groups of people. Others remain in their area by choice, even though they are physically surrounded by diverse people. William Kornhauser suggests that a person exposed to members of a variety of ethnic, class, regional, and other groups—to **crosscutting cleavages**—from an early age has a better chance of growing up to understand other groups' ideas and needs.[1] A person exposed only to his or her own cultural, regional, religious, and

ethnic group—to **cumulative cleavages**—may understand only that group's needs. *Cleavages* are divisions or splits; crosscutting cleavages allow a person to "cut across" divisions and gain knowledge of other types of people; cumulative cleavages allow a person to accumulate divisions around him or herself, cutting off contact with other groups (figure 12.1).

In rural areas (where high percentages of the populace live) in China, the post-Soviet republics, India, Nigeria, and Peru, few people have any opportunity to meet people different from themselves (that is, to be exposed to crosscutting cleavages). Transportation is poor and few can afford to travel; in rural China (and formerly in the Soviet Union), all citizens must receive official permission to travel or move, and foreigners are not allowed to visit most towns and villages.

Many people in urban work forces also are not exposed to crosscutting cleavages; the percentage who are is probably higher in the United States and the United Kingdom, where culturally diverse people have greater opportunity for spatial or social mobility than in the other seven systems.

In Germany, the post-Soviet republics, and China, school curriculums, radio and television programming, military service, and contacts with

Chinese are closely watched by gatekeepers surrounding their residences, and by neighborhood party officials, to determine that they are not contacting foreigners, citizens from differing ethnic groups, students, or others deemed suspicious. In the post-Soviet republics, where such pressures are easing, few can afford to travel, and tourists tend to visit only the major cities. Germany is largely composed of people whose families have spoken German and lived in the same region for centuries. Foreign guest workers and refugees from Eastern Europe have little social contact with Germans. Rural migrants to cities in Nigeria, Peru, and India often live in makeshift squatter colonies and have little contact with established urban dwellers.

Immigrants to the United Kingdom from India and Pakistan often live by themselves in isolated neighborhoods, but they do run small shops and restaurants, attend schools, and work in larger businesses which give them daily contact with people of British ancestry. Many black (West Indian) immigrants have more difficulty establishing such contacts. High percentages of the residents in London, Leicester, Birmingham, Bristol, and a number of other cities are likely to have some regular contact with people of other races, religions, and classes. Those contacts diminish as one moves into outlying suburban and rural areas.

It is hard to find any small town in the United States which does not contain a variety of immigrant groups, religions, races, and people born in different regions. Some communities host more variety than others; these groups may still have little close social contact with one another, but the opportunity for such contact exists. The opportunity for conflict, even violence, between these groups also exists.

varies greatly. People from differing cultures who have regular contact with each other may develop friendships or fight with one another. People from differing cultures who have no contact with one another, however, have little chance to discover common interests. The choices people who participate in politics make in regard to groups they identify with can thus make it easier or harder for political systems to fashion mutually acceptable solutions to social problems.

In China, India, Peru, and Nigeria, top political officeholders and leaders are usually well-educated. In China, such leaders come largely from provincial capitals or Beijing; in India, from New Delhi, or state capitals; in Peru, from metropolitan Lima or Arequipa; and in Nigeria, from metropolitan Lagos-Ibadan and Port Harcourt. Because these leaders grow up in the cultures of large cities, they have an opportunity to experience some crosscutting cleavages. However, they tend to mingle with people who largely cut themselves off from those in the countryside or from less prestigious schools, or (in the case of China) those outside the walled Zhongnanhai compound near the Forbidden City[2] in Beijing where the top Party cadres live. Thus, political leaders in these four nation-states often do not develop much sense of identification with the groups that form the majority of the populace. In the countryside, most people mingle primarily with their own group.

The United States, United Kingdom, Germany, and the post-Soviet republics offer more opportunities for political leaders from various regions to develop contacts and influence at both the regional and national levels. Because they grow up in various regions, interact with one another, and are exposed to media and school curriculums that introduce a variety of groups, some of these leaders are more likely to develop empathy for groups beyond their own and to promote government actions that benefit a variety of groups. They also can count on support from at least some people who participate in politics at the local level and who share this sense of empathy; most people probably fall between the extremes of narrow and broad group identification.

leaders can help compensate for limited exposure to other groups. In India, Peru, and Nigeria, smaller percentages of the populace are reached even by those contacts.

Hence, the opportunity for children to learn that groups from other races, regions, religions, and cultures are (in Prewitt and Dawson's terms) friends

Leaders from various parts of West Germany have interacted through school, bureaucratic and corporate hierarchies, and political contacts in the capital of Bonn. Party elites from various regions of East Germany interacted in Berlin, which was geographically close to all parts of that small country; many of those elites came from families of moderate means. But there was little contact between the elites of the East and West, resulting in considerable suspicion on both sides. Though Berlin is now the official capital of unified Germany, construction of new government buildings in Bonn continues, ensuring more segregation of the elites from the two zones.

In the Soviet Union, Leonid Brezhnev (who ruled from 1966 to 1982) expanded the chance for youths from rural and outlying urban areas to enter university and, subsequently, high positions in the Party. Moscow University and others experienced greater diversity in the student body, with opportunities for bright students from various parts of the Soviet Union to become friends and to keep contact as they were assigned responsible jobs. By the time Mikhail Gorbachev came to power, many such individuals had risen high enough in various professions and organizations to be promoted into positions of prominence. Since 1978, more young people from rural and outlying urban areas of China have reached university; they are gradually attaining prominence in local, regional, and republic politics.

Still, such empathetic leaders do not always emerge. Many top leaders in the Soviet Union were Great Russians; in China, Han; and in the United States and the United Kingdom, Anglo-Saxon. Some of them have broadened group identifications. Competitive elections in the United States, the United Kingdom, and the Federal Republic of Germany allow a variety of regional, ethnic, religious, or other groups to penetrate top leadership. At the same time, they let voters with narrow group identifications create and support some top leaders with similarly narrow identifications: For example, some East Germans, long forbidden to vote for unauthor-

ized splinter parties, have supported anti-Semitic and neo-Nazi leaders with narrow appeals since the reintroduction of multiple parties. East and West Germans alike have shown little sign of accepting the Africans, Asians, and other Europeans who have moved into their midst.

We sometimes assume that electing a black, a woman, or a Jew to a legislature will help blacks, women, or Jews. It may, if those individuals are determined to help those whose heritage they share. However, it is also possible that a white, a man, or a Gentile could be more interested in helping any of those groups; it all depends on the values of the person who is elected.

However, if blacks or women or Jews seldom voted, had no organized interest groups, and did not themselves seek office, the chances that any legislature would care about them would greatly diminish. Political leaders are surrounded by people who use political resources to influence their decisions. Even if they care about groups which are not politically active, it is easy to lose track of those groups in the midst of all the people hustling to influence them. If these groups are even a little politically active, they at least take a position to get attention from politicians who may identify with them—even politicians from other races, genders, or religions. However, if voters and current political leaders do not identify with blacks, women, or Jews and their issues, or if they are hostile to these groups, the groups still have little chance to influence political leaders. They may do well to try to get their own people, or at least others who identify with them, recruited into positions of political leadership.

This reinforces what we learned earlier. In China, India, Peru, and Nigeria, political leaders have little opportunity to develop empathy with the public at large. That public, in turn, has little chance to be recruited into leadership or to develop empathy for leaders. In the other nation-states, leaders are more likely to feel empathy for people from differing backgrounds, and to recruit them for political leadership—in the United States, the United Kingdom, and Germany, much more likely. But as we are about to see, another factor may also serve to broaden (or narrow) the groups with which individuals identify; that factor is ideology. When people feel compelled to learn more than simple ideology about their government and public issues, their empathy for other groups may rise.

WHAT PEOPLE LEARN ABOUT GOVERNMENT AND POLITICAL ISSUES

We know that political leaders and active participants in politics read and watch news, have a sense of efficacy, have access to information about government and political issues, and are motivated to determine whether policies aid or harm the groups they identify with. They may be interested in how various government institutions affect the interests of those groups. They may also be interested in how they as individuals can benefit from this information.

However, as we just discussed, we cannot assume that this segment of the populace will always identify with groups beyond their own. Even political leaders may have very narrow group identification. Furthermore, we cannot assume that those in leadership necessarily understand government policies, and the issues relating to them, in depth. They may understand a great deal about how to interact with other political leaders, and how to use resources and institutions to influence those leaders, without knowing much about the issues and policies themselves.

An individual with little knowledge may easily conclude that the legislature, the chief executive, the courts, or political parties are doing a good or bad job for the groups that individual identifies with. It requires little knowledge to decide that the government should—or should not—regulate trucking, help people obtain medical care, or lower taxes. A competent public relations firm can devise political speeches or television spots targeted to the group identities of particular people; they are designed to help the target audience reach such conclusions even without much information.[3] If a person likes group A and dislikes group B, and you want to arouse his

or her anger at the legislature, you can suggest in a television commercial or speech that the legislators are favoring group B at the expense of group A. Many people need not be told much more than this if the speaker looks good and sounds persuasive.

This is the sort of raw material a person processes to form **ideology**—one's vision of how politics, economics, and society should be regulated.[4] Ideology develops as a person characterizes policies, symbols (flags, monuments, insignia, holidays, music), organizations, people, and ideas as harmful or helpful to him or herself and to the groups he or she identifies with. People who describe themselves as having the same ideology do not always agree on what it means, or on what groups they wish to see protected.[5] Some may describe themselves as agreeing with an ideology on the basis of sparse and casual knowledge, while others subscribing to the same ideology may demand to know much more about issues than simple characterizations. The same ideology can sometimes be adapted to support opposite sides of a political issue. Some people—even people who feel efficacious—are satisfied to know little about government beyond simple characterizations and are convinced that their ideology is the only truth and that following it will effect great progress. Others do not describe themselves as agreeing with any particular ideology, preferring to characterize themselves as ''in the middle.'' However, those same people may still identify with symbols and words associated with ideologies. When individuals learn little more about politics than ideology, and identify with words and symbols they relate to that ideology, political leaders can use those words on television and in speeches to command the support of those individuals.

Nationalism itself—the belief that what one's nation-state does will inherently promote progress—can be an ideology. **Pan-nationalists** argue that members of their own ethnic or religious group should unite behind a nation-state which includes all members of their group but excludes members of all other groups. They may also believe in eliminating state organs that allow various religions to exist side-by-side and replacing them with institutions led by their own religious or ethnic leaders. They sometimes advocate abandoning the nation-state to form a new one, crossing over other national boundaries to include members of their own group; or they may want an existing nation-state to expand and unite one group, excluding all others. In 1992, pan-nationalist Serbs began a process of "ethnic cleansing" after declaring their territory in the former Yugoslavia separate and sovereign; they invaded adjoining territory, systematically killing or forcing the evacuation of non-Serbs. Their troops even captured large numbers of Muslim women, raped them, and forced them to bear children of Serbian blood, utterly humiliating them under Muslim traditions. Nationalism and pan-nationalism are sometimes hard to distinguish. Conor Cruise O'Brien says nationalism is a "conglomerate of emotions" that "cluster around landscape, ancestors, language, traditions and cultural patterns, often including religion."[6]

Liberalism in the classical sense is an ideology espoused by seventeenth- and eighteenth-century writers.[7] These writers argued that all individuals should be free to assert themselves politically and to compete in the marketplace while the government protects the right to private property but does not interfere in other ways. Some modern liberals do feel the state should help the poor and protect the environment, even if it interferes with private property and the marketplace. Others, who call themselves conservatives, adhere more to liberalism in its classical sense. They are less likely to believe government should intervene in the marketplace, even to assure that the marketplace is not controlled by monopolies.[8]

Communism is an ideology based on the core belief that the working class should unite to control government and commerce[9] and to limit economic and political freedom so other classes will cease to exploit them. Vladimir Lenin founded the Soviet Union on that ideology, as Mao Zedong did the PRC.

Socialism calls for some government control over commerce; leaders such as Jawaharlal Nehru, the founding prime minister of India, combined that ideology with a belief in liberalism and nationalism to provide India with a modern vision.

Adolph Hitler's Nazi Party in Germany acted on a pan-nationalist ideology it called **National Socialism,** arguing that "Aryan" Germans are a superior race which should be united under one state completely controlled by the Nazi party. The party tried to eliminate non-"Aryans," or physically imperfect "Aryans"; organized large industry to create military might and high consumption for all true "Aryans"; annihilated all opposing political (especially nationalist, communist, and liberal) movements; and sought to achieve military domination of the world.

These ideologies clearly conflict sharply with one another, as do those who adhere to them in a simplistic and dogmatic fashion. However, ideology can also serve to broaden a person's group identification, by making the individual feel part of a larger nation, class, or culture. It can make people feel ethically responsible for helping people that they are not like or that they have no contact with. The leaders of China may be isolated, yet their ideology suggests that they should support workers and peasants. Villagers around the world may be isolated, yet they may feel they must support others in their nation or those who share common class interests. That support, though, is sometimes only skin deep. Its depth can also decline after a revolutionary movement; after ideologists struggle and sacrifice to achieve power, they may be succeeded by generations of people who are attracted to office largely for personal gain. It is easy to use ideology to legitimize supporting others who have the same skin color, religion, customs, and attitudes. It is easy to pretend that you are helping others by using words and symbols, when in fact you are not. And it is hard to stir people's empathy for others unlike themselves; ideology alone seldom does that. A former *People's Daily* reporter explains how ideology can be obscured among citizens and leaders in China by their obligations to one another:

> In Ping county, you simply cannot clearly figure out the guanxi among people. It seems that in everyone's body there is a particular switch. If you touch a person, it will unexpectedly affect a large number of persons. . . . There are complicated and overlapping

relations between and among people, weaving a thick and tight social web. Whatever 'isms' or principles, whatever policies or program guidelines, as soon as they touch this social web, they lose their function immediately, like being electrocuted.[10]

In China, the Soviet Union, and East Germany, ideology was often used as a mask to cover one's real feelings, which might be quite different from the obligatory ideological phrases which floated in and out of fashion. People often spoke the words, knowing that their listeners did not believe them any more than they did. And as liberalization set in, this could result in remarkable statements. The first elected president of Kyrgyzstan, a scientist and former polytechnic professor, declared:

Although I am a communist, my basic attitude toward private property is favorable. I believe that the revolution in the sphere of economics was not made by Karl Marx but by Adam Smith.[11]

In free societies, and among a small minority in closed ones, some people really do passionately believe in ideology. Ideology can blind true believers to their own self-interest as they focus on a symbol or an issue, ignoring whether political decisions are actually aiding them. Your ideology may tell you to always keep property public (or private), to allow (or suppress) free speech, to support (or question) national leaders, to accommodate (or resist) other ethnic groups, or to follow other simple rules; this does not mean that when you follow these dictates, you are actually helping yourself or others. Ideology surrounding conflicts between class and religious groups, and the nationalist frenzy which often occurs during wartime, can cause people to passionately support actions harmful to themselves and others without pausing to think about the consequences. When people vote on the basis of emotional symbols manipulated by television advertising, ignoring what the candidates intend to do, they may also actually harm their own or others' interests.

Many political thinkers, however, have suggested that well-regulated political systems need both citizens and leaders who know more about government policy issues and identify with groups beyond their own. John Stuart Mill proposed that a democratic society needs discussion among people with differing viewpoints to arrive at policies acceptable to all.[12] William Kornhauser wrote of the importance of having contacts with people of differing backgrounds and interests (the crosscutting cleavages we just discussed), affording exposure to a variety of viewpoints. Aristotle spoke of the virtue of a mixed constitution with various institutions to represent various segments of the society, backed by families concerned about the common good.[13] C. Wright Mills distinguished between the public—the middle level of power, who understand and can respond to opinions they hear—and the mass, which simply hears opinions from the media.[14] Robert Dahl suggests the importance of developing an attitude of compromise, so mutually acceptable solutions can be devised for political issues.[15] And as we saw in chapter 6, Gabriel Almond and Sidney Verba explore the existence of a "civic culture" which features

1. *a substantial consensus on the legitimacy of political institutions and the direction and content of public policy,*

2. *widespread tolerance of a plurality of interests and a belief in their reconcilability, and*

3. *a widely distributed sense of political competence and mutual trust in the citizenry.*[16]

All of these characteristics require a willingness to compromise with other citizens or other leaders. To develop this willingness, people must gain tolerance for a variety of groups and viewpoints and welcome and respect diversity. They must become sensitive to how policies—even those espoused by their own ideology—affect various groups of people. They must try to resolve issues so that both their own objectives and those of others are attended to. They not only need to be willing to hear opposing viewpoints, but, if necessary, to change their viewpoint and objectives to accommodate the interests and needs of other groups.

Ironically, as people learn to think this way, they learn to look after their own self-interest as well; they see more clearly what harms and what helps the groups they support. To develop a perspective of this kind, people must have information about issues and some basis for empathy with a variety of groups. All nine systems contain segments of the populace with enough knowledge about issues to make such judgments. However, only a portion of them will develop a perspective like this. Most people who know little about political issues wish to benefit groups they identify with; as they decide which policies will best benefit those groups, they are likely to follow the lead of others.

The family is probably the most important socializer of efficacy, tolerance, and policy information. Children often emulate their parents. If the parents do not exhibit these traits, then another relative, a teacher, or someone else the child has close contact with (including a peer) may serve as a role model. Without such a role model, the child is unlikely to develop these traits.

As we just learned, it is hard for leaders in China, India, Peru, and Nigeria to develop a sense of identification with the groups that form the majorities in their nation-states. And few members of those majority groups know much about policy, feel a sense of efficacy, or trust in institutions or other social groups. This makes it difficult to develop compromises that benefit a variety of groups.

As we shall see in coming chapters, various leaders of India, Peru, and Nigeria have espoused ideologies which advocate assistance to the less privileged. Under the Cultural Revolution (discussed in chapter 21), China's leaders decreed that people from working class families should be promoted more often than those from other social backgrounds; since 1978, they have advocated that all classes work together and allowed increasing numbers of peasants and workers into universities. Leaders in all four of these systems, while favoring certain ethnic groups over others, have made strong efforts to encourage cooperation among various cultures. Top leadership in these systems, however, remains confined to a narrow range of families and

social groups who tend to exhibit little tolerance for a diversity of viewpoints. In China, and in Nigeria and Peru under military rule, opposing ideas may not even be publicly expressed within government; legislatures in India, Nigeria, and Peru include members with highly conflicting views who have great difficulty reaching agreements.

The communist systems in the Soviet Union and East Germany also encouraged cooperation among groups. Communist leaders censored people who sought to prevent ethnic and cultural groups from working together; since the introduction of a freer press and free assembly, ethnic pan-nationalists, anti-Semites, advocates of monarchy, and others have emerged who have actually made reconciliation and compromise among various groups more difficult. But although the communist leaders wanted groups to cooperate to achieve communistic goals, they did not believe in a plurality of interests freely competing to express their views.

The United States, the United Kingdom, and West Germany all have a free press; precisely because of this, people may choose to read and listen to viewpoints which argue against a civic culture. At the same time, these nation-states have many leaders and citizens who do share the traits conducive to a civic culture. And they have other leaders and citizens who do not. Policy outcomes often depend on how these two groups interact. When both leaders and broad portions of the citizenry believe in the civic culture, it is easier to effect compromises than when (as is the case in some regions) neither group does.

People who pride themselves on their broad-mindedness are sometimes lacking, nonetheless, in civic culture. Ideology, in fact, often helps cover up one's lack of tolerance and trust in others.

For example, in the United States, many liberals regard themselves as having *broad group identification* because they believe the government should aid the poor, protect the civil rights of women and minorities, press for the human rights of people in foreign lands living under authoritarian regimes, allow workers to organize unions, and allow everyone free speech. Many conservatives also feel they have broad group identification because they believe that everyone should have the right to work and to benefit from their own labor, that we should help people in foreign lands living under communism, that women and minorities should have the same rights as everyone else, that the government should refrain from interfering in our lives, and that everyone should have the right to better themselves and to keep most of what they earn.

Yet some of those, both liberals and conservatives, who believe strongly in such tenets *distrust the government,* because they believe it is not living up to their principles. Some therefore feel helpless about working within the system (even when they are recruited into government) and may even be willing to break the law to achieve their ends. Some *distrust anyone they perceive to have a different ideology* and refuse to cooperate with them politically. Some explain virtually all public policy stands they take in terms of one or another of these principles, and refuse to compromise their position because that would mean going against principle. They may even stick to this position when people they claim to want to help are in fact being harmed.

Such people obviously are not part of the civic culture. They also may not have as broad a group identification as they think. Take the example of your own family. If you have a parent or brother or daughter you profess to love, but whom you refuse to obey or compromise with or listen to because you feel you know better what is in the family's best interest, are you really identifying with the interests of your family? Are you prepared to identify with groups beyond your family? Are you helping prepare others in your family to do so?

Now think about someone you know who is extremely liberal or conservative. Is he or she truly tolerant of the viewpoint of a person at the opposite extreme? Does he or she effectively compromise with people who disagree with his or her views?

We have seen that the leaders of India, Nigeria, and Peru tend to come from a narrow range of groups. A civic culture, with the ability to reconcile a plurality of conflicting viewpoints, could compensate for that disadvantage. However, such an environment is less firmly rooted in India, Nigeria, and Peru than in any of the other nation-states. The United States, the United Kingdom, and West Germany are farther ahead in this regard. But respect for diversity, and a sense of efficacy and mutual trust, do not come easily anywhere.

SUMMARY

People identify with certain groups, and they generally want government to help the groups they support and identify with. Through personal contacts and a growth in understanding the view of others, some people develop tolerance and respect for groups they do not personally feel a part of. People also develop ideologies—visions of how politics, economics, and society should be regulated. Ideological thinking can become oversimplified and be used as a justification for protecting and supporting only the groups one identifies with. When both leaders and citizens lack tolerance and adhere tightly to ideologies that protect one group at the expense of another, it is difficult to effect compromise. When that happens, groups who are not represented in political institutions are poorly positioned to receive benefits from government. Even when leaders and citizens are tolerant and subscribe to ideologies that recommend including other groups in political compromise, benefits will not accrue to those groups unless officials are willing to learn how policies affect people's lives. That requires exposure to information about government, policies, and other people's viewpoints.

NOTES

1. Kornhauser maintains that ". . . non-elites are bound by multiple group affiliations of their own choosing in pluralist (e.g. liberal) society. . . . Modern urban life . . . provides a variety of contacts and experiences that broadens social horizons and the range of social participation." William Kornhauser, *The Politics of Mass Society* (Glencoe, Ill.: Free Press, 1959), pp. 228, 237–38.

2. The Forbidden City is the compound in which Chinese emperors used to live. Tiananmen Square lies in front of it.

3. James Fishkin, *Democracy and Deliberation* (New Haven: Yale University Press, 1991) argues that four out of five American citizens do not have stable opinions; they have "non-attitudes" or "pseudo-opinions" they present to pollsters in the form of "yes" or "no" answers to questions.

4. For a number of definitions of ideology, see Max J. Skidmore, *Ideologies: Politics in Action* (San Diego: Harcourt, Brace, Jovanovich, 1989), pp. 2–7.

5. For example, in the 1984 National Election Survey (NES), 79 percent who called themselves liberals thought we should "become less involved in the internal affairs of Central American countries;" 53 percent who called themselves conservatives responded in the same way. A majority from both groups agreed on the same approach. But 65 percent calling themselves liberals thought government should provide "more services even if it means an increase in spending," while only 30 percent of conservatives thought so. On that subject the two groups differed strongly and in keeping with their ideologies. Robert S. Erikson, Norman R. Luttbeg, and Kent L. Tedin, *American Public Opinion: Its Origins, Content, and Impact,* 3d ed. (New York: Macmillan, 1988), p. 79.

6. *New York Review of Books* (summer 1991). Benjamin R. Barber finds it a "powerful irony" that nationalism, which can be "a force of integration and unification, a movement aimed at bringing together disparate clans, tribes, and cultural fragments under new assimilationist flags" can also become "more a reactionary and divisive force, pulverizing the very nations it once helped cement together. "Jihad vs. McWorld," *The Atlantic* 269, 3 (March 1992): 60.

7. John Locke, who wrote in the seventeenth century, said in his *Two Treatises on Government* that by mixing labor with nature's riches, individuals earned the right to own private property, and the only proper role of the state is to protect the property rights acquired in this way. He did not believe the state had the right to infringe on those natural property rights in order to accomplish other goals. In the eighteenth century, Adam Smith's *An Inquiry into the Nature and Causes of the Wealth of Nations* suggested that the social good requires all individuals to be free to compete in the marketplace, and any interference with this by government disrupts the natural common good. Neither discussed what to do if some participants in the marketplace restrict the chance for others to compete.

8. An NES survey during the 1984 American elections asked people to describe liberalism and conservatism. Those who might describe themselves as conservatives described modern liberals as "socialist," and "extremist," charging that they "favor federal control," are "wasteful," and "help blacks." Similarly, those who might describe themselves as liberals referred to conservatives as "uncaring," "moralists," and "extremists," opining that they "do not help blacks," "look to the past," and are "for the rich." Positive terms respondents used to describe modern liberals include the ideas that they "look to the future," are "open-minded," "care," "help blacks," are "for the poor," "for people like me," and "for freedom." Positive terms respondents used to describe modern conservatives include the notions that they are "for free enterprise," "thrifty," "for state's rights," "for people like me," and "for freedom." Robert S. Erikson et. al., *American Public Opinion*, p. 78.

9. Chapter 8 discusses how communism accomplishes that control.

10. Li Pin-yen, *People's Literature*, (September, 1976): 34–35.

11. Daniel Sneider, "Askar Akayev: 'All of a Sudden I Become President'", *Christian Science Monitor,* January 10, 1991. See footnote 7.

12. See especially *A System of Logic* (1843), and *On Liberty* (1859); J. M. Robson, *The Improvement of Mankind: The Social and Political Thought of John Stuart Mill* (1968).

13. Ernest Barker, *The Politics of Aristotle* (New York: Oxford University Press, 1958).

14. *The Power Elite* (New York: Oxford University Press, 1959).

15. *A Preface to Democratic Theory* (Chicago: University of Chicago Press, 1956); *Who Governs?*

(New Haven, Conn.: Yale University Press, 1961); *Modern Political Analysis,* 4th ed. (Englewood Cliffs, N.J.: Prentice-Hall, 1984); *After the Revolution* (New Haven, Conn.: Yale University Press, 1970); *Polyarchy: Participation and Opposition* (New Haven, Conn.: Yale University Press, 1971); "On Removing Certain Impediments to Democracy in the United States," *Political Science Quarterly* 92 (1977): 1–20; *Dilemmas of Pluralist Democracy: Autonomy vs. Control* (New Haven, Conn.: Yale University Press, 1982).

16. Gabriel Almond and Sidney Verba, *The Civic Culture* (Boston: Little, Brown, 1965); *The Civic Culture Revisited* (Boston: Little, Brown, 1980).

EXERCISES

Think about the book thus far:

1. The introduction to chapter 11 lists four aspects of the process by which people decide how they will participate in politics. Which of those aspects is discussed in chapter 11? Which two does this chapter discuss? Look ahead to chapter 13. Which aspect will it discuss?

2. How do those four aspects of political socialization relate to the five characteristics of influence outlined in chapter 5?

KEY WORDS AND PHRASES

Define the following terms:

group identification   nationalism   socialism
crosscutting cleavages   pan-nationalism   National Socialism
cumulative cleavages   classical liberalism
ideology   communism

Answer each of the following questions (1–6) in one sentence:

1. How do schools, military service, and jobs teach group identification?

2. What are some conditions which help broaden a person's group identification?

3. Which nation-states offer few people the chance to develop contacts and identification with groups other than their own?

4. Why do ethnic, religious, and social groups not necessarily benefit when their members become government officials?

5. Do any of the ideologies discussed in this chapter broaden group identification?

6. How does group identification relate to civic culture?

THINKING IT THROUGH

Choose three systems to focus on. List an aspect of each system that assists the establishment of a civic culture. List an aspect of each that hinders the development of a civic culture.

System	Assists	Hinders
1.		
2		
3.		

Which of the three systems you selected has the best opportunity to develop a civic culture? Why?

chapter 13

POLITICAL SOCIALIZATION
HOW SHOULD I USE INFLUENCE?

In chapters 11 and 12, as well as in this chapter, we are inquiring into why some people acquire characteristics which let them exert influence and why they develop particular objectives in politics. We have examined why people support those they do to rule them, what people want from government, and what they are willing to learn about government and political issues. Now we will try to determine why and how a person might use (or not use) his or her influence.

We have learned that people develop attitudes toward their political system through the process of political socialization. We have also learned how people acquire certain traits or political resources that give them the potential to exert influence in the political system. But having the potential to exert influence does not mean actually using it. Why and how do people use influence? In this chapter, we will explore how people decide **whether to use influence, and if so, in what manner, to what ends, and to what extent.**

POWER AS MEANS AND ENDS

As we discussed in chapter 12, citizens and leaders may use their influence to benefit only the groups they belong to, or they may seek (or at least accept) compromises which benefit many groups. Citizens and leaders may approach politics with substantial knowledge about policies and issues, or with little. They may enjoy exerting influence, or they may dislike doing so.

Power is successfully exerting influence. Power can be an end in itself—it can provide fame, security, or just the intrinsic reward of a "sense of power." People who seek power must be able to formulate personal political objectives and develop

skills in using resources and institutions effectively. They must start with a sense of efficacy; but such individuals may at the same time have a low sense of self-worth, a dislike for other groups, little respect for the nation-state's institutions, and little knowledge about issues and how they affect people. People seeking power for its own sake may be oblivious to which groups are helped or harmed by the policies they advocate. If it suits their purposes, they may be willing to side with any narrow group interest; or they may try to see that a great variety of viewpoints and groups are accommodated in the political process. Such a person might just as easily seek a position outside government, as a leader in an opposition party or in a group trying to overturn the system. The position the individual exercises power from is less important than simply having—and guarding—that power. For this person, power is an end in itself.

Other individuals may look upon power as a means to an end. They may want government policy to aid some particular groups of people and decide that seeking a particular position—in the government or in an organization lobbying the government—will help accomplish that objective. When they are fortunate enough to gain such a position, they will (if the pursuit of power has not caused them to lose sight of their goal) attempt to implement the desired policy. People who seek power as a means to an end may be more likely to compromise with others if they believe the compromise will be advantageous to the groups they wish to aid. If their initial efforts fail, they are likely to try other initiatives to help the groups. They are willing to revise their programs in response to new information about how they are affecting people, even if the new programs seem to weaken their power. If they believe they could be more effective by stepping down or taking another post, they will do so. Such individuals use power as a means of achieving their political objectives.

A person seeking power in itself may feel comfortable in a consensual political party, which is oriented toward seeking compromise among a variety of viewpoints. Splinter parties, which take strong continuing stands on particular issues, are more strongly goal-directed. But a person with a strong goal orientation may also join a consensual party in the belief that they will better achieve results; a splinter party usually cannot elect a chief executive or control the legislature.

An old axiom says that boys and girls go into politics to be something, while men and women go into politics to do something. Some who start out simply seeking power for its own sake may end up developing objectives that they feel transcend even their personal desire for power.

An individual who looks on power as a means to an end may desire to serve the common interest or may only be interested in serving a few narrow group interests. An individual motivated primarily by a sense of power may be more prone to switch sides. By the same token, an individual who looks on power as a means to an end may be prone to compromise or may avoid compromise. The same is true of an individual motivated primarily by a desire for power. A person who starts out looking upon power as a means to an end may come to value it as an end in itself, or a power seeker may become caught up in promoting some particular goals. All political systems contain leaders in both categories.

USING INFLUENCE TO SUPPORT LEADERS

If all groups in a nation-state are to develop a feeling that the government is serving their needs and should serve the needs of other groups as well, it is obviously desirable that leaders come from a variety of groups in society, have broad group identification, or have beliefs associated with a civic culture—or better still, have all three of these traits. In any given nation-state, some ethnic, religious, class, regional, or tribal groups have less opportunity to acquire political influence. If a group is not represented in government by its own people, it needs friends from other groups who are part of government.

Many participants in politics, we have discovered, have insufficient knowledge about issues, or have little time and motivation to do more than vote, attend a gathering, or contribute some money to a cause. These individuals can still influence politics by supporting particular leaders. Some may give their support in exchange for money or a personal favor. Most people are more prone to support someone they perceive as a friend of the groups they like, or perhaps someone who is an enemy of the groups they do not like. When people know little about policy, politicians can easily gain support by creating impressions—in other words, by the way they talk, dress, and behave, rather than by the policies they endorse.

As we have seen, many people in all nine systems support leaders for such reasons. In the United States, the United Kingdom, the Federal Republic of Germany, India, and Peru, voters with little knowledge of the issues can have an important effect on who becomes chief executive and on the composition of legislatures. In these nation-states, group identifications, and the people's belief or lack of belief in a civic culture, take on added importance. If their group affiliations are narrow and they have little tolerance for other groups, political leaders may respond by catering to those narrow values. If their affiliations and tolerance are broader, it is easier to fashion compromises that benefit a variety of groups.

When citizens believe a government has the right to make and enforce laws, that government has authority. That authorization may come through voting, through simple acceptance that the government has the right to rule as evidenced by the political latency of its citizens, through citizen agreement with the government's policies, or through personal affinity for the chief executive. Some regimes may gain justification or willing acceptance on the basis of tradition, and others on the basis of legal authority, the charisma of leaders, the fact that leaders have been chosen in free elections, or the government's adherence to a particular ideology or to particular policies.

The most efficient and stable political system would be based on all these factors at work in the minds of all citizens. Obviously, no system can fully secure the support of all citizens in all these areas. But when at least some leaders involved in policy formulation firmly identify with a variety of groups in the nation-state, the government is more likely to enjoy the broad support of the citizens and to have the authority to rule. All of these nation-states meet this criterion to some extent. If many of the voters in a particular system have broad group identifications, the government is even more likely to have authority and stability and to serve the needs of many groups.

DECIDING TO USE INFLUENCE

An individual's political socialization has a huge impact on his or her use of influence. Socialization affects a person's sense of efficacy, and ability to exert influence. People who do not feel efficacious have little incentive to (1) understand the complexities behind issues or (2) use resources to influence their resolution. They are also unlikely to (3) seek access to the institutions where issues are resolved, or (4) develop clear objectives for resolving issues. High percentages of the populace in India, Peru, and Nigeria probably have little sense of efficacy in these four areas; this leaves them unable and unwilling to use influence.

In India, Peru, and Nigeria, political leaders also have unusually little opportunity to develop empathy

with the public at large. That public, in turn, has little opportunity to recruit leaders from its ranks or to develop empathy for groups beyond their own. In the other nation-states, recruitment and empathy are more likely to occur.

Few citizens in any of the nine systems, however, have the ability and inclination to use influence effectively. In the United States, the United Kingdom, and West Germany, more of the few who do use influence are willing to reconcile a variety of conflicting viewpoints—to foster a civic culture—than in the other systems. The communist system in China (as was true in the Soviet Union and East Germany) operates with a paradox in this regard. The consensual party has tried to include a wide spectrum of groups within itself, but it allows no opposition parties or interest groups.

Keep in mind that all we have been discussing thus far is how people acquire influence and the inclination to use it—not how they actually do exert influence. Do leaders actually formulate solutions to the social and economic problems presented to them? Do they compromise with one another, or do they more often end up in deadlock? Do they preserve their present political system or transform it? We will discuss those issues as we move to part 3: Using Influence.

PUTTING IT ALL TOGETHER: POLITICAL RECRUITMENT AND SOCIALIZATION

At this point, we can differentiate three categories of nation-states on the basis of the groups from which they recruit people into influential roles (chapters 7–10), and on the basis of the socialization experiences of the populace (chapters 11–13).

The political systems of the United States, the United Kingdom, and West Germany (1) recruit leaders of government, political parties, and interest groups from a wide variety of groups and families. These systems often draw political leaders from people with higher education; those individuals were often raised by parents with higher education. Some racial, religious, ethnic, class, and other groups may find it more difficult to obtain higher education and to acquire other traits that increase the chances that they will be recruited into political leadership. Yet many people acquire higher education despite the barriers. Moreover, in these systems, (2) many who achieve higher education come to identify with groups which have little opportunity to be recruited.[1] Many voters are exposed to socializing experiences which give them an opportunity to broaden their group identifications. For example, high percentages of citizens believe that women and racial minorities deserve equal rights (though they often qualify this belief with "ifs" and "buts"); lower percentages express tolerance for groups such as homosexuals.[2] Another characteristic of these three nation-states is that (3) few people are socialized to develop all the traits needed to achieve political influence. Many of those who do acquire influence also acquire some of the attitudes that help develop a civic culture, while many who do not acquire civic culture attitudes are among those who do not vote or otherwise participate in politics. Finally, in the United States, the United Kingdom, and West Germany, (4) voters are able to choose which party will control the position of chief executive. These four factors make it possible to produce compromises benefitting a wide variety of groups.

This does not mean that such compromises come easily. While some voters and leaders foster a civic culture, others may identify largely with their own racial, religious, ethnic, and class group. Moreover, many voters know little about issues and policies. These factors can work to the disadvantage of groups who are not represented at the highest levels of influence, even if leaders are oriented toward creating policies to benefit them. When leaders make compromises, it is easy to forget or ignore such groups, especially when they play little role in providing goods and services, or when leaders want to quiet the opposition among participants with narrow group identities.

The political systems of the CIS, China, and the former East Germany (1) have been recruiting leaders of government, political parties and interest groups from a more restricted set of groups, people whose class and cultural backgrounds may be diverse, but who have the proper connections and ideology. In recent years, political leaders are increasingly drawn from among those with higher education; in China, the more highly educated often have parents who had higher education. All three of these systems have excluded those whose political views were deemed unacceptable; that has ceased in the CIS and the reunited Germany. Some racial, religious, ethnic, class, and other groups have less access to both secondary and higher education, and to the traits they need to be recruited into political leadership. But large numbers of cadres recruited during China's Cultural Revolution have little education. Also, in these systems, (2) censorship, curriculums, and academic environments in higher education may discourage leaders from identifying with excluded groups. Fewer citizens are exposed to socializing experiences which give them an opportunity to broaden their group identifications. Another factor affecting influence in these three systems is that (3) few people are socialized to develop all the traits needed to acquire political influence or any of the traits associated with a civic culture. Leaders tend to make compromises that benefit only the groups who contribute leaders to the political process. Finally, in China, the former Soviet Union, and the former East Germany, (4) voters do not help choose the chief executive. This may be compensated, somewhat, by the need for government to acquire goods and services from groups which do not help choose political leaders. Government also may need these groups to keep peace in the border regions where many of them live. In addition, increasing numbers of the leaders in the post-Soviet independent republics are now elected. However, those who succeed in winning leadership positions in these elections are often people with prior influence.

The political systems of India, Peru, and Nigeria (1) recruit their government, political party, and interest group leaders largely from the more highly educated portions of the urban population, who have little contact with the great majority of the populace (the rural populace and the urban squatters). These

Table 13.1

Political Recruitment and Socialization: Three Categories

USA UK FRG	PRC USSR/CIS GDR	RI RP FRN
1. Recruit leaders from a wide variety of groups and families.	1. Recruit leaders from a wide variety of groups, but lack of family connections limit access.	1. Recruit leaders from a small minority of the populace.
2. Expose many people to socializing experiences which help them broaden group identification.	2. Expose fewer people to socializing experiences which help them broaden group identification.	2. Expose few people to socializing experiences which help them broaden group identification.
3. Socialize few people to develop all traits needed to achieve influence; those who do gain influence often have some civic culture attitudes.	3. Socialize few people to develop all traits needed to achieve influence or any traits associated with a civic culture.	3. Socialize few people to develop all traits needed to achieve influence or any traits associated with a civic culture. Few are motivated to place limits on the influence of leaders.
4. Allow voters to choose chief executive. Many participate in voting and the formal economy. Many political nonparticipants play minor roles providing goods and services in the formal economy.	4. Do (or did) not allow voters to choose chief executive. Many political nonparticipants play important roles providing goods and services in the formal economy.	4. Allow voters to choose chief executive, but limit choices because of the narrow group identifications of leaders and voters. Except for voting, only a small minority of the populace participates either in politics or in the formal economy.
Result: Compromises benefitting many groups are possible, but seldom easy.	*Result:* Compromises benefitting many groups are more difficult to arrive at.	*Result:* Compromises benefitting many groups are very hard to arrive at.

systems narrowly restrict access to the educational institutions leaders are recruited from. Also, in these nations, (2) geographical and social isolation, censorship, curriculums, and the urban environment make it difficult for leaders to identify with ethnic, religious, class, racial, and other groups beyond their own. Moreover, few citizens are socialized either to broaden the groups they identify with or to (3) develop the traits needed to acquire political influence, or to place limits on those who have it.

Finally, in these three nation-states, (4) the voters, except during military takeovers in Peru and Nigeria, help choose the chief executive; but many who select candidates, and many voters, have narrow group identifications. This can cause leaders to compromise largely among themselves and their own groups. Few outside their ranks control needed goods and services to help prevent this exclusive form of governing. (Table 13.1 summarizes these characteristics of each group of nation-states.)

On the basis of what we have learned up to this point, then, it would appear that the United States, the United Kingdom, and West Germany offer the greatest opportunity for a variety of social and economic groups to be recruited into political leadership roles, while India, Peru, and Nigeria offer the least. Likewise, leaders and citizens in the former group of nation-states have more opportunity to broaden their group identifications. It still remains for us to examine, in the next part of the book, whether members of such groups actually are recruited into positions of government leadership, whether those who are really do have broad group identifications, and whether the systems maintain enforceable limits on government authority. Then, in the remainder of the book, we shall see what bearing all this might have on people's lives.

USING INFLUENCE: SEEKING INDIVIDUAL INTERESTS VERSUS THE COMMON GOOD

America prides itself on its **individualism.** We each like to think of ourselves as charting our own course, as being independent even from our families, as competing with every man and woman, as owing nothing to anybody.

Aristotle took a different view. He emphasized the common good over the rights of the individual:

The civic body in every polis is the sovereign; and the sovereign must necessarily be either One, or Few, or Many. On this basis we may say that when the One, or the Few, or the Many, rule with a view to the common interest, the constitutions under which they do so must necessarily be right constitutions. On the other hand the constitutions directed to the personal interest of the One, or the Few, or the Masses, must necessarily be perversions. Either the name of citizen cannot be given to persons [whose interests are not regarded] or . . . they must have their share of the benefits.[3]

In Aristotle's view, a "Kingship" which looks after the common interest is superior to a perverted "Democracy" which looks out for the poorer classes but disregards the needs of others.[4] The smallest association we are a part of, he argued, is the family; the largest is the polis, or the full set of associations self-sufficient to afford their members the good life. But that good life, which results when government makes decisions that consider everyone's interest, must begin with all the members committing themselves to seeking the **common good** for one another—not the good of the individual.[5] This does not happen simply because people live on a common site, setting up laws and exchanging goods and services. To achieve a good life, Aristotle wrote, the members of a family (and ultimately, of society as a whole) must be committed to the common good of one another.[6] He suggested that this common good must begin with parents who exhibit temperance, courage, justice, and wisdom in running the household, dealing with one another, and raising children.[7] From the family spring the virtues needed by those who hold power.

In a good political system, Aristotle argued, those who display these virtues are citizens and rulers, and those who do not display them are not: "the goodness of a good man and that of the good citizen of the best state, must be one and the same."[8] Setting up a government which allows everyone to share in the duties of citizenship when only a few have the necessary virtues will result in a "perverted" constitution, Aristotle believed, as will setting up a system where many have these virtues but only a few share in citizenship.

Aristotle suggests that larger political bodies are no better than the families they are composed of. Families looking after their own common good are apt to be interested in the good of the broader community as well. Families whose members are trained to look out only for their own personal self-interest will not be interested in the common good of either their family or the broader community. So good families will support a good constitution, with leaders who care about the common good; families whose members do not treat one another with respect will support a perverted constitution, allowing leaders to manipulate people to achieve their own selfish objectives. The character of the family, then, affects the character of the civic body.

Aristotle believed that good constitutions would be backed by those with better educations and middle class status.[9] As we have seen, that is not always true; both poor and rich people may share the traits of good families, and many educated people from the middle class have some of what Aristotle called perverted traits. Some people whose parents had the character traits of good families fail to develop those traits themselves, and vice versa. And many people run entirely counter to Aristotle's premise by caring greatly for their own families, while caring little about anyone else.

When we discuss "broad group identifications" and "civic culture," we are looking at modern reformulations, with some added insights, of Aristotle's notions about character lying at the root of politics. In our reformulations of his premise, we in the late twentieth century tend to shy from directly using value-laden words such as *character* and *family*. By doing so, we lose sight of the important question Aristotle was posing: Can a political body achieve the common good when families do not seek their own common good? Can an individual truly seek the common good of the broader political community without seeking the common good of his or her own family?

We might also do well to keep in mind a question which concerned Aristotle's teacher, Plato: How do you keep the family's quest to achieve its own common good from standing in the way of everyone else's welfare?

SUMMARY

This chapter posed the question, "How should I use influence?" Some seek public office simply because they want power, and others because they seek to use power to accomplish goals; those two objectives may meld. Some leaders and citizens identify broadly with many groups, or at least believe that the interests of many groups can be reconciled, while others identify with a narrow range of groups and are intolerant of others. In some systems, most groups and high percentages of the populace are represented in politics, while in other systems, only a few groups and a minority of the population are represented. If the goals of leaders and their followers are compatible with the goals of other groups, and if high percentages of a populace are represented in politics, the sovereignty and authority of government—and the chance for a wide variety of groups to benefit from compromises—is enhanced. Even under these circumstances, however, citizens whose objectives are compatible with those of government leaders have an advantage.

NOTES

1. Robert S. Erikson, Norman R. Luttbeg, and Kent L. Tedin, *American Public Opinion: Its Origins, Content, and Impact,* 3rd ed. (New York: Macmillan, 1988), pp. 172–74, 187–94, presents data showing that support for women's rights is higher among the upper middle class than within the working class, and that members of religious groups whose membership often comes from higher socioeconomic groups (for example, Congregationalist, Jewish, Episcopalian, and Presbyterian) have more tolerance for atheists, communists, homosexuals, militarists, and racists than members of denominations whose membership often has a lower average income (for example, Baptist and Assembly of God).

2. In a 1981 survey, 33 percent of Americans, 54 percent of Britons, and 58 percent of West Germans, said that homosexuality is "sometimes justified"; in the United States and West Germany, those percentages are increasing. Two-thirds of Americans support an equal rights amendment to protect minorities, though lower percentages support affirmative action, busing, racial quotas, or "special privileges" for minorities. High percentages of West Germans and Britons believe women should have equal rights, but majorities of men in these nation-states think women should be responsible for housework and men should have preference when employers hire. Russell J. Dalton, *Citizen Politics in*

Western Democracies (Chatham, N.J.: Chatham House, 1988), pp. 105–12. In another survey repeated over the years, fewer than a third responded favorably to women's rights issues in 1970, while over half did by 1980; this survey showed little difference between men and women, or between high school- and college-educated men, but found that college-educated, employed women gave the most favorable responses. Keith T. Poole and L. Harmon Ziegler, *Women, Public Opinion, and Politics* (New York: Longman, 1985), pp. 21–24.

3. Ernest Barker, *The Politics of Aristotle* (New York: Oxford University Press, 1958), p. 114.

4. The three perverted forms: Tyranny, ruled by one person; Oligarchy, ruled by the rich; and Democracy, ruled by the poor.

5. Aristotle argued that "the polis is prior in the order of nature to the family and the individual . . . Not being self-sufficient when they are isolated, all individuals are so many parts all equally depending on the whole. The man who is isolated . . . must therefore be either a beast or a god." Idem., p. 6.

6. "What constitutes a polis is an association of households and clans in a good life, for the sake of attaining a perfect and self-sufficing existence . . . Those who contribute most to an association of this character have a greater share in the polis than those who are equal to them in free birth and descent, but unequal in civic excellence." Barker, *Politics of Aristotle*, p. 120.

7. Men, women, and children all exhibit these traits in differing ways. "The society of husband and wife, and parents and children, are parts of the household. The goodness of every part must be considered with reference to the goodness of the whole." Aristotle would examine "the nature of the goodness proper to each partner in these relations; the character of the mutual association of the partners." "A child is immature, and his goodness is obviously not a matter of his relation to his present self, but his relation to the end [which he or she will attain when mature] and to the guiding authority [parents]." Idem., pp. 36–37.

8. Aristotle qualifies this elsewhere by stating that there is no "single absolute excellence," so "it is possible to be a good citizen without possessing the excellence which is the quality of the good man." And "it is impossible for a state to be composed entirely of good men" but "each citizen of a polis must discharge *well* the function belonging to him." Barker, *Politics of Aristotle*, pp. 102, 152.

9. "Those who belong to either extreme—the over-handsome, the over-strong, the over-noble, the over-wealthy; or at the opposite end the over-poor, the over-weak, the utterly ignoble—find it hard to follow the lead of reason . . . the best form of political society is one where power is vested in the middle class, and, secondly, that good government is attainable in those states where there is a large middle class—large enough, if possible, to be stronger than both the other classes." Idem., pp. 181–82.

EXERCISES

Think about the book thus far:

1. Chapters 11 and 12 discussed the first three of four factors in political socialization. What is the fourth factor, discussed in this chapter?

2. How does this fourth factor relate to the five characteristics of influence introduced in chapter 5?

3. How do political recruitment and political socialization relate to acquiring influence?

KEY WORDS AND PHRASES
Define the following terms:

power
individualism
common good

THINKING IT THROUGH

Answer each of the following questions (1–5) in one sentence:

1. Is compromise more likely to occur when political leaders see power as a way to satisfy their own needs, or when they view it as a way to satisfy the needs of others?

2. Do consensual parties attract power seekers, those with strong ideological goals, or both?

3. Under what type of government do the group identifications of voters take on the most importance? Why?

4. Even under the type of government you identified in question 3, why might the group identifications of voters still not matter when policy is formulated?

5. What is the most stable basis for authority?

Now, ask yourself:

6. Why is it possible for elected leaders in all nine systems to carry out policies which do not benefit a wide variety of groups?

7. In which of these systems has the civic culture made the most inroads, and why?

8. What factors present in the United States, the United Kingdom, and Germany increase the possibility of producing compromises that benefit a wide variety of groups?

9. How does Aristotle's ''good constitution'' relate to the ''civic culture''? Is the civic culture compatible with individualism?

part 3

USING INFLUENCE

Now that we have examined recruitment and socialization processes, let's take a closer look at how political participation actually takes place in these political systems. We shall begin by exploring the political culture which participation occurs in. Then we will examine how people participate, or use influence, in political parties and interest groups, and within government institutions themselves—executives, legislatures, judiciaries, and bureaucracies.

The fact that people acquire the ability to exert influence does not mean they will use that ability. People with influence have some ability to protect their own interests; that does not mean they will try to do so. What groups use influence? How do their actions affect the ability of political institutions to compromise and to effectively solve the problems of a variety of citizens?

In part 2, we indicated that when a high percentage of citizens accept their government because they believe it accords with tradition, has legal authority, affords opportunity for many groups to participate in politics, is chosen by free elections, and has an ideology and policies they agree with, that government is in a good position to survive and accommodate the needs of a variety of people. In part 3, we shall examine more closely how many people in each of these nine systems believe their government has these traits, and how the influence of those who have (and do not have) these beliefs affects the functioning of their political institutions.

We have already learned that many people do not have the potential to exert much influence; now we shall examine more closely why it is more difficult to change this in some systems than others, because of their political cultures. As Aristotle noted, opening up the privileges of citizenship to wider portions of a populace by changing constitutions and political institutions does not necessarily improve the chances for the common good to be served if those wider portions of the populace are not ready to take on the responsibilities of citizenship. And citizens who do participate may have a tendency to assure that their system serves either the common interests of many, or only the narrow interests of a few. We shall view the political institutions of these nine systems in that context.

Are the people in each of these nation-states who have the potential to participate effectively in politics, and who identify with a wide variety of groups, actually recruited into politically meaningful roles? Both the political culture and the political institutions of a nation-state help to determine whether that is so, or whether recruitment is limited to those with narrower group identifications. Both culture and institutions also help determine whether such individuals can transfer their inclinations into policies which help more than a limited circle of groups.

What about other members of the populace; are they likely to support limits on government when authorities step out of line? Their political culture helps to determine whether they will. How do political institutions, both within and outside government, interact? Political culture helps determine this, too. How much influence do the political leaders themselves have? Can they ignore everyone else's interests? That, too, is an outgrowth of political culture and the institutions of the political system.

Let's begin our look at political culture and institutions with one important aspect of culture: national identity.

chapter 14

POLITICAL CULTURE

NATIONAL IDENTITY

Chapters 11 through 13 examined how people acquire their political attitudes and inclinations. This chapter, and the next four, examine political culture—what those attitudes and inclinations are. Chapter 11 examined why *people think as they do about their nation; this chapter discusses* what *people think about their nation.*

People's knowledge of, feelings toward, and judgments about their political system constitute **political culture.**[1] We have already discussed some aspects of how people are socialized into the political culture—aspects such as whether they are prone to obey or disobey authority, how attached they become to their systems, what groups they identify with, and how efficacious they feel. These attitudes and orientations grow out of both the historical experiences that affect an entire nation-state and the personal experiences of individuals. People filter both historical experience and personal experiences in different ways—factors such as family size, social class, ethnicity, community size and location, how much television one watches, what one reads, who one's friends are, and so on affect that filtration.

Insofar as its people differ in their knowledge, feelings, and judgments, a nation-state contains subcultures. Knowledge, feelings, and judgments about the political system shared by virtually everyone constitute a common political culture.

There are obviously many aspects of political culture we can discuss. We analyze the following aspects in this and the coming chapters:[2]

1. National identity
2. Beliefs about equality
3. Beliefs about who should be recruited into political institutions
4. Attitudes toward power and authority
5. Beliefs about legal protection
6. Assimilation into modern institutions

The first five of these attitudes relate to the political system; the sixth is an attitude toward and involvement in modern institutions that springs from the first five attitudes and from physical living conditions. How do people develop these attitudes? How do they affect the ways people acquire and use influence?

In this chapter we will discuss the first of these sets of values, attitudes about national identity. Chapter 15 discusses beliefs about equality and political recruitment; chapter 16, attitudes about power and authority; chapter 17, beliefs about the legal system; and chapter 18, attitudes toward and involvement in modern institutions.

NATIONAL AND SUBNATIONAL IDENTITIES

Ernest Renan defined allegiance as "the actual consent, the desire to live together, the will to preserve worthily the undivided inheritance which has been handed down."[3] It is that desire and will to live together inside the same territorial boundaries, with a sense of a common past and a common future, which constitute **national identity**—the heart of the nation-state.[4] Individuals who do not feel part of a system may not be able to place limits on it or to be recruited into its institutions.

Individuals may feel this sense of national identity because of long-held feelings of common cultural ties. They may also feel a sense of identity because of economic ties and the belief that authority derives from the people. As we saw in chapter 8, the idea that the nation consists of all its citizens, from whom all its authority arises, and that its government should promote commerce and technical progress, grew during the nineteenth century. Initially, most systems gave the vote to those who acquired property through success in business and commerce. They thought the nation deserved their loyalty because they helped make its laws by choosing legislatures and chief executives. They encouraged the nation to build roads and railroads, and to develop uniform weights and measures, contract laws, and other measures which would unify a national economy. By the twentieth century, some nation-states had become strong enough economically to affect the commerce and government of other nation-states. Some people united to revolt against their governments because they wished to establish control over their own governments and commerce, which had been increasingly dominated by outside nation-states or had stayed under the control of nobility and monarchs; they were asserting national identity.

Nearly all citizens of the United States have developed a strong sense of national identity. Most speak the same language and have a favorable attitude toward the flag and other symbols which date back to the Revolutionary War or the immigration of their ancestors. This is probably true among Great Russians as well, who were long united by loyalty toward the Russian Orthodox Church, the tsar, their common language, and other institutions and symbols; at least the pomp and carefully refurbished churches and palaces of past eras stand as proud symbols of that tradition.

The United States began its nationhood divided between slave and free states; many felt more allegiance to their individual state than to the federal union, although they joined that union voluntarily. Abraham Lincoln offered Robert E. Lee command of the Union Army; he chose instead to lead the army of Virginia. Between 1861 and 1865, Americans fought a bloody Civil War which left a legacy of hatred on the part of many participants. Yet even Generals Lee and Grant held a long and cordial conversation during the surrender at Appomattox, and Confederate General Johnston, who fought against General Sherman's march to Atlanta, served as a pallbearer at Sherman's funeral. The civilian population soon learned to compromise in similar ways; subsequent talk of splitting the nation again has found little support.

Nearly half the population of the former Soviet Union is not Great Russian, including many of the citizens of Estonia, Latvia, Lithuania, the Ukraine, Moldova, Georgia, Armenia, and large Muslim and Buddhist regions to the south and east.[5] These citizens represent over a hundred different nationalities. As we saw in chapter 11, they have many reasons not to identify with Great Russians, who originally conquered them, gave them little membership in national institutions, and long forced them to conduct their schools and businesses in the Russian language, with Great Russian staff occupying the highest positions. Their emotional attachment to their own regions or republics, like the attachment of many Americans to their own states, is fervent. In addition they have much less opportunity than Americans to move from region to region. Each region is identified with its own ethnic group and with that group's religious traditions and leaders.

Inhabitants of the Baltic republics—Estonia, Lithuania, and Latvia—had little reason to identify with the Soviet Union or the CIS. Estonians share a language heritage with Finland, whose television they watch. Since the fourteenth century, Latvia and Estonia existed under the dominance of others—the Swedes, Teutonic knights, Polish, Germans, and Russians. They have been within Russia's political sphere since the eighteenth century, with brief periods of shaky independence from 1918 to 1940. Lithuania became one of the strongest medieval states, but later merged into Poland, and eventually passed into Russia in the eighteenth century.

Lithuania, Latvia, and Estonia all have their own languages and strong nationalist movements, reinforced (as we saw in chapter 11) by religion. Rather than benefitting from inclusion in a larger national economy, they suffered economic setback when Russia removed them from the sphere of a more vibrant European economy. They resisted studying the Russian language. Many Soviet factories were built in Estonia; these factories were accompanied by considerable pollution and large numbers of unwelcome Russian immigrants who failed to learn Estonian. Estonia had to send most of its food to other parts of the Soviet Union at low prices and import consumer goods at high prices. In 1988 and 1989, the legislatures and Communist Party of these Baltic states began declaring autonomy. In 1991 referenda, with 85 percent of voters appearing at the polls, 70 percent of Latvians and 80 percent of Estonians supported independence. They broke from the Soviet Union before its final demise.

Estonians, like Latvians and Lithuanians, suffered severely under German occupation in World War II; even during the short periods of independence, the governments were often repressive. Thirty four percent of the population of Latvia and 30 percent of Estonia is Great Russian;[6] over half their economic output has been exported to or imported from republics of the CIS. All their oil comes from CIS republics. All these factors complicate the desire to go it alone. Only a small fraction of Great Russians living in Estonia meet its stringent new citizenship requirements, so few were eligible to vote in its first parliamentary elections in 1992.

Lithuanians have a history as a strong independent state. More than half are practicing Roman Catholics (a religion identified both in Poland and Lithuania with nationalist independence movements).[7] Only 17 percent (mostly Russians and Poles) are not Lithuanian; in the 1991 referendum on independence, 91 percent voted for independence, including most of those in regions where Russians and Poles predominate. The Polish regions bordering Lithuania are relatively more prosperous. The Soviet government severely restricted the freedom of the Church and other activist groups in Lithuania. That made Lithuanians especially eager to break away. It, and the other Baltic republics, must now find ways to end their economic dependence on the CIS or to continue it on a more equal basis. Although newly privatized businesses are rapidly expanding trade with Finland, industrial production in all three Baltic republics has plummeted. They cannot afford extensive imports from Western Europe and remain dependent on CIS republics for fuel.

Eighty five percent of Ukrainians voted for independence in 1991; in 1992, the Crimea voted for independence from Ukraine. The Moldavian Parliament asserted independence; many Moldavians (now generally called Moldovans, the Romanian form of the word) wish to merge with Romania, which they were once a part of and share a common culture with, while in the east along the Dniester River, Russian separatists have declared a state of their own. Fierce fighting broke out over these continuing divisions. In a 1991 referendum, with 90 percent of eligible voters participating, 99 percent of Georgians voted to separate from the Soviet Union. The southern Ossetians, in turn, fought to secede from Georgia; the Abkhazians, in an autonomous republic, also voted to secede from independent Georgia, and Russian troops intervened in the fighting there, which grows increasingly intense.

But there are reasons why people may wish to maintain some form of broader union. Many remember the horrors of World War II, during which Hitler's armies came close to occupying the Soviet Union's major cities and killed many of her people. They are thankful that the danger of such invasion has substantially declined. People along southern frontiers generally enjoy a higher living standard than their counterparts across the border. They are aware that their limited economic development, and need for relief after natural disasters like earthquakes (however inadequate that relief may be), make it hard to go it alone. In all the republics except Russia, trade with other parts of the former

Soviet Union accounts for 35 percent to 80 percent of economic output; without free trade across borders, they would have to pay for imports in hard-to-obtain U.S. dollars.[8] Republics along the Chinese border would also be vulnerable to Chinese incursion if they were not part of some larger security arrangement, and those to the west may fear the spread of regional conflicts like that in Bosnia-Herzegovina. Russia itself could be surrounded by, or contain within itself, a system of weak and disorderly states.

The Sakha-Yakut Autonomous Republic, lying within the Russian Republic, is as large as all of western Europe. Its population of 1.6 million is only 34 percent Yakut (an ethnic group closely related to North American Eskimos); the rest are Great Russians. In 1992 Russia's president, Boris Yeltsin, signed a Russian Federation Treaty with autonomous republics, granting them increasing control over mineral rights and other matters. The leaders of Sakha-Yakutia, which produces 98 percent of Russia's diamonds, negotiated a deal giving them a partnership with the central government in the diamond-mining company. But by 1993, some members of Russia's Congress of People's Deputies were advocating adoption of a new national constitution which would wipe out the Federation Treaty and such revenue sharing with autonomous republics, or extend more autonomy to other regions as well. Sakha-Yakutia's leaders vowed to strongly resist such moves; they want still more autonomy.

The autonomous republics of Chechen-Ingush and Tatarstan refused to even sign the Federation Treaty. When Chechen-Ingush sought to break from Russia, President Boris Yeltsin sent in troops. The locals forced these troops to retreat, and the Russian legislature voted not to support Yeltsin's action. In 1992, two-thirds of voters in oil-rich Tatarstan indicated a desire for autonomy over their taxes, trade, and industry.

With many extremely diverse nationalities spread across the republics and mingling with one another, the obstacles to forming pan-nationalist, independent, ethnically homogeneous nations are virtually insurmountable. Sixty million former Soviet citizens live outside their own ethnic areas. Although 83 percent of the population of the Russian Republic (which occupies 6.6 million of the former Soviet Union's 8.6 million square miles) is Great Russian, over half of Russia's territory is occupied by the 21 autonomous republics, which are seeking greater self-determination. The Great Russians themselves express ambivalence about their identity; in 1991, 43 percent identified themselves as Russians, and 43 percent as Soviets, to pollsters.[9] Many Great Russians may consider themselves Slavic nationalists, speaking of the "Russian soul," the tsar, the Russian Orthodox Church, and their superiority to the other races Russia has conquered. Some Slavic nationalists want to retain control over the groups they conquered, while others would prefer that they retreat and turn their energies inward. But since Slavs are spread across the border into Belarus and the Ukraine, and parts of Russia contain high percentages of other nationalities, even turning inward to a "Slavic homeland" can be complicated.

The Ukrainian Republic, too, faces divisions. Those who live in the east (which contains 11 million Russians along its border with Russia, out of a total Ukrainian population of 52 million) and south fear dominance by those in the west. The western Ukraine itself is divided between Russian Orthodox believers and Roman Catholics.

Along the southern borders of the CIS Shi'ite Muslims live next to Sunni Kurdish Muslims; historically, the two groups have frequently battled one another.[10] The autonomous republic of Dagestan (located within Russia) contains ten different nationalities—mostly Muslim, originating from Turkey, Iran, and the Caucasian mountains, plus Russians and Ukrainians. Kurds there want to unite with Kurds scattered in several nation-states across the border. Each of these groups adhere strongly to their own traditions. The Republic of Kyrgyzstan is 13 percent Uzbek and 22 percent Russian; attempts by its government to take collective farm land from Uzbeks and give it to homeless Kyrghiz in 1990 resulted in riots. In Tajikistan, a bloody civil war rages, pitting communists and an Uzbek minority against reform-ists and a fundamentalist Islamic movement, sup-ported by neighboring Iran and Afghanistan. This warfare could spread to Uzbekistan, which contains many Tajiks. Only three of the twenty-three bounda-ries separating independent republics are not con-tested; in 1991, border disputes produced half a million refugees.[11]

Armenian Christians live adjacent to Georgian Christians, who belong to a different church. The Armenians' old enemy, Turkey, is across the border; mass killings of Armenians took place in Turkey in 1915.[12] Until they began to win, Iran sided with the Armenians against its fellow Muslim country, Azer-baijan, for fear of nationalism among the many Aze-ris within its own borders. Azeris are ethnically close to Turks. Moldova contains a Turkic Gagauz minority who have declared themselves independent of Moldova and chosen their own president.

All these factors can enhance a desire to be part of a larger entity. Ethnic and human rights are not inherently safer in a smaller political entity than a large one. Economic independence is harder to maintain in the small entity than the large. In-creasingly, local people are heading party organs, bureaucracies, and economic institutions. The cor-ruption exhibited by some of them reminds people of the dangers of allowing the government to be en-tirely controlled by locals. Independent republics can crush dissent from minority ethnic groups with-out outside interference. So there are reasons why many people in these regions may ultimately balk at breaking completely away from union. Their attach-ment to the larger union, however, is often halting and tenuous. The Baltic republics have refused to take any part in the formation of the Commonwealth of Independent States, and the Ukraine, Moldova, Turkmenistan, Georgia, and Azerbaijan have resisted signing its charter.

These republics have been shut off from the outside world for a long time. If their citizens choose to be loyal only to other Slavs or Muslims or smaller ethnic groups they identify with, the possi-bilities for conflict are great. It will be hard for even the individual republics to unite their own people

Armenians in the Armenian Republic are Christian, while Azeris, the dominant ethnic group in Azerbaijan, are Shi'ite Muslims, the same segment of Islamic faith practiced by the supporters of the Ayatollah Khomeini and his successors across the border in Iran. Each of these groups has fierce ethnic loyalty. The Armenians, who have always been more prosperous than the Muslims, once controlled all this territory. When the Russians took control of the region in 1920, Azeris felt the Russians sided unfairly with their fellow Christians, the Armenians. But under Stalin, the Soviet Union made a region within Azerbaijan largely inhabited by Armenians—Nagorno-Karabakh—into an "autonomous region" (with little power) within Azerbaijan. In 1988, Armenians demonstrated to express their desire to make this region part of Armenia. Some Azerbaijanis responded by attacking and killing Armenians. When the local police did not interfere, large numbers of Nagorno-Karabakh's Armenian population fled to Ar-menia as refugees; fearing retaliation, many Azeris within Armenia and Nagorno-Karabakh responded by fleeing to Azerbaijan's capital, Baku. Moscow then sent in troops, but they were largely unable to stop the at-tacks and demonstrations. After Azerbaijan and Arme-nia received independence, the fighting escalated. When Armenians were resettled in Uzbekistan, Tajiki-stan Muslims rioted. Nagorno-Karabakh's Armenians declared themselves independent in 1992 and invaded Azerbaijan. Azerbaijan's new reformist-led Popular Front government, unable to hold back Armenian at-tacks, soon found itself fighting its own rebels, who re-turned the prior communist leader to power. In 1900, half the world's oil came from the Baku oil fields. New drilling contracts with foreign oil companies could revi-talize the economy of Azerbaijan's capital city. That raises the stakes in the continuing civil war.

and open them to the economy and politics of the outside world; people will continue to distrust other groups both within and outside their borders. With their economies and cultures so intertwined, and so many borders under dispute, even national identity which involves a desire to live together with all ethnic groups who reside in one's republic will need to include a willingness for the republics to cooperate in figuring out how to go their separate ways. Each republic needs the others for food and manufactured goods, which cannot be obtained in abundance without contacts throughout and beyond the Commonwealth; this need, and long habits and history of being together, will counterbalance the strong tendencies to fly apart.

Citizens of England have developed a strong sense of national identity. Though the people of Scotland, Wales, and Northern Ireland identify with the symbols of their own nations, most of them speak English and also identify with the British Crown. Some 33 percent of those in Wales, and 35 percent in Scotland, describe themselves as British, rather than Welsh or Scottish. But 86 percent in Scotland, Wales, and England answered affirmatively when asked by 1980 pollsters whether they were proud to be British. Though 67 percent of Northern Irish Protestants actually described themselves as British, only 15 percent of Northern Irish Catholics did; the bitter fighting there has alienated many in the latter group.[13]

Germans strongly identify with Germany as an ethnic group; they share a joint inheritance in language and customs extending back to the tribes of Gaul. However, Germans still demonstrate regional loyalties and ambivalence about whether they should form one nation; the eleven *Laender* (states) were artificially created by the Allies after World War II, although some, such as Bavaria, have long histories as distinct entities. East Germany attempted to diminish regional loyalties by failing to set up state governments; when Germany reunified in 1990, five new states were formed in the East around old cultural regions such as Saxony.

Germans express less pride in their country than Americans and Britons. Eighty seven percent of Americans indicated in a 1985 poll that they were very proud of their country, while 58 percent of Britons and only 21 percent of West Germans did so. Only 1 percent of Americans indicated that they were not very or not at all proud, while 32 percent of West Germans did so.[14]

It is hard to gauge the effects of the Hitler period (with its emphasis on order, national pride, camaraderie, social well-being, and leadership) and the postwar separation in dampening German national pride or arousing Germans' suspicion of old intellectual traditions about fatherland and nationalism. Even before reunification, East Germans were legally citizens of West Germany. But many in the West disapproved of communism, while citizens of the East absorbed attitudes associated with the communist social and economic system. Some West Germans, fearing increased taxes and differences in habits and attitudes, expressed reservations about reuniting so quickly, but the rapid absorption was possible because Germans on both sides of the Wall had long expressed hope that the East could reunite with the West.

Many East Germans lost their jobs and economic security as a result of reunification, and West Germans faced a 7.5 percent income tax increase to help pay for the high cost of adapting their economy. The immediate and massive economic reconstruction program on roads, railroads, sewers, the telephone system, schools, homes, stores, and factories did not turned around the pessimism which set in on both sides of the former border at that point.[15] The over one million people put out of work by the changes may become more optimistic as new jobs open. Yet they continue to receive lower pay, and often feel the "Wessis" look down on the "Ossis"—terms which have become popular to describe inhabitants of the East and West.

Many Germans cooperated with the Nazis; some may still sympathize with the goals of that regime, which did not include loyalty to the legal organs of the state. Many find it difficult to accept the presence of gypsies, Romanians, Czechs, Poles, Vietnamese, Turks, and others as permanent residents (who receive German government subsidies, and sometimes beg on the streets, at a time when many Germans are out of work) as a result of the changes in the region.[16]

China's unity has centered around the Han. For keeping order, settling disputes, and supervising public works, Chinese have traditionally deferred to individuals with higher education chosen for their jobs by the central authorities. These individuals were the only ones who could speak and write in Mandarin and thus transcend regional dialects. They worked with their minds, but not with their hands. The ruling authorities were expected to keep the state united and to provide for the well-being of all inhabitants. Children were expected to obey their families, and families the authorities. Hence, the Chinese developed a strong sense of national identity by adhering to these rules; the present regime retains them. These traditions are lacking only among some of the outlying non-Han peoples to the north and west (as we saw in chapter 11). Those regions are economically marginal as well. In Tibet, the traditions are not only lacking, but much of the populace disdains them. Tibet was ruled by its own Dalai Lama and had its own cultural and national identity before China conquered it in 1950. It has continued to be bitter about Chinese rule and to dislike Chinese culture, which has been forcefully imposed on it.

China's sense of identity has been reinforced by the events of the past century and a half, as outside powers conquered Chinese territory and forced it to comply with their demands. By the end of the last century, Russia dominated Manchuria, Britain controlled Shanghai and Hong Kong and the commerce of other Chinese port cities, Germany obtained the lease of the Shandong Peninsula, and France leased the Bay of Guangzhou. The United States forced China to make the same trading concessions to other nation-states as they had been forced to make to those which first arrived, letting us open businesses and mines on Chinese territory. After losing a war with Japan, China was forced to give the Japanese Formosa, the Pescadores, and the Liaodung peninsula. Soon China found itself overrun with foreign factories and investments, and with warlords who diverted abroad agricultural produce once used for domestic consumption. Then, in 1937, just as Jiang Kaishek was beginning to bring all the warlords under the control of a central government, the Japanese (who already had taken Manchuria in 1931) attacked China and occupied many major cities and a considerable portion of the hinterland. During the succeeding period of Japanese occupation, millions of Chinese were slaughtered. This provided the Chinese people with strong incentive to reassert their own national independence.

Hence, all these nation-states—the United States, the CIS republics, the United Kingdom, East and West Germany, and China—have long histories of national identity among at least a strong central portion of their populations.

IMPERIALISM AND CONFUSED NATIONAL IDENTITY

India, Peru, and Nigeria have no strong traditions of national identity. In pursuing their empires, Russia and China attempted to absorb conquered regions into one unified system of state rule. England also did so with Scotland and Wales, though not with Ireland. As the United States expanded, it allowed citizens of the new territories to establish co-equal states. People in the newly acquired regions of these different nation-states did not always fare as well politically and economically as those who purchased or conquered their territories, and they did not always like becoming part of the larger entity; they were, however, considered equal citizens of the growing nation-state. But when Spain, Portugal, Holland, England, France, Germany, Italy, Belgium, and the United States began from the sixteenth century forward to conquer and colonize portions of Latin America, Asia, and Africa, they did not bring the inhabitants of those regions into their political systems as equal citizens. Rather, they used the economies of the colonies to benefit the "mother" (colonizing) country.[17]

The French allowed some African delegates to sit in the French parliament, declared Algeria a department of France, and thought of their subjects as sharing in French civilization. In contrast, the British declared that their "indirect rule" did not seek to spread the benefits of British civilization to all subjects, but allowed subjects to continue their traditional laws and customs. In reality, colonial administrators from all these imperial powers allowed subjects to continue adhering to some traditional laws and customs, but radically altered others. None of the colonial subjects, however, were extended the full rights of citizenship which applied back in Europe.[18]

The British created a Commonwealth, an extension of the United Kingdom that encompassed its colonies and (in the style of France and Holland) extended Commonwealth British citizenship to some of the native inhabitants most educated in the customs and manners of Britain. The colonies were not considered full parts of the nation-states which ruled them; nor were they permitted to seek independent sovereignty for themselves. They also were forbidden to develop commerce (as we shall see in part 5) unacceptable to the colonizing country. The subjects who were trained to assist in rule were educated in the institutions of the colonizer; the same people usually led the eventual independence movements. Once the colonized people broke from the mother country and took sovereign control of their own lands, they were often more zealous than the former colonial powers about imposing foreign institutions, laws, and ideas upon others in their own country (as we shall see in the next few chapters). It was only at this point that they could begin to infuse their subjects with notions of national identity. Before this, the people were taught that they were both part of their own traditional, often regional, culture and part of the culture of the imperial ruler—not part of a unified individual nation. No one pretended that they had chosen or were consenting to live together, and the people as a whole had no undivided inheritance they could be asked to preserve.

India is an example of that. For thousands of years, traditional Hindu villages in India were strictly divided into castes. Each owed obligations to the others, and no one could change their caste. The villages as a whole owed taxes to the regional authorities. Thus, by following the same religious rules and deferring to regional authorities, people developed a sense of national culture but habits of deference to regional political authorities. Over the centuries, Aryans, Alexander the Great of Greece (Aristotle's private pupil), Mauryans, the Gupta Dynasty, Afghans, Moghuls, and then the British all sought to unify India by leaving local and regional authorities intact but asking people to declare loyalty and pay taxes to a central authority. However, whether the region was integrated into a larger political unit was a matter of indifference to villagers. By the time India gained independence in 1947, as we saw in chapter 11, India was divided into 860 different political entities, and princes presided over 562 of them. Many groups, such as the Bengali (around Calcutta) and the Narthex (around Bombay) were intensely loyal to their own regions, though they were members of the Hindu religion.

Members of other religions often strongly distrusted the Hindus. When the British granted independence, some Muslim-dominated regions broke away to form the separate nation-state of Pakistan. About 20 percent of India's population come from religious traditions other than Hindu, and an additional 6 percent are from scheduled tribes; many of these people have difficulty identifying with the Indian nation-state, which designates **Hindi** (spoken by 42 percent of the populace) as the national language and whose leadership is largely Hindu. The 15 percent of the populace from untouchable castes, who continue to face prejudice and have even been deprived of the traditional obligations other castes once owed them, are often alienated as well. In Jammu and Kashmir many Muslims want to break away to join Pakistan. India's people now speak at least eight hundred separate languages and dialects; the Dravidian languages of the south, entirely unrelated to Hindi, are divided into four language groups unrelated to one another.

As we have seen, many people undergo little socialization likely to break down the barriers between groups and draw them together to support one nation. The majority of the populace remains poor and is unexposed to economic development promulgated by the national state; thus they have no economic incentive to support the state, either. And groups like the Sikhs of Punjab (who are among the wealthiest groups in India but are not Hindu) and Nagas (who identify with Burmans across the

Machu Pichu, a former Inca community in Peru.
Bob Gamer

border) contain militant extremists who want their regions to break away so that they need not share with or be controlled by the rest of India. Guerilla fighters also operate in Assam and Kashmir.

Many caste and religious leaders and their followers—unlike the separatists—want India to continue as a nation-state. But they find little that binds them to other groups within the nation.

The people of Peru, too, held regional loyalties as well as loyalties divided between three cultures. Until about the middle of the thirteenth century, warfare was common between valleys and regions of Peru. About that time, the city of Chan Chan united the people into the Chimu political system, which collected taxes from a wide territory without effecting much change in political structures or regional loyalties. Around 1471, Cuzco began to conquer the Chimus and many other groups to form the Inca Empire. This empire was overthrown by the Spanish conquerors, beginning in 1533. Thus, there was little time—just over a half-century—to develop a sense of Inca national identity. The Spanish relied on the labor of the **Aymara** peoples (from around Lake Titicaca), the **Quechua** (from much of the rest of the Inca Empire), and some imported blacks but

did not accord them political rights. The Spanish born in America (*criollos*) did acquire some limited power to govern the towns. They led a revolution in the nineteenth century to obtain freedom from Spain; once they were successful, they forced the Quechua and Aymara to sell much of their best land, and did not give these groups voting rights until 1979. Later in the nineteenth century, Chile won a war against Peru, and immigrants took over much of the urban commerce in Peru. None of this helped instill a sense of national identity. As we have seen, many in the rural areas are still not exposed to socialization agents which could change this, and most operate in the informal sectors of the economy, which have no stake in whether the nation and its institutions continue. Moreover, the recent urban immigrants with economic power have little reason to invest their money or their loyalty in Peru.

Nigeria also has no traditions of national identity. Three tribal groups—the **Hausa** in the north, **Ibo** in the southeast, and **Yoruba** in the southwest—comprise about half the population of Nigeria. The other half of the population is divided among some 250 different ethnic groups. If, in the past, individual villages were incorporated into a larger political entity, it usually involved only members of their own ethnic group. Thus, villagers had no sense of national identity when, late in the nineteenth century, the British laid out the boundaries of the present nation-state encompassing all these tribes. They governed the nation through four separate regional administrative units, with different procedures for each; again, none of this helped Nigerians develop a sense of national identity. Since winning its independence, the nation-state has weathered a number of military coups, with leaders from one tribal group overthrowing those from another. The Ibo region even broke away from the federation in 1967, precipitating three years of bloody civil war. Elections—as we shall see presently—have also been marred by intertribal rivalries. Major-General Babangida succumbed to pleas from ethnic groups when he created eleven new states in 1992 (raising the number to thirty); consolidating those groups into separate territories may tempt politicians to appeal to separate ethnic interests when running for legislatures, further hindering a sense of national identity. Finally, Nigerian villagers have little money to buy and sell goods produced in a national economy. This, too, makes a national identity a difficult goal to achieve.

CONCLUSION

The United States, the United Kingdom, and China all have strong traditions of national identity; Welsh, Scots, and Northern Irish Catholics also have strong regional loyalties within the United Kingdom. Inhabitants of the various republics that used to be part of the Soviet Union often feel national loyalties to their own ethnic groups; they also have reasons to desire continuation of some sort of union among the republics. The national and ethnic identity of Germans remains strong despite the fact that it was undercut by the forty years of division into two nation-states with very different constitutions and economic systems. But a sense of national identity is far less developed in India, Peru, and Nigeria.

People who lack a sense of national identity are often the least integrated into the national economy and political institutions. They may have a strong belief in placing limits on the authority of public officials. It is difficult, however, for them to obtain the support of those who do have a sense of national identity—these individuals often resent the prospect of weakening the nation's unity and threatening its economy. Among the nine nation-states, then, the United States, the United Kingdom, Germany, and China appear to have the highest percentages of people with a strong sense of national identity.

SUMMARY

Some citizens develop a strong sense of national identity, while others do not. National identity depends on many factors: When leaders and citizens speak the same language, believe in a civic culture, share similar values, participate in national institutions, have a long history as part of the nation, are economically interdependent, face hostile forces across national borders, and have suffered military conquest by outside powers, this sense of national identity may be enhanced. Conversely, cultural, political, geographical, or economic isolation of different groups of people may hinder the development of a sense of oneness as a nation.

NOTES

1. See Talcott Parsons and Edward A. Shils, eds., *Toward a General Theory of Action* (Cambridge, Mass.: Harvard University Press, 1951), pp. 58ff. These three dimensions are cognitive (knowledge), affective (feeling), and evaluative (judgment) orientations toward political objects.

2. Gabriel Almond and Sidney Verba's *Civic Culture* focuses on six complexes of attitudes about the political system: sense of national identity, trust of government, class consciousness, political effectiveness, belief in freedom, and belief in equality. (See footnote in chapter 5.) Robert Dahl is interested in whether people believe in voting, and in partitioning power among several branches of government that can be forced to compromise with one another. Karl Deutsch, *Nationalism and Social Communication*, rev. ed. (Cambridge, Mass.: MIT Press, 1966), studies the assimilation of people into modern social groupings. We discuss these aspects of political culture in this text.

3. *Qu'est-ce qu'une Nation?* (What is a Nation?), Paris, 1882. Translation from *The Poetry of the Celtic Races, and Other Studies* (London: 1896).

4. A nation-state must have all the attributes we defined in the first chapter. One of those attributes is that at least a portion of the populace must have this sense of nation.

5. Less than a fifth of those living outside the Russian Republic are Great Russians, but Great Russians often are among the most urbanized. Robert A. Lewis, Richard H. Rowland, and Ralph S. Clem,

Nationality and Population Change in Russia and the USSR: An Evaluation of Census Data 1897–1970 (New York: Praeger, 1976), p. 132.

6. The percentages for the various republics come from Goskomstat, *Natsional'nyi sostav naseleniia* (Moscow: Information-Publication Center, 1989).

7. In a Gallup poll, 45 percent of ethnic and 50 percent of other Lithuanians said they consider themselves a "religious person," versus 62 percent in Western Europe and 81 percent in the United States. Fifteen percent of ethnic and 12 percent of other Lithuanians reported attending church at least once a week. Lithuanians expressed a higher level of confidence in the Church than any other institution; Hungarians ranked it second to the press, which helped pave the road for the revolution there. George Gallup, Jr. and Jim Castelli, "Religious Feelings Still Strong in Eastern European Countries," *Kansas City Star,* January 5, 1991.

8. "Russia's Future," *The Economist,* December 7, 1991.

9. Among Boris Yeltsin's supporters, 57 percent identified themselves as Russians and 30 percent as citizens of the Soviet Union. Roman Szporluk, "The End of an Empire, The Birth of a Nation," *Washington Post National Weekly Edition,* September 2–8, 1991. In a poll taken in February, 1992, 62 percent of Russians regretted the breakup of the Soviet Union, while 24 percent were glad. *Kansas City Star,* August 18, 1993.

10. Nadia Diuk and Adrian Karatnycky, *The Hidden Nations: The People Challenge the Soviet Union* (New York: Morrow, 1990), p. 181, argue that even the Shi'ites, though sharing their sect of the Islamic faith with Iranian leaders, are concerned about Iran's persecution of its Azeri minority and are not attracted to Iran's form of the fundamentalist religion.

11. The Academy of Science's institute of geography has counted seventy-six disputes over location of boundary lines. "Soviet Reformers Face a Staggering Task," *The Economist, Kansas City Star,* August 4, 1991. Zhores A. Medvedev, "Before the Coup: The Plot Inside the Kremlin," *Washington Post,* September 1, 1991. In 1991, eleven republics signed an accord at Alma Ata to cooperate economically and freeze present republic boundaries for fifty years; that agreement could be broken at any time.

12. Death estimates for these mass killings range from 600,000 to 1.5 million. Museums in Armenia are filled with memorabilia of the massacre. New towns and villages are named after the Armenian lands lost on the Turkish side of the border. The Soviet government encouraged nationalist feelings among the Armenians so that they would see the advantages of Soviet, rather than Turkish, rule.

13. Richard Rose, *Understanding the United Kingdom: The Territorial Dimension of Government* (London: Longman, 1982), pp. 12, 14. Schools in Northern Ireland have not been teaching civics classes. That probably reinforces the tendency of Northern Irish Catholics to identify with Ireland. However, it would probably be difficult to devise civics courses which would make British control of Northern Ireland's economy and politics appear attractive to Catholics, who lack economic opportunity.

14. In a *New York Times*/CBS poll, November 6–10, 1985, 87 percent of Americans said they were very proud to be an American: only 1 percent said they were not very proud or not at all proud. The European figures come from an October-November 1985 Gallup International poll. E. J. Dionne, Jr., "Government Trust: Less in West Europe than U.S.," *New York Times,* February 16, 1986.

15. A year after reunification, a public opinion survey found two-thirds of East Germans optimistic about the future—twice the percentage who expressed optimism six months earlier. Stephen Kinzer, "East Germans, Nurtured by Bonn, Take Heart and Begin to Prosper," *New York Times,* September 29, 1991. A survey two years after reunification found only 30 percent of westerners and 11 percent of easterners saying they felt closer to the "other" Germany. George Rodrigue, "Happy Anniversary? Not for Germany," *Kansas City Star,* October 4, 1992.

16. Germany has had a law which says that refugees from Eastern Europe who succeed in crossing the border may stay to become citizens, and that the 2.3 million ethnic Germans in the former Soviet Union are still citizens (though some no longer speak German or know much about German culture) and can return "home." Germany spends about 4 billion marks a year on these immigrants. In 1992 and 1993, that was tightened to place greater restrictions on immigration.

17. On this topic see J. A. Hobson, *Imperialism* (London: G. Allen and Unwin, 1938); Ernest Barker, *Ideas and Ideals of the British Empire* (Cambridge: Cambridge University Press, 1941); Mary E. Townsend, *Rise and*

Fall of Germany's Colonial Empire (New York: Macmillan, 1930); Rosa Luxemburg, *The Accumulation of Capital* (New Haven: Yale University Press, 1951); V. I. Lenin, *Imperialism: The Highest Stage of Capitalism* (New York: International Publishers, 1939); Rudolf Hilferding, *Finance Capital* (London: Routledge and Kegan Paul, 1981); and E. H. Dance, *The Victorian Illusion* (London: W. Heineman, 1928).

18. Many twentieth-century novels reveal insights into these relationships; for example see E. M. Forster, *A Passage to India* (New York: Harcourt, Brace, 1924); Paul Scott, *The Raj Quartet* (London: Heineman, 1976) and *Staying On* (New York: Morrow, 1977); Rudyard Kipling, *Kim* (London: Macmillan, 1901); Raja Rao, *Kanthapura* (New York: New Directions, 1963); Kamala Markandaya, *Nectar in a Sieve* (New York: J. Day, 1955); Joseph Conrad, *Lord Jim* (New York: Modern Library, 1931), *Heart of Darkness* (Garden City, New York: Doubleday, 1901), and *The Rescue* (New York: New American Library, 1950); George Orwell, *Shooting the Elephant* (London: Secker and Warburg, 1950); Eugene Burdick, *The Ugly American* (New York: Viking Press, 1957); Graham Greene, *The Man from Havana* (New York: Harcourt, Brace, 1950) and *The Quiet American* (New York: Viking Press, 1958); Paul Montgomery, *The Death of Eva Peron* (New York: Pocket Books, 1979); Naguib Mahfong, *Place of Desire* (New York: Doubleday, 1991); Gabriel Garcia Marquez, *Love in the Time of Cholera* (New York: Knopf, 1988) and *One Hundred Years of Solitude* (New York: Harper & Row, 1970); Mario Vargas Llosa, *The Real Life of Alejandro Mayta* (New York: Vintage, 1936); Carlos Fuentes, *The Old Gringo* (New York: Farrar Straus Giroux, 1985); V.S. Naipal, *Bend in the River* (New York: Knopf, 1979); Alan Patton, *Cry the Beloved Country* (New York: Scribners, 1948); Nadine Gordimer, *July's People* (London: Cape, 1981) and *My Son's Story* (New York: Farrar Straus Giroux, 1990); Doris Lessing, *Collected African Stories* (London: Joseph, 1973); Isak Dinesen, *Out of Africa* (New York: Random House, 1938); and Frederick Forsythe, *The Dogs of War* (New York: Viking Press, 1974).

EXERCISES

Think about the book thus far:

1. Part 2 of the book is about acquiring influence, while part 3 is about using influence. Why is political socialization discussed in part 2, and political culture in part 3?

2. Why is national identity an appropriate topic to discuss in connection with political culture?

3. Must one be a nationalist to have national identity?

4. Does a pan-nationalist have national identity?

5. Must one believe in civic culture to have national identity?

6. Are some inhabitants of some systems likely to be tempted to endorse more than one pan-national ideology?

7. How may economic realities divide pan-national movements?

8. How does pan-nationalism harm the nation-states we are studying? How does it help them?

KEY WORDS AND PHRASES

Define the following terms:

political culture

national identity

Hindi

Aymara

Quechua

Hausa

Ibo

Yoruba

THINKING IT THROUGH

1. Complete the chart by listing a factor which strengthens, and weakens, national identity in each of the nine systems:

	Strengthens	Weakens
USA		
CIS		
FRG		
GDR		
UK		
PRC		
RI		
RP		
FRN		

Now, ask yourself:

2. Does everyone in each of these systems have the will to live together? In which of these systems is national identity most firmly rooted? In which system is it the least rooted?

3. The summary at the end of chapter 13 and the introduction to part 3 refer to a greater base for authority and group influence in the United States, the United Kingdom, and West Germany than in the other six systems. How might that base affect national identity?

chapter 15

POLITICAL CULTURE
EQUALITY AND RECRUITMENT

Some people think everyone should be equally entitled to participate in all aspects of commerce and govern-ment and to rise as high in society and politics as their talents might take them. Others feel that we are born into certain social and economic positions and we should not stray too far from them; these individuals often believe that political posts are best commanded by people with social standing in their communities. In to-day's world, people sometimes feel torn between the two positions. But, without doubt, people's beliefs about equality and recruitment affect who actually is recruited to participate in a political system.

We are examining six aspects of political culture— people's knowledge of, feelings toward, and judg-ments about their political system. Chapter 14 dis-cussed attitudes about national identity. This chapter discusses **beliefs about equality, and about who should be recruited into political institutions.**

EQUALITY AND RECRUITMENT: OLD SYSTEMS

Every country includes people who have and earn more money, live in bigger and more substantial houses in neighborhoods with higher prestige, attend higher-status schools and land higher-status jobs, come from more "established" families, and/or rise higher in political institutions than others. Most of us regard these differences as natural, but we differ in our assessments of who these people should be. Should a person born without these attributes have an **equal opportunity** to acquire them—the same opportunity as the offspring of those who already have them? Should this opportunity extend to every person, regardless of social class, sex, race, religion, physical fitness, personal beliefs and habits, or fam-ily background? Should government guarantee a minimum level of these necessities and privileges

even to those who cannot or will not themselves ac-quire them? Should it reserve jobs and other bene-fits for groups who have not had the opportunity to acquire them in the past? These questions can spark disagreements at any corner gathering in any coun-try; the last question is likely to ignite the most con-troversy. But the general approach to the discussion will differ from one political culture to another.

Schools, the media, and personal conversations in both the United States and the former Soviet Union often espouse a belief in equality and equal opportunity. **Class consciousness,** the awareness and acceptance of class differences, is deemphasized in these two cultures. Americans do recognize class differences; one study found that when they were asked by an interviewer to identify which social class they came from, Americans differed little in their responses from the British. But even that study concludes that Americans are not inclined to orga-nize political resistance on the basis of class and that increasing percentages of Americans identify themselves as middle class.[1] In fact, in the United States, people like to think of themselves as part of a "middle class" country; in the former Soviet Union, people thought of themselves as part of a "working class" country. Leaders, in turn, like to show that they identify with those "middle" or "working" class values. America abolished titles of nobility and stressed the value of individual initiative in getting ahead, regardless of one's social background; gender, race, and religion are not supposed to bar people from economic, social, and political activity in the United States. In a 1960s poll, 98 percent agreed that "everyone in America should have equal opportunities to get ahead."[2]

Russia has a history of class consciousness; it has also long entertained the notion of equal opportunity. Until 1917, Russia had titled nobility who monopolized many of the top positions in society and government. Yet, even then, many people felt these positions should be open to anyone, regardless of their social standing at birth. Great Russians have exhibited ambivalence about nobility for centuries. During the Kievan period in the tenth to thirteenth centuries, the portions of Rus (the name given to that region and its inhabitants in those days) not subjugated to the Tatars, Poles, or Lithuanians were ruled by various princes. They gave the title of **boyar,** and land, to soldiers from families of merchants, farmers, and peasants. In 1462 (just thirty years before Columbus discovered America), Ivan III became the prince of Moscow, and set out to subjugate all the other princes so that his successor could take on the title of tsar. The tsars, to help consolidate their power, gradually reduced the power of the boyars, and Peter the Great outlawed them altogether. However, the tsars continued the tradition of granting nobility to favorite soldiers, thus adding people of humble origin to the ranks of the nobility. Sometimes they even used the nobility they had created to challenge the older nobility.

Clergy, lesser nobility, merchants, and peasants also owned land. At the end of the sixteenth century, in response to declining agricultural production, laws were tightened to tie the peasants closer to estates; these peasants became **serfs** who owed the estate owners free labor and could not leave without their permission. In the south, the **barshchina** system had peasants working on large estates they could not leave. Still, **Cossacks**—groups of peasants who had run away to occupy free

Rus was very small during the reign of Ivan III. In the seventh century, Slavic people lived in villages and tilled their own land. Between the eighth and tenth centuries, Norsemen began to marry tribal leaders, raise armies, and set up trade. Wars over control of trade developed between Kiev and Novgorod, and classes of princes and boyars arose. Some peasants fell into debt to large landowners, and princes seized some land and (later) entire villages, whose inhabitants became the property of the new owners. Still, even by the twelfth century, most villages and villagers remained free.

Then, in the thirteenth century, the Tatars under Genghis Khan laid the major towns to waste. They encouraged loyalty to Moscow and the Russian Orthodox religion to counter the influence of Poland and its Roman Catholicism, and supported the right of princes (into whose families they married) to collect taxes. Ivan III eventually expelled the Tatars. During the following century, Russia began to expand widely and rapidly.

lands—remained important allies of future tsars as they expanded Russia's boundaries to the east and south. In the north, under the **obrok** system, peasants paid landowners a percentage of their crops in exchange for individual plots of land and could engage on their own in crafts and industries. That gave them greater freedom than in the south, but they still could not leave the land.

For centuries before that, peasants tilled their own land. By the fifteenth century, some peasants had become wealthy as merchants. Peter the Great's encouragement of industry at the end of the seventeenth century allowed even more to move into these pursuits. Neither the tsars nor those without titles of nobility viewed society as automatically deferring to those with wealth or established rank.[3] Common people could receive titles of nobility. In 1861, Tsar Alexander II freed the serfs. All this set the stage for Marxist ideas about equality among the classes. The 1917 Revolution killed the Tsar and his family and caused many among the nobility to flee. But it had precedents in promoting workers and peasants to positions of leadership.

Soviet society exhibited a **reverse class consciousness** during periods when workers were thought to have "good" class backgrounds, while bourgeois (middle class) families were "bad." From the 1970s on, this was deemphasized. Party members, many from families of workers and peasants, enjoyed special privileges and status which they passed along to their children. As before the Revolution, many who did not enjoy those privileges resented them and thought them unfair.[4]

From the time the Great Russians first began to conquer outlying areas in the sixteenth century, however, they found it natural to dominate the ethnic groups they conquered. As Great Russians continued to dominate many top positions, other ethnic groups thought that unfair. Russia did not experience the Reformation, which eventually helped various religious groups earn tolerance in Western Europe. The communist regime alternated between outlawing religion entirely and favoring the Russian Orthodox church at times under Stalin; it consistently discriminated, however, against giving important political positions to people who practiced a religion, and it also closed places of worship and destroyed religious shrines.[5] It argued that by doing so it would erase the basis for intolerance and disunity; instead, it roused deep resentments. The communist regime did draw women into higher education and a great diversity of jobs and professions and gave them equal political rights; as you will see in part 4, corresponding changes in attitude come slowly. When the individual republics were finally able to assert their independence in 1991, they wished to overthrow Great Russian domination. Latvia immediately voted to exclude Russians from citizenship.[6] Other republics sought to take control over their own affairs. That often meant discriminating against Russians and other nationalities living within their borders.

Equality as a goal does not always translate into equality in practice. In America, slavery, subsequent discrimination against blacks and other minorities in hiring and political participation, and refusal to allow Jews and other minorities into country clubs and other social organizations testify that not everyone practices equal opportunity. Women's struggles to earn suffrage and overcome other inequalities are further evidence of the gap between belief and action. While both Americans and CIS republic citizens agree that anyone should have the right to rise to the top, government's attempts to help certain groups do so (for example, by promoting people of "good" backgrounds in the Soviet Union, or by enacting affirmative action and sexual harassment laws in the United States) can rouse the anger of people with historically easier access to the top.

The two cultures differ profoundly, however, in their attitudes toward those who attempt to better themselves. Americans tend to applaud their peers for seeking better education, jobs, and income; in contrast, CIS republic citizens often express resentment when their peers do this.[7] The long period of serfdom, and the Marxist system of guaranteeing everyone work, have offered few opportunities to develop personal initiative. They also encouraged a widespread notion that everyone is entitled to a job, housing, health care, and other amenities provided by government. The latter notion profoundly divides Americans; some agree that government should guarantee such necessities, while others would have government provide only minimal unemployment or poverty assistance.[8] Few Americans endorse the notion that everyone should be guaranteed a job. And, while Americans have gradually come to accept the idea that the major political parties should include all racial and ethnic groups,[9] opposition parties in the CIS may even win elections on the premise that their ethnic group should dissociate itself from other ethnic groups. Among these groups in the CIS, there is no widespread agreement that all races should have equal opportunity to participate in political institutions.

Still, both cultures believe that people from all classes should be recruited into positions of political influence. In the United States, we assume that people are represented as individuals—not as members of formal subgroups of society. Formal subgroups may organize interest groups around ethnic identity, areas of common concern (for example, the environment), business (for example, farmers or bankers), trade unions, or single issues (gay rights or abortion). But these interest groups are not directly represented as part of a political party or the legislature. A culture which deemphasizes class consciousness, and purports to ignore race and religion in politics, may not find a need to allow such groups formal representation. As Alexis De-Toqueville observed:

> They have not the slightest notion of peculiar privileges granted to cities, families, or persons; their minds appear never to have foreseen that it might be possible not to apply with strict uniformity the same laws to every part of the state, and all its inhabitants.[10]

From the earliest days of settlement, members of American legislatures were thought of as individuals rather than as formal representatives of particular groups. As we shall see later, this may leave women and some ethnic, class, and other groups underrepresented in the various institutions of government.

Russia had a long theoretical tradition that even peasants could appeal directly to the tsar. Its eleventh century Novgorod-style town councils, which died out during the thirteenth century, represented individuals as well as groups (mostly merchants, investors, and tribal leaders). In the fifteenth and sixteenth centuries, the Duma of Boyars replaced the councils; to compete with it in the sixteenth century, Ivan IV briefly created the *Zemsky Sobor,* a national assembly composed of lesser nobility, upper clergy, landed gentry, and urban merchants. During the nineteenth century, Tsar Alexander III created *zemstros*—district and provincial councils—with percentages of seats formally apportioned to landowners, newly freed peasants, and town dwellers. All of these assembly and council members represented particular groups. The first national legislature with authority to make laws did not come into being until 1907.

The Communist Party's Central Committee was almost entirely composed of Great Russians; at the end of 1988, only two members were not of Great Russian descent. But during one-party rule by the communists, the national legislature was carefully built of an array of individuals from all walks of life, with special seats for particular ethnic, cultural, and economic groups.[11] There was historic precedence for doing this. Soviets and CIS citizens have not confused equality with uniformity; they like living in a society that celebrates cultural and intellectual diversity, and private passions.

> *Many [CIS] intellectuals return [from America] dismayed by what they see as a superficial culture and by "political correctness," militant feminism, self-conscious egalitarianism and other manifestations of what they identify with the very intellectual conformity and intolerance that they spent their lives fighting against . . . the absence of "spirituality" and [of] the intensity of Soviet intellectual life.[12]*

Class consciousness is greater in the United Kingdom and Germany than in the United States. Individuals with titles—either of nobility or academic distinction—are still accorded considerable deference in both these nation-states by people from all social classes. Those with wealth and title try to distinguish themselves from those with less rank. People have a tendency to distinguish among social classes when identifying themselves and others, without expressing resentment over those distinctions. Voters find it natural to elect higher-status candidates to represent the interests of ethnic, religious, and occupational minorities.

This is reflected in representative institutions. The United Kingdom's upper house in the legislature (the House of Lords), as we saw in chapter 2, consists primarily of nobility (such as dukes and earls) and **life peers** (commoners to whom the king or queen grants titles of nobility, not transferrable to offspring, as a reward for personal accomplishment). Even the lower house (the House of Commons) and the cabinet, as we saw in chapter 10, have until recently included few business or union people who were not Oxford or Cambridge graduates. East Germany's parliament had formal representatives from various sectors of society, such as farmers and the clergy.[13] The Federal Republic of Germany's upper house represents the states, and some representatives also represent certain sectors of society. The lower house has proportional representation, which allows greater representation of minorities, but not necessarily underprivileged ones; it contains many representatives of business, unions, and the civil service, who retain their positions as leaders of those groups while serving in the legislature. With 60 percent of the Bundestag composed of such representatives, the proportion of white collar workers, farmers, and other professions and businesses has declined markedly.[14]

The earliest German nobility probably dates to before the time of Christ; Frankish kings conferred estates upon their warriors during the seventh and eighth centuries A.D. After that time, they tended to marry within their own class and to pass land along to their heirs. They ruled the countryside until the nineteenth century, with some competition from kings and chartered towns. From the fourteenth through seventeenth centuries, these towns gained some power, and leaders of town guilds sometimes married into aristocratic families. After the Treaty of Westphalia in 1648, most towns lost their charters to the princes, who used a **Reichstag** (legislature) they controlled themselves to compete with the power of the king and tighten their grasp on land. These families continued to intermarry, and (unlike Russia's princes) faced no competition from newly created nobility. The rulers of Prussia who united Germany in 1871 were members of the nobility, which retained great power in the new regime. As of 1913, 80 percent of cavalry, 48 percent of infantry, 42 percent of field artillery officers, 83 percent of chief provincial officials, 50 percent of presidents of government boards, and 40 percent of Reich ministers were nobility.[15] Unlike in Russia, the nobility retained strong influence clear into the twentieth century, with little competition from a king with the power of a tsar or a British monarch.

Furthermore, the German nobility supported and strongly affected (together with church allies) the public education curriculum.[16] This allowed many commoners to engage in commerce and manufacture after receiving an education which emphasized deference to the authority of the established rulers. Public primary education began in Germany during the sixteenth century[17] and was made mandatory in Prussia during the eighteenth century. By the 1870s, mandatory public education was in force throughout Germany.[18] There was little public primary school education in Britain until the nineteenth century; it was not made mandatory until the end of that century. Hence, Germany made better progress in attracting children of commoners into commerce and industry. Prussia also worked closely with such groups to develop commerce and industry. As a result, commoners obtained faster and firmer access to political institutions in Germany than in Britain.

In 1066, William the Conqueror crossed the English Channel and took control of England. His Norse cohorts quickly intermarried with and replaced the Anglo-Saxon nobility, who had previously been gaining ascendency. England was then organized into a tightly feudal society centering around king and nobles. When the barons forced King John to sign the **Magna Charta** in 1215, the House of Lords, which still exists today, was born. Subsequent kings came to rely on the **gentry**—the educated landowners of common (non-noble) origin—and the town leaders, who organized into a House of Commons, to resist these nobles. Each of these classes tended to marry within its own ranks. The gentry and town leaders later formed the base for the present middle class. In England, unlike Germany, the nobility thus experienced steady competition from both a king and commoners; as in Germany, it played an important role in all aspects of people's lives.

Both the United Kingdom and Germany developed clear **class hierarchies,** which delineated responsibilities and obligations for each class, and few people crossed over class lines. During the nineteenth and early twentieth centuries, rules were gradually changed to allow other classes to fill university classrooms, jobs, concert halls, political offices, and other positions formerly reserved exclusively for the nobility and the highest ranks of the gentry. Alexis DeToqueville commented on the suspicions this change aroused in the British, in contrast to Americans, who "are very ready to frequent the same places and find neither peril nor advantage in the free interchange of their thoughts" because "privileges of birth never existed":

If two Englishmen chance to meet in the Antipodes . . . they first stare at each other . . . then turn away . . . if one accosts the other, they will take care to converse with a constrained and absent air . . . whilst he seeks to raise himself into a higher circle, [the Englishman] is always on the defensive against the intrusions of those below him.[19]

Current citizens of both of these nation-states are likely to respond that people should have equal opportunities to rise in society, the economy, and government. The United Kingdom has had a grocer's daughter and a circus performer's son as prime minister.[20] Most nobility, and many with higher education, fled East Germany before it was established, allowing a great amount of social mobility there. However, new attitudes have only gradually been acquired as a result of the introduction of free enterprise, communism, and expanding suffrage within representative institutions. The notion of equal opportunity coexists with a sense of clear class hierarchies in the minds of many people; the hierarchies have not been destroyed by the process of opening up equal opportunity.

Furthermore, as we shall see in part 4, both Germany and the United Kingdom have passed laws to assure that wide portions of the populace acquire housing, medical care, pensions, and other benefits. Students with good academic records can receive free educations through the university level, helping them acquire good jobs regardless of their social backgrounds. Princes, dukes, kings, and town guilds were obliged to provide some such services; after the onset of the Industrial Revolution, these services were resumed on a national level with strong backing from those same leaders.[21] In West Germany and the United Kingdom, benefits supported by all major political parties include unemployment compensation and universal medical care. In East Germany, they were extended to include

guaranteed jobs, and many there probably still believe that this is their right.

Yet nobility continue to own over a third of the land in the United Kingdom[22] and large tracts in West Germany. The upper military officer's corps in those two countries still contain many officers from titled noble families; after reunification, the nobility began reclaiming titles and ancestral homes in East Germany. These titled families have a tendency to associate with other aristocrats, send their children to exclusive schools, maintain a distance from those who are gaining social mobility and those they feel are beneath them socially, believe in old (but not new) monopolistic privileges, and share a number of other ideas incompatible with equality of opportunity. In response to the continuation of this system of nobility, prominent members of both the Conservative and Labour parties have proposed doing away with Britain's House of Lords and replacing it with an elected upper house.

The United Kingdom accorded Commonwealth status to former colonies, extending citizenship to some colonial subjects. As a result, many Pakistanis, Indians, West Indians from the Caribbean, and other ethnic groups have migrated to the British Isles. They have not been welcomed by all segments of the populace, but they have been accorded equal rights under the law. In Northern Ireland, Catholics complain that Ulster protestants deny them equal rights. The West Germans admitted many Turks, Yugoslavs, and others to ease former labor shortages of unskilled and semiskilled manual labor. The government created some social programs for these groups, who tend to have a much lower standard of living than German citizens. The strong reemergence of anti-Semitic, anti-gypsy, and anti-Polish sentiments in East Germany is a reminder that the regime there did little to counteract those attitudes; efforts to do so in the West have not prevented strong resentment of the East Europeans seeking asylum there, either.

Russia began with class hierarchy; tsars tightened and loosened their control over the serfs and occasionally let serfs become nobles. This made Russia's class hierarchy less clear than those in

Britain and Germany. All three of these nation-states have, during the last two centuries, gradually created equal opportunities for all classes of people to engage in commerce and enter political institutions.

China, in contrast, long ago devised a system in which all Han boys had equal opportunity to rise to the highest political offices, while a rigid class hierarchy was maintained without noble classes. China outlawed feudal serfdom in the third century B.C. and introduced imperial courts (palaces with emperors and their officials) ruled by the teachings of the philosopher Confucius and speaking a dialect of the Chinese language eventually called Mandarin. The emperors ruled in conjunction with **literati,** scholar-officials who achieved their positions by passing rigid examinations in Mandarin language and culture (and who were therefore themselves sometimes called Mandarins). The literati could come from any class; those who passed the exams were usually sons of literati or came from educated urban families, but some were peasants.[23] In theory, anyone could petition the emperor, directly or through these literati, if they thought the literati were abusing their privileges. In addition, commoners could rise to prominence by becoming the wives[24] or concubines of emperors, or by becoming eunuchs in the imperial court. If drought, famine, or other hardship struck the land, people might decide the emperor had lost the Mandate of Heaven (heaven's blessing) and follow a revolt led by a soldier or ordinary citizen, who would overthrow the emperor and found a new dynasty. Thus, there was considerable chance for common people to rise to the top. But under Confucian traditions, people have always been highly conscious of their social roles and have given great deference to those in authority over them: children to parents, wives to husbands, younger brothers to older brothers, families to community leaders, community leaders to literati, literati to the emperor's court. No one would dare organize a political grouping to challenge any part of that hierarchy, except in secret.

Today these traditions largely continue, with some modifications. One major modification is in the role of women in the family and community. In traditional Confucian thought, women had no standing other than subordination. The emperor married common women; after the death of an emperor, his wives and heirs (other than the next emperor) no longer enjoyed high social status. Women, even from families with wealth and status, were expected to defer completely to their husbands, who were permitted to physically and psychologically mistreat them. They could own no property, received no education, and were expected to do the most menial work. The Communist Revolution attempted to give women greater status, at least in theory. Single women acquired jobs within townships, cooperatives, and factories, just as men did. They are entitled to own property, seek redress from the community if their husbands maltreat them, hold political office, help conduct community affairs, and strive for higher education and high-status jobs. In rural areas, their progress in these realms has been slow. But among the more educated urban Chinese, these new ideas are becoming firmly rooted; we shall look at some of the results of these new attitudes in part 4. Yet most of the highest village, town, city, provincial, and national leadership positions still go to males, and these councils govern most aspects of people's lives.[25]

Beyond this, current approaches to ensuring equal access to political institutions are quite traditional. Han do not view themselves as having individual representation in politics. In any given situation, one's behavior and rights depend on how one is related to the other person. Sons simply do not disobey fathers, and subjects do not disobey rulers. Interest groups may not challenge those in the political hierarchy; they may not even form without its permission. And individuals may not disobey the decisions of those who lead their groups. Rather, individuals identify with social groups as their primary point of reference, beginning with the family. Members of the family obey family leaders, who in turn develop social networks with other kin, villagers, and the like, and conform to their norms. One's place of work—village, cooperative, or factory—deserves cooperation; it, in turn, concerns itself with the behavior and well-being of workers and their families. The family can address the political system through community and work organizations, and the political system addresses the family through the same mechanism; that is a communist addition to the hierarchy.[26] Those elected to office are expected to be educated enough, and moral enough, to represent the interests of the family, community, and work place. In reality, most top political leaders come from the small group of urban families with social standing and *guanxi* (bonds of obligation to one another), while middle cadres often come from peasant or working families; they promote their own friends for vacant positions in the party and government.[27] One author points out that as Westerners:

We tend to see people as individuals . . . basically we have one code of manners for all . . . Chinese, on the other hand, instinctively divide people into those with whom they already have . . . guanxi . . . and those with whom they don't.[28]

During the Great Proletarian Cultural Revolution,[29] in a deliberate effort to eliminate *guanxi,* or the tendency to be loyal to a group one feels an obligation to, those of higher social standing were declared of ''bad'' class background; those from ''good'' worker and peasant backgrounds were even encouraged to divorce their mates from ''bad'' backgrounds. Gradually, those from ''bad'' backgrounds regained their rights. Today, under the responsibility system and with the establishment of cooperatives and stock markets some families may, once again, become wealthier than others[30] and send sons and daughters to university at government expense. But few workers, rural people, or ethnic minority members are likely to attain the education and *guanxi* needed to enter the rigid political hierarchy, and those who have not entered it are not free to challenge it. Only those with top political status can expect to be included in control of joint ventures and other lucrative business enterprises as China explores free enterprise. The graded hierarchies of the literati tradition continue,[31] excluding the vast majority of the populace from rising high in politics, commerce, or social status.[32] They also

stand in the way of introducing representative political institutions, which have existed historically and function today in the United States, the United Kingdom, Germany, and Russia.

Muslims, Tibetans, Buddhists, Cossacks, and other ethnic minorities in China have no standing in China's hierarchical social traditions. They are largely excluded from Chinese political, economic, and cultural institutions. The government encourages them to stay in villages and on assigned land, though they are eligible for housing and other forms of assistance. Until the 1970s, their places of worship were converted to other purposes or torn down.

Communism allowed people of low birth to gain political stature in China and East Germany, and to a lesser extent in the Soviet Union; but it only allowed them to do so if they worked their way up through a system of tightly supervised rules and institutions. Former Soviet and East German citizens have been more inclined to challenge those rules and institutions than the Chinese. While Germans and Britons defer to social hierarchies, they are also ready to accept those of low birth into high social, economic, and political positions. Americans are more likely to ignore social hierarchies and have a long tradition of advocating equal opportunity. West Germans, Britons, Americans, and many former Soviets and East Germans believe that the system should recruit people for political office through free choice and elections, and that political office should be open to all citizens in good standing.

Citizens of the communist and former communist systems are more convinced than those in the other systems that government should guarantee all citizens jobs, housing, and other needs; governments in the other systems do provide some such supports because substantial percentages of their citizens agree that this should be done to assist portions of the populace who need them. Some post-Soviet and Chinese citizens (like some Indians, Peruvians, and Nigerians) would prefer to resort to harsh measures to quell protest rather than set up a system which guarantees all ethnic groups equal political and economic rights; India and Peru may have developed even more advocates of the latter position than those two systems have. The periods when the Soviet Union, China, and East Germany discriminated against those who were from the ''better'' classes undercut the concept of equal opportunity; the speed at which that discrimination ended after those periods were over indicates that attitudes of reverse class discrimination did not penetrate deeply. It is more common for the ''better'' classes to have the upper hand. Those at the top may or may not encourage those beneath them to climb. Increasingly, though haltingly, they give that encouragement.

EQUALITY AND RECRUITMENT: NEW SYSTEMS

All the systems we just discussed show considerable continuity in their traditional and current thought about class hierarchies. While beliefs about equal opportunity have evolved slowly, wide portions of the populace have accepted them.

In contrast, traditional India held views about class hierarchies very different from those of its modern leaders. Many Indians still subscribe to those traditional views and reject modern notions of equal opportunity.

In traditional India, people did not believe all individuals were equal; instead, they were born into different levels of society called castes. Each caste was associated with an occupation, and children were expected to take up the same occupations as their parents. High-caste members of the community sought to assure that all people in the community had livelihoods, a share of the food, special assistance in times of famine, seed and implements for the tasks they performed, help in building temples and celebrating holidays, materials to build houses, and gifts for personal occasions such as marriages and deaths.[33] Caste leaders met with one another to sort out these obligations. Beyond the community level, rajas and other conquering rulers governed entire regions. All levels of society owed obligations to one another, and no one rose above the traditional occupation associated with their caste. The lowest scheduled castes had such low status they could not touch members of other castes or the food they ate;

Guard at the entrance to the rajah's palace, Jaipur, India.
Bob Gamer

as ''untouchables,'' they could not associate in any way with members of other castes.

Modern urban Indians, however, consider it acceptable for even those from untouchable castes, both male and female, and from all ethnic groups, to rise high in commerce and politics. Only a small, educated segment of the populace has been socialized into this modern view, which British administrators introduced to English-educated Indians. Many of those administrators came from the British working class and believed in their own and others' right to social mobility; they treated Indians as social inferiors, yet applauded efforts to end caste and other social barriers within India. Many English-educated Indians rose from lower positions in society to become wealthier than some higher-caste Indians (who sometimes resent this).[34] While they want social barriers removed, these modern Indian citizens give little support to programs which would assist those without access to food, clothing, and shelter. To emphasize that they are still a part of society, these individuals who have abandoned traditional caste roles often observe Hinduism in rituals and personal habits; ironically, in abandoning the caste system, they have also abandoned the traditional Hindu obligation to assure the well-being of those in the lower, less fortunate castes.

Most Indians remain highly sensitive to caste in their dress, eating habits, and social practices, and have little social contact with people who practice other religions. Even traditionalists who believe in caste, however, may be losing their sense of obligation to the lower castes; they no longer feel it necessary to assure that people of all castes have access to jobs, food, land, and assistance in times of emergency.[35] Nor do they think the national government should be involved in assuring those rights, especially to untouchables. Thus, neither view, modern or traditionalist, advocates a firm belief that humans should be equal. Nowhere is that more obvious than in the uneven status of Indian women, who are revered in some regards, downtrodden in others. Especially in the south of India, many ancient religious traditions survive. Female goddesses are thought to have great power; this belief is perhaps a vestige of the period before the Aryan conquests from the north imposed greater male control on a society which gave women great latitude. Among the Nayars of Malabar in Kerela, women could have multiple husbands, and they were not permitted to live in her house. At the other extreme, many high caste princes practiced **sati;** their wives and concubines were burned alive with them on their funeral pyres. In their efforts to gain control of India, the British were quick to outlaw the Nayar women's multiple husbands, but slower to outlaw sati (practiced by princes who were their political allies).[36]

The Congress party, taking its cue from the British, recognized that its ability to stay in rule depended on walking a tight line between modern notions of equal opportunity and traditional caste hierarchies. A coalition of parties led by V. P. Singh upset Congress-party rule in 1989 and raised this dichotomy to a major political issue. Though the parties in his coalition believe in a return to traditional religious values, Singh strongly advocated equality; he wanted to give special quotas of government jobs and university admissions to lower castes. He also resisted the demands of his own political partners, the Bharatiya Janata Party (BJP), that a Muslim mosque be removed from atop an ancient Hindu temple site at Ayodhya. Singh even sent troops in to stop BJP supporters who were attempting to tear the mosque down. The BJP advocates a return to traditional Hindu principles and a rejection of conquering Muslim influences, rather than equal opportunities for all groups. They have many supporters, even among modernized Indians. Singh soon lost the confidence of the Parliament and was replaced. In the 1991 election, his Janata Dal party dropped from 142 to 46 seats, while the BJP rose from 11.5 percent of the popular vote and 86 seats to 23 percent of the vote and 102 seats. No party won a majority of seats.[37] The dramatic events that then transpired are discussed in chapter 17; they make it clear that equality issues—such as whether old mosques will be torn down to build new Hindu temples, or whether untouchables and Muslims will have political rights—are likely to remain unsettled for the indeterminate future.

There is no solid basis for class or ethnic equality in India. Few from villages or urban squatter slums gain higher educations or achieve political office; even the leadership of the BJP and the communist parties are highly urbane and educated. The BJP's urban constituents are often those of high caste who resent establishing quotas to give jobs and educations to untouchables; although the party taps votes from traditional villagers, it does not recruit them into political institutions or advance programs to economically assist this portion of its constituency.

Peru presents a picture of a different sort. Its traditional villages combined notions of class hierarchy and equal opportunity; its modern leaders subscribe to a different notion of class hierarchy while largely rejecting equal opportunity. Traditional highland peasant villages were marked by class divisions. They were ruled by indigenous village authorities chosen by the heads of families. But the village authority saw to it that all families had land. Families often cooperated to mend fields, build one another's houses, repair roads and bridges, and plant and harvest in a work-sharing system called **minka,** which encouraged cooperation among community members to spread benefits to the community. They maintained religious structures, and assumed responsibility for the sick and the elderly. Higher-status families had houses built of better-finished stone and wore better clothing and jewelry; their living conditions were otherwise similar.[38]

The Spanish introduced a system in which they had higher status than all Quechua and Aymara. They even made themselves superior in status to the Spanish born in America (**criollos**). The Spanish did at least recognize the Quechua and Aymara individuals who had descended from leading families in the former empire as having higher status than others from their ethnic backgrounds. Nineteenth-century immigrants from other parts of Europe who established large commercial firms also viewed themselves as having higher social status; but, as we shall see in chapter 17, they removed some of the privileges the Spanish accorded to some of the Quechua and Aymara and left many landless. In the pre-Conquest society, *minka* had symbolized cooperation among equals to benefit the entire community. In the post-Conquest society, it was used to conscript the labor of landless workers who had no community or political rights. The new rulers used the free labor of highland peasants to work mines and *haciendas,* and to build the new road system during the 1920s, calling the conscripted labor *minka.* Thus, the status system of the post-Conquest society replaced that of the former society. Leaders neither believed in equality for all, or in the obligations of those of higher status to those they deemed

below them. As we have already learned, Quechua and Aymara who did not learn Spanish were not even allowed to vote until 1979. They still have not begun to enter the nation-state's political institutions beyond the village level. As we shall see in subsequent chapters, the rare government programs designed to assist them economically have received little support from the Spanish-speaking community.

Within Nigerian villages, families largely perceived and treated one another as equals. Family elders and headmen ruled the villages and (though they themselves had some privileges) made sure that all members had land or equal access to hunting and gathering. All lived in fairly similar houses. They formed societies to cooperate on building houses, conducting ceremonies, planting and harvesting, hunting, and other tasks. But they often viewed other tribal groups as inferior, and at times took members of some of these groups as slaves. Though they could not hold office and had lower social status, these people took part in community associations, tilled their own patches of land, and shared in other community resources along with their owners. Tribes in the north developed more sophisticated empires than those in the south, with classes of warriors and nobles who had hereditary titles and Muslim scholar-officials with status in the courts.[39] Many who received higher education during the nineteenth and twentieth centuries came from the south, especially from among the Yoruba and Ibo, and were not exposed to the sort of hierarchical structure that had evolved in the north. They might think of their own tribe as being socially superior to others, but they tend not to have strong beliefs that one social class should have more privileges than another. Ibo have also allowed women to play strong social and economic roles. But the concept that all tribes should have equal opportunities and rewards, imported from Britain, had little chance to reach villagers. And many of those first exposed to British education, whether offspring of headmen or of less influential parents, have sought to pass education and political offices along to their own children and thus exclude others from social mobility.

The hierarchies created by the Nigerian army, bureaucracy, and other political elites are all very recent imports. No one social elite commands deference. The notion that people from all tribes are equal is incomprehensible to many people. Most people have not become part of a national economy and know little about national laws or institutions. They are more inclined to continue observing traditional social and political obligations and to let themselves be represented in national politics by those who held high positions in their tribes or social groups. As leaders of such isolated and insular groups, those leaders have little incentive to advocate modern ideas about equal rights or national government assistance for all groups and classes. And the national hierarchies of the army and bureaucracy easily lose contact with those at the local level; programs to provide health care, emergency economic aid, or other economic benefits to villagers and urban poor have been occasional and minimal.

Hence, in India, Peru, and Nigeria, large portions of the populace have no opportunity to be recruited into politics. No national programs are in place to assure that jobs, food, shelter, medical care or other necessities will be made available to those who need them.

CONCLUSION: BELIEFS ABOUT EQUALITY AND RECRUITMENT

We have established that the United States and the CIS republics have long traditions emphasizing equality for all classes; in the CIS republics, these traditions evolved even when the society operated under a tsar and nobility. Ideas about equality for all ethnic groups have probably advanced more rapidly in the United States than in the CIS republics. The United Kingdom and Germany have more socially stratified societies but have gradually introduced equal opportunity for all groups to seek political office. The United Kingdom is more liberal about admitting outside ethnic groups into citizenship. East Germany did little to combat anti-Semitism,

anti-gypsy, anti-Polish, and other ethnic prejudices, and West Germans have expressed concerns about the influx of eastern European immigrants during the early 1990s. The traditional Chinese hierarchy allowed for the continuous infusion of fresh recruits from lower levels of society; this system continues, but seldom extends to those from minority ethnic groups or allows lower classes to reach the top. India, Peru, and Nigeria experience less continuity than that. India has a socially and ethnically stratified society; portions of its central leadership oppose that stratification, while others strongly desire to retain it. Peru has several layered social strata; they do not relate clearly to one another, in a hierarchy, but instead coexist without much political or economic intercourse. Parts of Nigeria observe traditions emphasizing relative class equality, while other parts have traditions emphasizing hierarchical social stratification; the national political and bureaucratic hierarchy is separate from both groups, and no political party has developed to bring together those who advocate equality among classes and races.

Americans like to think that individuals can enter politics without representing any particular group. Britons and Germans, and citizens in the CIS republics, while sharing that view, also think in terms of providing different ranks of people with formal representation at various levels of government. The right of an individual from a particular group to vote or enter political institutions is different from the right of that individual's group to be represented; the latter three systems (the United Kingdom, Germany, and the CIS) make provisions to assure that certain groups are represented in legislatures, in keeping with long-held traditions.

China has no tradition of representing groups or individuals in politics. The Chinese do believe that individuals from any social background should be able to become public officials if they acquire the proper education. Those officials then have obligations to look after the welfare of all families. Groups outside the family, work place, bureaucracy, and ruling party may not organize to influence those public officials.

India, Peru, and Nigeria fit neither of these scenarios. Although groups and individuals have traditionally been represented in community politics, those traditions do not relate to contemporary national politics. Leaders' attitudes about representation differ from those of much of the populace. It is easier for leaders to identify with the few people in the countryside they perceive to have "modern" ideas about equality, mobility, and authority than to those who seem to prefer older systems of stratification. And the majority who prefer the older systems have little opportunity to be recruited into national political office.

SUMMARY

Belief in a social hierarchy and in equal opportunity are not necessarily mutually exclusive; people can respect those above them in a social hierarchy and still believe in equal opportunity to rise socially, educationally, politically, and economically. In the United States (where people are often not very conscious of social class) and in the United Kingdom and Germany (where they are), people from increasingly diverse backgrounds compete and achieve a base level of benefits in these four realms. Many people in these systems believe in equal opportunity to improve one's status but disagree about how far government and society should go in encouraging it. Over the past few decades, the Soviet Union and China have made intense efforts to help people from a variety of ethnic groups and social classes improve their status, though lingering ethnic traditions often thwart the provision of equal opportunity for all ethnic groups. In contrast, Indians, Peruvians, and Nigerians often respect local elites who have no standing in national politics, cannot help them enter political institutions or obtain other benefits, and do not believe in equal opportunities for all groups. And national elites who profess to believe in equal opportunity try to disrupt the social hierarchies these local elites emerge from. These two sets of elites even disagree on the meaning of social, educational, and economic opportunity.

NOTES

1. Reeve Vanneman and Lynn Weber Cannon, *The American Perception of Class* (Philadelphia: Temple University Press, 1987), pp. 129, 153.

2. In a 1942 Gallup poll, 98 percent said they did not think it was a good idea to have "titles like Lord, Duke, and Sir in this country the way they have in England." In a poll conducted during the 1960s, 98 percent agreed that "everyone in America should have equal opportunities to get ahead." Herbert McClosky and John Zaller, *The American Ethos: Public Attitudes toward Capitalism and Democracy* (Cambridge, Mass.: Harvard University Press, 1984), pp. 74, 83.

3. For novels, plays, and short stories that offer insight into these attitudes, see Count Leo Tolstoy (a member of the nobility who later in life tried to give up this status), *Master and Man* and *Resurrection*; Anton Chekhov (himself the grandson of a serf) *The Cherry Orchard, Uncle Vanya, The Peasants, Gooseberries, In the Ravine, Daydreams, At the Mill,* and *An Encounter*; Ivan Turgenev (son of landed wealth) *Fathers and Sons* and *Virgin Soil*; Nikolai Gogol (son of a Cossack) *Dead Souls* and *The Inspector General*; Feodor Dostoyevsky (whose father owned serfs) *Poor Folk*; and Maxim Gorky (orphaned from a peasant mother) *The Smug Citizens* and *The Lower Depths*.

4. During the 1990s, pictures of tsars returned to the walls of many homes. Families who resented the privileges of communist *nomenklatura* could without contradiction look back fondly to the tsars, who were often perceived to side with the people against the privileged nobility who held power and rank.

5. In 1991, the Communist Party adopted a charter which for the first time endorsed freedom of religion.

6. Only those who were citizens June 17, 1940, when the Soviet Union invaded Latvia, and their offspring, could be citizens.

7. Russian humor is filled with references to this resentment. For example, in one joke, a French

person, a Briton, and a Russian are asked what they would like if they could get one wish. The French citizen chooses a chalet, and the Briton a country cottage. The Russian replies: "My neighbor has a goat; kill the neighbor's goat." Yet, a poll early in 1991 found 43 percent thought inequalities in wealth were justified; a poll after the attempted coup later that year found 75 percent thought them justified. "Russia's Future," *The Economist,* December 7, 1991.

8. A 1991 Times-Mirror poll found only 23 percent of Americans, versus 68 to 70 percent of Lithuanians, Ukrainians, and Russians, 64 percent of East Germans, 45 percent of West Germans, and 62 percent of Britons, agreeing that "it is the responsibility of the government to take care of very poor people who can't take care of themselves." Thirty-four percent of Americans, 9 percent of Britons, and 13 percent of Germans disagreed with the statement that "the government should guarantee every citizen food and basic shelter." *Christian Science Monitor,* November 22, 1991.

9. In surveys during the 1960s, 95 percent of Americans agreed that every citizen should have an equal chance to influence government policy, and 91 percent agreed that everyone should have an equal right to hold public office. McCloskey and Zaller, *American Ethos,* p. 74. Yet in 1958, only 40 percent of poll respondents indicated they would vote for a black for president "if he[!] were qualified for the job"; in the 1980s, 85 percent responded that they would. Seymour Martin Lipset, "Blacks and Jews: How Much Bias?" *Public Opinion,* July/August 1987, p. 5.

10. Richard D. Heffner, ed., Alexis DeToqueville, *Democracy in America* (New York: Mentor, 1956), p. 291.

11. As we saw in chapter 2, a third of the deputies in the Congress of People's Deputies were chosen to represent certain social and economic groups.

12. Serge Schemann, "U.S., Soviet Illusions About Each Other Fade," *Kansas City Star,* July 29, 1991. Schemann also records this anecdote: 'One Soviet woman went to an American doctor and tried to strike up a conversation about Toulouse-Lautrec,' said Tatyana Tolstaya, a writer who spends much of her time in the United States. 'She was shocked that he had no idea who he was. Our doctor typically would have known all about Toulouse-Lautrec, though he would have only a vague idea where her liver is.'

13. See chapter 4.

14. Forty nine percent of the members of the first Bundestag in 1949 were manual or lower-level white collar workers. John D. Nagle, "Elite Transformations in a Pluralist Democracy: Occupational and Educational Backgrounds of Bundestag Members, 1949–1972" (manuscript, Syracuse University, 1974), quoted in David P. Conradt, *The German Polity* (New York: Longman, 1978), pp. 130–31.

15. E. Sagarra, *Social History of Germany 1648–1914* (London: Methuen, 1977), p. 186. See also Hans Rosenberg, *Bureaucracy, Aristocracy, and Autocracy: The Prussian Experience, 1660–1815* (Boston: Beacon Press, 1966).

16. See chapter 11.

17. In 1525, just after the start of the Protestant Reformation, only 5 percent of the populace was literate in northern Germany. By 1675 in New England, 95 percent of the populace was literate (though few were literate in the American South). Over the subsequent two centuries, literacy spread elsewhere in Europe. Robert Marquand, "Bible Reading Altered History," *Christian Science Monitor,* November 13, 1991.

18. Bavaria gave public support to Catholic education; elsewhere, children were educated in public schools.

19. Heffner, ed., DeToqueville, *Democracy,* pp. 221–22.

20. After they leave office, prime ministers are normally awarded life peerages. Prime Minister John Majors's father was a circus performer; Margaret Thatcher, Majors's predecessor, grew up above her father's corner grocery store. After she left office, Queen Elizabeth gave Thatcher's husband Denis the hereditary title of baron and made Thatcher an hereditary countess, the first created in two centuries. Upon the death of Countess Thatcher, her son Mark will become a Viscount. That could set a precedent to award hereditary peerages to future retiring prime ministers.

21. The Conservative Party under Disraeli introduced many of these reforms in Britain during the 1870s; Bismarck did the same in Germany during the 1880s with the cooperation of Emperor Frederick III and of conservatives in parliament.

22. See chapter 8.

23. The literati examinations were open to anyone. Chinese villagers might help a bright youth from

their village obtain the time and tutoring necessary to study for them.

24. Sometimes the wife would remain on as Empress Dowager while her young son took the throne; Empress Dowagers wielding power behind the scenes are a common part of Chinese history. Emperors had more than one wife, plus concubines. If the son of another wife took the throne, it would end the power of an Empress Dowager. Other offspring of these wives and concubines did not become nobility.

25. The movie *Ju Dou* concerns the wife of the owner of a cloth dyeing mill, who is severely abused by her husband and falls in love with and has a son by one of his poor relatives. In the end, the son and the village council of elders side with the abusive husband. Though the story takes place during the 1920s, it has been heavily criticized by the current leadership, who fear that audiences might imagine such actions and attitudes continue today.

26. See Andrew G. Walder, *Communist Neo-Traditionalism: Work and Authority in Chinese Industry* (Berkeley: University of California Press, 1986) and Vivienne Shue, *The Reach of the State: Sketches of the Chinese Body Politic* (Stanford: Stanford University Press, 1988) for two differing views on this.

27. See chapter 10. Mao Zedong's social origins were relatively humble, but most other leaders of the new regime came from educated families. Many of these are still in power, or just retiring.

28. Fox Butterfield, *China: Alive in a Bitter Sea* (London: Coronet, 1983), pp. 74–75.

29. See chapter 21.

30. Before 1978, former landlords were classified as class enemies, and thus found themselves restricted from economic and political advancement. Since that time this distinction has been erased, and some of them have become heads of production teams and excelled in production on their land, which they now may lease. Hence, there is some continuity between those peasants who were wealthy, and those who are now (provided they lived through the killings of the 1950s discussed in chapter 21). John P. Burns, "Chinese Peasant Interest Articulation," in David S. G. Goodman, ed., *Groups and Politics in the People's Republic of China* (Cardiff, England: University of Cardiff Press, 1984), p. 141.

31. Cadres and bureaucrats are expected to have more education than most others in the community. Formerly, the education consisted of learning the Confucian classics, language, and decorum; today, it is expected to include Marxist ideology, science, management, and other modern subjects.

32. See John Wilson Lewis, *Political Networks and the Chinese Policy Process* (Stanford: Northeast Asia-United States Forum on International Policy, 1986); Susan Shirk, *Competitive Comrades* (Berkeley: University of California Press, 1982).

33. See E. Kathleen Gough, "Caste in a Tanjore Village," in E. R. Leach, ed., *Aspects of Caste in South India, Ceylon, and North-West Pakistan* (Cambridge: Cambridge University Press, 1969), pp. 11–60.

34. For insight into this, see Paul Scott's novels, *Staying On* (New York: Morrow, 1977) and *The Raj Quartet* (London: Heineman, 1976).

35. It is common for Indian citizens to engage in individual charity, regularly setting out food for a family of unemployed untouchables or giving to certain beggars. But entire castes are no longer deemed to have a legal or moral right to food, clothing, and shelter.

36. Joanna Liddle and Rama Joshi, *Daughters of Independence: Gender, Caste, and Class in India* (London: Zed, 1986).

37. Government in India has been increasingly fractured in recent years. In 1989, Janata Dal ran in 243 districts, while in 1991 it ran in 317; during the same period, BJP more than doubled the number of districts it contested, from 227 to 479. The Congress party rose from 197 to 217 seats, but the increase in activity from other parties forced its leader, P. V. Narasimha Rao, to rule in a coalition government. Hamish McDonald, "Fractured Mandate," *Far Eastern Economic Review* 152, 26, (June 27, 1991): 10–12. During the 1991 election campaign, the Congress party leader Rajiv Gandhi was killed by a Tamil militant protesting Gandhi's cooperation in putting down the Tamil rebellion in Sri Lanka. Gandhi's mother, Prime Minister Indira Gandhi, was killed by her own Sikh bodyguard in retaliation for her storming a Sikh temple to rid it of arms being used for rebellion in the Punjab. Later, Sikh leaders who tried to seek compromise in the rebellion were

assassinated. In the 1991 Punjab elections, over twenty moderate candidates were assassinated to prevent them from defeating militants who ran for office from their jail cells. When, after five years of emergency rule, elections for a state legislature were held in 1992, the militants threatened to shoot anyone who went to the polls. Turnout was 28 percent of voters—less than half the previous record low.

38. See Sally Falk Moore, *Power and Property in Inca Peru* (New York: Columbia University Press, 1958), and Christine Hastorf, *Resources in Power: Agriculture and the Onset of Political Inequality before the Inca.* (New York: Cambridge University Press, 1993).

39. See H. A. S. Johnston, *The Fulani Empire of Sokoto* (London: Oxford University Press, 1967); Siegfried F. Nadel, *A Black Byzantium* (London: Oxford University Press, 1951); Daryll Forde, "The Governmental Roles of Associations Among the Yako," in Ronald Cohen and John Middleton, eds., *Comparative Political Systems* (Garden City, N.Y.: Natural History Press, 1967), pp. 121–41; Sara Berry, *Fathers Work for their Sons: Accumulation, Mobility, and Class Formation in an Extended Yoruba Community* (Berkeley: University of California Press, 1985); Michael Watts, *Silent Violence: Food, Famine, and Peasantry in Northern Nigeria* (Berkeley: University of California Press, 1983); Ikenna Nzimiro, *Studies in Ibo Political Systems: Chieftaincy and Politics in Four Niger States* (Berkeley: University of California Press, 1972); and G. I. Jones, "Councils Among the Central Ibo," in Audrey Richards and Adam Kuper, eds., *Councils in Action* (Cambridge: Cambridge University Press, 1971), pp. 63–79.

EXERCISES

Think about the book thus far:

1. This chapter discusses the second and third of what six attitudes?
2. Are the systems with political cultures that most support equality those where the highest portion of the populace identify with their nation-state?

KEY WORDS AND PHRASES

Define the following terms:

equal opportunity	obrok	class hierarchy
class consciousness	reverse class consciousness	literati
boyar	life peer	sati
serf	Reichstag	minka
barshchina	Magna Charta	criollos
Cossack	gentry	

Answer each of the following two questions in one sentence:

1. What do boyars, Cossacks, literati, gentry, and some English-educated Indians have in common?
2. Why is it hard to introduce representative institutions in China?

THINKING IT THROUGH

1. Fill out the following chart by giving an example of something that promotes equality in each of these systems, and something which discourages it.

	Promotes Equality	Discourages Equality
USA		
CIS		
FRG		
GDR		
UK		
PRC		
RI		
RP		
FRN		

Now, ask yourself:

2. The text suggests that leaders in Peru, India, and Nigeria have different ideas than most of their citizens about who should be recruited into prominent social and political positions. Is that a bigger obstacle to equality than some of the points you just listed in the right-hand column? Does it promote equality?

3. Is it more even handed to represent groups, or individuals, in legislatures?

4. Contrast attitudes toward equality in the CIS republics and the United States with those in Germany or the United Kingdom.

chapter 16

POLITICAL CULTURE

POWER AND AUTHORITY

In examining political culture, we have thus far explored the extent to which people identify with their nation and believe other citizens have a right to share in ruling the nation and in the benefits it affords. Now we will focus, in this chapter and the next, on people's attitudes toward government and leaders. This chapter looks at the way people view those who exert influence and how they confer authority in their own minds. The next chapter examines the way people approach the law.

We turn now to the fourth of the six aspects of political culture, attitudes toward power and authority. **How do attitudes toward power and authority affect the ability of citizens to place limits on the authority of political leaders?**

The leaders of all these systems argue that authority derives from the people. Elections are held and laws passed to legitimate certain institutions—to give them **legitimacy,** or the legal authority to exercise sovereignty. The word *legitimacy* derives from the Latin *legis,* which means law. Sovereignty is sometimes exercised in accordance with law, and sometimes not. But, ultimately, the legitimacy of laws or elections depends on whether citizens and other nation-states recognize their validity. Citizens may have three attitudes toward the laws which legitimate authority:

1. They may feel they should obey laws, and those who make and enforce them, but perhaps not obey officeholders who do not comply with the law.

2. They may feel they should obey laws, but sometimes withhold authority from those legitimately entitled to it while authorizing others to exert sovereignty unlawfully.

3. They may feel they need not obey laws because those exercising sovereignty have no authority to make them.

Influence, as we have defined it, is the capability to change the attitudes and behaviors of others; one can have such a capacity without actually using it. Power, as we defined it in chapter 13, is success at exerting influence. And authority (viewed from this angle) is the influence conferred by others' willing acceptance of one's right to make laws and issue commands and to expect compliance with them.[1] Clearly, citizens who fall in categories (1) and (3) feel that those successful at exerting power in government and political institutions do not always have the right to do so, especially when they fail to obey the laws they themselves make. Those in category (2) may be ambivalent—simultaneously attracted and repulsed—in their attitudes toward persons with such power; that may at times give leaders authority even when they are not obeying the law or remove authority from them even when they are.

LEGITIMATE AUTHORITY AS LAWFUL EXERCISE OF POWER

For differing reasons, citizens of the United Kingdom and Germany tend to feel (as in category 1) that officeholders should rigidly adhere to laws.

Citizens of the United Kingdom normally show little interest in seeing people with authority, such as the prime minister,[2] and are reserved as to what they anticipate such individuals will accomplish.[3] They often view politics as a clash between parties organized around class, but they are willing to vote for parties associated with a class other than their own. British citizens view power as shifting not from one person to another, but from one party philosophy to another. They are willing to accord considerable authority to the leader of the party which controls the Cabinet and the House of Commons without placing complicated restrictions on that authority. They know a new election or vote in Parliament can remove that leader from power at any time and that he or she operates under the legal limits discussed in the next chapter. So the system itself limits the authority of their leaders. One observer comments:

> They do not have the habit of making life difficult for government, especially a strong government. . . . This preference, which is for strong government over accountable government, is seen in the ascendancy of executive over legislature, in the whipped passivity of parliamentary parties, in the vast range of things government does under the most vestigial democratic control.[4]

Germans are more reticent than the British to talk about or become involved in politics. Germany's traditions of deferring to civil servants and other authorities, and of presuming they will act for the common good, seem to be firmly entrenched among older people but declining among the

young.[5] During the seventeenth century, the Thirty Years War ravaged Germany. Catholic and protestant princes declared war on one another, and Sweden and France took sides with some of them. Half the population of Germany was killed. Much of the northeast was devastated. The princes burned the free towns, looted their wealth, and took them over. Kings ceased to exercise the few powers they formerly had. It became clear that to survive, one had to quietly support whoever had a firm hold on and the ability to write laws for one's territory. The war left behind 1,800 separate German states; later wars consolidated them.

These historical experiences taught Germans to be cautious about participating in politics,[6] retain a rigid **hierarchy** (a structure with clear ranks, each submissive to the one above it) in government and civil service, and allow their leaders long terms in office. West Germany has had six chancellors since World War II; in the same period, Britain has had eleven prime ministers, India eight prime ministers (one of whom served twice), and the United States ten presidents. The German people do not seem disturbed by the notion that a lot of power might reside with one individual for a long period of time. The national parties are organized somewhat around class lines, but seek to incorporate all major interests within their ranks. East Germany's ruling party also sought to do this.

Both the United Kingdom and Germany partition authority between various levels of government in an orderly manner. The "King (or Queen) in Parliament" presumably holds the highest authority in the United Kingdom. In practice (as we have seen), the prime minister, consulting with the cabinet and Parliament, exercises this authority. In many ways, this division is convenient; one can question the judgment of the prime minister without feeling unpatriotic because the king or queen, who does not direct policy, is the ceremonial head of the nation. Some authority also resides with the cabinet, civil service, political parties, and local levels of government. The civil service, which promotes within its own ranks independent of the cabinet and organized interest groups, is traditionally consulted on impor-

This portion of the East German side of the Berlin Wall became a mile-long art gallery during the final months of East Germany's existence. Artists filled it with political commentary. This poster portrays East Germany's former leader Eric Honecker ardently kissing former Soviet leader Leonid Brezhnev. The caption reads ''God help me to survive this deadly love affair.''

© *Gary Widmar*

tant cabinet decisions. Political parties formally organize outside of Parliament and pass resolutions at party gatherings which sometimes influence the cabinet. Cities and towns have some decision-making authority, as do the governments of Scotland, Wales, and Northern Ireland. The courts may review certain government actions.

West Germany's ministries, chancellor, two houses of parliament, judiciary, states, and cities all have legal authority. The same was true of East Germany's prime minister, parliament, and cities; reunification required little change in this arrangement beyond the addition of states. The responsibilities of each of these German institutions are clearly and carefully defined, and they change infrequently and only after extensive deliberation—though sometimes individuals deviate from them on an informal

basis. While West Germany's competitive elections afforded more chance for people to choose their leaders, other clearly defined rules assured citizens in both East and West that initiatives supported by various groups of people would be carried out. This formal system of laws and rules reinforces public willingness to confer authority without additional limits and for long periods of time. It is clear who has legitimacy to write and execute laws, and how to review their actions in the courts; citizens accept that.

The Chinese, too, recognize the absolute right of their leaders to write laws and command obedience. In times of peace and general prosperity, the people are disinclined to question this authority, though they may sometimes ignore it in practice. They have a saying: ''Heaven is high, and the emperor is far away,'' meaning that people are obedient to authority, but less obedient when that authority is not directly present. The Chinese like to cite rules, yet they also like to break them. They may outright refuse to obey an emperor who has proved inadequate to handle China's problems. Historically, when China suffered war, fights between the civilian and military authorities, foreign conquest, or famine, people sometimes rebelled, threw out the emperor, and replaced him with a new one. But then they returned to an attitude of trust in and absolute refusal to question the authority of the new leader.

The authority conferred in this way partitions power by dividing responsibilities, but not in terms of assigning exclusive privileges to different levels of government. Politics, in Confucian thought, should create harmony between the family at one end and the national leader at the other. That leader has a personal ''Mandate from Heaven'' to lead, quite apart from any human institutions. Rather than partitioning power into separate spheres of authority, with different levels of government authorized to check one another, the Chinese view power as a continuum. Each level of government has responsibilities and is expected to exercise discretion in carrying them out. Periodically, the central government may ask for shifts in bearing the responsibilities.[7] In practice, the *literati* and their successor government officials have always developed special *guanxi* relationships—bonds of mutual obligation—with tightly entrenched local leaders who seek privilege for themselves and their regions.[8] The period when warlords flourished during the decades prior to World War II strengthened this tendency even more. The connections of the late General Xu Shiyou with survivors of the Long March shielded Jiangsu province from some of the excesses of the Cultural Revolution; the connections of the father of the Governor of Guandong has helped it secure special treatment.[9] But the participants in such dealings understand that the decisions made are subject to review both from above and below; decisions can be overruled or ignored. This reinforces the tendency to obey lower officials, who are closer at hand, even when they momentarily disagree with the central

government, or emperor, who is far away. People may sometimes ignore the top leader, but they are prepared to obey without reservation when he calls for obedience. This happens even after abrupt shifts in policy emerge from the top.[10]

Tibetans, and many Turkic and Mongolian people, do not share in that perception of authority. They would prefer not to be part of China, and they do not confer authority to the Chinese government in philosophy or in practice.

Britons and Germans have great respect for laws. In the United Kingdom, Germany, and China, most citizens feel that the officials who occupy formal positions in the hierarchy have the right to exercise sovereignty; when they speak, people obey. Han Chinese (for reasons which will become still clearer in chapter 17) have more respect for those officials than for any particular laws, and respect those officials more in their presence than when they are far away; this leaves some leeway for officials to exercise power unlawfully.

AMBIVALENCE ABOUT POWER, AUTHORITY, AND LEGITIMACY

Americans, in contrast to Britons, Germans, and Chinese, prefer a government structure without hierarchy—without ranks making one part of government submissive to the one above it. Americans prefer to scatter authority among various institutions not clearly submissive to one another. In some situations, this results in confusion—no one knows for sure who is authorized to exercise sovereignty in a given situation. Moreover, citizens themselves sometimes withhold authority from individuals and institutions entitled by law to exercise sovereignty, and instead give authorization to individuals or institutions exercising power unlawfully. Americans show ambivalence toward power and authority; they are both repelled by it and attracted to it. They show much interest in media stories about people with power in all kinds of realms (government, business, entertainment, media), and they like to see such people when they come to town. They can develop enthusiasm for candidates largely on the basis of personality and image, accompanied by high hopes as to what such an individual can accomplish. Their trust in government—and in individual leaders—veers up and down.[11] But in response to questions about whether they trust the government with regard to particular issues, or whether they trust particular institutions, they often respond negatively.[12] They surround their leaders with restrictions; yet they want to see those leaders act forcefully and vigorously. They do not feel comfortable cleanly vesting authority in Congress and the president; in what some analysts call an "unspoken conspiracy," voters frequently gave control of the Congress to Democrats and the presidency to Republicans.

During the nationally televised Irangate hearings in the late 1980s, the public response to Lieutenant Colonel Oliver North mirrored this ambivalence. North was accused of carrying out a scheme devised by a few high public officials to secretly trade arms to Iran in exchange for American hostages. The conspirators were also accused of diverting profits from the arms sales to covertly aid rebellious Contra forces in Nicaragua, an action Congress had rejected. North testified that he was in the habit of saluting smartly and carrying out the command when a superior ordered him to do something. He believed that what he and others did was not wrong, even though his immediate supervisors did not think he had legal authority from Congress, and even though President Reagan and North's immediate superiors contended that he was acting on his own and not carrying out the commands of the president. Although Congress had passed legislation requiring they be consulted, North argued that the president had the right to act in foreign affairs without consulting Congress; yet he also contended he had done no wrong in setting up a stand-alone agency to carry out foreign missions for the United States, staffed by private people who did not even report to the president.[13] He indicated that it was necessary for him to take matters into his own hands because Congress had been using its authority irresponsibly.[14] He also asserted that his actions were lawful, despite the fact that his supervisors disagreed; North claimed he was surprised that he was being charged with unlawful activities, since he had done what he thought was right. He said he did not inform those with formal authority of some of his actions for fear that the Congress and his immediate superiors would act irresponsibly if he did.[15]

North's comments demonstrate Americans' ambivalence about power and authority; he felt there was nothing wrong with exercising sovereignty outside the limits of the law if those with legitimate authority were acting irresponsibly. A segment of the public seemingly agreed with his actions. In polls, a third of respondents said they believed North's actions were justified and regarded him as a real patriot.[16]

Alexis DeToqueville wrote in the nineteenth century that Americans consider the majority sovereign, and government entrusted with protecting that majority. They set up "a network of small complicated rules, minute and uniform, through which the most original minds and the most energetic characters cannot penetrate, to rise above the crowd." At the same time, the government sees itself as "an immense and tutelary power, which takes upon itself alone to secure Americans' gratifications and to watch over their fate."[17] We may be critical of individual portions of our government because we are convinced that somewhere amid the complexity of the whole—it does not much matter where—the will of the majority will emerge.

The French, under the old monarchy, held it for a maxim that the king could do no wrong; and if he did do wrong, the blame was imputed to his advisors. This notion made obedience very easy; it enabled the subject to complain of the law without ceasing to love and honor the lawgiver. The Americans entertain the same opinion with respect to the majority.[18]

Many Americans find it hard to decide whether a leader claiming to act on behalf of the majority or a morally motivated minority has the authority to exert sovereignty unlawfully. Many cannot even decide which leader has the legal right to do what. Americans are often confused about legitimate authority and ambivalent about those who exercise it.

The people of the former Soviet Union are ambivalent about power and authority as well. Consider the following:

- The retreat from Stalin's era of one-person-rule into an era of rule by a directorate of leaders met warm public response. Yet Stalin was still viewed as a strong leader, and Gorbachev's efforts to point out Stalin's crimes received a cautious response from many.[19]

- Power in the Soviet Union was divided at all levels between party and governmental leaders. As opposition parties took over the governments in the union republics, autonomous republics and regions, and cities, confusion reigned as to who was in charge. In the western Ukraine, for example, the Democratic Bloc party took every seat for the region in the Ukrainian legislature (which promptly declared itself sovereign and autonomous from Moscow) and took nearly all seats in the regional and city councils themselves. But, under a decree issued by Communist Party predecessors just before they turned power over to the new leaders, the KGB, directors of collective farms, interior ministry, television stations, and Russian Orthodox churches refused to take orders from the new governments.[20]

- Everyone knew that Gosplan (the central economic planning agency), the military, and other units of government had the power to resist initiatives from top political leaders. Gorbachev's 1988 government reorganization, which strengthened the power of the president, also referred to the American concept of "checks and balances" in emphasizing that those units would still reserve powers to themselves.

- After the 1991 coup attempt against Gorbachev, the republics declared sovereignty but (except for the Baltic republics) continued to function under a central government. Finally their leaders met without President Gorbachev and declared that the nation-state he led was dissolved. The republics had not followed the laws that spelled out procedures for declaring independence and that allowed only the legislature to amend the Constitution. When the Soviet legislature refused to meet, Gorbachev tried to convene the Congress of People's Deputies, even though it had dissolved itself after the coup. Finally, Gorbachev simply declared that the reign of the Soviet Union was over.

- Leaders of the individual republics, like Gorbachev as President of the Soviet Union, sometimes pass laws through the legislature, and at other times simply issue decrees in place of passing laws.

The media show leaders of the Soviet Union and the post-Soviet republics acting assertively and without hesitation; yet we all know that change is always very slow. There is undoubtedly more confusion than ever in people's minds about where power and authority reside now, and where they should reside.

As we shall discuss in part 4, Russians are fascinated by the contrast between absolute power and anarchy. During the "Time of Troubles" in the seventeenth century, many peasants revolted by simply running away from their owners and emigrating or becoming Cossacks, and princes revolted by ignoring the tsar; it took time for central power to reassert itself. Russia's greatest strides forward came under leaders who used their power aggressively; Russian citizens like to follow such strong leadership but also like to secretly resist it. They have few traditions that lead them to try to directly exert influence on leaders. Traditionally, all authority rested with the tsar; power at other levels was not legitimate. When things went wrong, people believed it was because the tsar's advisors had misinformed him.

The United States Constitution formally partitions authority between the states and the national government. It also formally partitions authority among the three branches of the national government—Congress, the president, and the judiciary. Power can shift from one body to another when individuals who occupy the positions assert themselves. Because Americans have not made up their minds firmly about where final authority should lie, they may allow it to shift in their own minds to whomever is successful at exercising power within these various parts of government. Because everyone understands that authority is dispersed, the system can withstand these shifts in power. Laws spell out who has what powers; this makes divided authority legitimate. People believe in those laws, but they are often confused as to what they mean; the people allow an independent Supreme Court to sort out that meaning and support its right to do so. That is what makes the U.S. system of divided authority work.

Authority has never been understood to be dispersed in Russia. While people may feel ambivalent about it, and sometimes even be prone to defy it, authority has always resided at the top of a rigid hierarchy. Plans since 1988 to formally partition power among various institutions in the Soviet Union and, later, in the republics, frequently alter. In the past, people who exercised power independently of the tsar or the Communist Party were viewed as anarchists, acting outside authority.

The Union of Soviet Socialist Republics did two things to confuse the rigid hierarchy. First, as a gesture to various ethnic groups who did not like Great Russian domination, the communists alleged that they were creating a union of fifteen "sovereign" Union Republics (which, in turn, contained the "autonomous" republics for ethnic minorities), with authority divided between these republics and the central government. Then Moscow proceeded to control all those regions just as tightly as in the past. The Communist Party Politburo, dominated by Great Russians, had the last word on exercising all authority. So, even though authority was shared on paper, it was difficult for Soviet citizens to think of this arrangement as a real division of authority. But the republics had their own legislatures and would eventually declare independence. The second action the Soviet Union took that confused the issue of authority was to divide power between the organs of the political party and the organs of government, and between leaders of state industries and party functionaries; leaders at each level of government and the economy had corresponding political party functionaries. Neither set of leaders had full power over decisions, and both watched one another. This was because the Communist Party initially was suspicious of the hierarchical power exercised by the tsar and his bureaucracy, and they wanted to watch it. In doing so, they dispersed power among many of their own units at all levels. This often made it unclear who had authority to do what. As new rules are made in the republics to take power from party functionaries, it is difficult to tell where that power will now be exercised.

Both the United States and the CIS republics, then, disperse power among a number of persons and institutions. Americans accord more legitimacy to the notion of shared power than CIS citizens do. Both show ambivalence toward the exercise of power and authority, alternately applauding and decrying it. Yet CIS citizens are more uncomfortable than Americans about partitioning legitimate authority to various institutions. They may permit it to shift from a tsar to a centrally controlled communist party to a president and then perhaps even to some other supreme commander; they are reticent to confer authority upon competing institutions it cannot legally be taken away from. This makes it hard to create institutions through which citizens can exert influence and limit their leaders. Whatever their ambivalence, Americans tend to defend the proposition that particular institutions with legitimate authority have the right to keep it. They are equally prone to assert the proposition that citizens have the right to remove the leaders of those institutions, directly or indirectly, through elections. Thus, Americans expect to exert more influence through political institutions and leaders and feel more need to assure that all those institutions have power.

Legitimate and Illegitimate Authority

Traditionally, Indians have not felt ambivalence about authority. Authority was formally partitioned between regional and national government. Even those who ruled from Delhi left nobility in charge of many regions and ruled indirectly through them;[21] except in the areas of taxation and security, these nobles were largely left to control their own regions and administer the laws. Usually the laws stemmed from their own religions and clearly spelled out obligations and responsibilities, thus providing a strong basis for authority. National, regional, and local leaders all agreed on what constituted legitimate authority, and what did not.

The British and the central government they helped create altered this basis of legitimacy. Hindus ordered their authority on the basis of caste; those of higher caste had the authority to give orders to those of lower caste, on a strict hierarchical basis. As we have seen, the British, and especially the central government since India became independent, have tried to change these rules. The new government outlawed caste and declared all people equal; that was a bold affront to those who still believe authority derives from one's caste position. At the same time, the government formally removed the obligations of higher to lower castes, and asserted that all people should have access to political institutions, regardless of the caste to which they formerly belonged. They shifted to the national level many powers formerly reserved to regional government, and they reduced the former 860 different political entities to fourteen states. So, in India, there is a clear difference between modern and traditional concepts of authority and legitimacy. The modern leaders do not recognize the authority of traditional leaders; villagers and their traditional leaders often do not recognize the authority of the national leaders. Each may see the authority of the other as illegitimate; it is hard for them to see one another's viewpoint. Those who exercise sovereignty may find little need or occasion to listen to the views of those practicing politics in more traditional ways. The traditionalists do not comprehend how to exert influence in the new institutions.

Before the Spanish conquered Peru, authority was formally partitioned among the local, regional, and national levels. During the short period of Inca rule, the nobility and regional governors were entitled to their own fields and mines and to the part-time labor of villagers to grow their crops and work the mines. The Inca (as top ruler of the empire) conscripted some young men into military service for limited terms, allowing each family to retain an able-bodied man at home to work the fields; villagers helped the Inca to obtain metals, food, and wool, and he helped them obtain metal plows, statues for their shrines, and other useful artifacts. The Inca also had the last word over the distribution of land among villages and matters relating to security. But villages largely governed their own affairs and controlled their own land. A system of roads connected them with other villages throughout the Andes.

The Spanish conquest ended all that. After a full century of resistance by Quechua and Aymara, the Spanish completely destroyed this system. They built new towns atop the old and allowed the roads and irrigation terraces to decay. The Inca was replaced by a viceroy and a set of regional governors—always Spaniards born in Spain. Quechua and Aymara nobility were retained by the Spanish as intermediaries in their interactions with the villages. But during the 1570s, the Spaniards arbitrarily moved many villagers to **reducciones**—resettlement villages closer to Spanish settlements—and used Quechua and Aymara labor for fields and mines without the formal limits the Incas had applied earlier. Many of the best fields were taken over by **encomiendas** (Spanish-style landed estates making use of free labor from native Americans), and Peruvian villages became isolated, without the resources previously supplied by the outside political structure. Towns grew up around the *criollo* (descending from the Spanish conquerors) businessmen, civil servants, and Catholic clergymen, who created their own town councils and felt they had no obligations to Quechua and Aymara. So in Peru, as in India, there is a clear difference between older and newer conceptions of authority. That dichotomy continues. In the process, local village government has largely been wiped out, leaving villagers and urban slum dwellers out of contact with the new governmental institutions intended to replace the old ones.

In traditional Nigerian villages, authority was formally partitioned within the community between various societies and their leaders, but regional political entities had little interaction with villages except to collect taxes. Everyone had access to the local political leaders through frequent and lengthy discussions, and all villages had strict mores and customs to regulate the behavior of villagers and leaders. Today, 80 percent of Nigerians still live this way. But there is one major difference: The local leaders who are chosen locally often have little ability to affect the daily lives of villagers. Village leaders chosen from outside can make money and exercise power without regard to the needs of the villagers.

Some tribes consolidated control over a number of villages and collected taxes from them to support kingly towns; the villages still continued to run their own internal affairs. In the north, many of these rulers became Muslim. As late as the 1920s, fewer than five thousand British maintained rule over Nigeria by allowing these rulers to share—often in the form of salaries—in the taxation of the lucrative trade the British had established to export palm oil, peanuts, cotton, cocoa, and other commodities. Rather than let villages choose their own leaders in the traditional manner, in some regions the British designated whom they would recognize as leader, making the position hereditary. In the south, sons of the village headmen were often trained to assist in operating the British trading firms. A Nigerian army was created to deal with insurrection.

These changes became the roots of the more modern political culture. As in India, British schools taught Nigerian children about the British parliamentary traditions. And the British were careful to meet challenges to their rule with decisive force. British rulers stressed loyalty to modern government as opposed to tribal leadership. Yet people who happened to hold positions of authority in tribal governments, or who lived near British ports, were often given more opportunity than others to receive modern education; this created unequal access to modern government power and allowed some local leaders to ignore their traditional obligations to their villages. Village leaders could now govern without the careful reciprocities that formed the basis of their authority before.

Nigeria was formally partitioned into four parts—Hausa, Ibo, Yoruba, and river tribes—but without any clear demarcation of authority between the regional and national levels. Today, regional governments, under the close supervision of the central government, have taken most responsibilities away from local leaders. So, in Nigeria too, modern concepts of authority clash with traditional notions.

CONCLUSION

India, Peru, and Nigeria, then, have less continuity in their conceptions of political power than the other nation-states do; modern conceptions about authority contradict, rather than reinforce, traditional ideas.

In the other nation-states, traditional conceptions differ, but modern concepts of authority have evolved from traditional ones. Citizens of Germany, the United Kingdom, and China believe in a clear hierarchical system of authority and obey the leaders installed in top positions. Citizens of the United States like authority to be dispersed in a less clear hierarchy; people in the CIS republics show confusion about how hierarchical authority should be exerted. They have lived this way for centuries. But in India, Peru, and Nigeria, people traditionally had a clear idea of where authority lay. Today, legitimacy has shifted to entirely different institutions without their authorization. The new institutions which modern urban dwellers perceive to have authority may be very different from those that villagers and urban squatters confer authority upon. Because they continue many traditional cultural practices, these modern urban dwellers themselves sometimes find it hard to choose between the two approaches to authority. As DeToqueville observed, "customs are useful to people; for their chief merit is to serve as a barrier between the strong and the weak, the ruler and the ruled."[22] When customs become obscured, those barriers fall.

SUMMARY

Some people confer authority on those the law says should have it; they want clarity about where authority lies. Others confer authority on those legally entitled to it, but want power or authority spread between enough separate individuals and institutions to prevent any one person or institution from gaining too much power; this may obscure the lines of legal authority. A nation-state trying to mix both those traditions, or to replace one clear hierarchy with a new one, may find that people from one tradition withhold their authority from those holding sovereignty under the other system.

NOTES

1. Jack C. Plano and Milton Greenberg, *The American Political Dictionary,* 8th ed. (Fort Worth: Holt, Rinehart & Winston, 1989), p. 14, says that "legitimacy is based on the conversion of the exercise of political power or the assumption of a political position into a situation of 'rightful' authority."

2. The monarch is the ceremonial head of state, who presides over public occasions. People do like to see the royal family and read about the intimate details of their personal lives.

3. The October-November 1985 Gallup International poll showed 5 percent "almost always" trust the government "to do what is right", 25 percent do "most of the time," 43 percent do "some of the time," and 25 percent "almost never" do. E. J. Dionne, Jr., "Government Trust: Less in West Europe than U.S.," *New York Times,* February 16, 1986.

4. Hugo Young, "Giving a Hoot, Mon, for Democracy," *Manchester Guardian Weekly,* September 25, 1988.

5. See chapter 11.

6. West Germans were asked in public opinion polls, "Do you have the feeling that one has, as a citizen, influence upon the federal government, or is one powerless?" The percentage who answered "powerless" ranged from 55 to 48 percent between 1975 and 1978. Yet, on another question, fewer than 25 percent indicated that they had too little influence in government; apparently Germans are content with a perceived lack of power. Those indicating they would be willing to join a party seldom exceeds 15 percent. Gordon Craig, *The Germans* (New York: Putnam, 1982), p. 293.

7. In 1978, the government began to shift responsibilities formerly held by communes and factories to local governments. For example, in 1971, the Secretary of the Party Committee of the Beijing Woolen Mill was supervising family disputes, childrens' school problems, and water temperatures in bath houses. By the 1980s, attempts were made to move such problems into the hands of local government officials. Tony Saich, "Workers in the Workers' State: Urban Workers in the PRC," in David S. G. Goodman, ed., *Groups and Politics in the People's Republic of China* (Cardiff, England: University College Cardiff Press, 1984), p. 168.

8. Residents of Chinese villages often share the same surname, attend school together, and belong to the same production team. If one becomes a cadre, or moves to town to start a business, he or she can use the name to obtain special favors from the village or may grant special favors to the villagers. These favors may involve falsifying production reports, bribery, withholding grain from the market, or stealing fertilizer and other supplies; such actions are winked at by both sides.

Heads of large families with many able workers often emerge as informal village leaders; they also have the greatest opportunity to excel under the post-1978 responsibility system, which gives an edge to those with enough workers to achieve maximum production on their plots.

T'ung-tsu Ch'u, *Local Government in China under the Ch'ing* (Stanford: Stanford University Press, 1962), discusses similar practices during the eighteenth and nineteenth centuries.

9. Robert Delfs, "Saying No to Peking," *Far Eastern Economic Review* 151 (April 4, 1991) 14: 22.

10. See chapter 21 for a discussion of such shifts.

11. In chapter 11, we discussed the relationship between trust and efficacy. Here we are discussing how one person's trust rises and falls over time. To gauge trust, American pollsters ask people how much they trust their government to do what is right; in 1958, only 25 percent said "some" or "none"; since 1974, this figure has never been less than 50 percent. They also ask whether the government wastes tax money; whether people running the government know what they are doing (in 1958, 28 percent said "quite a few of them don't seem to know what they are doing"; in 1980, 63 percent); whether people running the government are "crooked"; and whether the government is run by "a few big interests looking out for themselves" or "for the benefit of all the people" (in 1958, 18 percent said "big interests"; in 1980, 77 percent; in 1988, 64 percent). Still, this expressed distrust is moderated. A 1972 poll found, for example, that 74 percent of those expressing strong distrust on all these questions said they were "proud of many things about our form of government"; 43 percent would "keep our form of government as it is." Such findings partly reflect confidence in the particular government in power rather than in our system of government. In 1974, during the Watergate scandal, only 34 percent expressed trust all or most of the time; during the Iran hostage crisis in 1980, this figure dipped to 28 percent.

The percentage of people disagreeing with one or both of the following statements rose over time, indicating heightened trust: "Sometimes politics and government seem so complicated that a person like me can't really understand what's going on"; "Voting is the only way that people like me can have any say about how the government runs things." The numbers disagreeing with these statements rose from 40 percent in 1952 to 53 percent in 1980 among whites, and from 22 to 36 percent among blacks. Meanwhile, over the same years, the percentage of whites disagreeing that "public officials don't care much what people think" and "people like me don't have any say about what the government does" declined from 55 to 45 percent, while blacks disagreeing rose from 30 to 35 percent; by that index, confidence was rising more among blacks than whites. Paul R. Abramson, *Political Attitudes in America:*

Formation and Change, (San Francisco: Freeman, 1983), pp. 135–36, 143, 175–76, 194ff.

In West Germany in 1974 (when the Social Democrats were in power with a coalition government of the left), 46 percent said that the government can be trusted to do what is right only some or none of the time; in 1985 (with the Christian Democrats in power), 55 percent responded this way. The decline in trust was largely expressed by Social Democrats and others to the left. Those shifts are less radical than the shifts in the United States, which cut across party lines. Warren E. Miller, Arthur H. Miller, and Edward J. Schneider, *American Election Studies Data Sourcebook 1952–1978* (Cambridge; Mass.: Harvard University Press, 1980), pp. 257–59; Everett Carll Ladd, *The American Polity* (New York: Norton, 1991), pp. 342–43, 348; E. J. Dionne, Jr., "Government Trust." *American National Election Studies Data Sourcebook 1952–1988* (Ann Arbor: Center for Political Studies, University of Michigan).

12. As of 1984, 47 percent expressed a great deal of confidence in the U.S. military (versus 28 percent in 1980 and 62 percent in 1966); 28 percent in the Congress (versus 9 percent and 42 percent); 13 percent in organized labor (versus 14 percent and 22 percent); and 21 percent in major companies (versus 16 percent and 55 percent). In 1982, 24 percent expressed great confidence in the executive branch, and 25 percent in television news. Seymour Martin Lipset and William Schneider, *The Confidence Gap: Business, Labor, and Government in the Public Mind,* rev. ed. (Baltimore: Johns Hopkins, 1987),pp. 48–49.

13. "Maybe I'm overly naive, but I don't see anything wrong with that," North declared. He indicated that his stand-alone agency was the idea of the Director of Central Intelligence. This agency could procure a ship to stand off the coast of a foreign nation when the CIA and the military could not, due to a lack of authorization from the president. It was not necessary for North's agency to report this action to the president or anyone else: "If the Director of Central Intelligence directed me to do so, that is good and sufficient." Yet North's immediate superior, Admiral Poindexter, had specifically ordered him in a written memorandum not to divulge his activities to the Director of Central Intelligence; Poindexter reasoned that the CIA director directed another agency, not the White House which employed both Poindexter

and North, so North need not answer to the central intelligence director. (Taken from the nationally televised hearings)

14. "Plain and simple," North argued, "Congress is to blame because of the fickle, vacillating, unpredictable, on-again, off-again policy toward Nicaraguan democratic resistance." (Nationally televised hearings)

15. "I didn't want to show Congress a single word of the whole thing." North said he was willing to be the "fall guy," to "take the rap" for many of the actions: "Every centurion had a group of shields out in front of him—a hundred of them." But he was only willing to take the rap politically, not legally. Toward the end, North and CIA Director William Casey decided that North's immediate supervisor, Admiral Poindexter, should take the rap; North did not indicate that he told Poindexter of this decision. When Poindexter told North the president had not approved some of their memos explaining their actions, North did not find this disconcerting. "I'm not in the habit of questioning my superiors. If he [Poindexter] deemed it not to be necessary to ask the president, I saluted smartly and charged up the hill." (Nationally televised hearings)

16. The New York Times-CBS News poll asked: "At one time, Congress prohibited the government from giving military assistance to the Contras. Was Oliver North justified in doing what he did to aid the Contras then because he believed it was right, or should he not have done it?" Thirty five percent said he was justified, and 50 percent said he was not.

When asked whether North behaved "as if he were above the law," 46 percent said yes, 44 percent no. Sixty percent trusted Congress more than the president "to make the right decisions on foreign policy," and 24 percent trusted the president more than Congress. Sixty four percent regarded Col. North as "a real patriot," though only 18 percent saw him as "a national hero." A third both saw his actions as justified and regarded him as a real patriot; a fifth saw his actions as unjustified and did not

regard him as a hero. *New York Times,* July 11, 1987. In a 1992 Times-Mirror poll, 63 percent said America needs a strong leader to take direct action "without worrying about how Congress and the Supreme Court would feel"; only 27 percent thought that dangerous.

17. Richard D. Heffner, ed., *Democracy in America* (New York: Mentor, 1956), p. 303. Children, DeToqueville said, are raised to respond to persuasion rather than punishment and to consider themselves on par with adults. But those in power try to keep the people happy as one would keep a child happy. "Men are seldom . . . forced to act, but they are constantly restrained from acting." "The principle of equality has prepared men for these things; it has predisposed men to endure them and often to look on them as benefits."

18. Idem., p. 113.

19. "It is not uncommon to hear Soviet citizens complain that Gorbachev is moving too fast to liberalize society and that what's really needed is a stern disciplinarian like Stalin to crack the whip. . . Photographs of Stalin hang in many taxis and trucks, and moviegoers sometimes break into applause when images of Stalin flicker briefly on the screen." Philip Taubman, *New York Times,* March 16, 1987. Gorbachev encouraged the publication of books and articles exposing Stalin's crimes. Earlier, Khrushchev had attempted to expunge Stalin from history books, while Brezhnev sought to rehabilitate him by emphasizing his strong leadership and ignoring his crimes.

20. Linda Feldmann, "Democrats Take Over in Lvov," *Christian Science Monitor,* August 28, 1990.

21. Even in 1931, at the height of British rule, there were only 50,000 British in India as civilian officials, and 70,000 in the army. George Rosen, *Democracy and Economic Change in India* (Berkeley: University of California Press, 1966), p. 51.

22. Heffner, *Democracy,* p. 310.

EXERCISES

Think about the book thus far:

1. This chapter discusses the fourth of six aspects of political culture: people's beliefs about power and authority. What are the first three aspects we discussed?

2. What are the three main categories of people's beliefs about power and authority outlined at the beginning of this chapter?

3. If a person is confused about their national identity and issues related to equality, will they therefore fall into that third category of belief about power and authority?

KEY WORDS AND PHRASES

Define the following terms:

legitimacy   hierarchy   reduccione   encomienda

Answer each of the following questions (1–4) with one sentence:

1. Where does authority derive from?

2. What is the difference between authority and legitimacy?

3. What is the difference between power and authority?

4. How do the "Irangate" hearings demonstrate Americans' beliefs about authority and legitimacy?

THINKING IT THROUGH

1. What are some differences between traditional and modern conceptions of authority in India, Nigeria, and Peru?

2. How do Confucian ideas about authority differ from ideas in the United Kingdom and Germany?

3. Who has sovereignty in the CIS and the United States? Are those who hold sovereignty the same as those with legitimate authority?

4. Give an example of a group discussed in this chapter with attitude (a); with attitude (b); and with attitude (c):

    a. Citizens may feel that they should obey the laws, and those who make and enforce them, but not obey officeholders who do not comply with the law.

    b. They may feel they should obey the laws, but sometimes withhold their authority from those legitimately entitled to exercise it while authorizing others to exert sovereignty unlawfully.

    c. They may feel they need not obey the laws because those exercising sovereignty have no authority to make them.

5. Is it important that power be exercised with authority, and that authority be legitimate? Why or why not?

chapter 17

POLITICAL CULTURE
LEGAL PROTECTION

Like chapter 16, this chapter examines attitudes about government and leaders. We saw in the last chapter that laws are passed to confer legitimacy on government and its rules and actions and that people sometimes do not find it necessary to obey the laws. In this chapter, we look at how attitudes about laws—how they should be enacted and enforced—affect citizens' ability to seek protection from harm caused by government or other citizens.

This chapter surveys the fifth aspect of political culture, beliefs about legal protection.

PRESCRIPTIONS FOR PRESCRIPTIONS

Political culture is citizens' knowledge of, feelings toward, and judgments about their political system. Physicians also operate within a culture—the knowledge of, feelings toward, and judgments about medicine they share with their medical colleagues. When your doctor gives you a prescription, he or she is laying down, as a guide, rules of action you must take if you are to get well; go to the drugstore and get this medication. That prescription is given within the context of another prescription—the prescription of the medical profession about what to do when someone has symptoms like yours. The American medical profession (not to mention the public) tends to frown on the use of leeches to cure respiratory ailments, but to endorse the use of antibiotics; those attitudes are general rules of action that underlie the more detailed rule of action on the piece of paper you take to the drugstore. They are prescriptions for writing your prescription.

Laws, as we saw in chapter 1, are rules of behavior prescribed by government institutions (which, unlike your doctor, can force you to act on their rules). **Do the citizens of a nation-state prescribe rules for lawmakers to follow when they write laws? And do those prescriptions include any limitations on the behavior of political leaders?**

Jerry Hough thinks Soviet political culture provided such "prescriptions for prescriptions." He comments on a mindset shared by state bureaucrats, economic administrators, party officials, and probably much of the public in the Soviet Union. It constitutes a prescription for the behavior of political leaders writing laws, a prescription one would expect citizens to "write" for these leaders:

> *One would certainly expect the overwhelming majority to take for granted the wisdom of governmental ownership and planning of industry and agriculture; the desirability of a political order which avoids the factional squabbling and 'irresponsible' criticism of a multiparty system; the desirability (if perhaps not the absolute necessity) of writers and artists providing moral inspiration to the citizens and particularly the youth; the need of 'society' to protect itself against those malcontents who spread 'malicious lies' about it; the need of the Soviet Union to protect itself against 'American imperialism'; and the desirability of supporting those foreigners fighting against private-ownership social systems.*[1]

All but the last of these attitudes (fear of America and private ownership is now subsiding into a strong minority viewpoint, which could return to prominence if reforms fail) have held sway in Russia for several centuries.[2] As we shall see in part 4, these notions continue to color the mindset of Russians and other CIS republic citizens, breaking down slowly even among those who think of themselves as reformers. In the United States, we have our own prescriptions for the laws. One can expect top bureaucrats, businesspeople, and party officials to support our centralized private-enterprise system,[3] our compromise-oriented two-party system, our governmental checks and balances, teaching patriotism in our schools, "responsible" intellectual freedom, and (until recently) the fight against Soviet imperialism in a similar fashion; we have been socialized to believe in such ideas.

During the twelfth century, the German merchants on Gotland Island formed an association, or hanse, for exporting northern European goods to Slavic regions and Slavic goods back to Europe. Cologne had a similar association for its merchants in London. Over seventy cities—mostly German—followed suit and eventually formed the Hanseatic League.

The United Kingdom has seen centuries of cooperation among **hansas** (merchant leagues), chartered companies, and the government (a different mix from our centralized private enterprise); three centuries of a two-party system within parliamentary government; traditions of intellectual freedom, combined with the obligation of the educated to provide moral leadership; and a long military tradition of protecting its overseas investments, public and private. Germany has known long cooperation between governments and hansas (and government assistance in establishing joint stock companies during the nineteenth century); a multiparty system within a parliament since the nineteenth century; several centuries of close ties among educators, religious leaders, and government; and centuries of battle against

outside political divisions on the European continent. When legislators write, executives enforce, and jurists interpret laws, they take into account those cultural attitudes, which constitute "prescriptions for their prescriptions."

COMMON LAW VERSUS HIERARCHICAL LAW

In all four of these political systems—the post-Soviet republics, the United States, the United Kingdom, and Germany—people have widely shared cultural attitudes which affect the way they write and apply laws. The political cultures of the United States and the United Kingdom, however, share the unique notion that individuals should be protected by law from undue government interference. This attitude has deep historic roots.

Prior to William the Conqueror's arrival in 1066 A.D., Saxon England seems to have been divided into vills, sokes, and demesnes. A **vill** was the land surrounding a village. That land often had many owners. When disputes arose among those owners or their tenants, they often submitted them to a soke for adjudication. The **soke,** a term referring both to a person and his land, might be an important landowner, a nobleman like an earl, or the king himself, as well as the land area he administered; the boundaries of sokes and vills often overlapped. A family that did not pay taxes or owe labor services to a particular soke might still turn to it to rule on a dispute. It was conceivable, for instance, for people living on a royal soke to take adjudication to the king's courts while paying taxes to an earl in an adjoining soke in exchange for protection. An earl might even have a soke without the privilege of using a portion of royal forest (the hunting ground for the king) which lay within his soke. People who submitted themselves to the tax jurisdiction of a soke could remain freemen and landowners. Furthermore, the heads of such families participated in the governance of the vill. Several vills contributed to a governing council called the **hundred**; the principal leaders of several hundreds came together to form meetings of the **shire.** They could also take disputes

Figure 17.1   Britain has long had overlapping jurisdictions.

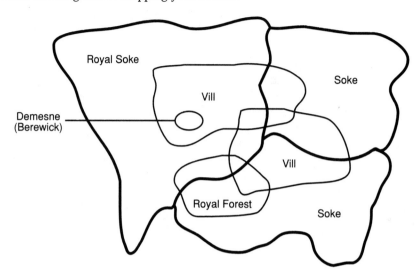

to those jurisdictions. All these overlapping territories and governing arrangements meant that kings, nobles, and township councils could exist side by side without clear hierarchies.

The nobility themselves, along with some who did not hold titles of nobility (but who may have served in the nobles' armies) had farmsteads called **demesnes,** which occupied a minority of the land. A demesne consisted of a manorial house, often rectangular with a high wood-beam ceiling, and adjoining land worked by tenants who owed labor services, and perhaps worked by some slaves as well. These tenants, too, might submit to adjudication by a royal soke and were thus not entirely under the jurisdiction of the demesne.

The Norman invasion in 1066 brought changes. William killed people in regions where his armies met resistance or rebellion. He moved large numbers of people from other regions to occupy the lands formerly held by those he killed. In regions where he met less resistance, he seems not to have taken land from freemen or earls or the Church. He in fact sought to increase the power of the earls and the Church over the populace, and then forced them to give allegiance to him. But the Norman kings introduced this feudalism without destroying any of the

When the Normans arrived, the Church probably occupied a third of England's arable land. The Normans reduced this acreage. The remainder of land was occupied by individual landowners, the king, and the nobility.

old institutions. The sokes, demesnes, and vills and the freemen, hundreds, and shires endured. So did the overlapping boundaries among demesnes, vills, and sokes. It even remained possible to have several demesnes (more commonly called manors during this period) within a single soke. However, in most instances, adjudication and taxation within each soke were now carried out by either the Church or a nearby earl. All these **overlapping jurisdictions** (overlapping boundaries within which jurists or people with authority could hear cases under laws) made it clear that the people were subject to law, and that those who administered the law were subject to others; more than one authority might try a case in any given place, so people were not subject to the control of only one authority.

In the medieval period, English kings developed a theory that the law applying in the king's court

Even today, many English villages are surrounded by land belonging to nobility.

Bob Gamer

should represent the "**common law** of the realm." This meant that these laws derived from, but also took precedence over, law and custom in the individual manors or demesnes. Higher courts cited the older laws and court cases as **precedents** (preceding guidelines) for their decisions; they, in turn, expected lower courts to treat their new decisions as precedents. Thus, the common law assures that common traditions and habits in the practice of law must continue to be observed. No one wrote a set of laws into a code book, declaring them the only laws to be followed. But precedent assumed a strong role in English common law. One can still cite cases from the king's courts in medieval days, which in turn cited demesne law, as precedents; new laws and court decisions are still expected to befit the traditional laws. A solicitor defending a person in court today for owing debts can refer back to the procedures used by the hundredmen in a vill to decide on such a case. He or she can cite the way the king's court interpreted such a case in the medieval period and argue that current procedures give the defendant fewer rights than the earlier ones. The court must address this argument in its ruling, at least explaining why the new procedures are as fair as the old. Thus, the new law did not destroy or expel the old; it absorbed it.

The Norman kings also stabilized the system of obligations to assure that those of higher status maintained their responsibilities to those of lower status, and vice versa. People without land could take on jobs for lords, or for the king or vill, as bailiffs, sheriffs, and reeves (roughly, rent collector and overseer of a manor). That made people of high status dependent on their servants to collect the obligations owed them. If the person of high status were declared bankrupt or removed from their position by royal command, the same servants enforced that decision against their employers. The courts, which played an important role in enforcing this system, also recruited people of relatively low status as members of **juries,** bodies of citizens who decided the guilt or innocence of anyone accused of a crime or involved in a dispute. The middle class often bought their way out of the obligation to serve on juries. People of low status, who could not buy their way out, were probably cooperative with efforts to make bankrupt manor owners live up to their obligations to sell their land to the owners of even larger manors. This helped establish a tradition that even people of low rank could preside over the fate of the mighty. People had more than one place to seek redress of grievances and could pit one person of status against another; they themselves were part of the system through which redress was sought. And juries, like hundredmen, might have some empathy and understanding in cases with defendants of their own rank.

These traditions carried over to the American colonies, whose British appointed governors were expected to abide by British common law and to work with elected legislatures. Church elders and town councils presided over the early colonies; their decisions were to be obeyed as law. Gradually, additional overlapping units of government, overseeing everything from schools to water service, became as confusing as the British overlay of sokes and demesnes. From the British, the United States adopted the notions of common law and trial by jury. However, unlike in Britain and Germany, different states can pass different laws on matters such as bankruptcy, divorce, and various criminal offenses.

The founders of the United States wrote a constitution late in the eighteenth century which was expected to serve as the fundamental law of the land. The Supreme Court has become the highest authority in interpreting this document, ensuring that chief executives, laws passed by legislatures, and common law are in line with it. The Supreme Court may even go so far as to declare laws or acts of the president null and void if they conflict with the Constitution. This court is the highest **court of appeal** in the nation-state, meaning that the parties to a case already decided in a lower court can try to appeal that decision all the way up to the Supreme Court for a final determination. In its decisions, the Court cites as precedents its own past cases, English common law, and the cases of inferior courts in an attempt to bring all laws into conformity with the Constitution. Citizens who feel their constitutional rights have been violated may seek redress by citing such cases as precedents for their claim. Citizens of the United Kingdom, too, may appeal cases to the British High Court, which takes all the same factors into consideration, except a constitution.

The Commonwealth of Independent States has no such traditions. The Russian tsar had absolute authority. He or she could have anyone, anywhere, executed at will. He need not refer the case to court or cite any precedent. The tsar needed the Russian Orthodox church, the nobility, the army, government-licensed merchants and manufacturers, boyars, Cossacks, and others to implement policy, and these groups therefore gained some independence and developed their own organized institutions to lead them. But there were no formal legal limitations on the power of the tsar over groups, individuals, or institutions. In 1864 Tsar Alexander II tried to introduce jury trials and judicial reforms, but the bureaucracy strongly resisted. During the twentieth century, the Soviets introduced law and written constitutions, but there is little depth in the support for them. The Soviet Union tried some experiments to legally protect individuals from one another, but they developed little experience in legally protecting individuals from the government or in using the laws to limit the activities of public offi-

cials. "As first secretary of the Stravopol region," Mikhail Gorbachev told a 1990 gathering, "I could decide everything, without thinking or answering to the law or the constitution. I decided, and that was that!"[4]

In the United States, political parties and interest groups are seldom outlawed.[5] In the Soviet Union until 1990, only the Communist Party and officially sanctioned interest groups were permitted to function. In the United States, the Supreme Court may order even the president to cease doing something it declares unconstitutional; the courts in the Soviet Union had no such power. The Soviets did create the Committee on Constitutional Oversight in 1988; the Congress of People's Deputies chose the members of the Committee to review laws and assure they adhered to the Constitution, but the Committee's powers were never tested. The individual republics will have to develop judicial oversight for themselves.

Another difference between the U.S. and Soviet legal systems is that the American president is expected to refrain from interfering in court decisions; there was no such expectation in the Soviet Union. If it can be proven that a person has been illegally imprisoned in the United States, the person goes free. In the Soviet Union, people could be imprisoned without legal justification and without a trial. In the final days of the Soviet Union, trials were guaranteed, but the independence of the court—or even the continuance of the system—was not. The Supreme Court was chosen by the Supreme Soviet for a ten-year term instead of the former five; those former Soviet judges now serve Russia and the other CIS republics.[6] New measures for judicial review will have to emerge in the republics, even though the older ones had yet to prove their effectiveness. In 1992, former Soviet President Gorbachev refused to cooperate when Russia's Constitutional Court summoned him for a trial of the banned Communist Party; in 1993, President Yeltsin stepped back from asserting emergency rule after the Constitutional Court declared that action unconstitutional and the Congress of People's Deputies threatened to vote him out of office.

The United States has had over two centuries to fine tune its presidency, Congress, Supreme Court, and state government systems. Various institutions within the bureaucracy, along with political parties, have had time to evolve. Among the public there is wide acceptance of these institutions and the roles they perform; the public would in fact resist attempts to alter these formal roles. Russia's professional civil service extends back to the time of Peter the Great, but the institutions and political party which ruled the Soviet Union were all born during this century. Russia's first national legislature did not come into being until 1907, and had not been through a single free election when the Revolution took place in 1917. The roles performed by each of these institutions have shifted dramatically with the succession of new leaders. The public's support for all of them is shallow; their roles can continue to shift with little public resistance.[7] Russia's Congress of People's Deputies makes constant changes in its constitution (for example, 250 changes between August 1991 and December 1992).

The common law tradition, with its many jurisdictional layers, its reliance on past precedents when making decisions, and its history of allowing people of low status to decide cases involving people with higher status, gives the individual recourse when government steps on individual rights or acts in an unlawful manner. The hierarchical legal tradition, which allows the ruler and his courts to define the law as they see fit, does not give the individual such rights.

ADAPTING HIERARCHICAL LAW TO INDIVIDUAL RIGHTS

Germany, like the CIS, has no common law traditions. Its territory was divided into many jurisdictions without overlapping boundaries. Some areas belonged to kings and queens, some to barons, some to other nobles, some to the Church. Each had nearly absolute control over his or her own territory. Cities, too, had charters which gave them complete control over their own territories. Emperors tried to exert influence over these independent entities, but with only partial success; the barons, nobles, and free cities often turned to armed combat before they would accept outside jurisdiction. To mobilize their defense, the people sometimes were forced to submit to the rule of others in their territory. People became used to living within only *one* jurisdiction, which made its own rules and was subject to no outside restraint, but which did spell out in contracts and law books the rights and obligations of ruler and subjects. The separate baronies and free cities also developed their own court systems and wrote laws rooted in the old Roman legal codes. After unification in 1871, these laws were codified and the same laws applied throughout the land. From then on, judges had to refer to this code in their decisions; they could not cite older laws or other court cases as precedents.

In the duchy of Prussia, Frederick William I created a central administrative service along professional lines in the eighteenth century. As his successors gradually unified Germany, this service came to enforce the laws. Thus, there was one set of laws and one enforcement agency.

Even in Britain, the laws in the king's courts took precedence over those in sokes, demesnes, and manors. Today, laws may be changed by Parliament at will. No other unit of government has jurisdiction over the law; the Parliament can pass any laws it likes without interference by the courts. Yet the Parliament must not depart radically from common law traditions. And its rulings must be filtered through many jurisdictional layers to be implemented. The courts can look far back in time to common law cases, or quote prior parliamentary legislation and the courts' interpretation of it, in citing precedents to interpret how new legislation should be enforced. This takes some enforcement control out of the hands of the prime minister, who might not always agree with the courts' interpretation of how the law is meant to be applied. German courts had less discretionary, or interpretive, power; the ruler made the laws, and the courts enforced them. Under Hitler, the courts had to enforce laws outlawing opposition parties, seizing Jewish property, and allowing the deaths of millions of people.

The British legal system differs from the American tradition, which bases law on a written constitution. For instance, in Northern Ireland, under an Act of Parliament pertaining only to Northern Ireland, police seeking to keep order can simply lock up anyone they like and remove that person's right to avoid self-incrimination if he or she refuses to supply the police with requested information. In the United States, the courts would probably declare such a law unconstitutional for depriving Northern Ireland of "due process and equal protection under the law"—phrases in the Fourteenth Amendment to the Constitution of the United States. The U.S. Supreme Court has decided that this means the procedures which apply to one region must apply to all. The British Parliament is not subject to such review by any court. But laws are written in ministries by lawyers trained in the common law. And the House of Lords and House of Commons both count many jurists among their members. If they find a proposed piece of legislation deviates too far from the common law, by tradition they help rewrite the law to bring it into conformity. It is up to the courts to determine how these laws apply to particular cases. But the courts do not have the power to declare laws to be against the common law, and therefore null and void, as the courts in the United States do with regard to the U.S. Constitution.[8]

After World War II, a West German constitution, the **Basic Law,** was written (under supervision of the occupying Allied Forces) to combine elements of both the British and United States systems. The Basic Law, which was adopted in 1949, was a document similar to a document used by the Weimar Republic, which Hitler had overthrown. The German chancellor's cabinet proposes laws, as in the United Kingdom, but these proposals must pass two houses of the legislature (the Bundestag and Bundesrat) and then undergo the courts' interpretation, as in the United States.

Most courts in the Federal Republic of Germany exist at the state level and are appointed by state authorities. Unlike the courts in the United Kingdom and the United States, these courts need not (but may) compare new laws passed by legislatures to old laws and court cases (that is, they may, but are not required to, refer to precedents); and they need not hold jury trials in criminal cases. The German courts refer to the many-volumed legal code created at the end of the nineteenth century and revised gradually since; the same code applies in all the states. The judge's role is to assure that all the facts about a case can be assembled, so that they can be interpreted in terms of what the laws, code, and Basic Law say. Because judges look only at those three elements, and not at one another's decisions, two judges may come up with different conclusions about cases involving similar facts. Moreover, because the judges are not supposed to decide whether laws violate the code or the Basic Law, it is difficult for most defendants to challenge the validity of the laws under which they are tried. But such individuals can appeal decisions to the Federal High Court, which tries to assure that laws have been interpreted uniformly and settles disputes between *Laender*. Citizens can also appeal bureaucratic decisions to the Administrative Court.

West Germany's written constitution, the Basic Law, contains many protections for individual civil liberties. A separate, independent federal Constitutional Court[9] is charged with reviewing legislation and government actions and settling disputes between various units of government. When cases raise questions about the constitutionality of laws or of government officials' actions, about the interpretation of the Basic Law, or about disputes between various units of government, this court can decide on those questions. It has declared about a hundred national and state laws unconstitutional and therefore not enforceable. It has also outlawed some political parties. In 1990, it came to the defense of East Germany's communists by outlawing an agreement which would have required them to amass 5 percent of the vote throughout united Germany to win a seat in parliament during the first election after reunification. Once the Constitutional Court has declared a law constitutional, state and federal courts must enforce that law, but they may limit its application to a particular case on the ground that the Basic Law would require them to limit it; these cases may not be appealed to the Constitutional Court.

East Germany adopted a Constitution in 1974; this document also spelled out many individual rights. But the East lacked a Constitutional Court and let the People's Chamber recall executives and judges at any time. Thus, the legislature could pass laws interfering with individual liberties without any fear that these laws would be overturned. Since judges were not independently appointed, and operated under a one-party system, they could not declare actions taken by government or party officials invalid. In the absence of jury trials, there was little to check the judgments of individual judges in their findings regarding criminal defendants.

West Germany's Bundestag and Bundesrat, and East Germany's Volkskammer, with its formal representation of different recognized groups, have their roots in the nineteenth-century Volkshaus and Staatenhaus. These, in turn, descended from **diets,** which grew out of earlier tribal assemblies. Traditionally, however, the nobility, church leaders, civil service, hansas, and guilds had more power than the diets. Hence, the concept of a legislature as the supreme lawmaking body is relatively new to Germans.[10] In Britain, these groups were all represented within the House of Lords and House of Commons (which grew out of factions surrounding nobles on the one hand and the king on the other since the days of the Magna Charta), which worked with the king or queen to pass laws. The King in Parliament was the supreme law of the land. The two legislative bodies (representing nobles and gentry) provided the basis for a two-party system, with two competing parties operating everywhere in the land. Germany, on the other hand, had a tradition of allowing only one party to survive in each of its duchies; the concept of free-party competition is new to Germans. Germany's lawmaking tradition does not firmly include the notions that laws should be made by representative bodies and reviewed by courts. Its traditions do include the idea that regional government should gain input from a variety of factions, and should be based on clearly written laws spelling out the rights and obligations of groups and individuals and subject to interpretation by independent courts.

LI AND FA

Chinese ideas about status and political representation also involve their own conceptions about law. **Li** were ritualistic duties, rules of decorum, which regulated activities of the emperor and the literati (the Confucian scholar-officials). These ritual duties, which were based on wisdom, reason, propriety, and justice, were written into administrative codes which evolved from dynasty to dynasty. Ultimately, it was the emperor who decided whether his own behavior, or that of one of his officials, broke the code. In short, as long as they performed their ritual duties with what the emperor felt was proper decorum, the emperor and officials could do whatever they chose to do and ask others to abide by their rules of propriety as well. In contrast, **fa** were laws prescribing punishments, written by the emperor and the literati, to restrict the behavior of the common people. Local magistrates and the literati, rather than courts, often deliberated disputes, with the disputants arguing before them and other gathered community members. Sometimes they would apply the gentler li, asking the defendants to right their behavior, and sometimes they would apply fa, prescribing punishment. The community's sense of propriety and justice was the foremost consideration in such deliberations. Punishment was often harsh; the emperor had to review capital punishment decisions. China never developed anything equivalent to legislatures to interfere in these processes; the emperor, the literati, and the community leaders ran civic affairs and decided what the law would be. Emperors served for life; even today the top party leader receives absolute obedience from the people, cadres, and officeholders until his death.

Today, the Chinese supplement li with Western concepts about commercial and criminal law, as well as with socialist ideas about civil procedure. Guided by li, community leaders still deliberate many local cases on their own, stipulating actions defendants must take to rectify their errors. Courts handle more serious cases, again often recommending actions to rectify behavior. Sometimes they deliver sentences more in keeping with fa, specifying punishments. For less serious offenses, community leaders and members sit in judgment of their peers, demanding that the defendants admit their crimes, apologize for them, and reform their behavior to remove shame from their families.

Neither fa nor li ever limited the behavior or power of central government in its dealings with individuals. Central government has always had wide discretion to change the rules of li and fa. It can outlaw groups, imprison people, rearrange government institutions, and closely restrict intellectual freedom. It has never succeeded, however, in replacing civilian and military leaders wholesale.

Therefore, in China—as in the United States, the United Kingdom, Germany, and the CIS republics—there is continuity between older and newer conceptions of law. Unlike the Russian tsar, the Chinese emperor shared the interpretation of the law with a professional class of officials with some similarity to Prussia's bureaucracy. As in Prussia, the law could be made and enforced without interference by legislatures or competing units of government. Throughout history, China was without any clear set of laws for individuals to follow; rules changed with the whim of the officials. Those traditions continue, leaving the individual with little recourse against the state's unfriendly actions; but at least community leaders take part in enforcing and administering some laws.

OLD VERSUS NEW SYSTEMS OF LAW

India has no clear continuity of tradition in its system of law. In 1935, the British colonial government passed the Government of India Act; the Indian Constitution which went into effect in 1950 contains large verbatim extracts from it. The section on fundamental rights in the Constitution guarantees eight rights known in Britain—equality, freedom against exploitation, freedom of religion, cultural and educational rights, the right to property, and the right to constitutional remedies. This Constitution, largely written by the British and by English-educated Indians, was adopted by the leaders the British had allowed to occupy the legislative institutions when it granted independence. Since then, the people who have taken control at national, regional, and local levels continue to be those who learned rules of political culture different from those governing the villages. The people who operate the bureaucracy, parliament, courts, army, professions, and business establishments live in cities. They are educated in English-speaking schools. They are conversant with British history and institutions. They know little about the lowest levels of Indian government, but they are knowledgeable about Indian central government and its relations with state governments. And they want the laws passed by parliament—laws passed and printed in English—to be the ultimate law of the land.

Thus, government leaders in India are concerned that the national institutions, political parties, interest groups, and laws be preserved. But they are very different from England's Norman invaders, who took great care to incorporate old soke, demesne, and vill law into the newly evolving common law, so that even today barristers can cite those early precedents to support their cases. Instead, India's English-speaking leaders are willing to destroy local traditional political institutions, obligations, and customary laws in favor of rules that often stem from British colonial education and government and the British common law. For example, national leaders pass laws which allow private urban investors to purchase and control land without any obligations to villagers; many villagers remember the traditional system in which entire communities, or their highest caste members, owned all the community land and distributed proceeds among all villagers. Similarly, village governments are affected by British ideas; several parties compete at the village level, and the same village may split its vote among several of them, instead of deciding unanimously as was traditionally the case.[11] The national

Muslims constitute only 12 percent of India's population, but for centuries they dominated India and built mosques atop the sites of former Hindu temples. In recent years, as we saw in chapter 15, Hindu radicals have sought to tear down such mosques and rebuild temples on these sites; those same radicals do not favor giving special privileges to lower castes, nor do they advocate reinstating the traditional caste obligations.

Controversy has focused on an unused sixteenth-century mosque atop the site where the Hindu Lord Rama is reputed to have been born in the city of Ayodhya. Prime Minister Indira Gandhi's attempts to prevent the destruction of this mosque led to riots among Muslims and Hindu radicals; her son Rajiv, who succeeded her after such confrontations with Sikh radicals led to her assassination, retreated from such controversy. In 1985, the high court ruled that the site was a Hindu temple, and not a mosque, causing the Hindu zealots to renew their assault on it. In another controversial ruling that year, the court declared—in contrast to traditional Muslim law—that divorced Muslim women were entitled to compensation from their former husbands under a law passed by parliament.[12] In the face of violent objections from Muslims, Prime Minister Gandhi backed away from enforcing this law.

In 1989, V. P. Singh of the Janata Dal party convinced Muslims and the Bharatiya Janata Party, a middle-class, upper-caste party which contains a minority faction of Hindu fundamentalists (the Vishwa Hindu Parishad), to create a coalition advocating a return to religious values. This coalition upset the Congress party at the polls and formed a Government. In 1990, Prime Minister Singh (who is himself high-caste) lost the loyalty of the Bharatiya Janata Party and many intellectuals in his own party when he tried to raise the quotas of lower castes employed in government service and admitted to universities, and when he blocked Hindus from destroying the Ayodhya mosque to build a temple. Thousands died in rioting, and his Government was toppled by a vote of no confidence. He handed power to a socialist,[13] Chandra Shekhar, who received strong backing from industrialists whom Singh had angered when he vigorously investigated them for corruption. Shekhar, in turn, was succeeded by P. V. Rao of the Congress party after the 1991 elections.

The fight over the temple and mosque site continues. Singh attempted to forge a compromise by seizing the land under eminent domain[14] and proposing that Hindus build a temple next to the mosque, so that both Hindus and Muslims could have shrines at the site. His ideas were rejected by both the Hindus and the Muslim All-India Masjid Action Committee; both groups argued Singh was setting a dangerous precedent of asserting the state's rights over religious places. Chastened by that, Prime Minister Rao sought to settle the issue through negotiations among party leaders. In 1992, the Bharatiya Janata Party issued another ultimatum threatening to topple the mosque. Rejecting a negotiated agreement, demonstrators tore down the mosque while thousands of troops looked on passively.[15] The bloodiest rioting since independence broke out all over India, followed by a spate of terrorist bombings; several thousand people died.

Since first coming to power in 1977,[16] the Janata party has struggled to retain a balance between members who belong to traditional, antagonistic religious groups, and members who espouse modern ideas of socialist equality and toleration among religious groups. Like the Congress party, it has found that hard to do. The civil unrest following the destruction of the Ayodhya mosque causes Indians to wonder whether any party can strike such a balance.

legislature has outlawed the caste system, with all associated social obligations. But the Congress party has been cautious about guaranteeing the rights of the lowest castes and religious minorities. Article 29 of the Constitution protects the right of any group to protect its culture; in practice, politicians and courts have often interpreted this article in ways that destroy community traditions. To the consternation of many Hindus, Muslim marriage and other traditional laws regulating social customs are often recognized, while Hindu dowries and many other customs are denied by law.

India has two very different traditions of political culture. Most people continue to reside in villages. They have more contact with, and more respect for, local and regional authorities (who speak the local dialects) than national authorities. People of higher caste have abandoned many traditional social and economic obligations to the entire community and have restricted themselves to giving personal assistance to a few families who beg food from them. Some families of high caste are reduced to dire economic straits. Though it is against the law to discriminate against the lower castes, lower-caste people must walk their bicycles through high-caste neighborhoods and use separate glasses at roadside tea stalls. Yet, as in the past, people of lower caste tend to elect people of higher caste to political office. They also continue to obey traditional religious and social laws the central government attempts to set aside, and they often resent government interference with the few privileges those religious laws confer on them, and with their own attempts to repress other religious groups. Thanks to regional party politics, these villagers are aware that many of the new laws and ideas sprang from alien British rule, including infringements on religious laws, the special privileges of people affiliated with central government to use land for commercial agriculture, and the emphasis on strengthening national (and weakening regional and local) institutions.

The two cultures are not entirely separate in people's minds. Villagers often show more interest in national election campaigns than in regional and local ones. The lowest scheduled castes, in keeping with the central government's values, frequently assert their newly established caste rights against those of higher castes. In reaction, and to assert traditional values, higher-caste members sometimes riot to protest the modern rights given to lower castes; Hindus also riot to protest privileges and protections given to religious minorities. It is often unclear whether people are asserting a secular belief that people should be treated equally, or a religious belief that traditional caste rights and obligations should be recognized. The tendency may be to support one or the other according to what currently suits one's own interests; few people consistently advocate the tolerance and protection of rights implied in a civic culture. Even educated professionals sometimes ally with linguistic, ethnic, and religious groups to vote for parties representing them to give themselves a social identity. The laws passed by the central government take precedence over the traditional religious laws; the government does not attempt to blend the two traditions.

A similar dichotomy occurs in Peru. The laws under which the colony of Peru operated were not always clear, and it could take as long as three years to receive instructions from Spain. This placed considerable discretion in the hands of the viceroy, provincial governors, and town councils (composed of people of European extraction), who could test their power against subordinates and one another. These shifts in power, in turn, created great ambiguity about the law.

The achievement of independence in 1821 did little to affect this. Rather than absorbing them into a national culture, the Spanish had always preferred that highland peasant villages have communal land tenure and govern their own internal affairs. Under new laws passed after independence, millions of acres of community land were sold to latifundia and haciendas, great landed estates. For the first time, many highland peasants moved into towns and cities governed under different rules; those who did not speak Spanish would not receive the vote until 1979. Moreover, the external boundaries of Peru continually shifted. Until a reformist military coup took place in 1919, access to political institutions was limited almost exclusively to large landowners and businesspeople. These same individuals controlled politics at both the national and provincial levels.

From 1821 to 1872, six civilians (none of whom had been elected) served a total of five years as president, and twenty military leaders occupied that role after an assortment of coups and uprisings. The country has operated under ten constitutions, including the one written in 1979, which was to be replaced after President Fujimori suspended it in 1992. From 1872 to 1919, the nation-state generally operated under elected leaders (for seventeen years, under elected military leaders). But during those years, Peru had twenty-five separate presidents and underwent at least five coups. Since that time, there have been six coups and thirty-seven years of military-backed regimes. Fifty-two of Peru's eighty-one presidents, as of 1993, were military officers. Judges, legislators, bureaucrats, and military officers all conduct their business in Spanish.

Meanwhile, the remaining highland villages continue to govern most of their own affairs, control their own land, and provide their own social services. Community members perform cooperative labor projects and carry out many other customs which date back to pre-conquest days.

In Peru, as in India, there are two very distinct political cultures. In Peru's case, the line rather cleanly draws the population in half: half speak only Quechua or Aymara and live in the mountains, while the rest of the population can speak Spanish. While power resides with the Spanish speakers, the limits and continuity of that power are far from clearly established.

The Spanish ruled Peru by directly establishing their own cities, farms, and mines under the complete control of Spaniards and Spanish emigrants, keeping them entirely separate from the people and culture which had prevailed there before. The British ruled Nigeria in an indirect manner, bringing in few British people but instead working through established local and regional authorities. Laws attempted to preserve village ownership of land and encouraged loyalty to traditional regional rulers. Those rulers helped the British export their local resources in exchange for cash. They were also allowed to send their sons to British universities, where they learned about British institutions. But in Nigeria, the British did not introduce competing parties at a central level, with opposition and the right of the people to determine their own leaders. The

political parties that formed were centered around small Westernized groups who came from differing tribes. Although this prevented Nigeria from developing a harsh contrast between central and tribal governments and from displacing people from their land, it also provided no basis for cooperation among tribal groups within a modern state.

When Nigeria gained its independence in 1963, it tried to introduce parliamentary government with universal suffrage to bring together the various tribal groups. The position of prime minister was created, but powers were also formally partitioned to the Ibo, Yoruba, and Hausa-dominated regions. The first prime minister was a Hausa; when it became obvious that Hausa had tampered with the first census, conducted the following year, to exaggerate their numbers and thus their privileges under the Constitution, Ibo leaders strongly dissented, and controversy ensued. By 1966, the army staged a coup to stop the civilian turmoil. In 1967, the Ibo seceded to form Biafra and bloody civil war began.

After the Ibos lost the war, new ground rules were created to end this formal partitioning of power. The central government formed new, smaller states, which it hoped would be correspondingly weaker. Popular elections were established for the governing bodies of villages, towns, cities, and states, to end traditional clan leader domination; these newly elected bodies were given few official powers or duties. However, the central government has been under the control of civilian leaders for fewer than four years since that time, while the 80 percent of Nigerians who still live in villages continue to choose and heed their own traditional leaders. Frequent riots in northern cities challenge central government policies which traditional leaders and their followers believe interfere with their religious and social practices. So in Nigeria, too, there is a rift between the laws espoused by national leaders and those espoused by local and regional officials. After heavy debate, the 1992 Constitution—which to date has still not been adopted—was written to allow appeals under traditional Muslim law to the national courts, reaffirming national dominance over local or religious leaders.[17] As Nigerian, F. Aribisala, writes:

> *I certainly know of no values that I can describe as being widely accepted without contradiction in Nigeria . . . values such as excellence, merit, equality, and justice . . . continue to be questioned . . . while in other societies they are accepted as matters of faith. . . . Until we reach a consensus about national values to which we can appeal or refer without fear of contradiction we will not be able to establish solid constitutions and mechanisms to protect and promote our national interests.[18]*

Conclusion

Of the nine systems, only the United Kingdom and the United States have strong traditions of protecting the individual from the power of the state, both through the law and through the institutions that implement it; these old traditions have been carefully blended into the new. Germany, the post-Soviet republics, and China have long traditions giving individuals legal recourse against one another; among these, only Germany has been able to extend these rights to include protection against the power of the state as well. Traditions in all of these systems, however, gave considerable discretion to authorities; similar processes, with similar rules, continue.

In India, Peru, and Nigeria, older regional traditions for settling disputes are being superceded and ignored by new legal systems and institutions. These new laws may provide individuals with protection against the state, but they do not formally protect the families and groups many individuals identify with. The new systems involve rules and customs very different from those which many people still observe and practice, and these rules are enforced by institutions which high percentages of the populace have no effective access to. In the name of newer notions such as property rights and contracts or equality under the law, court decisions often trample traditional community rights and village social practices.

An Indian, Manvendra Singh, who believes India's roots are Hindu—not Muslim or British—expresses his bitterness over that situation:

> *A state can be multicultural, but not a nation . . . just as roots are the source of a tree, and need to be watered for survival, the commencement of a nation's identity also requires attention. . . . Multiculturalism, which is now an industry, disregards the foundation of national identity . . . the notion that India has been created by marrying many cultures will stand exposed. India could only be created by Indian thought and culture; the import of architectural designs and cholesterol-rich [orthodox Hindus are on a low-fat, vegetarian diet] recipes are, after all, later additions. It is inherently faulty to restructure cultural influences and distribute an equality amongst them. That is not how India was made. . . . India must have a cultural peg to set forth from.[19]*

Summary

In some political systems, individuals are protected from government by the law. In others, laws may change at the whim of government officials, leaving individuals without legal protection against the government. Most systems also have laws to protect citizens from one another. However, no system has protective laws unless citizens and their leaders believe such protection is important. In systems where citizens and leaders have long believed in individual rights, newer laws uphold the old traditions. In systems where citizens identify strongly with local groups and customs, and where group identity is more important than individual rights, traditional group loyalties and customs may clash with newer notions of limited national government and equal individual rights; just writing and enforcing new laws based on those new notions will not necessarily protect individuals from government or one another.

NOTES

1. Jerry F. Hough, "The Party Apparatchiki," in H. Gordon Skilling and Franklyn Griffiths, eds., *Interest Groups in Soviet Politics* (Princeton, N. J.: Princeton University Press, 1977).

2. With regard to the first attitude: As we have already seen, government always took an active role in deciding who received commercial monopolies; it also founded industries under Peter the Great, and the tsar owned land. But centralized planning and ownership of *all* industry and agriculture began after 1917.

3. In a 1958 survey, 84 percent of the general U.S. public and 88 percent of influentials agreed that private ownership of property is necessary for economic progress. In a 1978 survey, 87 percent of the general public and 74 percent of influentials agreed that private ownership of property is as important to a good society as freedom. Also in a 1978 survey, 82 percent of the general public and 82 percent of influentials agreed that the main features of communism, if adopted in the United States, would make life worse for most Americans. Herbert McClosky and John Zaller, eds., *The American Ethos: Public Attitudes toward Capitalism and Democracy* (Cambridge, Mass.: Harvard University Press, 1984), pp. 135, 140.

4. David Remnick, "Gorbachev Lives Out His Legacy," *Kansas City Star,* December 16, 1990.

5. National surveys taken in 1954 found that only 27 percent of Americans would allow an admitted communist to speak in their community. A 1965 survey of University of Michigan students and their parents found that 84 percent of seniors and 72 percent of parents would agree to let a communist speak. Only 36 percent of seniors and 28 percent of parents agreed with the statement "If a communist were legally elected to some public office around here, the people should allow him to take office." A replication of the 1954 study conducted in 1978 found that 53 percent would allow the communist to speak.

    As these figures show, "community influentials" and "legal elites" express much greater tolerance than the general public on these answers. Over 90 percent of respondents endorse the statement that "competitive elections may not be perfect, but no one has yet invented a better way to choose leaders in a free country." A 1974 study found that only 25 percent of those with low political trust, 9 percent of those with medium political trust, and 5 percent of those with high political trust felt a big change is needed in our form of government. That form of government includes institutions and procedures which can protect individual liberties even when tolerance is low. See Paul R. Abramson, *Political Attitudes in America: Formation and Change* (San Francisco: Freeman, 1983), pp. 201, 241–59; McClosky and Zaller, *American Ethos,* esp. p. 213.

6. Lower court judges were appointed by the unit of government just above (for example, republic-level judges were appointed by the national government) so that they could not easily support laws passed by a republic legislature seeking autonomy.

7. Gorbachev's 1988 reorganization of government institutions took place in a dramatic new atmosphere. He claimed that over four hundred thousand people had written letters offering suggestions. In stark contrast to former Soviet practices, there were even votes cast against the reorganization in the formal bodies that approved it. Estonians openly challenged the new plans, and some alterations were made. But the changes, which constituted fundamental rearrangement in the powers of various individuals and institutions, were adopted after brief formal debate shortly after they were announced, meeting with little resistance.

8. For prominent expositions on these interpretations in the United Kingdom, see A. V. Dicey, *An Introduction to the Law of the Constitution,* 10th ed. (London: Macmillan, 1959); Sir Ivor Jennings, *The Law and the Constitution,* 5th ed. (London: London University Press, 1959); Geoffrey Marshall, *Constitutional Conventions* (Oxford: Clarendon, 1984); and Nevil Johnson, *In Search of the Constitution* (Oxford: Pergamon, 1977). Geoffrey Marshall, *Constitutional Theory* (Oxford: Clarendon, 1971) compares the United Kingdom's judiciary system with those of the United States, Nigeria, and India.

9. A justice on the federal Constitutional Court cannot be removed except by the president with the approval of the Constitutional Court itself. Its staff is entirely

separate from other courts. It draws up its own budget and presents it directly to parliament. Half of the judges are chosen by the Bundestag, and half by the Bundesrat.

10. Nearly a fifth of West Germans indicate in public opinion polls that they do not consider legislatures a necessary part of government.

11. In traditional Indian villages, it was common after strenuous discussions for the village leader to simply state the consensus of the group, rather than taking a vote that would divide everyone.

12. Under Muslim *sharia* law, the woman's blood relatives, and religious bodies, would be responsible for supporting her.

13. Shekhar was head of the Janata Dal-Socialist party.

14. The doctrine of eminent domain declares a government's right to seize property for socially useful projects after compensating the owners.

15. Prime Minister Rao had assembled sixteen battalions of troops, but, under what he thought was a negotiated agreement that authorized only a symbolic demonstration, left them under the command of the state government, which was controlled by the

Bharatiya Janata Party and the Vishwa Hindu Parishad. The fundamentalist Vishwa Hindu Parishad, which led the demonstrations at the mosque and resisted all attempts at negotiations, contends in its literature that Hindus whose ancestors were coerced into other faiths by invaders should acknowledge their Hindu identity so they can practice their religion freely.

16. The Janata Dal party tried unsuccessfully to pass legislation banning Christians from seeking converts. They also tried but failed to ban textbooks which pointed out flaws in Hinduism or ignored the flaws in former Muslim rulers.

17. If a person is convicted or acquitted in a local trial under Muslim *sharia* law, a Nigerian national court may overturn that decision on the basis of its own criteria.

18. F. Aribisala, "Nigeria's National Interest and Values," *African Concord,* May 31, 1988.

19. Manvendra Singh, "The BJP in Transition: the Importance of the Millennial and the Mundane," *Indian Express,* November 25, 1992.

EXERCISES

Think about the book thus far:

1. This chapter discusses the fifth of six attitudes that affect political culture: people's notions about legal protection. How might a person's attitudes about the law relate to his or her attitudes about (1) national identity, (2) equality, (3) recruitment, and (4) power and authority?

2. How does an individual's political socialization affect his or her attitudes about legal protection?

3. Are any of the people mentioned in this chapter pan-nationalist? How might that affect their attitudes toward legal protection?

4. To support equal protection under the law, must a person believe in civic culture? Why or why not?

KEY WORDS AND PHRASES

Define the following terms:

hansa	demesne	court of appeal
vill	overlapping jurisdictions	the Basic Law
soke	common law	diet
hundred	precedent	li
shire	jury	fa

THINKING IT THROUGH

Answer each of the following questions (1–11) in one sentence:

1. Give an example of a "prescription for prescriptions" that differs in two of the systems discussed. (In other words, describe how the people in two different systems require their governments to enact laws with different outcomes.)

2. Why is it important to the rights of individuals in the United Kingdom today that the boundaries of sokes and vills often overlapped? Why was a tenant on a demesne not entirely subject to control by the noble who owned that demesne?

3. Why
   a. does citing precedent make it difficult to ignore the diversity of past laws?
   b. might it help an individual to cite past laws and court cases in his or her own court action?
   c. does the need to cite only a legal code (as opposed to precedent) give a court more freedom to ignore the rights of individuals?

4. Point out two differences between the legal systems of the United Kingdom and the United States.

5. How does the German Federal Constitutional Court differ from the United States Supreme Court?

6. How do the United Kingdom and Germany compare in the roles legislatures and courts take in creating and interpreting laws?

7. Point out a difference between the legal systems of East and West Germany.

8. List two differences between legal traditions in the United Kingdom and the former Soviet Union.

9. Point out a similarity, and a difference, between Chinese and German legal traditions.

10. How did the Normans' approach to establishing common law differ from the manner in which the British set up India's laws?

11. Why do language, education, and differing legal traditions make it difficult for villagers in India, Peru, and Nigeria to protect their traditional rights?

Now, ask yourself:

12. How do bailiffs, sheriffs, reeves, and juries help assure that the law will be enforced for all classes of people?

13. Is a constitution necessary to assure that laws will be obeyed by leaders and subjects? Why or why not?

14. Compare the relative "fairness" of these systems. In which would you rather be tried for a crime? Why? In which would you have the best chance of gaining redress for an action the state has taken against you? Again, why do you believe this is so? Is it fair to apply European-type laws in India, Nigeria, and Peru?

chapter 18

POLITICAL CULTURE
ASSIMILATION INTO MODERN INSTITUTIONS

This is the last of five chapters devoted to examining political culture. The five characteristics discussed in the prior chapters relate to the questions of economic integration discussed in chapters 8 and 9. People not integrated into the national economy may not develop national identity, belief in equality, recruitment into political institutions, trust in national authority, and belief in legal protections. That leaves them with weak influence unless a sufficient number of political leaders believe in a civic culture.

After we eat, our body will (we hope) **assimilate** part of the food, or absorb it into the body's substance. People, too, become assimilated into communities and groups when they come to identify with those communities and groups and are absorbed into them. They also may become assimilated into the economic and political institutions of the modern nation-state when they work for, buy from, or are recruited into those institutions. We have been discussing beliefs—beliefs about national identity, equality, who should be recruited into political institutions, political power and authority, and legal protection. All these, as we shall see in this section, help determine the ability of individuals to be assimilated into the political system and, ultimately, to protect their own well-being. That is because these beliefs affect (and are affected by) another belief: whether a person believes they belong to their political system and its institutions. When people feel they do not belong to their political system, or when those with influence feel they do not belong, that set of people may be excluded from benefits when compromises are made. Such people are not likely to be assimilated into the political system.

As chapter 9 indicates, about a third to a half of the American work force is employed by large corporations, a fourth by various units of government, and the rest by smaller businesses. Participants in each of these sectors have considerable interaction with the others—shopping at retail businesses, sending the kids to school, renewing their driver's licenses, and the like. They want their sector to be prosperous, and they recognize that this requires prosperity among the other sectors as well. To this end, they often share many attitudes toward work—placing value on showing up on time, dressing and acting in accordance with the wishes of their employers, and cooperating with fellow workers. They tend to adapt well to technological innovation (with some grumbling and occasional strikes). Even among those protected by civil service status, unions, or academic tenure, these values are required for survival and promotion at their jobs. People usually aspire to remain employed or advance within the organizations they work in, or to change to a similar job in a similar organization.

Most citizens of the post-Soviet republics are employed by government-owned businesses and farms and by the civil service and military. Once hired, people can usually keep their jobs as long as they don't seriously offend their supervisors, who are rarely permitted to fire anyone. Continuing in their jobs also helps them obtain and retain public housing, vacations, and other benefits. They, like U.S. workers, often want to remain employed at the organizations where they work and are wary of any political reforms which might cause them to lose their jobs. Employers and employees in these republics tend to be conservative about technological innovation, but they do not wish to return to simpler forms of technology.

In both the United States and the post-Soviet republics, then, most individuals are assimilated into modern economic institutions. Neither system recognizes nobility or has many people employed by religious institutions. Attitudes toward work in both nation-states are, however, affected by religion. That effect is not always out of keeping with assimilation into large modern economic institutions. Judaism, as well as many protestant groups such as the Presbyterians, Congregationalists, and Methodists in the United States, often encourages its members to work hard and increase their status within the organizations where they work. The Russian Orthodox and Roman Catholic churches, protestant denominations like Lutherans and Anglicans, and Muslim leaders traditionally encourage people to fulfil their obligations to landowners, employers, and political leaders when those individuals are of the same religious faith.

In both the United States and the CIS republics, though, there are people who live in extended families, among others who share religious and cultural traditions. Those traditions often differ from the traditions of those who dominate the government. Sometimes these people are largely self-sufficient, providing their own food, clothing, and shelter (or are at least able to get by without formal employment). This means that some of them have little contact with modern economic institutions such as grocery stores or work places where you punch a time clock or sell goods to a large marketing firm. People with strong religious and ethnic traditions that isolate them from the formal economy are scattered throughout rural areas of the CIS; Georgians, Moldovans, and the Buddhists and Muslims to the south and east probably include disproportionate numbers of such individuals among their ranks. To some degree, so do American blacks, Irish, hispanic Americans, Native Americans, Italians, Poles, Jews, and certain other ethnic groups.

The extent to which such tradition-oriented individuals become assimilated into modern government and economic institutions may affect the ability of a political system to achieve compromise and effectively solve the problems of a variety of citizens. We have discussed the concept of civic culture, which involves the belief that one's political institutions and their policies are legitimate, tolerance of other viewpoints, and a personal sense of competence and mutual trust in politics. As we saw in chapter 10, those who do not work for government or large organizations, and who buy few goods beyond those made by their neighbors, are unlikely to be involved with or knowledgeable about institutions and policies or to have much contact with opposing viewpoints. These individuals often do not identify with groups beyond their own or have other civic-culture supportive attitudes. This does not make them inclined to **compromise**—to make concessions to reach mutually acceptable agreements—with people in other groups. They may, however, have a strong ideology, and they may vote. If they vote for candidates who share their views, they can actually disrupt the civic culture by making it more difficult to reach compromises, resulting in fewer policies that solve the problems of a variety of citizens.

Such individuals remain unassimilated into modern economic institutions. Through voting, they potentially assimilate themselves into political institutions. But there is a catch. If the person they vote for to be a member of the legislature shares their values, this legislator might find it necessary to reject compromises with groups who offend the folks back home. If this representative does not learn to compromise within the legislature, he or she will not be assimilated into it—such an individual will be ignored by other members when deals are struck, his or her constituents will have no effective representation in the legislature. On the other hand, if this representative joins in compromise, he or she may cease to share the characteristics and values of those back home—again, leaving those constituents largely unrepresented.

In actuality, it is not uncommon for a representative to have grown up with friends, values, and economic advantages completely alien to those of the voters. This person may be elected because people are used to voting for certain types of candidates, or because they like what the candidate says and does around them. Since voters who are not assimilated into modern economic institutions have little idea what kinds of advantages and disadvantages political institutions are able to pass out when settling conflicts, they may assume that a mosque, an outhouse, an outdoor schoolhouse with an occasional teacher, a water well left unattended after construction, or a bribe of a few cents before an election represents the full extent of what the system can give them. That leaves their representative free to ignore them when the important compromises are made.

ASSIMILATION AND COMPROMISE

From what we have discussed thus far, one can rank the nine systems according to the percentage of their populace which is assimilated. Obviously, Nigeria has many citizens who are not assimilated into either economic or political institutions, while West Germany has few such citizens. Figure 18.1 rates each nation-state's degree of assimilation in rough order.

From the figure, we can see that Nigeria has a high percentage of people who potentially lie outside the circle of those who benefit from the political system, while West Germany has a low percentage. But another factor helps determine how many people actually benefit. Unless those not assimilated are represented in politics by people who identify with their needs, government can ignore their concerns; and, conversely, when such individuals are represented by people who understand their needs, government may be more responsive to them.

The United Kingdom and Germany contain people who bond to extended families, religious and cultural traditions, and habits of self-sufficiency in running their farms, households, and neighborhoods. In the United Kingdom, many of these people are

Figure 18.1   Degrees of assimilation.

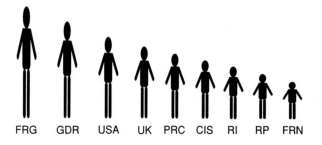

Highest Percentage of
Populace Assimilated

Lowest Percentage of
Populace Assimilated

FRG   GDR   USA   UK   PRC   CIS   RI   RP   FRN

Northern Irish Catholics, Scots, and Welsh, who rarely speak English. Such people also inhabit older neighborhoods and rural areas throughout England. In Germany, they are largely Germans who live in small towns and less productive rural areas. Those in the United Kingdom often engage in handicrafts or service jobs, or are unemployed, giving them minimal involvement in the national market both in terms of jobs and purchases. This is less true in Germany, where many who live in traditional or rural settings nonetheless work for large businesses, farms, or the government, making them at least partially assimilated.

In West Germany, the state governments and the upper house of parliament, which is chosen by state legislatures, contain some people who come from and continue to identify with these kinds of voters. In East Germany, only those with "progressive" leanings could seek office; individuals who identified with supposedly "unsocialist" attitudes of traditional voters (for example, lack of desire to fit into the modern work force) were often excluded from seeking office. The United Kingdom, too, offers little opportunity for people with such values to run for office. Members of Parliament—the national legislature for England, Scotland, and Wales—are generally approved by party headquarters in London; those who insist on discussing in the legislature the most sensitive cultural concerns of their constituents would not be as likely to be tapped to run for office. Northern Ireland is an exception to this rule. From 1921 until 1972, it had its own legislature which, with the aid of extensive gerrymandering, was dominated by the Scotch-Irish Protestant Ulster Unionists. The Unionists, though dominant in the region's economy, were not assimilated into the national politics of the United Kingdom. They promoted protestant education in the schools and excluded Catholics from housing and employment. This conflicted with national policies. After the Catholics began to organize new opposition to these measures, violence ensued. The national government closed down the legislature and brought in troops to restore order. Efforts since that time to create a new government based on a sharing of power have been slow and halting. Those who refuse to compromise with other groups continue to block settlement; Catholics remain largely unassimilated into either the economy or political institutions, and Northern Irish representatives in the House of Commons bring the narrow concerns of their groups with them.

In the United States, state legislatures and the Congress contain some individuals who come from urban ethnic neighborhoods or isolated rural districts. The Communist Party in China (as in East Germany and the Soviet Union earlier) screens its candidates to be sure that none will be disruptive. Even many who are assimilated into economic institutions have refused to participate in these limited groups and, hence, have not been well represented. At least, they may have more of the other prerequisites for exerting influence. When the Soviet Union opened up its voting to other parties, an explosive array of candidates, both from assimilated and unassimilated groups, appeared to provide a voice for those who felt their ethnic groups had been excluded from politics and the economy; many now sit in republic legislatures. Unemployed East Germans without experience in democratic politics constitute a volatile and unpredictable group in the politics of the unified Federal Republic of Germany; they are capable of winning seats in legislatures.

In India, Peru, and Nigeria, where high percentages of the populace are unassimilated, candidates never come from families without education and modern means of livelihood. Representatives from

Squatter shacks on a Bombay street. Streets and vacant lots of Indian cities contain millions of makeshift structures like this. They "house" people who have been unable to make a living in the countryside and cannot afford a place to live in the city.

© *Dolores Potts*

rural areas are often large landowners, or merchants whose own personal interest in acquiring land, low-cost labor, raw materials, debt repayment, and other assets from unassimilated families make them unlikely to support compromises which would return such assets to their voters. Growing up outside the villages, and educated in a different language and cultural milieu, they are also not well prepared to understand the religion and customs of the villagers. But, as we have seen already, they sometimes use narrow ethnic concerns to win votes and disrupt compromises.

All nine systems contain people not assimilated into modern economic institutions. Such people are often isolated from other groups and have cultural habits different from those more assimilated into modern institutions. They are sometimes in conflict with groups better assimilated and represented in political institutions. If people within conflict-resolving political institutions discuss these controversies, the rhetoric can become heated. Because such individuals may not be inclined to compromise, it may be difficult for officeholders to make the concessions needed to resolve such conflicts. It is tempting to simply exclude people with such views from governing institutions and thus avoid having to resolve these conflicts at all. And since those not assimilated lack the traits needed to exert influence, it is easy to keep them out.

The systems where disruptive views are more likely to be represented in legislatures are often countries where the people holding such views constitute small percentages of the populace. Political officeholders may conclude that such minority groups can be included (and thus quieted a bit) without causing major social disruptions or diverting large amounts of physical resources. This helps legislatures reach consensus and compromise. If the unassimilated people in a system comprise a much higher percentage of the populace, they have little chance to be represented; officeholders are likely to conclude that their inclusion would make it difficult to govern, especially if many of these people are very dissatisfied. This leaves portions of the population unrepresented, ignored when political compromises are made—and sometimes seething with rage. They may decide to organize outside the normal political processes or to resort to violence to get the attention of those with influence. Survival of the CIS and post-Soviet republics depends on whether they can find effective new means to exclude disruptive voices from the legislatures, while at the same time controlling protest.

PROTEST

Some groups, though unrepresented, do retain a potential for exerting influence. If they constitute sizable percentages of the populace concentrated in the same region, they can cause trouble for the government. It also helps if they are organized. Religion can provide such an organization, led by clerics who share (and possibly provoke) the separatist attitudes of their followers. Northern Ireland's Catholics, ethnic minorities to the south and east in the CIS, ethnic minorities to the north and west in China,

people in rural areas in India, highland peasants and some urban dwellers in Peru, and some tribal and religious groups in Nigeria include concentrations of people with the potential to cause trouble.

People like these are often frustrated because they have not achieved influence in national politics, and they may identify with their own group more than the nation as a whole. They usually distrust other groups and have no concept of social equality or equal opportunity. They often do not trust the laws, do not support imposing legal limits on government or individuals, and do not understand or desire compromise.

Some Northern Irish, religious and linguistic minorities of India, and the Sendero Luminoso and Tupac Amaru movements in Peru have been involved in violent antigovernment activities for years. As the Soviet Union liberalized, leaders of similar groups there increasingly promoted violence to achieve their ends.

Political institutions can respond by formulating policies that attend to the needs of such groups. They can respond with police and military force. Or they can do both.

Protest leaders need the capacity to rouse people with grievances to anger. Government leaders, in contrast, need the capacity to resolve conflicts. Military force may defer or squelch conflicts, but it does not resolve them. To resolve conflict, government leaders must desire to learn why people are angry and seek compromises which alleviate the anger-provoking conditions.

Those least willing to compromise are often people who have never received much benefit from compromise. Because they have not been included in past compromise, they do not recognize its value. When they lack the capacity to effectively exert influence within the political system, they exert force against the system from outside. That does not mean they would not respond to compromise if it were offered. The leaders who are capable of formulating objectives for them, and of devising strategy to meet those objectives, often have enough education and experience to become assimilated into the political system. If even part of those who lead the revolt are drawn into such contact, the leadership may split. But at least partial assimilation offers some slim hope for groups to gain benefits from their political system.

The scores of separate nationalities in the CIS and other post-Soviet republics present a strong obstacle to assimilation. Some were integrated into the economy, but not the politics of the Soviet Union. Some have used their new independence to fight the assimilation of other groups into the politics of the new nation-states. The leaders of the Soviet Union sought to give small ethnic groups at least token representation in government institutions; leaders of the new, smaller nation-states may be more inclined to ignore and suppress them, leaving violence as their only recourse.

After any period of civil war or revolution, control is likely to return to those who have experience exercising authority. After citizens stormed the headquarters of the state police in Leipzig, East Germany, they set up a group of sixteen volunteer investigators to identify the names of secret police agents and informers; nine of these volunteers subsequently turned out to be members of the communist party. The people who appear to set up new governments after old ones have fallen always include a strong contingent of former participants in the old government. New participants must quickly learn on the job if they are to compete with those experienced in governing.

IMPOTENCE

People cut off from political and economic institutions who do not resort to violence, or nonviolent combined protest, cannot exert influence. If, at the same time, those within political institutions fail to formulate policies that benefit these people, they are left out of the political process altogether and depend on people within the process who simply believe in helping those left out. As we noted in chapter 13, all these systems have individuals involved in their political institutions who seek to help those without influence. Yet there are many more who primarily look after the interests of the groups they represent. If there are not many who support tolerance and reach for chances to include marginal groups in compromise, it is hard for a system to arrive at such policies. Yet the systems with the highest percentages of unassimilated people—Nigeria, Peru, India, and the CIS—are among those least likely to have proponents of civic culture as leaders in political institutions. That leaves the unassimilated, already without access to social and economic institutions, out of the political system as well. They are not part of the "regular pattern of human relationships through which competition over goods and services and conflicts over cultural traditions, ideas, and other values are conducted and resolved" in the nation-state. All nine systems contain politically unassimilated people.

Increasingly, because they are politically weak, such individuals are either being pushed from the land and forced to work for absentee landowners, go entirely unemployed, or face cultural challenges from other groups who wish to expel them from their regions or alter their living habits. Those who work for someone else have a political resource the unemployed lack. However, that resource ceases to serve either an economic or a political purpose if a person's labor is no longer needed by an employer or can no longer support the family. When people have no land or jobs, their community disintegrates, and they even lose the bases for protest we just discussed.

James C. Scott studied the efforts of poor Malaysian peasants facing just that prospect.[1] The owner of the land they worked on planned to bring in agricultural machinery which would replace most of them. These peasants decided to use their jobs as a political resource. They found several ways to resist, such as walking off the job; blocking a combine-harvester from entering the fields; refusing to break strikes; slaughtering livestock; moving field boundary markers; threatening that fields would not be harvested unless wages were raised; refusing to compete with one another for jobs; stealing; refusing to report stealing; engaging in malicious gossip and character assassination; spreading rumors; flattering potential employers; and helping organize electoral activity. All these activities are examples of exerting influence, making use of jobs and elections as political resources. But they are also examples of influence exerted by people with little education, information, or access to institutions. Such influence may or may not be sufficient to reduce the disruptions in their lives. Scott does not tell us whether the peasants were replaced by the agricultural machinery. If they were, their exertion of influence was without effect.

In this case, resistance took the form of not absorbing the values of their employers, of interacting with them as little as possible, of making annoying disruptions in their lives and making them depend on the peasants in small ways. None of this was likely sufficient to stop the employers from making the fundamental changes which would destroy the peasants' community and livelihood. In a situation like this, if you cannot make yourself important as an employee or customer, gain access to the political institutions that run the state apparatus, or seek legal redress to stop the changes, your traditions of life and livelihood may be endangered and out of your control. When people lose their land and cannot find other work, there is little they can do. No one with political or economic prominence depends on them for anything any longer. There is no need to compromise with them. They must enter government institutions, or at least find people within government institutions who identify with them enough to try to help, even if doing so may put their own political positions at risk. Such leaders virtually do not exist in Nigeria, Peru, and India.[2] Their presence in the other systems is muted. For a politician, there is no reward in helping the helpless.

Passions cool. People cannot often keep up the momentum of resistance for long periods of time. If they do not use the opportunity to obtain information, gain access to institutions, and develop other attributes needed for influence, their chance for change may pass. Even when the entire political system changes rapidly, with new leaders coming to the fore, as in former communist systems, those taking control of the new institutions are likely to give more attention to those wielding influence. They may depend on temporary crowds, or resistance, from people not otherwise equipped to exert influence. In the long term, however, they must give ear to those who regularly exercise influence if they are to survive as leaders.

If unassimilated individuals are to receive benefits from the political system and avoid being harmed by those more powerful, they have little choice but to acquire traits associated with influence. They need to become assimilated into the political system. Sporadic resistance by groups which constitute a high portion of the populace but have few other traits which might give them influence may ultimately be counterproductive to their well-being, like a wasp that stings a man without flying away. Those in charge may simply double their resolve to exclude them from institutions and compromises.

ASSIMILATION AND LEGAL PROTECTION

To be represented in the political system, one need only take part in modern economic institutions. Because so many Americans, British, Germans, CIS citizens, and Chinese are part of such institutions, they are part of the process by which their political systems resolve conflicts over goods and services; the institutions where they work and buy are represented in politics, and so, indirectly, they are. Those institutions, of course, may look after their own needs more than the needs of their workers and customers. To balance that, individuals can join various interest groups—if they are allowed to do so. These interest groups will look after their needs. But there is no substitute for personally acquiring the traits that give one influence; anyone with an education is in a position to do so.

The competition between various individuals and groups is even more balanced if people believe in social equality and equal access to political institutions. Clear legal rules for operating national institutions that protect the rights of various groups and individuals also broaden influence to greater proportions of the population.

The political cultures of the CIS republics, China, India, Peru, and Nigeria have neither of those last two characteristics. The minorities which are assimilated in India, Peru, and Nigeria, though they have learned to compromise with one another, always face uncertainty about their jobs, property, and liberties. The majorities assimilated in the CIS and China are finding it difficult to expand their rights; it is uncertain that laws will be enforced to benefit those they are claimed to benefit.

In China, at least, families remain strong. Children continue to be socialized under Confucian standards to obey their parents, and strong pressures keep husbands living with wives. Community leaders enforce these standards. In contrast, family life is under great stress in the CIS republics. As we shall see in chapters 25 and 26, alcoholism, abortion, divorce, and separation are common; few social institutions bind people together.[3] India, Peru, and Nigeria face tensions among racial groups and a decline in the power of community leaders. That compounds the difficulty of achieving social equality, equal access to institutions, and clear legal rights.

Among those who are assimilated, the more people share a sense of national identity, a belief in equality, a belief that access to political institutions should be widely shared, and a belief in legal protections for both groups and individuals, the greater the nation-state's ability to reach mutually beneficial compromises. Among the nine nation-states, higher portions of the populace may share these attitudes in the United States, the United Kingdom, and West Germany. East Germany's sense of national unity included West Germany, and its beliefs in equality and access to political institutions may be stronger than those in the West; however, East Germans have little experience with legal protections and are uncertain about their role in reunified Germany. The former Soviet Union and China have also socialized people to believe in equality. Great Russians and Han have strong feelings of national identity, but also an inclination to place only their own people in positions of high authority. Neither system has a tradition of legal protection. The populace and leadership in India, Peru, and Nigeria share none of these beliefs. Hence, the latter three nation-states would appear to have significantly less opportunity to create mutually beneficial compromises. Since these nation-states have the highest percentages of unassimilated populace, they also have many inhabitants who can be left out of the compromises they do make.

A perfect eighteen–hole golf course is useless to someone with no clubs or golf balls; similarly, a perfectly designed set of government institutions is of no use to those without influence. Even for individuals with the motivation and resources to acquire influence, government institutions are no better than the values they are built on. A set of institutions designed to protect personal liberties cannot do so unless the people involved with them have the desire and ability to protect liberties.

Britain's common law tradition is clearly of benefit in protecting the liberties of British and American citizens. Exported to India and Nigeria, the benefit of British forms of government is less clear. The traditional belief in equality helps great varieties of Americans access educational and governmental institutions; without that belief, similar institutions do not afford the same liberties to Peruvians or Nigerians. The lesson is clear: The laws and institutions themselves do not create liberties; such institutions allow *expressions* of liberty when they are backed by widespread belief in the importance of law and equality. Political culture establishes the boundaries in which institutions are created and used.[4] The best institutional design is worthless if the political culture does not support concepts such as social equality, equal access to institutions, and well-defined legal rights.

SUMMARY

Individuals are more likely to be included in compromise if they (1) desire to live within certain territorial boundaries together with others who live there; (2) are accepted as equals by those who rule the nation-state that governs that territory; (3) are able to organize politically and be elected or appointed to public office; (4) recognize and trust in the authority of those with sovereignty; (5) can turn to the law for protection; and (6) are involved in the formal economic institutions recognized by law. When none of those conditions apply, there are only two ways for such individuals to benefit from the policies of their nation-state: At least some of the citizens and leaders with influence must feel that these individuals belong and must reach out to extend benefits to them, or the individuals must offer sustained resistance to restrictions on their right to organize and protest. Those with sovereignty will feel more comfortable including such individuals in compromise if their numbers are small, so that they will not gain too large or strident a voice.

NOTES

1. James C. Scott, *Weapons of the Weak: Everyday Forms of Peasant Resistance* (New Haven, Conn.: Yale University Press, 1985), chapter 5.

2. Lloyd I. Rudolph and Susanne Hoeber Rudolph, *In Pursuit of Lakshmi: The Political Economy of the Indian State* (Chicago: University of Chicago Press, 1987), pp. 253, 364–92, discuss political pilgrimages (in which people walk from village to village in a demonstration), shutdowns, roadblocks, and lock-ins (where workers lock themselves into a place of work) as means of political protest. They argue that most protest movements include many who own some land and are involved in selling some crops, and hence emphasize concerns such as market prices more than wages and jobs for farm workers, but that poorer laborers join to protest destruction of their property, molestation of their female members, unacceptable terms of employment, and other grievances. Ultimately, voting gives the poor their greatest impact. Rudolph and Rudolph conclude: "Laborers who lack assets, income, and bargaining advantages also often lack that sense of self-worth and efficacy that they need in order to believe that they can influence their fate through collective action. . . . Our account of mobilization of the rural poor has shown not only that it occurs rarely, but also that the prospects are dim for it to be a vehicle of revolutionary transformation." Still, these writers point out, "Despite the appropriation of benefits by better-placed cultivators and landowners, targeted programs designed to enhance the assets, incomes, or employment of the rural poor have become and are likely to remain an imperative for party support and state legitimacy." They do not discuss the effectiveness of the programs targeted to the poor.

   Michael Watts, *Silent Violence: Food, Famine, and Peasantry in Northern Nigeria* (Berkeley: University of California Press, 1983), pp. 363–67, 683, discusses protests in Nigeria. "The colonial period ushered in a new social field of force in which the surplus was appropriated and fought over in profoundly new ways. Famines indicated that these struggles had been decisively lost by the peasantry in spite of their dogged resistance."

3. One of the first new films to emerge from the Soviet Union under *glasnost* was "Freeze, Die, and Come to Life," which won the Camera D'Or Prize at the Cannes Film Festival for the Best First Film. Its director, Vitaly Kanevski, grew up in the town of Suchan, near Vladivostok, and served eight years in a labor camp. He made the film in Suchan, graphically depicting the breakdown in social life.

4. "Democracy grows from the bottom up and cannot be imposed from the top down. Civil society has to be built from the inside out. The institutional superstructure comes last." Benjamin R. Barber, "Jihad vs. McWorld," *The Atlantic* 269, 3 (March 1992): 63.

EXERCISES

Think about the book thus far:

1. This chapter about assimilation concludes the discussion of political culture. It discusses the sixth of what six attitudes?

2. According to the introduction to chapter 14, how does assimilation relate to the other five aspects of political culture?

3. For a person to be assimilated into the political system, how must he or she relate to these other five aspects?

KEY WORDS AND PHRASES

Define the following terms:

assimilate
compromise

THINKING IT THROUGH

Answer each of the following questions (1–7) in one sentence:

1. Political culture exists where?

2. How are people economically assimilated into a nation-state?

3. Why can voting be a means of assimilation into the political system?

4. This chapter points out that it may be easy for a representative from a district where voters are largely unassimilated into economic and political institutions to engage in compromises that barely benefit those back home. Why is this true?

5. Why may people without influence not understand compromise?

6. What is the danger of excluding people who do not know how to compromise from political institutions? What is the danger of including them?

7. Why is it hard for the unassimilated to mount effective protests against injustices that affect them? Is their case strengthened if they keep their protest nonviolent?

Now, do this:

Figure 18.1 ranks countries according to the percentage of citizens who are assimilated. Those with the highest percentage assimilated appear to the left and those with the lowest percentage to the right. Try a similar ranking, drawing on what you have learned in chapters 14–18, by filling out the following chart.

Following is a list of the traits we have discussed in the last five chapters:

a. people with national identity

b. people who believe in equality of opportunity for all classes and ethnic groups

c. people who can be recruited into public office

d. people who confer authority on their government

e. people who believe all citizens have a right to legal protection from the state and other citizens

f. people who are assimilated into political and economic institutions (use figure 18.1, or create your own rank ordering)

In vertical column 1, you will list the names of the countries where each of these six traits is strongest; in column 9, you will list the countries where each trait is weakest. In between, rank the nations in order. For example, focusing on the first trait: Based on what you know, which country might have the greatest portion of its populace sharing a strong national identity? Put the name of that country in the first box under column 1. Which country has the smallest portion of its populace sharing a sense of national identity? Put its name in the first box under column 9. Then rank the others in between. (For the CIS, think in terms of citizens identifying with their own republics.) Perform the same steps for the other five traits, leaving the final column (headed "Importance") blank for now. (Hint: The fourth from the last paragraph of this chapter may help you determine how to complete the chart.)

	I			II			III			Importance (%)
	1 (Greatest %)	2	3	4	5	6	7	8	9 (Lowest %)	
a. National identity										
b. Social equality										
c. Equal access to institutions										
d. Authority of government										
e. Legal protections										
f. Assimilation										
							Percentage from other factors:			
									Total:	100%

Now try tabulating your results in two different ways. First, analyze the raw numbers. Write down the number of the column in which a system appears for each of the six traits (a–f). For example, if you have placed USA in column 1 for a, and 3 for b, assign it a "1" and a "3" in each of those columns below. Then add up the total for each system across all nine rows.

By Raw Numbers:

	a	b	c	d	e	f	Total
USA							
CIS							
FRG							
GDR							
UK							
PRC							
RI							
RP							
FRN							

Now try a second way to tabulate. Notice that the columns are divided into groups I, II, and III. Every time a system appears in category I, give it one point; give it two points for category II, and three points for category III. Again, add across each row to come up with a total for each system.

By Divisions I, II, and III:

	a	b	c	d	e	f	Total
USA							
CIS							
FRG							
GDR							
UK							
PRC							
RI							
RP							
FRN							

The text contains the following hypothesis: Among those who are assimilated, the more people share a sense of national identity, a belief in equality, a belief that access to political institutions should be widely shared, and a belief in legal protections for both groups and individuals, the greater the nation-state's ability to reach mutually beneficial compromises. That hypothesis may not be correct; your rankings of the nation-states may also be inaccurate; (the afterword on scientific method speaks to that). But if both the hypothesis and your rank orderings are in the right range, you can expect the countries with the lowest scores to be more likely to benefit wide portions of their populace in compromises.

Perhaps some of these criteria are more important than others. If a nation-state is to arrive at mutually beneficial compromises, is it more important that high percentages of its populace identify with the nation as a whole, or that high percentages of its populace are assimilated into the national economy and political institutions? Perhaps some criteria not charted in these boxes are even more important, such as whether national leaders (rather than particular percentages of the populace) share some of these beliefs, or whether the nation-state has free elections or some of the arrangements of government institutions we will discuss in the next six chapters. You might want to try assigning percentages in the ''Importance'' column on the chart to indicate the relative importance of each of the six factors. Would you give 10 percent to a, or 5 percent or 20 percent? How much would you reserve for the other traits? How might this affect your judgment about the hypothesis and the scores?

AN AFTERWORD ON SCIENTIFIC METHOD

You might want to think a bit more about scientific method. First, it is important to base comparisons on criteria which you can share with others and which they can test for themselves. Criteria are not charts or statistics, but judgments about factors which seem important in determining whether something might exist. What is one criterion you applied to all nine of these entities in assessing the percentage of populace who identify with the entire nation? in assessing the percentage who believe in equality, or in legal protection?

Next, it is necessary to decide how to weigh or quantify a criterion, and how many criteria go into deciding whether a phenomenon exists. The phenomena we are discussing here are not easy to measure because they are ideas in people's minds. You cannot see into a person's mind to know whether they do or do not identify with their nation. You can set up some criteria to measure this: their tendency to obey their government, their rejection of parties dedicated to regional separation, the length of their history together, the types of interaction they have. You may be able to gather some statistics about this and assign scores, but ultimately you must make subjective judgments about how to score each criterion and how important each of these criteria are in determining whether particular people feel attached to their nation. You can never be sure of how they feel; you can only share the thoughts and information you used to make the judgments and assign the scores.

To compare, you need to create some categories. Here we have created two such categories for rank ordering: by raw numbers (presumably, each successive nation-state in column a contains a smaller percentage of the populace who identify with the nation as you move from left to right on the chart and is thus assigned a number from 1 to 9), and by portions of the sample (top third each gets one point, middle third two points, and lowest third three points). This could also be done by deciding that if a country has over 80 percent of its populace with (or rating a certain score on) a certain characteristic it gets 1 point, 60 percent to 79 percent, 2 points, and so on. Or one can categorize in other ways.

Once you have quantified the phenomena you are investigating, you must think about what the results might signify. Usually this is done by creating hypotheses, or assumptions, about how these phenomena might affect other phenomena. As we move along in the book, we shall examine more information needed to test the validity of our hypothesis about the relationship between assimilation, attitudes, and compromises. If the hypothesis is valid, which of these nation-states seems to best meet the criteria for creating widely beneficial compromises, based on your judgments about those phenomena and the two methods of quantification we have created here?

One final question to ponder: Are those who believe in traits b, c, and e generally from among people with traits a, d, and f? Why or why not? How does this relate to the idea of a civic culture?

chapter 19

PARTIES, INTEREST GROUPS, AND ELECTIONS

POLITICAL PARTIES

Now that we have explored political culture, we turn our attention to political institutions. We shall see that similar institutional arrangements can produce different results, depending on the political culture and dispersion of influence within a nation-state. The next three chapters discuss the input side of the political system—political institutions and processes outside government; the subsequent three chapters discuss the output of the political system—political institutions and processes inside government. Let's begin by focusing on political parties, raising the question of whether allowing voters a choice between two or more parties increases the chance that a variety of groups will have input into compromises.

The political system in each of the nine nation-states includes political parties, though these parties may go underground during periods of military rule. Some systems allow these parties to compete freely, while others do not, as we discussed in chapter 3. Allowing free competition does not necessarily assure that the parties that form will represent the full diversity of citizens; some will try to appeal to a great variety of people, while others are narrower in their appeal. In either case, political parties may not represent the full spectrum of citizens if the political culture does not afford the right climate. **In a political system where influence is not widely dispersed and the political culture does not support a civic culture, can particular types of parties, or free competition between parties, make it easier to arrive at compromises which benefit wide portions of the populace?** We approach that question here.

We learned from the past several chapters that these systems vary widely in the extent to which they disperse influence. They also differ in the degree to which people believe in the legitimacy of political institutions and the direction and content of public policy, tolerate a plurality of interests and believe these interests can be reconciled, and feel efficacy and mutual trust. These aspects of political culture affect the types of political parties that form and the ability of parties to arrive at mutually acceptable solutions. Can leaders construct party systems which overcome the obstacles posed by the absence of these attitudes?

Some people acquire enough influence to become involved in political institutions, while others do not; that is a fundamental factor in politics. An individual who simply learns about those institutions, without developing a sense of who participates in them and how, gains little knowledge of how politics functions. But now that we have an idea of who does participate and how they do so, it is time to find out more about the institutions they participate in. The institutions, political and otherwise, which develop in a nation-state will affect the group identities people develop and the sorts of issues placed on the political agenda. And it is within those institutions that people debate issues and resolve conflicts—or in other words, determine policy outcomes. In chapters 19 through 21, we shall examine one set of political institutions involved in this process—political parties and interest groups. These institutions exert influence on government institutions, which we shall examine in chapters 22 through 24.

The most conspicuous political institutions people participate in in modern nation-states are political parties. We defined parties in chapter 1 as institutions which choose nominees to run in elections for public office, and which try to keep those in public office cooperating on a variety of shared objectives.

If political parties are to help voters promote shared objectives, nominees must first offer clear policy alternatives on issues important to voters and then, once elected, attempt to pass these policy alternatives into law. Political parties can help officeholders gain and organize public support for compromises they must make in passing laws. They can help the public put pressure on officeholders to change their behavior. They can help officeholders cooperate in passing legislation and developing compromises among themselves. Or they may help citizens organize to overthrow the government by force.

Maurice Duverger suggests that modern political parties had their origins in cliques emerging within legislatures.[1] Some of these cliques were composed of legislators from the same region. Occasionally they were composed of legislators who shared similar views on policy. These cliques helped legislators make compromises with one another to pass legislation; because they were friends, they were disposed to work well together.

As suffrage was gradually extended during the nineteenth century, legislative cliques within political parties took on a new purpose; the members of these cliques helped one another gain votes. Some could appeal to one segment of the population and others to another. They could tell voters that, once elected, they would get legislation passed because of the number of friends they had in the legislature. Outsiders without political party backing could not make similar promises. In the process of gaining

votes, party leaders could organize branches and committees composed of private citizens. Parties like this which emerged from cliques inside legislatures, and which added such private committees as well, could hope to work out compromises on legislation and gain public support for these compromises. Some parties also organized outside the legislature. These parties posed a threat to those organized inside, and as a result, at least some of the insiders resisted them. Parties emerging from within legislatures can better influence policy than those which originate, and remain, entirely outside.

Parties vary in their attitudes toward the entire political system. A **prosystem party** wants to make the existing system work; an **antisystem party** wants to fundamentally change the way the system operates. Antisystem parties are likely to start outside legislatures, but when they elect even a few members, they can interrupt proceedings. However, once inside, antisystem party members may find themselves defending the system against their more radical supporters.

As we discussed in chapter 3, parties also vary in the variety of groups they attempt to include. A consensual party attempts to include as many members as possible, even though their views may differ. Parties whose members are rigid in their support of a certain ideology, or of a few special policies or interests—splinter parties—appeal only to certain narrow segments of the populace. Splinter parties may be able to cooperate temporarily to rule a nation-state. Consensual parties are more likely to develop compromises and effectively solve the problems of high percentages of citizens, and thus they are more likely to produce long-lasting, stable rule. However, the presence of consensual parties does not assure compromise. Without civic culture attitudes, it is hard to form competitive consensual parties. Even with it, consensual parties may sometimes fail to appeal to certain minorities, who must turn to splinter parties; in either case, it is hard to represent minorities who have no influence. But systems with single consensual parties, or only splinter parties, in political cultures that lack a civic culture, can leave many minorities, and many concerns of the majority, out of the political process.

This 1990 West German election poster reads, "When men recognize our dignity, there will be enough kindergartens. Men ought to vote for this woman. Carola Von Braun, the intelligent alternative."
© Gordon Seyffert

CONSENSUAL AND SPLINTER PARTIES

Seven of the nine nation-states (all but Nigeria and the post-Soviet republics) contain prosystem consensual parties. In the United States, the Republican and Democratic parties fit this description. West Germany has the Christian Democratic Union and the Social Democratic Party; the United Kingdom, the Conservative and Labour Parties. So these three nation-states each have two prosystem consensual parties, which control the chief executive's post most of the time. The Republican, Christian Democratic Union,[2] and Conservative parties have close ties to the business community, civil servants, and wealthier social groups. The Democratic, Social Democratic,[3] and Labour parties have associations with leaders of labor unions and other interest groups representing working people, women's groups, and immigrants and racial minorities. But all these parties try to appeal to people from all classes, racial groups, and regions. As we have seen, the groups most likely to vote and take part in politics include disproportionate numbers of people who have completed secondary or higher education, pay some attention to politics, and are well integrated into the economy. So these consensual parties try to appeal to such middle-class individuals.

The Communist Party of the Soviet Union was, and China's Communist Party is, an example of a prosystem consensual party, as are the Indian National Congress in India, and APRA (the American Popular Revolutionary Alliance) in Peru. Each of these nation-states, as well as East Germany, has (or had) only one prosystem consensual party. Before Mikhail Gorbachev implemented reforms in the late 1980s, the Communist Party of the Soviet Union allowed no other parties to organize; after the failed 1991 coup attempt, when hard-line communists tried to oust Gorbachev, the party itself was forced to disband. East Germany's ruling communist party, the Socialist Unity Party, contested elections in concert

These posters from East Germany's 1990 election call for "Freedom, equality, brotherhood, and social security," along with jobs for both East and West Germans. The scowling man advertises Leipzig's alternative newspaper.

© *Bob Gamer*

with closely allied splinter parties in the National Front; China's Communist Party does the same in conjunction with the "democratic parties." These communist parties claimed to be the "vanguard of the working class" and in the Soviet Union, "of Soviet society." Since they alone ruled and contested elections, and tried to maintain support among all ethnic groups and all types of "workers," these parties had to formulate objectives that would benefit a wide variety of groups. In China, that still happens.

In their first free election in 1990, voters in East Germany voted primarily for West Germany's two consensual parties. Since Germans feel a strong national identity, and East Germans had hopes of integrating into the prosperous West German economy, their votes are not surprising. If economic integration succeeds, that trend is likely to continue. But if high unemployment continues without a visible improvement in the standard of living, splinter parties could draw votes. Conversely, many people in the Soviet Union did not have a strong sense of national identity in support of the entire union; that is one reason it eventually broke down. Now parties formed within the individual republics where competition is allowed must see whether any of them can emerge as consensual parties.

India and Peru allow other consensual parties, but so far none has emerged. However, coalitions of other parties have frequently succeeded in electing chief executives. During recent years, civilian rulers in Peru have all come from such coalitions except for APRA's Alan Garcia; such coalitions have seldom toppled India's Congress party from rule, but they have been increasing in strength in recent years.

Table 19.1 lists the consensual party or parties in each nation-state. All of these consensual parties, except for the two in Nigeria and the Soviet Union's Communist Party which was recently disbanded, have survived for a considerable time. The Democratic Party in the United States grew out of committees of correspondence created shortly after the United States was formed; the Republican Party entered its first election in 1855.[4] The Soviet Union's Communist Party was founded in 1898,[5] as was China's in 1921,[6] as an antisystem splinter party.

Table 19.1

Consensual Parties

	Workers, Women, Racial Minorities		*Business, Civil Servants*
USA	Democratic		Republican
USSR	Communist Party (outlawed 1991)		
CIS			
FRG	Social Democratic		Christian Democratic
GDR	Socialist Unity Party		
UK	Labour		Conservative
PRC	Communist Party		
RI		Congress	
RP		APRA	
FRN	Social Democratic		National Republican

Germany's Social Democratic party was founded in 1875,[7] and the Christian Democratic Union immediately after World War II (as was East Germany's Socialist Unity Party). The United Kingdom's Conservative Party, founded in 1832, has roots in the seventeenth century; the Labour Party, founded in 1906 out of earlier parties, eclipsed the Liberal Party (founded in the 1840s) as the Conservatives' major competitor.[8] The Indian National Congress party was established in 1885,[9] and Peru's APRA in 1930. Both patterned themselves after workers' parties such as the United Kingdom's Labour Party or Germany's Social Democrats but fell under control of leaders with close ties to business firms. All of these consensual parties have been heavily represented in legislatures and have elected or appointed chief executives (though APRA did not succeed in electing a chief executive until 1985 and then suffered a major decline in support in the 1990 election).

Nigeria has not been able to establish a consensual party. Its parties have centered around its three largest tribal groups—Hausa, Ibo, and Yoruba. Dating from 1940, 1944, and 1951 respectively, these parties have changed their names over the years.[10] Sometimes two of them have formed a coalition for an election, but never all three; these elections were won by coalitions of splinter parties. In 1983, the Hausa-based party led by President Shagari claimed to win reelection with 47 percent of the vote, and over 25 percent of the votes in sixteen of the nineteen states; in actuality, vote fraud was rampant in that election. The military regime led by Major-General Mohammed Buhari, which soon overthrew Shagari, uncovered hundreds of thousands of duplicated names on the voter lists, vast quantities of extra voting cards, and hundreds of nonexistent voting stations which sent in voting returns.[11] The 1992 Constitution outlaws all parties except the National Republicans and Social Democrats, created by Major-General Ibrahim **Babangida** (who overthrew Buhari in 1985). It also requires that a presidential nominee receive a majority of overall votes and at least a third of the votes cast in two-thirds of the states.[12]

Prosystem splinter parties play a role in all these systems. As just noted, this type of party was the only kind of political party in Nigeria until 1992, when splinter parties were banned. From 1977 through 1980, and again in 1989, coalitions of splinter parties unseated India's Congress party from the chief executive's position; in 1991, it returned to power in a shaky coalition with a splinter party. Janata Dal, Janata Dal-Socialist, the Bharatiya Janata Party, the Communist Party of India, and the

Communist Party of India (Marxist) contest elections throughout India. Within different states, several splinter parties contest elections and sometimes control the legislatures, including the Dalit Mazdoor Kisan party and the All-India Anna Dravida Munnetra Kazhagam, Telequ Desam, the Indian People's Front, Akali Dal (among Sikhs in the Punjab), the National Conference, Buhajan Samaj (composed of "untouchables"), and others. In Peru, where parties often form or coalesce around individuals seeking the presidency, there are about forty political parties. With the exception of APRA's 1985 victory, Peru's general elections have been won by temporary coalitions of splinter parties which break up after the term of office expires.

East Germany's Socialist Unity Party shared legislative seats with splinter parties representing farmers, churches, Liberal and National Democrats, women, youth, trade unions, and cultural concerns. These parties did not run against each other, and they combined in the legislature as a coalition called the National Front.[13] A similar coalition helped China's Communists when they first came to power, and members of these "democratic parties"[14] are still permitted to run for some Chinese legislative seats. In 1990, the Soviet Union allowed new parties to form, and these parties immediately began to win local, regional, and republic elections. New political parties in many of the republics, such as RUKH (Ukrainian People's Movement for Perestroika), the Armenian National Party, the Reformer's Democratic Party of Tajikistan, and National or Popular Fronts (or Democratic Blocs), were formed by intellectuals seeking a more open system of government. In Russia, Democratic Russia helped elect Boris Yeltsin president; Popular Accord, a coalition of three parties including the Democratic Party of Russia, broke from it, and soon democratic free-market reformers had formed eight additional splinter parties. Other parties formed: groups such as Tajikistan's Rastokhez Popular Movement and Islamic Renaissance Party, the Azerbaijani Popular Front, and a dozen small Russian parties (foremost among them, Pamyat and Sobor and the National Salvation Front, which reveres both Hitler and Stalin) became

vehicles for the expression of regional ethnic separatist sentiment. By 1991, the situation had become even more complex. The outlawed Communist Party had reorganized itself into individual parties within the different republics (the Socialist Party of Tajikistan, the People's Democratic Party of Uzbekistan, and so on). New parties keep forming as old ones split and elections require coalitions.

In West Germany, the Free Democratic Party,[15] founded after World War II, has frequently formed coalitions with the two consensual parties, which are so evenly matched in electoral support that they need the Free Democrats' help. The Christian Social Union of Bavaria allies with the Christian Democrats.[16] The environmentally conscious Greens, founded in 1980, held forty-six seats in the Bundestag—nearly the same number as the Free Democrats—after the 1987 election, though they lost them all in 1990 because they won less than 5 percent of the vote. The Party of Democratic Socialism, founded after the collapse of East Germany, combines remnants of East Germany's National Front. It received 10 percent of the vote in the 1990 election. The new German People's Union (DVU) advocates expelling all non-Germans.

In the United Kingdom, the Liberal Party (now the Liberal Democratic Party) persists as a stable competitor, increasing its share of votes from 3 percent in 1951 to over 25 percent in 1983 and 18 percent in 1992, always retaining a few seats in the House of Commons. The Ecology Party, Communist Party, Socialist Workers' Party, the National Front, the Natural Law Party (of Maharishi Mahesh Yogi), and the British National Party, along with a few other parties and independents, contest parliamentary seats, but seldom win one. The Abstention Party refrains from running candidates, in protest against the system. A variety of regional parties compete with the Conservatives, Labour, and the Liberal Democrats in Scotland, Wales, and Northern Ireland.[17] In the United States, the Prohibition, Socialist, Progressive,[18] Farmer-Labor, Libertarian, and Liberal parties have all existed for many years, and periodically run candidates for various seats. Some win seats in a single state, but they almost never take a seat in the Congress. Occasional independent candidates, such as Ross Perot in 1992, also run for president.

These nation-states also contain antisystem splinter parties, some of which are officially banned. China and Nigeria have banned all opposition parties not allied with their leadership. China Spring and other groups try to organize Chinese living abroad to overthrow the Communist government, and rebels in Tibet and western provinces have some underground organized leadership. In the United States, the Socialist Workers, Socialist Labor, Communist, Militant Workers, and Workers' World parties contest elections with the expressed goal of overturning the present system of government; they never receive many votes. Many opposition groups in the Soviet Union united prior to glasnost and later evolved into some of the legal splinter parties in existence today. In West Germany, communist groups have been permitted to contest elections, but neo-Nazi groups like the Free German Workers party have not. East Germans formed underground groups which helped organize the demonstrations that led to the downfall of the communist regime. In united Germany, the Autonome and other neo-Nazi groups, such as German Alternative and the National Offensive, organized frequent demonstrations to protest unification; though they were banned in 1992, their clones continue to pop up. Stasi, the former secret police of East Germany, are suspected of collaborating with the long-established Red Army Factions to promote terrorist acts of violence.

In the United Kingdom, The National Front, British National Party, Constitutional Movement, Communist Party, Communist Campaign Group, New Communist Party, Workers' Revolutionary Party, and Socialist League all voice sentiments for fundamental change. The Militant Tendency is a group which attempts to infiltrate constituency organizations within the Labour Party so as to make party policy more militant. Sinn Fein is the mechanism through which the terrorist Irish Republican Army competes in elections; the Revolutionary Communist Party supports Marxists within the Irish Republican Army.

Groups operating among Sikhs, Kashmiris, Nagas, and in Assam and Jammu advocate violent separation from India. During the 1991 elections for the Punjab state assembly, jailed Sikh militants ran for office, while other militants killed over twenty nominees from opposing parties in districts where those nominees seemed destined to win and determined to resist the militants. In Peru, both Sendero Luminoso and Tupac Amaru conduct terrorist activities from the mountains and urban neighborhoods. All splinter parties remain outlawed by Nigeria's military government, but their old leaders remain prominent and organized just beneath the surface. The Northern Elements Progressive Union (NEPU) became the People's Redemption Party in the 1979 elections; it appealed to farmers protesting compulsory labor, resettlement for large agricultural projects, uneven distribution of credit and fertilizer, uniform taxes on all adult males, and other policies. Many of its leaders were arrested in 1981, while civilian rule was still in effect.

WHAT SUPPORTS CONSENSUAL PARTIES?

Consensual parties have had difficulty establishing themselves in Nigeria and Peru, but India, another Third World nation-state, has long been dominated by one. The consensual party in a communist system has proven unstable once other parties are allowed to compete. Yet the present consensual parties in the United States, the United Kingdom, and the Federal Republic of Germany have been major players for decades, despite competition from numerous groups. Do some systems provide a better environment for consensual parties than others? What factors might affect this?

In chapter 3, we examined a factor that affects consensual parties—election rules that require a candidate to obtain a *plurality* or *majority* of votes to win. It is easier for nominees from consensual parties to reach either of these goals than for independent candidates or nominees of splinter parties, who often appeal to a narrow segment of the electorate; but splinter party nominees may often come in second in a race. Furthermore, if voters know such a candidate can win a seat by coming in second, they have more incentive to vote for them. Election rules that let more than one officeholder represent a district therefore help splinter parties win legislative seats. For example, in the United Kingdom's 1992 general election, the Liberal Democratic Party won 18 percent of the popular vote, yet took only 20 (3 percent) of the 650 seats because in other districts it failed to achieve a plurality; the Conservative Party won only 42 percent of the vote, but received a majority (336) of the seats in the House of Commons and formed its own Government. By contrast, under West Germany's system of proportional representation, the Liberal Democrats would have received 18 percent of the seats and the Conservatives 42 percent, forcing the Conservatives to include the Liberal Democrats in their Government.[19]

India's single-member seats with plurality win help the consensual Congress party. Even the populations in districts reserved for scheduled caste candidates seldom have more than 30 percent untouchables, so the Buhajan Samaj party, which largely appeals to them, may garner fewer votes than the Congress or coalitions of other parties; with multimember districts, the untouchables would have a good chance to come in second in those districts and gain seats. Though the Lok Sabha regularly contains around seventy members who are untouchables belonging to other parties, Buhajan Samaj seldom wins a seat.

In Nigeria, Major-General Ibrahim Babangida's military government attempted to create election rules that would support consensual parties. As we will see shortly, by *banning opposition parties* other than the two government-created parties and by *demanding that presidential candidates receive a portion of votes from voters or legislators throughout the nation-state,* Babangida forced future presidents either to cheat or to genuinely cooperate with groups around the country in order to win. This move may not insure the emergence of a consensual party, but it does hold splinter parties in check.

Communist parties have also used the tactic of banning all opposition parties to keep their consensual coalition alive.

In chapter 2, we looked at two other factors that affect consensual parties—whether the executive is chosen by the legislature or directly by the voters, and how much control the executive has over the legislature. *Parliamentary systems* (in which the executive is chosen by the legislature and controls its votes) may help consensual parties by making it easier for the executive and legislature to cooperate and by forcing candidates for legislative seats and party leadership to agree on election platforms. Since such systems function best when one party has a majority in the legislature, they create an incentive for consensual parties to grow.[20]

Presidential systems may help consensual parties by giving individual legislators freedom to vote as their constituents want them to, allowing a consensus to grow as the various committees bargain with one another and with the president. When the system makes use of primaries, it also allows people not connected with legislatures to run for president and introduce new ideas into politics. Parties in presidential systems, then, can incorporate many viewpoints, which encourages the development of consensual parties; but they also have little discipline to carry through on promises.[21]

During the nineteenth century, even though the United Kingdom had a parliamentary system, parties there exhibited little party responsibility. Parliament often voted against measures the prime minister presented; unlike today, this did not cause the government to fall. Yet voters generally supported the two major consensual parties.[22] Rules were gradually tightened to induce the present party discipline, and the trend of voting for two major consensual parties continued (though the Liberals declined, while Labour grew, after suffrage was extended). This history raises questions about how important a role party discipline plays in inducing people to vote for consensual parties. In both the United States and the United Kingdom, people tend to vote for consensual parties, with or without strong party discipline.

As we shall note in a moment, that may have more to do with being socialized to seek compromise than with rules regarding party discipline.

Both presidential and parliamentary systems work best when one or two major consensual parties are in control. As we have seen, Nigeria has tried both types of systems, along with election rules that force candidates for chief executive to seek broad support. These steps have not been enough to create consensual parties. When the military regime of Major-General Babangida initiated the creation of two new consensual parties by ending military rule and once again legalizing civilian politics in May 1989, a month of rioting ensued. Thirty parties organized; the best organized was a successor to the Hausa-based party which had ruled from 1979 to 1983.[23] Babangida refused to recognize any of the parties, saying they were "the old political wolves in new sheepskins;" he forbade individuals who had formerly held political office from running in the first elections. The National Republican Convention Babangida then set up was soon called the party of the North, and his Social Democratic Party the party of the South.[24] Babangida forbade candidates to appeal to race or ethnicity in gathering votes.

Politicians from the old parties maneuvered for positions of leadership in these parties, providing campaign contributions and promoting close associates to run for the seats.[25] The first test of the new parties took place in the 1990 local elections. Fearing violence, only 15 percent of those eligible voted, and critics claimed massive voting fraud had again taken place. The Social Democrats won a majority of local councilors in fourteen of the twenty-one states existing in 1990. Before the 1991 elections, the number of states was increased to thirty.

Primary elections for state governors and legislatures in 1991 were also marked by ethnic violence, killing hundreds. Primary voters had to stand in a line marked by the name of the person they wanted to vote for; some voters were bribed to switch lines.[26] Babangida ordered a revote in parts of nine states and arrested some politicians working behind the scenes. The general elections proceeded without violence, but the later revelation that election rolls contained twenty million bogus names brought the validity of this and all prior elections into question.[27] The Republicans won sixteen governorships and the Democrats fourteen. Some states with Republican governors work with assemblies controlled by the Democrats, and vice versa. Each party controls states in the south and north.

Following the 1991 elections, Babangida opened the national elections to former politicians, who were back in the forefront of the 1992 presidential primaries and election. They will determine whether a two-party system can work in Nigeria, or whether the factions that already divide the Republicans and Democrats will tear them apart. After massive fraud in the first 1992 presidential primaries, the National Electoral Commission cancelled primaries altogether.[28] As all these problems in Nigeria demonstrate, a nation-state cannot create consensual parties simply by establishing a parliamentary or a presidential system.

Along with election rules and type of government system, *political culture* has a strong bearing on whether a system can support consensual parties. When people identify strongly with a particular ethnic group, region of the nation-state, religion, or social class, it is easy for them to identify with a splinter party representing that group, region, religion, or class. If they are adamant about all these affiliations, splinter parties of all kinds may develop to, for example, represent such minute groupings as members of the same church congregation. Splinter parties thrive on narrow group identification.

A consensual party can quickly emerge in this situation if the political culture has socialized people to compromise. They can continue to maintain all their group attachments, while expanding their willingness to compromise with other groups. If a party reaches out to include new groups which present members refuse to compromise with, it risks losing present members. If every citizen of a nation-state has large numbers of groups they refuse to compromise with, it becomes difficult to create any consensual parties. Conversely, if large numbers of citizens refuse to compromise with one particular group, it is hard for that group to be represented within a consensual party. That group must resort to forming or joining in the activities of splinter parties. In some nation-states, one party emerges to win the support of a large number of people who have learned to compromise with people from other ethnic groups, regions, religions, and classes. Members of certain ethnic, religious, and regional groupings who have not learned to compromise remain relegated to splinter parties. In other nation-states, two consensual parties may emerge, or none at all.

As we saw in the discussion of political culture in chapters 14 through 18, people exposed to cross-cutting cleavages and modern economic institutions are perhaps in the best position to learn how to compromise. By definition, they are also in the best position to learn to form consensual parties. And once such parties work within legislatures, they further enhance their ability to effect compromises and perpetuate themselves. Alexis DeToqueville believed that Americans were developing compromise to an extreme:

> . . . as long as the majority is still undecided, discussion is carried on, but as soon as its decision is irrevocably pronounced, every one is silent, and the friends as well as the opponents of the measure unite in assenting to its propriety . . . I know of no country in which there is so little independence of mind and real freedom of discussion as in America . . . the majority raises formidable barriers around the liberty of opinion; within those barriers, an author may write what he pleases, but woe to him who goes beyond them . . . he is exposed to continued obloquy and persecution.[29]

Splinter parties are persecuted if they cannot criticize the compromises that have been made; but some degree of compromise is needed to support competing consensual parties. (Consensual parties are based on consensus—consent to compromise and reach agreements.)

If a party, by legal or illegal means, gains control of a legislature, it may be tempted to outlaw all other parties. If high percentages of people believe this action is unconstitutional and illegal, the government may have to use force to get its way. If it succeeds in outlawing all competitors, it may become so dependent on force that it rules without a broad base of support, as a splinter party. On the other hand, it may retain support from many groups despite their disapproval of its move to outlaw other parties. If high percentages of people feel it is legal and constitutional to outlaw other parties, it may even be able to rule without force by maintaining an assortment of groups within its ranks and working out compromises among them. Such a party has a strong incentive to remain a consensual party, seeking compromises among a variety of groups; if large numbers of people in a variety of groups are entirely ignored, they can cause unrest and require the government to continuously exert force. A simpler strategy is to accommodate the wishes of some of the leaders of these groups in exchange for their cooperation in controlling their followers.

It is easier for a political system to sustain more than one consensual party when much of the populace believes that more than one political party has a constitutional and legal right to exist. It is also easier to effect compromises among various groups when this belief exists.

ELECTION RULES AND COMPROMISE

The fact that some people with cooperative natures can come to the fore within consensual parties does not mean they cooperate with everyone. They do not need to cooperate with those who are left out of politics. They need not cooperate with all splinter parties either, especially those that are not good at compromise or are excluded by election rules from sending members to the legislature.

Rules and procedures can affect who is in a position to engineer compromises and therefore be included in them. A decentralized party, which gives power to members outside the legislature, may develop coalitions with other parties and interest groups at the local level that differ from its alliances at the national level. A centralized party, which is run by members within the national legislature, is less likely to do so.

If those in charge of party membership have a narrow, exclusive vision of who should join the party it does not matter how the party is organized—it will remain narrow. It thus makes a great deal of difference which level makes decisions about membership; if party leaders at the national level have a broader vision of who should join the party than leaders at the regional level, they may try to attract people with broader vision into membership. The same is true if major differences of opinion over membership exist between party members inside the legislature and those outside.

With primaries, it is possible for candidates who have no party experience to run under a party's name. Party caucuses also make this possible, but less likely, except in years of exceptional voter unrest and activism; this is because those attending caucuses and being elected as delegates to the conventions usually have experience working in the party. When party officers, permanent staff, or members of the legislature control nominations, they are likely to choose only candidates with experience in the party to run for office. Here, again, these procedural differences matter when outsiders are either more or less prone than insiders to compromise on ideological stances. They also matter if you happen to be an outsider and want to run (or support another outsider) for office.

Presidential systems raise the cost of political campaigns because the campaigns last longer and each candidate emphasizes a different package of issues supported by a different variety of interest groups. These systems also raise the cost and complexity of influencing policy. Those who want influence must deal separately with various members of the legislature and the president. If (as in the United States) different members are financed by different sources in connection with different issues, a party must remain loosely organized to reach a consensus; it must not try to make all its members vote the same way on every issue. So-called campaign reform laws in the United States even limit the amount that political parties can contribute to individual candidates, strengthening candidates' reliance on individual contributions and weakening the influence of political parties.

Primaries, caucuses, and presidential systems loosen party discipline and increase the likelihood that campaign financing will be widely dispersed, with funds going to individual candidates rather than to parties themselves. This works to the advantage of groups with much money to spend on lobbying and campaign contributions. It works to the disadvantage of groups which do not have much money, including splinter parties, which often find it hard to raise money because they have little chance of controlling government. If it takes little money to reach voters with one's message, and if voters do not expect gratuities in exchange for a vote, then opposition political parties may form and compete without much money. As we saw in chapter 4, this can happen in Germany, the United Kingdom, and the CIS republics, where opposition candidates can get subsidies and some free time on the air waves; it may also occur in Peru. But splinter parties and opposition candidates have a hard time reaching voters in the other systems.

MEDIA AND COMPROMISE

Television and radio play an increasingly important role in reaching voters. Decentralizing control over them may either benefit or harm opposition parties. When such parties control state governments, they can benefit from decentralized, state control of the media. When they control no level of government, they benefit from systems like those in the United Kingdom and Germany, which donate television time to forums by nominees from all parties. Otherwise, it is hard for opposition parties to gain media access (see figure 19.1).

In both West Germany and Nigeria, state-level government controls radio and television. As we saw in chapter 4, in West Germany, even small regional splinter parties that do not hold prominent positions in their regions may compete, partly because they are guaranteed some air time on radio and television. In Nigeria, opposition parties have not been given air time; that rule remains to be tested under the 1992 constitution. Moreover, campaign costs are lower in West Germany than in Nigeria, and they can get government subsidies. All these circumstances help

Figure 19.1   Control of radio and television in each system.

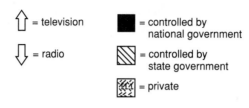

*now controlled by individual republics

assure that a greater variety of parties may enter politics. It does not, however, assure that every party's views will be reflected in the compromises government makes to form policy. Disciplined, competitive, consensual parties are in a better position to develop compromises than decentralized consensual parties or coalitions of splinter parties. But when leaders of parties can pick nominees without requiring them to raise large amounts of money in order to procure the nomination, the chances increase that party policies will even reflect the views of groups who do not have extensive funds to contribute. When, in addition, splinter parties are able to procure legislative seats, the range of groups entering into compromise promises to broaden even more.

ECONOMIC INTEGRATION AND COMPROMISE

A disciplined, two-party consensual party system which also lets splinter parties win seats in elections may still exclude the interests of many people from compromises. Some officeholders may even have civic culture attitudes which make them try to include everyone in compromise, and the system may still prove insufficient to respond to the interests even of groups with access to office if those groups

are not part of the national economy. People who are not part of the economy are not easy to include in compromise. In Nigeria, Peru, and India, much of the populace is not economically integrated. They may be excluded from compromises, regardless of whether parties are centralized or decentralized, whether competitive elections are allowed, and whether splinter parties compete.

In the United States, nearly all citizens are intimately exposed to new technology and obtain their jobs and basic goods and services from the same interconnected complex of businesses that serves government and backs the two consensual parties. The educational system affords most people the chance to acquire skills needed for economic mobility. Even that minority which lacks rudimentary skills and cannot find work has some level of influence inside the two main political parties. In a presidential system with decentralized parties, there are many levels at which different groups may be represented. When government deals with issues relating to fiscal matters, education, or employment in mainstream businesses, it at least potentially impacts on high percentages of the populace, who can vote for the other party if they do not like the government's policies or for a legislative or local-level candidate whose views differ from the views of the president.

Table 19.2

Characteristics that Increase a Group's Inclusion in Compromises

Group Characteristics

	Part of National Economy	Officeholders Include Group's Members	Officeholders Sympathetic to Group	Free Party Competition	Competition within Ruling Party Coalition	Group's Chances of Being Included in Compromises
Has all these	x	x	x	x	x	increased chance
Has these four	x	x		x	x	
Has these four	x	x	x		x	↑
Has these three		x	x		x	
Has these two	x				x	
Has these two	x			x		
Has these four		x	x	x	x	
Has this one	x					
Has these three		x		x	x	↓
Has these two		x			x	
Has none of these						decreased chance

As table 19.2 indicates, free party competition among parties like those in the United States, which encompass competing groups within themselves, is more useful to groups incorporated into the national economy than to those which are not. The latter groups might actually be better off under a system ruled by a single party which allows no competition but has leaders sympathetic to these groups; such leaders can force more influential groups to share resources with less influential ones.

Like their counterparts in the United States, less advantaged portions of the populace in the United Kingdom are at least partially assimilated into the economy and party politics, and hence would not fall in the bottom row of table 19.2. The United Kingdom has a parliamentary government with a centralized party system, combined with a large middle class and skilled labor force. This made it possible for the United Kingdom's Conservative Government to promote modernization of industry and service firms and help large numbers of people in the process. But many people in the north and west are less easily drawn into modern economic activities due to their lack of assimilation into the modern economy and their distance from London, the center of commerce. As old industrial plants closed to accommodate the new investments, many lost their jobs and lacked the education to replace them. As a consequence, people working in the small shops and service firms where these workers shopped in turn lost their livelihoods, and entire cities lost their revenue bases and began to deteriorate. Yet many of these economically displaced individuals vote and are active in party politics.[30] They continue receiving government assistance checks and participating in government-sponsored programs, elect municipal government leaders, and threaten to help elect the leader of the opposition consensual party as a new prime minister.

In contrast, many citizens of the CIS and other post-Soviet republics do fall at the bottom of table 19.2. They live in villages and towns far removed from the modern economy. These villages often have mud streets, a small selection of items for purchase in their stores, and little contact with the outside world aside from television. Towns and regional cities are often bleak industrial areas, centering around antiquated manufacturing or processing plants or around the distribution of agricultural commodities in jobs requiring heavy physical exertion but little skill. The few residents who finish higher education often do not return to their home cities. Those who remain behind strongly identify with their own regions and are often suspicious of other cultures and nationalities. They also tend to support political candidates and leaders from their own class and region, whether they are poor farmers or industrial workers. For decades, small groups of people, closely tied to leading family clans, controlled local political branches. Because those local leaders had to work within the Communist Party, they hid their rejection of other cultures and their promotion of local class interests; in public, at least, they asked their local followers to identify with all groups in the nation and cooperate with the leaders of work units. They could guarantee their constituents jobs, some access to land, and continuing sustenance by assimilating their work units into the centralized national economy. Their families and close associates benefitted most; they could move out of the most remote and economically deprived regions.

Glasnost let leaders voice suspicions of other nationalities and advocate breaking from the union; in the short run, taking this stance could make them popular with local citizens. But as reformers start their own businesses, charge higher prices, and transfer labor-saving equipment into local plants (allowing them to lay off workers and leaving workers facing unemployment for the first time), they frighten many who like guaranteed jobs and low prices; ironically, many of these reformers are

former Communist Party officials, while those complaining about job security were initially supporters of reform. While people may want more freedom for their ethnic group and region, they do not want to lose economic security by dismantling the old centralized economy. Even national leaders such as Russian president Boris Yeltsin, who broke away from the Communist Party to represent both economic reformers and ethnic separatists, found it difficult to balance the widespread desire for change against the widespread fear of the disruptive effects of change. Some regional nationalists among these reformers and former Communists resist economic change; some economic reformers deplore regional parochialism. Some want a free market in theory, but not in practice. Some want freedom for their nationality, but not a free market or freedom for other nationalities.

Regardless of people's opinions, the post-Soviet republics do share a common economy they must maintain or reform; they cannot escape it simply by declaring independence. Whether leaders move decisively toward change or hold back, they face resistance from within their own ranks and from citizens of other republics. Consensual parties cannot emerge unless they bridge these gaps. They must please those who resist economic change and distrust other nationalities, while at the same time support the reform of the interdependent economy shared by all the republics. Obviously, this is a tough order to fill. As a result, separate splinter parties are emerging to unite the nationalists on the one hand and the economic reformers on the other; parties created by former Communists have been more agile than new reform parties at attracting both types of voters, or both types of attitudes within the same voter. The Movement for Democratic Reform, an umbrella party for reformists all over the new Commonwealth, advocated rapid economic change and attacked regional parochialism. It soon found itself fading, along with the prospects of the Commonwealth. In 1992, the Civic Union made a new attempt to unite Russia's main parties led by dissident reformers with parties led by former Communists. The Union had little success at bringing together Russia's several dozen splinter parties. None of these movements have much to offer the large numbers of people who lie at the margins of the economy. Many will waste their votes on small regional splinter parties who sponsor candidates they share little common ground with, or on candidates without party allegiances. And their future role in national economies remains uncertain.

East Germans were more exposed to modern technology than most citizens of the Soviet Union; the single party which controlled them for decades provided most citizens with technical skills and jobs in mechanized agriculture or industry. Even many in the most rural areas had West German television beamed into their homes. Since reunification, West Germany is extending both its political and economic system to the East; most Germans identify culturally with Germany. While they must change their work habits, much of the East's populace is prepared to take jobs within the modern system of the West; when jobs are not forthcoming, they can vote (though they constitute only 10 percent of Germany's total population) for established opposition parties, which welcome membership and participation from all levels of society, and for newly created parties as well. Their representatives within the Bundesrat will have veto power over some changes in their territory. West Germany wants a place of prominence in the new European Economic Community and influence over the future of the former Soviet Union. This gives it incentive to succeed in modernizing the East, so the people in the East are likely to be represented and included in modern economic and political institutions.

The vast majority of China's people have little contact with high technology but are nevertheless integrated into the national economy; what improves that economy improves their lives. They are part of the ruling consensual party, providing it with many cadres. They have the skills, the land, and the tools needed to participate in a call for individual entrepreneurship, higher productivity, and a television set in every home. They responded enthusiastically to the responsibility system for individual land cultivation and to forming cooperative manufacturing enterprises. Meanwhile, the small number of educated elite in the cities want even greater strides toward high technology, and cultural minorities want greater autonomy; to achieve both these ends, they must battle the mass of peasants in the party who fear that too many changes may harm their lives. Those country peasants with their sandals and manure carts are a political force to be reckoned with.

Thus, in all these countries—the United States, the United Kingdom, the former Soviet republics, Germany, and China—consensual parties have been able to effect changes beneficial to wide portions of their populations. In the one-party systems, ruling consensual parties have been able to stifle dissent based on class or ethnic attachments. That has served to keep these nations intact, but it has impeded technological innovation advocated by the emerging middle classes and slowed the cultural aspirations of many minorities. It has also aided some groups with little influence; the future of such groups is uncertain as the post-Soviet republics loosen their grip and allow competing voices to be heard.

India presents a stark contrast. The membership of the Congress party and its rivals is largely composed of rural landowners and urban professionals, old and young, who want automobiles, VCRs, irrigation equipment, and much of the paraphernalia of the modern world. Meanwhile, most of the populace lives in villages in houses with mud floors or in urban slums. They buy little made outside the villages, aside from food. Government efforts to start new industries, encourage entrepreneurship, and promote high technology have little relationship to their lives. Only the most severe famine is likely to arouse government to assist them (and even then, prominent party members with access to food often hoard it and then sell it for profit). Unlike the people in the north and west of the United Kingdom, and those in rural areas of the CIS, rural Indians are largely excluded from membership in parties. This, combined with a centralized parliamentary system, allows leaders to make rapid, sweeping changes without interference from such groups and without accommodating their interests.

Nigeria and Peru are in a similar situation. Much of their population is cut off from the modern economy and totally excluded from membership or participation in political parties and politics. The portion of the populace absorbed into the modern economy is smaller than in India, and it has little contact with those who are not. Leaders are free to exploit oil, copper, gold, and other resources and divert profits to themselves at a cost and pace which disrupts even the modern economy. Much of the populace remains in poverty. They are not part of the national economy, of political parties, or of legislatures.

A consensual party can benefit people more widely when the bulk of the populace is assimilated into the national economy and the party system and is generally agreeable to change. At that point, a centralized party is useful for achieving that change, whether in a system with one consensual party (as in China or East Germany) or two (as in West Germany or the United Kingdom).

When there is disagreement about how change should proceed, however, a single consensual party can act decisively only if it excludes those who disagree and thereby insures that their needs will be ignored. It will be a party capable of working out compromises more quickly than competing splinter or consensual parties in the same climate of disagreement, but those compromises may at times exclude much of the populace. The single centralized party must include many factions who resist challenges to their positions and fight with one another. But such a party has little need to include groups lying outside the national economy unless it needs their labor to expand agriculture and industry, or is ruled for a time by leaders who believe strongly in drawing these groups into the system.

In systems like our own, Germany's, the United Kingdom's, or the systems evolving in the post-Soviet republics, with most people at least partially assimilated into the economy and substantial disagreement about government policies, a parliamentary system with two or more consensual parties can effect change quicker than either a presidential system or a system with only one consensual party (with or without free elections). In a presidential system, it is hard for party leaders to exert centralized control and steer policy from the top. When voters have a choice between electing one consensual party and several splinter parties, the choice is between a known party watering down its promises to attract a majority of votes or seats, and a coalition of parties whose exact composition can only emerge after the election. A system led by one consensual party that allows no competition is often held back from change by the many factions it must balance to keep afloat. In systems with two centralized parties, by contrast, people with opposing views can move to the other party, leaving the first able to act more decisively; voters have a clear choice between two parties, either of which can direct policy.

Whether rapid change is desirable is another question. Regardless of their political system, people who are comfortable with their lives are not likely to think change is desirable. Nor are those who want changes different from the changes they see proceeding. In either case, it is clearly useful for such individuals to be able to influence or slow down the changes in progress. A person not assimilated into the national economy or able to exert influence within a consensual political party is in a poor position to do so; substantial numbers of Indians, Peruvians, and Nigerians find themselves unable to effectively slow, block, or encourage change.

CONSENSUAL PARTIES, SPLINTER PARTIES, AND CIVIC CULTURE

Whether consensual parties will emerge, then, is rooted in how people are socialized and assimilated. If few people desire to cooperate with other groups, consensual parties cannot emerge. Yet government itself is premised on cooperation: Without cooperation, government cannot exist. If some people desire to cooperate with some other people, there is a basis for government. Party organization and election rules can facilitate that cooperation if they are created to give influence to those people who do desire to cooperate. This means that no one form of organization or set of rules works best in all nation-states. For consensual parties to develop, government procedures must be patterned to assist those who are willing to cooperate and compromise; the same rules which bring this about in one nation-state may obstruct it in the next.

All modern nation-states contain individuals who seek cooperation. People who develop control over economic resources could not do so without the ability to cooperate. They are likely to also develop skills that enhance cooperative activity—skills in speaking, organizing, retrieving information, and conducting human relations. This gives them qualifications to create consensual parties, or to build cooperation among splinter parties. It also gives them the skills to adapt party organization and electoral rules so that they allow those with cooperative skills to control the party. Modern nation-states also contain people who do not like to cooperate; if they control political institutions, they may make rules which exclude people with cooperative skills from party leadership.

Even when rules tend to draw people with cooperative natures to the forefront, it does not mean they will cooperate with everyone. They need not cooperate with people who are not involved in politics. They need not cooperate with all splinter parties either, especially those which are not good at compromise themselves. And their ideologies may cause them to resist cooperating with many of their political adversaries. Yet, such people often enter politics because they can then control goods and institutions; this gives them an incentive to continue to arrive at compromises so they can retain control and preserve the system.

A two-party consensual party system which also allows splinter parties to compete in elections has greater potential to accommodate a variety of interests than a one-party system, a system with only splinter parties, or a two-party system with rules that make it difficult for other groups to compete. But such a system may not be able to accommodate many groups in compromises if party decision makers and the voters who back them are not disposed to compromise with those groups. Bringing previously excluded groups into political institutions can make those institutions less capable of compromise, rather than more, if the new groups are not

willing to compromise. Splinter parties need to do less compromising within their own ranks because they include a narrower range of views than a consensual party, but they may also be freer to clearly express that narrow range of views. Nigeria has banned (along with all splinter parties) the People's Redemption Party, which led peasants in creating roadblocks and other acts of resistance during the 1970s to protest encroachment on their land by large agricultural schemes. It remains to be seen whether the views the party represented—views held by poor peasants and small farmers—will be left out of new civilian institutions or brought into the two new consensual parties.

Leaders of consensual parties are experienced at forging compromise; they are also experienced at excluding those who do not exert influence from compromise. We asked at the outset of the chapter whether particular types of parties, or free competition among parties, make it easier to arrive at compromises which benefit wide portions of the populace. When wide portions of the populace are prepared to participate in politics and to compromise among one another, consensual parties which encourage free competition appear to advance that goal more than one-party systems or systems with only splinter parties. But when a nation-state lacks a national identity, and when there is not a common desire among large portions of its citizenry to compromise with one another and to extend benefits even to those who do not participate in politics, it is hard to compensate for these deficiencies by simply creating a competitive party system. In fact, such competition could pull the nation-state apart.

SUMMARY

When (1) influence is widely dispersed, (2) people believe in the legitimacy of political institutions and the direction and content of public policy, (3) most citizens tolerate a plurality of interests and believe conflicts can be reconciled, and (4) efficacy and mutual trust are high, competing consensual parties are more likely to emerge, and those parties are more likely to accommodate the interests of wide portions of the populace. When those attitudes are present among political participants, and when a system is a two-party system with competing consensual parties and rules which allow splinter parties to take seats in legislatures, the system's ability to effect compromises is enhanced. When political participants do not have such attitudes, compromise may still be effected by a consensual party which has established a one-party system; its chances to form compromises

that benefit large portions of the populace may be less than a consensual party in a two-party system with splinter parties taking seats, but better than a system composed entirely of competing splinter parties. In any case, it is hard for those who do not participate in politics or the national economy to achieve representation and inclusion in political compromise; leaders need not worry about the needs or desires of these portions of the populace.

NOTES

1. Maurice Duverger, *Political Parties*, 2d ed., (New York: Wiley, 1959).

2. Forty percent of the members of the Christian Democratic Union are from business and the civil service, 6 percent are students, and 11 percent are manual workers. Twenty percent are women, and 65 percent are Catholic. Gordon Smith, "Federal Republic of Germany," in *World Encyclopedia of Political Systems and Parties*, vol. 2, 2d. ed. (1987), pp. 396–405.

3. Twenty-eight percent of the members of the Social Democratic Party are manual workers, 9 percent students, and 34 percent from business and the civil service. Twenty percent are women, and 50 percent are under age 30. Idem.

4. During the period from 1801, when Thomas Jefferson became the first Democratic president, until 1855, the first race Republicans ran in, the Democrats controlled the presidency for forty-seven years, the Senate for forty-nine years, and the House of Representatives for forty-five years. In its early years, the Democratic Party was called the Republican Party.

5. The Communist Party in the Soviet Union was founded in 1898 by student and worker groups as the Social Democratic Labor Party. They divided into two factions, the Bolsheviks (led by V. I. Lenin), who worked outside the system, and the Mensheviks, who competed in elections; in 1912, these groups formally split into two parties. The Kerensky government, which the Bolsheviks overthrew by force in 1917, contained Menshevik ministers. The Mensheviks did not oppose the Bolsheviks in

the civil war which followed, but nevertheless, they were abolished in 1921.

6. China's Communist Party came to power in 1949 via a revolution against the Guomindang after first helping them come into power in Beijing in 1928. A few months after the Guomindang attained power, they purged the communists from their coalition and began a campaign to annihilate them. A long civil war between the Guomindang and the Communists ensued, against a background of Japanese occupation; at times, both groups paused to fight the Japanese.

7. The General German Workers' Association, founded in 1863, and the Social Democratic Labor Party, founded in 1869, merged in 1875 into the Social Democratic Party; by 1912, it had become the largest party in the Reichstag. Between 1933 and 1945, Hitler banned all parties except his own National Socialist party. In 1946, the Social Democrats in East Germany were forced to merge with the communist party into the ruling Socialist Unity Party. In West Germany, the Social Democrats were the only major prewar party to reemerge after the war. A new party, the Christian Democratic Union, formed the first postwar government in 1949.

8. The Roman Catholic Duke of York threatened to accede to the throne in 1679; his supporters were called Tories, and his opponents Whigs. Both held seats in Parliament. In 1832, the Tories became the Conservative Party. The Whigs became the Liberal Party during the 1840s, and merged with some other groups to form the Liberal-Social Democratic Alliance during the 1980s; the Social Democrats disbanded in 1990, returning the Liberals to the

name Liberal Democratic Party. The Labour Party was founded among workers in 1906, growing out of predecessors which began in 1869, and soon overtook the Liberals as the second major consensual party.

9. The Congress party formed in India to contest elections to legislative councils.

10. The Northern People's Congress (NPC) was founded in Nigeria in 1940, the National Council of Nigeria-Cameroons (NCNC) in 1944, and the Action Group (AG) in 1951—each largely based in a different tribal region (Hausa, Ibo, and Yoruba, respectively). They formed a coalition around the first president (an NPC). In 1964, NPC and NCNC joined to form the Nigerian National Alliance (NNA). The AG joined some other parties to form the United Progressive Grand Alliance (UPGA). The NNA won the election, but was overthrown by a military coup in 1966. The next election in 1979 was won by the National Party of Nigeria, the successor to NPC, with UPGA's successor, the Unity Party of Nigeria coming in second. All parties were again outlawed after the 1983 and 1985 military coups. The National Republican Convention, set up by General Babangida in 1992, is bringing out remnants of the National Party of Nigeria, while the Social Democratic Party has roots in the Unity Party of Nigeria.

11. Richard A. Joseph, "The Overthrow of Nigeria's Second Republic," *Current History* 83, 491 (March 1984), and Larry Diamond, "A Tarnished Victory for the NPN," *Africa Report* 28, 6 (November–December 1983) relate some examples of vote fraud in the 1983 elections. Troops and hired thugs prevented the agents assigned to watch the vote counts from doing so; students were bribed and given ten or twenty registration cards each and sent to vote all over town; booklets of fifty ballots were on sale at voting stations to be thumbprinted and stuffed in ballot boxes; and a young man saw his brother accept thousands of naira to change the results of a senate election. Soldiers stopping a funeral party even found the casket full of stuffed ballot boxes.

12. Should no one attain the necessary majorities on the first round, the Election Commission will call for a runoff election. The winner must receive a majority of the total votes and a third of the votes cast in a majority of the states. If no one succeeds in winning the runoff election, the National Electoral Commission will call all the members of both houses of the National Assembly and state assemblies to form an electoral college, which votes on the same day. If someone receives a majority of electoral votes, he or she becomes president. If that fails, they will vote again on another day.

13. The National Front parties drew up a joint list of nominees to present to East German voters, who could either accept this single list or reject it.

14. The Revolutionary Committee of the Guomindang, the Democratic League, the Democratic National Construction Association, the Association for Promoting Democracy, the Peasants' and Workers' Democratic Party, the Zhi Gong Dang, the Jui San Society, and the Taiwan Democratic Self-Government League helped the Communists come to power in 1949, initially formed a coalition government with them, and are still active largely among intellectuals.

15. Forty-four percent of Free Democrats are from business or the civil service, while 5 percent are manual workers. Smith, "Federal Republic."

16. The Social Democrats, Christian Democrats, Christian Social Union, and Free Democrats have collectively received over 90 percent of the vote in each national election since 1961.

17. The Scottish National Party, founded in 1934 to rally for Scottish independence, is the principal competitor in Scotland. It received the second largest number of Scottish votes and several seats in the 1974 election, but has declined since. Plaid Cymru, founded in 1925, supports Welsh independence and its language and traditions and holds about two seats in each successive Parliament. The divisions between protestants and Catholics in Northern Ireland are reflected in highly divided splinter parties there, which together receive high percentages of the vote. The Ulster Unionist party has been the principal organ of the protestants for many decades, together with the more militant Democratic Unionist party. The Catholics are divided in their allegiance to the Nationalist party (which helped bring about Irish independence), the Alliance party (which seeks peace with protestants), the more militant Social Democratic and Labour Party, and Sinn Fein (the political arm of the Irish Republican Army).

18. At their height, the Progressive Party received 27 percent of the presidential vote and the Socialist Party 900,000 votes.

19. Proportional representation can help minorities in other ways as well. In 1983, women won 4 percent of directly contested seats in the Bundestag while they occupied 16 percent of the seats filled by the party list.

20. For a discussion of parliamentary systems, see S. H. Beer, *Britain Against Itself: The Contradictions of Collectivism* (New York: Norton, 1982); Sir Ivor Jennings, *Cabinet Government* 3d ed. (Cambridge: Cambridge University Press, 1969) and *Party Politics,* 3 vol. (Cambridge: Cambridge University Press, 1960–62); and Douglas Ashford, *Policy and Politics in Britain: The Limits of Consensus* (Oxford: Basil Blackwell, 1981).

21. For a discussion of presidential systems, see James Bryce, *The American Commonwealth* (New York: Macmillan, 1916); Donald L. Robinson, *"To the Best of My Ability"* (New York: W. W. Norton, 1986); and Woodrow Wilson, *Congressional Government: A Study in American Politics* (Baltimore: Johns Hopkins University Press, 1981; originally published 1885).

22. Walter Bagehot's *The English Constitution* (Ithaca, N.Y.: Cornell University Press, 1966) discusses the period just prior to the 1867 reforms. See R. H. Crossman's introduction to the 1964 edition.

23. The National Party of Nigeria. See footnote 10.

24. At the National Republican Convention, northerners promised the vice-presidential position to millionaire politician Hyd Onuaguluchin in exchange for his assistance in splitting the vote of delegations from the west and east. This meant a southerner could be picked as party chairman, clearing the way for a presidential candidate from the north in 1993. Olugbenga Ajeni, "Another Step Forward," *West Africa,* July 20–August 5, 1990. The Social Democrats chose a presidential candidate from the south.

25. Commenting on Babangida's contention that the "new breed" of political leaders and the new political parties constitute a "clean break" from the old ones, the Chairman of the Social Democratic Party in the state of Kano said: "Making a 'clean break'? That's purely academic. It's only normal that one bows to the people, resources, and expertise of the old order." Former legislator and millionaire businessman Arthur Nzerjbe, arrested for twenty days for addressing an

election rally in his home added: "I'll tell you who the new breed is. He's a known crook and vagabond, he has no background, he is a wheeler-dealer, and he is a politician. Ever since independence he has been going for election and losing." Michael A. Hiltzik, " 'Banned' Politicians Continue to Exert Influence in Nigeria," *Minneapolis Star-Tribune,* June 16, 1991. In 1993, Nzerjbe sponsored billboards in the capital city calling for a continuation of military rule. Nobel Prize winner Wole Soyinka calls these arrangements "voodoo democracy." "Attention!", *The Economist,* October 26, 1991.

Committees like the Middle Belt Forum, Yoruba Elders, and Northern Elders were set up to control politics from behind the scenes, and tell villagers how to vote.

26. "Attention!", Idem. Robert M. Press, "Nigerians Set to Vote in Primaries in Step Toward Civilian Rule," *Christian Science Monitor,* October 18, 1991. This "open balloting" lends itself to bribing before the election; those giving the bribes can see whether the individual votes as agreed.

27. Worse yet, it raised questions about the authenticity of the 1991 census, on which apportionment of legislative seats is based. That census found millions fewer people than prior ones; how there were still 50 million registered voters, but only 35 million adults. Names of 15 million dead people remained on the election rolls, even though 20 million had been removed.

28. In 1992, the two parties held conventions organized by the National Election Commission and attended by unelected delegates, and they chose presidential nominees. As expected, the Republicans picked a northerner and the Social Democrats a southerner. Both were millionaires and Muslims; one was a banker and the other a shipper. The Republicans promptly picked a Christian Ibo as vice-presidential candidate to balance the ticket. The choice of a running mate was harder for the Social Democratic presidential candidate, a Yoruba; a Christian Hausa would be an unpopular choice in the north, and the Social Democrats needed support there to avoid being another "party of the south." The Republican nominee was almost unknown to the public, even among his own Hausas in the south. The Social Democrat won the 1993 general presidential election

by a landslide; when Babangida declared the election void, riots ensued and Babangida appointed an "interim" civilian-military Government led by one of his close associates.

29. *Democracy in America*, Richard D. Heffner, ed. (New York: Mentor, 1956), pp. 117–18. DeToqueville goes on to say that these tendencies "are as yet but slightly perceptible in political society; but they already exercise an unfavorable influence upon the national character of the Americans."

30. In 1987, the Conservatives lost eight Scottish seats, reducing them to five. Nearly all the north is represented by the Labour Party, while nearly all the south is represented by Conservatives.

EXERCISES

Think about the book thus far:

1. How do chapters 19–24, on political institutions, relate to chapters 14–18, which discuss political culture?

KEY WORDS AND PHRASES

Define the following terms:

prosystem party   antisystem party   Babangida

THINKING IT THROUGH

Answer each of the following questions (1–8) in one sentence:

1. Which of these systems contain consensual political parties?
2. Which consensual party is the oldest?
3. Which parliamentary systems have more than one consensual party?
4. In which system do splinter parties have the greatest opportunity to win legislative seats?
5. What attitudes are most conducive to supporting consensual parties?
6. What distinguishes decentralized from centralized parties?
7. Under what circumstances can party membership limit participation in politics?
8. How can splinter parties help—and harm—minorities?

Now, ask yourself:

9. How does each of the following affect consensual parties?
   a. proportional representation
   b. presidential system
   c. parliamentary system
   d. party discipline
   e. political culture

10. Under what circumstances do consensual parties
    a. promote compromise?
    b. inhibit compromise?
    c. exclude groups from politics?
    d. help include new groups in politics?

11. Why are some groups left out of compromises within and between consensual parties? How do campaign financing and control of the media affect this? Does assimilation into modern institutions play a role?

chapter 20

PARTIES, INTEREST GROUPS, AND ELECTIONS

INTEREST GROUPS

Some countries offer citizens great freedom to organize interest groups, though many people fail to take advantage of the opportunity. Others tightly restrict freedom to organize. A third group of countries allows interest groups to form fairly freely, but only among social groups to which few people belong. Those which restrict the freedom to organize largely leave out people who have less education and less efficacy. Those with social rather than political restrictions on joining interest groups leave out their poorest citizens.

We learned in chapter 1 that people with common interests who are not within government, or even within political parties, create institutions which pressure government leaders to adopt and implement policy favorable to their interests. Political scientists call these institutions interest groups. Such groups may serve other purposes as well—they may act as trade unions, business associations, recreational clubs, or what have you. Or they may be set up strictly for the purpose of influencing government policy. Some may last only long enough to push for a single policy initiative. Occasionally a "group" forms without any organization at all—for example, when large numbers of people write their legislators about some issue and thus create groups of people pro and con, or when a street riot begins spontaneously.

Everyone belongs to groups from birth, beginning with their family; not everyone tries to influence policymakers. Those who do may first try to influence them as individuals; they soon discover it is easier to influence a policymaker as a member of a group than as an individual. Suppose a good friend is elected to the legislature, and you approach him or her asking for support on a piece of legislation. Your friendship alone is likely to give you some influence, especially if you can make a persuasive argument for your case and if you and your friend share some common interests. That influence might be greater if your family and your friends have developed ties. But unless your family has ties with other types of influential groups, your influence could easily be outweighed by people in groups. Various civic groups may oppose your piece of legislation—groups who could influence voters in the next election. Civil servants needed to implement the legislation after it passes may threaten to sabotage the law if they do not like it. Businesspeople whose contributions are needed in the next election may oppose the legislation or may be able to field an opposing candidate. Groups like these tend to have more influence on legislation than individuals do.

Those groups most likely to try to influence policy are those which contain individuals who were socialized to be politically active and who have experience influencing policymakers. Groups which last only a short time can easily be forgotten once they disband. Groups which have lasted for a long time but have never tried to influence policy may be successful the first time they try, but they will quickly find themselves competing with experienced groups.

To win elections (in systems with competitive elections), and to pass and implement legislation, policymakers in all nine nation-states need the support of groups who will furnish time, money, energy, information, and other resources. Such interest groups may be **institutional interest groups**[1] connected with government or a political party, or they may be independent. In either case, the policymaker must do the group favors to keep its support. One such favor might be to restrict the organization of other competing interest groups. Such restrictions aid the policymakers by making it difficult to organize competing political parties which might attempt to remove them from office. Restrictions also aid the interest groups by reducing competition and making them the only ones policymakers owe favors to. But restrictions on interest group formation do not always aid individuals, because individuals lose the right to decide which interest groups they wish to join or support. In systems where legal protection for individual rights is not a firmly established part of the political culture, it is easy to create such restrictions by writing and enforcing laws. In systems whose political cultures do not recognize equality among races and social classes, those viewed as having lower status (who therefore have fewer economic and material assets) also meet social barriers to organizing. **Legal, social, and economic barriers can restrict an individual's ability to acquire and exert influence. Social and economic barriers are more difficult to remove than legal ones.**

In the United States, the United Kingdom, the Federal Republic of Germany, and (except during emergency decrees) India, interest groups may form freely. Legal restrictions on interest groups in the CIS have greatly diminished, but not completely disappeared. East Germany had such restrictions. Except during periods of military rule, laws in Peru and Nigeria let groups form rather freely. But, as we just pointed out, laws alone do not tell the whole story. The political cultures in the United States, the United Kingdom, and West Germany give influential citizens strong convictions that such laws should (usually) be enforced; the political cultures of the other systems are less firm about this. Political cultures in the United States, the United Kingdom, East and West Germany, and the CIS support the notion that all ethnic groups and social classes have the right to organize politically; in China, India, Peru, and Nigeria, that idea is far less established. Except in India, Nigeria, and Peru, high percentages of the populace engage in economic transactions that affect the national economy. That makes it harder to pass laws that restrict individual rights to organize in the United States, the United Kingdom, and West Germany and easier to use social taboos to restrict organization in India, Peru, and Nigeria.

LEGAL PROTECTION

The United States has both social and legal barriers to organizing interest groups. We have already seen that various citizens feel certain ethnic and social groups should not have equal access to political institutions. Many people feel that communists should not be allowed to speak in schools, that drug users, homosexuals, or people who have AIDS should not have certain legal rights, or that their own religious or ethnic group has the right to restrict the public expressions and actions of others. Many blacks were lynched earlier this century for attempting to exercise their rights. The Supreme Court upheld the jailing of labor leaders for opposing World War I and backed legislative restrictions on the right of labor organizations to strike. Japanese-Americans were corralled into camps during World War II simply because of their ethnic origins. During the 1950s, Senator Joseph McCarthy used the House Committee on UnAmerican Activities to force people out of their jobs and cost them their civil rights simply because they were alleged to have joined or sympathized with the Communist Party during the 1930s; some states passed laws requiring loyalty oaths, and affidavits affirming no membership in communist or communist ''front'' organizations, as a requirement for employment in public agencies and educational institutions. During the 1960s, civil rights activists were killed by police and private citizens. The Federal Bureau of Investigation infiltrated civil rights and antiwar organizations during the 1970s. Passports were withheld from some organizers who opposed intervention in Nicaragua in the 1980s. Unpopular groups often find it difficult to get media attention unless they deliberately cause disturbances.

At the same time, the United States Constitution states that

> *Congress shall make no law respecting an establishment of religion, or prohibiting the free exercise thereof; or abridging the freedom of speech, or of the press, or the right of the people peaceably to assemble, and to petition the Government for a redress of grievances. . . . No state shall . . . deny to any person within its jurisdiction the equal protection of the laws.*

The Supreme Court periodically shifts the meaning of these terms with reference to particular actions. Over the years it has created precedents which make it unlawful for other units of government, or private citizens, to abridge these rights as well. Any citizen who feels their rights have been abridged may take their grievances to court for a hearing. Private groups like the National Association for the Advancement of Colored People and the American Civil Liberties Union regularly defend groups and individuals whose rights they feel have been abridged. While the public sometimes becomes angry over defending the rights of unpopular people and groups, it generally supports the right of any individual to take such a case to court and of the courts to render independent judgment. Congress periodically conducts inquiries into the undercover activities of government agencies which interfere with the rights of private citizens. At times, it passes resolutions to exonerate or make restitution to people whose rights were trammeled decades earlier by overzealous prosecutors or presidents, as with the Japanese jailed during World War II.

The result is that a broad array of groups, representing people from all walks of life, petition U.S. officeholders to change policy. Some of these groups have more political resources than others. Some fight social discrimination and work to change laws which periodically bar them from particular forms of participation. Institutional interest groups within political parties and the government have an inside track, because policymakers often need them: for example, the Defense Department, and social welfare and civil engineering bureaucracies, spur the economy in Congressional districts across the country and reduce unrest among some social groups by distributing money. Associational interest groups who have large amounts of money to contribute to campaigns, or who are needed to keep the economy healthy, are also in a good position to be heard. In 1990, 75 percent of the lobbies registered with the United States House of Representatives represented corporations and trade associations, 1 percent labor unions, 3 percent state and local governments, 10 percent citizens' groups, and 11 percent groups in other categories.[2] Such groups spend money to support the election campaigns of presidential or Congressional candidates favorable to their interests. They make friends with high-ranking members of the bureaucracy. They hire well-trained legal counsel to defend their position in the courts. They orchestrate campaigns to exert public pressure (letters, demonstrations, and the like) on decision makers.[3]

The United Kingdom and West Germany, too, place some social and legal restrictions on organizing. Groups deemed too radical may be outlawed under Germany's Basic Law, with the blessing of the Allied Forces which oversaw the formation of West Germany's government after Hitler's defeat in World War II; that was partly to compensate for the system of proportional representation which makes it easy for small groups to gain seats in Parliament. As late as 1962, the editor of *Der Spiegel,* one of Germany's leading newspapers, was arrested and imprisoned for a month for publishing an article critical of the army (though the article forced the Minister of Defense to resign). In the United Kingdom, governments have frequently invoked the Official Secrets Act of 1911 to stop publication of memoirs by former ministers or to stop racial incitements. The Government of Prime Minister Margaret Thatcher banned the performance of a play,[4] several books, and a television report on terrorism. In

Northern Ireland, the British army has arrested terrorist suspects under laws which allow them to be held for years without a trial. The High Court has upheld these measures.[5] The Labour Party has proposed creating a bill of rights, and prominent members of the Conservative Party would make the European Convention on Human Rights part of British law, to place greater limits on government in these regards.

British people are not loath to express their opinions. They do so publicly, in places like Speakers' Corner in Hyde Park, and privately at home and in the corner pub. It is British tradition to allow either Parliament or the courts to deal with matters of law and adjudication. Bans on free speech are created directly by the prime minister and Parliament, operating under specific laws. When Americans began picketing abortion clinics in 1993, they were promptly arrested and deported; British laws do not permit that kind of public confrontation. The United Kingdom has almost no quasi-judicial bodies similar to the American regulatory agencies empowered to make decisions about rates, routes, safety of plants, union disputes, money supply, interest rates, and other matters.[6] In the United States, no one except courts of appeal can reverse the decisions made by these semi-independent agencies because, though appointed by, they need not answer to the chief executive. In the United Kingdom, such matters stay within the regular courts or ministries, and the prime minister can at any time change decisions these bodies have made. Some limited agencies have been set up to regulate land use and social security; many British fear this will set a precedent for creating further agencies which could interfere with their freedoms. They prefer allowing the prime minister to directly interfere with such freedoms—but only within the glare of public debate. Both the public and Parliament feel free to withhold support from decisions which seem sharply out of step with common law traditions.

The United Kingdom's common law tradition has developed, through legal precedents, considerable protection for individual rights and freedom to petition government officeholders. It is traditional

Spycatcher, a book by a former British secret agent which alleged that there were Soviet double agents in the British government, was banned in the 1980s by Prime Minister Thatcher under the 1911 Official Secrets Act. The ban on publication was challenged in court by the press. Meanwhile, Member of Parliament Anthony Wedgewood Benn regularly appeared in Hyde Park and defied the ban by reading portions of the book aloud to gathered crowds. British tourists in the United States helped make the book a bestseller there, and no copies were confiscated when the Britons returned with them through customs.

When another former agent tried to make similar allegations about double agents high in the secret service, the government also banned publication of his book. A private member's bill introduced by a Conservative Member of Parliament proposed changes in the Official Secrets Act; the Government opposed the bill. Though it lost, eighteen Conservative Members of Parliament broke ranks to vote for it, and an additional eighty Conservative Members abstained. Unless there is a clearly demonstrable threat to national security, the Official Secrets Act permits governments to keep all their acts secret, as do two subsequent bills introduced by Thatcher and passed after the private member's bill was defeated.

In this case, serious allegations relating to national security were raised, implicating a former prime minister and a head of an intelligence agency, among others; these allegations could not even be discussed in the press. No other agency of government was in a position to investigate the charges, much less end the ban of free press discussion of them. The lower courts ruled that the ban was not appropriate under the act, and the Government appealed the case to the Law Lords. They held that the book was already published abroad and could not easily be recalled, but that the Act still stands.

for the cabinet to consult with appropriate interest groups when drafting policy. Leaders of such groups are often old friends of government officials—classmates in public (that is, private grade and high) schools, Oxford and Cambridge, and other universities. They often have long-standing positions as suppliers of commodities to the Crown, Government, and the public. Nobility occupy the House of Lords. Unions are a formal part of the Labour Party. That gives all these groups some advantage in approaching officeholders. Other groups have considerable legal and cultural protection in their right to form and express themselves.[7]

The civil service in the United Kingdom is supposed to be neutral in politics; that is meant to prevent them from taking advantage of their position as an institutional interest group when competing with other groups. Each ministry is headed by a permanent secretary who is expected to serve politically appointed ministers in successive cabinets, regardless of party. Members of the House of Commons are not seen as representatives of particular interest groups. In West Germany, however, getting ahead in the civil service has meant joining, and cooperating with, a major political party; as we saw in chapter 4, leaders of trade unions, businesses, farmers' organizations, environmental groups, and various regional interest groups also campaign for parliament with those affiliations in plain view. The proportional representation system lets individuals affiliated with other groups enter parliament as well. Furthermore, such groups literally become a part of government within bureaucratic institutions like the Bundesbank, labor courts, social insurance funds, the church tax, and other institutions jointly run by them and government.[8]

These traditions of wide group access to the political process have evolved more slowly in the United Kingdom and West Germany than in the United States. Prior to the American Revolution, Americans could own land and start businesses. Major commodity trading, however, was licensed to firms favored by the colonial governments. And restrictions made it difficult to open factories which would compete with those in Britain. Except for slaves and indentured servants, people could move where they chose. Few worked for large firms, so labor unions had not yet formed. Puritans and other religious dissidents who came to America were part of the Reformation which protested the Pope's dominance; some of the colonies established one religion, but other nearby colonies had other established religions or complete religious freedom. The press was censored, but people were free to gather and exchange ideas. The American colonies partitioned power among legislatures, governors, and courts, giving them independent powers and applying common law to insure legal protections of contracts.

As the American Revolution approached, many colonists questioned the special licenses given to trading firms; the Boston Tea Party was one response. Revolutionary leaders who were in the publishing business questioned press censorship. The Revolution forced holders of the major trading monopolies into exile and brought an end to press censorship and established religion. Now the legislatures and courts would operate without taking directions from a king and his governors. Americans settled frontier land. Not everyone benefitted. Indians were killed or displaced to poorer territories. Blacks remained slaves in the South until the Civil War, and some other ethnic groups contained disproportionate numbers of indentured servants or poor workers. Early immigrants from Britain and northern Europe retained considerable influence in political and economic institutions. But as new states were created, they fell under the control of their own citizens, who exhibited considerable independence in establishing their own institutions and cultural traditions. Americans were infected with notions about human equality; these notions were reinforced by emigration to a new land where all faced a harsh wilderness, which treated nobility and commoners alike under the law, and where citizens achieved consensus without having it imposed from the top.

Many of these ideas were to carry over to France, and eventually to the rest of Europe. Prior to this, much of Europe's business had been carried out by guilds, hansas, royal charters, and other groups with a monopoly on trade. Only nobility, clergy, ranking businesspeople, and other select and privileged groups could participate in politics. Most people were tied to the land or towns where they were born by social, legal, and economic bonds; each area had its own religion. Press censorship was common. Leading social classes controlled the bureaucracy, army, and religious hierarchies. All this severely restricted the groups which could organize and compete in politics. Then came the Reformation, which brought freedom for new religious groups to form and practice, and the Renaissance and Enlightenment, which encouraged people to explore science and to raise questions about established beliefs and social practices. The French and Industrial Revolutions created pressures to open trade and legislatures to new social groups. Gradually suffrage expanded. By the twentieth century, both the United Kingdom and Germany had seen the decline of guilds and monopoly trading groups and the rise of corporations and proprietorships headed by individuals who had not been part of the dominant agricultural and town elite. Under new laws, the nobility was sharing bureaucracies,[9] legislatures,[10] army high commands, universities, and land ownership with social and religious groups which had formerly been shut out. Many aristocrats were killed in World War I. At the end of it, U.S. President Woodrow Wilson encouraged the winning Allies and the new League of Nations to create a Republic in Germany which assured that political parties representing all social groups could participate, while at the same time asking Germany to pay heavy reparations for the damage inflicted by the war. The Republic was founded in the city of Weimar. Worldwide depression followed.

While some groups benefitted from these changes, others were harmed. Scholars studying votes for and membership and leadership in Hitler's National Socialist Party in 1932 have found the party primarily attracted people who were watching others gain social and political power while they themselves lacked or lost such power. These people included small farmers who were suffering from inflation, falling produce prices, steeply rising taxes, and lowered subsidies under the Weimar regime; lower-level bureaucrats and industrial workers facing job layoffs;[11] small shopkeepers who were harmed by inflation, weak currency, and unavailability of credit and goods, and who were losing business to large department stores exempt from the government regulations applied to smaller businesses; craftspeople suffering from the end of the guild system and competition from factory goods; pensioners, disabled veterans, small investors, and others on fixed incomes; lower-level white collar employees with uncertain job security; and students and unemployed youth.[12] The National Socialist party also attracted support from aristocrats seeking a return to the days of national power and order, from big business, and from some unionized workers.[13] Except for the aristocrats and former guild members, these people were all from the ranks of those who had benefitted most from the broadened participation in politics since the French Revolution. They were not from the poorest portions of the populace. Their vote for Hitler supported a major period of setback in the growing movement toward broad participation in politics. After World War II, the Allies once again helped write the terms for a highly representative form of government in West Germany, this time accompanied by prosperity which helped bring the populace into agreement with its rules. Big business and unions both amassed considerable power, but the door remained open for many types of groups to participate in politics.[14]

Social groups which have had long control of various interest groups do not step aside to admit other groups without a struggle. In the United States, the United Kingdom, and West Germany, that struggle has been in progress for a number of decades. As a result, new social classes and ethnic groups have entered established interest groups, and new interest groups have been able to form representing a great variety of people. As we saw in chapter 10, only a minority of citizens take advantage of entering such groups, especially from classes and cultures which have risen most recently. But laws assuring all social groups access to education, jobs, bureaucracy, and political participation in these three nation-states have grown progressively stronger, and so has public opinion backing them.

LEGAL BARRIERS

The post-Soviet republics have neither a social nor a legal climate supporting universal entry into interest group competition. From the days of Kiev and Novgorod, buying and selling in Russia has been strictly limited to those licensed by government. It was not unusual for one person to be given a monopoly on an entire commodity. Factories only arose under Peter the Great, under strict government license. Peasants were generally not permitted to leave the estates where they were born. Jews lived in ghettoes and separated villages. Russian Orthodoxy was the established religion. Unions were outlawed. Russian became the official language of those who were conquered, and local elites in many regions were replaced by Great Russians. The press was strictly censored. The Reformation, Renaissance, and Enlightenment passed by Russia; many intellectuals infected by the ideas of these movements were exiled to Siberia.

During the nineteenth century, more and more foreign investors were allowed to develop large urban factories and modernized farms in the Ukraine and the Crimea to grow export crops, and after 1906, an increasing number of peasants were allowed to invest in land independently of the *mir* (the peasant communities to which Tsar Alexander transferred land in his emancipation of the serfs), *barshchina* (the system in the south, where peasants worked on large estates), and *obrok* (the system in the north, where peasants paid the owners a percentage of the crops in exchange for individual plots of land). Free primary education spread. The new urban professional and working classes became increasingly resentful of the commanding role of the nobility and the Church in politics and began electing representatives to the new legislature. But land, bureaucracy, and commerce were still inaccessible to most people.

In the 1917 Soviet Revolution, the Communist Party seized the monopolies on land, power, culture, and commerce held by the tsars, the nobility, and the Church, and kept them. It had some help from workers and soldiers, who were weary of fighting

World War I, but the party was opposed by many groups during the months of civil war which followed. It initially encouraged individual agriculture and claimed to give nationalities more cultural autonomy. These two initiatives did not last long. For the most part, the new regime returned to the pattern of restraints Russia had known in the past. Manufacturing, buying, and selling came under strict government license. Foreign investors and *kulaks* (peasants who became private landowners after the emancipation of the serfs) were removed from ownership, and landholding returned to modified patterns of *barshchina* and *obrok* (but without the nobility) as state and collective farms. People were tied to their farms and factories. Great Russians dominated. Religion was restricted or suppressed if it did not fit the official line (this time, not Russian Orthodoxy,[15] but Communism). Jews remained in the ghettoes. The press was censored. The Komitet Gosudarstvennoy Bezopasnosti—KGB, or Committee for State Security—kept files on one in six Soviet citizens and sent anyone who showed any tendency to express freedom of thought to the dreaded Gulag camps.[16] The KGB released imprisoned scientists after the war to develop atomic and hydrogen bombs within its own laboratories and even spied on members of the Politburo and, later, President Gorbachev, through their personal bodyguards. Past restrictions continued.

The most radical departure from the system under the tsars, besides exiling and killing the tsar and nobility and suppressing the Russian Orthodox Church, was removing foreign investment and shifting agricultural production from export to the domestic market. Whereas wheat and sugar and cotton from the mechanized farms had primarily been destined for export, under the Soviets it was sold on the domestic market at controlled prices the public could afford. The production turned out by large factories was also for domestic consumption. This gave Soviet citizens access to consumer goods they had not had before. But it could not produce the new classes of independent entrepreneurs, gravitating into legislatures and prone to expand political rights, which resulted in the American Revolution.

Workers on the state and collective farms, and in state factories, were organized; but they would experience neither progressive modernization as technology improved, nor the right to use that organization to question the policies of officeholders.

Independent legislatures and courts had feeble roots in Russia. Movements advocating religious freedom never arose. Since Catherine the Great, little land has been privately owned by commoners. Those not Great Russian have known little cultural freedom. The government has tightly coordinated and regulated commerce. Laws restrict movement within the nation-state and abroad, as well as the flow of information. That provides little basis for free interest group participation.

Institutional interest groups—such as defense and consumer industries, agricultural collectives, the military, and *apparatchiki* and officeholders in cities and regions—commanded much of the Soviet Union's economic and political resources and often differed over policy. In addition, the Communist Party created a number of interest groups to speak for workers, women, students, and other segments of the populace through the Communist Party. While it thereby brought into politics social elements which had little access to political institutions before, it outlawed all groups not a part of government or created by the party itself. Approved interest groups had representatives within the Communist Party, whose primary organizations operated within all major industries, unions, government bureaus, army units, state and collective farms, and other institutions. Members of approved groups were also elected to legislatures; even judges and arbitrators could hold legislative seats. To exert influence, they had to bargain with the *apparatchiki* and the Politburo in a variety of ways—by failing to meet production quotas until they obtained specified concessions, offering to support the careers of particular Politburo members, developing support for their positions among other primary organizations in their towns or regions, and the like.[17] Gorbachev's *glasnost* was an attempt to expand the groups which can participate in politics to include those which disagree with government leaders; the political cul-

ture provides little historic basis for such groups to compete freely. Increasingly, the leaders of republics and municipalities and of the Supreme Soviet were being elected from opposition political parties; republics and municipalities won control of buildings, transport, industries, mines, and other assets with which they could exert influence. That, in turn, can shift the focus of interest groups seeking to influence officeholders in the post-Soviet republics.[18]

One of Boris Yeltsin's first moves after being elected President of the Russian Republic was to pass legislation banning the formation of political party organizations within work and military units; this attempt to remove Communist Party *apparatchiki* and KGB officials from their monopoly on forming party cells within the places where people work, and their control over these bodies from within, was roundly resisted by the army (which itself contained 37,000 party branches)[19] and the Communist Party. After the aborted 1991 coup, the Communist Party was banned throughout the Soviet Union; its operatives still retain jobs and connections in the CIS republics. The KGB, the internal security police, the four million members of the armed forces, and the civilian bureaucracy were absorbed by the governments of the republics. So these institutional interest groups continue to exert influence. Many new interest groups are now forming among the general populace to fight for improved ecology, various personal freedoms, and political change. They have their work cut out for them as they attempt to challenge the institutional interest groups already entrenched.

After World War II, the Soviet Union established a similar system in East Germany. That region had been the home of the Prussian landowning nobility, which had begun setting up the strong bureaucratic hierarchies on which German unity had been based in 1870. The businessmen along the Rhine who had begun the modern industries came from within what was then West Germany; those trapped within East Germany after the war generally fled. Hence, the eastern part of Germany had less of a basis for open economic, social, and political competition than the western part. Having experienced

In 1978, this billboard greeted foreign "bourgeois" capitalists emerging from the railroad station of Guangzhou (Canton), China, as they arrived from Hong Kong to explore investment opportunities under Deng Xiaoping's new reforms. Erected by opponents of the reforms (who are still active in China, with counterparts in the CIS republics), it indicates their dislike of market freedoms: "Why did Lenin speak of exercising dictatorship over the bourgeoisie? It is essential to get this question clear. Lack of clarity on this question will lead to revisionism. This must be known to the whole world."

© *Henry Mitchell*

the Reformation, the Renaissance, and Enlightenment, several decades of rule under elected legislatures, and considerable contact with other European countries, East Germany was more prepared than Russia to allow freer interest group competition. By introducing separate party organizations through which unions, industry councils, youth organizations, and others could join into the National Front, rather than forcing all groups to compete within the communist party, it offered one element of competition absent in the Soviet Union. The East German government allowed churches to own land, print publications, broadcast Sunday services, collect a tithe (using the government bureaucracy), and run hospitals and nursing homes. But the government strictly censored the press and airwaves, arrested people without trial, forbade unauthorized groups from forming and meeting, deported intellectuals they did not like, shot those attempting to cross the Berlin Wall, and otherwise restricted freedom of thought and debate. When East Germans stormed the archives of Stasi (the secret police) after the fall of the regime in 1989, they found files on 15 percent of the population.[20]

Though the tsar retained tight control, tsarist Russia allowed the Church, universities, the nobility, *zemstros* and *Zemsky Sobors* (legislative councils), courts, and foreign and domestic cartels to create their own hierarchies and receive protection for their activities. In China, such groups were not even permitted to organize. As we have seen, under Confucian traditions all power to make and enforce laws rested with the emperor and the *literati* (who themselves did not constitute a separate, organized class, since they received their jobs through competitive examinations). The populace was expected to obey these laws without question. That left no room for any social group to organize interest groups.[21] Even the bureaucracy was unified around the literati. During the nineteenth century, a few intellectuals read and discussed ideas from the Renaissance and Enlightenment in the West. The emperors and literati, and the warlords and Guomindang military rulers who followed them, resisted such liberal ideas about the right to organize and govern yourself through representative institutions.[22] They allowed organization, but only if they controlled the groups that organized. The communists organized in work units, in townships, mines, factories, stores, army units, professions, and neighborhoods. All of these organizations have representation in the party and in various levels of government through Peoples' Congresses and elsewhere. But party leaders do not allow members to express their views publicly outside the strict rules they lay down, and they only allow bargaining to take place in secret, with tight procedures as to who may bargain with whom.[23]

Until recently in the Soviet Union and East Germany, the leaders of party- or government-approved interest groups faced virtually no competition. Individuals were not free to organize competing groups. Hence, such leaders could use their power to enrich themselves through black market operations, bribes, kickbacks, perquisites, and grants to one another. They had no incentive to improve their operations. Rank-and-file members of enterprises, party organizations, cultural organizations, and other groups found it hard to oppose the initiatives of their leaders. So while high percentages of people were represented in groups, group members had little control over the policies those groups would espouse. Still, because these agricultural units, defense and consumer industries, producers, urbanites and rural dwellers, members of various professions, and other groups often had interests opposed to one another, they competed within the system on issues affecting high percentages of the populace. In China, they still monopolize group competition, but the introduction of the responsibility system and joint ventures between provincial governments and foreign enterprises, as well as the rise in outside contacts by

universities and students, has made these strict bargaining rules harder to enforce. Tight legal restrictions on bargaining remain.

All of these groups are important to the economies of their respective nation-states, which depend upon them to produce goods and weapons and to sell to one another. High percentages of the populace work for these groups. As we saw in chapter 10, few people from any of the nine systems are actively involved in interest groups. But many work for, buy from, and depend in other ways on organizations which operate effectively as interest groups.

SOCIAL AND ECONOMIC BARRIERS

India, Peru, and Nigeria have adopted legal rules growing out of the Industrial and American Revolutions. But just as the economic growth spurred by the Industrial Revolution has not spread widely, neither have the political reforms of the American Revolution. These three nation-states have free elections (interspersed with military rule in Nigeria and Peru), courts with a degree of independence to counter the actions of officeholders, press and media with a good deal of independence, and rules which give individuals considerable latitude to form interest groups. Yet the dominant economic organizations, which involve much smaller portions of the populace than in the other six systems, tend to monopolize interest group competition. Many villagers do not feel free to organize or belong to interest groups separate from their communities, and they tend to vote for higher-status community members to represent them in existing bodies.

A small percentage of Indians belong to organizations. Because India's political parties are so centralized, it is necessary for interest groups to coordinate with their central leadership to exert influence. And the national economy depends on only a few organizations to function.

Within villages the strongest groups are the **panchayati raj,**[24] or elected village councils, and the cooperative societies. Villagers usually elect larger landowners to hold seats in those bodies; these landowners have converted them into effective interest groups to lobby state and national government. Occasionally, regional organizations such as the Tamil Nadu Agriculturalists Association, with a membership of three million smaller farmers, do involve additional rural dwellers in politics. At the national level, the Congress Kisan for peasants, the Youth Congress, and the Indian National Trade Union Congress[25] are all affiliated with the Congress party and largely controlled by its central leadership. Today there are some seventeen thousand unions in India with about ten million members. They include government workers and professionals, as well as blue collar workers. Workers often switch from one union to another, and the unions have four separate national federations; this leaves their influence fragmented. With the largest union federation associated with the Congress party, and high percentages of both professional and blue collar workers working for government or government-owned firms, unions often function as institutional interest groups associated with government.

Besides the *panchayat* and cooperative membership, the other most effective interest groups are business-related. India's largest **managing agency** (a corporate holding company controlling numerous business enterprises) is the House of **Tata** in Bombay. It operates the Forum of Free Enterprise and the Fair Trade Practices Association. Though Tata was one of the major contributors to the Congress party during the 1890s, in recent years it has given heavy assistance to other parties as well. It built India's first steel mill in 1907, and it manages scores of companies. The next five largest managing agencies dominate the Federation of Indian Chambers of Commerce and Industry, founded in 1927. This federation is represented on about a hundred government commissions and councils and has paid lobbyists to deal with the bureaucracy, the parliament, and the prime minister. The Federation has worked closely with the Congress party since its inception. India's second largest managing agency, House of **Birla,** from Calcutta, is closely consulted by the Congress leadership. Birla was a close friend of Nehru's Deputy Prime Minister Patel, and the Birla managing agency has helped select all of the

nation-state's finance ministers (including Morarji Desai, who later was prime minister under the first brief Janata Government, and the finance minister under the Janata Dal Government which served from 1989 to 1991). Mahatma Gandhi was a guest at the Birla family estate when he was assassinated. The House of Birla controls 25 percent of the votes of the Federation of Indian Chambers of Commerce and Industry and publishes New Delhi's leading newspaper, the *Times,* along with a journal, the *Eastern Economist,* and a number of other newspapers. Along with three other newspapers owned by industrialists, the *Times* consumes a third of all newsprint in India. The top seventy-five managing agencies control about half of the nation-state's capital assets not in banks or government.

Medium-sized firms and British firms are represented in two other federations, and other businesses are represented in a variety of other organizations. **Bakshish,** the payment of bribes to governmental officials in exchange for services, is an established part of Indian life; it is sometimes called "license raj" because the bureaucrats and political party officials use their right to grant licenses to demand payments and lord it over licensees.[26] All businesspeople have contact with government in this manner. This system rewards those who have money to pay.

Among the five million students past high school, about a hundred thousand are active in organizations. There are also about five million unemployed graduates of higher education, some of whom are politically active. With over one million members and two hundred thousand in reserves, the army is effective in lobbying for appropriations, though it has scrupulously followed British army traditions by refraining from intervention in political affairs.

To sum up, fewer than a million larger and middle landowners take part in interest group politics as members of *panchayats* and cooperative societies; most activists in political parties are also within these ranks. Several million more belong to some agricultural or urban squatter organizations which organize civil disobedience. Some ten million Indians own businesses, most very small; two or three percent of these are organized into interest groups. About a hundred thousand students are active in organizations which occasionally involve additional students in strikes and demonstrations. Ten million Indians belong to trade unions. The bureaucracy also contains ten million. Some Indians are leaders of religious groups and castes. Beyond this, few of India's 850 million people belong to any kind of organization other than a religious group, even though they are legally free to form any kind of organization they like. Most are outside the formal economy. The caste organizations which once operated at the local level are largely in decline, and religious leaders are usually far removed from their followers and discourage them from joining other groups.

Kerela, a state at the southern tip of India, was a site of early British development of plantations and trade. For many centuries, ships have brought settlers to Kerela from the Mediterranean and from other regions across the Indian Ocean. Decades ago, high percentages of its populace became actively engaged in associations resisting caste, and in trade unions, tenant farmer associations, and radical political parties. Its literacy rate is nearly double the national average. Though it remains one of the poorest regions of India, its state government, under pressure from active interest groups, has led the way in land reform, school lunch programs, food ration shops, village health centers, pensions, and other programs. It ranks first among all Indian states in providing villages access to schools, post offices, buses, food ration shops, health dispensaries and hospitals, credit cooperative banks, newspapers, and other services. With 97 percent of its villages served by electricity (versus a national average of 33 percent), it ranks number three. A higher portion of Kerela's populace is active in interest groups than is true of the rest of India.[27]

Except for the period from 1985 to 1990, Peru has not been ruled by well-organized, established political parties. Interest groups have had to directly lobby the president, the cabinet, or the bureaucracy. Major business groups generally have actual members in these positions. At times, factions of the army do as well.

Within Lima, trade unions are organized among workers, and squatter colonies have neighborhood associations. Presidents Odria and Velasco, seeking their support, allowed large wage increases. All presidents have distributed small gifts of money and other favors among workers. At other times, workers have resorted to strikes.

Other interest groups have little regular access to government. There are no formal ties between the assemblies and administrative councils in the peasant villages and the national political leadership. Provincial, district, and regional town leaders often have few political or economic contacts with the Lima elite. Only 9 percent of the labor force is in the modern sector. The principal legal export businesses—copper mining, sugar, petroleum, and cotton—employ only a portion of those modern sector workers, and the modern sector exports little. The *haciendas* and import firms that supply food to Lima and other cities employ only a portion more. Government revenues largely derive from these workers and activities.

Much of the populace engages in subsistence agriculture or barters goods and services. They largely lie outside the formal money economy and the taxation structure. The portion of that group most likely to organize is the many graduates of the new regional universities who come from peasant families and cannot find satisfactory jobs in the modern sector after leaving school. The underground terrorist organization *Sendero Luminoso* seems to have attracted many of these graduates, who sense that legal organization is unproductive.

During the 1920s the regime of President **Leguia** for the first time brought professionals, middle class businesspeople, civil servants, and *hacienda* owners into government circles; they have continued to be included. However, the prominent families which had dominated politics up to that point also continued to do so. Other groups have failed to achieve important political roles.

From 1968 to 1976, a military reform regime begun by General **Velasco** distributed land to workers on estates and attempted to organize them, along with residents of squatter colonies, into production cooperatives and administrative councils. Velasco also outlawed APRA, the political party which had previously tried to organize such workers. With the resumption of civilian rule, APRA returned, but these cooperatives and administrative councils largely fell into abeyance. In 1987 President Alan Garcia, of APRA, introduced a new scheme to increase the influence of peasant communities. Communities were given title to their lands,[28] and regional legislatures with village representation were established.[29] However, these units had no budget authority; the villages were made part of a new decision-making process without power to spend money. As inflation soared and the economy deteriorated further, little came of this. The real decisions remain in the hands of units of government where only the most prominent interest groups wield influence. President Fujimori's decrees allow the army to disrupt interest group activity when it thinks such activity endangers security, and they also allow employers to bypass laws which prevent the dismissal of workers.

Few Nigerians belong to formal organizations. The most significant interest groups in Nigeria are civil servants, public development corporations, trade unions, and the armed forces.

In 1985, Nigeria (with a population of about 80 million) had about one hundred fifty thousand high-level civil servants and over a million middle-level bureaucrats or school teachers. The first civil service union was formed in 1921, and the first railroad workers' and teachers' unions in 1931. During the 1970s, these unions and the (at that time) one hundred fifty thousand industrial workers were incorporated into a National Labor Congress supervised by the government. (There are now triple that number of workers.) This gave them leverage to strike for pay increases. The highest civil servants have higher educations and operate expensive development projects. Since Nigerians highly respect education and the thirteen leading universities are operated by the national government, top academics are recruited into prominent positions in both civilian and military regimes.

Since the expansion of universities in 1976, students have become a larger factor in Nigerian politics. Prior to this, all graduates could hope to find good jobs; with the rapid increase in the number of students, this was no longer the case. Whereas the old National Union of Students had been at the center of establishment politics, the new Students Union finds reasons to criticize it. Many students welcomed the 1983 military coup. However, hunger strikes had been prevalent in the expanded number of "post-primary" institutions as students protested tuition, refectory food, poor instruction, religious discrimination, and other grievances. The new regime closed the Executive offices of the Student Union, abolished all private universities (which had sprung up in some places), and sent home students on campuses where strikes were being held.

Many students are sponsored by their local communities, who expect to receive some patronage from them after they get good jobs. Student protests thus have some relation to local communities as well.

Civil servants within individual agencies in Nigeria try to position themselves so as to have the ear of the government in power. For example, in 1978, when political party activity was resumed, many agencies split into factions supporting one party or another. The cities of Lagos, Oyo, Ondo, Kano, Kaduna, and Sokoto, which have been favored by recent regimes, have road, rural electrification, health, medical, water, and housing projects. Different units of government vied for the opportunity to handle these funds, which eventually were funneled to those most supportive of the government. The Green Revolution Program, the National Accelerated Food Production Project, the eleven River Basin Development Authorities (with a 1980–85 budget of $1.5 billion), the Commodity Boards for marketing agricultural commodities, Operation Feed the Nation, the Agricultural and Cooperative Bank (1973–83 lending: $270 million),[30] the Agriculture Credit Guarantee Scheme,[31] and the Fertilizer Company handled billions of dollars and could favor those who lent political support. Customs inspectors had considerable power to enforce, or not enforce, customs laws, allowing extensive smuggling upon payment of **dash**—the folded bundle of currency which accompanies most transactions with government officials, soldiers, or police.

As of 1972, some 70 percent of all industries, and a much higher percentage of industrial production, were in control of foreign firms. That year, the Nigerian Enterprises Promotion Decree mandated that Nigerians be included among the owners of these companies. In 1977, Nigeria nationalized about two-thirds of oil companies, in partnership with the foreign firms. This offered new opportunities for very small numbers of highly placed civil servants and politicians, from the tribal groups which control national government, to serve on the boards of these companies and become part owners. As the percentage of business controlled by these firms under this system increased, the position of independent Nigerian businesses declined. Large numbers of Lebanese and Chinese small businesspeople were, in fact, expelled from the country in 1983.

Because it rules much of the time, the Nigerian army, with over one hundred fifty thousand members, has considerable influence. Civilian regimes cannot afford to offend it, and hence reward it with funds and favors. The army, in turn, cannot ignore the wishes of other interest groups. The military regimes which took power from 1975 to 1976 and 1983 to 1985 were aggressive about cracking down on special privileges in many established interest groups; these regimes were soon overthrown by other military officers and replaced by regimes that cooperated with those interest groups. They still allowed highly placed millionaire-officials to retain special import licensing monopolies and provided heavy subsidies to keep gasoline prices low for urban motorists and air passengers. The regime of Major-General Ibrahim Babangida, which took power in 1985, allowed some businesses to return to 100 percent foreign ownership, but they still had to obtain permits by bribing officials with dash. In 1988, the army seized the National Labor Congress to stop its demands for wage increases and featherbedding during economic downturn. That allowed it

to raise the price of gasoline a bit, deeply devalue the currency so as to discourage imports, and continue cutting the number of civil servants. Frequent strikes and disobedience ensued, along with attempted coups. In Nigeria, then, as in Peru and India, small numbers of well-placed individuals in interest groups continue to wield extensive influence.

CONCLUSION

In any system, interest groups which perform functions needed by the national economy and government are likely to have influence with political leaders. Certain ethnic groups, social classes, and regions may have advantages in this regard. In the case of India, Peru, and Nigeria, groups with historic advantages nearly monopolize interest group competition; few people perform functions needed by the national economy and government. Those integrated into the economy are not strongly protected by law; those outside it often cannot even read or be reached by mail, roads, or television and can be cut off from contact with groups that offend local elites. China and the Soviet Union removed the historic advantages of some groups, but kept or created advantages for others; they do have high portions of their populace involved in the national economy and government- or party-affiliated interest groups. In all systems, it is hard to generate competition against established interest groups. The United States, the United Kingdom, and Germany have created laws and economic integration which help people from many walks of life attempt it.

SUMMARY

The American and Industrial Revolutions extended the variety of social and cultural groups which can participate in national economic and political activities. That extension of participation is most pronounced in systems which have experienced the effects of both of those revolutions. Some systems have widened individual participation in the economy without creating a new legal framework to encourage independent political participation. Others have created a legal framework without broadening participation in the economy. Both of these types of systems narrow the range of individuals able to compete within interest groups. That range is especially hard to widen when economic participation in the formal economy is limited to small portions of the populace.

NOTES

1. Gabriel A. Almond and G. Bingham Powell, Jr., eds., *Comparative Politics: A Developmental Approach,* 2d ed. (Boston: Little, Brown, 1978), p. 176, use this term. Almond calls the groups which grow up spontaneously "anomic" or "nonassociational" groups, and those organized outside political parties and government "associational" groups.

2. Everett Carll Ladd, *The American Polity,* 4th ed. (New York: Norton, 1991), p. 308. During the 1978 Congressional campaigns, Political Action Committees (PACs) of corporations and trade associations donated $21.4 million, of labor unions $10.3 million, and of other organizations $3.4 million to federal candidates. *Congress and the Nation,* vol. 4, (Washington, D.C.: CQ), p. 76.

3. See V. O. Key, *Parties, Politics, and Pressure Groups,* 5th ed. (New York: Crowell, 1964); David B. Truman, *The Governmental Process* (New York: Knopf, 1951); R. Golembiewski, "The Group Basis of Politics," *American Political Science Review* 54, 4 (December 1960): 962–71; T. L. Gais, M. Peterson, and J. Walker, "Interest Groups, Iron Triangles, and Representative Institutions in American National Government," *British Journal of Political Science,* 14, 2 (April 1984): 161–86; and D. Yates, *Bureaucratic Democracy* (Cambridge, Mass.: Harvard University Press, 1982).

4. The play Thatcher's Government banned was *Perdition,* about the Nazi atrocities; it is strongly anti-Zionist and suggests that some Jewish leaders collaborated with the Nazis.

5. See Max Beloff and Gillian Peele, *The Government of the UK: Political Authority in a Changing Society,* 2d. ed. (New York: Norton, 1985), pp. 377–98, for an overview of this.

6. The Independent Television Commission banned broadcast of the miracle-healing portion of a weekly program by Morris Cerullo, successor to Jim and Tammy Bakker, on grounds that it contained claims of "special powers and abilities" which could not be substantiated; that violated the code drawn up by the commission. *Kansas City Star,* August 14, 1991. In the United States, such a ban would be appealed to the Supreme Court on grounds that it violated the First Amendment to the Constitution, guaranteeing free exercise of religion.

7. See Michael Rush, ed., *Parliament and Pressure Politics* (Oxford: Oxford University Press, 1990); S. E. Finer, *Anonymous Empire* (London, 1966); C. C. Hood and M. Wright, eds., *Big Government in Hard Times* (Oxford: Martin Robertson, 1981); D. Marsh, *Pressure Politics: Pressure Groups in Modern Britain* (London: Junction Books, 1983); A. G. Jordan and J. J. Richardson, *British Politics and the Policy Process* (London: Allen & Unwin, 1987); Geoffrey Alderman, *Pressure Groups and Government in Great Britain,* (New York: Longman, 1984); B. Sedgemore, *The Secret Constitution: An Analysis of the Political Establishment* (London: Hodder & Stoughton, 1980); Hugo Young and Anne Sloman, *No Minister: An Inquiry into the Civil Service* (London: BBC Publications, 1982); M. T. S. Holmes, *Political Pressure and Economic Policy* (London: Butterworths, 1982); R. Taylor, *The Fifth Estate* (London: Routledge, 1978); P. Taylor, *Smoke Rings: Politics of Tobacco* (London: Bodley Head, 1984); F. Field, *Poverty and Politics* (London: Heinemann, 1982); P. Whiteley and S. Winyard, "The Origins of the New Poverty Lobby," *Political Studies* 32, 1 (March 1984): 32–54; R. King and N. Nugent, eds., *Respectable Rebels: Middle-Class Campaigns in Britain in the 1970s* (London: Hodder & Stoughton, 1979); and P. Lowe and J. Goyder, *Environmental Groups in Politics* (London: Allen & Unwin, 1983).

8. See Philippe C. Schmitter and Wolfgang Streeck, eds., *Private Interest Governments* (Los Angeles: Sage, 1985); Peter J. Katzenstein, *Politics and Policy in the Federal Republic of Germany: The Semi-Sovereign State* (Philadelphia: Temple University Press, 1987); Gordon Smith, William E. Paterson, and Peter H. Merkl, eds., *Developments in German Politics*

(Durham, N.C.: Duke University Press, 1989); Peter J. Katzenstein, ed., *Industry and Politics in West Germany: Toward the Third Republic* (Ithaca: Cornell University Press, 1989); Joseph Esser, "State, Business and Trade Unions in West Germany after the 'Political Wende,'" *West European Politics* 9, 2 (April 1986): 198–214; Wyn Grant, William Paterson, and Colin Whitson, *Government and the Chemical Industry: A Comparative Study of Britain and West Germany* (Oxford: Oxford University Press, 1988).

9. Civil service laws passed around 1870 opened the bureaucracy to all classes in the major European countries, but nobility continued to dominate it at all levels for several decades thereafter.

10. The percentage of nobles in the House of Commons dropped from a sixth in 1860 to a twelfth in 1905, but the House of Lords retained its veto until 1911. Germany retained a system of class voting until near the end of the nineteenth century. In this system, each social class had the same number of seats in the legislature.

11. Unemployment in Germany grew from nearly nothing before World War I to 1 million in 1930 to 6 million in 1932. Between 1929 and 1930, utilization of industrial capacity dropped by 50 percent. Between 1927 and 1932, unemployment pay dropped from 30 to 16 reichsmark a month in cities, while inflation caused the reichsmark to be worth a fraction of its former value. Almost half of working-class families were on social welfare; many of them voted for Communist party candidates rather than National Socialists. Joseph Rovan, *Le Monde*, July 22, 1991.

12. See Thomas Childers, *The Nazi Voter: The Social Foundations of Fascism in Germany 1919–1933* (Chapel Hill: University of North Carolina Press, 1983); Timothy A. Tilton, "The Social Origins of Nazism: The Rural Dimensions," in Michael N. Dobkowski and Isidor Wallimann, eds., *Towards the Holocaust,* (Westport, Conn.: Greenwood Press, 1983), pp. 61–72; and Seymour Martin Lipset, *Political Man: The Social Bases of Politics* (Garden City, N.J.: Doubleday, 1960).

13. Richard F. Hamilton, *Who Voted for Hitler* (Princeton: Princeton University Press, 1982); Peter Merkl in Stein Ugelvik Larsen, Bernt Hagtvet, and Jan Petter Kyklebust, eds., *Who Were the Fascists?* (Bergen, Germany: Universitetsforlaget, 1980); John Nagle, "Composition and Evolution of the Nazi Elite," in Dobkowski and Wallimann, *Holocaust,* pp. 75–92; Henry Ashby Turner, Jr., *German Big Business and the Rise of Hitler* (New York: Oxford University Press, 1985); and Michael H. Kater, *The Nazi Party: A Social Profile of Members and Leaders 1919–1945* (Cambridge: Harvard University Press, 1983). Kater and Turner, who follow the period after 1933, found that after the burning of the Reichstag and the massacre of Ernst Roehm's SA storm troops by Heinrich Himmler's SS blackshirts, giving Hitler firm control over the Gestapo's secret police and unleashing its reign of terror, support from aristocrats, business, and unions quickly subsided, except among some who benefitted most directly, such as big business owners. All these studies indicate that Hitler's staunchest support came from the groups discussed here. Hannah Arendt, *The Origins of Totalitarianism* (New York: Harcourt, Brace, Jovanovich, 1973), pp. 326–40, also discussed this "Temporary Alliance Between the Mob and the Elite."

Klaus Scholder, *The Churches and the Third Reich,* vol. 1, 1918–34 (Philadelphia: Fortress Press, 1988) documents the close ties of both protestant and Catholic church leaders to Hitler. These leaders liked Hitler's invocation of both God and nationalism. Some of these church leaders who originally welcomed his arrival split away later to become adamant foes.

14. See Gerard Braunthal, *The Federation of German Industry in Politics* (Ithaca, N.Y.: Cornell University Press, 1965); J. Esser, "State, Business and Trade Unions in West Germany after the 'Political Wende,'" Katzenstein, *Industry and Politics in West Germany:* Schmitter and Streeck, *Private Interest Government;* Peter Swenson, *Fair Shares: Unions, Pay and Politics in Sweden and West Germany* (Ithaca, N.Y.: Cornell University Press, 1989); and Kathleen Thelen, *West German Unions and Industrial Adjustment: A Case Study of the I. G. Metall* (Berkeley: University of California Press, 1988).

15. However, Stalin allied with the Russian Orthodox Church for a period of time.

16. For a good overview, see Amy W. Knight, *The KGB: Police and Politics in the Soviet Union* (Boston: Unwin Hyman, 1990).

17. See H. Gordon Skilling, "Interest Groups and Communist Politics," *World Politics* (April 1966): 435–51; H. Gordon Skilling, "Interest Groups and Communist Politics Revisited," *World Politics* 36, 1

(October 1983): 1–27; H. Gordon Skilling and Franklyn Griffiths, eds., *Interest Groups in Soviet Politics* (Princeton: Princeton University Press, 1971); William Odom, "A Dissenting View on the Group Approach to Soviet Politics," *World Politics* (July 1976): 452–567; Andrew Janos, "Group Politics in Communist Society: A Second Look at the Pluralist Model," in Samuel P. Huntington and Barrington Moore, eds., *Authoritarian Politics in Modern Society* (New York: Basic Books, 1970); Alexander Yanov, *The Drama of the Soviet 1960s* (Berkeley, Calif.: Institute of International Studies, 1984); and Theodore H. Friedgut, *Political Participation in the USSR* (Princeton, N.J.: Princeton University Press, 1979).

18. The KGB, for instance, drew closer to the military and to new political parties which opposed liberalizing the economy and politics.

19. According to the top Communist party official in the Soviet army, General Mikhail S. Surkov, in announcing his intention to ignore the ban, since the army was controlled by the national government and not the state. *Kansas City Star*, August 11, 1991.

20. David Remnick, "Liquidating the Fearsome KGB," *Washington Post National Weekly Edition*, September 2–8, 1991.

21. See Andrew Nathan, *Chinese Democracy* (New York: Knopf, 1985).

22. Yuan Shikai, the Chinese general who ruled briefly after the overthrow of the emperor, said: "Under the pretext of freedom of association [the people who hold that liberty is something sacred] are free to plot rebellions; relying on the freedom of speech, they are free to spread rumors." Quoted by Qin Xiaoying, "Jumping Out of the Vicious Cycle of History; China's Third Polemic over Authoritarianism," *Beijing Jiangjixue Zhoubao*, March 12, 1989. In *China's Destiny*, Jiang Kaishek, the leader of the Guomindang, wrote: "Liberalism will turn the country and nation into a state of disunity, and the national economy into anarchy."

23. See Lucien Pye, *The Dynamics of Chinese Politics* (Cambridge, Mass.: Oelgeschlager, 1981); Marshall Goldman, *China's Intellectuals* (Cambridge, Mass.: Harvard University Press, 1981); Peter Ferdinand, "Interest Groups and Chinese Politics," in David S. Goodman, ed., *Groups and Politics in the People's Republic of China* (Armonk, N.Y.: M. E. Sharpe,

1984); and Alan P. L. Liu, *How China Is Ruled* (Englewood Cliffs, N.J.: Prentice Hall, 1986), chapter 4.

24. Villages in India traditionally had *panchayats*, which were councils of the caste elders. After independence, the Congress party wished to establish a noncaste version of these councils by instituting elected councils. But villages tend to support the candidates of large landowners and caste leaders to serve on these councils.

25. In 1918, Mahatma Gandhi organized The Ahmedabad Textile Labour Association—a union dedicated to finding reasonable compromises between workers and owners. Meanwhile, Socialist Congress members were organizing unions using violence and calling for an end to capitalism. The National Trade Union Federation, founded in 1920, split in 1929 (with Jawaharlal Nehru, who would later become India's first prime minister, as its head) when the nationalists left, and again in 1931 when the communists withdrew. By 1945, the communists had full control of the federation. The Congress then set up their own federation.

26. Chapter 33 discusses Indian Prime Minister Rao's attempt to end these licenses; he was strongly opposed by those collecting the bribes.

27. Richard Franke and Barbara Chasin, *Kerela: Radical Reform as Development in an Indian State* (Berkeley, Calif.: Institute for Food and Development Policy, 1989).

28. *Ley General de Comunidades Campesinas*, no. 24656; *Ley de Deslinde y Titulacion*, no. 24657; promulgado por el Señor Presidente Constitucional de la Republica en la Case de Gobierno el dia 13 de Abril de 1987.

29. *Regionalizacion*, leyes 23878 (Plan Nacional de Regionalizacion) y 24650 (Ley de Bases de la Regionalizacion), Centro Bartolome de Las Casas, Cusco, 1987.

30. Its average loan was $85,000. Michael Watts, ed., *State, Oil, and Agriculture in Nigeria* (Berkeley: University of California Institute of International Studies, 1987), p. 22.

31. Of the $8.5 million it lent in 1980, 80 percent went for the ranching, poultry, and mixed farming projects of large farms. Michael Watts, *Silent Violence: Food, Famine, and Peasantry in Northern Nigeria* (Berkeley: University of California Press, 1983), p. 503.

EXERCISES

Think about the book thus far:

How do chapters 19 and 20, on political parties and interest groups, relate to assimilation into modern institutions?

KEY WORDS AND PHRASES

Define the following terms:

institutional interest groups	House of Tata	Leguia
panchayati raj	House of Birla	Velasco
managing agency	bakshish	dash

THINKING IT THROUGH

Imagine that you are a member of one of the following groups, and you want to change a government policy. What are some obstacles you would need to overcome? In which of the nine systems might you expect to encounter the least number of obstacles?

  a. a small businessperson from a cultural minority
  b. a peasant in subsistence agriculture
  c. a blue collar industrial worker
  d. a retired person

chapter 21

PARTIES, INTEREST GROUPS, AND ELECTIONS
CONSENSUAL PARTIES AND CHANGE

All of us belong to groups; not all of us become involved in interest groups and political parties, even when we are allowed to. During the past two centuries, some countries have expanded the groups allowed to exert influence on officeholders; others have reduced or restricted the groups able to do so. Competitive, and even noncompetitive, consensual political parties have helped widen participation in the former countries; in the latter, they have failed to reverse the narrowing of participation which results from reducing, rather than expanding, the percentage of people who play roles in the national economy.

All of us are born into groups. Other people also place us into groups in their own minds, based on skin color, language, accents, habits, place of residence, and other traits. As we saw in chapter 12, we place ourselves into certain regional, tribal, ethnic, religious, cultural, class, and occupational groupings by deciding that we belong to them. In subsequent chapters, we examined how some of these groups are better able than others to exert influence—because they have had influence in the past, are accepted by those with influence as legitimate participants in political institutions, and/or are in the habit of acquiring traits needed to exert influence.

In chapter 20, we discussed how some groups have increased their influence during the past century as a result of economic activities and governmental policies which allowed groups which formerly had little influence to form and participate in political parties. In this chapter, we continue that discussion, focusing on when and why those changes took place and how they relate to political parties. **Do consensual parties expand participation? Do they benefit from expanded participation?** These are the questions we will discuss in this chapter.

POWER REALIGNMENTS, PARTY DEALIGNMENTS, AND EXPANDED PARTICIPATION

As we saw in chapter 20, the United States, the United Kingdom, and West Germany have all expanded suffrage during the past two centuries and relaxed other barriers to allow a wide variety of groups to participate in politics. The Soviet Union and East Germany abruptly removed some classes of people from their countries, while organizing other classes within economic and political institutions that have increased their influence to some extent. All these events have been accompanied by party realignments and dealignments.

Sometimes members of an ethnic group or age group or region leave one party and shift their votes and their loyalty to another party; this is called **party realignment.** Sometimes such groups may leave one party and begin to shift their votes back and forth among parties, with little loyalty to any one party; this is called **party dealignment.** Either phenomenon, or the extension of suffrage to new groups, can cause a dominant party to become a minority party. For example, in the United States, the Democratic Party controlled both the presidency and the Congress until the Civil War; during the period from 1801 to 1855, the Democrats controlled the presidency for forty-seven years, the Senate for forty-nine years, and the House of Representatives for forty-five years. During the seventy-two years from 1860 to 1932, by contrast, the Republicans controlled the presidency for fifty-six years, the House for fifty-two years, and the Senate for sixty-two years. From 1932 until 1992, the Democrats again controlled the presidency for thirty-two years, the House for fifty-six years and the Senate for fifty-two. The U.S. population, in each of these shifts, realigned or dealigned its support for one party over the other.

Those swings were accompanied by increases in suffrage, shifts in the groups individuals identified with, and events which changed people's attitudes about the policies each party was associated with. For example, the Democratic Party advocated free trade and monetary standards which made borrowing easy and supported rules which allowed the expansion of slavery. That pleased settlers who were moving to the Western frontier to begin small farms, and Southern planters, who needed to borrow money for their farms and wanted no barriers to exporting their agricultural produce. It did not please industrialists, who wanted protection from competition with European imports, nor settlers who wanted to cross into the territories West of the Mississippi after it became impossible to decide whether they would be slave or free. The Republican Party was formed in 1854 to appeal to those groups. A settler who might earlier have supported the Democrats because of their monetary policy and ignored their stand on slavery now turned to the Republicans because they opened the land and railroads to the West and ushered in new kinds of goods and industries in those territories. Yet, by the 1890s, fluctuating market prices for crops, tight credit, high interest rates, and resulting farm foreclosures caused some of those Western farmers to swing back to the Democratic Party. Other realignments have occurred since. Some ethnic minorities who supported the Democrats during the 1960s because they advocated civil rights (a reversal of the party's stand a century earlier) found themselves attracted to the Republican Party during the 1980s because the Republicans proposed lowering taxes. After the 1960s, some workers also shifted from the Democratic Party, which they had supported because it brought them out of the Great Depression, to the Republican Party, which was less inclined to promote minorities competing for workers' jobs. Thus, in the 1980s, there was some dealignment as the Republicans gained some former Democrats as supporters.

Now voters are less predictable. The Democrats were the majority party until the 1970s, when many voters began to shift their votes from one party to the other in different elections, or to vote for candidates from each party, and regular supporters of both parties began to even out in number.[1] In 1992, many voters—now less attracted to either party—turned away from the Republicans to endorse the Democrats and independent Ross Perot.

But change in voter loyalties is only one reason why support for particular parties waxes and wanes. During the past two hundred and fifty years, the United States has experienced a Revolutionary War, wars against Spain and Mexico, the Louisiana Purchase, Indian Wars, and the Civil War, many of which involved an expansion in territory and the exile (voluntary and involuntary) or demotion of people with property and influence. Some of the merchants who were most influential prior to the Revolutionary War fled to Canada and elsewhere when the war began, as did prominent officials and traders from the former French and Spanish colonies. Most Native Americans and Southern plantation owners could not flee, but experienced drastic changes in their living standards and their ability to exert influence; the lands and the Senate seats they had occupied fell under the control of others. All these events involved **realignments of power,** as people are removed from high positions they hold and replaced by people from other groups in society, or as some institutions are favored at the expense of others that have fallen out of favor. Economic depressions, too, can bring such shifts, both by stripping individuals of their fortunes and by creating new programs which shift spending patterns; the Great Depression and Franklin D. Roosevelt's policies aided the consumer and defense industries, and encouraged the growth of various government agencies designed to prevent depression from recurring, while harming many who had invested heavily in land or stocks. The latter were often old settlers; the former—new consumer and defense industries—welcomed the participation of newer immigrant groups which had previously been reduced to working for others in small firms.

Party realignments or dealignments can themselves result in some realignments of power if the party which gains office changes policies to help one group at the expense of another. Sometimes power realignments occur because a party comes to office with a willingness to end a controversy by taking a firm stand harmful to the groups who lost the election; the Civil War began because the new Republican President Abraham Lincoln was willing to end the impasse over slavery and westward expansion by refusing to allow the South to leave the Union. That was an unusually bold move. Such radical changes are more likely to occur if the party acceding to power does so by force rather than election. Lincoln's settlement involved force; when the Congress and military high command refused to cooperate with his intent to fight the Confederacy, he bypassed them. Normally, a consensual party does not act this decisively, precisely because it tries to find consensus among the groups involved. On the whole, except for the historic breaks discussed in the last two paragraphs, the United States has experienced a rather gradual expansion of influence to new groups, while groups which have influence tend to retain it. In the United States, party realignments have been accompanied more by an expansion of those with power, rather than a realignment of power from one group to another.

The communist parties of the Soviet Union, East Germany, and China came to power by force. As we have seen, they promptly expropriated land, industry, and titles from the people who owned them, often taking their lives as well, and turned these assets over to newly formed government agencies and party officials. Peasants and workers, often against their will, were recruited into factories, mechanized farms, schools, the military, and other institutions. This actually enhanced their ability to exert influence, though they were strictly forbidden to do so in unauthorized ways. That represented a sharp realignment of *power*.

Since that time, war and economic change have caused *party* realignments within the Communist Party in the Soviet Union. Immediately after their takeover in 1917, the Communists' Red Army faced resistance from the White Armies, which enjoyed support among many peasants. After the White Armies were quelled, the government initiated the New Economic Policy with its emphasis on aiding farmers and consumer industries. Later, Stalin quelled threats more brutally by murdering high officials and ordinary citizens, frequently and randomly. He responded to external threats and continuing peasant resistance by emphasizing heavy industry and gearing farm production toward creating food for the cities, urging city workers to sacrifice on consumer goods. Khrushchev responded to public pressures for consumer goods and greater benefits for farmers, while Brezhnev steered back again toward greater emphasis on defense production. Gorbachev's reemphasis on agricultural and consumer production was accompanied by new methods of controlling the economy and politics.

Each of these changes involved shifts in the composition of the Politburo and in the relative influence of various interest groups; these realignments within the Communist Party were realignments of power, for various social groups, though less profound than the realignment which took place in 1917. Rather than resulting from realignment in the party preferences of voters, these power realignments came from the changing preferences of party and government officials as they struggled to control policy within the single ruling party. *Glasnost,* which brought freer party competition, allowed voters to shift their votes to other parties; they did so with a vengeance.[2] As a result, the Communist Party changed its charter to allow new members: people who did not believe in a communist economic system, who desired private property, and who were not members of the "working class" were admitted to party membership for the first time. The party hoped to use this, and its control of assets like hotels and resorts with exclusive membership, to stop the rapid downturn in its membership and voter support; more types of people would now be welcome to join their "club," which monopolized all the privileges. Meanwhile, *apparatchiki* were busy forming banks and businesses with money they had personally diverted from state enterprises. This left them ready and able to enter new capitalist enterprises, and to continue to dominate politics and bureaucracy, when the Communist Party was outlawed following the 1991 coup attempt. Rather than joining the "club," many people supported ending its monopoly of privileges.

The Soviet Union's realignments of power may be less profound than they appear on the surface. The tsar and his family were killed after the Revolution, and many nobility fled. Many lost land, businesses, and buildings. But many families of intellectuals, scientists, and the middle class continued to send their children to university, even during the height of the Stalin era. Most peasants and workers still did not have the chance to do so. Some did become prominent in the Communist Party. And those in the Communist Party are in a position to reap economic and political benefits through newly organized parties and businesses now that the party has been banned. Thus, there were changes in the social groups exerting power, but the slowness of social mobility during and after the communist era attests to their subtlety.

As suffrage expanded in the United Kingdom during the nineteenth century, the nation-state experienced frequent party realignments. As the new middle classes grew, they moved into the Whig party to challenge the aristocratic Tories; the Whigs later became the Liberal Party, and the Tories the Conservative Party. The Conservative Party attracted new working-class voters under Benjamin Disraeli, who emphasized imperialist expansion abroad and welfare projects at home for workers. William Gladstone rallied middle-class votes for the Liberal Party, with a call for less foreign adventurism, free trade, expansion of education, and competitive admission to the civil service. As working class suffrage grew further, the Labour Party was formed and eventually came to attract more working- and middle-class votes than the Liberal Party. Labour Governments after World War II sought disengagement from the empire into closer ties with Europe and the expansion of welfare programs; during the 1980s, Thatcher's Conservative Government broke with her party's tradition by moving into the European Economic Community, and won working- and middle-class supporters away from Labour by expanding job opportunities in business.[3] This caused the Labour Party to modify its positions on welfare spending, nationalization, and concessions to unions in order to win back these voters; that weakened the position of labor.[4] These minor realignments of power were accompanied by an expansion (but little realignment) of groups in a position to exert power.

Germany's aggressive push to industrialize in the late nineteenth century pushed many peasants from the land into industrial jobs and hence, initially, into radical political parties which bemoaned their working conditions and lack of political rights. During the 1880s, Germany's government sought to soften that opposition by creating strong welfare programs and outlawing radical parties. When they were again legalized in 1890, these parties formed the Social Democratic Party, which quickly became the leading party of the German Reichstag (legislature). The party presided over the rapid industrialization of Germany, trying to create cooperation between labor and capitalists.[5] After World War I, it was challenged by Socialists and Communists on the left, and, later, National Socialists on the right. When National Socialist leader Adolph Hitler seized power, he banned all parties except his own, and geared industrial production toward military ends. Jews were wrenched from prominent positions and sent into exile and death camps. After World War II, the Social Democrats faced their chief competition from the Christian Democrats, a party moderately to their right with some roots in prewar parties. Those two parties have alternated in power up until the present.[6]

East Germany, under communist rule, did not experience major swings in emphasis after its inception. But the most recent party chairman, Erich Honecker, was a skilled politician and led his nation-state through a number of policy shifts which involved major changes in party leadership. In the first election after the 1989 fall of the Berlin Wall, however, his party won few votes. East German voters turned to the Social and Christian Democrats and their allies.

Germany's biggest realignments of power came from seizures of power by political parties in 1933 and 1945; for East Germans, 1990 reunification constituted another such realignment. For Jews, 1933 represented a profound realignment as Hitler ascended to power. Middle-class flight to the West in 1945 catapulted many peasants and workers into prominent positions in East Germany; after reunification, armies of bureaucrats returned from the West to remove many of them from those positions, and former owners came to reclaim land and buildings. Most other Germans did not experience radical shifts in their ability to wield power over these years.

Consensual parties in all these systems have largely continued to draw votes from the same pool of voters, though the portion of those eligible to vote gradually expanded; during this century, they have not drawn on large new pools of voters since the introduction of female suffrage and the civil rights laws opening voting to blacks in the United States. Except for the Hitler period, rule in the United States, the United Kingdom, and West Germany has tended to alternate between consensual parties which tried to appeal to the same groups of voters. Rather than experiencing major realignments of the loyalties of various groups of voters from one party to another, these systems have experienced some dealignment—a tendency for voters to cease having strong loyalty to any particular party and to instead shift their vote between parties.[7] No one yet knows which parties will benefit from the shifts in loyalty away from the communist parties of East Germany and the Soviet Union. In all these systems, the number of groups which can participate in politics has grown extensively during the past two-hundred years. But expansion of power for some is seldom accompanied by a radical decline in power for others. Economic and social changes bring changes in opinions; a consensual party with competition has incentive to respond to those changes by changing their views to correspond. Party realignment and dealignment is thus more prevalent than realignment of power.

POWER REALIGNMENTS, AMATEUR PARTY REALIGNMENTS, AND EXPANDED PARTICIPATION

As in the Soviet Union, communist rule in China brought a major realignment of power as former landowners, manufacturers, and officials were forced to give up their power and assets to institutions which would greatly expand the economic and political involvement of workers and peasants. Since coming to power in 1949, the Communist Party in China has been through several realignments which have affected the relative power of various groups. These realignments have involved an element not experienced in the other nation-states—the creation of amateur parties and interest groups to compete with real ones and bring groups of people into political competition who did not have prior influence. That unusual phenomenon bears closer examination; it highlights some aspects of realignment which are unique to China, and some which may be found in the other systems as well. The creation of amateur parties caused an unusually large number of uneducated peasant and worker cadres to rise to power within the ruling party (as we discussed in chapter 10). But, far from resulting in a major realignment of power among groups, this shift has made difficult the sort of party dealignment occurring in most other former communist countries. The realignment of power has brought many new people into politics but gives them little incentive to seek party realignment.

China's Communist Party came to power in 1949 by fighting a civil war with the ruling Guomindang party (table 21.1). The communists had actually split from the Guomindang during the 1920s. By 1949,

Table 21.1

Important Dates in China's Realignments

1949	Communists take over
1955	Collectivization
1957	Great Leap Forward
1958	Reversal of Great Leap Forward
May 1966	Great Proletarian Cultural Revolution begins
January 1968	Mao creates revolutionary committees

China had been through several decades of factional fighting between warlords and occupation by and war with Japan. From 1949 to 1954, the party ruled through a United Front government, which included leaders of nine political parties backed by five army units, whose commanders befriended local elites. The new regime moved rapidly to stabilize the currency, repair railroads, distribute food and clothing, create public health and sanitation programs, and develop heavy industry. They let cooperative landlords and factory owners run their farms and businesses, welcomed technical specialists to work in them, and purchased equipment to modernize factories and the army. This resulted in increased power for the army, businesspeople, landowners, and local officials.[8] Except for the loss of power among wealthy landlords and officials who had fled to Taiwan after the Communist takeover, this represented little power realignment.

However, though heavy industry was booming, agriculture was in a state of stagnation. Peasants could not obtain credit to purchase seeds, fertilizer, and equipment. Poor peasants were being forced to sell land, while wealthier peasants evaded government regulations, and officials accepted bribes and special privileges. That, too, represented little difference from before the Communist takeover. Mao Zedong, who believed in a society where everyone would share equally in economic rewards, resolved to make changes. In 1955, as both chief of state and party chairman, he instituted a rapid program of farm collectivization which constituted a major realignment of power. All landowners and peasants were asked to turn over their land to large collective farms, which they all would work for. Many landowners resisted turning their property over to the collectives; as a result, nearly a million were killed. Many slaughtered their animals, destroyed their farm implements, and neglected their fields in resistance. By 1956, 100 million families were collectivized. The immediate result was an increase in agricultural output, caused by the distribution of better fertilizer and farm implements, combined with an end to warfare and the fortune of good weather; by 1957, production was 15 percent higher than in 1950.[9] But many peasants, and many members of the party hierarchy, were displeased with the social disruptions and loss of former personal income. The other members of the Politburo, who had opposed the collectivization in the first place, removed Mao Zedong from his post as Secretary General of the Secretariat and gave this position to Deng Xiaoping. They hoped, in this manner, to end Mao's control over the day-to-day operations of the party. They also created the Standing Committee of the Politburo, composed of the Chairman (Mao), four vice-chairmen, and the Secretary General. In this way, they hoped to end one-person rule.[10]

Mao quickly responded by producing a new set of competing institutions led by peasants. This was an attempt to get around the power of the bureaucrats by turning over production and management to peasants; this first attempt was to prove short-lived, but it would be repeated nine years later with more long-lasting effect. The idea was to destroy all family, bureaucratic, military, and political structures, and shift the power to run the economy and politics directly into the hands of peasants and workers. No longer could rich peasants, bureaucrats, and party cadres conspire to keep power and privilege in their own hands. Mao hoped to effect an enormous realignment of power, shifting it to the lowest levels of society. Within a year, in his **Great Leap Forward,** he had placed 500 million peasants into "people's communes." All their property was confiscated. They ate together in hastily constructed mess halls. They formed military brigades, which held frequent "self-rectification" sessions (gathering in the evenings to criticize anyone with doubts about what was transpiring); and, in addition to working the fields, they moved about building projects such as roads and small dams. Thus, peasant counterparts were created to the professional civil service, party officials, and the army. Mao had effected a unique *party* realignment by generating new party and state institutions outside the party and state, run by new social groups.[11] This realignment would be short-lived.

The results were disastrous. For a time, the party leaders went along. Peasants were caught up in Mao's bold rhetoric. Soon, however, major factories closed. Bad weather followed. Water management facilities, normally run by public officials, were poorly supervised. Communes used up seed stores they could not replace. The fertilizer market ceased. Crops dwindled, and food intakes returned to the levels they were at during the war; as many as 30 million people may have starved.[12] The exhausted peasants sometimes staged raids against the state granaries. The black market, especially in food, began to thrive. Far from ending corruption and special privileges, the Great Leap Forward created more.

Toward the end of 1958, the party leadership quietly began to strike back. They passed word to local officials to simply ignore private gardens and food sales (designed to get around the Great Leap Forward). They returned to wages and incentive pay. And they removed Mao from his position as head of state (leaving him with only the party chairmanship). This gave them the opportunity to place their own people at all levels of the party and governmental structures. Thus fortified, they proceeded with a new approach to agricultural development, ordering heavy industry to turn out insecticides, irrigation equipment, farm implements, and fertilizer. They began heavy imports of fertilizer and wheat, and set up twenty-five thousand workshops to repair small farm implements. Production teams were created within the communes, with the power to decide how to divide profits among members. Now peasants were free to cultivate their private plots and bargain for larger ones. Leading officials openly indulged in luxuries. Party leaders, wealthier peasants, and bureaucrats (though, for the moment, not the army) were back in positions of power. The attempt at a major power realignment had failed.

Mao had lost control of the party hierarchy, but he kept control of media, school curricula, and other organs of indoctrination, which he used to stir up support for "class struggle" against "capitalist roaders" in the party. And the army was headed by one of Mao's supporters, Lin Biao.[13] He set out to recruit two-hundred thousand political commissars into the army, carefully screened to be sure that they were loyal to Mao's ideas about realigning power downward. He promoted loyal officers and ordered special food rations. To emphasize equality, he abolished rank insignia and titles (though not rank itself, or special privileges for officers). He urged his troops to be resolute in their ideology and lead the people. The rest of the high command, who resisted these initiatives, realized that their call for a more professional, less egalitarian and ideological army would only be heeded if the army were needed to defend the nation-state. They became increasingly vocal about the need to help the North Vietnamese fight the United States in Vietnam. Mao recognized that actual military involvement would force the army to emphasize professionalism and weapons procurement and would end its role in resisting the internal party organization; Mao and Lin Biao resisted these attempts to enter the conflict.[14] They wanted to use their armed forces instead to upset the power of the party leadership.

Mao's stature in the party grew from the fact that he, before World War II, when other party leaders rejected the strategy, had organized millions of peasants to resist the Japanese invaders, take land from landlords to produce food for their own use, and eventually capture Beijing. His success in doing so made it difficult for others to personally attack him. He now decided to use his prestige to begin removing Party officials by personally attacking them. His first target was the Mayor of Beijing, whom he attacked late in 1965 because of a play written by a Deputy Mayor which, Mao said, constituted a personal attack on himself.[15] As Mao persisted in his attack, he noted that others failed to support the Mayor for fear of placing themselves in direct confrontation with Mao. Furthermore, he had created a group of supporters among students and his political commissars in the army, who were angry at corruption and the decline of ideals. Mao had organized mass mobilization campaigns before, inducing young people to harass others to make them conform. None had the effects of this round. These students began to taunt the mayor in public with "big character posters." Under fire and without supporters, the Mayor resigned in May, 1966; the **Great Proletarian Cultural Revolution** had begun.[16]

Soon students all over the country were becoming bold and active, organizing themselves into cliques called Red Guards. They first turned their attack on university administrators and closed the universities, which (together with elementary schools) would not reopen for many years. Then they turned on people at all levels of the party, the military, the government, the media, and the various national federations. They would arrive at the homes of these individuals, drape demeaning banners around their necks and place dunce caps on their heads, parade them through the streets, and jail them in pig pens or place them under house arrest. Red Guards brought former officials to "people's trials" and refused to recognize any authority. Tens of thousands of people, faced with this harassment and humiliation, committed suicide. Bureaucrats and youths from "bad" (that is, bourgeois) social backgrounds were sent to the countryside to do manual labor, purportedly to cleanse their thinking and renew their ties with the people. Some cadres fought back by organizing their own Red Guards, and one group would end up fighting another. Mao ordered Lin Biao's army units to take part in the confrontations, to side with his Red Guards; they often sided with more than one of the factions, which were by this time fighting one another like street gangs. Universities, factories, government offices, and marketing firms ground to a standstill.[17] Worse still, these creators of an "all-round dictatorship over the bour-

Mao Zedong with Lin Biao.
From Edgar Snow Papers Collection, Archives— University of Missouri at Kansas City.

geoisie" were supposed to be ending *guanxi* and all special privileges; instead, they were using their new positions to enrich themselves and their friends by looting and taking privileges for themselves. Confronted with this, and with a large Soviet buildup on one border and the Vietnam War on another, Mao, in January 1968—only twenty months after the Cultural Revolution had begun—ordered the Red Guard workers and students (now former students since all schools were closed) to rejoin the very party officials they had been fighting, and with army officers, to create revolutionary committees which would restore order. By 1969, over half the Politburo of the Party's Central Committee was composed of Lin Biao's army officers, and the Ninth Party Congress proclaimed the Cultural Revolution; what had begun as a revolt against the party had become official party policy. The amateur party realignment ended as a broadening of participation and realigning of power within the ruling Communist Party.

During the several years that followed, army and party leaders worked to restabilize China. While the highest echelons of the party (and local party chapters which were allowing admission of the Red Guards) contained the rebels, the old party hierarchy gradually reasserted control. That was made more difficult by the presence of the large numbers of new members who did not wish to cooperate; but they were carefully stroked and watched by their elders, who could use both age and *guanxi* as cultural factors to request deference and could rely on their education and experience to outsmart the newcomers. It took several years to reopen the universities, rebuild party organizations and government bureaucracy, and put the economy back on track. Corruption was rampant. Workers were told to emulate the commune at Dazhai; pictures showed it prospering because of the peasants' self-reliance, when in reality, Mao was rewarding its leader with massive state aid and his relatives with promotions to high positions.[18] Gradually, many of the old party and government leaders returned to power, uniting under the old Secretary General of the Party, Deng Xiaoping. These leaders, in turn, began to exert control over the army. This was only after the party, the government, and the military had been filled with millions of cadres from among the Red Guards and other backers of the Cultural Revolution. As we saw in chapter 10, these cadres do not rise high in the party, but they keep its middle ranks from supporting moves that might realign power to certain groups. These groups include enterprising peasants, small businesspeople, members of industrial cooperatives, workers with advanced technical skills, women, and westernized intellectuals who have been recruited into the party since 1980. Over a third of cadres are still from among Cultural Revolution-era recruits, many of whom come from poor families which never before had influence and who lack education because of school closings during that era. These cadres work hard to continue to promote others from their social ranks. This represents a long-term realignment of power emanating from Mao's attempts to bypass the normal avenues of power.

Mao died in 1976. In 1978, Deng Xiaoping recaptured power and allowed China to begin making economic reforms. Because they promote private industry and a new generation of students much better educated than the old leadership, those reforms threaten the power both of older cadres and of those recruited during the Cultural Revolution. These two groups now have a common fear of seeing their power usurped by this new generation. Ironically, these groups were able to use the student street demonstrations of 1987 and 1989 to their advantage. They invoked fear of a return to the Cultural Revolution as an excuse for slowing the advance of this new, well-educated generation within the power hierarchy. Since Chinese have traditionally obeyed authority without question and have not been permitted to organize independent parties and interest groups, they have long used "spontaneous" street demonstrations as a form of protest. As we have seen, during the Taiping Rebellion in the nineteenth century, such demonstrations led to a civil war involving millions of people, and demonstrations brought the Ming dynasty into existence. After the excesses of the Cultural Revolution, people were leery of any activities which might again cause social disorder. In defending his decision to respond forcefully with his crackdown at Tiananmen Square, Deng Xiaoping said he feared the reemergence of groups which would try to wield power apart from government. In 1989, he told U.S. President George Bush:

If we seek nominal democracy, we will neither promote democracy nor develop our economy in the end. This can only lead to a situation of chaos and laxness. . . . Each and every person might have his or her own views. If this group of people stage a demonstration today, and that group do so tomorrow, there will be demonstrations 365 days a year . . . it would be impossible to carry out economic construction.[19]

That leaves the ruling party elite in power, with little chance to displace them. Many more peasants and workers have a greater basis for exerting influence than before the Communist Revolution, in organizing production, sending their children to school, and controlling their own agricultural output; but they have little chance to break into the power structure. The rigid bureaucratic and party hierarchy has few members and offers no chance to organize independent interest groups; unlike the Communist Party in the Soviet Union, it has been presiding over economic improvements affecting all segments of society, with the aid of outside investors who are willing to work with all these factions. With citizens socialized to flee, rather than resist, when challenged by government authority, it is hard for protestors to transform demonstrations into permanent groups promoting particular policies. Change can only come if the party leadership promotes people with a variety of views within its highest ranks. Since *guanxi* demands that one support the views of the person who promoted you, party leaders are still unable to present their views openly; policy is likely to shift around with little explanation as one faction leader after another gains favor at the top. This habit of avoiding normal channels and "walking through the back door" is widely condemned in public, but shows no sign of subsiding until it can once again be challenged from outside the normal channels of power.[20] Meanwhile, new business enterprises are absorbing the modern generations of the educated elite, which should help divert them from protest. Many are entering the ranks of the party cadres themselves. But growing numbers of unemployed might be prepared to support future efforts at amateur realignment.

POWER REALIGNMENT, PARTY DEALIGNMENTS, AND NARROWED PARTICIPATION

The United States, the United Kingdom, Germany, the CIS, and China, by very different means, have all brought greater portions of their populace into political institutions during the past two centuries. In addition to arising from wars, revolutions, and other significant political events, realignments of power have occurred by more subtle means, such as the gradual rise of the middle and industrial working classes. The social mobility of these classes, combined with increased education and suffrage, have brought them into positions of greater political prominence. Their maneuvering for position helps explain many of the party realignments we have just discussed. They now share power with groups that had it previously, within political systems that expanded their influence gradually (with the exceptions of China's collectivization and Cultural Revolution and the reigns of Hitler and Stalin, discussed in chapter 23). Most social classes have experienced periods of setbacks or advances in their power; those deviations tend to be slow and modest, and to continue.

India, Peru, and Nigeria, in contrast, have experienced more radical shifts in status that affect all segments of the population; many of those shifts have been downward. Major realignments of power took place between one and five centuries ago, when Europeans changed ownership of land and reordered commerce to shift control of resources and politics into the hands of small portions of the populations and of immigrants. It is difficult for additional realignments of power to take place in these nation-states.

For over five-thousand years, India has had highly developed cities and settled agriculture in the Indus River valley and habitation in other regions as well. Between 2700 and 1500 B.C., Indo-Aryan peoples moved in from the north and gradually assimilated with the darker races and civilizations they found there. They had more advanced metals and weapons and raised cattle. Like their predecessors, they settled in communities along river banks. Husbands served as warriors and priests, and kings ruled over regions. Writings of the period divide Aryans into nobles, Brahmin priests, traders, and peasants. Beneath these on the social scale were non-Aryan wood hewers, lesser tradespeople, and slaves. These distinctions were later to evolve into a caste system which gave a specific place to every person in every community, complete with responsibilities and privileges.

In northern India, each Hindu community was controlled by a high-caste family which was descended from some early conquering group. Beginning with Alexander the Great, countless leaders from the eastern Mediterranean and central Asia were to lead successive conquests of India. None would make a significant dent in this landholding system. As it evolved, major caste leaders took charge of community lands, devising means to feed all members of the community and paying taxes to the ruling kings of the day. The invaders brought along their own courtesans, and tended not to intermarry with the locals. These foreigners, in turn, would be swept away by successive invaders who established their own courts. The social order in the countryside changed little; land ownership remained within the individual communities. The caste leader would incorporate all members of other castes into the community, assigning them roles appropriate to their caste, such as tending fields or cattle, or being potters, barbers, blacksmiths, or carpenters. They were all provided with a portion of the crop and other personal needs, and they all exchanged services with one another. A village *panchayat,* with leaders of all castes represented, met regularly to govern the village. The emperors or princes assigned hereditary rights to collect taxes to **zamindars** and **talukdars;** these taxes were paid in the form of a percentage of the crop, directly from the community caste leader.[21]

In the south and in some of the hill regions, some communities were governed without regard to caste. They chose their own leaders, and each family of the community was allotted a piece of land to raise its own crops. Then, abruptly, during the eighteenth century, the system of land ownership and taxation was to change profoundly all over India.

By 1750, when the British began to conquer India, the tax collectors and wealthy merchants had developed the habit of making personal loans to peasants, often placing them in permanent debt and forcing them to give up large portions of their crops in repayment. The emperors let these lenders take children, as debt-servants, but never land, in repayment of loans.

The last Muslim emperors and the British changed this rule, allowing land to be seized in repayment. By British standards of morality, as it was evolving toward the eighteenth century, it was more criminal to take a person's child than to take their family's only means of livelihood, their land. Suddenly government civil servants and merchants, who had been personally lending money (often simply taxes which had not been passed along by *zamindars* to the government) took possession of great quantities of land. Land which for thousands of years had been collectively owned by communities for the service of those living there passed into the hands of urban investors who lived elsewhere and who had never before wielded such social, economic, and political power. *Zamindars* and *talukdars* themselves became owners of much land in this fashion.

Furthermore, these urban investors speeded the process of diverting land from producing crops for domestic consumption to producing crops for export. To facilitate this, the British sponsored massive irrigation projects, roads, and bridges. They deforested the land to acquire lumber for these projects, lowered the water table by pumping, and salinized fields by flooding them. This drastically curtailed production on much of the land still retained by communities.

These social disruptions destroyed the guarantees of food and livelihood community life had provided. They encouraged people to have more children to establish personal security in later life. At the same time, improved medicine forestalled epidemics and allowed the population to soar. India's 1920 population of 250 million was probably at least triple that of two centuries earlier. It continued to rise at increasing rates each year, growing to 850 million by 1990.

In Madras, and some other areas in the south, land was distributed to those who happened to be tilling it at the time. It no longer belonged to the entire community to be continually redistributed. Those owning it could sell it to anyone they wished, and others in the community would go without land.

As a result, by the time India achieved independence from Britain, 57 percent of the total farmland belonged to 17 percent of families owning sixteen acres or more; only a tenth of these owned more than seventy-five acres.[22] Some eighty-thousand families (out of 100 million) had declared annual incomes over fourteen thousand U.S. dollars. Most of these families descended from nobility, or from merchants and imperial tax collectors who had never owned land in past centuries. Many are related to one another. In an effort to end this dominance by a few elite, the Congress party instituted an active program of land reform during the 1950s, giving compensation to *zamindars* in exchange for their land, which was transferred principally to their tenants but sometimes to other large landowners;[23] Prime Minister Nehru, influenced by Mao, even gave thought to collectivizing the land. As a result, the proportion of those classified as tenants declined from 60 percent to 25 percent.[24] Many large landowners were politically active in the state governments which carried out the reform and used false titles and other means to avoid giving up their land. By 1970, 10 percent of rural families controlled 53 percent of land.[25] Politics, and land ownership, centers around this group; all members of the community once shared in both. But the concentration was not as great as in 1950; over those two decades, a new group of peasants with smaller landholdings became active in politics and in mechanized farming.

During the land reforms, some absentee *zamindars* evicted their tenants and claimed to be the cultivators themselves, and thus eligible to retain the land for their personal cultivation. To get around laws which specify limits on how much one family can own, relatives and tenants can be listed as owners when they are not, especially when they are heavily indebted to the notable and must cooperate with him or her. Statistics now list who controls (lives on and cultivates) land, meaning that tenants can be listed as controlling land even though their former landowners still own it.

Meanwhile (in 1970), 27 percent of rural families owned no land at all; 45 percent of landowners owned or tenant-farmed under 2.5 acres,[26] providing little more (and often less) than subsistence. As we saw in chapter 8, only a portion of the 18 percent of peasants with 5 to 10 acres, and the 22 percent with 2.5 to 5 acres, can produce surpluses or fully sustain themselves, not to mention achieve enough income to purchase other goods for themselves.[27] Indira Gandhi's efforts at additional land reform during the 1960s and 1970s were stalled by large and medium landowners influential in state politics. Her extensive programs to help those with dry, unirrigated land of under 7.5 acres made over 50 million eligible (out of 60 million landowners); fewer than seven million received any aid under the many programs instituted at that time.[28] Some of those who received help may have been able to introduce elements of technology to their food production under those and later programs. But mechanized agriculture and manufacturing generate few jobs, paying very little.[29] Only 7 million out of 850 million people in India make enough money to pay personal or corporate taxes.[30] The nation-state thus has little working capital. Those with little or no land, in parched areas, have largely been removed from active political participation.

Early in the eighteenth century, virtually all Indians were guaranteed access to land, food, and various community support services. Their communities had sufficient influence to keep these supports alive despite centuries of conquests and imperial change. Today, that influence is gone. And the influence of many princes and merchants who held power in that era has been superceded by new social groups which came to prominence during the eighteenth and nineteenth centuries.

So India experienced a rapid shift in power among social groups. These changes in power affect everyone. The result was not an expansion of the numbers of people within effective interest groups but, rather, a marked reduction. And there has been little change in this situation since.

Peru, too, experienced a dramatic power realignment during the nineteenth century. By 200 B.C., Peru's villagers had become highly skilled at irrigation. Great cities developed, but land ownership remained within communities. During their thirty-nine years of rule, the Incas did not disturb this pattern. Then, in 1532, the Spanish *conquistadores* overthrew the Inca Empire and rewarded the soldiers with encomiendas. The soldiers, now **encomenderos** (operators of *encomiendas*) did not formally own the land, but they could assess animals, food, and labor services from the highland peasants who lived there. Spanish towns were built, sometimes on the sites of former Inca towns, and the more prosperous encomenderos lived there. In the 1570s, many highland peasants were transferred from their traditional communities, where all had owned land and participated in community affairs, into *reducciones*— newly built settlements which each contained the inhabitants of several former communities. These new communities were often close to the main valleys, where the *encomenderos* maintained their fields, so that more labor would be available.

The highland peasants still retained community land, but it was often on lower hillsides where water was less plentiful than when they had been higher up. Armed conflict, exposure to mercury in the mines, and European diseases such as smallpox took a heavy toll. When the Spanish arrived, they found six million inhabitants in the Inca Empire.[31] The census of 1790 found 600,000 Quechua and Aymara, 400,000 of Spanish extraction, and 80,000 blacks.[32]

Over the years, the land of the *encomenderos* was partly divided among their offspring. Some was given as a reward to new groups of soldiers or was sold to new individuals; other land was given to Jesuit or Dominican orders of the Catholic church. Other Spaniards also settled in to become landowners.

After Peru's Spanish descendents (*criollos*) declared independence in 1821, they changed the laws so that land would be distributed to individuals in the communities, and these individuals would then be free to sell their share. Soon the highland peasants were forced by economic necessity, or persuaded by economic reward, to sell their land to the *criollos*. Millions of acres were acquired at bargain-basement prices by giant new *latifundia*. When, in the 1920s, community land was once again declared inalienable,

> The Spanish supported the continuation of communal land ownership for the Quechua and Aymara population. This made those highland peasants self-sufficient and a controlled source of labor and taxation and insured that the *criollos*, of Spanish extraction, did not achieve too much political and economic control over their regions.

little existed; many highland peasants had lost their land or were surviving on much less of it.

After Peru won its independence, Lima largely fell into the control of the army. The *cabildos* elected a central Congress, which often chose a military leader; others came to office by military coup. One of these, Ramon Castilla, helped landowners establish an extensive guano trade (guano is nitrogen-rich bird droppings used for fertilizer)[33] along with sugar estates, mining, industries, and banking. When guano deposits ran out, the government had to borrow heavily from British investors, and was later overthrown and conquered by Chile. As a result, new British, Italian, German, and United States immigrants acquired substantial business interests in Lima.

By 1965, some 80 percent of irrigated land on the coastal plain was occupied by 920 giant *latifundia*, largely owned by *criollos* and by some immigrants and foreign corporations as well.[34] Just forty-four families owned 23 percent of coastal cultivated land; twenty-six of them (including *criollos*, Germans, Italians, and British) also had investments in urban real estate, banking, and manufacturing; twenty-one had insurance holdings; seventeen, commercial firms; and a few were in mining, commerce, heavy industry, and fishmeal. This was the heart of "the oligarchy." In addition, 181 families owned about 60 percent of the tillable land in the mountains.[35] About half of the nation-state's families owned land; of these, only 12 percent owned a parcel large enough to completely support even their own family.[36] There were few jobs for landless families or to give extra income to those with inadequate amounts of land. Many people were unable to support themselves adequately.

The military regime which took power under General Velasco tried to redress this imbalance, but with little success. From 1968 to 1976, it carried out land reforms transferring a fourth of tillable land to about eighty thousand families—mainly former tenants and workers.[37] The former owners received payment; many of the smaller owners were left with few resources, while the largest shifted their concentration to urban enterprises. The new owners often had to abandon the land for lack of water and capital. Those left often cannot move beyond subsistence farming. Others without land, or with inadequate land to support themselves, were unaffected by the reforms. Those among the landless who poured into the slums of Lima found few jobs awaiting them in the formal economy there.

Thus, Peru, too, has experienced extreme changes in the political status of all sectors of the populace. The resources and organization available to highland peasants dwindled markedly. The influence and wealth of many *encomenderos* and *criollos* waxed and then waned. Many recent immigrants have achieved high prominence in business and government. The military, with its prominent position in government, has recruited new social classes into its ranks, but has not been able to help the large numbers of urban and rural poor.

The result has been upheaval in the relative power of all groups within society, and a reduction in the relative power of most groups. The new pecking order has largely been frozen in place.

Prior to arrival of the British, the regions now occupied by Nigeria contained many tribal groups speaking over 250 different languages. To the southwest, the Yoruba extended their course westward into what is now Togo; the town of Benin ruled over a number of tribes; and inland, the Hausa and some other Muslim tribes controlled a number of smaller tribes. Otherwise, except when they engaged in occasional raids to take slaves for themselves, each tribal group tended to preside over its own territory. Some of the larger tribal groups had their own kings, who collected percentages of crops for taxation and even sometimes owned (or allowed their nobles to own) entire villages. Most land was controlled by members of the community that occupied it. Villages normally owned their own land, which was distributed to all members, and generally governed their own affairs.

In 1861, Britain took possession of Lagos Island. In 1880, two French trading companies opened about thirty trading posts along the lower Niger River. They soon encountered the United African Company, founded by a Briton in 1879, and sold their rights to it in 1884. In 1885, Britain established a protectorate over the lower Niger River, and the United African Company became the Royal Niger Company. The company concluded treaties with the Hausa and other inland Muslim groups. On January 1, 1900, all continental territories were transferred to the British Crown, and in 1906, Lagos became the colony's capital.

As of 1930, only five thousand Britishers resided in Nigeria; most were in Nigeria on only short tours of duty. The British ruled through local subjects. They trained friendly tribespeople—often from the North—as soldiers, and used these troops to fight tribal groups which resisted the new protectorate. Once opposing tribes were subdued, the hostile leaders of these tribes were replaced with friendly leaders willing to give the British control of land and taxation policy. Africans—especially from among the Ibo, Yoruba, and ethnic groups in the southwest—were sent to Oxford and Cambridge to become high administrators within the British hierarchy. Initially, many were sons of chiefs, but they were soon joined by sons of those engaged in cash-cropping. Only a handful were selected at a time. Many came from families that had not been socially prominent or influential.

The British governors decided most land should continue to be owned within communities. However, the village head traditionally held the land in common for the entire community, continually redistributing it to assure all families some land. Now much of the land was converted to raise export crops, and individual villagers could permanently own parcels that would no longer be redistributed by chiefs to members of the village. Credit, banking, and marketing were in the hands of firms commissioned through Lagos to carry out these transactions. These firms dealt with village chiefs, who chose which lands would be used for which crops and decided how lands and profits would be distributed. When this did not work, the British sometimes created new chiefs (as among the Ibo) or allowed community families who raised more crops (as in the southwest) to develop more influence. In addition, some land, especially after Nigeria achieved independence in 1963, was sold to investors—some in small parcels to individual farmers within villages, some in large parcels which became plantations worked by foreign laborers, and some to companies for mining, oil drilling, and cattle raising. Some land changed hands through development rezoning around northern cities, where farmers were forced to sell land to the city; the city could then resell the land to investors at high prices. Control of that land thus shifted from villages into the hands of a few individuals from a few favored tribes.

The Nigerian government also established **marketing boards** for the sale of all the cocoa, cotton, peanuts, and palm oil grown by the new export farms. These boards (now dissolved) had the power to set prices paid to farmers, to force farmers to sell exclusively through them, to control credit to farmers, and to retain a considerable portion of selling prices for themselves. The British gained great wealth from these boards. After independence, those profits went to the rulers in Lagos, who shared them with the state governments. They used the money to increase the size of the bureaucracy and public service sector and to encourage foreign companies to set up subsidiaries to produce goods for the Nigerian market. That created new classes of white- and blue-collar workers.

In 1973, the Organization of Petroleum Exporting States, which Nigeria is a member of, radically raised the price of oil. Nigeria's oil production rose along with the prices. In 1964, petroleum made up 3 percent of Nigeria's Gross Domestic Product; in 1974, 46 percent. Oil's contribution to federal revenues rose from 4 percent to 80 percent during this period.[38] Meanwhile, agricultural exports plummeted downward, and total GDP rose as Nigeria became one of the world's ten largest petroleum-producing countries. Nearly all the revenue flows directly through Lagos. The government contracted for seven new university campuses, extensive housing for the military and bureaucracy, new weaponry, office buildings, coastal roads, airports, agricultural development, and other expensive projects. It invested $1.5 billion in joint ventures with foreign firms to create oil wells and refineries, automobile assembly plants, cement plants, sugar and paper pulp plants, steel rolling mills, and mines.[39] This happened in Western Europe during the nineteenth-century Industrial Revolution. In Europe, the production continued to expand. But many of Nigeria's projects were poorly conceived, built, and operated. They could not compete on international markets, and their product often cost more than imports. The new construction brought a temporary burst of urban employment, but the new plants did not generate additional employment on their own.

Control over Nigeria's principal assets thus shifted to a new set of leaders in Lagos or Port Harcourt. These individuals often have little social contact with the rest of the country; their children grow up in the city, go to university in Ibadan or abroad, and then return to Lagos to find a position in the bureaucracy, petroleum production, commerce, or industry. Most people remained on their own land, but since much production was now geared toward commodities, they depended on outsiders for supplying loans, seed, and fertilizer and setting market prices.

Traditional Hausa rulers still retain prominence in their regions and in the army; that has helped them compete with the new entrepreneurs from the south. In many other regions, the influence of former regional leaders has dwindled; whereas local leaders formerly could look to them for political assistance, they now must turn to centrally-appointed bureaucrats with no local roots and who often do

In 1976, the World Bank initiated Agricultural Projects, aimed at improving production for peasants with small and moderate amounts of land. One of the first three projects was at Funtua, in an area with about eighty-five thousand farming families. The plan centered around distributing fertilizer at low, heavily subsidized prices, as well as providing improved seed, herbicides, and pesticides. Meanwhile, the government was building one of its River Basin Projects at Bakolori on a tract of about one hundred square miles of land, with the announced intent of creating farmsteads of 12.5 acres each.

The Bakolori project was contracted to an Italian firm, which brought in five-hundred Italian, six-hundred Portuguese, and fifty-five thousand Nigerian construction workers and laborers to tame the river with a dam and irrigation channels, at a cost of over $225 million. They displaced forty villages, resettling thirteen-thousand people. Upon the advice of outside consultants, they divided most of the project land into farms of 1.3 square miles each. Between 1976 and 1979, the portion of farms in the valley with less than five acres grew from 36 to 47 percent, mostly on higher and drier land; and at the same time, the floodplain peasants planted crops in during the dry season had been destroyed by the project. The original intent was to plant wheat and sugar. Wheat cost more to produce than the imported wheat it was intended to replace, and the sugar cost so much it could not compete on international markets. So most production turned to corn, which brought low market prices because Nigerians prefer to eat sorghum. Most of the large holdings went to officials and urban business owners; within a year, many with smaller holdings were selling their plots because they could not repay debts. As of 1979, only 186 families had plots of over one hundred acres.

At nearby Funtua, the World Bank pilot project was distributing fertilizer to local villagers. An anthropologist in an adjoining town studied how this functioned. An agricultural instructor married a daughter of a village head and lived in the town, borrowing money from wealthier farmers to supplement his salary. District and village heads, the leaders of the Local Government Authority, wealthy urban merchants, and other wealthy absentee landowners bought the fertilizer at the low, government-subsidized prices, though they had to add the cost of bribes to officials. The anthropologist selected twenty-four farmers to study. He found that those with over twenty acres (representing less than 10 percent of total farms in the area but occupying over a third of the land) received over 85 percent of the fertilizer, while those with less than five acres received 6 percent. The 70 percent of farmers around Marmara who had five or less acres occupied about 15 percent of the land, so these farmers received far less subsidized fertilizer per acre.

One of the biggest landowners in the area (with fifty acres), frozen out of the distribution because he was a leader of the radical People's Redemption Party (PRP), joined with three other larger landowners and some urban traders to complain about the corruption and bribery in the Marmara fertilizer distribution. At Bakolori, the PRP helped peasants displaced by the irrigation project organize to blockade roads, disconnect sprinklers, and otherwise obstruct farm operations. The police attacked, killing and wounding hundreds and burning villages. In the 1979 elections, the PRP won the governorships of Kaduna and Kano states, where these projects were located. In 1979, the Federal Agricultural Development Project sought to distribute the fertilizer more equitably; that year, those with over twenty acres in the Marmara sample received about 55 percent of the fertilizer, while those with five or fewer acres received about 10 percent. The government dropped plans to increase taxes on peasants to repay the costs of the Bakolori project, and it found that fertilizer subsidies for the project were costing $10 million a year.[40] The 1983 military coup drove the PRP from office.

not even speak the same language. Villagers no longer have control over the best land, and export agriculture is largely in abeyance (though improving for large landowners since 1987). The politically well-connected often benefit from attempts to reform agriculture. Much of Nigeria's income now derives from petroleum production; the bureaucrats most directly involved with this, as well as the leaders of the armed forces, are in the best position to acquire resources and exert influence.

Nigeria's land distribution is more equitable than India's or Peru's. But, like the latter two nation-states, Nigeria experienced a realignment that reduced the power of most segments of the populace and elevated the power of a few.

In the United States, the United Kingdom, Germany, the CIS, and China, many of the social groups exerting influence today had influence two centuries ago. Some other groups have lost influence since then; but these losses are counterbalanced by the increase in influence of groups representing larger percentages of the populace (in China, some of these groups have increased their influence markedly).

India, Peru, and Nigeria present a different picture. There, the groups with the greatest influence often come from sectors of society not prominent two centuries ago. And the portion of the populace that can effectively exert influence has been shrinking rather than expanding.

Furthermore, because so few participate in influential interest groups in India, Peru, and Nigeria, and because much manufacturing is controlled from abroad, foreign institutions play an important role in interest group politics as well. In India, seventy-five managing agencies (as discussed in chapter 20) control half the nation-state's assets not in banks or government agencies; a third of these agencies' capital comes from foreign investors. The government borrows heavily from the World Bank, and formerly received military assistance from the Soviet Union. As of 1968, 50 percent of Peru's manufacturing assets were controlled by foreign firms; current figures are hard to find, but this figure is still substantial.[41] Peru borrowed extensively from the World Bank and commercial banks, and has received foreign aid from the Soviet Union, the United States, and elsewhere. Ninety-eight percent of Nigeria's export revenues come from oil;[42] most industries are reverting back to foreign control because of International Monetary Fund pressures to stabilize the economy after $30 billion in foreign borrowing. Thus, not only have new groups within these nation-states grown in prominence; outside interest groups play an important role as well.

CONCLUSION

We have suggested that influence is more widespread when the government and high percentages of families rely on the same economic institutions for jobs, goods, and services; when diverse segments of the populace are recruited into the legislature, executive, judiciary, and bureaucracy; and when people are socialized to believe in placing limits on the authority of public officials.

High percentages of the populace and the government do rely on the same economic institutions for their jobs, goods, and services in the United States, the United Kingdom, East and West Germany, the CIS, and China. Similarly, diverse segments of the populace are recruited into political parties, interest groups, legislatures, executives, judiciaries, and bureaucracies in the United States, the United Kingdom, East and West Germany, and—to a lesser extent—the CIS and China. People in the United States, the United Kingdom, and West Germany are socialized to believe in placing limits on the authority of public officials. The populations of China, the CIS, and the former East Germany are not.

India, Peru, and Nigeria have dual economies. Large segments of the populace rely on economic institutions separate from those that provide jobs and goods and services to government and those with formal educations. Furthermore, these segments of society have few representatives in political parties, interest groups, government, or bureaucracy, and they are not socialized to believe in placing limits on public officials. Strong consensual parties have not developed in Peru and Nigeria; India's consensual Congress party faces increasing difficulty holding itself together.

When we take all these circumstances into consideration, we might expect it to be easier for political parties and interest groups in the United States, the United Kingdom, and West Germany to devise policies which benefit large portions of the populace than for parties and interest groups in China, the CIS, and East Germany to do so. But parties and interest groups in all six of these nation-states should find it easier to do so than their counterparts in India, Peru, and Nigeria. Consensual parties in the first six nation-states have expanded participation over the past two centuries. In the other three, the proportion of the populace involved in politics and formal economics has decreased significantly over the past centuries. Though it has ruled most of the years since independence, India's consensual Congress party has not held back that decline.

Summary

Consensual parties in the United States, the United Kingdom, East and West Germany, the CIS, and China have pulled increasing portions of their populace into modern political and economic institutions. In China, that assimilation took place by opening normal political and party channels from the outside in. But India, Peru, and Nigeria—between one and five centuries ago—all experienced a sharp decrease in the portion of the populace owning economic assets and participating in politics. This situation has changed very little in the past century.

Notes

1. In CBS/New York Times polls during the first half of 1991, 31 percent of respondents said they identified with the Republicans and 34 percent with the Democrats. That compares with 19 percent and 39 percent in 1976.

2. In their first free elections, several republic legislatures immediately fell under the control of competing parties. The 1991 election of Boris Yeltsin as the first elected president of the largest republic, Russia, had a decisive effect; he won a majority of votes on the first ballot against prominent Communist Party opponents. Poll results in mid-1991 showed that more than half of respondents did not believe the Communist Party had great influence anymore, a third believed it should be dissolved, and two-thirds thought it was concerned only about its own interests and properties. Gorbachev disclosed that the party had lost 4.2 million members during the prior eighteen months, reducing its membership to fifteen million. David Remnick, "Overhaul Aimed at Regaining Lost Confidence," *Washington Post,* July 26, 1991.

3. William L. Miller, *How Voters Change: The 1987 British Election Campaign in Perspective* (Oxford: Clarendon, 1990), analyzes survey data which indicate that large portions of the British electorate change their party allegiances frequently—a profound dealignment.

4. See Bo Sarlvik and Ivor Crewe, *Decade of Dealignment: The Conservative Victory of 1979 and Electoral Trends in the 1970s* (Cambridge: Cambridge University Press, 1983); Dennis Kavanaugh, *Thatcherism and British Politics: The End of Consensus?* (Oxford: Oxford University Press, 1987); John McIlroy, *Trade Unions in Britain Today* (Manchester: Manchester University Press, 1988); Stuart Hall and Martin Jacques, eds., *New Times: The Changing Face of Politics in the 1990s* (London: Verso, 1990); and Patrick Dunleavy and Christopher T. Husbands, *British Democracy at the Crossroads: Voting and Party Competition in the 1980s* (London: Allen & Unwin, 1985).

5. See Geoffrey Barraclough, *The Origins of Modern Germany* (London: Basil Blackwell, 1946); Geoff Eley, *Reshaping the German Right: Radical Nationalism and Political Change After Bismarck* (New Haven, Conn.: Yale University Press, 1980).

6. One study of United States congressional elections from 1952 to 1984, and parliamentary elections in the United Kingdom and West Germany from 1953 to 1987, found that the percentage of working class people voting for parties of the "left" did not vary more than 11 percent in any of these systems over that time period. The middle class increased its tendency to vote for those parties in the United States (rising from 42 percent in 1952 to 54 percent in 1984) and West Germany (from 29 percent in

1953 to 51 percent in 1987). Russell J. Dalton, *Citizen Politics in Western Democracies* (Chatham, N.J.: Chatham House, 1988), p. 156.

7. The percentage of strong partisans has declined from 45 percent in the 1960s to 20 percent in the 1980s in the United Kingdom; from 18 percent in 1970 to 10 percent in 1983 in West Germany; and from 35 percent in 1950 to 30 percent in 1985 in the United States. Dalton, *Citizen Politics*, p. 189. Also see Russell J. Dalton, "The German Voter: Dealignment or Realignment?" in Gordon Smith, et al., *Developments in West German Politics* (London: Macmillan, 1989).

8. After the austere egalitarianism of the Communists before the war, they now began awarding themselves special privileges. Army officers built themselves elaborate clubs with extra food rations. Local officials could accept bribes. Businesspeople paid themselves large salaries. Landowners sought to withhold crops from the government marketing boards to sell on the black market.

These trends disturbed Mao Zedong. They not only offended his egalitarian principles. They also made it difficult for the party to exert influence from the center and thus reunite China. In fact, he said that China was slipping back into military warlordism.

9. Vaclav Smil, "China's Food," *Scientific American* (December 1985): 116.

10. Mao, however, remained chief of state and party chairman. At this time, Khrushchev was in the process of revealing many of Stalin's crimes and calling for greater freedom. Early in 1957, Mao called for freer speech in China as well. He recalled two classical Chinese slogans encouraging greater discussion of ideas: "Let a hundred flowers bloom; let a hundred schools of thought contend." Predictably, a number of intellectuals quickly began to voice complaints. Within three weeks, Mao called an end to the free speech and began to arrest those who had dissented. He had made the point that the "experts" could not be trusted. His tactic went beyond this. He used the occasion to begin an extensive purge of "rightists" from all levels of the party.

11. See Kenneth Lieberthal, "The Great Leap Forward and the Split in the Yenan Leadership," in John K. Fairbank and Roderick MacFarquhar, eds., *The Cambridge History of China* vol. 14 (Cambridge: Cambridge University Press, 1987).

12. Smil, "China's Food," p. 116.

13. Michael Ying-mao Kao, ed., *The Lin Piao Affair: Power, Politics, and Military Coup* (White Plains, N.Y.: M. E. Sharpe, 1975); William Whitson, *The Chinese High Command: A History of Communist Military Politics, 1927–71* (New York: Praeger, 1973).

14. See Stanley Karnow, *Vietnam: A History* (New York: Penguin, 1984), pp. 453ff; Gerald Segal, "The Military as a Group in Chinese Politics," in David S. G. Goodman, ed., *Groups and Politics in the People's Republic of China* (Cardiff, England: University of Cardiff Press, 1984), pp. 83–101.

15. *The Dismissal of Hai Rui* was about a Ming dynasty official who returned land to peasants—land he claimed had been illegally confiscated by a despotic emperor. The emperor then fired the official. The play was written and performed at the height of the Great Leap Forward's seizure of property from peasants and had some resemblance to Mao's firing of a popular defense minister.

16. See Ahn Byung-joon, *Chinese Politics and the Cultural Revolution* (Seattle: University of Washington Press, 1976); Anita Chan, Richard Madsen, and Jonathan Unger, *Chen Village: The Recent History of A Peasant Community in Mao's China* (Berkeley: University of California Press, 1984); Lowell Dittmer, *Liu Shao-ch'i and the Chinese Cultural Revolution: The Politics of Mass Criticism* (Berkeley: University of California Press, 1975); Lee Hong Yung, *The Politics of the Chinese Cultural Revolution* (Berkeley: University of California Press, 1978); Roderick MacFarquhar, *The Origins of the Cultural Revolution*, 2 vol. (New York: Columbia University Press, 1974 and 1983); and Ezra Vogel, *Canton Under Communism* (Cambridge, Mass.: Harvard University Press, 1969).

17. See Gordon Bennett, *Yundong: Mass Campaigns in Chinese Communist Leadership* (Berkeley, Calif.: Center for Chinese Studies, 1976); Charles P. Cell, *Revolution at Work: Mass Campaigns in China* (New York: Academic Press, 1977); Richard Baum, "Revolution and Reaction in the Chinese Countryside: The Socialist Education Movement in Cultural Revolutionary Perspective," *China Quarterly* 38 (April-June 1969): 92–119; Harry Harding, *Organizing China* (Stanford, Calif.: Stanford University Press, 1981); Frederick Teiwes, *Politics and Purges in China* (Armonk, N.Y.: M. E. Sharpe, 1979); Lee Rensaleer III, "The Hsia-fang System:

Marxism and Modernization," *China Quarterly* 28 (October-December 1966): 40–62; Stanley Rosen, *Red Guard Factionalism and the Cultural Revolution in Guangzhou* (Boulder, Colo.: Westview Press, 1981); and Lynn White, "Workers Politics in Shanghai," *Journal of Asian Studies* 36 (November 1976): 99–116.

18. See Alan P. L. Liu, *How China Is Ruled* (Englewood Cliffs, N.J.: Prentice Hall, 1986), p. 244.

19. *Renmin Ribao (People's Daily)*, June 24, 1989.

20. A 1988 survey in Shanghai and surrounding rural areas asked: "Suppose you have a problem. If you follow the normal channels, it will take a long time, and the result may not be satisfactory. Do you think you should go through some connection?" A great majority—71.7 percent—of respondents said they would "first try some connections." Forty-six percent of young people, versus 35.1 percent of older people, said that connections are "very important," while only 5 percent of the young and 13.6 percent of the older said they were "not very" or "not at all" important. However, 59.1 percent said that *guanxi* is the "least important" qualification for a work unit, and 82.2 percent would refuse to vote for someone simply at the request of a good friend. For them to ever have the chance to vote for someone without connections, their attitudes toward connections might need to change. Gordon Chu and Ju Yanan, *The Great Wall in Ruins: Cultural Change in China* (Honolulu, Hawaii: East-West Center, 1990), pp. 58, 66.

21. Sirajul Islam, *Bengal Land Tenure: The Origin and Growth of Intermediate Interests in the Nineteenth Century* (Calcutta: K. P. Bagchi, 1988): and Dilbagh Singh, *The State, Landlords, and Peasants: Rajasthan in the Eighteenth Century* (New Delhi: Munohar, 1990) chronicle the rise of *zamindari* power since the eighteenth century.

22. Charles Bettelheim, *India Independent* (New York: Monthly Review Press, 1968), pp. 25–27, 54–59.

23. Lloyd I. Rudolph and Susanne Hoeber Rudolph, *In Pursuit of Lakshmi: The Political Economy of the Indian State* (Chicago: University of Chicago Press, 1987), pp. 340, 354.

24. Rudolph, *Lakshmi*, p. 315. Land reforms placed 20 million peasants into the status of "controlling" the land they farm—much of it dry and unirrigated. From 1960 to 1970, the number of tenants declined by 15 million; but the number of day laborers also rose by 20 million. B. L. Sukhwal, *India: A Political*

Geography (Bombay: Allied Publishers, 1971), p. 41. Frances Moore Lappe and Joseph Collins, *Food First: Beyond the Myth of Scarcity* (Boston: Houghton Mifflin, 1977), p. 129. The Green Revolution requires irrigation, hybrid seeds, and fertilizer, which only wealthy owners can afford; this encourages land consolidation and reduces the need for labor.

25. Only 6 percent had over fifteen acres, constituting 39 percent of agricultural land. Rudolph, *Lakshmi*, pp. 336, 409–10.

26. See chapter 8, footnote 5, and Rudolph, *Lakshmi*. As the prior paragraph indicates, at least a fourth of these are probably tenants.

27. Only 12 percent of long-term commercial bank loans for farm improvements went to the 45 percent of owners with less than 2.5 acres of land, 13 percent to the 22 percent with 2.5 to 5 acres, and 19 percent to the 18 percent with 5 to 10 acres. But the 15 percent of landowners with over 10 acres received 56 percent of the loans. Sixty-two percent of loans from cooperatives went to the 33 percent of owners with over 5 acres. This only tells the number, and not the size, of the loans, which go disproportionately to those with larger parcels of land; the amounts lent to the larger owners are probably greater as well. And the government figures fail to indicate the total number of loans, so one cannot tell the percentage of landowners receiving them.

"Households operating five acres or more constitute only 24 percent of rural holdings but include 75 percent of the land. Their holdings are large enough to generate the capital or secure the credit to pay for the inputs of the new technology. The 49 percent of rural households that operate less than five acres, on the other hand, often cannot generate the capital or obtain the credit to invest in the new technology." The other 27 percent of households have no land. Rudolph, *Lakshmi*, pp. 324, 373.

28. Rudolph, *Lakshmi*, p. 328.

29. Prosperous Green Revolution areas like the Punjab use a lot of seasonal day laborers during the peak of the harvest season, but even farms with twenty to thirty acres use few hired hands even then. Most smaller producers hire only relatives. See Rudolph, *Lakshmi*, pp. 353, 386.

30. Principally, those making over 100,000 rupees (US $3,906) a year must pay taxes; their tax rate is over

50 percent of income. Hamish McDonald, "Wind of Change," *Far Eastern Economic Review* 155, 10 (March 12, 1992): 37.

31. Edward P. Lanning, *Peru Before the Incas* (Englewood Cliffs, N.J.: Prentice-Hall, 1967), p. 115.

32. The Viceroyalty of Peru included what is now Peru, Colombia, Ecuador, Bolivia, Chile, and Argentina. There were few Spaniards, however, in the regions farthest from Peru.

33. On islands along the Peruvian coast, fish-eating birds had left these droppings in accumulations hundreds of feet thick, which provided a major source of rich fertilizer to support the newly mechanizing agriculture in Europe and elsewhere.

34. Solon Barraclough, ed., *Agrarian Structure in Latin America: A Resume of the CIDA Land Tenure Studies of Argentina, Brazil, Chile, Colombia, Ecuador, Guatemala, and Peru* (Lexington, Mass.: D. C. Heath, 1973), p. 252.

35. John Stephen Gitlitz, "Impressions of the Peruvian Agrarian Reform," *Journal of Inter-American Studies and World Affairs* 13, 3–4 (July–October 1971): 466.

36. Celso Furtado, *Economic Development in Latin America* (Cambridge: Cambridge University Press, 1970), p. 54.

37. See Robert E. Gamer, *The Developing Nations: A Comparative Perspective*, 2d ed. (Boston: Allyn & Bacon), p. 303.

38. O. Oyediron, ed., *Nigerian Government and Politics Under Military Rule 1966–1979* (New York: St. Martin's, 1979), p. 69.

39. Michael Watts, *Silent Violence: Food, Famine, and Peasantry in Northern Nigeria* (Berkeley: University of California Press, 1983), p. 477.

40. Bjorn Beckman, "Public Investment and Agrarian Transformation in Northern Nigeria," in Watts, *Oil*, pp. 110–37; Richard Palmer-Jones, "Irrigation and the Politics of Agricultural Development in Nigeria," in Watts, *Oil*, pp. 138–67; Paul Clough and Gavin Williams, "Decoding Berg: The World Bank in Rural Northern Nigeria," in Watts, *Oil*, pp. 172–200; Watts, *Silent Violence*, pp. 482–514.

41. Since the Velasco reforms, statistics such as these have been hard to acquire. Forty percent of the capital in textile industries, and much capital in mining and oil drilling (through which a considerable portion of the nation-state's legally obtained revenue is derived) comes from foreign sources. E. V. K. Fitzgerald, *The Political Economy of Peru 1956–78: Economic Development and the Restructuring of Capital* (Cambridge: Cambridge University Press, 1979), p. 274.

42. "The Economic Puzzle," *The Economist*, August 21, 1993. Jon Kraus, "Economic Adjustment and Regime Creation in Nigeria," *Current History* 88, 538 (May 1989): 233. As of 1979, oil constituted 35 percent of GDP and 91 percent of exports. Since 1974, it has accounted for four-fifths of government revenue.

EXERCISES

Think about the book thus far:

How does the topic of this chapter—consensual parties and shifting influence—relate to assimilation into modern institutions?

KEY WORDS AND PHRASES

Define the following terms:

party realignment	Great Leap Forward	encomendero
party dealignment	Great Proletarian Cultural Revolution	marketing boards
realignments of power	zamindars and talukdars	

THINKING IT THROUGH

1. When did the most radical realignments of power take place in
    a. the United States, the United Kingdom, and Germany?
    b. the Soviet Union?
    c. China?
    d. India, Nigeria, and Peru?

2. Could the Cultural Revolution happen in the United States? Why or why not? Do the problems Mao was addressing with the Great Leap Forward and the Cultural Revolution arise in the United States? If so, do you think we have better ways to solve them?

3. Reread the first and last paragraphs in the conclusion of this chapter. How do the two relate? Is the last paragraph "true"? Why or why not?

chapter 22

GOVERNMENT INSTITUTIONS

LEGISLATURES AND EXECUTIVES

A nation-state needs a chief executive and bureaucracy strong enough to implement policies, but restricted enough that they will be honest and remain sensitive to the needs of their citizenry. That requires a delicate balance: Legislatures and political parties must be independent enough to restrain the power of the chief executive and bureaucracy, but submissive enough to let the chief executive and bureaucracy draft and implement coherent policy. This is easier to achieve when two consensual parties exist than when there is only one, or none at all.

We have been examining how people outside government exert influence. Now we will see how those inside government wield authority. Chapter 1 indicated that a government with the ability to direct and control the people of a nation is sovereign. A sovereign government is composed of a number of institutions cooperating with one another to decide how to direct and control people, and how to distribute goods and services, as well as how to implement those decisions once they are made. Sometimes we prefer that our top leaders not have much power. Without power at the top, however, it is difficult to hold a nation-state together and to achieve objectives its people agree on. Some ways of holding it together may contribute to achieving widely supported objectives; others may principally help small, powerful groups of people.

DECIDING GOVERNMENT POLICY

Who decides what policy decisions government will make? Who should decide, in order to make honest, sensitive, and coherent policy? Webster's defines **decide** as "to terminate a controversy by giving the victory of rendering judgment." An individual or institution does not have power to render a definitive judgment unless they can follow through

to implement and enforce the decision, to either ensure or prevent certain activities. A judgment not obeyed does not settle controversy.

In chapter 2, we examined various restraints on the ability of a chief executive to exert sovereignty. We learned that, while some chief executives share sovereignty more extensively than others, none decides on and executes policy alone. They all join with other individuals and institutions to direct and control the people of their nation. The strengths and weaknesses of those other individuals determine how much the chief executive shares in sovereignty.

All nine of these nation-states have (at least part of the time) legislatures which make written laws prescribing rules of behavior. Not all those legislatures can decide what these laws will be; some just give the laws a formal stamp of approval. In all these nation-states, at least some legislators help decide policy, if only because of their contacts with executives or party leaders. In all except Nigeria and Peru under military rule, voters have some choice as to who enters legislatures. They exist at both the national and lower levels. In addition to its national legislature, the United States has local, county, and state legislatures; in the post-Soviet republics, legislatures at the local, and **oblast** (district or region) or autonomous republic level make laws;

in the United Kingdom, local and county; in West Germany, local and state; in East Germany, local; in India, local, district, and state; and in Peru, local (district), provincial (county, first elected in 1990), and regional (state) levels of government have elected legislatures.

In all these countries, different parties may control or at least hold seats in each of the legislatures. The absence of party discipline at the national level in the United States and Peru gives these legislators especially great latitude, even when they are members of the same party as the chief executive; so does Germany's complex system of choosing party officers and candidates. The 1992 Nigerian constitution allows for legislatures at the local and state levels, with only two "national" parties competing in each; it is unlikely that party leaders will control those parties from the top. In China, local, county, and provincial party secretaries control the legislatures; though these secretaries are appointed by national leaders, they are difficult to remove and can resist central pressures to some degree. These legislatures are limited to voting on subjects the national government permits them to decide. These usually include matters relating to roads, education, health, police, housing, pollution control, public utilities, and welfare.

Once bills are passed into law, they must be implemented by the executives and the bureaucracy. So while some legislatures may be decisive about rejecting bills, none is really decisive about settling controversies, because the issues may reemerge in the executive, bureaucracy, or courts. If a bill is not passed, the executive branch may try to initiate government policy that does not require a bill. If a bill is passed, there are still people at other levels of government who must decide exactly what it means. Even when a chief executive does not give a legislature discretion in passing bills, or eliminates the legislature altogether, he or she must still give the bureaucracy some discretion. As we saw in chapter 2, the extent to which the national chief executive controls the bureaucracy, or shares control with executives at state or lower levels of government, also varies.

Chief executives face a paradox in bureaucracy. If they have little bureaucracy, they lack power to implement policy. But as bureaucracy expands, so does its power. All these systems have many separate units of bureaucracy whose members are scattered throughout the nation-state. Their employees and constituents have many diverse interests. They develop permanent alliances with nongovernmental interest groups, government and party leaders, and other units of bureaucracy. Because they are responsible for implementing policy, it is not easy for legislatures and chief executives to end controversy without the bureaucracy's cooperation. Discord can continue to brew as these various bodies and groups attempt to influence the manner in which the bureaucracy carries out government policy.

As we have already stressed, then, no chief executive or elected official makes decisions alone. Except in the military regimes in Nigeria, all must consult or share decision-making powers not only with the bureaucracy, but with activists in their political parties, representatives of interest groups, members of their legislatures, and elected officials at other levels of government. This shared sovereignty has advantages and disadvantages. When a chief executive or legislators try to end controversy in favor of broad segments of their populace, their attempts may be sabotaged by power sharing; but attempts by a chief executive or legislators to harm various groups may also be thwarted by it. Groups without influence in any of these institutions are certainly at a disadvantage.

AFFECTING DECISIONS ABOUT GOVERNMENT POLICY

As we have seen, members of legislatures, executives, and bureaucracies cannot easily make authoritative decisions which settle controversies about government policy. But they do engage in a wide variety of activities that affect policy, and their roles vary in different systems. Furthermore, all these systems offer many chances for political parties and interest groups to interact with those involved in creating government policy. Parties and interest groups, as well as each of these units of government, may have political resources such as legitimacy, public support, money, various skills, needed supplies, access to information and media coverage, weapons, or technology. The distribution of any or all of these resources may affect the relative balance of power among institutions.

The distribution of power has great impact on who makes government policy. Certain factors weaken or strengthen government bodies and groups as they interact with one another. The relative strength of each unit, in turn, affects the ability of these government bodies to distribute resources among themselves and to different segments of the public. We will look at the way power is distributed between three groups. Two—legislatures and executives—are a part of government. The third is crucial to the strength of each of these government bodies: they depend on political parties to organize support for their policies.

Legislatures

A law must be written and formally introduced into a legislature as a bill. If a legislature's members have the right and ability to write, propose, introduce, amend, and ultimately pass or defeat bills—determining whether they become laws—that legislature has a strong role in deciding policy. In the United States, the Soviet Union from 1990 until 1991, Peru until 1992,[1] and Nigeria from 1979 to 1983 and under the proposed new constitution, both houses of the legislature can propose, reject, and amend bills. The same holds true of the legislatures of the post-Soviet republics. In parliamentary systems, legislatures have varying amounts of power to reject and amend bills but seldom propose them. Because proposals for legislation emerge largely from the cabinet and usually become law, the executive can plan with confidence that most laws will be passed.

The legislatures with the least power to make decisions are those subjected to strict party discipline; in such a system, the chief executive or some other party leader tells the members of the legislature how to vote. If voters choose the legislature in competitive elections and candidates present clear promises, this can help assure that their promises will be carried out. In a parliamentary system, the legislature will pass legislation proposed by the chief executive but can remove him or her if the legislation proves unpopular. Chief executives of the United Kingdom, Germany, and India can command discipline from their legislators, at least in the lower house, but that discipline is tempered by the legislature's ability to remove the chief executive. On the other hand, if the legislature is chosen in noncompetitive elections and the legislature cannot remove the chief executive—as in China, or formerly in the Soviet Union and East Germany—party discipline simply gives leaders the power to carry out policy without interference from the legislature. Figure 22.1 shows differences in various legislative powers in the nine nation-states.

In Peru, the United States, the post-Soviet republics, and Nigeria, the chief executive's control is less rigid. Once a law was passed by the Peruvian legislature, it could not be vetoed by the president. However, in 1992 President Fujimori simply disbanded the legislature, held elections for a new one under his own rules, and called for a new constitution. Although presidents in the other systems do have veto power, presidential vetoes in the United States, in the Soviet Union (from 1989 to 1991), in Russia and most other post-Soviet republics, and in Nigeria under the proposed civilian government can be overridden by the legislature. Furthermore, individual members are free to vote their own consciences. In Peru, they must keep in mind that they were chosen to run by their party's leader, but the legislature (even the new one) contains many parties, preventing any one from taking control. The new Nigerian constitution specifies that a member will lose his or her seat if they switch from one of the two authorized parties to the other; that is an attempt to impose party discipline, but, as we have seen, it will be difficult to create centralized parties in Nigeria. From 1989 to 1991, Soviet president Gorbachev proposed most legislation and presided over and mingled with the Congress of People's

Figure 22.1   Differences in legislatures' powers in the nine nation-states. Arrows pointing up indicate features that strengthen legislatures. Arrows pointing down indicate features that weaken legislatures.

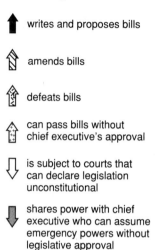

Legislature

↑ writes and proposes bills

amends bills

defeats bills

can pass bills without chief executive's approval

is subject to courts that can declare legislation unconstitutional

shares power with chief executive who can assume emergency powers without legislative approval

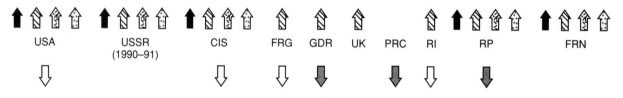

Deputies, giving individual legislators some chance to work on changes directly. Legislatures of the individual post-Soviet republics can also amend and vote down legislation proposed by their presidents.

Constitutions can limit legislatures' power, especially if combined with the doctrine of judicial review (as in the United States, the Federal Republic of Germany, and India), which permits the courts to declare acts of the legislature unconstitutional. A legislature not subject to judicial review has more freedom to act; but constitutional limits can also help protect legislative power from infringements by chief executives. In 1992, President Fujimori of Peru first bypassed the legislature, which rejected his tax reform and other major bills, and simply issued laws by decree; then he disbanded the legislature entirely and held elections for a new unicameral one under new rules which stripped the legislature

of all power. Under the old constitution, he was permitted to dissolve the lower house, but not the Senate. He could get by with this because the army, large businesses, and much of the public, approved of his economic and antiterrorist programs.

Former Soviet President Gorbachev issued frequent decrees on monetary and other important matters which might be presumed to be covered by law. Without clear constitutional standards, and with no procedures for judicial review by an independent judiciary,[2] it was difficult to prevent Gorbachev from taking such actions. Presidents of individual CIS and post-Soviet republics issue frequent decrees without consulting their legislatures. Russia and other post-Soviet republics operate under the same constitution they had under the Soviet Union; attempts to rewrite it meet political resistance, and even new documents are frequently amended.

Table 22.1

Can the Chief Executive Declare a Peacetime Emergency?

	Power to Declare Emergency	Power to Override or Approve Declaration
USA	no	
USSR (1990–91)	yes	Congress of People's Deputies
CIS	yes	Legislatures of Republics
FRG	yes	President and Bundesrat
GDR	yes	
UK	yes	Parliament
PRC	yes	
RI	no	President and Parliament
RP	yes	
FRN[1]	yes	
FRN[2]	yes	National Assembly

Table 22.2

Size of National Legislatures

	Lower House	Upper House
USA	435	100
USSR 1989–91	2,250	542 (in two chambers)
USSR 1991	450	
CIS	varies in different republics	
FRG	663	63
GDR	400	
UK	650	no fixed number
PRC	2,977	
RI	542	250
RP (–1991)	180	60
RP (1992–)	80	
FRN[1]		
FRN[2]	453	64

The constitutions of Peru and Nigeria[3] are reinterpreted, rewritten, or abandoned whenever there is a military coup. The very fact that units of the military can succeed in overthrowing civilian leaders and take control shows that constitutions do not limit sovereignty; constitutions may simply be changed by new sovereigns. There has been little chance to test whether they can effectively place limits on chief executives in these nation-states.

Even legislatures operating under constitutions have reduced authority if (as in Peru and China) the executive can declare emergency powers without legislative approval in times of war, disaster, or civil unrest. In Nigeria,[4] the United Kingdom,[5] India,[6] Germany,[7] and the Soviet Union and post-Soviet republics,[8] they can do so only with the approval of the legislature; the latter two countries (as the next chapter discusses) have bitter memories of what happens if a chief executive seizes such powers without legislative approval. In the United States, Congress must declare a war emergency, and an emergency cannot be declared in peacetime.

Table 22.1 summarizes the chief executive's emergency powers in each nation-state. Table 22.3 sums up other factors that weaken or strengthen legislatures as bodies, or that weaken or strengthen individual legislators.

A legislature is ineffective if it cannot meet. Without a declaration of emergency, a chief executive can neutralize a legislature by failing to call it into session or by closing a session in progress. The president of India calls the Parliament into session (which may thus not choose its own time to meet) and may dissolve the lower house (thus ending its session without its consent). The national legislatures in the United States, Nigeria's proposed constitution, and formerly in Peru decide for themselves when to meet or adjourn. Those in the United Kingdom and West Germany decide on their own calendars, but their schedules are subject to party discipline; this is also true in China and was formerly true in East Germany.

Legislatures are strengthened in dealing with the chief executive if the chief executive does not enjoy

Table 22.3

Factors that Strengthen or Weaken Legislatures and Individual Legislators

Factors Strengthening Entire Body	*Factors Weakening Entire Body*	*Factors Strengthening Individual Legislators*
Right to write, propose, introduce, amend, and defeat bills	Right of individual legislators and committees to write, propose, introduce, amend, and defeat bills	Right of individual legislators and committees to write, propose, introduce, amend, and defeat bills
	Strict party discipline Lax party discipline	Lax party discipline
Right to question ministers		Right to question ministers
Right to call own sessions		
Specialized committees	Specialized committees No specialized committees	Specialized committees
Constitutional limits	Constitutional limits No constitutional limits	No constitutional limits
Professional staff		Professional staff
Long terms of office	Short terms of office	Long terms of office
	Emergency declarations	
Popular head of legislature	Popular chief executive	Unpopular chief executive
	Public apathy	Public apathy
	Private obligations of legislators	Money from private contributors
	Large number of members	

public support, if legislators find it easy to cooperate in arriving at decisions, if the legislature's size is small enough that they can hold manageable meetings, and if they meet frequently. Under one-party communist systems, legislatures were generally large and met for less than a week a year (table 22.2). Russian President Boris Yeltsin hopes to create a bicameral legislature with fewer members to improve efficiency.

Legislatures are strengthened as a working body if (as in all but the one-party communist systems) they have committees with specialized knowledge about all major activities they deal with. But committees can also weaken the synergy of a legislature. Individual members of a legislature who head committees are more powerful than members who do

not, and they can sometimes resist the attempts of party leaders to exercise party discipline, especially if some of those committees grow to have much more power than others. Committees may also be able to hold hearings to examine the activities of the chief executive, cabinet, and bureaucracy.

The right to question the chief executive and ministers frequently and at close range is a restraint on corruption and bad judgment. The parliaments of the United Kingdom, West Germany, and India regularly question their chief executives on the floor of the house in face-to-face exchanges with members of their parliaments. The chief executives of China, the former East Germany, and the United States are not accessible to the legislature for this type of questioning. The legislatures of the Soviet

Union of 1990–91 could only question the president when he chose to call them into session. That still holds true in the post-Soviet republics.

The legislature is strengthened if its members do not change frequently, so they have time to acquire experience; during that time, they can also forge alliances with interest groups and various units of the government's bureaucracy and rise to power within committees. If the next Nigerian legislature bans former members from running, as General Babangida at one time proposed, it will be the only one among these nation-states without long-serving members. Term limits on the U.S. Congress might also have the same effect. A legislature with strong powers (like that in the United States) but short-term membership might be especially easy for interest groups to manipulate; some of those groups have long experience lobbying Washington.

If a legislature has power to make decisions, then some legislators will have more power than others. However, the power of the institution as a whole is not always enhanced when individuals within the institution acquire power. Thus, some of the very factors which strengthen the power of *individual* legislators may weaken the ability of the legislature to work as a body—and vice versa.

Individual legislators are strengthened if (as in the United States Congress or the Indian Lok Sabha) they have their own professional staffs so they do not have to rely entirely on outside bureaucracies and interest groups for information; yet personal professional staff and offices can weaken the unity of the legislature as a whole by giving legislators greater independence from one another.

Personal power will be especially enhanced—and the coordination of the legislative body as a whole weakened—when the individuals who head important committees operate under rules which let them kill or amend bills and if the legislature is not subject to party discipline. Both of these factors are true of the U.S. legislature. Personal power may be further enhanced if (unlike in the United States) constitutional limits and judicial review do not apply to the legislation in which powerful members have an interest. The power of these legislative

The Rules Committee of the United States House of Representatives has much influence over whether bills are amended before the final vote is taken.

Courtesy of Nona Bolling

leaders is also enhanced if the president has not declared emergency powers and is unpopular, if they have access to professionals to gather information but the legislature as a whole does not, and if the public knows and cares little about the legislature's concerns.

If (as in the United States) legislators with personal power within a legislature owe heavy personal obligations to any groups—for example, if groups helped them secure nomination to office, finance and conduct campaigns, gain votes, or pass legislation—these personal obligations can weaken the ability of the legislature to serve other groups.

If legislative or party leaders within the legislature of a presidential system are popular, they may be able to arouse support for particular bills by appealing directly to the public, over the heads of committee chairs. Such individuals can seldom command as much attention as the chief executive. In a

Table 22.4

Factors that Strengthen or Weaken Chief Executives

Factors Strengthening Executive Power	Factors Weakening Executive Power	Factors Weakening Executive Ability to Aid Wide Portions of the Populace
Party discipline		
No constitutional limits	Weak judiciary	Weak judiciary
Can declare emergency		
Popularity		
Weak legislature	Weak legislature	Weak legislature
Large personal staff		
Patronage	Patronage	Patronage
Large bureaucracy	Small bureaucracy	Large bureaucracy

parliamentary system, such leaders can invoke party discipline because they are associated with the cabinet and prime minister, or potentially may be after another election. That makes it easier for them to get legislation passed, but weakens the legislature in relation to the chief executive.

Even legislatures which seem weak often contribute members to cabinets or other units of government. They attend meetings with members of the executive branch. And they help, at least on occasion, to draw up legislation. Members expressing private displeasure on occasion may cause the chief executive to back away from a bill, or to amend it. The more powerful a legislature becomes, the more its chief paradox becomes evident: a legislature is composed of numerous individuals, and power cannot be distributed evenly among them. That can lead to friction and grid-lock. As a single individual, the chief executive is better able to exert leadership.

Executives

Legislatures are sometimes weak; chief executives always have some power to make decisions. The most powerful chief executives can enforce party discipline, are not subject to constitutional limits, can declare emergency powers, and are popular. Chief executives are strengthened in their freedom

to make decisions when members of their legislatures find it difficult to cooperate with one another, are not popular with the public, change members frequently, and have weak committees. The chief executive's power is further increased when he or she is part of the military, or has a large paid staff and a patronage[9] system for bureaucracy and even the judiciary. But even without these characteristics, executives may have much power because people look to them for decisions. Table 22.4 sums up factors that affect a chief executive's power.

Some conditions which strengthen the chief executive's power may also weaken it. For example, a patronage system may open the door for corruption within the bureaucracy. A weak legislature and judiciary leave a chief executive without assistance in gathering information and keeping bureaucracy under control. Instead, he or she must rely on bureaucrats for information, and they may bias their reports to suit their interests. With no independent body to oversee bureaucratic activities, corruption may increase, and morale may decline among those truly trying to carry out their assigned functions. Chief executives may need to bypass those with the highest merit when making bureaucratic appointments to return favors to friends and associates. All this increases the likelihood that problems will fester and create public dissatisfaction, eventually eroding the chief executive's power. In short, a chief executive who does not share power is not necessarily a strong chief executive.

Any chief executive with such conditions is likely to owe obligations to groups inside and outside government. A bureaucracy powerful enough to feed, clothe, and shelter the people needed to defend the nation-state and mobilize the people needed to cooperate with government is also powerful enough to make demands on the chief executive. A chief executive without a bureaucracy capable of performing these functions cannot rule unless he or she can find groups outside government to do them. In this case, the chief executive becomes obligated to those outside groups.

If the groups the chief executive depends on represent large numbers of people and wide segments of the populace, these groups may cause more equitable distribution of influence among the populace, and the chief executive would have reason to include all those segments in compromises.

But if such groups contain only small portions of the populace, the chief executive need not consider wide segments of the populace in making compromises. In that case, the only recourse for these less influenced segments would be to become active in political parties to affect future elections for the chief executive and the legislature, or to become active in interest groups that influence the bureaucracy.

Political Parties

The effectiveness of a government in catering to the needs of the populace is heavily dependent on its party system.

The power of political parties to make or influence decisions is potentially strengthened if parties are disciplined, so national party leaders can formulate cohesive policy knowing it will be supported at all levels of the party. If no constitutional limits exist, those policies cannot be resisted or overturned by the courts. A large legislature which subjects itself to party discipline, and which has weak committees, small staffs, and high turnovers, is easier

for leaders to direct. When the formal chief executive has a small staff and no independent access to media, is appointed from outside the legislature rather than elected, and has no powers of patronage, yet controls the judiciary or lets the political party control it, the power of party leaders is potentially enhanced; they can direct from behind the scenes. In this setting, it is easier for a party to seize control of information sources, the bureaucratic hierarchy, the chief executive, the legislature, and the courts and close down all opposing political parties and interest groups. This is the situation in China, and until recently, in East Germany and the Soviet Union.

This kind of power lets a political party suppress and ignore many interest groups. It also creates a new set of interest groups in and around the party and bureaucracy, who use these groups to seek to direct benefits to themselves. Without opposing political parties and interest groups, or a free press, those special interests are free to help themselves and any other portions of the population they wish to help.

Another system may have a strong independent legislature and chief executive, which weakens party discipline but strengthens the freedom of political parties and interest groups to form and govern themselves as they like. This can help assure that a wide variety of groups are represented in politics. It can also allow small sets of powerful interest groups to influence policy decisions by aiding individual legislators, bureaucrats, executive officeholders, and others who help make policy decisions.

A parliamentary system with strong, disciplined competing parties gives much authority directly to the formal chief executive, who is responsible for policy and can be voted out of office if the public does not like that policy. This strengthens accountability. But if one majority consensual party wins frequent reelection, and some groups find little representation in any consensual party, many people can be bypassed by government policy for long periods of time.

To satisfy the needs of broad portions of the populace, a nation-state needs an executive strong enough to articulate and carry through with policy, yet responsive to public criticism. To establish this responsiveness, the public needs access to individual elected leaders. That implies a freely elected legislature with some independence yet also with enough discipline and unity to carry through with coherent policy. Without strong, competing consensual parties this balance is unlikely to occur. Competing parties give legislators and executives incentive to cooperate on carrying through with promises so they will not be voted out of office.

Even strong parties without competition must accommodate the people needed to defend, feed, clothe, and shelter the groups that support them and to induce the public's cooperation with government. This makes it hard to serve the groups that the party does *not* require for those purposes, unless those groups participate in party activities.

Weak parties, on the other hand, make it difficult for individuals to gain representation in politics by voting for leaders offering policy alternatives they want implemented. Even electing a legislator you like does little good if he or she belongs to a splinter party with only a few seats in the legislature. Weak parties do make it easier for well-organized interest groups to influence individual legislators or bureaucrats by working behind the scenes. Thus, compromises may not reflect as great a variety of interests when political parties are weak.

All in all, political parties find it difficult to help interest groups which otherwise lack influence to achieve effective representation in politics. To successfully arrange compromises beneficial to a wide variety of groups, political parties need a degree of strength. Specifically, they need at least some party discipline, enough constitutional and legal limits to guarantee their right to compete and to ensure the integrity of government decision-making institutions, a legislature small enough to deliberate easily but large enough to represent a variety of groups and ideas, competition from other consensual and splinter parties in the legislature, legislative committees strong enough to challenge the chief executive without disrupting compromise, some control over the choice and financing of candi-

dates, and the ability to expose and challenge the behaviors of officeholders and bureaucrats.

If these postulates hold true, the solution to finding compromises among groups representing wide segments of the populace lies neither in very strong, nor in weak, parties. It involves some subtle, hard-to-achieve balances in the relationships between governmental and nongovernmental institutions. Among the most perplexing is creating a chief executive and bureaucracy powerful enough to create and implement compromises but not so strong as to distort them.

If many groups with relatively equal resources have power over the legislature, and the legislature shares power with other units of government, no one group will control the legislature or the rest of government. Instead, legislators will be able to work out compromises among the various groups and units of government. As important as the number of these groups, however, is the question of whom they represent. If they do not include, or care about, many of the nation-state's citizens, those citizens will not be represented.

To successfully arrange fair compromises beneficial to a wide array of groups, a legislature might ideally have the following:

1. Moderate party discipline—enough to keep members united, but not so great as to exclude input from members

2. Constitutional or legal limits on the powers of all groups and institutions

3. Small enough size to deliberate easily but large enough size to represent a variety of groups

4. A balance between two consensual parties (to allow for compromise) and splinter parties (which represent minority interests)

5. Committees with enough staff to gather independent information

6. The ability to independently question the chief executive

7. Members not dependent on only a few groups to finance their election campaigns

The question of how power is shared still depends, above all, on the relative power of interest groups. Groups who have influence with a variety of government and nongovernment institutions have more power than those who can influence only part of them. Groups restricted from participation in politics, or without resources or willingness to do so, operate at a distinct disadvantage. But acquiring resources and the willingness to participate requires a particular political culture: one that encourages group members to develop the traits they need to assert influence.

As we saw in part 2, interest groups differ greatly in their composition. In some nation-states— notably the United States, the United Kingdom, and West Germany—groups may speak for high percentages of the populace; in others, for only a few. In some systems—again, notably the United States, the United Kingdom, and West Germany—diverse segments of the populace are recruited into the various units of government; in others, only a few are. That may have a stronger bearing on the fairness of a political system than the specific roles played by individual governmental units. It may also help account for why the characteristics of a legislature discussed in the prior few paragraphs might better create fairness in those three nation-states than in some others, where representation is less broad. It is like the chicken-and-egg dilemma. When diverse segments of the populace are recruited into various units of government, those units can develop compromise, balance, moderation and limits; without the recruitment of diverse people, this balance cannot be created. The types of balance we have been discussing cannot be created by writing a constitution with rules and an organization chart. They can only be created by public participation in politics.

China's legislature is obviously weak in its power to make decisions; it has virtually none of the characteristics of a strong legislature, nor of the seven characteristics which might enhance compromise. It also has only one strong consensual party, which excludes competitors. Yet the Chinese system has some basis for broad group representation. Many party cadres come from among peasants and workers. And the government must acquire food from a great number of independent producers and other necessities from labor-intensive industries. It thus has an incentive to provide these producers with some economic security. At the same time, it has no way to deal with corruption of special interests that divert resources to themselves. Strong, centralized party control also stifles modernization and personal freedom.

Legislatures and political parties in the other nation-states all have strengths and weaknesses; in the United States, the United Kingdom, and West Germany, they perhaps have more (in no case all) of the seven characteristics which might enhance compromise. The Soviet Union was so weakened at the end that none of its organs commanded much power; they could not resist when the presidents of the individual republics seized them in 1991. India, Peru, and Nigeria have very restricted group representation, and exhibit few of the seven characteristics that enhance compromise. Their parliamentary and presidential systems find it hard to effectively serve broad elements of their populations.

CONCLUSION

All of us harbor a bit of anarchy in our hearts. We do not really like the fact that others can make decisions which affect us. We are a bit jealous of their power, and we enjoy seeing them tripped up. Some of the decisions they make harm us, but others underlie our very existence. Acquiring security and food requires collective decision making; and living in a war-torn or starving nation is not good for the body or the spirit. Our refusal to grant power to government leaders can easily backfire; it can force indecision when decisions are needed. A sensible nation-state limits the authority of its leaders, but limits that authority in measured ways.

A powerful legislature with no party discipline may simply use its power to aid its own members and the groups they are close to—which will always include bureaucrats and groups needed to keep the formal economy functioning, but may exclude much of the populace.

As a single individual with strong instruments of force and the ability to shift resources from one group to another, a powerful chief executive not answerable to a political party, legislature, or courts is in greater danger than a legislature of being unaware of who is offended by his or her actions. Powerful groups who are ignored may conspire with the military, bureaucracy, legislature, and others to ignore and perhaps even throw out the chief executive.

A powerful chief executive answering to a circle of leaders in a party with narrow membership is less likely to be isolated; that circle will keep him or her aware of complaints and ways to appease or silence complainers. Yet, because their party is not broadly based, they may leave out the wishes of many groups when creating policy.

Measured power requires that political parties represent diverse segments of the populace in an atmosphere conducive to compromise. The seven characteristics that help a legislature successfully achieve compromise, as discussed in the last section, suggest elements that atmosphere might include. They give the chief executive enough power to implement policies, but provide some assurance that those policies will win acceptance beyond the ruling circle. They require compromise, but not to such a degree that bargaining ends in stalemate. They constitute ways not of organizing government, but of operating it. They grow out of habits, attitudes, and—ultimately—influence which must be acquired by the people of a nation before those habits and attitudes can become a part of the way government operates. Government is always sensitive to the needs and wants of its own members and of especially influential people it relies on; it can become sensitive to the needs and wants of wider segments of the public only when those individuals involve themselves in effective party organizations and interest groups and make demands. But one more precondition remains: The demands people make must include an insistence that government both limit itself and get on with the business of creating policy that will benefit as many people as possible.

SUMMARY

Shared authority among government institutions can both encourage and restrain the abuse of power. It can give more groups the opportunity to exert influence on government policy, but it may also strengthen the influence of select groups inside government or with close ties to it. Groups who have influence over all aspects of the political system have more power than those who can influence only part of them. Groups restricted from participation in politics, or without resources or willingness to do so, operate at a distinct disadvantage. Constitutional limits and party competition help assure that a wide variety of interests will help decide public policy but can do little to assist groups who have no influence.

NOTES

1. The Peruvian president had the right to be consulted when bills were revised, and could also submit bills.

2. A Constitution Supervisory Committee declared Gorbachev's prohibition of a rally by political opponents in 1990 unconstitutional; he simply ignored them.

3. The 1992 Constitution may be revised with approval of two-thirds (for some articles, four-fifths) of the members of both houses of the National Assembly, and a majority vote in two-thirds of the state legislatures.

4. In Nigeria, under the 1992 Constitution, the president may declare an emergency, but it can be overturned by a two-thirds vote in the National Assembly.

5. Northern Ireland has been under emergency rule since 1972, with a special administrator replacing normal civilian authorities, and special suspensions of rights for people suspected of terrorism.

6. When Parliament is not in session, the president of India may promulgate ordinances which have the full effect of law until Parliament returns, and may even suspend the constitution and bring parts of the country threatened by civil unrest under direct federal control for up to two months. With the consent of Parliament, he or she may take control of a state for up to three years, suspending all state government except the judiciary. Prime Minister Indira Gandhi asked the president to declare a state of emergency for the entire country between 1975 to 1977. The Janata Government which followed her amended the constitution to require approval of two-thirds of both houses of Parliament, rather than a simple majority, with a mandatory revote every six months. And if 10 percent of the members of the Lok Sabha call for reconsideration of the emergency at any time, a revote must be taken.

7. Germany's federal president can declare a state of emergency which allows the chancellor to rule by emergency decree, but only with the approval of the Bundesrat. After the 1930 parliamentary elections brought many of Adolph Hitler's National Socialists, and Communists, into the Bundestag, and it was difficult to maintain a majority in Parliament, the chancellor and president ruled by emergency decree. In 1933, Hitler seized the chancellorship by force, closed Parliament entirely, and ended the Weimar Constitution.

8. The president of the Soviet Union could declare a state of emergency in any area without the consent of local authorities, but only with subsequent approval of the presidiums of the legislature(s) of that republic or a two-thirds vote of the Supreme Soviet. The president could dissolve the Supreme Soviet and rule by decree, but the Congress of People's Deputies theoretically could recall him or her for breaking the law. In 1991, they gave President Gorbachev power to rule by decree. In 1992, Russia's Congress of People's Deputies gave Boris Yeltsin similar powers for a time.

9. Patronage is the ability to hire and fire bureaucrats at will, and replace them with friends. See chapter 23.

EXERCISES

Think about the book thus far:

1. How do chapters 19–21 differ in focus from chapters 22–24?

2. How does the topic of this chapter—how chief executives and legislatures wield influence—relate to the topics in chapters 19–21? (how groups outside of government exert influence)?

3. How does the topic of the chapter relate to the discussion of institutional interest groups in chapter 20?

KEY WORDS AND PHRASES

Define the following terms:

decide
oblast

DISCUSS THE CHAPTER

Answer each of the following questions in one sentence:

1. Would you have more respect for the United States Congress if its members were free to vote as they wished, or if they had to vote as their party leaders told them, as legislators do in Germany and the United Kingdom? Why or why not?

2. If the legislature is not chosen through competitive elections, how can party discipline strengthen its authority? weaken its authority?

3. How can constitutional limits strengthen the sovereignty and authority of a chief executive? a legislature?

4. Imagine legislatures with 40, 100, and 1,000 members.

    a. In which would it be easiest for members to share their views with one another?
    b. In which would it be easiest for constituents to share views with their legislative representative?
    c. In which would small minorities with moderate influence have a better chance to be elected?

5. Will a legislature be in a better position to pass legislation appealing to a wide diversity of interests if it contains

    a. one political party?
    b. two consensual parties?
    c. two consensual parties and small numbers of representatives from splinter parties?
    d. only splinter parties?

6. If legislatures are to assist a wide variety of groups, what might be an advantage of having weak committees combined with party discipline making legislators answerable to the chief executive? What might be a disadvantage of this system?

7. Do the following factors strengthen or weaken the sovereignty of a chief executive?

    a. a weak judiciary
    b. a weak legislature
    c. weak legislative committees
    d. a large bureaucracy
    e. party discipline
    f. competitive elections

8. Do the following factors strengthen or weaken the authority of a chief executive?

    a. a weak judiciary
    b. a weak legislature
    c. weak legislative committees
    d. a large bureaucracy
    e. party discipline
    f. competitive elections

THINKING IT THROUGH

Let's return to the question posed at the end of chapter 3: Do factors which strengthen the sovereignty of a chief executive strengthen his or her authority? Try approaching this question by answering the following:

1. For public policy to reconcile the interests of people from a wide variety of backgrounds, is it advantageous for a chief executive to share or monopolize sovereignty?

2. Are people without influence better off if the chief executive shares, or monopolizes, sovereignty?

3. In which systems—those with the strongest or the weakest chief executives—is the chief executive in the best position to receive the authority that derives from substantial consensus on the legitimacy of political institutions and the direction and content of public policy? Are citizens more inclined to accept compromise and support public policy when the chief executive retains a lot of decision-making power, or when he or she shares it with many other members of government? Review your scores in the Chapter 3 exercise if that helps you focus on this question.

4. The seven characteristics of a legislature able to form successful compromises, discussed in this chapter, suggest that a chief executive has the greatest authority when he or she shares some sovereignty, but not too much. Do you agree? Why or why not?

chapter 23

GOVERNMENT INSTITUTIONS
BUREAUCRACY, MILITARY, PLURALISM, AND CORRUPTION

This chapter is about participation, and what happens when it comes to a halt. Except in rare times of madness, government officials, bureaucrats, and their close associates participate in politics. How can participation, and its rewards, extend beyond these few?

Corruption sets in when a government's actions differ from its announced intentions. Most governments announce their intentions to serve all the people of a nation-state. Some people in or closely associated with government, however, prefer to implement policy in a manner which serves their own ends more than those it is publicly proclaimed to benefit. **Bureaucracy and the military share in governmental decision making. Powerful bureaucracies and militaries can restrict systems to a minimal amount of pluralism; minimal pluralism is often associated with corruption.** A military government can sometimes bring bureaucracy, and corruption, temporarily under control. But real pluralism requires a free press, independent courts, competitive political parties, and freely elected legislatures and executives capable of controlling corruption in the military and bureaucracy.

BUREAUCRACY

In all nation-states today, bureaucrats far outnumber legislators, executives, and officials in judiciary and political party leadership posts.

The bureaucracy in a centralized economy offers an extreme example of how central a role bureaucracy can play in politics. Numerous government bureaucratic organizations in China, the Soviet Union and post-Soviet republics, and until recently in East Germany, control agriculture and industry,

the media, publishing, sports, the arts, and many other aspects of life. The Soviet Union's chief economic planning organization, **Gosplan,** decided what percentages of two thousand raw materials would be allocated to which ministries, and reserved approval for all development schemes. It had separate committees in each of the fifteen republics and in regions transcending republics. Another agency, Gossnab, presided over customer-supplier relations for commodities. Still another agency, the State Committee for Prices, set prices for over two-hundred thousand commodities and products. Their work and that of other agencies was supervised by one-hundred-fifty to two-hundred thousand Party apparatchiki at the national, republic, oblast, and local levels, as well as by the Communist Party's Politburo and the top bureaucratic unit, the Council of Ministers. Individual bureaucrats answered to several planning committees at once, as well as to party officials. For example, materials-moving equipment was made by 380 factories operating under thirty-five different ministries.[1] Obtaining raw materials, permission to build factories, and markets involved considerable overlap in areas of authority. The party apparatchiki had to work out conflicts with leaders of primary party organizations. The military, industrial, and agricultural bureaucracies were all heavily dependent on one another for supplies, orders, and support.[2]

Under such a system, it is hard for top leaders to effect major changes in procedures.[3] When Gorbachev came to power in the 1980s, he replaced various government and party leaders with individuals loyal to him and then proposed decentralization of bureaucratic procedures under his **perestroika** (economic restructuring) program.[4] In 1992, the central government was eliminated and its bureaucracy transferred to the individual republics. But the bureaucracy is large and contains people who have held their positions many years. These bureaucrats have resisted at every turn attempts to further loosen prices, end subsidies to force plants to produce better products, allow businesses to seek their own markets and freely hire and fire, and otherwise reduce bureaucratic controls.

Since 1978, China's economy and political system has become increasingly decentralized. In 1978, seven hundred kinds of producer goods were allocated by central planners; in 1991, twenty. Forty percent of coal and 45 percent of steel was being distributed outside the control of central planners by 1991. Deng Xiaoping's moves toward decentralization were opposed by leaders of the State Council and the State Planning Commission and the Party's Control Commission for Inspecting Discipline. When loosening controls led to raw materials shortages, price increases, shortfalls in transportation and energy production, and government budget deficits, the State Council banned the price increases, placed lids on capital spending, suspended all new projects raw materials were not guaranteed for, and reintroduced other centralized controls. In recent years, cities and provinces along the seacoast have begun to derive extensive revenues by forming joint-ventures with foreign businesses. Because reforms gave industries and provincial authorities more capital to work with, they can ignore centralized directives. Many groups are competing for power and resources.[5] The emperors' policy was to avoid stationing literati in the towns where they were born and to move them frequently so they could not become entrenched enough to resist demands from the central government. More recent government attempts to shift governors and other high cadres often are simply ruses allowing central officials to promote people from their own provinces and to expand their power base.

Since so many levels of the society and economy are involved in these interactions, the bureaucracy is a major arena for conflict. Various units of bureaucracy compete with one another for scarce resources. Different levels of the bureaucratic hierarchy are pressured by different levels of the party and government, often presenting conflicting demands; the bureaucracy can then sort out these demands and make up the rules by which conflicts are resolved. This also opens the door to a good deal of corruption within the bureaucracy, which is answerable to no one with direct power.

In most systems, government bureaucrats play roles in fewer realms than the bureaucracy in China or the Soviet Union. But their impact can still be considerable. Some of their tasks involve reporting on activities of private citizens, institutions, or other units of bureaucracy. Other roles involve bringing such entities into compliance with rules, including rules made by the bureaucracies themselves. Bureaucracy may attempt to educate or to represent the public or various interest groups. Bureaucracy may manufacture, mine, grow, transport, and/or distribute raw materials and products. It may also consume such products. It may coordinate the activities of various institutions and individuals. It may produce, consume, and distribute money. Armed forces or police may kill, injure, or incarcerate people. Bureaucracy may also entertain, threaten, or tempt citizens, as well as provide them services.

Bureaucracy has become such an annoying part of modern life that many people view bureaucrats as holding virtually absolute power to make decisions. They are powerful, as we just learned, when the chief executive is powerful, because he or she must rely on them for services. Bureaucratic power may also be considerable if the chief executive is weak and does not have the power to oversee the bureaucracy's activities. If a system is federal, with executives at different layers, yet just one set of bureaucracy responding to all these executives, bureaucracy can play one executive against another. If there is more than one layer of bureaucracy, one layer can blame the other for actions which they themselves take.

The power of bureaucratic agencies also increases when legislatures have little ability to oversee bureaucracy; on the other hand, strong oversight committees often include long-standing members who have accumulated numerous contacts with bureaucrats they do not wish to offend. If political parties have little cohesion or internal discipline, bureaucratic power is also enhanced. Parties that do have cohesion and discipline still must rely on bureaucracy to gain information and to execute policy. In short, bureaucracies have power regardless of the way governments are arranged.

A **merit system,** which selects bureaucrats on the basis of ability, knowledge, and skills in open competition, and which protects them from arbitrary dismissal, allows bureaucrats to entrench themselves and develop tight chains of command. They can then resist orders from chief executives and nurture relationships with special interests. A **patronage system,** which allows chief executives to hire and fire at will, permits individuals to disobey orders from their immediate superiors if it suits the chief executive who hired them, and weakens the solidarity of bureaucratic units as a whole, can help chief executives entrench themselves along with insubordinate bureaucrats.

So, regardless of the composition of the government system, bureaucracy exerts considerable influence. If an otherwise weak group wishes to exert more influence, entering the bureaucracy is a way to do so.

MILITARY RULE

One portion of bureaucracy is in a position to go farther than any other. Because it controls weapons, troops, and other elements of physical force, a military is at times able to turn aside legislatures and executives and take over sovereignty in a nation-state.

China,[6] Germany, the United Kingdom, Russia, and the United States have long histories of military officers remaining loyal to civilian authorities. So did India under empire, and the British tried to continue that tradition. During World War II, a member of the Congress party named Subhas Chandra Bose (educated at Cambridge University) assumed command of some of the Indian National Army troops captured by Japan when they seized the island of Singapore and declared his intent to take over India by military force. After the war, his troops were banned from the Indian Army. Pakistan, which split from India at independence, has undergone periods of military rule. But India's army has remained strictly professional and subordinate to civilian rule.

We saw in chapter 17 that military leaders have ruled Peru for ninety-six of the years since Peru achieved independence in 1821. From the time it became a republic in 1963, Nigeria has only had seven years of elected civilian government; the rest of that time, it was under military rule.

Peru's military officers were once the sons of **latifundistas** (owners of *latifundia,* landed estates) and businesspeople, so the army protected the interests of those groups. Since World War II, with radical politics threatening security and newly educated people needing employment, military academies have been opened to train young men from less prosperous or prominent families as officers. These new officers often found themselves in an ambivalent position. As military officers, they did not like the instability the more radical workers' parties threatened to cause. Yet they sympathized with the parties' objectives of broadening political and economic opportunity. They found themselves promoting reforms while suppressing the political parties of reform. They prevented established families from losing control of the government and economy, even though those families would not let military leaders join the most exclusive social clubs.

As we have seen, during the military reform regime from 1968 to 1980, General Velasco upset this balance by forcing *latifundistas* to sell their workers most of their holdings. Velasco set up national banks to lend to peasants, nationalized oil and mining, and otherwise reformed businesses. He was able to do this because, as a military leader, he could bypass regular bureaucracy and even his own cabinet (Council of Ministers), which was composed of high-ranking military officers. He had an inner council of radical colonels, who listened to the more radical reformers under the prior civilian regime and reported regularly to General Velasco.[7] They formed two supraministerial commissions of civilian bureaucrats to circumvent the regular bureaucracy, and special agrarian courts to bypass the regular judiciary controlled by local landowners. Then they integrated all this into one supraministry (SINAMOS), which proceeded to institute the reforms over the objections of much of the military high command and the regular ministries.

Civilian presidents Alan Garcia, and especially Alberto Fujimori, have subsequently attempted to use agencies outside the regular bureaucracy to promote reforms. They had to face harsh criticism in the legislature and the press, along with frequent strikes and civil disobedience, and they had little control over the business community. This weakened their ability to promote change. Velasco faced such resistance in the form of inability to obtain adequate investment and foreign aid, bureaucratic mismanagement of state enterprises, failure to enforce his decrees, and grumbling within the ranks. Massive foreign debt and food shortages led to strikes. In 1976, he was forced to turn power over to another general, who softened the reforms. The civilian government which followed in 1980 abandoned the reform process and returned many expropriated urban properties to their original owners; during the 1990s President Fujimori eliminated the last of the state-owned companies. Velasco had, however, changed the face of Peruvian politics by doubling employment in the public sector, destroying the old landowning elites, distributing a third of agricultural land to peasants, recruiting many middle- and lower-class individuals into political participation, and strengthening the power of unions and neighborhood organizations.

The eighty thousand families receiving land under these reforms were not from the lowest classes and had been politically organized under civilian rule. To circumvent the regular bureaucracy, Velasco's supraministries worked with organizations composed of tenants on the large estates, who subsequently became the recipients of the land and shut out surrounding peasants from benefits. By one respectable estimate, the poorest half of the populace was unaffected by the military's reforms, while the lowest fourth was even worse off.[8]

Since this time, wealthy Peruvians have looked upon the military with some distrust, and military leaders have feared that attempts to take power would make them the prime target of Sendero Luminoso[9] terrorism and promote civil war.[10] To fight Sendero Luminoso, however, President Fujimori turned control of much of the countryside over to the military. He enjoyed their support when he dissolved the courts and the legislature in 1992.

In contrast to Peru, officers of the Nigerian army largely come from middle-class urban families. They do not tend to support radical change. Most of Nigeria's coups have purported to shift control from one tribal group within the military to another and to clean up corruption. Yet every civilian and military regime in Nigeria has been heavily influenced by the Hausa. The 1975–76 and 1983–85 military leaders (Murtala Muhammed and Mohammed Buhari), who aggressively cracked down on many established interest groups, were soon overthrown and replaced by military rulers cooperative with these interest groups;[11] even those reformist regimes were less aggressive about cracking down on corruption among Hausa than in other regions. The 1966–75 regime of Colonel Gowon was as corrupt as any civilian regime.[12] Major-General Babangida, who took power in 1985, shared with his predecessors (President Shagari, who was overthrown in 1983, and Major-General Buhari, who overthrew Shagari) the frustration of losing support from key factions when trying to enforce economic austerity measures after a period of cooperation with and permissiveness toward economic elites.

A military bureaucracy is strong only when well supplied with food, equipment, and weapons; it is often dependent on other units of bureaucracy to help obtain these necessities. It is even possible for civilian bureaucracies to be largely dependent on other civilian bureaucracies for their supplies. In most nation-states, they rely on nongovernmental groups as well. Once again, the composition and attitudes of all those groups affect who is served by government—they help determine whether compromises among bureaucratic units serve many people or only a few. Military rulers must cooperate with such groups in order to rule. Romiti T. Suberu believes that civilian politicians are better than military leaders at "mediation and moderation of religious and regional cleavages by competitive political bargaining."[13]

Both Peru and Nigeria have become heavily dependent on imported food and on earning income by exporting copper, gold, oil, and other products which involve few people in production. It has not been necessary for the governments of these two countries to assist large portions of the populace to maintain the needed economic and bureaucratic interactions. Neither nation-state has been impelled to reform by threats from bordering countries, either. So while military governments have forced other units of government to implement some equalizing reforms to aid the poor and ethnic minorities, these reforms have been short-lived. It is hard to control people and institutions needed to supply basic services and resources. While a military can act quickly with force, it may find it hard to quell disagreements within its own ranks or to resist pressure from groups or nation-states it relies on for money and weapons. Military chains of command are good at creating large institutions. In the civilian realm, they may feel most comfortable issuing orders to and through large institutions as well, thus strengthening the larger over smaller ones. None of this helps military rulers promote egalitarianism among people who largely lie outside the national economy.

Furthermore, military rule stifles courts, the press, and political parties. Without these institutions, it is hard to stop corruption either in the military or among its allies in other bureaucracies and the private sector. When people cannot express discontent, the problems that cause their displeasure often go unattended.

In systems which have experienced military rule, the armed forces can play a special role even during civilian rule. When President Alan Garcia moved to nationalize Peru's banks and insurance companies in order to make more money available to rural and small business development projects, the business community was angered, and the courts ruled that he needed the legislature's consent. The army, however, signalled its approval, helping Garcia to proceed. Unfortunately, the move did not accomplish its purpose. The leading bank lost its credit lines, and private investment crawled to a standstill. As with similar moves under General Velasco, the initiative failed. One of the first moves of Garcia's successor, Alberto Fujimori, was to dismiss a number of army officers he felt might disagree with his more moderate approach; after that he cooperated closely with the military, even giving it broad powers to control other institutions. Nigeria's nationalization of oil and other industries took place during General Obasanjo's 1976–79 period of military rule; it had a similar effect, slowing investment, and was rescinded when General Babangida returned oil production to private ownership in the late 1980s.

PLURALISM AND CORRUPTION

In part 2, we examined how people acquire influence. Part 3 has been exploring how people use it. When influence is widely distributed among different ethnic, religious, economic, and cultural groups, when these groups compete freely with one another in shifting patterns as new issues arise, and when government provides a favorable climate for debate and compromise to occur, a political system exhibits **pluralism.**

At its heart, pluralism depends upon people's ability to identify policies they support and to influence institutions to adopt those policies, even in the face of other institutions' objections. If an all-powerful government leader could stop all groups from identifying and promoting their own interests, pluralism would cease. Instead of incorporating a diversity of interests, government would allow people to identify only with the leader and the principal institution to which he or she belonged. There would be no institutionalized basis for the public to participate in politics.

Mussolini first used the term *totalitarian* in a 1925 speech, referring to "our fierce totalitarian will." Giovanni Gentile, the official philosopher of his movement, had used the word earlier that year in reference to a state which would unite state and society in "a total conception of life." During the 1930s, English and American journalists began to apply the word, often without clear definition, to the regimes in Russia, Germany, and Italy, and sometimes others; after World War II it came into common usage. George Orwell's *Animal Farm* and *1984,* and Arthur Koestler's *Darkness at Noon,* which described the complete loss of personal identity and the omnipresence of the leader in personal life, played a major role in bringing the term to popular attention.

Totalitarian[14] regimes attempt to destroy group identities by transforming people into masses who identify only with the state and its leader. Historically, various groups competed for power within regimes such as Russia and Germany. But Stalin in the Soviet Union and Hitler in Germany set out to destroy group identities and group competition. They wanted no institutions or loyalties to rival the power of the party and the nation-state. Their principal weapon was uncertainty. They made it hard for people to trust anyone. And nothing a person did could make him or her safe unless that person was especially needed to defend or operate the nation-state.

As Commissar of Nationalities, Stalin had traveled throughout the Soviet Union and acquired loyal supporters. He used these individuals in his rise to power and they, in turn, used him to obtain favors for themselves and their supporters. Thus, influence was exerted in predictable ways. Trotsky, Zinoviev, Bukharin, and other rivals for Stalin's party leadership after the death of Lenin also had supporters, who were gradually edged out of prominent positions. That, too, was initially predictable. Then Stalin initiated a policy of purge and terror, in which even his own prominent supporters in high positions might be suddenly removed from power and executed without warning.[15] That ended predictability.

With the terror Stalin was attempting to induce in the population a climate of psychological unease that would render it as amenable as possible to manipulation from the centre. Since no one was safe from denunciation and arrest, a patron's ability to protect and a client's ability to support were constrained by mutual knowledge that either or both might lose position, liberty, and even life, with no warning and no apparent reason. He made decisions without consulting a legislature, interest groups, the regular bureaucracy, or units of his political party. They depended upon the whim of the supreme arbiter, Stalin.[16]

Hitler did not remove and execute his leaders in the same arbitrary fashion. However, the SS and SD security officers (secret police) who were controlled by Hitler's small coterie of colleagues infiltrated virtually every group in society. Hitler put his own supporters in charge of many private organizations. People suspected of disloyalty to the regime were arbitrarily arrested, and executed or imprisoned, without legal recourse. Gangs of youths were sent to break windows, burn houses, and beat up resisters, who were horrified to discover that no police or private citizens would come to their rescue. Soon it was possible for Hitler's private SS storm troops to drag anyone—regardless of how high their position in society or government—off to a cell or concentration camp without interference from civil authorities or the public.

These two regimes were different in many ways. Their ideologies, organization, goals, allies, and achievements were very dissimilar. Even their methods of suppressing participation differed. They did not entirely succeed at ending participation but were able to gradually stifle it; the victims of Stalin's prison camps and of Hitler's concentration camps and extermination squads were completely cut off not only from participation, but from their own identities as members of social groupings or even as human beings. Hitler designated certain entire categories of people (Jews, homosexuals, other nationalities) to be casually rounded up and sent to concentration camps simply because of who they were. Millions of them were crammed into railroad boxcars and cells, stripped of all possessions and dignity, forced to work long hours and fight like animals for food and even air, and then murdered. Some workers and inmates were given privileged positions in factories and concentration camps to cause dissension and divide the loyalties of other workers and inmates; after being given special status, these individuals might be killed at any time. Writers were forced to write in praise of the system and then sent to prison for what they had written. Children spied on their parents. The industries and military establishments the regimes relied on for their expansion and defense were kept intact, for a price. Hitler forced big business to heavily bankroll his power grab in 1933, then disbanded or took over their interest groups, forced them to fire Jews, persecuted those who hesitated, and treated them with great rudeness before public audiences. Other groups received similar or worse treatment. Politically active people saw that any attempts they made to organize and exert influence on the state—even through the Communist or National Socialist parties—would be futile, not because the state would crush the attempt, but because it did not respond predictably to pressure; it simply acted erratically as it pleased. But they also knew that if they acquiesced while other groups were crushed, they would be, for the time being, safe and successful, at least until they or their group suddenly became a target. So no one was safe; nothing you did could protect you, nor would anyone else.

Under such circumstances, political participation is a meaningless concept. Regular patterns of human relationships, and rules and procedures, are destroyed. There was little basis under Stalin or Hitler for competing over goods and services, or over cultural traditions, ideas, and other values; there was little opportunity for government decisions to resolve such competition to the advantage of any group or groups. These regimes could be trusted to do nothing they said they would do; they were corrupt to the core.

Hitler's movement was destroyed by the Allied Forces in World War II. Stalin survived until 1953; after his death, the purges and terror ended. Leaders of various bureaucratic and party institutions were able to compete with one another again. But people became entrenched in their new positions, and it grew increasingly difficult to remove them. From here, they could support regional and personal interests. Those entrenched individuals developed ties with local leaders and groups throughout the Soviet Union. The party was in charge of all institutions; it consisted of many leaders at many levels. The party and government controlled information from the center and often made arbitrary administrative decisions without giving clear reasons for their actions. The Great Russians dominated the other nationalities. This took place in an atmosphere of far greater *predictability* than under Stalin. The secret police no longer could arrest leading party members and were generally (but not entirely) subservient to the Politburo. After Khruschev was removed from office in 1963 (after seven years of attempting to introduce greater freedom of expression), the KGB began arresting intellectuals who were calling for greater human rights, trying them before handpicked audiences and sentencing them to a maximum of seven years in labor camps and five years in exile. Some intellectuals and writers stayed safe by avoiding dissent. Political participation was now predictable; dissent meant prison terms, and avoiding dissent meant escaping them. Though activities were still supervised, the state encouraged people to organize groups and celebrate the customs of their nationalities.

Predictability and state encouragement to organize restored, once again, the possibility of group identities and group competition. An institutional basis existed allowing people to identify their own interests and to participate in politics under predictable rules and procedures. This competition, to be sure, took place within rules different from those in the United States—many of them rules long familiar in Russia. The state (guided by the Communist Party) controlled information, the economy, and political organizations from the center and imprisoned its critics. Leaders were prepared to listen to those who controlled agriculture, industry, the army, and other bureaucracies, and work out compromises among them; they suppressed the organization of nationalities, religious groups, or other groups who wanted radical change in policies. But the Soviet Union had moved from a period dominated by terror and ideological indoctrination to one dominated by bureaucracy.

> *Instead of the preeminence of police terrorism, the system recognized the 'leading role' of the communist party nomenklatura. As the members of this political class acquired political immunity from indiscriminate police behavior, islands of legality began to develop. Emphasis on the total mobilization and control of the society was gradually replaced by a form of 'social contract' between the nomenklatura and the rest of society . . . it was also a sign of the beginning of 'posttotalitarian civil society,' . . . **safe social places.** Gradually, the dissident movement developed its underground press and universities and festivals. Like those in classic guerilla warfare, many of these resisters managed to avoid being captured by simply melting into the society. Obviously, the posttotalitarian state still punished its opponents harshly, but as a rule, people no longer disappeared into an Orwellian 'memory hole.'*[17]

Bureaucracy itself supplies one aspect of pluralism by creating competing institutions and centers of power, even when civilian legislatures and executives are lacking, or when single political parties outlaw all forms of competition. But without pluralist competition in the form of a free press, independent courts, competitive political parties, and elected legislatures and executives, bureaucracy easily becomes corrupted. These institutions help assure that all groups and individuals can enter the competition under similar rules. This is the system Gorbachev and Yeltsin tried to create. Entrenched groups and bureaucrats are prepared to resist those initiatives and retain their power.

Citizen groups can organize to express opposition to bureaucratic activities, from the operation of waste dumps to foul-ups in school bus schedules. They may pressure political leaders to intervene in such matters. Newspaper and television reporters sometimes expose bureaucratic irregularities. Groups

A month before the Berlin Wall opened, these shoppers are waiting in front of an East Berlin "convenience store" called "Early and Late." The store's shelves were filled with many jars of beans and a few other items. Notice the dingy exterior caused by heavy air pollution and decades of neglect.

Bob Gamer

may take complaints to the courts when they seem to involve bureaucratic breaches of the law, or to interpret whether groups have been treated with equity. Individuals can vote for public officeholders who have pledged to make changes.

The need for exposure is great in all systems to restrain bureaucratic corruption and abuses of power. The United States president can staff all the highest levels of bureaucracy with his or her own people and has a large personal staff. Still, it is difficult for the president to supervise the bureaucracy. The U.S. bureaucracy gathers its own information, is large, and is primarily composed of merit appointees who know that if they protect one another they will be in office longer than any president and his or her political appointees. Many of these bureaucrats have long-standing contacts with interest groups who contribute to political campaigns. Important independent regulatory commissions, such as the Federal Reserve Board, do not take orders from the president. In addition, the president does not control bureaucracy at the state or local levels; these bureaucracies may receive commands from governors, counties, and municipalities that differ from the directives the president gives to the national bureaucracy.

In the United Kingdom, individual ministers are given charge of their ministries, and may be considered "soft" if they cannot keep their budgets healthy. They also may conflict with one another on policies which affect ministries differently. But as politicians, they have little time or expertise to supervise the daily affairs of their departments. Each department is headed by a permanent secretary, a civil servant who will keep his or her job after any given Government leaves office. Top civil servants often attended school together at Oxford and Cambridge and have close ties to one another. Because they are required to consult with appropriate interest groups, bureaucrats sometimes form alliances with them to pursue common goals. The National Farmers' Union, the Confederation of British Industry, teachers, road haulers, doctors, police, and other groups have strong ties to the ministries which affect them. Individual bureaucrats often have obligations both to the national government and to local governments headed by different political parties. This makes bureaucracy difficult to control, even though pluralism exists.

Germany, too, has pluralism and institutions capable of exposing bureaucratic corruption. This nation-state, smaller in area than Montana, is divided into separate states, governmental districts, regional administrations, counties, cities, and over fifteen thousand local communities. Most plans affecting the entire nation-state must pass through both national and state legislatures and involve negotiations among various bureaucratic agencies. Bureaucrats are free to run for seats on legislatures and often have close contacts with interest groups. Furthermore, the government holds stock in a number of major corporations. Ministries are divided into four levels, with five classifications of employees. There is little communication or coordination between different levels, classifications, or ministries. Experts carrying out policy at the bottom cannot discuss problems with policymakers at the top, who also have close contact with interest groups. All of this makes the German bureaucracy difficult to control.

Early in 1991, the people of Latvia and Lithuania demonstrated one way to control bureaucracy. Amon, a black beret unit affiliated with the KGB and Soviet army, rolled tanks through the streets to overthrow the republic's government in the name of a "National Solidarity Committee." They were greeted by a mass of citizens who had gathered in an all-night vigil to stop them. Scores of people were wounded and killed, but the street crowds prevailed in holding Amon back. The next morning, Gorbachev professed not to have known what was happening; Amon backed off from further confrontation. A crowd of half a million took to the streets of Moscow in response to threats by the army during that same period. Among the south Ossetians of Georgia, the army instigated revolt against the Georgian republic and then patrolled the streets along with Georgians to stop it. On numerous occasions when army, Politburo, or KGB leaders threatened to clamp down on new freedoms, crowds with hundreds of thousands of citizens appeared in the streets to defy them. Later in 1991, the practice paid off when thousands took to the streets in Moscow, Leningrad, and elsewhere to successfully defy the communist hardliners' attempted coup. That is a direct way to block bureaucratic initiatives. As we have seen in prior chapters, such defiance is in keeping with national character. In East Germany, crowds in Leipzig openly defied government orders to back down; when the government failed to fire on them, the door was opened for the dissolution of the nation-state.

In China, as we saw in chapter 21, Mao led another effort to use people directly against bureaucracy during the Cultural Revolution. Had the arbitrary attacks on bureaucrats, high party officials, and private citizens continued with full support from Mao, and with all others afraid to assist the victims, they could have led to an era of totalitarianism. Mao prevented that from happening by calling upon bureaucracy to reassert authority. Once it had done so, efforts to organize outside bureaucracy faltered. China does not have traditions which permit individuals to defy authority in independently organized groups; when demonstrators took to the streets in 1979 and 1989 in defiance of government leaders and bureaucrats, they ran for cover and returned to their homes after the government sent in troops to return order.[18]

These are dramatic events which occur only occasionally. They do not stop bureaucracy from quietly getting its way in day-to-day activities. A free press, competitive parties and elections for executives and legislatures, freely formed interest groups, and independent courts do help hold the bureaucracy more accountable. They allow citizens who are not bureaucrats, and not closely associated with bureaucracy, a chance to find out whether they approve of what is happening and to pressure officeholders to make changes if they disapprove. In the United States, the United Kingdom, and West Germany, those institutions are in place. They can render independent judgments. Large portions of the public vote, and most feel free to shift their support to different nominees. Ordinary citizens join in communicating with their elected officeholders and in other interest group activities. This gives them some chance to control bureaucracy. In the CIS, and even in East Germany, where former Stasi secret police still hold some bureaucratic positions, it remains an open question whether courts, the press, and political competition can give people such control.

In India, Peru, and Nigeria, much smaller portions of the populace participate in politics. Many who do are closely associated with bureaucrats. And close social ties bind the press, political parties, officeholders, and the courts. That makes it more difficult to supervise the activities of government and bureaucracy.

Peruvian bureaucrats often have direct blood ties to people with leading interests. In Peru, highland peasant villagers are organized around families. The heads of families occupy the village assemblies. The 1,662 districts are headed by towns, which usually contain a few hundred inhabitants. Each town has a mayor and an elected council, often composed of village notables like storekeepers or wholesale purchasers of local products, truck owners, or landowners large enough to hire labor. The 150 provincial capitals have two or three thousand inhabitants. Their mayors and elected councils are drawn from the ranks of larger merchants, wholesalers, truck owners, and labor contractors. The capitals of the twelve regions are towns with many thousands of inhabitants. Their principal streets are lined with fine houses belonging to families of latifundistas, immigrant businessowners, doctors, lawyers, and other professional people often educated in Lima or abroad. The councils and mayors of the district capitals, and the prefects and governors of the provinces, are often drawn from the ranks of these professionals and businesspeople.

The political elites at these four levels—village, district, province, and region—have little in common. And the elite in Lima, drawn from the top ranks of the most successful latifundistas and immigrant businesspeople, has little in common with those in the regional capitals. The ties that do bind them are often personal and informal. It is common for villagers to select a member of the district elite to be a godparent to their children. When the ceremony is held to cut the child's first locks of hair, the godparents give gifts; they may later help the child through school and eventually to become a closely affiliated civil servant. Likewise, district elites may seek godparents among provincial elites, and provincial elites among regional elites. The sons and daughters of regional elites often marry into families of latifundistas and successful immigrant business families in Lima. Thus they have a system of obligations to one another.

These traditional ties also help some youth to move from highland peasant families into teaching and lower-level civil servant jobs. As just mentioned, a godparent may help a child through school and into a civil service position. Relatives who moved from village to town may allow a bright rural nephew to live with them and help with the housework while he attends secondary school and university. Thus, traditional social customs aid social and economic mobility. Such mobility is not sufficient in itself, however, to allow such an individual to achieve political or economic prominence.

As civil servants, they will need to work closely with the local elite who sponsored them.

Army officers, police guards, agronomists, and other government officials sent from Lima are not part of this system and are often viewed with suspicion. Even now, with universal suffrage, the informal system is still at work to select political candidates from among traditional elites. While these Lima-based officials direct some decisions on security, crops, marketing, and finances, they cannot wrest the power to select candidates and local bureaucracy from the elite clubs of the regional capitals. Thus, they must learn to cooperate at both ends of the system. Orders do not flow down from the chief executive and top bureaucrats if they conflict with the wishes of local elites.

The ties between bureaucracy and other elites are also close in India. Indian bureaucracy plays a similar role of mediating among elites at various levels. About two-thirds of the three thousand members of the top Indian Administrative Service work for states;[19] these civil servants are well educated and largely come from good families (though a fourth are lowest-caste untouchables or come from minority tribes). India's states have their own bureaucratic structures and hire most of India's ten million bureaucrats—often individuals with close ties to local elites. Over half of India's police work for state governments. The bureaucracy works closely with the business community and the larger landowners and merchants who dominate the *panchayati raj* (local councils) and *zila parishad* (district councils). They have contacts with New Delhi both through political party organizations and the bureaucracy. National political leaders must work closely with all such groups, who also influence recruitment to the judiciary. Supreme Court justices are chosen from among state high court judges. When Indira Gandhi, early in the 1970s, passed land reform and other legislation to aid the poor, her reforms were frequently declared unconstitutional by the Supreme Court, which accused Gandhi of interfering with property rights. Attempts to use the bureaucracy to carry out policies unfavorable to local elites can meet with resistance. Bureaucrats do not want to upset the local groups with whom they must work and from whom they need support. All these groups share a commitment to technological advance, but not necessarily advances which harm their own positions.

Nigeria's bureaucracy has greater social distance from the villages than the bureaucracies of India and Peru. But its ties to parties, the military, and businesses are strong. In Nigeria, villages are often ruled by councils composed of families who would have been king and nobles in tribal days. These councils control land distribution in the village and have good connections with bankers and political leaders in nearby towns. As the economy increasingly centered around oil production, and centrally appointed administrators took jobs in state capital cities that were formerly performed by the local aristocracy, bureaucratic power grew. The central government could collect oil revenues and pass them on to these administrators, who in turn could spend them; that increased the power of these bureaucrats, who could share oil wealth with local political leaders in return for favors. Petroleum-related businesses and urban real estate developers attracted workers to the cities, where they acquired a taste for food and goods imported by other businesses; all these businesses must pay "dash" to bureaucrats and soldiers, who also collect taxes distributed by the central government and recruit additional friends and relatives into their ranks. Under civilian rule, local political party leaders preside over these revenue distributions. Under military rule, local commanders supervise. Federal revenues returned to states often support military or party leaders (such as the administrators) with lavish homes and cars.[20] Simultaneously, local Muslim religious teachers (**mallams**) and their students, and the vast majority of the populace who are self- or unemployed, find their real income shrinking and traditional privileges impacted. With the support of the bureaucracy, unions, the business community, local political leaders, and others who share in oil income, troops repeatedly suppress frequent rioting emanating from such groups. At least five thousand people were killed in such incidents during 1991 and 1992 alone.

Bureaucracy in all three of these systems develops ties which permit it to resist reforms aiding nonparticipating portions of the populace. In Peru, India, and Nigeria, as in one-party systems, local political party leaders have close personal ties with bureaucrats capable of responding to their requests. Those same individuals have control over newspapers and interest groups in their regions, and over judicial appointments. The ties among social elites, bureaucracy, and the institutions capable of controlling bureaucracy are rigidly and tightly intertwined. Because the same circle of people controls recruitment both into bureaucracy and into the organizations capable of directing it politically and exposing its corruption, it is hard for chief executives to make and enforce laws unfavorable to that circle of people. Because the circle is likely to include leaders of major ethnic, religious, economic, and cultural groups, it is hard for their members to form independent organizations of their own. So ethnic, religious, economic, and cultural groups cannot compete and cooperate with one another in shifting patterns, as pluralism—with subordination of bureaucracy to law and to supervision by elected officeholders—would demand.

EPILOGUE

The post-Soviet republics are going through dramatic changes in their political institutions. Attempts to shift power downward, away from the old Communist Party, will bring many new institutional experiments. But, as we saw in chapter 10, 2.25 million Soviet citizens belonged to fifty thousand elected soviets. Some 15 percent of the populace was involved in street and house committees, councils, volunteer militias, comradely courts, factory brigades, and other groups which ran virtually every institution. The KGB had a million members and many additional informers. All this involvement is in addition to the full-time apparatchiki and bureaucracy.

Virtually all these people now declare themselves "reformers," just as they declared their allegiance to all prior initiatives of national leaders. They are often not keen on changing the institutions they have long been running. As long as the institutions they run remain intact, they are likely to use them to resist sharing power with other groups. When these groups are disbanded and replaced by others, the same people will join the new groups overnight, bringing along their tight social networks and lifetimes of experience at controlling meetings and institutions. It will not be easy for novice political participants to wrench power away from these individuals. When institutions change, people with influence scramble to control the new ones, as they did the old. By mid-1993, some 80 percent of top-level bureaucracy in the new republics was still composed of former Communist Party *nomenklatura;* chief executives in 11 of the 15 republics were former senior officials in the Communist Party. To counter their experience, new participants need the help of a free press, free elections to legislatures, courts which can ensure that bureaucrats obey the legislatures' laws, and safeguards for the rights of all groups to organize peacefully. These reforms can only take root if public opinion supports them. Real pluralism calls for new participants to roll up their sleeves and enter the fray.

SUMMARY

Bureaucracies accumulate power and privileges for themselves and their close associates. When one powerful unit of bureaucracy, the military, takes over the exercise of sovereignty, it can try to assist the powerless but cannot easily interfere with the privileges of the bureaucracy it relies on to implement its rule. Totalitarian leaders may use unpredictable terror for a time to squelch the power of the bureaucracy. Sometimes ordinary citizens rise in the streets to resist it. A more effective way to resist, and to assure a favorable climate for various groups to compete in, is to maintain pluralism through a free press, competitive parties, elected executives and legislatures, and free courts. If those groups do not exist, or are too closely intertwined with the bureaucracy, it is difficult for ethnic, religious, economic, and cultural groups to compete and cooperate with one another in shifting patterns as new issues arise.

NOTES

1. Jerry Hough, *The Soviet Prefects* (Cambridge, Mass.: Harvard University Press, 1969), p. 164.

2. For a discussion of competition within the Soviet bureaucracy, see Zbigniew Brzezinski and Samuel P. Huntington, *Political Power USA/USSR* (New York: Viking Press, 1964); Zbigniew Brzezinski, *Between Two Ages* (New York: Viking Press, 1970); Robert V. Daniels, "Soviet Politics Since Khrushchev," in John W. Strong, ed., *The Soviet Union Under Brezhnev and Kosygin* (New York: Van Nostrand-Reinhard, 1971); Thane Gustafson, *The Soviet Gas Campaign: Politics and Policy in Soviet Decision-making* (Santa Monica: Rand report R-3036-AF, June 1983); Susan Gross Solomon, ed., *Pluralism in the Soviet Union: Essays in Honour of H. Gordon Skilling* (London: Macmillan, 1983); Jiri Valenta and William C. Potter, eds., *Soviet Decision-making for National Security* (London: Allen & Unwin, 1984); Peter Juviler and Henry Morton, eds., *Soviet Policy Making* (New York: Praeger, 1967); J. Schwartz and W. Kiech, "Group Influence in the Policy Process in the Soviet Union," *American Political Science Review* (Sept. 1968): 840–51; "Soviet Politics in the Brezhnev Era: 'Pluralism' or 'Corporatism?' " in Donald R. Kelley, ed., *Soviet Politics in the Brezhnev Era* (New York: Praeger, 1980), pp. 1–26; Jerry Hough, *The Soviet Prefects* (Cambridge, Mass.: Harvard University Press, 1969); Jerry F. Hough, "The Soviet System: Petrification or Pluralism?" *Problems of Communism* 21, 2 (March-April 1972): 25–45; William Taubman, *Governing Soviet Cities* (New York: Praeger, 1973); Joseph LaPalombara, "Monolith or Plural Systems: Through Conceptual Glasses Darkly," *Studies in Comparative Communism* 8 (August 1975); Jerry F. Hough, *The Soviet Union and Social Science Theory* (Cambridge, Mass.: Harvard University Press, 1977); Theodore H. Friedgut, *Political Participation in the USSR* (Princeton, N.J.: Princeton University Press, 1979); and John Lowenhardt, *Decision Making in Soviet Politics* (New York: St. Martins Press, 1981).

3. Gosplan was long reluctant to divert resources into establishing a major chemical industry. Khrushchev made this a personal goal. He was successful in introducing one new plant.

4. The reforms associated with perestroika are discussed in chapter 31.

5. See A. Doak Barnett, *Cadres, Bureaucracy, and Political Power in Communist China* (New York: Columbia University Press, 1967); Paul Wong, *China's Higher Leadership in the Socialist Transition* (New York: Free Press, 1976); Martin Whyte, "Bureaucracy and Modernization in China: The Maoist Critique," *American Sociological Review* (April 1973): 149–63; David M. Lampton, *The Politics of Medicine in China: The Policy Process, 1949–1977* (Boulder: Westview Press, 1977); David M. Lampton, *Paths to Power* (Ann Arbor: University of Michigan Center for Chinese Studies, 1986); David M. Lampton, ed., *Policy Implementation in the People's Republic of China* (Berkeley: University of California Press, 1987); Benedict Stavis, *The Politics of Agricultural Mechanization in China* (Ithaca, N.Y.: Cornell University Press, 1978); and Lester Ross, *Environmental Policy in China* (Bloomington: Indiana University Press, 1988).

6. In China's long history, military officers occasionally led a popular rebellion against an empire (never simply taking over by a coup). If a military takeover was successful, a military leader became emperor and returned to civilian rule.

7. See Alfred Stepan, *The State and Society: Peru in Comparative Perspective* (Princeton, N.J.: Princeton University Press, 1978); Peter S. Cleaves and Martin Scurrah, *Agriculture, Bureaucracy, and Military Government in Peru* (Ithaca, N.Y.: Cornell University Press, 1980); and Gregory J. Kasza, "Bureaucratic Parties in Radical Military Regimes," *American Political Science Review* 81, 3 (September 1987).

8. Adolfo Figueroa, *Capital Development and the Peasant Economy in Peru* (Cambridge: Cambridge University Press, 1984).

9. See chapter 27.

10. Cynthia McClintock, "The Prospects for Democratic Consolidation in a 'Least Likely' Case," *Comparative Politics* 21, 2 (January 1989): 138–40, surveyed military officers. Seventy-five percent said democracy was "most adequate for a country such as ours," versus the 7 percent who endorsed military rule. The majority expressed fears of civil war under military rule.

11. General Olusegun Obasanjo, who succeeded Muhammed, has been accused of fixing prices and

other misconduct by human rights organizations, whom he sued for $5 million. Cliff Edogun, "The Structure of State Capitalism in the Nigerian Petroleum Industry," in Claude Ake, ed., *Political Economy of Nigeria* (London: Longman, 1985), p. 98; "'Attention!'," *The Economist*, October 26, 1991. *The Economist*, August 4, 1984, reported that during the "clean" Buhari regime, policemen checking cars for smuggled goods were seen accepting "dash" from drivers with expired licenses. The drivers threw the money into bushes. Uniformed men with submachine guns were also seen begging for food and cigarettes and accepting biscuits.

12. Colonel Gowon did pass the 1971 Indigenization Act, which gave the Nigerian National Petroleum Corporation 60 percent equity in all foreign oil companies. While the company placed Nigerians (who, together with bureaucrats in charge of the NNPC, were in a position to acquire great personal wealth) in top management, foreigners continued to manage the corporation. Under Babangida, the petroleum companies were returned to foreign ownership.

13. Larry Diamond, "Nigeria's Third Quest for Democracy," *Current History* 90, 556 (May 1991): 230.

14. Hannah Arendt, *The Origins of Totalitarianism*, new ed. (New York: Harcourt Brace Jovanovich, 1973), pp. 107–9, 316–26, distinguishes between the *people*, who are the average representatives of all classes of society, and the *mob*, which is the residue of people who have been excluded from all those classes—outcasts, revolutionaries, "armed bohemians," failures, adventurers—and which therefore hates the classes from which it has been excluded. Representatives of the mob, she contends, are those who lead totalitarianism; they try to transform the people from those who identify with various strata and classes of society into *masses* who identify only with the state and its leader.

Carl J. Friedrich, "The Evolving Theory and Practice of Totalitarian Regimes," in Carl J. Friedrich, Michael Curtis, and Benjamin R. Barber, *Totalitarianism in Perspective: Three Views* (Praeger: New York, 1969), p. 153, and Leonard Schapiro, *Totalitarianism* (Praeger: New York, 1972), p. 124, both write of totalitarian features such as an elaborate ideology, a single mass party led by one person, a system of arbitrary terror, a monopoly over mass communication and weapons, and central control and direction of the entire economy, which could exist alongside pluralist features in particular regimes. Friedrich suggests that it is difficult to keep entire regimes alive on such principles, since relatively independent army, police, and economic institutions are needed to keep a regime stable. Thus "it is quite meaningful to speak of totalitarian features in terms of more or less, and . . . it is meaningful also to speak of totalitarian trends. Such trends actually manifest themselves even in regimes which are definitely not totalitarian, such as de Gaulle's or some of the one-party systems in underdeveloped countries; indeed, they are not absent in constitutional democracies such as the United States." Schapiro emphasizes that all systems contain some totalitarian elements and that totalitarianism "is not a fixed or immutable form; it can change and evolve, as well as end in collapse and overthrow. . . . It can coexist . . . with an independent church, as in Poland . . . with dissent, incipient pressure groups and some pluralism of institutions in the Soviet Union."

15. Arthur Koestler's *Arrow in the Blue* (New York: Macmillan, 1952–54) and *Darkness at Noon* (New York: Macmillan, 1941) offer powerful insights into Stalin's actions.

16. R. H. Baker, "Clientism in the Post-Revolutionary State: The Soviet Union," in Christopher Clapham, ed., *Private Patronage and Public Power: Political Clientism in the Modern State* (London: Frances Pinter, 1982), p. 42.

17. Pavel Machala, "The Post-Communist State," *PAWSS Perspectives*, 1, 2 (December 1990): 2–3.

18. See Jonathan Unger, ed., *The Pro-Democracy Protests in China: Reports from the Provinces* (Armonk, N.Y.: M. E. Sharpe, 1991); Robert E. Gamer, "From Zig-Zag to Confrontation at Tiananmen: Tradition and Politics in China," *UFSI Field Staff Report* 1989–90, no. 10.

19. In 1984, Indira Gandhi revealed that 70 percent of the Indian Administrative Service bureaucrats worked in their state of origin, where they are more susceptible to the influence of local elites.

20. The 1992 Nigerian constitution requires that all officeholders declare their personal assets and liabilities upon taking their oath of office.

EXERCISES

Think about the book thus far:

1. What does pluralism have to do with the five characteristics that contribute to a person's influence (discussed in part 2 of the book)?
2. How do the discussions of bureaucracy and military rule in this chapter relate to the discussions of institutional interest groups in chapter 20 and of bureaucracy in chapter 22?
3. How does the discussion of bureaucracy in this chapter relate to the discussion in chapter 2?
4. What are some examples of corruption discussed in prior chapters?
5. Is totalitarianism an ideology as defined in chapter 12?

KEY WORDS AND PHRASES

Define the following terms:

corruption	merit system	pluralism
Gosplan	patronage system	totalitarian
perestroika	latifundista	mallam

Answer each of the following questions in one sentence:

1. Why is it hard for
   a. China's State Council to control provincial authorities?
   b. military rulers to control bureaucracy?
   c. Soviet chief executives to change bureaucratic procedures?
   d. Peru's chief executives to control local bureaucracy?
2. How does totalitarianism destroy group identities and group competition?
3. Why are regular rules and procedures needed for pluralism to flourish?
4. How can pluralism and totalitarianism control bureaucracy in different ways?
5. How do both the United States and China exhibit some degree of pluralism?
6. How do the bureaucracies in Peru, India, and Nigeria inhibit pluralism?

THINKING IT THROUGH

Discuss each of the following statements. Are they accurate? Why or why not?

1. A system does not necessarily become totalitarian just because the government and economy are controlled by a single mass party led by one person who does not allow opposition parties to form.
2. It is difficult for chief executives—even under military rule—to control bureaucracy, except through totalitarianism or pluralism.
3. Free political competition does not always spawn pluralism, but pluralism cannot survive without free political competition.

4. Pluralism does not mean everyone has equal influence or opportunities.

5. Pluralism cannot be achieved simply by changing election rules and the rules of operation for political institutions.

6. Some institutional arrangements work better than others to benefit people with little influence.

7. A regime that will predictably ignore the law in certain ways is less corrupt than a regime whose actions are completely unpredictable.

chapter 24

GOVERNMENT INSTITUTIONS
LAW AND PUBLIC POLICY

Chapter 23 contended that pluralism requires an independent judiciary. This chapter examines that point, and questions whether an independent judiciary can come into being without the presence of a civic culture.

Pluralism **requires an independent judiciary that impartially administers the law. An independent judiciary, in turn, requires attitudes that support pluralism.** All nine nation-states have judiciaries. All provide means for trying civil and criminal cases against individuals. All, too, handle cases in which they must make judgments about government policy. But, not all have independent or impartial judiciaries.

Since judiciaries involve trials, and trials involve issues with two sides, judiciaries always involve at least two separate units, one containing prosecutors and one containing judges. Prosecutors or procurators charge people with breaking laws and bring together the evidence needed to support the case. Judges try cases and determine punishments.

Police, which form a third unit, find and arrest lawbreakers. A penal system, sometimes part of the same unit as the police, sometimes in a separate, fourth unit, incarcerates individuals before and/or after judges pronounce sentences (terms of punishment).

Lawyers may assist individuals involved in trials. Sometimes trials involve lawsuits between two private individuals, or between an individual and a business or government. Both sides in a lawsuit usually find lawyers to represent them. Prosecutors are usually lawyers. Judges are almost always lawyers. Legal aid is sometimes available to assist defendants who cannot afford to hire a lawyer.

Trials may be held in front of a judge, who decides on cases by himself or herself, or before a jury

and judge. A jury is composed of private citizens called to serve for one trial only. The jury might make the decision as to whether the defendant is guilty or innocent, leaving it to the judge to decide the sentence. They determine whether laws have been violated—laws promulgated by executives and legislatures, and judicial precedents set by courts interpreting those laws in prior cases. In China, private citizens serve as assessors who determine guilt *and* pass sentence.

All these systems, then, use judiciaries to interpret government policy. However, not all are allowed to interpret policy in a manner which conflicts with the chief executive's wishes. Not all can protect individual freedoms against incursions by the government or other individuals, or protect the rights of citizens to organize politically. In the United States, the United Kingdom, and Germany, courts periodically hand down decisions that chief executives don't agree with or decisions that protect individual freedoms from government interference; government must comply with these decisions. The American Supreme Court and the Constitutional Courts in Germany and Russia can declare legislation unconstitutional. While the United Kingdom has no constitution, its High Court can declare that the prime minister has not properly followed the procedures dictated by law. The U.K.'s High Court bases its decisions on precedents; precedents change slowly. Similarly, the Constitution of the United States is difficult to amend;[1] it is easier to amend

Germany's Basic Law, but no amendments may be made to the portions spelling out basic civil rights and dividing the country into states.[2]

In the Soviet Union, new procedures were introduced after 1989 to protect defendants' rights in trials, but the courts did not attempt to challenge the actions of the president. The constitution could be amended simply by a two-thirds vote of the Congress of People's Deputies; it was in such a move that the Congress of People's Deputies permanently disbanded itself after the aborted 1991 coup. The constitution adopted in 1977 (to replace one written under Stalin in 1936) was amended frequently after 1988 to radically shift power from the Communist Party to the president and legislature, and from the central government to the governments of individual republics. In 1991, it was abandoned altogether as presidents of the republics declared that their republics would rule themselves.[3] Legal limits on power remain tenuous in the post-Soviet states. Russia's constitution has been amended over two hundred fifty times. When the Constitutional Court declares an act of the legislature unconstitutional, the legislature can amend the constitution.

India's Supreme Court frequently declares legislation or executive actions unconstitutional, often on the grounds that they conflict with the Fundamental Rights of citizens. The Parliament may override the Court's decision by passing a new constitutional amendment by a two-thirds vote of those present and voting in both houses. When the Peruvian courts ordered President Alan Garcia to cease nationalizing banks until he could get a formal bill through Congress, he complied by passing a formal law. Such incidents are rare in Peru; presidents are not often inclined to upset elites. A separate body, the Court of Constitutional Guarantees, determined whether individual rights guaranteed in the constitution were infringed on, and a National Judicial Council reviewed complaints against Supreme Court justices, which it could pass along to the Attorney General for investigation. That weakened the powers of the regular court system. In 1992, with the economy rapidly deteriorating and terrorism on the increase, President Fujimori suspended the constitution, dissolved the Congress, censored the press, and fired much of the judiciary. He had the backing of the army.

Nigeria adopted a constitution in 1979, ending a long period of military rule, but a military coup ended it four years later. The proposed new constitution is intended to be hard to amend,[4] but it would come into effect after more than thirty-three years of independence including only seven years of civilian rule. Nigerian courts often jail journalists or politicians for making what they consider rash statements, but usually only for a few days or weeks. The proposed constitution requires that the president and governors appoint judges; it does not indicate how long judges serve or how they may be removed. That can limit their independence by leaving their positions vulnerable to the whims of the president and governors.

As we saw in chapter 22, all these systems except the United States have formal emergency peacetime procedures to temporarily suspend the laws in some cases. Courts can interpret the extent of those powers. When Indira Gandhi's president declared an emergency between 1975 and 1977, using the procedure specified in the Indian constitution, she passed a bill through Parliament which declared "no limitation whatever on the constituent power of Parliament" to amend the constitution and stated that the courts could not declare acts of Parliament invalid.[5] These provisions were overturned after the Janata Government took power in 1977. The Supreme Court is again able to exercise judicial review, though it continues to dismiss cases which charge sitting prime ministers with personal wrongdoing. Courts in the CIS and Nigeria have not yet clearly tested their freedom to challenge other units of government. Those in China would not dare. Peru's President Fujimori arrested judges who resisted his exercise of emergency powers.

A court's freedom to censure political leaders affects its ability to root out corruption. The chief protection against corruption in China lies with the party's Central Commission for Discipline. It is easier for this commission to investigate officials at the provincial level than the national level because it has greater regular contact with leaders at the national level. It has no direct connection with the courts. The Central Committee of the Communist Party contains a Political and Legal Commission which coordinates with **procurators,** officials who decide when to make arrests and who serve as prosecutors at trials. That political party connection reduces the freedom of procurators to act independently. China has only fifty thousand lawyers, so attorneys are far from universally available to defendants. Defendants are expected to plead guilty at trials and then ask for lighter sentences in exchange for repentance. At the local level, trials are often held with untrained private citizens serving as ''assessors'' whose main purpose is to pressure people to conform to community standards. Periodically, political leaders have given orders to execute petty thieves, arsonists, embezzlers, and others (some of whom may be political dissidents) as a deterrent to crime; at other times, the same offenses draw light sentences. This system is not conducive to protecting civil liberties or allowing judicial review of government leaders' actions.[6]

The chief protection against corruption in the former Soviet Union lay in the office of the Procurator-General. This official's principal task was to fight corruption. The procurators watched not only bureaucrats, but judges and lawyers as well, for signs of impropriety. Judges did not have the power to rule over major economic disputes, to declare laws unconstitutional, or to participate in many equity cases (seeking formulas or principles to provide fairness to all parties in cases such as child custody battles, states fighting for water rights, and the like). Any legal interpretations judges made could be overruled by the Presidium of the Supreme Soviet. As legislatures of the individual republics passed new laws that openly defied national laws, the courts could not resolve the contradiction. The Procurator-General himself was hesitant to interfere with the activities of especially powerful agencies because the law itself was so unclear and subject to reinterpretation by the bureaucracy. In each of the post-Soviet republics, judicial officials remain cautious. However, while trials at the lower levels in the Soviet Union often resembled those in China, defendants are increasingly allowed to plead innocent and obtain lawyers to challenge the procurators in the newly independent republics.

The United Kingdom, the United States, and West Germany have advanced further than the other systems in giving the judicial system power to protect individuals and institutions against the power of the state.

LEGAL SAFEGUARDS FOR PEOPLE WITHOUT INFLUENCE

The real test of the strength of a judiciary is its ability to rule in favor of people without influence, even at the expense of the politically influential. Courts in China, Nigeria, the former East Germany, and the CIS republics probably do not stand up well to that test; those in India and Peru may not either. The courts in these nation-states might side with powerful private citizens when they resist executive and legislative initiatives, but not with weak minorities. If courts are to have the freedom to protect the rights of weak minorities against strong minorities, bureaucrats, and government officials, they need a political climate which encourages the rule of law.

Judiciaries are freer to uphold the law in accordance with their own judgments when constitutional guarantees and the rule of law are widely recognized by the general populace. This freedom may be enhanced when judges serve for life, rather than for limited terms followed by a reelection campaign or a search for another job.

In any case, judges have no powers of enforcement, so they must seek cooperation from other units of government. Even when judges, prosecutors, and police all cooperate, they must still seek funding, and recognition of their legitimacy, from the government agencies which create laws. Ultimately, the chief executive and bureaucracy enforce the law. Their desire to abide by and enforce the law determines how effectively the nation-state is ruled by laws. And the need for their cooperation can cause judges to treat them with care, so they will continue to cooperate.

The role local and regional party leaders play in recruiting India's and Peru's judiciaries is reflected in their courts' willingness to challenge the national legislatures and executives, while they are unwilling to interfere with the prerogatives of local elites and bureaucracies. In Nigeria, people with national connections appoint judges, which may serve to bias cases in the opposite direction—against local and regional rather than national defendants. Newspapers discuss the double standards that sometimes result. But without a broad consensus on the need to apply the law uniformly, and without widespread participation in party and interest group activity, it is difficult to change the systems.

As we have seen, public attitudes in the United States, the United Kingdom, and Germany favor upholding the rule of law. But even in these nation-states, legal protections do not always help those who lack influence. Although the judiciaries protect individual liberties, the question is whose liberties are guaranteed. Juries may favor one group over another. There may be no substitute for actually acquiring influence oneself to ensure one's liberties, or at least assuring that judiciary and other public officeholders respect a plurality of interests.

The following five characteristics of a political system might be useful in protecting limited government and individual rights. They are not always successful in protecting everyone in a nation-state.

1. *Constitutional guarantees.* If a system offers no recourse to rights under the law, an individual may be subject to the whims of government or other citizens, free commerce is not secure, weaker institutions may be excluded from the political process, and corruption can flourish. Constitutions sometimes guarantee special privileges to certain groups.[7] If these groups have little influence, equality may increase (provided the groups have enough money to take cases to court); if the groups have great influence already, constitutional guarantees of their rights may come at the expense of others and can interfere with the power of executives and legislatures to end inequalities.[8]

2. *Belief in equality.* Political cultures which believe that privilege is natural and acceptable may find it hard to spread resources among the underprivileged. A belief in equality makes it easier to broaden participation in free elections. Yet, ironically, mass publics voting in elections sometimes support candidates who advocate interfering with other groups' freedom and equality of opportunity.

3. *Willingness to compromise.* This willingness shows when one group treats another's views as equal to their own, both worthy of consideration. It is an especially helpful quality when combined with a strong belief in equality. But without a commitment to widespread equality, compromise between two groups may take place at the expense of a third group.

4. *National identity.* A sense of national identity can help promote a spirit of willingness to help all sectors of the nation-state. But it can also lead to blind nationalistic appeals whose symbolism diverts people from noticing inequalities and injustices. Either approach may be refuted in court decisions.

5. *Partitioning of power and federalism.* Partitioning sovereignty among several governmental units increases the number of points at which groups may approach government and seek action. One unit of government can extend the liberties another denies. On the other hand, partitioning can also render ineffective enforcement of the laws. In upholding the principle of separation, courts may defend the privileged against political leaders who attempt to restrict privilege, or vice versa.

A strong, independent judiciary is necessary to preserve freedoms over time. In making its decisions, however, a judiciary has the power to expand or restrict freedoms. It can shift the definition of freedoms and limit the power of legislatures and executives to act in support of popular initiatives. It can protect groups deprived of resources and freedoms, and deprive groups of resources and freedoms they already have.

Ultimately, the preservation of liberties depends on the attitudes and involvement of citizens. Judges reflect their cultures. Their willingness to take on powerful forces in defense of a legal principle depends on the support they will receive from political leaders and the populace.

CONCLUSION

In chapter 18, we suggested that when high percentages of citizens in a nation-state are assimilated into modern economic and political institutions, and share a sense of national identity, a belief in equality, and a belief in legal protections for both groups and individuals against the power of the state, that nation-state's ability to reach mutually beneficial compromises is enhanced. This chapter raised some cautions about the potential benefits of such beliefs. However, the dangers of not having such qualities and beliefs are much greater.

When a nation-state does not have a broad sharing of beliefs in freedom and equality, weak groups must depend on friends in high places—top officeholders who believe in helping the weak—to protect them. Those top officeholders are surrounded by bureaucracy which seeks to divert goods, services, and protection of rights to itself and its friends, despite officeholders' intentions to benefit the weak. And, of course, some of those top officials might not care about the weak and therefore cannot be relied on to protect them.

In such a situation, weak groups might turn to free elections, a free press, competitive parties and interest groups, and constitutional guarantees to protect them. The competition between different institutions and groups, however, may give advantages to those who know how to and are able to participate in using them; those participants may then use them to harm the weak, rather than help them. Unless

there is public support for guaranteeing and enforcing the laws which define how competition takes place, freedom-enhancing institutional arrangements may not last, or the system may exclusively admit into participation those the powerful favor.

Only those assimilated into the modern economy are likely to develop attributes which give them the capacity to participate in politics effectively. Only when wide portions of the populace identify with the nation and feel that all citizens have an equal right to participate in its politics and its benefits, and that all citizens and leaders of the state should be both protected by laws and expected to abide by them, is there strong assurance that political institutions will stay intact and laws will be enforced. That gives the weak a fighting chance. They still may lose battles, but they also may find on occasion a champion to take on their case, using the legislature, the press, and the courts to push it through.

In the United States, the United Kingdom, and West Germany, high percentages of the populace are assimilated and share such beliefs. In India, Peru, and Nigeria, few are assimilated and few share them. These nation-states cannot change the situation by adopting new rules for running elections and political institutions. It can only change if political and economic assimilation—and widespread attitudes—also change.

SUMMARY

Individual liberties depend on an independent judiciary. To be effective, an independent judiciary must be supported by influential people who believe in an independent judiciary and in laws which protect individual liberties. This is essential—but not sufficient in itself—to protect individual liberties. If individual liberties cannot be protected, even against the power of the state, the rights of many people to compete in politics and secure a livelihood will be in jeopardy.

NOTES

1. Amendments to the U.S. Constitution must be proposed by two-thirds of each house of Congress, or by a convention called by two-thirds of the state legislatures; proposed amendments must be ratified by the state legislatures of (or conventions in) three-fourths of the fifty states.

2. Amendment of the Basic Law requires a two-thirds vote in both the Bundestag and the Bundesrat. Between 1949 and 1985, it was amended thirty-one times; reunification brought further minor amendments. The East German Constitution could be amended by a simple majority of the Volkskammer.

3. President Gorbachev called the Supreme Soviet into session to formally vote the Soviet Union out of existence, but only a handful of members turned up for this final vote.

4. Amendments to the proposed Nigerian constitution require approval by two-thirds to three-fourths of the members of both houses of the national legislature, and a majority of the legislators in two-thirds of the state legislatures.

5. Michael Henderson, "Setting India's Democratic House in Order: Constitutional Amendments," *Asian Survey* 19, 10 (October 1979).

6. See Susan Ogden, *China's Unresolved Issues: Politics, Development, and Culture* (Englewood Cliffs, N.J.:

Prentice-Hall, 1989), pp. 187–234; Robert C. Goodwin, Jr., "The Evolving Legal Framework," *The China Business Review* (May-June, 1983): 42–44; and Alan P. L. Liu, *How China Is Ruled* (Englewood Cliffs, N.J.: Prentice-Hall, 1986), pp. 179–87.

7. Aristotle wrote: "Rightly constituted laws should be the final sovereign. . . . But what rightly constituted laws ought to be is a matter that is not yet clear; and . . . law itself may have a bias in favor of one class or another. . . . The one clear fact is that laws must be constituted in accordance with constitutions." Ernest Barker, *The Politics of Aristotle* (New York: Oxford University Press, 1958), p. 127.

8. James Madison's Federalist Paper #10 states: "The latent causes of faction [which] are thus sown in the nature of man . . . have . . . inflamed them with mutual animosity, and rendered them much more disposed to vex and oppress each other than to cooperate for their common good . . . a body of men are unfit to be both judges and parties at the same time; yet what are many of the most important acts of legislation but so many judicial determinations. . . . And what are the different classes of legislators but advocates and parties to the causes which they determine . . . the most powerful faction must be expected to prevail."

EXERCISES

Think about the book thus far:

1. How does the topic of this chapter—the judiciary and people's attitudes toward it—relate to political culture?

2. Compare the conclusion and summary at the end of this chapter, the epilogue and summary at the end of chapter 23, and the final paragraphs and summary at the end of chapter 22. What does each passage say about public opinion and the law?

3. What do the summaries at the end of chapters 17, 19, 20, and 21 tell us about why some systems have widened participation and others have narrowed it?

4. What do all these chapters say about how political culture affects institutions?

KEY WORDS AND PHRASES

Define the following term:

procurator

Answer each of the following questions in one sentence:

1. How do the roles of prosecutors and judges differ?
2. How may courts limit executives and legislatures?
3. In which of the nine nation-states do judiciaries have the power to set such limits?
4. How can a judiciary's inability to enforce laws affect its judgment about cases?

THINKING IT THROUGH

Illustrate your answers to the following questions with information about specific countries:

1. In chapters 6 and 12, we talked about a civic culture. A civic culture is characterized by
   a. a substantial consensus on the legitimacy of political institutions and the direction and content of public policy,
   b. a widespread tolerance of a plurality of interests and belief in their reconcilability, and
   c. a widely distributed sense of political competence and mutual trust in the citizenry.

   Chapter 14 discusses national identity. Is that needed for characteristic *a* to develop?
   Chapter 15 discusses a belief in equality. Is that needed for characteristic *a* to develop?
   Chapter 16 discusses acceptance of authority. Is that needed for characteristic *a* to develop?
   Chapter 17 discusses belief in legal protections. Is that needed for characteristic *c* to develop?

   Chapter 18 discusses assimilation into economic and political institutions. When influence is widely distributed among ethnic, religious, economic, and cultural groups, which cooperate and conflict with one another in shifting patterns as new issues arise, and government provides a favorable climate for this to occur, a political system exhibits *pluralism* (discussed in chapter 23). Does pluralism depend on large portions of a populace being assimilated?

   If large portions of the populace are not assimilated, can pluralism be achieved by creating rules which allow free competitive elections, independent organization of political parties and interest groups, a free press, and courts with the power to reverse decisions made by bureaucratic units and chief executives when they conflict with the laws? Can these rules be enforced? Can they help those not assimilated? Would it help if officeholders have civic culture attitudes?

2. Can officeholders in a system without free elections or pluralism develop and use civic culture attitudes to protect those who are not assimilated? How will bureaucratic corruption affect advantages those attitudes might bring to the unassimilated?

3. When a system lacks pluralism and a civic culture, are some institutional arrangements (of parties, interest groups, and government institutions) more likely than others to distribute goods and rights fairly? Think about the pros and cons of one-party, two-party, parliamentary, presidential, and military-rule systems in this regard.

4. Among these nine systems, are the United States, the United Kingdom, and the Federal Republic of Germany in the best position to distribute goods and rights fairly? Why or why not? Are India, Peru, and Nigeria in the worst position to do so? What about China and the CIS? Explain your answers.

part 4

INFLUENCE AND PEOPLE'S LIVES

Parts 2 and 3 discussed who acquires influence, how, and the ways influence is exerted within the various institutional arrangements of these political systems. Now we shall look at how people actually live in these countries. We shall look at four aspects of human existence: degree of equality in the distribution of material goods, jobs, and other benefits; amount of freedom; protection of the environment; and personal and national security. Then we will discuss how influence, political culture, and political institutions may affect these conditions. Are some systems better for people than others?

chapter 25

EQUALITY

MATERIAL WELL-BEING

In part 3, we concluded that some political arrangements and beliefs might serve better than others to help citizens receive the rewards they seek. In part 4, we shall see whether some of the nine countries actually distribute rewards better than others. We begin in this chapter with the most basic rewards people seek—food, clothing, shelter, health care, and consumer goods.

For two dozen chapters, we have been looking at the political systems of several countries. We turn now to examining how people actually live in these countries. In this chapter, we ask, **Do the people in all these systems have food, housing, health care, and consumer goods commensurate with their needs and desires?** In the next chapter, we will examine whether they have equal opportunity to develop skills and to achieve higher earnings and social mobility with improved performance.

FOOD

A century ago, food production was abundant in both the United States and Russia. In the United States, much of that abundance was consumed at home; in Russia, much of it was exported. American farmers and townspeople ate better than their Russian counterparts.

Today the CIS countries are net importers of grain, while the United States both feeds its citizens and exports surplus grain. Soviet citizens generally ate better than their ancestors did a century earlier. They got adequate amounts of grain in their diet; bread was readily available at low prices supported by heavy government subsidies. Meat and dairy products were often in short supply and thus were

During the nineteenth century, much land in the Ukraine and other productive growing regions was used to raise wheat, cotton, and other crops to export to other countries. When Russia's grain production in the Ukraine and Siberia was modernized, grain exports tripled. The most prosperous farmers were Great Russians who had crossed the Urals to take lands from other nationalities. Districts supplying only their own internal consumption were not modernized. After Tsar Alexander II freed Russia's serfs in 1861, peasants were taxed heavily. They often had the poorest land. They could not easily leave land fallow to replenish it and also afford seeds and equipment. About a fourth were without a horse for plowing, transportation, and fertilizer. Peasants had little part in the money economy, and their consumption was low, though Emancipation did give them somewhat more buying power. In 1904, annual per capita consumption of cotton in Russia was 5.3 pounds, versus 39 in Britain and 20.4 in the United States. In 1897, per capita consumption of kerosene in Russia was 11.2 pounds, versus 41.8 pounds in Germany. Russians were consuming 10.5 pounds of sugar apiece, versus 92 in Britain. A high percentage of workers' income went for food.

sometimes rationed; because of subsidies and selling through state stores, meat sold at less than half the cost of production, but one waited in long lines to obtain it, and quality was generally low. Meat from private markets was of better quality, though much more expensive.[1] Soviet families all generally spent half or more of their income for food. When prices were freed in 1992, that percentage rose. Americans spend about an eighth of their income on food.[2] Figure 25.1 summarizes comparisons in daily and annual consumption and in the import-export ratios for different nation-states.

You can see from figure 25.1 that caloric intake is also high in the United Kingdom and Germany. Meat and eggs cost about twice as much (in terms of minutes worked to earn them) in East Germany as in West Germany, and the meat was of much lower quality. Bread and potatoes (subsidized by the government) cost less in East Germany than in West Germany, and milk and vegetables were also plentiful. There was no variety. Since reunification, the quality and selection of food has greatly increased, while price increases have been moderate. West Germans spend about a fourth of income on food, tobacco, and beverages.[3]

Note that average calorie consumption is lower by a third or more in China, India, and Nigeria, and still lower in Peru. China and India are both self-sufficient in grain production, but in China[4] grain is more equitably distributed than in India.[5] China has extensive government programs to help people buy food; India has no regular programs for this. It is commonly argued that about half of Indians have insufficient income to sustain an adequate diet, though some scholars place as little as 15 percent of the populace in that category.[6] Nigeria's average per capita caloric consumption has hovered just above the World Health Organization's minimal standard of 2080 per day ever since 1960, but the portion of both protein and fat in that diet has been declining. Between 20 and 40 percent of the rural population, and between 10 and 20 percent of urban dwellers, consume below the WHO standard.[7] Grain imports rose from 106,000 tons in 1968 to 2.3 million tons in 1984.

During the 1987 drought, Gujarati peasants in India had to sell their cattle to keep them from dying—a last resort to a Hindu. This left them without milk, crops, or animals to plow future crops. Meanwhile, the government gave assistance to landowners with irrigation (which lowers the water table for adjoining farms) and released 23 million tons of grain (potentially, 60 pounds per person in India) from emergency warehouses run by bureaucrats closely affiliated with those landowners, who were thus in a position to hoard all food supplies until prices soar. Then it spent about 1.6 billion U.S. dollars (2 U.S. dollars per Indian) to buy grain on the open market to distribute. Whole regions were without any crops at all; the government called it the worst drought of the century. In years without famine, there are no government programs to cope with high food costs and malnutrition.

Few Indian workers, even in white collar jobs, earn over 50 rupees ($1.90) a day; many manual laborers earn 7 to 15 rupees (25 to 50 cents) for a twelve-hour workday. A very basic meal consisting of unleavened bread with some ground vegetables and yogurt costs at least 2 rupees (8 cents), so feeding three such meals a day to a family of five would take 30 rupees. Even after a day of heavy toil by several family members, many cannot afford to eat that much. In addition, many men are alcoholics (as many as 90 percent in some villages).[8] Village-brewed arrack and toddy claim much of their wages; a bottle of whiskey costs about 30 rupees.

Peru produces about half a pound of grain per capita per day; that is much less than India's 1.5 pounds and China's 2.3.[9] It imports about four-tenths of a pound of grain per capita per day. Nutrition levels are constantly declining due to lower per capita production of food (down 24 percent between 1970 and 1985) and declining personal income.[10] Between 1970 and 1981, food production grew 13 percent, while population grew 36 percent;[11] in that period average caloric intake per person declined by a fourth. In the mountains, 54 percent of families have a calorie intake, and 43 percent a protein intake,

Figure 25.1   Differences in food production and consumption. (a) Each bar indicates total daily per capita calorie consumption, 1980–83. Shaded areas indicate daily per capita calories from meat, 1980–83. (b) Annual meat consumption in selected nations. (c) Grain imports and exports for USA and USSR.

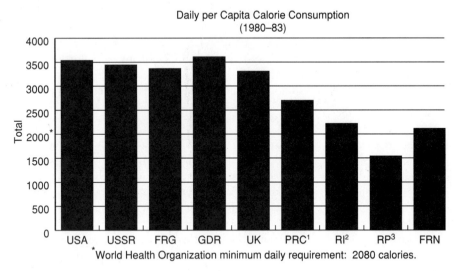

Daily per Capita Calorie Consumption
(1980–83)

*World Health Organization minimum daily requirement: 2080 calories.

*Figures not available.

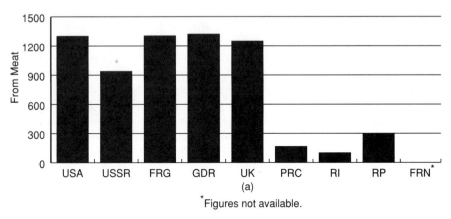

(a)

Meat Consumption (in annual pounds per capita)	
USA	207[4]
USSR	123
PRC	39[5]

(b)

Grain Imports & Exports (in million metric tons)		
	Imports	Exports
USA	.2	93.9
USSR	20.2[6]	2.4

(c)

[1]1983. Vaclav Smil, "China's Food," *Scientific American* (December 1985): 119,122. In 1985, production of meat, fish, vegetables, oil-bearing plants, and sugar was up substantially. From 1978–85, annual per capita consumption of grain jumped 28 percent to 554 pounds, edible oil consumption nearly tripled to ten pounds, and pork consumption rose 70 percent to 28 pounds. Robert Delfs, "Collective Efforts are Overwhelming State Enterprise," *Far Eastern Economic Review (FEER)* 131, 12 (March 20, 1986): 77–78.

[2]1983.

[3]1980, down from 2,031 calories in 1974. Thomas G. Sanders, "Peru's Population in the 1980s," *University Field Staff International Reports (UFSIR)* 27 (1984): 8.

[4]*Kansas City Star*, October 23, 1980, USA and USSR.

[5]1988. *China Statistical Abstract 1990 (CSA90)*.

[6]1978, the year when the Soviet Union began its policy of making up for shortfalls in grain production by imports, saw one of the best Soviet grain harvests in years. Since then, grain imports have ranged from 25 to 55 million tons per year. Rick Atkinson, "Grain is the Tie That Binds U.S.-Soviets," *KCT*, November 20,1982. *KCS*, March 30,1986. *KCT*, July 1, 1987. In 1981, a Soviet Central Committee study leaked estimates that 20 percent of the Soviet Union's grain, fruit, and vegetable harvest, and up to 50 percent of its potato crop, is lost each year from late harvest and poor storage, transportation, and distribution. Part of the problem with the potatoes is the overuse of nitrates as fertilizer to meet production quotas, producing potatoes that rot easily. Some 11 to 12 million tons of grain are also used annually to produce vodka. *Department of State Bulletin (DOSB)* 85 (September 1985): 71. Rick Atkinson, "Soviet Agriculture: An Unfulfilled Promise," *KCT*, November 15, 1982.

One-fourth of Soviet farms have no roads connecting them with rural centers. There are virtually no frozen foods, and only peas, fish, and stewed fruit are commonly available in cans. Robert Gillette, "Creaking Economy Needs More Than a Little Repair," *KCT*, November, 26, 1987.

below prescribed minimums; a 1971–72 study found 29 percent of coastal children under the age of six, and 40 percent of mountain children, to be malnourished.[12]

From 1980 to 1985, Peru's inflation averaged 80 percent and more a year. The devaluation of the currency that accompanied this raised the cost of imports. During the 1970s, the military government began subsidizing the cost of rice, the principal staple cereal in the cities. During the 1980s, the cost of those subsidies rose so high that they were considerably reduced, and then dropped altogether in 1990 to be replaced by government-sponsored (and often nonexistent) free soup kitchens for the seven million poor. Thus, Peru has faced constantly rising food prices coupled with steady unemployment and low wages. By repudiating repayment of Peru's international debt (discussed in part 5) and reemphasizing oil production, price controls, and government subsidies, the government of President Alan Garcia reduced inflation and raised incomes from 1985 to 1987; when government assets were depleted, the economy went out of control, and inflation had reached 3,000 percent by the time Alberto Fujimori took office in 1990. Within a year he lowered inflation to 150 percent, but a recession began that left only 5 to 10 percent of the work force fully employed— and at fixed wages amid the rampant inflation.[13] That left a third of the populace living on less than 30 U.S. dollars a month, though it would take 417 U.S. dollars a month to adequately feed a family of four.[14]

INCOME

In the Soviet Union, a number of black marketeers became millionaires.[15] By one estimate, only 2.3 percent of Soviet citizens could be called wealthy, and only 0.7 percent of those earned their income lawfully.[16] East Germany had about one hundred legal millionaires, while West Germany had about eighteen thousand. The new joint ventures in China offer the chance for some party officials and others to become very wealthy. During the 1980s, the United

States had one hundred thousand new millionaires every year;[17] in 1986, 28.5 percent of America's wealth was in the hands of 3.3 million people (about 0.5 percent of families with a combined net worth of $3.8 trillion.[18] Top managers in major American firms earn between forty and ninety-five times the incomes of the average worker, versus twenty-three to twenty-five times in Germany and thirty-five in Britain.[19] By 1976, 10 percent of West Germany's adults owned 50 percent of its productive capital.[20]

Konstantin Simis, a lawyer in the Soviet Union, defended dozens of underground millionaires in court. Typically, they were managers of publicly owned plants making artificial leather goods, knitwear, shoes, sunglasses, records, bags, costume jewelry, and the like. They undersized the goods they were making for official purposes, and shorted them on dye, beads, and other raw materials. They then paid their workers higher wages to make goods for the black market and sold these goods under-the-counter to clerks in public retail stores. Party and public officials were bribed to look the other way. In this manner, families could amass hundreds of millions of rubles. They might dress simply and even make duplicate meals (of poor food) in their public housing flats so as not to rouse suspicion; if they were on good enough terms with the entire local party hierarchy, they might live in an elegant home and invite party officials to banquets. Most were Jewish, carrying on trades long familiar to them; many were barred from rising as high as they otherwise could have in professions and party life. After being caught for their illegal business activities, they were sentenced to fifteen years or more of hard labor, or death.[21]

Money does not constitute the only form of remuneration. A million or fewer[22] top *nomenklatura* in the CIS, like those in China and the former East Germany, have access to much better housing than is available to average workers; they also receive bonuses for surpassing production quotas, special vacation pay, and chauffeured automobiles, can shop at special stores with subsidized prices on goods unavailable to most of the populace, have access to special restaurants and health clinics, may send their children to the top universities, and have other privileges that, in reality, considerably increase their pay and that of their offspring. The Soviets who held about twenty-three thousand top ministerial and party posts could derive incomes above a thousand rubles ($1,400) a month, with access to limousines, luxurious estates in the countryside,[23] and other perquisites which place their living standards far above average. Today, these types of individuals are well-positioned to take advantage of free market business opportunities in all three of those systems.

Extra benefits may also add to the incomes of those not at lower levels of the earning scales. In the United States and Western Europe, many employees receive retirement, health, and other compensations in addition to their regular pay. In both East and West Germany, many factories supplied kindergartens, clinics, holiday facilities (1.6 million package holidays in East Germany in 1976), apartments (or help in getting one), and other services for many of their workers; the quality of such benefits was markedly higher in the West. West German workers receive an average of two months paid leave annually. Every year Soviet factories and youth organizations rewarded workers who performed according to plan by sending several million adults on vacations and several million children to camp free or at subsidized rates (while leaving many million others at home).[24] Profits from collective farms and factories are partly used to build recreation centers for the workers. In the United States, millions of families have incomes high enough to take such vacations and engage in recreation on their own. "Private" plots of land on state and collective farms provide about a third of income for rural Soviet citizens.[25]

Chinese working for government or state industries receive labor insurance, welfare, medical care, social security, housing, ration coupons, meal service, child care, food rations, paid leaves, bonuses, loans, and other services through their place of work.

Some elements of society are less prosperous than others. A 1966 study, for instance, found that peasants in Estonia had incomes at 191 percent of the Soviet Union's national average, while the incomes of Tajikistan peasants were at 61 percent of the national average;[26] that imbalance continues among the post-Soviet republics.

In 1984, the net worth (possessions minus debts) of the typical white American household ($39,135) was twelve times greater than that of a black household ($3,397) and eight times greater than that of a hispanic household ($4,913).[27] In 1989, nearly half of rural black American households (mostly in the South) lived in poverty,[28] as did 40 percent of black and 32 percent of hispanic children.[29] By 1991, 35.7 million Americans (mostly white) lived in poverty.[30] Between 1985 and 1992, the number of Americans suffering from hunger rose from 20 million to 30 million.[31]

The United Kingdom has some entire regions (and cities, such as Liverpool) that are economically depressed, as well as neighborhoods of citizens who are living in an impoverished state,[32] but it also has more programs to aid the poor than the United States does.[33] About 2.5 million people from various parts of the Commonwealth—notably South Asia, Africa, and the West Indies—have moved to England; many are economically disadvantaged.[34] West Germany has about 2 million foreign workers. They and their families live crowded together in the worst sections of cities, paying high rents; they are provided some social services such as government-sponsored health care.[35] In 1992, most of West Germany enjoyed a Gross Domestic Product (GDP) of $23,800 per person, while the GDP for most of East Germany was $8,000 per person.[36]

Because the western parts of China (where ethnic minorities predominate) are less urbanized and have benefitted less from sales to urban markets than the eastern regions, the disparity of income between those two portions of China has increased.[37] Average 1989 per capita income in the coastal city of Shanghai was seven times that of the southern inland province of Guizhou and urban incomes continue to grow faster than rural incomes.[38]

All these countries have a number of unemployed citizens. The Soviet Union once guaranteed

A report issued in 1986 by the Harvard University School of Public Health identified 150 "hunger counties" across the United States with high rates of malnutrition and low government assistance. A 1987 report from this same source estimated that about 24 million Americans— mainly blue collar workers whose job status had been reduced, children, and the elderly—suffered from inadequate food intake. A 1986 study by a lobbying group, Public Voice, funded by the Ford Foundation, identified 13.5 million rural poor (36 percent more than in 1979) who were seriously malnourished, suffered disproportionate rates of infant death (with a rising infant mortality rate) and stunted growth (also impairing learning abilities), and received little government assistance. They listed the 85 poorest counties, mostly in the south, the far north, Appalachia, the Ozarks, the Rio Grande, and on Indian reservations. They found the numbers of poor to be larger and their nutritional problems more severe than among their urban counterparts. Public Voice also identified 12.9 million urban poor.

In the United States, one out of eight adults and one out of four children were living below the poverty level in terms of income (that is, they had, at the time of the study, a combined family income of less than $11,580 for a family of four, before taxes and benefits were counted). In 1990, 9 percent of births in the United States were to unmarried teenage mothers. Studies indicate that 96 percent of teenage mothers keep their babies, rather than releasing them for adoption. Fewer than half of these mothers finish high school. One study reported that 96 of every 1,000 American teenage girls becomes pregnant.[39]

A 1987 study (*The People, the Land, and the Church*) by the Church of England's Hereford diocese, which involved two thousand rural consultants in several regions of England, concluded that 25 percent of rural families there were living at or below poverty levels. None of the regions examined were in the extreme north and west, where poverty is even more serious. One Herefordshire village lost more than 50 percent of its five- to fifteen-year-olds because their parents could not find employment; they left the area, leaving grandparents to fend for themselves. Many of the poor live in remote cottages, away from sources of social services. A 1990 study found 63 percent more people in the north living at below half of average income than in the southeast. And unemployment among males in urban housing estates is often four times the national average—as high as 25 to 30 percent.[40]

everyone jobs for life; now, in the post-Soviet republics, unemployment is increasing. A third of Russians now live below the poverty line.[41] Six to 12 percent of the work force in the United States is usually unemployed. East Germany had negligible unemployment; since reunification, a third or more of the populace has become unemployed or semiemployed as Germany copes with the economic transition.[42] Even before reunification, West Germany had begun to experience a rising unemployment rate.[43] Unemployment levels of around 10 percent of the work force have become endemic in the United Kingdom;[44] government benefits accounted for 96 percent of the 1985 gross incomes of the poorest 20 percent of United Kingdom households.[45] A growing portion of China's labor force cannot find work.[46]

The only study comparing Western incomes (after government benefits and taxes) with communist-country incomes (including all the kinds of extra benefits discussed) found that the top 10 percent of individual income earners in the Soviet Union earned 8.5 times as much as the bottom 10 percent.[47] In the United States, that ratio was 9.9, in the United Kingdom 4.7, and (for household incomes) in East Germany, 6. Using data derived from different sources, we can get an idea of how the top fifth of wage earners compare with the bottom fifth in several of these countries when taxes and benefits are not included (see table 25.1). Because the sources and time frames involved vary widely, and for other reasons explained in the footnotes, it is better not to directly compare one country with another on this chart. But the figures do show that there is a definable range between the lowest and highest fifths of the populace in terms of earnings.

Table 25.1

Comparison of High and Low Earnings in Different Nation-States (in U.S. dollars)

| | Average Incomes | | |
	Highest Fifth	Lowest Fifth	Ratio
USA	$94,101[1]	$9,133	9 times[2]
USSR	9,380[3]	2,345	4 times[4]
UK	35,680	2,300[5]	15 times
FRG	22,900	4,570[6]	5 times
GDR	10,900	3,660[7]	3 times[8]

Note: This data was generally compiled by estimating the number of wage earners in a country, dividing that number by five, and then averaging the total amount of money earned by that fifth of wage earners in a year.

[1] 1986. *Kansas City Star (KCS),* November 7, 1988. *Information Please Almanac* (IPA) reports United States 1987 per capita income at $15,340. In 1987, the Census Bureau reported $12,287 per capita income, $13,031 ($15,265 by 1990) for whites and $7,499 ($9,017 by 1990) for blacks. By 1990, median *family* income before taxes and benefits was (according to the Council of Economic Advisors) $35,353.

[2] In 1986, versus eight times in 1982 and seven times in 1979. During the 1980s, the top fifth of American families increased their earnings by an average of $9,000 to $85,000 (adjusting for inflation; that is, figuring the totals in 1980 dollars), while the bottom fifth declined $576 to $8,880. The annual report of the House Ways and Means Committee on entitlement programs, the 1991 "Green Book," reports that between 1980 and 1989, the lowest three-fifths of families lost $600 to $800 in after-tax income, while the next highest fifth gained $1,700 and the top fifth gained $18,000. David S. Broder, "Bush 'Good Society' Vision Could In Fact Be Dangerous," *KCS,* May 20, 1991. Just 660,000 families (the top 1 percent, with $506 billion of income in 1989) got 60 percent of that gain. *Newsweek,* March 16, 1992.

According to the U.S. Census Bureau, in 1976 the top 20 percent of U.S. citizens had 41.1 percent of all income, the next fifth 24.1 percent, the next 17.6 percent, the next 11.8 percent, and the lowest 5.4 percent. By 1991, the top fifth had 46.5 percent, and the lowest fifth only 3.8 percent, of income. The Congressional Budget Office estimates that between 1977 and 1992, the top fifth gained 32 percent and the next fifth 2 percent in income,

while the middle fifth lost 7 percent, the next lowest lost 10 percent, and the lowest fifth lost 13 percent (in constant 1992 dollars, before taxes and benefits).

[3] *KCS,* November 7, 1988. *Kansas City Times,* June 29, 1987, reported average annual 1987 income in the USSR to be $3,700; the 1991 *World Almanac (WA),* $3000.

[4] In the late 1960s and 1970s, some of the wages of lower-paid occupations in the USSR rose faster than higher-echelon categories. In 1970, urban incomes exceeded farm incomes (including private plots) by 25 percent; in 1980, by around 10 percent. D. Gale Johnson, "Agricultural Productivity in the Soviet Union," *Current History* (October 1985): 321. Morrisson's figures are for 1973; the gap is 4.8 times if extra benefits are included.

[5] In ranking household incomes, Christian Morrisson found the top fifth in Britain had an average after-tax income 4.8 times that of the bottom fifth, based on 1978 figures. Christian Morrisson, "Income Distribution in East European and Western Countries," *Journal of Comparative Economics* 8, 2 (June 1984): 121–38. These 1985 figures bear that out; the $24,720 after-tax income of the top fifth is 4.6 times that of the after-benefits income of the bottom fifth. As these figures show, the disparity before taxes and benefits can be much greater.

A British government study found that average 1985 income for the lowest fifth of households was $2,300 before taxes and benefits and $5,420 after. For the top fifth, it was $35,680 and $24,720. The top fifth had 44 percent of pretax (38 percent after-tax) income in 1975, and 49 percent (41 percent after-tax) in 1985. The poorest fifth had 0.8 percent (6.6 percent) in 1975 and 0.3 percent (6.5 percent) in 1985; after government benefits, 7.1 percent in 1975 and 6.7 percent in 1985. Total income rose considerably during the period. Sarah Hogg, "Forty-Nine Percent of Income Goes to Top Fifth of Households," *The Independent,* August 18, 1987. *IPA* reports 1985 per capita income at $8,380.

[6] *KCS,* November 7, 1988, based on 1983 figures. *WA* gives per capita income for West Germany at $9,450 in 1985, $19,750 in 1988. Meanwhile, the exchange rate moved from 3.09 to 1.67 deutschmarks to the dollar.

[7] *KCS,* November 7, 1988, reflecting 1983 figures. *WA* reports 1984 per capita income of $8,000 (at a rate of exchange of 3.09 mark to $1.00), and $10,000 in 1987 (at 1.67 mark to the dollar).

[8] Without adjusting for extra benefits Morrisson showed the top fifth portion of East German households in 1972 earning 3.5 times that of the bottom fifth. With that adjustment, the ratio was 4.1.

The West German deutschmark was traded on international exchanges and worth its exchange rate. The East German mark was not traded at official exchanges but was claimed to be worth the same as the West German deutschmark. On the black market, one could obtain several East German marks for one West German deutschmark. So, in reality, East Germans were receiving pay several times lower than West German workers. When reunification took place in 1990, the West German government decided to set the official rate at two East German marks for one West German deutschmark. People who retained their jobs in the East continued to be paid the same amount in terms of marks, but received half as many deutschmarks instead. Their pay scales have been rising to about 70 percent of West Germans' pay.

It is also hard to compare Soviet incomes with those in the United States or other parts of the world. Soviet statistics were notoriously unreliable. And, until 1992, rubles could not be traded on international currency markets. The official exchange rate always made the ruble more valuable than the dollar, with the dollar exchanging for less than one ruble; one could obtain many rubles for a dollar on the black market. To confuse matters further, rates varied according to the type of transaction; some goods and services were valued at different rates than others. Foreigners visiting the Soviet Union had to pay for most services in dollars. In 1991, the official rate was .58 rubles to the dollar, commercial rates were generally 1.76 rubles to the dollar, and the government competed with the black market by letting banks give tourists 27.6 rubles to the dollar, with almost daily adjustments to keep even with the black market, which gave 32 rubles to the dollar. To pay its bills, the government rolled new rubles off the printing press. By the time the ruble could be freely converted in international markets, in January 1992, rubles exchanged at about 100 to the dollar; by 1993, the rate was 650 rubles to a dollar, and inflation exceeded 2,000 percent a year. Even though wages kept rising, this left workers making about five U.S. dollars a month. Those wages bought 40 percent less than the lower wages a year earlier—so real income dropped. Many people have taken to selling goods at weekend markets, where they may average 100 rubles or more an hour of supplementary income. Only 1 percent had incomes over 10,000 rubles (about fifteen dollars) a month.

Because of government subsidies, bread still costs 5¢ a loaf, and a three-room apartment a dollar a month. Chicken legs cost 65¢ a pound, an orange 25¢, sturgeon $6 a pound, a bottle of vodka 50¢, and a German refrigerator $1,000. Just bread and housing can easily use up a quarter of a family's income, even with those subsidies. Ten thousand rubles of savings—enough to buy a car in 1992—would buy one ticket to see the Bolshoi ballet in 1993.[48]

During the 1970s, China's economy experienced a 3.3 percent annual growth rate; between 1981 and 1991, annual growth was above 7 percent and by 1993 surpassed 15 percent. This was at a time when the economies in East Germany and the Soviet Union were stagnating. China experienced inflation exceeding 20 percent a year, but wages and peasant earnings rose faster than that.[49] The purchasing power of the Chinese was on the rise. Since 1992, rural incomes have been rising more slowly than either prices or urban incomes, and unemployment continues to rise; growing economies create imbalances.

As you can see from table 25.1 and its footnotes, the difference between three and fifteen times between the upper and lower fifths is hard to compare and depends to a great degree on how the data is measured; inflation, and exchange rates among currencies, can make the data fluctuate quickly. But these differences between top and bottom are minor compared to the situation in the other three countries. Disparities of income and living standards are far greater in India, Peru, and Nigeria, than in the nation-states on table 25.1, or in China. The United Nations Development Program estimates that in 1992 the fifth of the world's populace in countries with the highest per capita incomes earned 60 times more than those in the lowest fifth.

A 1953–54 survey in India reported that seventy thousand urban Indians had annual incomes over $2,500 (in U.S. dollars). Some three-hundred thousand earned between $720 and $2,500. An additional 6 million, designated as lower middle-class, earned in a range below $720 a year. Everyone else—over 440 million people in a country which already had over 450 million people—earned less than that.[50] Since then, wages have risen; but official surveys still show that a fourth of India's populace lives below the poverty line.[51] Because of the Green Revolution, larger landowners, and some with only three or four acres, can earn more income than they did before; a fourth to half comes from government subsidies, and much of it may go to repay loans. Professionals, some bureaucrats, and small businesses producing agricultural equipment and services benefit. But landowners who formerly let their land be sharecropped have now turned to mechanization, and they no longer need the sharecroppers or much seasonal labor; those without land, or with inadequate land, can find little income.

In Indian towns, mechanization of industries also reduces the need for labor. The large number of landless people makes labor readily available and keeps down wages, even for union workers. Large numbers of people are unemployed and must beg, pick trash on streets or in garbage dumps, sell small items, or barter services to earn enough for bare subsistence. Well over a fourth of the populace earns less than twenty-five U.S. dollars a month.[52]

Higher education, and better professional jobs, go largely to India's (sometimes extremely wealthy) landowners, businesspeople, or professionals. The only wage and salary earners with incomes that will buy even slightly more than bare necessities are the most prosperous of the Green Revolution farmers (probably not over 15 million), 2.5 million businessowners, perhaps 3 million of the best-paid workers in larger businesses and industries,[53] perhaps 2 million bureaucrats (who are among the better paid, or are in a position to receive *bakshish*); another 8 million bureaucrats who are poorly paid, and a million professionals. All these people and their families constitute less than 100 million[54] out of a population of 834 million. Two million of them have annual household incomes above $2,240, another 4 million have incomes above $1,600, and 14 million more live in households with incomes above $1,000. They are the only ones with access to medical care,

social security, housing, leaves, bonuses, and other such benefits; they also benefit from the extensive underground economy through bribes and illegal money changing. The richest of them buy cars and modern housing, and the rest motorcycles and scooters. It is they who buy packaged food, refrigerators, telephones, air conditioners, and color TVs. An additional 80 million people live in households with annual incomes above $500 (35 rupees a day); one survey estimates an additional 250 million people may live in households earning 35 to 50 rupees a day. The rest of the population receives very low or no income and no fringe benefits. The average income is $275 per person per year.

Peruvian incomes remain low. The Ministry of Labor estimates that 68 percent of the rural work force was underemployed in 1983.[55] The half of the population which lives in remote mountain areas almost universally owns twelve or fewer acres of land high on rocky mountain slopes, or no land at all; the latter group is increasingly moving to towns or cities, and those who stay are seldom able to cultivate all the food they need. Those in the countryside also graze a few head of sheep, llamas, alpacas, or cattle on the common pasture land which surrounds the fields. With no fences, it is not possible to control breeding or to prevent overgrazing; the animals are often scrawny. The small amount of income derived from this source, or from selling occasional vegetables or grain, must be used to purchase or barter for other food or to pay for family festivals. During the 1970s per capita rural income in Peru fell 20 percent; from 1980 to 1986, it fell an additional 11 percent.[56]

About a third of Peru's population lives on the outskirts of towns and cities. They have often illegally occupied land and built shelter from whatever materials are available. They have no income from either land or herding and seldom find regular employment. They do odd jobs or construction work as day laborers, make or vend small items produced in informal factories, scavenge, work as domestic servants, and carry out other menial tasks to support their families. Their communities are often well organized, dispensing food to those who have none and performing other social services—entirely outside the regular economy.[57] In 1989, Lima's half million informal street vendors made an average of $58 a month—four times the legal minimum wage—but 70 to 90 percent of workers in the informal sector are un- or underemployed.[58] The austerity program initiated by President Fujimori in 1990 raised the number of those living in extreme poverty from 7 to 12 million; a third of the populace lives on less than $30 a month and much of the rest on little more.[59] With seven million people, Lima counted only 124,000 individuals (5.3 percent of its economically active population, and about 1.7 percent of its total population) as having "adequate employment" in the formal economy in 1991.[60]

With a population of 22 million, Peru has at most four or five million "economically active" workers; if even 10 percent of them were "adequately employed" (that is, earning more than minimum wage), that would mean only half a million wage earners (supporting perhaps a tenth of the country's families) have formal incomes over $40 a month, the current minimum wage. As we saw earlier in the chapter, that amount of income falls far short of what it takes to even feed one's family. A few people own small stores and artisan shops, which provide a place to live and a modest income. Some own one of Peru's 165,000 trucks and derive income from hauling; others own vans or cars giving informal taxi and bus service. About half a million people work in modern sector factories, mines, and farms, though not many of these make more than $40 a month. Another million have white collar jobs with government, banks, hospitals, universities, and business firms which also often pay salaries of less than $40 a month; a very small percentage of these make more. This portion of the population—from shopkeeper to white collar worker—is especially vulnerable to the constant high inflation, high tariffs, devaluation of currency, and wage freezes which have reduced their purchasing power to almost nothing. Those fortunate enough to reside in homes their families have owned at least may live in respectable poverty; if not, they must take refuge in the squatter colonies at night and clean up to go

Provision shop in Azpitia, Peru, 1986. The village of Azpitia is located in a fertile valley near the coast. © *Kip May.*

to the office in the daylight. They also moonlight at informal-sector jobs. Only the highest executives (a few of whom are multimillionaires), who have inside information, social standing, and liquid assets, can shift investments to guard against such economic changes before they take place. To help keep their wages up, unionized workers must resort to strikes or threats to withhold support at elections; their threats have frequently precipitated military coups.[61]

Opportunities for higher education, which could be expected to lead to a job paying more than $100 a month, are largely reserved to the sons and daughters of salaried workers and executives with the highest social standing. Though increasing numbers of Peru's peasant children receive university degrees, those degrees seldom lead to good jobs. Modern medical care, pension plans, bonuses, government housing, and other fringe benefits largely go to the university and military academy graduates with the best jobs. Hence, few workers receive those benefits.

Between 1980 and 1986, real Nigerian rural household income fell 27 percent, while real income in cities fell by over 50 percent. Urban unemployment rose from 4.7 percent in 1976 to 11.9 percent in 1986.[62] Per capital annual income dropped from $1,000 (in U.S. dollars) in 1980 to $300 in 1989.[63] A 1982 study in Kano found that 52 to 67 percent of the population were living at the ''absolute'' poverty level, earning less than the $472 per capita annual income to which the average had shrunk.[64] The United Nations has reclassified Nigeria as among the most economically disadvantaged countries. Many uneducated workers who had migrated to the cities during the oil boom of the 1970s returned to their villages and resumed production of sorghum, millet, yams, cocoyams, cassava, and maize—the basic subsistence crops which make up half of Nigeria's (and the great majority of poor rural dwellers') caloric intake.[65] Because high percentages of the populace retain access to village land, they can support themselves on this.

Drought and shortened growing seasons in northern Nigeria threaten production there; sorghum and millet adapt to these conditions better than maize and the new strains of ''miracle'' wheat. Prices for fertilizer and consumer goods have been rising, and producers of these crops have little access to credit. Government programs to aid agriculture are for growers of cotton, ground nuts, cocoa, rubber, wheat, and maize; these farmers constitute less than 1 percent of the workforce. Though 90 percent of export crops are grown by smallholders, most government aid has gone to the large projects of very rich, politically well-connected, people.[66]

With a potential labor force of around 35 million, about 350,000 Nigerians can earn some income from market agriculture, 5 million from formal and informal sector manufacturing, and 1.5 million from public employment.[67] Only a portion of those receive fringe benefits such as pensions and health plans or earn enough to buy more than basic necessities. Fiscal austerity and low oil prices have produced layoffs in all sectors of the formal economy. In 1986, 46 percent of those with secondary educations were unemployed.[68] The 1990 upturn in oil prices eased that problem a bit.

HOUSING

About two-thirds of CIS citizens live in subsidized public housing or in housing they pay little or no rent for.[69] The housing units tend to be small and poorly built; over 20 percent of urban families share bathrooms and kitchens. These units are generally larger (about ten feet by ten feet per person) than aging private housing, but they are not being built at a rapid rate; young couples must often wait years to get an apartment of their own. The southern and eastern regions contain higher percentages of private housing. Rural post-Soviet communities seldom have sewers or running water and have inadequate public bathhouse facilities.[70] As of 1970, 12 percent of cities and 30 percent of suburbs in the Soviet Union had no running water, and 40 percent of cities and 75 percent of suburbs had no sewers; that situation has improved, so that 9 percent of cities were without water and 11 percent without sewerage in 1985.[71] Rural electrification increased markedly during the 1960s. About a third of Moscow's citizens have a plot of land outside Moscow to raise vegetables (especially valued as food prices rise); some have a small dacha—a summer cottage—adjoining their plot. Potatoes, pickled cabbage, and stewed fruits from these plots may account for half of a family's food consumption.

When Moscow party chief Boris Yeltsin visited a housing project as part of Gorbachev's policy of exposing problems, he was invited in to see leaking roofs and broken sewers—problems which repeated pleas to party officials had failed to remedy. In one high-rise, raw sewage was knee deep in the basement, and all ground floor tenants had requested transfers to avoid the stench. In another, pipes had burst when the temperature was 30 degrees Centigrade below zero, and they had still not been fixed by summer. Yeltsin saw leaking roofs, fist-wide cracks in walls, and rat-infested piles of rubbish in children's play areas.[72]

A much higher percentage of Americans live in private housing,[73] which tends to be larger,[74] has at least one bathroom and a kitchen for each family, and uses up at least a third of family income. Mortgages cost more and are harder to obtain for some ethnic minorities.[75] Housing is abundant in the United States, but the cost of rent keeps a portion of the populace living with marginal shelter or none at all. Between six-hundred thousand and 9 million Americans are homeless. The post-Soviet republics, too, have homeless people. Their press discusses the *bozis* (people without definite direction or work) and *bombzhis* (people without a definite place of residence). One to three million people sleep on park benches and around train stations and try to head south during the cold winters; these citizens are products of many of the same social problems which create homelessness in America—housing shortages, joblessness, divorce, drug addiction, drunkenness, mental illness, and the like.[76] More than an additional million are homeless because they are refugees from ethnic unrest in their home regions.

A higher percentage of West Germans and British own their own homes than in East Germany; all three nation-states have subsidized housing and rent controls, but the average cost of rent as a percentage of income was lowest in East Germany.[77] So is the quality of the housing. Much of West Germany's housing has been built since World War II (because of the more extensive bombing there); much of it is well designed, with modern amenities. High percentages of the housing in the United Kingdom and East Germany predate World War II. All three areas experience housing shortages. In 1971, 58 percent of East Germany's houses had no indoor toilet, and 61 percent no bath, versus 20 percent in West Germany and 7 percent in England in 1976. Between 1971 and 1982, 1.2 million flats (averaging twenty-five feet by twenty-five feet) were constructed and six-hundred thousand others modernized in East Germany, constituting a fifth of total housing; these units are often stark and poorly constructed.[78] Much older housing is dingy and in poor repair. Families could wait years for a new flat.[79] Many East Germans (and citizens of the Baltic Republics) have

built themselves tiny summer huts by lakes or woods to retreat to on weekends. Some live in housing which belonged to others before the war, but was then seized by the communist state; even though many made improvements, at least two-hundred thousand families were forced to return them to former owners after reunification.[80]

When Margaret Thatcher came to power in 1979, 54 percent of U.K. housing was owner-occupied; by selling public housing, she raised that figure closer to 67 percent by 1990 (the number rose from 4 million owner-occupied homes in 1951 to 15 million in 1990). Since then, there has been little emphasis on construction of new homes for lower wage earners, and the cost of housing has risen sharply. By 1987, 69 percent of homes had central heating. Between 1978 and 1987, the price of most housing in the south of England quadrupled, while most people experienced only modest increases in income. To remedy this, home mortgages were made available to many more people, and in greatly increased amounts, and the government has made money available for home improvement grants.[81]

Most rural Chinese live in houses they construct themselves, often using factory-made precast concrete floor sections and fired bricks. Many peasants use income earned through the responsibility system to build spacious, functional houses which compare favorably to those found in the United Kingdom and East Germany, not to mention India.[82] Communes used to furnish bathhouses and other amenities; increasingly, these must be produced by townships and individual initiative. The amount of electricity available to rural areas increased tenfold between 1965 and 1985; five-hundred thousand of the seven-hundred ten thousand villages have electricity, furnishing electricity to 60 percent of the total population.[83] The average urban housing had about six feet by six feet of space per person in 1978; by 1985, this had grown to about six feet by twelve feet.[84] On average, rural housing is now more than twice this large. About 10 percent of urban housing consists of shacks, 10 percent is classified as dangerous, and 30 percent is in ill repair; it is not uncommon for three generations to live in the same room. Less than 10 percent of urban housing is privately owned. Housing built by factories for workers tends to be newer and better and is thus highly coveted; it accounts for about half of urban housing. Municipalities and work units are building new units at a rapid pace. Rent constitutes about 2 percent of income, but low rents mean that building managers have little money to make improvements on older housing, which is often cramped and in bad repair. Chinese cities do not have squatter colonies. Some temporary housing has been built by people seeking employment in the rapidly developing new economic zones along the coast.

Most rural Indians live in simple housing they construct themselves from sun-dried mud bricks. In urban areas of India, millions of people live in houses they own or rent. Millions more live in squatter colonies; this means they use scraps of wood and metal, cardboard, plastic, and other materials to build shelter on vacant lots, sidewalks, and squares. Residents must carry water from public taps. Periodically, bulldozers clear away such colonies; they soon reappear. The public housing which has been built is occupied by government and factory workers. Many white collar and factory workers must live in the squatter colonies because their low pay is inadequate to pay high urban rents. In Calcutta, hundreds of thousands have no shelter at all. Villages have communal wells, which sometimes go dry during drought; thousands of villages have no working well, and villagers must walk miles for water. Some three-hundred fifty thousand of India's six-hundred thousand villages are reached by electricity, but most is used for irrigation; few peasants can afford a hookup. Less than 14 percent of the total populace has electricity.[85]

High percentages of Peru's urban dwellers build their own housing illegally.[86] Metropolitan Lima is blanketed with squatter colonies. Forty percent of Lima's population has no garbage collection services, 23 percent no potable water, and 51 percent no sewage facilities.[87] Only a third of the population is served by electricity. New hydroelectric projects to expand access to electricity remain largely uncompleted. Sendero Luminoso, the underground revolutionary movement, has periodically sabotaged Lima's power supply, cutting the metropolitan area's electrical service for minutes or hours. This sends a pointed message to the portion of the populace served by electricity.

Most Nigerians live in simple houses they construct themselves from mud bricks and other local materials. Nestled among new modern homes, stores, and offices, many urban dwellers live in cardboard shanty towns, or decaying buildings, without piped water or electricity.[88]

HEALTH CARE

The death rate among CIS adults has been climbing during recent years, lowering life expectancies; the causes probably relate, among other factors, to poor rural sanitation and health care, degradation of the environment, low priority given to producing pharmaceuticals or building blood supplies,[89] increased incidence of smoking,[90] and alcoholism. Over a million alcoholics served in Soviet labor factories after a third arrest for drunkenness.[91] Gorbachev's government instituted campaigns against both smoking and alcohol, but the increase in mortality continues, among infants as well as adults. The life expectancy of Americans is rising (see figure 25.2).

Medical services are free in the CIS, but there are fewer facilities and medical staffs in rural areas than in towns and cities (where these services are also free, but more advanced). Even in cities, drugs and equipment are often scarce. Contraceptive devices are largely unavailable and unreliable;[93] with housing and income uncertain, women submit to frequent abortions, generally without anesthesia.[94] Though promiscuous sex is prevalent, little information is disseminated about AIDS. The best hospitals are reserved for the elite.[95] With 1993 pay scales of about 50¢ a day—below the income of bricklayers, cleaning personnel, and auto mechanics—doctors have huge incentive to devote time to patients who can pay them privately.

F*igure 25.2* Life expectancy at birth, 1988: (a) males; (b) females; (c) males and females combined. (d) Life expectancies for blacks and whites in the United States, 1988.

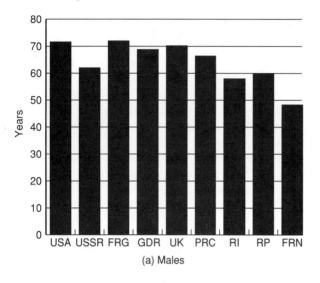

(a) Males

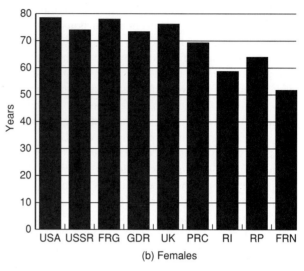

(b) Females

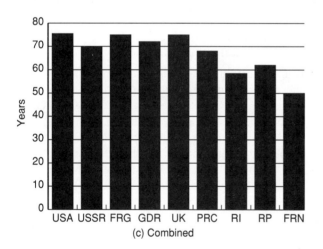

(c) Combined

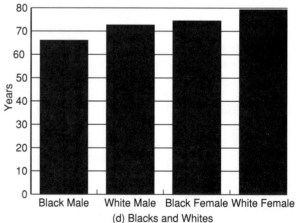

(d) Blacks and Whites

The United States has many fine hospitals, and pharmaceuticals are widely available. Some rural areas are not served by a nearby hospital or doctor, but transportation is usually available for emergencies. The 35 to 40 million citizens (including 12 million children, 20 percent of blacks, 26 percent of hispanics, and 12 percent of whites) without employer-provided health insurance plans, along with 70 million more who are underinsured,[96] cannot always afford treatment. The number of trauma centers in urban hospitals is shrinking across the United States because these units lose money from serving people without insurance. Twenty million Americans live in rural areas where there is no basic

The CIS may have the highest consumption of distilled liquor of any area in the world; it ranks fifth in total consumption of alcoholic beverages. One study indicates that half of all hospital beds in the CIS may be occupied by people with alcohol-related problems. A Soviet conference discussed estimates that 12 to 15 percent of the Soviet populace spends time each year in state-run detoxification or sobriety stations. A Duke University professor estimates that the Soviet Union contained 20 million alcoholics, mostly in the Russian and Ukrainian Republics. Under Gorbachev, the government greatly reduced the hours of liquor stores and restricted purchases. The program reduced one of the main sources of state taxes and increased the illegal home production of a popular moonshine liquor called *samagon,* brewed from the sugar available at the market at low subsidized prices. Long waits in line at the liquor stores also proved unpopular, and the restrictions were eased amid official admissions that consumption had not been reduced and that the country's sugar supply had been used up. In 1980, per capita consumption of pure alcohol via alcoholic beverages was 18 quarts, including 4.75 quarts of alcohol in *samagon* and homemade wines and beers. In comparison, other studies show that Americans and French consume about 4.75 quarts a year, and the British (according to figures from the liquor industry) have reduced consumption to 7. The Department of Health and Human Services reported that in 1988, 10.5 million U.S. adults showed signs of alcoholism, and an additional 7.2 million suffer from some form of alcohol abuse.

The CIS also has forty-nine thousand registered (plus uncounted numbers of unregistered) users of marijuana and semiprocessed opium. During the summer of 1987, two-thousand illicit poppy fields were destroyed in a sting operation. At the same time, an *Izvestia* reporter found drugs readily available in Moscow Metro stations late at night and even through the back doors of pharmacies. This problem is undoubtedly much larger than the government has admitted.[92]

medical care. Figure 25.3 compares availability of physicians and infant mortality rates in the nine nation-states.

East and West Germany, and the United Kingdom, have had national health care programs open to all citizens, who pay only nominal fees for treatment. Germany began national health care in 1883. The East German plan, which featured low pay for health care workers and publicly operated hospitals catering to workers with guaranteed employment, paid for abortions; mothers also received eighteen-week paid pregnancy leaves and a year off with pay after the birth of a child. Hospitals were equipped and supplied in a better manner than those in the Soviet Union, but they still did not meet the standards of those in West Germany and the United Kingdom. Care for the mentally ill in East Germany was very poor. The West German national health program—not yet extended to East Germans—has generous benefits, such as six weeks paid leave for each illness. Every West German family with an income below $36,000 must contribute to a private, nonprofit sickness insurance plan through a payroll deduction matched equally by their employer;[97] the government subsidizes the premiums of those without work or with lower incomes. At the time of unification with East Germany, only one-hundred thousand West Germans were without insurance, and government was paying only 14 percent of health care costs. In contrast, the United States federal and state governments pay (through Medicare, Medicaid, veterans', and other programs) 42 percent of their citizens' health care costs, yet nearly half of American citizens do not receive full coverage of medical expenses.[98]

China's communes were once responsible for providing medical services; now townships are in charge of these services. About two-hundred thousand physicians practice in rural areas; paramedics who have learned basic medical skills serve nearly all villages.[99] In cities, factories and other government-run work units provide free medical services with the assistance of one-hundred thousand trained physicians. Medical services are also available to the general public (including villagers, who are entitled to come in on referral from paramedics)

Figure 25.3   (a) Physicians per 100,000 population. (b) Infant mortality per 1,000 births, 1988.

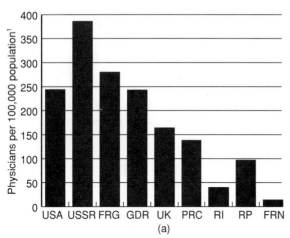

(a)

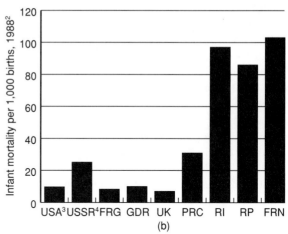

(b)

[1] Except for China, these figures come from *World Almanac* 1991. The China figure, taken from the *China Statistical Abstract 1988,* includes paramedics and nurses. The *World Almanac* indicates 170 physicians in China per 100,000. *Europa World Yearbook 1990* indicates USA 200, USSR 560, PRC 23, and RP 50.

[2] *World Development Report 1990,* World Development Indicators 1990, Table 28, 32, A.2.

[3] In 1989, infant mortality was 8.1 among whites and 18.6 among blacks in the United States (versus 8.6 and 17.9 in 1988). In 1960, the U.S. ranked twenty-sixth in the world; in 1980, twentieth; in 1989, twenty-fourth. The mortality figure declined 4.3 percent a year during the 1970s and 2.6 percent a year during the period from 1981 to 1984 to 8 per 1,000. It is now rising among blacks. *Kansas City Star,* January 30, 1986, August 29, 1991, and February 7, 1992; *Kansas City Times,* June 26, 1987.

[4] This figure is probably very conservative. In 1913, 268 of every 1,000 children born died before the age of one; by 1971, that rate had fallen to 26.2 (versus 19 in the United States). By 1974, when official statistics ceased, it had risen to 27.7, and the rate has been rising ever since. Increasing alcoholism and smoking among women, low pay for doctors, shortages of medical supplies, and poor sanitation contribute to this rate. *Department of State Bulletin,* 85 (September 1985): 74. David E. Powell, "The Emerging Health Crisis in the Soviet Union," *Current History* (October 1985): 339. Abel Aganbegyan estimates that 2 to 3 percent of the Soviet national budget went toward health care. *Daily Telegraph,* July 31, 1987.

The CIS is also the only industrialized area which has not wiped out diphtheria and whooping cough, despite the availability of vaccines. William J. Eaton and Dan Fisher, "Revolution of a New Sort is Underway," *Kansas City Times,* November 26, 1987.

at hospitals for very low fees. Hospitals for cadres are better equipped and staffed than those for the general public. With tobacco companies' heavy marketing, smoking is on the rise, as is consumption of saturated fat; half the world's increase in tobacco use is occurring in China, and respiratory disease causes a fourth of all deaths.[100] Smallpox, typhoid, pneumatic plague, malaria, diphtheria, polio, and whooping cough have nearly been eliminated through vaccinations and better hygiene.

In contrast, medical services other than those of traditional healers are generally unavailable in Indian villages. Periodically, jeeps bring medical teams which administer vaccinations and treat those who appear with complaints. Most of the two-hundred seventy thousand practicing physicians are in the cities; in 1980, ten thousand doctors were unemployed. India has no programs offering daily medi-

cal care to villages. Those in the city who cannot afford private care must wait for hours to receive treatment in emergency rooms. Hygiene is often poor. Most people obtain their water from open wells. Cholera, malaria, hepatitis, encephalitis, polio, typhoid, dysentery, rabies, and diarrhea all present serious health risks. AIDS, largely spread through prostitution, has been reported in twenty-one states.[101] There are over a million heroin and two million opium addicts.

In Peru, water is generally available from springs in the mountains, but scarce in the towns and cities. Many must procure it from public taps or buy it off tanker trucks. Lima has periodic typhoid epidemics spread through its water supply, and malaria and hepatitis infect many thousands. Peru's 1991 cholera epidemic was the first in the Americas since early in the twentieth century; cholera can be cured with inexpensive doses of tetracycline and IV rehydration, but these treatments are generally unavailable in Peru. Few doctors may be found in rural areas; they practice in the towns and cities. Entire provinces (which collectively have some 24 percent of the population) are without a hospital, clinic, or doctor, while other provinces have only a single doctor and clinic.[102] Two-thirds of the populace is served only by the Ministry of Health, which in 1980 had nineteen physicians per one-hundred thousand population; 70 percent of Peru's eleven thousand doctors live in Lima, which has a fourth of Peru's population.[103] Soap is generally unavailable and sanitation not practiced. Yellow fever and dengue (like malaria, spread by mosquitoes), Chagas' disease, tuberculosis, polio, and leprosy are endemic. Cases of bubonic plague have even appeared.

In 1983, Nigeria had 11,249 doctors, 37,112 nurses, 588 dentists, and 3,131 pharmacists, nearly all practicing among the middle class in cities. This left medical care in rural areas largely to practitioners of traditional medicine, or to 704 community health officers and 26,921 midwives.[104] As figures 25.2 and 25.3 show, Nigeria is far behind the other nation-states in its ratio of doctors to the total population, infant death rate, and life expectancy; even Haiti has twice as many doctors per one-hundred thousand people. In some regions of Nigeria, 60 percent of the populace are infested with guinea worm. A fifth of all Nigerian children die by their first birthday. Like much of the Third World, Nigeria is a heavy target for tobacco advertising, and smoking is on the rise.[105] In 1991, Nigeria experienced Africa's worst outbreak of cholera. The Babangida government inaugurated a Primary Health Care Project with a goal of inoculating half the populace, making oral rehydration kits (to prevent children from dying of diarrhea) and drugs available to village health workers. Though AIDS is spreading more rapidly in West Africa than in any other part of the world, with one in five of those tested among the general populace registering HIV positive,[106] no Nigerian government programs address it.

GOVERNMENT SERVICES

Both the Soviet Union and the United States have had programs to provide day care for children while mothers work outside the home. The Soviet program accommodated about a million children a year, and the United States fewer than that; this leaves millions of children with no or in private day-care arrangements.[107] Soviet parents have paid 15 to 25 percent of the cost of child care; sanitation is often deficient at the government centers, contributing to the mortality rate.

Soviet citizens were assured of minimum old age pensions of forty-eight rubles (sixty-five dollars) per month from all sources; those whose work record warrants it receive more.[108] Most, but not all, workers receive small pensions.[109] Retirement comes at age sixty for men and fifty-five for women.[110] Most urban pensioners must continue to live in their children's public housing, perhaps doing part-time work. Since 1991, inflation has destroyed the value of savings and of government pension funds. Pensions have increased, but not as much as the cost of living. Special departments for pensioners and veterans in state stores provide weekly parcels of butter, flour, cereals, and eggs for about 500 rubles (70¢) to help them fight inflation. Most Americans are entitled to Social Security benefits upon retirement; those who had the lowest earnings (and are least likely to have pensions or savings) receive the lowest payments. In addition, a third of workers are covered by pensions,[111] and some have voluntary insurance plans and accumulated savings. Workers commonly retire at age sixty-five. Medicare assists with retirees' medical costs. Over 60 percent of United States Government expenditures on entitlements go to people over age sixty-five.[112]

Over 61 percent of East Germany's children under age three went to nursery schools during the day, and 91 percent of those aged three to five could attend kindergarten (at a cost of 1.4 marks a day);[113] despite the fact that about a third of women in West Germany work outside the home, only 2 percent of children there have such government-run facilities available.[114] A 1992 law legalizing abortions will also expand public child care facilities.

Retiree carrying his caged bird as he spends the afternoon in Lu Xun Park, Shanghai, China. Many retirees gather in the park to play mah jong, do "tai chi" exercises, and talk.

Bob Gamer

About 17 percent of children attend public kindergartens in the United Kingdom.

Pensions in East Germany averaged a third of those in West Germany.[115] The East German government allowed some thirty-thousand people over sixty-five to emigrate each year to West Germany, which still recognized them as citizens and provided them with pensions. Even in West Germany, pensions do not allow for a high standard of living, though the government provides modern institutional care for many. The United Kingdom has government programs for the elderly; even after they receive benefits, many have incomes far below the norm. Studies show their incomes to be half those of workers, and they constitute 40 percent of the individuals on welfare rolls.[116]

In China, child care and retirement are not a serious problem in the villages, where older people are able to live with their children and look after grandchildren. State-run work units in cities, which most people nearing retirement age work for, have pension plans and let retirees retain their housing. They also provide child care to younger workers, though the quality is uneven.[117] Younger urbanites who do not work for state enterprises lack these services.

India, Peru, and Nigeria have no public day care programs, and no programs that care for the elderly, except for the small portion of the populace with better jobs in the public or formal private sectors.

CONSUMER GOODS AND SERVICES

Aside from a house, the most expensive item an average consumer may buy is a car. As you can see from figure 25.4, the portion of the populace owning a car in each of these countries varies widely.

Public transportation is heavily subsidized in the CIS, so people may move about cities very cheaply; some of that service is very poor, and some very good.[118] Most roads are unpaved and poorly repaired, so bus service is nonexistent or highly sporadic. East Germany also subsidized public transport; trains and buses were often crowded and behind schedule. China's cheap bus fares provide rides on buses heavily loaded with passengers. Many Chinese can afford bicycles, which are inexpensive.[119] They are especially useful in cities and in rural areas with roads good enough to pedal private crops to town markets; the loads they haul can stagger the imagination. But there are few rural roads, and those that exist are in poor condition; there is not even a national ministry to build roads. These communist transportation systems allow people to get to work cheaply (thus solving a problem which can cost those in other systems a great deal of money, whether they own a car or not), but they give them little opportunity to go elsewhere.

Private transportation is a more difficult proposition. Except for in Canton and Shanghai, few automobiles in Chinese cities belong to anyone other than work units; that is changing rapidly as the richest Chinese purchase Mercedes, Volkswagen, and other cars. Cars in the former Soviet Union are poorly designed and built; purchasing one involves long waits, high prices ($5,000 in 1993), and frequent repairs. Some East Germans ordered the small and highly unreliable Trabant cars; these cars were not redesigned after 1964 and had lawn-mower-sized

Figure 25.4   The 1988 figures for (a) automobiles per person; (b) television sets per person; (c) radios per person; (d) telephones per person; and (e) percent of populace served by electricity in each of the nine nation-states.

(a) The World Almanac 1991, *1988 figures. (b)* UNESCO Statistical Yearbook 1990, *1988 figures. PRC, RI, FRN* Television and Video Almanac 1993. *(c)* UNESCO Statistical Yearbook 1990, *1988 figures. (d)* The World Almanac 1991, *1989 figures.*

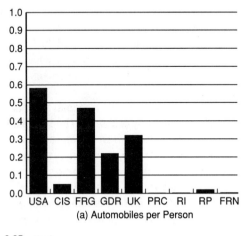

(a) Automobiles per Person

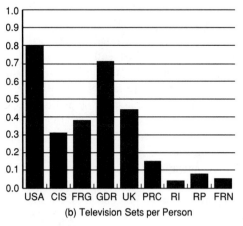

(b) Television Sets per Person

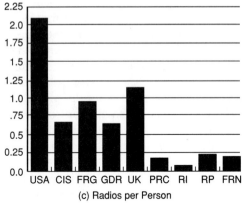

(c) Radios per Person

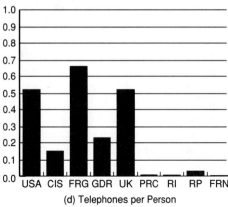

(d) Telephones per Person

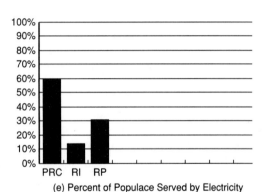

(e) Percent of Populace Served by Electricity

engines, yet buyers had to wait months to get them. West Germany, by contrast, produces cars that set standards for the entire world. During the weeks following reunification in 1990, more than a quarter of East German households are estimated to have purchased new and used cars brought in from lots all over Europe, at prices lower than they had paid for Trabants; within a year, virtually no Trabants could be found on the streets.[120]

As we have seen, the United States was already ahead of Russia in the nineteenth century in its distribution of consumer goods. That trend continues. The quality and technological sophistication of Soviet (and East German) consumer goods is far lower than in the United States or Western Europe;[121] service in retail establishments and in repair shops is often as shoddy as the goods themselves—slow, inefficient, and uncaring.[122] The choice between small consumer items is far less diverse; the Gorbachev regime reported that 15 percent of retail sales were alcoholic beverages before their antialcoholism drive, a fact which helps dramatize how little else the stores contained. Under *perestroika,* for reasons we shall explore in part 5, Soviet stores contained even less. In the countryside, selections were even poorer than in cities; rural Soviet citizens spent about a third as much per capita on nonfood items as did town dwellers and city folk. There were often shortages of consumer goods, and prices were high on nonessentials. Much discretionary spending went into clothing, which was readily available but bland and expensive. Clothing and other consumer purchases were often made on the black market, where both quality and costs were higher. Today, selection is improving, but (as we have seen) most people have little money for discretionary spending. China, in contrast, has a great variety of well-made, fashionable clothing and high-quality household goods for sale in the stores of towns and cities.[123] High fashion is spreading even to inland cities, and discretionary spending is flourishing on a constantly widening array of consumer goods.

Notice from figure 25.4 that India has few cars per capita. About two-thirds of India's cars are Ambassadors from Hindustan Motors of Calcutta. They are sturdy but fuel-guzzling vehicles made on dies of Morris Oxfords imported from Britain during the 1950s, and the designs have not changed since then.[124] They sell for about $9,000; gasoline sells for over $2 a gallon (a price the government deliberately set high to conserve domestic oil supplies). Bajaj (Vespa) motor scooters, Kinetic Honda motorcycles, and Suzuki Maruti automobiles, assembled in India, offer new lower-priced and more fuel-efficient alternatives to the most affluent urban dwellers. They bought over a million cycles and scooters, 165,000 cars, and 4 million television sets in 1991.

As the statistics on the other items in figure 25.4 hint, consumption is much wider in East Germany, China, and the CIS than in India. A third of India's, and a fourth of China's, villages lie away from a vehicular road. That greatly restricts the people's access to manufactured consumer goods. The 86 percent of Indians, and 40 percent of Chinese, who do not have electricity in their homes obviously cannot easily use items such as television sets, washing machines, vacuum cleaners, refrigerators, and space heaters, whose production is fast expanding in both countries.[125] China's electrification is proceeding more rapidly than India's at providing service to rural homes;[126] when electrical service reaches a village in China, it finds villagers who already have rising incomes from their own land which they can use to pay for electricity and for the appliances which follow it. Those who live in cities tend to have homes and jobs which bring in steady income; over 67 percent of China's urban households have washing machines, and at least two thirds have television sets.[127] By 1992, Chinese owned 160 million television sets; Indians owned 24 million.[128]

Citizens of the post-Soviet republics are struggling economically. But in 1983, the Soviet Union already had 87 radios per 100 households (versus 49 in 1963) and 85 television sets per 100 households (versus 15 in 1963). This would be impossible in India; high percentages of the populace cannot afford such items, and of course have no place to plug them in. The same holds true for Peru and Nigeria.

SUMMARY

Some of these systems distribute food, income, housing, health care, government services, and consumer goods more widely than others. Far more people go hungry in India, Peru, and Nigeria than in the other systems. Those three systems also have far greater portions of their populace with inadequate income, housing, health care, and government services. The communist systems in the Soviet Union, East Germany, and China have distributed food, housing, health care, and other government services to wide portions of their populace; the quality of those goods and services is often minimal. Quantity and quality of goods and services are greater in the United States, the United Kingdom, and West Germany. The distribution of them among diverse segments of the populace, however, is uneven.

NOTES

1. Soviet citizens had to work ten times longer than Americans to buy a pound of meat. David Remnick, "A Vast Landscape of Want," *Washington Post National Weekly Edition (WPNWE),* May 28–June 3, 1990.

2. Merwyn Matthews, *Class and Society in Soviet Russia* (New York: Walker, 1972), p. 69, says Russians spent 50 percent. A 1981 CIA study found the average Soviet family spent 46 percent of their income on food, tobacco, and beverages (including 17 percent on hard liquor) versus 17 percent for these three goods in the United States; a 1985 Soviet survey estimated Soviets spent 30 percent. *Kansas City Times (KCT),* November 27, 1981 and June 29, 1987.

3. A 1981 CIA study reported 27 percent of an average West German family's income was spent on food, tobacco, and beverages. *KCT,* November 27, 1981. In 1971, East Germans spent about 48 percent and West Germans 38 percent of income on food.

4. Agricultural production has risen an average of 8 percent or more a year since 1978. Peasants retain a portion of their output for their own use. Some they can sell directly to consumers. The government buys the rest, and sells it at reduced cost to city dwellers. This subsidy, plus grain imports and subsidies for cooking oil, used 28 percent of the entire government budget in 1982; it is being phased out. So the price of some food has risen in the cities, along with workers' incomes.

    Some 200 to 270 million Chinese were estimated to be living with inadequate food in 1978. "The Titan Stirs," *The Economist (TE),* November 28, 1992. A 1980 study of poorer Shanghai workers doing light to moderate work found average daily intakes of 1,715 calories and 37.2 grams of protein in diets including grain, meat, vegetables, and fruit. This adequate but minimal diet is available to nearly all Chinese through the subsidies, allotments, and grain and cooking oil rations. More prosperous families eat more. A 1983 nationwide survey found an average daily intake of between 2,200 and 2,380 calories. In a January 1984 article, quoting a government study, Deng Xiaoping said, "Eleven percent [90 million] of the rural population still have not resolved the problem of dressing warmly and getting enough to eat." Vaclav Smil, "China's Food," *Scientific American* (December 1985): 119.

5. Since 1970, per capita wheat production (subsidized by the Indian government) has considerably increased, but bean production has declined; with meat consumption low, both grain and beans are needed for adequate protein. Per capita protein and calorie figures have shown little change. Population growth continued at 21 percent per year between 1980 and 1986 (versus 1 to 1.3 percent in China during the same period). China has 2.3 children per family (versus 3.9 in India), and its birth rate drops each year, while India's rises.

6. Lloyd I. Rudolph and Susanne Hoeber Rudolph, *In Pursuit of Lakshmi: The Political Economy of the Indian State* (Chicago: University of Chicago Press, 1987), p. 365, cites several such studies.

7. Paul Collier, "Oil Shocks and Food Security in Nigeria," *International Labour Review* 127, 6 (December 1988): 714.

8. Molly Moore and John War Anderson, "Finally Fighting Back," *WPNWE,* April 19–25, 1993.

9. Smil, "China's Food," pp. 121, 122.

10. Thomas G. Sanders, "Peru's Population in the 1980s," *University Field Staff International Reports (UFSIR)* 27 (1984): 8. The Population Reference Bureau and U.S. Department of Agriculture found population rose 2.5 percent in 1986, while per capita grain production declined 24 percent from 1970–72 to 1985. Lester R. Brown, "Analyzing the Demographic Trap," *State of the World 1987*, p. 28. By 1991, the formal sector's minimum wage of forty dollars per month would pay for only a fifth of an average family's food. Nicole Bonnet, "Japanese Unmoved by Peru's Plight," *Le Monde (LM)*, July 28, 1991.

11. Between 1980 and 1986 population was rising at a rate of 2.5 percent a year.

12. Sanders, "Peru's Population," p. 8.

13. Nathaniel C. Nash, "Peru's President is Trying to Tame a Maelstrom of Inflation and Poverty," *New York Times (NYT)*, July 7, 1991.

14. J. Brooke, "Peru Struggles to Digest Free Market Reforms," *NYT*, April 30, 1991; "Peru: Dearer and Still Dearer," *TE*, August 18, 1990.

15. A Moscow newspaper reported that one-hundred fifty thousand individuals in the USSR had assets of one million rubles (US$25,000) or more; fewer had hundreds of millions of rubles. David Remnick, "New Soviet Masters of the Universe," *WPNWE*, July 15–21, 1991.

16. Only 11.2 percent of Soviet citizens could be called middle class, and 86.5 percent were poor. Anatoli Deryabin, writing in the official journal *Molodoi Kommunist*, as quoted by David Remnick, "A Vast Landscape."

17. *Fortune (F)*, September 1991, listed sixty U.S., twenty-three German, and three British billionaires (including Queen Elizabeth II, the world's richest woman, with US$10.7 billion in assets). The top 10 percent of U.S. families gained as much income from 1979 to 1987 ($543 billion) as the remaining 90 percent. The top 20 percent gained $23,620 a year, more than the average total income of the bottom 40 percent. Without an increase in the number of working women, the incomes of the bottom 80 percent would have fallen. David R. Francis, "Studies of Income Gap Multiply," *Christian Science Monitor (CSM)*, September 4, 1990. The University of Michigan Panel Study of Income Dynamics found that from 1978 to 1987, the portion of individuals earning over $55,000 (in 1987 dollars) grew from 8 to 13 percent. But the portion earning less than $18,000 rose from 17 to 20 percent. Richard Morin, "America's Middle-Class Meltdown," *Kansas City Star (KCS)*, December 4, 1991.

18. Internal Revenue Service study. The total Gross National Product that year was $4.1 trillion. The 26 percent of households in the lowest income group (earning below $900 a month) had less than 10 percent of total net worth. The 12 percent of households in the highest income group (over $4,000 a month) had 38 percent of total net worth. Married couples had an average net worth of $50,116, households headed by a female without a husband, $13,885, and by a male without a wife, $9,883. Average net worth of households headed by a person below age thirty-five was $5,764; between ages fifty-five and sixty-four, $73,664; and age sixty-five or over, $60,266. *Washington Post (WP)*, July 19, 1986. *KCS*, August 23, 1990.

A Federal Reserve Board study found the 2 percent of American families earning over $100,000 annually control 30 percent of assets, including 50 percent of all stocks, 71 percent of tax-free bonds, 39 percent of taxable bonds, 23 percent of money in checking accounts, 8 percent of money in savings accounts, 15 percent of funds in money-market accounts, and 20 percent of real estate. *KCS*, October 9, 1984.

Kevin Phillips (as quoted by Leslie Gelb, *KCS*, June 13, 1991) estimates the richest 2.5 million Americans earn as much as the bottom 100 million. The Congressional Budget Office estimated that the top 1 percent (660,000 families) increased pretax income, adjusted for inflation, from $314,526 in 1977 to $675,859 in 1992.

19. The $18.9 million earned by United Airlines' CEO in 1990 was 1,200 times the salary of a flight attendant. George Will, "Ripping Off Capitalism," *WP*, September 1, 1991.

20. David P. Conradt, *The German Polity*, 4th ed. (New York: Longman, 1989), p. 27.

21. Konstantin Simis, "Russia's Underground Millionaires: How to Succeed in Business Where Business is a Crime," *F*, June 29, 1981; *USSR, the Corrupt Society: The Secret World of Soviet Capitalism* (New York: Simon & Schuster, 1982).

22. Merwyn Matthews, "Top Incomes in the USSR: Toward a Definition of the Soviet Elite," *Survey* 21, 3 (Summer 1975): 1–27 argues that only 10,000 of the 625,000 government managers, 140,000 of the 400,000 party officials, and 30,000 military and police belonged to the privileged class at that time. But some perks are available to everyone in these categories.

23. Before the 1991 coup, many had already purchased these elegant dachas for around fifteen thousand rubles. Eleanor Randolph, "Soviet System of Privileges Examined," *Manchester Guardian Weekly (MGW)*, August 25, 1991.

24. Car owners sometimes drive south. In 1986, there were two-hundred fifty thousand reported accidents, due to drunken driving (in 20 percent of cases), bad roads, speeding, driving too long without a break, and other factors. Often drivers reach the seaside resorts and find them filled with booked tours, with roadblocks up to prevent entry. Tent camping grounds often lack sanitary facilities and are jammed. Mary Dejevsky, "Trail of Car Crashes as Russians Drive to the Sun," *The Times (TT)*, August 19, 1987.

25. A 1978 study found the average nonfarm wage was 159 rubles. *Kolkhozy* workers earned 98 rubles without and 124 rubles with private plot income. *Sovkhozy* workers earned 135 rubles without and 162 rubles with private plot income. Jane P. Shapiro, "Soviet Consumer Policy in the 1970s: Plan and Performance," in Donald R. Kelley, ed., *Soviet Politics in the Brezhnev Era* (New York: Praeger, 1980), pp. 107–8. Collective farms sometimes pay their workers, in part, by giving them agricultural products.

26. Matthews, *Class and Society*, pp. 161–62, 165.

27. U.S. Census Bureau. A third of black, a quarter of hispanic, and less than a tenth of white households had no assets at all or were in debt. Annual income of whites was a bit less than twice that of blacks or hispanics. In 1986, median income for a black family headed by a woman was $8,648; 6 percent of white males and 15 percent of black males were unemployed. Donald Kaul, "Problems of Black Families Should be No Surprise," *KCT*, February 7, 1986. By 1989, net worth of blacks was a tenth of that of white households, largely due to advances in income by the 14 percent of black families making over $50,000 a year; overall, average black income was 56 percent that of whites. *KCS*, August 9, 1991.

U.S. median household income in 1991 was $30,126, down 5.1 percent from 1989.

Between 1984 and 1989, the net worth of high-income families in the University of Michigan panel study grew from $167,700 to $305,400, while that of low-income families fell from $3,700 to $3,100. Morin, "Middle-Class Meltdown." A Federal Reserve Board study found net worth of families making over $50,000 a year rose from $176,100 in 1983 to $185,600 in 1989, while net worth of those earning below $10,000 fell from $3,800 to $2,300, and that of people with incomes of $20,000 to $30,000 a year stayed at $37,000. James Risen, "Wealth Gap Widened," *KCS*, January 7, 1992.

28. See Nicholas Lemann, *The Promised Land*.

29. Children's Defense Fund. Twelve percent of white children lived in poverty in 1989. Those figures had risen 11 percent since 1979. *KCS*, July 8, 1992. Between 1982 and 1990, average after-tax family income grew 26 percent, while average income for hispanics rose 70 percent; but their incomes still remained a third less than average. Scott Pendleton, "Downturn, Job Shortages, Trouble Hispanic Voters," *CSM*, February 20, 1992. Only 10.6 percent of those in poverty in 1991 were elderly, while 40.2 percent were children. The poverty rate among young families with children doubled from 20 percent in 1973 to 40 percent (68 percent among blacks) in 1990.

30. This compares to 31.5 million in 1989 and 33.6 million in 1990. Homeless people are excluded. In 1991, 14.2 percent lived in poverty, versus 11.4 percent in 1979 and 22.2 percent in 1960. By 1991, the poverty level was defined as below $13,924 annual income for a family of four, before taxes and benefits were considered. A total of 32.7 percent of black, 28.7 percent of hispanic, 13.8 percent of Asian American, and 11.3 percent of white households had incomes below this line. Since 40 million of America's 250 million people are nonwhite, most in poverty (11.3 percent of 210 million, or about 24 million) were white. About 38 percent in poverty owned houses worth over $100,000; half of those were elderly. Sixty-nine percent spend more than 30 percent of income on housing, and 40 percent at least half of their income. R. A. Zaldivar, "Reports Put Triple Whammy on Recovery Hopes," *KCS*, September 27, 1991. Clarence Page, "Lots Left Out of Statistical Peek at Poor," *KCS*, October 8, 1991. If

the poverty line for a family of four were $15,017, 13 million more would be classified as poor—one in four children (versus one in five) and one in four elderly (versus one in eight). Robert P. Hey, "U.S. Poverty Estimates Miss 13 Million Poor," *CSM*, July 20, 1990.

31. These figures are according to a Tufts University School of Nutrition Study. Robin Wright, "Three Faces of Hunger Haunt the World's Poor," *KCS*, December 20, 1992.

32. In contrast, East Germany's poorest region–Mecklenberg–was aided by an influx of tourism, new industry, and agricultural development projects. This is discussed further in chapter 33.

33. The Joint Center for Political and Economic Studies, analyzing 1986 mean incomes of households headed by twenty- to fifty-five-year-olds, found that 18.1 percent of United States households earned an income below the poverty line, versus 12.5 percent in Great Britain and 6.8 percent in West Germany. They defined the poverty line as 50 percent of the nation's median income after taxes and public assistance payments were figured in (in the United States, $15,000 annual income for a family of four–higher than the government's official 1986 standard of $11,203). "U.S. Falters in Help to Poor, Study Finds," *KCS*, September 19, 1991.

34. A study by Richard Layard in a Background Paper for the Royal Commission on Distribution showed that "Coloured" immigrants from the West Indies had earnings 13 percent below normal; other "coloured," 22 percent below normal; and Irish-born, 7 percent below normal. Samuel Brittan, "Poverty and Policy: A Cool Look," *Financial Times (FT)*, September 7, 1978.

35. See Gunter Wallraff, *Ganz Unten: Mit Einer Dokumentation der Folgen* (Koln: Kiepenheuer und Witsch, 1988).

36. "Germany: The Shock of Unity," *TE*, May 23, 1992.

37. The gap between east and west in average monthly rural income grew from thirty-six U.S. dollars in 1981 to ninety U.S. dollars in 1987. Robert Grieves, "China Woos Tibetans with Language Concession," *TT*, August 12, 1987. In 1990, the government still estimated that 50 million Chinese had incomes below 38 U.S. dollars a month. Ann Scott Tyson, "China's Remotest Regions Slip Deeper into Poverty," *CSM*, July 22, 1992.

38. Robert Delfs, "Saying No to Peking," *Far Eastern Economic Review (FEER)* 151, 14 (April 4, 1991): 22. All the coastal provinces except Hebei have higher per capita incomes than any inland province other than Heilongjiang. The World Bank estimates that 70 million peasants live in "absolute poverty" in inland provinces. In 1992, average per capita income in Shenzhen was 4,200 yuan, versus an average rural income of 710 yuan; though seventy percent of Chinese live in the countryside, urban dwellers held sixty percent of bank accounts. "Soaking the Rich," *TE*, June 6, 1992.

39. *KCT*, March 26 and 29, 1986; October 27, 1987. Terry Hughes, *KCS*, March 2, 1986. CBS Evening News, March 3, 1986. *KCS*, March 29, 1993.

40. Alan Pike, "Rural Poverty Research Puts Paid to Green and Pleasant Myth," *FT*, August 22, 1987. Sheila Gunn, "MP's Issue More Attacks on Poverty Figures," *TT*, May 24, 1990. "How the Other Tenth Lives," *TE*, September 12, 1992.

41. A million are unemployed. John Greenwald, "Why It Still Doesn't Work," *Time (T)*, December 7, 1992. "Getting Richer, Getting Poorer," *TE*, February 6, 1993.

42. Many former East Germans lost their jobs in state industries. New private owners have been hiring, and the government created 23 percent of the new jobs to rebuild roads, buildings, and other basic infrastructure. After a sharp dip, the portion of the labor force unemployed, on their former company payrolls without actually drawing full salary, or working part-time on a government-sponsored temporary job leveled at about a third of the East German populace. Francine S. Kiefer, "Germany Puts Easterners to Work," *CSM*, October 2, 1991. In 1992, the official unemployment rate in East Germany was 16 percent. "The Greenness Behind Germany's Power," *TE*, October 3, 1992.

43. Unemployment rose to 8 percent in 1986 (*KCS*, June 7, 1987) and 9 percent in 1987; in 1992, it stood at 6 percent and in 1993 rose to 8 percent. Andrew Fisher, "Unemployment in West Germany on Rise Again," *FT*, August 5, 1987. *TT*, January 9, 1988. *TE*, October 3, 1992. A decade earlier, it was virtually nonexistent.

44. From 1948 to 1966, nearly 3 million new jobs were created in Britain, and immigrants supplemented the growing domestic population. Unemployment averaged only 300,000. From 1966 to 1977, some

650,000 new jobs were created, and the number of people on unemployment passed a million; 1.2 million factory jobs were lost, and nearly two million service jobs added. David Freud, "A New Era for Women," *FT,* June 28, 1978. In 1981, unemployment passed 2.5 million; by 1987, 3 million (11 percent). By January 1993, it stood at 2.8 million–over 10 percent of the workforce. *KCS,* June 7, 1987; March 15, 1992.

45. *Economic Trends,* August 1987. Sarah Hogg, "Forty-Nine Percent of Income Goes to Top Fifth of Households," *The Independent (TI)* (London), August 18, 1987. The Diamond Commission (Royal Commission on the Distribution of Wealth) Report found that in 1976, 25 percent of U.K. families were "lower income"; of these, 60 percent had no income and lived entirely on government subsidies. About 1.1 million of Britain's 28 million families earned incomes below the poverty line, even after receiving all benefits due them; 40 percent were pensioners, and 40 percent families with children. The top 1 percent of the populace had 24.9 percent of the wealth; the poorest 90 percent had 39.4 percent of the wealth. David Freud, "Wealth of Top 5 Percent Rose in 1975–76," *FT,* July 12, 1979. *FT,* May 25, 1978.

46. William L. Parish, in a public address given March 25, 1986 at the University of Missouri-Kansas City, estimated 11 percent of China's workers were unemployed at that time. Some estimate that by 1991, 150 million people (about 15 percent) were unemployed.

47. Christian Morrisson, "Income Distribution in East European and Western Countries," *Journal of Comparative Economics* 8, 2 (June 1984): 121–38. The data compares incomes during the 1970s.

48. Martin Rosenberg, "Life in Moscow: Muddling Through," *KCS,* March 28, 1993. "Street Capitalism," *TE,* April 25, 1992. "Getting Richer, Getting Poorer," *TE,* February 6, 1993.

49. In 1976, the CIA estimated average Chinese per capita income at $340, rising from $153 in 1952. *China: Economic Indicators,* Washington, D.C., 1977 and 1978. Urban workers made 4.58 times more income than peasants in 1978. More prosperous peasants made four times the income of poorer ones. Gilbert Rozman, ed., *The Modernization of China* (New York: Free Press, 1981), p. 335. Between 1978 and 1984, real per capita income in rural households rose 2.5 times, due to the responsibility system and a 54 percent increase in state purchase payments to

farmers. Smil, "China's Food," pp. 116, 123. Rural incomes grew three times faster than urban, making average urban income 2.7 times that of rural. After 1990, urban incomes again began to grow faster than rural. Robert Delfs, "Collective Efforts Are Overwhelming State Enterprise," *FEER,* 131, 12 (March 20, 1986): 78.

50. George Rosen, *Democracy and Economic Change in India* (Berkeley: University of California Press, 1966), pp. 32, 39.

51. Kevin Rafferty, "Economic Survey," in *The Far East and Australasia 1980–81* (London: Europa Publications, 1980), p. 434. Rudolph and Rudolph, *Lakshmi,* pp. 266, 365–69, 375. The percentage of people living below the poverty line fell by more than half between 1957 and 1990 (from over 50 percent in 1977–78 to 25 percent today), but since the population has nearly doubled over the same period, the number living below the poverty line has risen by 20 million over that time (from 200 million to 220 million). Sara Adhikari, "873, 762, 705," The *Sunday Times of India,* November 1, 1992. V. G. Kulkarni, "100 Million, United by Affluence," *FEER,* 156, 2 (January 14, 1993): 46.

52. Bernard Weinraub, "India Peers at Its Future With a Sense of Gloom," *NYT,* July 14, 1991.

53. About 2.2 million Indians work in public sector firms, which constitute about 70 percent of the industrial labor force. Their average annual salary plus benefits is about US$3,250. *FEER* 139, 2 (January 14, 1988): 56, 59.

54. That figure is commonly used in newspapers as the size of India's middle class. See "A Democracy in Crisis," *WPNW,* May 27–June 2, 1991; Sheila Tefft, "Economic Woes Besiege India," *CSM,* June 4, 1991. It is based on two large scientific surveys conducted in 1990. Kulkarni, "100 million."

55. Thomas G. Sanders, "Peru's Economy: Underemployment and the Informal Sector," *UFSIR* 39 (1984): 3.

56. Brown, "Demographic Trap," p. 29. In 1971–72, 53.8 percent of rural families had 14.7 percent of rural income; 2.5 percent had 21 percent.

57. See chapter 8, and Hernando deSoto, *El Otro Sendero* (Lima, Peru: Instituto Libertad y Democracia, 1986).

58. Mark Falcoff, "The Only Hope for Latin America," *Commentary* 87, 4 (April 1989): 36; D. Wehrlich,

"Fujimori and the 'Disaster' in Peru," *Current History (CH)* 90 (553), 81. The legal minimum wage has since risen to $40 a month; with rapid inflation, the income of street vendors has also risen.

59. Nicole Bonnet, "Japanese Unmoved by Peru's Plight," *LM*, July 28, 1991; J. Brooke, "Peru: Still Dearer."

60. Essentially, adequate employment means earning more than the minimum wage. The 124,000 figure is an estimate of the Center for Parliamentary Studies. They found that 86.4 percent of the work force was underemployed in 1991, versus 66 percent who were adequately employed in 1980. Sally Bowen, "Peru's Fujimori Weighs in On Behalf of Street Sellers, *CSM*, March 4, 1991.

61. In 1991, the Peruvian union federations called a general strike to protest the government austerity program, which left only 5 to 10 percent of the workforce fully employed. Many of the few who had full-time jobs did not join the strike.

62. Collier, "Oil Shocks," p. 714.

63. *TE*, November 18, 1989.

64. Edmund Burke III and Paul Lubeck, "Explaining Social Movements in Two Oil-Exporting States: Divergent Outcomes in Nigeria and Iran," *Comparative Studies in Society and History* 29, 4 (October 1987): 653.

65. Collier, "Oil Shocks," p. 762.

66. S. J. Scherr, "Agriculture in an Export Boom Economy: A Comparative Analysis of Policy and Performance in Indonesia, Mexico, and Nigeria," *World Development* 17, 4 (April 1989): 553, 555, indicates that in 1982 only 17 percent of government spending on agriculture went to small growers.

67. Collier, "Oil Shocks," p. 274.

68. Idem., p. 278.

69. Some public housing in the CIS is built by factories or collective farms for their workers, and some by municipalities. Much is of low quality and poorly maintained. There were some innovations. The October Collective Farm in Krasnodar let workers pick the style of house they wanted from an album, and then lent them up to 10,000 rubles ($14,000) at .5 percent interest to have it built. Rick Atkinson, "Stalin's Legacy Guiding Force on the Farm," *KCT*, November 16, 1982.

Abel Aganbegyan, an economist at the Soviet Academy of Sciences, estimated the average Soviet family spent 3 percent of income on housing and communal services. Trevor Fishlock, "Tale of a Tipsy Russian Takes on Deep Economic Meaning," *Daily Telegraph (DT)*, (London), July 31, 1987.

70. The three-hundred fifty thousand Soviet settlements with less than 200 or so inhabitants, designated as "futureless," did not receive services, and their inhabitants (often numbering no more than three or four households) were encouraged to move into larger villages where it was easier to provide services. Fifteen million people, a sixth of the rural population, lived in such settlements. Under Gorbachev, the policy of phasing them out was reviewed; little happened. *Pravda* describes the village of Kuldzhinskoye, population 300, in southern Kazakhstan: "The village found itself without a kindergarten; its children had to walk three kilometers to school. It is a half hour's walk to a water pump. A canal that earlier permitted the spring rains to run off is now silted up, and spring floods are a frequent occurrence." Atkinson, "Stalin's Legacy."

71. In 1960, 62 percent of city housing lacked running water, and 65 percent lacked sewers. Marshall Goldman, *The Spoils of Progress: Environmental Pollution in the Soviet Union* (Cambridge, Mass.: MIT Press, 1972) pp. 165–66; "Human Rights," Department of State Bulletin (DOSB), 85 (September 1985).

72. *TI*, August 22, 1987. Mary Dejevsky, "Party Chief Staggered by Moscow in the Raw," *TT*, August 22, 1987.

73. In 1977, nearly 70 percent of American housing was privately owned. Michael Cassell, "Home Ownership: Still a Major Party Issue," *FT*, December 3, 1977. In 1980, 47 percent of young families with children owned their homes; in 1991, 31 percent.

74. In 1971, urban housing in the Soviet Union was generally about half the size of that in the United States (11.2 square meters versus 25 square meters). Robert A. Lewis, Richard H. Rowland, and Ralph S. Clem, *Nationality and Population Change in Russia and the USSR: An Evaluation of Census Data 1861–1970* (New York: Praeger, 1976).

75. A study by federal regulators found that 33.9 percent of blacks' credit applications were rejected, compared

to 21.4 percent for hispanics, 22.4 percent for American Indians, 14.4 percent for whites, and 12.9 percent for Asian Americans. "Home-Loan Denial Higher for Blacks," *KCS*, October 22, 1991.

76. David Remnick, "The Soviets Have Their Own Homeless," *KCS*, March 27, 1988; Jeri Laber, "A Vast Landscape," *NYT*, June 24, 1990; Sen. Paul Simon's committee, CBS Evening News, January 15, 1990.

77. In 1971, rent, gas, and electricity took about 5 percent of the income of an East German family, versus 20 percent of income for a family in West Germany.

78. *GDR Facts and Figures '83*, (East Berlin: Zeit im Bild, 1983), p. 43. The new flats were small, poorly constructed high-rises. In 1978, only 10.7 percent of units constructed in East Germany were for one or two families, versus 70.4 percent in West Germany and 73.9 percent in Britain. David Childs, *The GDR: Moscow's German Ally* (London: Allen & Unwin, 1983), p. 261.

79. Waiting time for flats in East Berlin was nine to ten years for single people and five to six for a woman with a child. Some old, empty properties were simply taken over by such individuals, with little resistance from authorities. Martin McCauley, "Power and Authority in East Germany: The Socialist Party (SED)," *Conflict Studies* 132 (July 1981): 10.

80. "East German 'Dream' Homes Reclaimed by West," *KCS*, October 13, 1991.

81. Michael Cassell, "Council Houses: The Tories' 'Sale of the Century'", *FT*, April 26, 1979. Peter Murtagh, "Britain Turns into Nation of Long-Lived and Languid Fat Cats," *The Guardian (TG)*, January 6, 1988.

82. Survey data shows that Chinese are nine times more likely to use their money on housing, food, clothing, and savings than for improvements on their land. Nicholas Lardy, public address at University of Missouri-Kansas City, March 24, 1986. The new housing is using up millions of acres of agricultural land each year, taking it out of grain production. Jonathan Mirsky, "Fear of Famine Surfaces as China Debates Rural Policy," *TI*, August 18, 1987.

83. Christopher Flavin, "Electrifying the Third World," *State of the World 1987*, pp. 91–92.

84. The average rural house grew from 8.1 square meters per capita in 1978 to 16 square meters in 1987. The average urban house grew from 4.2 to 8.6 square meters in that time. *China Statistical Abstract 1988 (CSA88)*. Some 15 percent of the urban populace has less than seven feet by three feet per person. William Parish, public address at the University of Missouri-Kansas City, March 24, 1986.

85. Flavin, "Electrifying," pp. 91, 93. Many villages listed as having electricity do not actually have it.

86. An estimated $7.2 billion (in U.S. dollars) in housing has been built in this manner. Geof Barnes, "Inca Cola", PBS "South American Journey" series.

87. Sanders, "Peru's Population," p. 8.

88. A Lagos slum, with half a million people, was demolished in 1990. The families of about seventy-five hundred landlords were resettled to partly finished flats many kilometers away. Other residents were not relocated–simply adding to the portion of the populace squatting in shelters made of cardboard boxes. Olugkenga Ayeni, "A Tearful Exodus," *West Africa*, July 30–August 15, 1990.

89. Even basic items like bandages, syringes, aspirin, and facilities for blood transfusions are often in short supply in the CIS republics. In an inventory in Novosibirsk, which has leading academic institutes and can be expected to have modern facilities, only 11 percent of 216 standard prescription drugs were available. "Human Rights," *DOSB*, p. 74.

   Former Soviet Health Minister Yevgeny I. Chazov told a television interviewer about an operation requiring an unexpected transfusion. There was no blood bank, so the anesthesiologist held out his hand and transfused his own blood to the patient. "This is a fact of our life, you understand," Chazov said. William J. Eaton and Dan Fisher, "Revolution of a New Sort is Underway," *KCT*, November 26, 1987.

90. One study found two-thirds of Soviet men smoked. In 1969, only one woman in ten smoked; by 1977, four in ten. The Soviet government placed "smoking is hazardous to your health" warnings on cigarette packets, increased production of filtered and low tar and nicotine cigarettes, produced public service films for school and television, banned advertising, prohibited smoking in public places, reduced smoking in movies and on television, and even tried paying bonuses to people who do not smoke in an effort to stem the rising numbers who smoke. David E. Powell, "The Emerging Health Crisis in the Soviet Union," *CH* (October 1985): 339. *KCT*, January 26, 1987.

91. One study estimated 30 percent of males in Moscow and its vicinity were alcoholics. The incidence of alcoholism among women is also rising. Powell, "Emerging Health Crisis," p. 328. One in three Americans says alcoholism has brought trouble to his or her family. Thomas V. Seessel, *KCT,* July 7, 1986.

92. Helene Carrere d'Encausse, *Decline of an Empire: The Soviet Socialist Republics in Revolt* (New York: Newsweek Books, 1979), pp. 53–57; Powell, "Emerging Health Crisis," pp. 326–28. *KCT,* January 1, 1982. Edward Townsend, "Britons Cutting Back on Alcohol," *TT,* August 11, 1987. *WP,* October 26, 1988. *KCT,* January 24, 1990. *KCT,* June 26, 1987. Mary Dejevsky, "Hundreds Arrested in Soviet Drive Against Drugs," *TT,* August 18, 1987.

93. For many years, Soviet gynecologists told women that contraception is dangerous.

94. Sociologist Dmitri Shalin estimates that a fourth of the world's abortions occur in the Soviet Union. The Koppel Report, ABC Television, December 19, 1990. Tatyana Mamonova, a feminist publisher, says in 1987 there were 115 abortions for every 100 live births.

95. Nikolai Ignatiovich, former chairman of the Soviet Commission on Privileges, says the average citizen received 60 rubles worth of free health care a year; the nomenklatura, 1,500. Randolph, "Soviet Privileges."

96. The Joint Economic Committee of the Congress estimated that in 1988, Americans spent $500 billion (12 percent of our economic output) on health care, including $125 billion for unneeded tests and procedures—among the world's highest per capita costs. In 1990, we spent $662 billion (still 12 percent), including $175 billion on paperwork and administration. In 1991, that rose to $738 billion (13 percent), and in 1992 to $838 billion (14 percent). In 1993, it was expected to reach $940 billion; by 1995, $1 trillion. But nearly half the populace cannot afford many procedures. *KCS,* October 2, 1989. CBS Morning News, December 3, 1991. Robert Pear, "President's Plans for Health Care Outlined to A.M.A.," *NYT,* January 9, 1992. *KCS,* January 5, 1993. Sixty percent of uninsured family heads are full-time employees, and 20 percent more work part-time. Even though a fourth of the poor are uninsured, Medicaid, the program giving health careto the poor, set an eligibility requirement at half the federal poverty line in some states. Canada, with a federal health plan covering all citizens, spent 8.6

percent of its economic output on health care in 1988 (with 11 percent spent on administration, versus 25 percent in the United States). West Germany also spends 8.6 percent of its economic output on health care. Bob Moos, "Another Big National Health Care Issue Must Be Tackled," *KCS,* October 2, 1989. Francine S. Kiefer, "Germany Holds Health Costs in Check," *CSM,* November 25, 1991.

97. The average premium is $100 a month from the employee, matched by $100 from the employer. Those with incomes above $36,000 receive less matching funds and pay a higher premium.

98. U.S. Health Care Financing Administration. Richard A. Knox, "Germany's Health Care for All Succeeds," *KCS,* May 20, 1991. Annual health care costs in the United States amount to $2,354 per person, versus $1,232 in West Germany, $836 in Britain, and $1,683 in Canada. David R. Francis, "Why the Medical Bill Keeps Growing," *CSM,* November 18, 1991.

99. Health care personnel at the village level in China dropped from 1 million in 1980 to 873,323 in 1989 (including 200,000 doctors), but their training and equipment improved markedly. Instead of less than a year of training, most of the remaining personnel have three, and township hospitals increasingly have modern operating theaters and radiology. Robert Delfs, "Stress Syndromes," *FEER* 149, 3 (July 26, 1990): 21.

100. Cerebrovascular disease, heart disease, and cancer claim 42 percent of Chinese who die. "Africa: Ashtray of the World," *The Sunday Times (TST),* May 13, 1990. Delfs, "Stress Syndromes," p. 21. Before 1950, infectious diseases and parasites were the major killers.

101. Harinder Baweja and Arun Katiyar, "The Indian Face of AIDS," *India Today,* November 30, 1992. "20 p.c. Deviancy among School Kids: Survey," *Indian Express,* October 30, 1992.

102. Sanders, "Peru's Population," p. 8. Pierre L. van den Berghe and George P. Primov, *Inequality in the Peruvian Andes: Class and Ethnicity in Cuzco* (Columbia, Mo.: University of Missouri Press, 1977), p. 180.

103. In 1981, Peru had one doctor for every 18,000 people in the highlands, and one for every 1,750 on

the coast. Cynthia McClintock, "The Prospects for Democratic Consolidation in a 'Least Likely' Case," *Comparative Politics* 21, 2 (January 1989).

104. K. Adeyomi and A. Petu, "A Health Strategy for Nigeria," *Long Range Planning* 22, 6 (December 1989): 57.

105. Idem., p. 61. *TST.*

106. Baweja, "The Indian Face of AIDS."

107. By one estimate, by 1992, 70 percent of American women with children under age five were working outside the home. CBS Evening News, February 5, 1987. A 1984 United States Census Bureau survey found that 7 percent of children aged five to thirteen, a total of 2.1 million, go home alone after school as "latchkey" children while their mothers work. Others estimate that 6.1 to 7 million children are in this category. *WP,* February 6, 1987. Nearly all CIS women work outside the home.

108. Before 1964, younger workers had to contribute to a fund which helped support their parents. Legislation passed in 1964 forced most industries and collective farms to create funds for minimum pensions.

109. There are over 31 million pensioners. An American journalist visiting a neighborhood of retired miners in Donetsk, the Ukraine, found them in crowded, squalid quarters, sharing a pump and outhouses. One told of persistent and unsuccessful attempts to get free coal for their stoves from officials, denied despite the fact that their pensions were below the assured minimum. Kevin Close, *WP,* February 16, 1981.

110. Agricultural workers often continue working and receive at least a partial pension as well. In regions with acute labor shortages, some in other professions may continue to work, too. Doctors and professors may do so, but at half pay.

111. About 28 million of 93 million American workers had pensions in 1988. Pensions of a retired federal government worker averaged $12,966, and of a private worker $6,512, in 1990. Money in pension funds is declining, and increasing numbers of retirees find they cannot collect on pensions. Donald L. Barlett and James B. Steele, "Don't Bet Your Retirement on a 'Guaranteed' Pension," *KCS,* November 28, 1991. Half of all elderly women living alone have incomes below $9,500 a year.

112. Richard D. Lamm, CBS Face the Nation, September 30, 1990. Between 1968 and 1988,

payments to or for the elderly rose from a sixth to a fourth of the national budget. Richard Reeves, "Old People Causing Big Problems for U.S. Society," *KCT,* December 16, 1988.

A World Health Organization study of sixty-five-year-old men in twenty-one countries found that their remaining life expectancy was 14.8 years in the United States versus 16.2 years in Japan. The men in Cuba, Greece, Switzerland, Canada, France, Spain, and Sweden all had higher life expectancies than the Americans. The study found disposable household income of U.S. men aged sixty-five to seventy-four was 99 percent of the national average for all ages. U.S. women aged sixty-five could expect to live for 18.9 more years, versus 20 years in Japan, 19.4 in France, and 17.3 in Greece. David Brindle, "A Poor Look-Out for the Old," *MGW,* November 13, 1988.

113. Childs, *The GDR,* p. 257. East Germany needed its women in the labor force, while West Germany could import workers; the presence of absence of the facilities probably had as much to do with the needs of the state as of the women.

114. Attempts by the West German government to pay mothers to take in children as "day mothers" were opposed both by women's movements and church groups. But day care centers must be registered by the central government and meet their standards; in the United States, if any standards are imposed on such centers, they come from the states.

115. Before the 1970s, East German pensions were even worse. Then they rose about a fourth. State institutions to care for the elderly were poorly financed and operated. Church-run nursing homes give somewhat better care, but together contained only eleven-thousand beds. Such homes cost around 100 marks a month. Handicapped people, too, were neglected; there were few programs for them.

People from certain professions deemed hazardous, important, or short of labor received higher pension benefits, as did survivors of Nazi concentration camps.

116. There may be some improvement in the status of British retirees. The proportion of the poorest fifth of households headed by a retiree dropped from 81 percent in 1975 to 64 percent in 1985. *TI,* August 18, 1987. But the WHO study cited in footnote 112 found that 8.5 million British elderly were

below the qualifying level for income reporting, and 2.7 million were less than 40 percent above that level. Those aged sixty-five to seventy-four had disposable household incomes equal to 67 percent of the country's average income; West Germany's elderly had a higher percentage. English and Welsh men aged sixty-five could expect to live 13.3 additional years, versus 12.8 in northern Ireland and Scotland, 13.8 in West Germany and 12.5 in East Germany. A sixty-five-year-old Scottish woman could expect to live 16.1 more years. Brindle, "A Poor Look-Out for the Old."

117. The new workers' congresses may help. Between the Septembers of 1979 and 1981, the workers' congress at Jiamusi Paper Mill in northeastern China received 435 suggestions from workers, built 21,000 square meters of living quarters and an auditorium, and set up a nursery for 700 children. Only a minority of plants have workers' congresses, and only a small portion of these function effectively. Tony Saich, "Workers in the Workers' State: Urban Workers in the PRC," in David S. G. Goodman, *Groups and Politics in the People's Republic of China* (Cardiff, England: University College Cardiff Press, 1984), p. 167.

118. The Moscow subway is truly a marvel. The underground stations are clean, with mosaics, stained glass windows, vaulted ceilings, and other beautiful features. Clean, modern, fast trains come every minute during rush hour, charging low fares. But buses are slow and overcrowded, with erratic schedules.

119. By 1987, China had 293 million bicycles, up from 188 million in 1985 and 75 million in 1978. This breaks down to 177 bicycles per 100 urban households. *CSA88*.

120. Mark M. Sheehan, "Car Sales Soar in Merged Economy," *CSM*, September 27, 1990.

121. Some Soviet economists estimated only 10 percent of output reached a level of quality and technological advancement found in products of other advanced nation-states. About 800 million pairs of shoes were made each year, piling up in warehouses while people lined up to buy the 100 million pairs imported each year. Defective television sets started 40 percent of residential fires in Moscow in 1986. Robert Gillette, "Creaking Economy Needs More Than a Little Repair," *KCT*, November 26, 1987.

122. Citizens of post-Soviet republics still spend an average of two hours each day standing in line to wait for the most basic purchases and services.

123. By 1991, many Chinese were going to Russia as tourists. Their fashionable clothes and cameras drew attention from Soviet passersby. By bringing along jeans, shoes, and shampoo to sell to Soviets, tourists could pay for their whole trip. Soviets crossed into China to buy thermos flasks, plastic buckets, cotton clothes, and food. The Chinese, however, found little to buy in the Soviet states other than caviar. Tai Ming Cheung, "Shampoo for Caviar," *FEER* 152, 26 (June 27, 1991).

124. But people everywhere in India know how to improvise repairs on Ambassadors, and nothing need be imported. *KCS*, January 21, 1988.

125. But a study done for the Ford Foundation by the Tata Economic Consultancy Services points out that India lags far behind China in producing goods for mass consumption.

126. In one village in Uttar Pradesh, controlled by one large landowner who made high-interest loans to villagers and ran the village panchayat, bureaucrats failed to supply a power line from the power cables a kilometer away; the landowner knew that villagers' purchases of electricity and its ancillary products would reduce their ability to repay loans and pay taxes and increase their ability to gather information from the outside world.

127. These figures are from 1987. Figures from the same year indicate that 64 in 100 urban households have a black and white TV, and 34 in 100 have color; 75 in 100 have a sewing machine, 103 an electric fan, 20 a refrigerator, and 57 a tape recorder. *CSA88*. Those percentages are now much higher.

128. "Soaking the Rich," *TE*.

Exercises

Think about the book thus far:

1. How does part 4—on how influence affects people's lives—relate to part 3 on using influence?
2. Look back at the conclusion of chapter 24 and figure 18.1. What might you expect to discover about equality and material well-being in this chapter?

Answer the following questions:

1. What deficiencies do you see in the availability of food, housing, and health care in these systems?
2. What advantages do some systems have in distributing these items equitably?

Thinking It Through

Choose one country, and compare it with the others in regard to the following questions:

1. How many people have enough to eat?
2. How many people can live adequately on what they earn?
3. How many have sufficient housing?
4. How many can get decent health care?
5. Do government services reach those who need them?
6. How widely distributed are consumer goods?

Does this comparison surprise you? Why or why not? If you were among the lowest fifth of the populace in terms of income, in which of these countries would you rather live?

chapter 26

EQUALITY

OPPORTUNITY

In chapter 25, we examined inequalities in the distribution of food, clothing, shelter, health care, and consumer goods. Now we will examine whether all members of society have an equal opportunity to develop and use their skills, to gain rewards for doing so, and to better themselves socially and economically.

As we saw in the last chapter, some people in the countries we are studying are paid much more than others. Are the highest-paid workers the ones who have the most skills and who work the hardest? Does everyone with comparable ability and willingness to work have an equal opportunity to obtain one of these higher-paying jobs?

As we saw in chapter 7, children tend to seek education, jobs, and marriages that keep them within the same earning status as their parents. But there are also people who rise above their parents in status.

Are earnings commensurate with jobs, skills, and willingness to work? Do all people have equal opportunity to develop skills and to move ahead socially and economically if they improve their performance? These are the questions we will explore as we discuss equal opportunity.

OPPORTUNITY IN THE USA AND CIS

In the United States, some descendants of Native Americans, nineteenth- and twentieth-century immigrant groups, and former slaves and sharecroppers have gained economic mobility.[1] The same is true of the descendants of many serfs in the CIS. Like Native Americans, many Ukrainians, Estonians, Latvians, Lithuanians, Poles, Jews, Cossacks, Buddhists, and Muslims had higher status in their own cultures

before outsiders conquered them. But it is often harder for individuals from such groups to advance than for Anglo-Saxon protestants in the United States or Great Russians in the former Soviet Union. Groups such as Jews and Lithuanians in the Soviet Union, like Japanese and other Asian-Americans in the United States, occupied a higher percentage of university seats and upper-level professional positions than was proportional to their percentage of population, but these minority members seldom reached the very highest positions. In inner cities and some regions of the United States, minority schools are often not as good as those available to other groups. The post-Soviet republics experience similar problems; but now some roles are reversed, as former ethnic minorities discriminate against Russians and other minorities within their territories.

One important difference between the CIS and the United States in this regard is that many groups who are not achieving social mobility in the CIS are nationalities which for centuries have done better economically than Great Russians. In contrast, the groups with the lowest mobility in the United States are generally among those which started with lower economic status.

In both systems, it is sometimes possible for people to climb to the top of bureaucratic ladders largely on the basis of their ability to use family contacts or make friends in the right places. But there is also considerable opportunity for those who do not have such connections if they will work to receive educations. Both nation-states have also opened up educational opportunities, and reserve some positions especially for minorities in economic and political institutions.

Women constitute more than half the populations of both the United States and the CIS. CIS women are encouraged to become teachers, secretaries, milkmaids, agronomists, economists, scientific laboratory technicians, journalists, and doctors.[2] Nearly all CIS women work outside the home to supplement family income.[3] Soviet pay scales are often lower in professions dominated by women;[4] these tend also to be professionals not held in high esteem by the public.[5] Women working jobs identical to men's may find themselves working harder for less pay at more sporadic intervals than their male counterparts; it is especially difficult for women to get jobs in industry, where wages are higher. Many women have manual labor jobs requiring strenuous physical exertion. Rural women, especially, find it hard to obtain good jobs.[6] Soviet men tend not to share in housework, so working women must work extra hours looking after aging parents and children, cleaning house, and spending an average of two and a half hours a day waiting in long lines to purchase necessities.[7]

In both America and Russia, women were introduced into the urban work force in the nineteenth century by manufacturers seeking cheap labor. It was often the wives of manufacturers and managers who led the women's rights movements seeking to end exploitation and give women the vote and greater freedom to leave the house. Ending the worst abuses of the sweatshops and making it more acceptable for women to step out onto the street in the daytime accelerated their ability to shop for both goods and jobs. Russia's huge workforce losses in both World War I and II, and America's entry into World War II, opened new job outlets to women. In both countries, educational institutions increasingly opened their doors to women.

American women have been encouraged to become secretaries, teachers, medical technicians, retail clerks, and computer programmers and operators. Many women must work to supplement family income, taking jobs with less pay than their husbands.[8] In recent times, American women have demanded acceptance into a wider range of professions at more equal pay scales; in 1986, the number of women in professions surpassed the number of men.[9] This does not mean that women hold jobs of comparable status within these professions; a 1990 study found that 3 percent of top executives in the thousand biggest companies were women and 1 percent were minority members.[10] Women still do not receive the same income as men with comparable educations, and they have experienced difficulty obtaining employment suitable to their educational accomplishments, although that is improving.[11] Women hold some posts on the cabinet, the Supreme Court, in legislatures,[12] and at the top of bureaucratic divisions and corporations. As of 1990, there were three women governors, six lieutenant governors, ten secretaries of state, three state attorney generals, and twelve state treasurers, and 3,867 women in local offices. Blacks held 6,829 and hispanics 3,300 local offices.[13] By 1993, seven of the 100 United States Senators, and 47 of 435 members of the House of Representatives, were women.

No similar progress is apparent in the CIS at the highest levels. Only two women were ever on the Politburo.[14] Since World War II, only two women have headed ministries. Only 3 of the 749 members of the National Academy of Science are women.[15] Two women have served as ambassadors. At the levels immediately below this, progress has also been slow, as in the United States. As of 1975, there were only 2 female department and sections heads (out of 200) on the party's Central Committee; since the 1920s, not more than 4.2 percent of its members were women. In 1975, 7 of 550 deputy ministers and deputy chairs of state committees were women. In 1976, 3.8 percent of the members of the party bureaus at the republic level were women. Some 23 percent of members of republic and regional, 29 percent of city and district, and 25 percent of primary party central committees were women, as were half of chairpersons of trade unions, 18 percent of staff of the Communist Party's Central Committee below the section level, 23 percent of Communist Party members,[16] and 32 percent of "leaders of organs of the state administration, Party and Komsomol, trade union and other public organizations, and their structural subdivisions." Women constitute 9 percent of enterprise directors.[17] No women head academic institutions. They are rarely included in delegations traveling abroad.

Glasnost did not improve employment and political opportunities for women. Only 5 percent of members of the Congress of People's Deputies were women.[18] Few women occupy high positions.[19] Many younger women wish to leave the dreary work places and devote their time to domestic activities; most cannot. Child leaves are rare, and husbands tend to give little help tending babies or cleaning house. With divorce and separation common, more than half of Moscow's families are headed by single parents—mostly women. State-sponsored day and health care programs have been reduced under budget constraints. Birth control devices, sanitary napkins, and many other products remain scarce. Women comprise 80 percent of those unemployed by layoffs in state enterprises. Independent feminist organizations began only in 1991 and have few members.

Both nation-states—the United States and the CIS—contain some groups which are underpaid and have little chance for social mobility; they also contain people of humble origins and average educational backgrounds who have risen to the highest levels. Some people with skills in both nation-states are unable to use them. Some do not have access to good elementary and secondary schools. With only 21 percent of CIS citizens in tertiary (college-level) education, versus 61 percent of Americans, that avenue is more open to Americans. Some CIS jobs require less education than similar positions in America. But both these nation-states contain many people who do not have much social mobility, even when they are offered educational opportunities.

Some groups can obtain the jobs they prefer with greater ease than others.

Thus, in both the CIS and the United States, some groups need to work harder than others to get the best jobs and to acquire the skills needed for those jobs, but educational paths are open for them to do so. Most people do not gain social mobility, but a few people from varied class, ethnic, and religious backgrounds do. Women and various ethnic and religious minorities have difficulty reaching the very highest rungs of their professions; that situation has been improving, but slowly. Those with the most frustration about acquiring new skills and higher-status jobs are those who wish to but cannot—who seek mobility but are frustrated about achieving it, or had a better job and lost it, or who are struggling to keep up with the skills and job levels of their parents.

In the United States, such people might include many women, people losing farm and factory and white-collar jobs, people whose skills exceed the demands of their jobs, and people who see those with fewer skills than themselves rising to higher positions. In our system, characterized by mass higher education, the trend for many jobs to become simpler and pay less, an active women's movement, and fast turnover in job markets, such frustrations may be rather widespread. They are probably offset, somewhat, by the generally high standard of living, the opportunities to launch one's own business, and recreational opportunities to occupy free time.

In the CIS, many rural people who are restricted in their movement to cities: Jews, inhabitants of the Baltic Republics, and others who seek advancement to the top levels of their professions but are not allowed to progress; and women, artists, intellectuals, and people with better educations may be among those experiencing the greatest frustration in acquiring new skills and higher-status jobs or the right to return to a home which affords them privacy and free time. Their numbers, too, may be large. They cannot turn to the same compensating factors as their counterparts in the United States. Many of these frustrated workers are probably among those supporting changes in the system.

OPPORTUNITY IN THE UNITED KINGDOM AND GERMANY

The most disadvantaged ethnic minorities in the United Kingdom tend to be the Welsh, northern English, Scots, Northern Irish Catholics, south Asians, and blacks. In Germany, those working the Junker estates in the eastern part of the country were among the slowest to receive the benefits of modernization. Even the Turks, former Yugoslavs, Italians, and Greeks who have been living and working in West Germany for decades, and their children who were born in Germany, cannot become citizens under German law. These are all groups which have been relatively disadvantaged over long periods of time.

West Germans and citizens of the United Kingdom do not experience extensive social mobility. However, with a longer history of universal education, and a larger number of giant business enterprises, East and West Germany provide more berths in middle management—recruited on the basis of merit—than the United Kingdom. Germany has also had more high-paying blue collar jobs and skilled workers to fill them. The East German school system allowed children of working- and peasant-class families to obtain higher education. Many of East Germany's factories, farms, and government institutions were led by people from such backgrounds, partly because many with more advanced skills and higher class origins emigrated to the West at the end of World War II. There is little sign of comparable mobility for the United Kingdom's ethnic minorities.

Most of the women working outside the home in the United Kingdom come from families at the lower end of the pay scale, though many middle-class women work. Sixty-eight percent of British women work, versus 10 percent in the 1930s.[20] On average, their pay is 65 percent that of males, and women heads of households have not kept pace.[21] In 1987, 10.5 percent of students enrolled in British university and polytechnic engineering courses were women. In West Germany in 1972, 26 percent of university students were female, mostly studying home economics, elementary teaching, and foreign languages. In 1971, 37 percent of West Germany's work force was women, yet they earned only 25 percent of the payroll. White collar males earned 55 percent more than white collar women. In 1988, women's hourly earnings in manufacturing were 73 percent those of men.[22] In professions men do not enter, this has caused labor shortages.[23]

In East Germany, about half the enrollment in technical colleges[24] and the work force has been women, and over 90 percent of women of working age had jobs (versus 55 percent in West Germany).[25] But as of 1978, women constituted only 25 percent of the technically trained work force outside the building trades.[26] Women predominate in health and social services, and in education and cultural activities—which are low-paid professions. Sixty percent of teachers, but only 25 percent of school heads, were women in 1973.[27] With little day care, most schools open half days, and stores closed evenings and Sundays, working women all over Germany encounter difficulties; a third of the female work force is part-time. A third of those enrolled in universities are women, but university graduates are generally paid little more than nongraduates. With a great labor shortage, East Germany was anxious to employ the skills of women. An estimated 20 percent of skilled workers were not employed at tasks commensurate with their qualifications. This affected women more than men. As of 1973, 35 percent of physicians and 37 percent of judges in East Germany were women; only 20 percent of physicians, 5 percent of professors, and 3 percent of judges in West Germany are women. However, 12 percent of West Germany's company presidents were women by 1980.[28]

About 12 percent of the Socialist Unity Party's Central Committee in East Germany were women, as were a third of party members;[29] in 1982, the East German Council of Ministers contained one woman, while the West German cabinet contained two.[30] In 1988 the Social Democratic Party mandated that 40 percent of its members and elected officers would be women. By 1992, a fifth of the members of the Bundestag were women, as were 11 to 35 percent of Laender parliaments and 20 to

42 percent of city and local council members. In the United Kingdom, Margaret Thatcher was the only woman in her cabinet. Thirty-five women were elected to the British Parliament in 1987; the three Afro-Caribbeans and the black Asian who won seats that year were the first blacks to serve since 1929.[31]

East and West Germany contain fewer people who may be disadvantaged in economic competition as a result of their ethnic origin than does the United Kingdom. Chances for social mobility may have been somewhat greater in East Germany than in West Germany or the United Kingdom. Education is widespread in all three, including 20 to 30 percent in tertiary education, but the best job positions go to those attending the best elementary schools, middle schools, and universities. Few people experience social mobility. Women have employment opportunities, though usually at lower pay scales; few achieve prominent positions. The assimilation of East Germany into Germany has caused widespread unemployment in the East; two-thirds of those losing their jobs were women.

Thus, in the United Kingdom and West Germany, fewer people probably experience social mobility than in the United States, the Soviet Union, or East Germany. Those that do must work hard to achieve it; one of the biggest hurdles is entering into the restricted system of higher education. Women and members of various ethnic and religious minorities have difficulty reaching the very highest rungs of their professions; that situation has been improving. As in the United States and the CIS, those with the most frustration about acquiring new skills and higher-status jobs are those who wish to do so but cannot—who seek mobility but are frustrated about achieving it, or had a better job and lost it, or who are struggling to keep up with the skills and job levels of their parents. East Germans, who were trained for jobs that no longer exist and are untrained for jobs that will exist, have strong reason to be frustrated.

In the United Kingdom, people at a disadvantage might include many unemployed skilled workers, lesser numbers of people whose skills exceed the demands of their jobs, and many whose real income is declining. Such people often live in areas with low living standards and few recreational outlets, and they often have little background or ability to start their own businesses.

West Germany used to have virtually no unemployment; today the unemployment rate largely reflects displaced East Germans, but it is also rising among West Germans. Some West Germans must wish to rise higher educationally than the system allows. But on the whole, West Germany has a smaller percentage than the United Kingdom of people who wish to acquire new skills and a higher-status job. In East Germany, where more people experienced social mobility, the greatest frustration used to affect those at the middle and top of their professions, who realized how much lower their earnings were than in the West and how little they could buy with them. Now, such people hope they can successfully compete with those in the West. Turks and other foreigners residing in Germany have twice the unemployment rate of German citizens, and only one in sixteen of their often gifted children (versus one in four German youth) finish the highest level of secondary school.

OPPORTUNITY IN CHINA

In China, only a small fraction of those with higher education come from peasant backgrounds; most are the sons and daughters of urban workers or people with higher education themselves. Virtually all of the best jobs at the national level go to university graduates; virtually all university graduates get high-status (though often low-paying) jobs. Only about 1 percent of young people receive a university education; that percentage is even lower among non-Han people. Under the responsibility system, peasants have been increasingly pulling their children from school early to help earn money; but an increasing percentage of university admissions come from peasants.[32]

Most people earn enough to take care of their basic needs. Most can earn extra money if they develop some skills in production, marketing, or manipulating the political system.[33] Very few achieve social mobility. Middle-level workers marketing agricultural produce, owners of small cooperative factories, workers in joint-venture enterprises, and the children of cadres probably have the greatest opportunity to do so.

Two members of the State Council are women; two other women hold ministerial posts (out of about fifty). About 21 percent of the members of the Sixth National People's Congress were women (13.4 percent of delegates were from ethnic minorities); women hold some posts at all levels of the Communist Party (which had 13 percent female membership in 1983).[34] A woman chairs the important Chinese People's Political Consultative Conference. Very few women hold other high-level posts in government. In 1981, women constituted 26 percent of the cadres, but only 3 to 6 percent of the high-ranking cadres.[35]

Primary education is universal for men and women. Many women go on to obtain higher education; many of them may take jobs as administrators or teachers or take other positions that offer some status but do not pay well.[36] Most schools and some bureaucratic units require higher entrance examinations scores for women than for men. In farms and factories, women work alongside men; one survey found their output to be higher, but their wages 30 to 87 percent those of men. Women do 60 to 70 percent of farm work. By 1985, women constituted 36 percent of the nonagricultural labor force as well.[37]

In Imperial China, since about a thousand years ago, even the peasants bound women's feet, women were forced to obey their husbands entirely, and women were not allowed to receive education or hold paying jobs. Their present position represents a dramatic change. Today, they go to school and work alongside men (though often at low-paying jobs); most women are employed outside the home.[38] However, in rural China, there is considerable reticence about acknowledging the birth of a female child[39] or teaching women technical skills or giving them land titles, yet little reticence about assigning them the hardest jobs, the lowest pay, and all household tasks.[40] Half of rural women are illiterate. Sale of women as concubines and prostitutes continues in some places. The "one child" policy has led to millions of forced sterilizations, and abortions, and IUD insertions. In urban areas, pay for comparable work is greater than in rural regions, but women are channeled into jobs with lower pay and fewer chances for advancement.[41] As state factories reduce staff to compete with joint ventures and cooperatives, poorly educated women are often the first laid off; two-thirds of the jobless are women.

In China, fewer people probably experience social mobility than in the United Kingdom, Germany, the United States, or the CIS. Those that do must work hard to achieve it; one of the biggest hurdles is entering into the restricted system of higher education. Women and various ethnic minorities have difficulty reaching the very highest rungs of their professions; that situation has been improving very slowly for ethnic minorities, and slowly for women. As in other nation-states, those with the most frustration about acquiring new skills and higher-status jobs are those who wish to do so but cannot—who seek mobility but are frustrated about achieving it, or had a better job and lost it, who are struggling to keep up with the skills and job levels of their parents, or who are comparing their status with people abroad. That might include people who lost jobs and educational opportunities during the Cultural Revolution, new generations of unemployed youths in the cities, youth who have gone to study in foreign countries, and youth who have been unable to pursue higher studies they aspired to, or have done so but cannot find challenging jobs. They probably do not constitute a high percentage of the population, but their education makes them politically volatile. To some extent, they also probably include many women, who constitute a high percentage of the populace.

OPPORTUNITY IN INDIA

Most of the five hundred thousand students studying in India's colleges and universities are children of the more affluent families. Most still study liberal arts, but enrollments in engineering, medicine, law, and agriculture have increased. The best jobs go to these graduates, but many of them remain unemployed. Disproportionate percentages of Sikhs, Marwaris, Parsis, Jains, Gujarati Vaisyas, Maratha, and members of certain other communities find the best educations and jobs; the same holds true for members of higher castes. Employers hiring people for important jobs also tend to recruit the children of workers who already hold the jobs. The daughters may go into medicine or teaching; the sons, in addition, may go into management in industry or the civil service. According to 1971 census data, 21 percent of those in medicine, 18 percent in teaching, 2 percent of industry executives, and 9 percent of management-level civil servants were women. Interviews with 120 women from these four professions revealed that 82 percent of their fathers were university graduates, compared with 1 percent of the population and 3 percent of urban males.[42]

The great majority of the population, however, have little chance to advance educationally and virtually no hope for social mobility. Poorer peasants have little opportunity for education or job advancement. Because boys bring in rather than cost dowries, many female babies are aborted in the second trimester—following detection by ultrasound scanning—or killed at birth by rural mothers,[43] and girls (like their mothers) are often fed less and receive less medical attention than boys. Most people do not earn enough to care for even their basic needs; they work long hours simply to subsist. Many teenage girls are forced to leave school early to do chores and then into early marriage. Others are sold into prostitution or slave labor. About 95 percent of boys enter first grade, and 35 percent enter ninth grade; 60 percent of girls enter first, and 10 percent ninth. The average woman has eight or nine pregnancies and spends most waking hours doing heavy work. Rural men often spend half their income on alcohol, leaving the women to fetch water and firewood and carry out all domestic tasks. Wife beating is common in villages and squatter colonies. Divorced or widowed women may not inherit land and are often left dependent on the mercy of their children. Many are cast into the streets. Those few,

male or female, who graduate from high school or university can seldom obtain jobs of any stature; the women among them often take low-paying jobs as school teachers or social workers. Government schools are often miserably housed, equipped and taught. Private schools are only within the reach of the upper levels of the middle class; few of even their graduates reach university.[44]

India had a woman prime minister for a number of years. A number of women have held ministerial posts at the national and state levels, including chief state minister.[45] The Congress party chooses women to run for a fifth to a sixth of its state legislative seats; women held 28 of 542 Lok Sabha seats in 1980. Few women hold other high posts in government.[46]

A few of India's many cultural communities contribute most of the people who receive the best educations and jobs. Few people experience social mobility. Only women from educated families have a chance to obtain higher educations; the range of jobs available to them is limited.

India, like China, has very little social mobility. Those that do move ahead socially must work hard to do so; one of the biggest hurdles is entering into the restricted system of higher education. Women, members of lower castes, and various ethnic minorities have difficulty reaching the very highest rungs of their professions; that has been improving slowly. Most people have no chance to rise above their present status. Those with the most frustration about acquiring new skills and higher-status jobs are those who wish to do so but cannot—who seek mobility but are frustrated in their attempts to move forward, or had a better job and lost it, who are struggling to keep up with the skills and job levels of their parents, or who are comparing their status with people abroad. These people might include youth who have gone to study in foreign countries, youth who have been unable to pursue higher studies that they aspired to, youth educated in Hindi and other non-English languages who want advanced training, or those with adequate training but inadequate caste and family connections. Largely because educational

The *Times of India* can be taken seriously when it calls itself one of the world's five great newspapers. Its world affairs reporting is sophisticated and witty. Its pages discuss the skirmishes between the United States Congress and president, European politics, the latest London plays, Paris fashions, rock music, and vacation paradises on the Mediterranean. Like the journalists at most Indian newspapers, its correspondents write in depth on problems facing India's women and their new and growing feminist movement. On Sundays—with separate listings for different religions, castes, regions, occupations, and those with green cards to study in the United States—its second to fifth pages are filled with classified "Grooms Wanted For" (and "Brides Wanted For") advertisements similar to the following:

North Indian Brahmin Indian Administrative Service or Private Executive businessman wanted for 26-year-old, very beautiful, brilliant convent-educated postgraduate (eye specialist) doctor girl from well-known Brahmin family of high social and political status. No horoscope needed. Send returnable photograph.

Good looking, 26 to 30, 170 centimeters tall boy with progressive outlook for good looking, fair, slim, Iyengar girl, 25, well-employed as software engineer, from decent, educated family. Groom in case from USA should possess H-1 visa status. Girl interested in studying abroad, and passed GMAT, TOEFEL in flying colours. Send horoscope.

Protestant parents want Born-again, qualified groom for daughter, 28, very fair, 147 centimeters, M.A. degree, drawing Central Government pay.

Anglo-Indian, 23/152 centimeters tall, pretty, postgraduate employed girl seeks Anglo-Indian Catholic groom.

Issueless [without child] divorcee Brahmin spinster, 35, architect, soft nature. Caste no bar.

Honey-complexioned, attractive-featured, domestically trained, Sunni Muslim with Ph.D. from a top university in the USA, employed in Washington, USA citizen, seeks professional, doctor, Ph.D., or engineer from respectable family. Visiting Delhi mid-December.

Some 98 percent of Indian marriages are arranged by families. Senior family members study the replies to advertisements or personal inquiries and choose candidates to interview. The prospective brides and grooms are given an interview with one another, and either may reject a candidate after the interview. In most instances, the bride's family must offer the groom's family a dowry or bride wealth, ranging from around 10,000 rupees ($400) for peasant families to hundreds of thousands of rupees for families like those represented in the previous ads. Families often borrow money and incur years of debt to pay off these obligations. Increasing numbers of cases are reported of husbands killing their wives in kitchen fires because of unsatisfactory dowry payments. But many Indians remark on how successful their arranged marriages have been; the system does bring together couples with similar backgrounds.

The law forbids the practice of Hindu traditions which demand that a bride's family pay a dowry, deny women property rights, and forbid widows to remarry. But these practices still continue openly. The government recognizes Muslim personal law, which permits a man to divorce his wife simply by saying "I divorce thee" and to have his daughter's clitoris removed with broken glass or razor blades to reduce her sexual pleasure and keep her chaste (an often-fatal practice even more widespread in Africa).*

See A. M. Rosenthal, "Genital Mutilation the Fate of Many Females;" "Women are Scarred in a Ritual of Violence," Kansas City Star, January 3 and August 1, 1993.

opportunities have never expanded more rapidly than job opportunities, such people probably do not constitute a high percentage of the population. But they may include increasingly large portions of the populace who have come to realize that they cannot share in the new prosperity enjoyed by the wealthiest members of the middle class because they are tied to their villages by perpetual debt, their inability to speak English, and reliance on landlords and bureaucrats for their subsistence.

Opportunity in Peru

Nineteenth-century Peruvian immigrants opened small businesses, banks, mines, vegetable farms, and real estate developments. Some **mestizos** (persons of mixed race, or Quechua who had adopted European dress and culture) moved to the coast or mining towns as workers on the sugar and cotton plantations, in mines, and in construction. Since that time, the descendants of these individuals have been able to better themselves through education and to assume leadership in the professions, smaller businesses, and white collar jobs, and through investments in *haciendas,* commerce, real estate, and industry. They represent a high portion of those in the modern sector of the economy. Between 1955 and 1972, Lima's share of Peru's industrial output grew from 60 to 73 percent.

During the 1920s, substantial numbers of highland peasants and mestizos moved to Lima on the new roads. Few of these have moved into the modern sector of the economy. Even Alianza Popular Revolucionaria Americana's popular universities[47] largely taught those who had arrived on the earlier waves of immigration.

Many of the one hundred sixty thousand Peruvian university students come from the old *encomienda* families and from among the nineteenth-century immigrants; but more than half come from highland peasant families. Some of the old encomienda families have not taken advantage of the new educational and investment opportunities and must live modestly. There are no programs to help highland peasants; mestizos with little education develop job skills which might help them enter the modern sector. To even complete primary education, a highland peasant must generally move to a district capital; then he or she must go to a provincial capital to obtain secondary education. However, highland peasants who move into towns and join mestizo culture have more opportunity today for higher education than their counterparts who moved to Lima two or three generations ago. They have more chance to develop personal ties to people who will help them enter the priesthood, the armed forces, bureaucracy, teaching careers, or a university.

Chola market women selling produce in Arequipa, Peru.
Bob Gamer

The daughter of a mestizo man and a Quechua woman is called a **chola.** Chola women, wearing white stovepipe hats, dominate the market stalls in provincial towns. They provide transport for food, small manufactured goods, wool, and other raw materials from their places of production and sell them to smaller buyers. They also extend credit to buyers and sellers and pay taxes and market fees. They invest their profits in educating their children, hoping that the children may become factory laborers or petty bureaucrats. Considered social inferiors by mestizos, chola and their families cannot fully join town society; but their contacts between town and countryside, and their command of both some Spanish and Quechua, assure them of income and make them indispensable to both bureaucrats and urban dwellers. They have also founded mothers' groups, collective cooking for poor families, *chicha* bars serving home-brewed maize beer, mutual help associations, syndicates, unions, and branches of political parties. They have money and influence, but social restraints keep them and their families from moving into higher positions in society. It is not surprising that their children are found among the ranks of Sendero Luminoso terrorists. Before their arrest, eight of the nineteen members of Sendero

Luminoso's central committee were women, who also lead many of its local guerilla bands.

No women have held cabinet posts in Peru. Some now hold congressional and mayoral posts. Far fewer women are educated than men. But women clearly wield influence within their own villages, and widows are permitted to vote in village assemblies in place of the deceased male head of the family. In contrast, among the highland peasants who move into towns and mestizo culture, it is often the men who learn Spanish, while the women speak only Quechua or Aymara dialects and play a retiring role. Hence, a disproportionate percentage of the highland peasants in universities are men. And the now-aborted land reforms further set back the position of women, because the land titles were issued to males, instead of to females as in the traditional system; also, few women became members of cooperatives, and their educational level is lower than that of males.[48]

Peru's best jobs are largely reserved for a limited array of families. Social mobility is increasing for other sectors of the modern economy. Most people, however, are not in the modern economy.

Peru has very little social mobility. It is perhaps most noticeable among village youth moving into regional universities and into the army. Women, highland peasants, and others of low social status have difficulty reaching the very highest rungs of their professions. Those with the most frustration about acquiring new skills and higher-status jobs are those who wish to do so but cannot—who seek mobility but are frustrated about achieving it, or had a better job and lost it, who are struggling to keep up with the skills and job levels of their parents, or who are comparing their status with people abroad. These people might include youth who have graduated from universities without finding jobs, people whose savings and earnings have been reduced by the rampant inflation, people whose farm income has ceased, those whose native crafts are being replaced by machine-made goods, those who have moved from formerly productive villages to the city and cannot find work, and children of chola women. They may represent a fairly large portion of the populace.

OPPORTUNITY IN NIGERIA

Less than a fifth of Nigeria's populace speaks English. Those who do often come from among Yoruba, Ibo, and Hausa who benefitted early from British education because of their proximity to port cities or because of their royal lineages. As we learned in chapter 7, only about a third of the populace are literate; many of those who are graduated from Muslim schools and were taught in Arabic. Fewer than 6 percent of rural youths attend high school. The fourteen universities draw their eighty thousand students largely from Ibo and Yoruba youth whose fathers already hold privileged jobs. Yet because of their strong influence in the army and politics, Hausa wield disproportionate influence. The army offers more social mobility to individuals from other tribal groups than the civil service or commerce and manufacturing, which are largely controlled by established Yoruba, Ibo, or Hausa families.

Women play little role in the army, national politics, or modern sector employment. One in four nominated local government councilors, two of seventy senior advocates before the Supreme Court, and the vice-chancellor of the University of Benin are women. Each state has a woman commissioner. A growing number of women serve in the senior civil service. Women have served in local and constitutional assemblies, as medical corps commanders, and as federal ministers. Of Nigeria's fifteen thousand lawyers, three thousand are women.

Most of the cassava, the subsistence crop of the south, is grown by women, who also sell crops or products sold in village markets. Yoruba women often pursue village trades independently of their husbands. This gives them some control over family finances; a few have accumulated vast fortunes. But, as with Peru's chola women, it does not give them or their families much access to other kinds of jobs or political status, and they remain subservient to their husbands, many of whom have multiple wives.[49]

An even smaller portion of Nigerians from peasant homes have been exposed to higher education than the peasants in Peru. A smaller portion have access to radio and television. While their villages are poor, they are not controlled by a single land-owning family, as is often the case in India. Many who do have secondary or higher educations but cannot find jobs are able to emigrate to England, the United States, or elsewhere. All this reduces the tendency for people to become frustrated with lack of opportunity. Those with advanced educations who are out of work, along with traditional Muslim leaders in the north (whose political control over their social groups is challenged by central government and military leaders from families of lesser social rank) are some of the most likely individuals to express discontent.

CONCLUSION

Most people in the United States, the CIS, the United Kingdom, Germany, and China are experiencing a better standard of living than they have known in the past. But some are not, and they have clear reason for discontent. The Soviet Union and East Germany underwent a period of economic improvement, but eventually their standards of living stalled and became stagnant; living standards are now rising in East Germany, while those in CIS republics remain uncertain. While some in India, Peru, and Nigeria are experiencing a better standard of living than they have known in the past, most are as poor (or even poorer) than their parents were. Their standard of living does not meet their needs; a far higher percentage of the populations of Peru, India, and Nigeria have reason for discontent with this realm of their lives than their counterparts in the other nation-states. A higher percentage of Indians have reason to feel content with their living conditions than Nigerians or Peruvians. A higher percentage of people in the United States, West Germany, and the United Kingdom have stronger reason to feel content than in any of the others.

Do earnings correlate with jobs, skills, and willingness to work? Do all people have equal opportunity to develop skills and to gain social mobility as they improve their performance? In all nine of these nation-states, social mobility is more the ex-

ception than the rule. In all, women tend to have fewer education and job opportunities than men, but educated women are entering job markets. All afford better job opportunities to those who achieve higher educations (though some individuals with good educations are not well paid). All contain citizens from certain ethnic groups and regions who experience more difficulty than others in obtaining jobs; all are attempting to improve educational opportunities for such groups, some more aggressively and successfully than others.

The majority of children in India, Peru, and Nigeria are offered such inadequate primary educations that they cannot hope to obtain even high school educations or jobs that provide anything beyond subsistence income, even if they have skills and determination. Primary education in China is also minimal, but the responsibility system and rural cooperatives nonetheless offer peasants prospects for increased living standards. So high percentages of people in India, Peru, and Nigeria barely satisfy their minimal needs for survival, no matter how hard they work. Boys or girls who work hard at school in China can usually hope to attain more than minimal occupational status; the same holds true in the United States, the CIS, Germany, and the United Kingdom. The United States affords more chances than the others for people with little education to achieve social mobility and high income; it also offers more opportunity than the others for children to obtain a complete education. The CIS, East and West Germany, and the United Kingdom extend opportunities for primary and secondary education to broad segments of the population; social mobility is still very difficult in these countries.

The nation-states that give people more opportunity to acquire influence may offer more opportunities for social mobility as well. Curiously, greater opportunity does not always lead to greater contentment. People who are efficacious enough to develop influence often feel frustrated when they encounter obstacles somewhere along the way. At times, those with fewer aspirations experience more contentment.

SUMMARY

Some of these systems offer more opportunities to women and ethnic minorities to achieve higher educations, better jobs, and higher social status, regardless of their social or economic origins, than do others. Education and involvement in modern economic institutions seem to be doorways of opportunity. Groups who have little access to either are unlikely to have the opportunity to improve their standards of living or social standing.

NOTES

1. Job opportunities for educated blacks and hispanics have increased in the United States in recent years; many do not receive quality educations due to social conditions in the inner cities and poor rural regions. In 1955, black women working full-time year-round had a median income equal to 51.4 percent of the income of white women; by 1982, that figure had risen to 90.8 percent. In 1955, black men had a median income equal to 60.9 percent of that of white men; by 1982, 75.2 percent. Comparable 1955 figures are not available for hispanics; in 1982, Hispanic women had incomes equal to 82.1 percent of those of white women; hispanic men had incomes equal to 70.1 percent of the incomes of white men. Francine D. Blau and Marianne A. Farmer, *The Economics of Women, Men, and Work* (Englewood Cliffs, N.J.: Prentice-Hall, 1986), p. 176.

2. As of 1975, 43 percent of Soviets in college-level teaching, 40 percent in science, and 45 percent in journalism and writing were women. Jerry F. Hough, *The Soviet Union and Social Science Theory* (Cambridge: Harvard University Press, 1977), p. 147. Twenty-four percent of those in transportation, 29 percent in construction, and 44 percent in agriculture were women, as were 40 percent of engineers. Some 85 percent of medical personnel and 10 percent of full professors were women. Gail Warshofsky Lapidus, *Women in Soviet Society* (Berkeley: University of California Press, 1978), chapter 6. In 1970, women were 74 percent of Soviet doctors (falling to 69 percent by 1979). Throughout the 1970s, 71 percent of teachers in general education schools were women. In 1975, 86 to 89 percent of economists and accountants were women. A third of all women who work outside the home are employed as agricultural laborers. "Human Rights," *Department of State Bulletin* 85 (September 1985): 71. In 1975, 20 to 23 percent of chief agronomists, zootechnicians, and

veterinary surgeons, 34 percent of agronomists, 53 to 58 percent of zootechnicians and 33 to 44 percent of veterinary staff on state and collective farms were women. But women held only 3 percent of technical and engineering jobs on state and collective farms in 1975 and 5.2 percent in 1980. Susan Bridger, *Women in the Soviet Countryside: Women's Roles in Rural Development in the Soviet Union* (Cambridge: Cambridge University Press, 1987), pp. 71, 76–77.

3. The Koppel Report, ABC Television, December 19, 1990, stated that 86 percent of Soviet women are employed outside the home. Ellen Hume, "The Same Old Men's Club," *Kansas City Star*, December 30, 1990, quotes an estimate of 92 percent. "Labor force participation in the USSR for women of prime working ages, between twenty and forty-nine, has for some time been close to 90 percent . . . 53.3 percent of the female workers were in the labor market only part-time (compared to 28 percent in the United States) and . . . women constituted only 31.2 percent of the full-time labor force" Blau and Farmer, *Economics of Work*, pp. 337–38.

4. Female doctors in the CIS generally receive less training and less pay than males. Surgeons and physicians with good reputations can often receive extra private payments from people who want them to perform operations or give treatment. Only 6 percent of surgeons are women. Fifty percent of chief physicians, 90 percent of pediatricians, and nearly all nurses are women. Lapidus, *Women in Soviet Society*, chapter 6.

5. "The majority of specialists, 56 percent of the total employed in rural areas in 1970, were women. . . . Women formed 75 percent of what Soviet sociologists term the nonproductive intelligentsia: that is, specialists in education, health, and culture. Amongst the productive intelligentsia, specialists

directly concerned with agricultural production, women formed only 32 percent of the work force. There is little reason to suppose that a radical change in this pattern of employment has taken place since this date." Bridger, *Women in the Soviet Countryside,* pp. 70–71.

6. Studies of rural workers find that women tend to be called to labor only at high season, while males can work throughout the year. Large families and inadequate child care facilities make it hard for women to work full-time. Men are allowed to use machines, which earns them higher pay and status in a society where workers on machines were constantly seen on posters and television, while women are left to work manually. "In 1970 . . . less than 5 percent of rural women worked in industry in Azerbaijan and the Central Asian Republics, with the exception of Kyrgyzstan. . . . One of the few sociological surveys of rural industrial workers was carried out in 1971 in Belarus. This found that the majority of rural industrial workers were men—a finding in line with national trends." Women working in industry were mostly younger; those achieving senior positions were mostly men. On surveys, more than twice as many men as women tend to state that they are working in the profession of their choice. Bridger, *Women in the Soviet Countryside,* pp. 68, 83.

7. See Francine du Plessix Gray, *Soviet Women: Walking the Tightrope* (New York: Doubleday, 1990). One group estimates that Soviet women do 90 percent of housework. Anne H. Cahn and Catherine M. Kelleher, "Women Professionals Face Obstacles in USSR," *Christian Science Monitor,* January 23, 1991.

8. A study by the Economic Policy Institute found the percentage of families with working wives increased from 55.4 percent in 1979 to 66.1 percent in 1986, causing family incomes to rise to 7.3 percent in that period. Wives' earnings increased 12.1 percent (from $14,064 to $15,768, adjusted for inflation), while those of men fell 4.2 percent (from $23,204 to $22,240). But families earning the lowest two-thirds of income were slipping behind inflation, probably because women in those brackets found less work, and men were reduced to jobs with less income. *Kansas City Star,* November 7, 1988. In 1960, 30 percent of women with children under age eighteen worked; by 1987, 65 percent did. But in 1973, median *family* income minus Social Security taxes was $31,687; in 1990, in constant dollars adjusted for

inflation, it was $32,648 (only $1,000 more, with more family members working). George F. Will, "In Economy of the 90s, More is Less," *Kansas City Star,* October 31, 1991.

9. *Kansas City Times,* March 19, 1986. Professionals include teachers, librarians, architects, engineers, mathematical and computer scientists, natural scientists, physicians, dentists, pharmacists, social workers, lawyers, public relations specialists, writers, artists, journalists, psychologists, and professional athletes. In February 1986, there were 13,847,000 people in such professions; 6,938,000 were women.

10. The Secretary of Labor stated that 7 percent of the positions above the level of vice-president are held by women and 3 percent by minorities. CBS Evening News, August 8, 1991.

11. Compare the median incomes of men and women working full-time, year-round, with equal years of schooling. Women in 1967 made 53.8 to 62.5 percent as much as men; in 1983, 61.7 to 67.2 percent. (For example, in 1967, men with one to three years of high school had median incomes of $6,891; women with the same amount of schooling had median incomes of $3,704, or 53.8 percent of the men's median. In 1983, women with one to three years of college made 67.2 percent as much as men with one to three years; women with four years of college made 61.7 percent as much as men with four years.) When women and men of the same age are compared, the results show the changes; women aged fifteen to nineteen have incomes much closer to their male counterparts than women aged sixty to sixty-four, with an even progression between. Blau and Farmer, *Economics of Work,* pp. 174–78. In 1991, women earned 70 percent as much as men; those twenty-four to thirty-five years of age earned 80 percent. Fourteenth Annual Survey, *Working Women,* December 16, 1992.

12. Women held 20 percent of state legislature seats in 1993. In 1984 they held 13 percent, and 5 percent in 1971. In 1984, women constituted 8.9 percent of big city mayors, versus 1 percent in 1971. Most of that increase came between 1971 and 1977. In 1983, there were twenty-one women in the House of Representatives and two in the Senate. Only 7 women have ever served as a governor. Keith T. Poole and L. Harmon Zeigler, *Women, Public Opinion, and Politics* (New York: Longman, 1985), pp. 151–52, 156. *Kansas City Star,* August 22, 1993. Twenty times

more women serve at the city and county level of government than at the state and federal levels combined. A total of 4,650 women held elected positions in municipalities and townships in 1975, and 14,136 in 1980—13 percent of the seats. In 1980, there were 1,444 elected women in county government. Most served in municipalities with populations below 25,000. Denise Antolini, "Women in Local Government: An Overview," in Janet A. Flammang, ed., *Political Women: Current Roles in State and Local Government* (Beverly Hills: Sage, 1984), pp. 23, 27.

13. J. L. Albert, *USA Today*, June 30, 1989. Seventeen hispanics were members of the House of Representatives in 1993.

14. Hough, *Social Science Theory*, pp. 141, 143, 147. In 1986, Gorbachev appointed the second.

15. Lapidus, *Women in Soviet Society*.

16. About a third of new members were women. By around 1980, 28 percent of party members were women, rising from 19 percent in 1960. John H. Miller, "The Communist Party: Trends and Problems," in Archie Brown and Michael Chaser, eds., *Soviet Policy in the 1980s* (Bloomington: Indiana University Press, 1982); Bridger, *Women in the Soviet Countryside*, p. 188. But different regions varied markedly in the number of women they admitted to party membership, again demonstrating that central policy directives had to filter through some pluralist decision-making processes. Ellen Mickiewicz, "Regional Variation in Female Recruitment and Advancement in the Communist Party of the Soviet Union," *Slavic Review* 36, 3 (September 1977): 453.

17. Lapidus, *Women in Soviet Society*. In 1980, of nearly 47,000 top management posts in agriculture, women occupied 817. Bridger, *Women in the Soviet Countryside*, pp. 78–79.

18. The Supreme Soviet had a Committee for the Protection of Women, and another Committee on Families. They contained no women.

19. One of the few who does, Svetlanta Goriatchev, a deputy to Russian Republic President Boris Yeltsin, advocates larger families with women returning to the home.

20. Over 60 percent of married women work outside the home. Women constitute 43 percent of the workforce. World War II brought many women permanently into the economy. Two-thirds of working women are married. David Freud, "A New Era for Women," *Financial Times*, June 28, 1978. *The Economist*, June 30, 1990. *Christian Science Monitor*, April 29, 1993. The percentage of the populace with university degrees is rising, as are jobs for them in businesses involving computers and other high technology. But jobs for women with lesser skills are declining relative to their numbers.

21. A Study by the Family Policy Studies Centre found that between 1979 and 1985, the average earned income of one-parent British families fell 38 percent, and their income after taxes and benefits fell 11 percent. Unemployment, very low wages, increasing divorce, and changes in the tax laws were cited as reasons. During the same period, the income of the richest fifth of families rose 9 percent. Peter Pallot, "Poorest Families Are Worse Off as Most Grow Richer," *Daily Telegraph*, January 4, 1988.

22. OECD, European Commission. That is up from 63 percent in 1955 and 71 percent in 1973. Blau and Farmer, *Economics of Work*, pp. 320, 326.

23. In 1988, the German federal association of hospital administrators estimated a shortfall of sixty thousand nurses. Nurses' pay is barely higher than that of casual laborers. Shortages of casual workers in hospitals have forced nurses to distribute food, empty bedpans, and make beds, in addition to operating sophisticated medical equipment, giving medication, and working as administrators; they seek more pay. Some males in the Christian Democratic Party have suggested all girls over eighteen should be forced by law to do a year of "compulsory social service." Anna Tomforde, "Germany Short of Nurses," *Manchester Guardian Weekly*, August 28, 1988.

24. David Childs, *The GDR: Moscow's German Ally* (London: Allen & Unwin, 1983), p. 254. In 1987, 10.5 percent of those enrolled in British university and polytechnic engineering courses were women, up from 7.8 percent in 1983. Kenneth Baker, "The Challenge That Britain Can Meet," *The Times*, August 6, 1987.

25. OECD, European Commission, 1988. Women constituted 39 percent of the labor force. But a 1988 poll of women aged eighteen to thirty-three showed that 82 percent of them wanted to work. Francine S. Kiefer, "Missing: Germany's Women Workers," *Christian Science Monitor*, April 29, 1993.

26. Childs, *The GDR*, p. 254.

27. Forty-five percent of trade union officials were women. Knowing it could not match salaries received by highly skilled technicians and physicians in the West, East Germany awarded them elaborate academic titles people address them with. Germans respect and like to use such titles. Martin McCauley, "Power and Authority in East Germany: The Socialist Unity Party (SED)," *Conflict Studies,* 132 (July 1981): 15.

28. Idem.

29. Idem., pp. 7–8.

30. Childs, *The GDR,* p. 252.

31. One of the blacks elected in 1987 was a woman. Blacks represent 4.3 percent of the total population. The last Asian was elected in 1922. *Kansas City Times,* June 12, 1987. Paul Gordon and Anne Newham, *Different Worlds: Racism and Discrimination in Britain* (London: The Ronnymede Trust, 1986), p. 6.

32. Because agricultural extension officers in China and other petty bureaucrats are poorly paid, while peasants can earn more by working their fields diligently, the incentive to pursue education so as to achieve a bureaucratic job is reduced. At the same time, there is a new incentive to go to school and move to town and urban jobs requiring more skills. Schools are no longer supported by collectives, and local government has little money to invest in them. Richer peasants either want to use their children in their fields or send them away to better schools in the towns. This leaves the poorer children in poorly run local schools.

33. Since 1978, there has been an increased emphasis on productivity as the basis for income. Prior to that time, younger temporary workers often made less and had fewer privileges than older permanent workers with job security and less incentive to produce. Now, pay increases are often based on written and technical tests, and the young often fare better on such measures. Jobs requiring technical skills pay more. Workers are sometimes hired on two- to five-year contracts giving higher pay and equal benefits; contracts are not renewed if performance is not high.

34. Women constituted 62 percent of the members of the Chinese Communist Youth League. Martin King

35. Whyte and William L. Parish, *Urban Life in Contemporary China* (Chicago: University of Chicago Press, 1984), p. 210.

35. Idem., pp. 210–11.

36. Some bureaucratic units require higher entrance examination scores for women than for men. William Parish, seminar, University of Missouri–Kansas City, March 25, 1986; John P. Burns and Stanley Rosen, eds., *Policy Conflicts in Post-Mao China* (Armonk, N.Y.: M. E. Sharpe, 1986), pp. 303, 304.

37. Survey data shows that with a grandmother at home, a Chinese woman does three to four hours of housework a day after returning from her place of employment; without a grandmother present, she does eight hours. William Parish, public address, University of Missouri–Kansas City, March 24, 1986. Men generally refuse to do household chores. Many homes are now acquiring washing machines, vacuum cleaners, and microwaves, and processed, packaged food is growing more popular.

38. Only five of the 100 urban women intensively interviewed by Margery Wolf said if they had all the money they needed to live on they would happily stay at home. Margery Wolf, *Revolution Postponed: Women in Contemporary China* (Stanford, Calif.: Stanford University Press, 1985), p. 57. One survey showed that a fifth of working women would prefer not to. Parrish, public address. Jung Chang, *Wild Swans: Three Daughters of China* (New York: Doubleday, 1992) gives an interesting account of changes in the lives of women during this century.

39. Under China's policy of allowing only one child per family, many peasants will place daughters up for adoption, leave them at the door of an official, give them to a childless woman, or even drown them at birth. Many women abort female fetuses identified with ultrasound scanning. While the world (and 1964 Chinese) average ratio of male to female births is 105 to 100, the 1990 census recorded 113.8 boys born for every 100 girls. That has risen to 118.5 per 100. In one province, eligible bachelors were reported to outnumber women their age 10 to 1. John Ward Anderson and Molly Moore, "The Burden of Womanhood,"

Washington Post National Weekly Edition, March 22–28, 1993. *Kansas City Star,* July 21, 1993.

40. Margery Wolf, in her study of five villages, found that the factory jobs, favored because of their higher pay and flexible hours, were predominantly held by men. Women were not given work during slack season and lost hours because they were sent home to cook for men. Nonetheless, their output on work teams was almost universally greater than men, though they were never assigned comparable work points. Their average yearly wages were 30 to 87 percent as high as those of the men. Wolf, *Revolution Postponed,* p. 97.

41. Wolf, *Revolution Postponed,* pp. 67–68, 72; Whyte and Parish, *Urban Life,* pp. 177–85, 206. Steven Mosher, *A Mother's Ordeal* (New York: Harcourt, Brace, 1993). Many joint-venture factories hire only illiterate young women working long hours at low pay, and lay them off after they reach 30.

42. Joanna Liddle and Rama Josh interviewed 120 women in these four professions. "In terms of class position, the education and occupation of our women's fathers indicate that they come from a very select group of families. Seventy-four percent of fathers' occupations were in the top two categories . . . [versus 13 percent of Chandigarh city heads of household] . . . The figures suggest that although women's professional employment is affected by both class and caste, socioeconomic class is a more stringent barrier than is caste, since all the castes are represented in our group, whereas only women from the most highly educated families with fathers in the top half of the occupational hierarchy have succeeded in entering the professions." People from lower castes have access to professions their parents have already entered. Joanna Liddle and Rama Josh, *Daughters of Independence: Gender, Caste, and Class in India* (London: Zed Books, 1986), pp. 124–25.

43. Anderson and Moore, "The Burden of Womanhood," report that a Community Services Guild Survey in Madras concluded that more than half the women questioned had killed babies. India's men outnumber women 100 to 93. Numerous city sign boards advertise facilities that identify fetuses' sex so girls can be aborted.

44. Only 2 percent of applicants are accepted in even mediocre colleges. In 1992, a hundred thousand applicants sought to take exams for 820 positions in India's senior civil services. Molly Moore, "India's Students Have All the Answers," *Washington Post National Weekly Edition,* April 26–May 2, 1993. Surveys show that over 90 percent of central government jobs belong to the two highest castes, who use their connections to recruit more of their own kind. Tagleen Singh, "Jumbled Up Priorities," *Indian Express,* November 29, 1992.

45. The chief minister of Tamil Nadu, a former movie star, died in 1987. There was disagreement within his party about a successor, so they chose his wife, also a movie star, who had no prior political experience. When Rajiv Gandhi was assassinated, the Congress party tried to choose his wife as his successor, to continue the family's control; she refused.

46. Tarlok Singh, *India's Development Experience* (New York: St. Martin's Press, 1974), p. 30.

47. To attract popularity among workers for its political movement, APRA set up free evening "communiversities" staffed by volunteer university students.

48. The few that did benefit from land reforms were often single. Since the cooperative rules dictated that only the head of household could be a member, women relinquished membership when they married. The only woman to become head of a cooperative, in Cuzco, resigned shortly thereafter due to family responsibilities. Carmen Dean Deere, "Rural Women and Agrarian Reform in Peru, Chile, and Cuba," in June Nash and Helen Safa, *Women and Change in Latin America* (South Hadley, Mass.: Bergin & Garvey, 1986), pp. 195, 198.

49. See David D. Laitin, *Hegemony and Culture: Politics and Religious Change among the Yoruba* (Chicago: University of Chicago Press, 1986); Sam Barty, *Fathers Work for their Sons: Accumulation, Mobility, and Class Formation in an Extended Yoruba Community* (Berkeley: University of California Press, 1985). Nigerians vote by lining up before the booth of the party or candidate of their choice. It is hard for wives to join a line separate from their husbands, or for employees to vote independently of their employers.

EXERCISES

Think about the book thus far:

1. How do chapters 7 and 10 relate to this one?

KEY WORDS AND PHRASES

Define the following terms:

mestizo
chola

THINKING IT THROUGH

Make three columns, using information from the chapter. List examples of:

1. Evidence of men earning more than women or holding better jobs than women with comparable training
2. Evidence of some ethnic groups earning more or holding better jobs than others
3. Evidence of economic opportunities for women, ethnic minorities, and children from poor families

1	2	3

Did your evidence come only from certain countries? If you were a woman from a poor family or an ethnic minority, and you wanted to develop skills and move up the social ladder, in which countries would you prefer to live? Why?

chapter 27

FREEDOM

In part 4, we are examining how people in each nation-state actually live—how equal they are in terms of obtaining goods, opportunity, their freedoms, their physical environment, and their personal and national security. We have looked at the issues of material well-being and equality of opportunity; we turn now to freedom. How much freedom do people have? And how is that related to the influence they exert?

A political system, as we have defined it, is the regular pattern of human relationships through which people compete to resolve conflicts over various *values*. Freedom implies an absence of restraint; we are free to behave as we please until somebody challenges us or something stands in our way—that is, until someone else begins to compete with our values and restrain our ability to achieve what we want. We saw that we could talk about equality without specifically discussing the political system; in fact, it is difficult to assess exactly how the political system affects the food, clothing, shelter, skills, and jobs people have. But a discussion of freedom cannot be separated from an examination of the political system. The political system is one boundary of freedom. The physical environment is another. Insofar as we are restricted by nature and inanimate objects, our freedom is unrelated to the political system. But when we are restricted by other *people,* we are restricted by the political system itself.

When people in political systems prevent or implement particular policies, the political system *may* affect equality. Policies do not always affect equality. But they always restrain someone from doing something, and thus they always affect freedom. Whenever people in political systems prevent or impose policy, then, they *always* affect someone's freedom.

A difficult problem to resolve is the effect certain forms of government—presidential, parliamentary, one-party, military rule, or a theocracy—have on freedom. Because freedom is also affected by factors such as socialization and political culture, political freedom depends on much more than simply a particular form of government. It might be possible to change a nation-state's political institutions and yet have little impact on certain freedoms. In a similar vein, two nation-states may have the same form of government, yet very different freedoms. **How much freedom do citizens have to buy and sell, carry on cultural traditions, and express thought?** This is the central question we will focus on in this chapter.

FREEDOM IN THE UNITED STATES AND THE CIS

Citizens of both the CIS and the United States experience restrictions on their freedom to participate in buying and selling, to carry on cultural traditions, and to express thought. But there are sharp differences in the nature and severity of these restrictions.

Most rural and some urban citizens of the Soviet Union were allotted small private plots of land; some did their own herding or farming. They could sell goods produced on their private plots on the open marketplace. After it came to power in 1917, the communist government confiscated all land and businesses. Under Gorbachev in the 1980s, Soviets were eventually allowed to organize a few privately owned businesses, including hairdressing and meat shops, taxi services, and small manufacturing firms; but even the governments of the post-Soviet republics remain hesitant to allow farming and farm land to fall into private hands.[1] Private firms also must still get permission from many layers of bureaucracy to set up business. CIS citizens have little choice in consumer goods and face frequent shortages in stores on even the most basic items. Those with money to buy more exotic goods must purchase them on the underground black market, which sells everything from appliances to recreational drugs. By one estimate, a fourth of the Soviet Union's Gross National Product was diverted to the black market;[2] with increasing disorder since the creation of the CIS, that percentage has grown. Top *nomenklatura* had a much greater variety of goods available to them through special stores, medical services, holiday retreats, chauffeured cars, and other privileges reserved for them; some of those privileges persist.

Any American may own land and start his or her own business. Though Americans must abide by government regulations and pay many taxes to do so, the bureaucratic restrictions they face are tame in comparison to those in the CIS. They may produce whatever products they like, subject to regulations for health and safety; as a result, only rare goods and services such as illicit recreational drugs and prostitution are sold underground. Few people own productive land or their own businesses. Americans have a wide choice in consumer goods; richer Americans can afford far more of them.

Americans may move about without restriction, and their widespread access to cars and good roads makes this easy to do. Nearly all Americans can obtain passports to leave the country, and millions travel abroad. Until 1990, few citizens of the Soviet Union could;[3] they still must obtain passports to cross the borders of the post-Soviet republics, and passports for world travel cost three hundred dollars—a prohibitive sum for most people.[4]

Most Americans must find jobs and work for others. Americans can choose among unions to represent them at their plants and can strike; they may also choose not to join a union. Many firms do not have unionized labor. Government has at times used force to break strikes or prevent unions from organizing; it helps arbitrate labor disputes. Soviets were not able to choose among unions or strike; new laws in 1990 freed unions from government control. Most CIS citizens are still guaranteed jobs but cannot choose them. Their work places are often filthy and unsafe, with antiquated machinery requiring heavy physical labor.

Most Americans live in a house or apartment large enough to afford them privacy, with one family in each unit. Many CIS citizens live in small apartments shared by other families they are often not even related to. This affords them little privacy.

CIS citizens envy the American standard of living. But it is common for them to express unease about the stress, fast pace, and lack of security they perceive to be associated with economic life in the West.

As we have seen, half the Soviet Union's citizens were not Russians; they are of other nationalities, religions, and customs. These members of other groups did not have their own schools or compete for prized jobs. They were encouraged to celebrate cultural holidays, teach their own languages, perform their own theater and music, and the like. They were expected to learn Russian, and to study a basic curriculum of physics, math, history, and chemistry up to the eighth grade, at the same pace, everywhere. Those who identified too closely with any religion could not hold positions in the party (and thus advance themselves professionally in government jobs). Now, people associated with religious institutions are once again free to worship,[5] and the separate republics are seizing the opportunity to express their cultural differences.

Jewish people, as special targets of Stalin's anti-Semitism, lost the right to publish, perform in their own theater groups, teach their language, and organize at the national level. Until recently, they could print only ten thousand copies of their prayer book and publish only one Yiddish literary journal. This prevented them from adequately teaching Yiddish, their literature, or their customs, though they could worship at their synagogues and celebrate religious holidays. These restrictions have now been lifted, and Jews are free to emigrate. Those not active in synagogues can rise high in professions, although they still cannot attain top positions.[6]

Forty to fifty million Muslims had only five hundred registered mosques, about a thousand *mullahs,* and two theological schools with a total of eighty students. Organized Buddhism was virtually destroyed. But both faiths had thousands of underground brotherhoods and popular adherence to underground leaders. Azerbaijan in 1969 had only sixteen registered mosques, but clandestine ones probably exceeded one thousand, along with three hundred places of pilgrimage. In a district with only one official mosque, *sovkhozy* and *kolkhozy* (state and collective farms) built seven new clandestine mosques in 1970 alone. By 1987, with religious freedom advanced under *glasnost,* enormous crowds began gathering at mosques on Muslim religious holidays.[7] The rise in religious freedom has been accompanied by violence and bloodshed, as religious groups have begun fighting among one another.

Many citizens express concern over the quality of education and social services, crowded buses, high prices, poor food in markets, alcoholism, and breakdowns in urban life. Under glasnost, newspaper and television reporters and members of the legislature were encouraged to expose laziness, inefficiency, and corruption. The state sponsored rock concerts featuring heavy metal groups attacking bureaucratic sloth. Party chiefs fired corrupt and inept managers and party leaders (but often replaced them with others of equal stature). Stalin's crimes were exposed in newspapers and television documentaries. The government admitted textbooks printed deliberate lies; in 1988, examinations for 53 million students were postponed until texts could be rewritten. Cartographers admitted maps were deliberately distorted; correct ones were released. Jamming of Radio Free Europe broadcasts ended.

Americans are free to discuss social and political problems freely, but we often do not take advantage of the opportunity. Often we cannot do much about them, either. But we are able to organize meetings, to make speeches, and to write about them. The U.S. Constitution guarantees our rights to free speech and assembly, and our court system has acted to preserve such rights; at times, it has placed limits on free speech. Control of schools and many other matters is left to state governments, which can use their money and laws to help preserve cultural traditions if they so desire. The right to criticize leaders is supported by all major institutions, both governmental and private.

The pattern of freedom in these two systems is deeply grounded in their political cultures and systems. Their current systems carry forward habits which long predate them. Changes do not come easily. Before glasnost, the Soviet government—like the tsars before them—heavily censored the news,[8] though popular magazines frequently carried complaints about factory work conditions and individual bureaucratic behavior. Glasnost broadened this to allow complaints against the system itself. That criticism mushroomed in 1989 after Andrei Sakharov, inventor of the Soviet hydrogen bomb and an outspoken critic of the government since 1966 (released from exile by Gorbachev in 1987), used the seat he had won on the new Congress of People's Deputies to call for popular demonstrations. Because the sessions of that body were televised, and Gorbachev allowed him and others to use its podium to freely speak their minds, their words were heard by millions.

Foreign policy, government ideology, environmental pollution, and standing in never-ending lines to buy goods and obtain services all became targets of popular criticism on street corners or television. People also criticized unsanitary conditions and shortages of drugs and equipment in clinics, hospitals, and day care centers. They asked government service agencies to rehabilitate Stalin's victims. Women's rights and religious education were espoused at meetings and in the press. Gorbachev's support of rock music drew heavy criticism, even from intellectuals who sought freedom of expression. The press in Belarus discussed the propriety of exhibiting the works of favorite son Marc Chagall, the Russian Jewish forerunner of surrealist painting whose works were formerly out of favor. Crowds demonstrated daily against the privileges accorded leading party members and such officials' pretentious spending, despite officials' opposition. Shoppers rioted. Pickets blocked rail lines. Strikes broke out constantly; police and the KGB sometimes intervened and sometimes helped organize them. Smokers marched against cigarette shortages. Prisoners rioted. Bandits broke into army depots. Complaints grew as the prices of formerly subsidized basic foods, housing, education, mass transit, and fuel began to rise.[9] Nationalities demanded their rights; though they were officially discouraged, their protests gathered increasing force; street gatherings often turned violent. Armenians organized independent paramilitary militias which battled one another in the streets.

Most importantly, when the government sent armed military units to break up such activities, hundreds of thousands of people took to the streets in defiance. When the KGB and top government officials staged a coup attempt to remove Gorbachev in 1991, it was too late; they faced masses of angry people who stayed in the streets of Moscow, Leningrad, and other cities around the clock until the coup leaders (whose orders were even defied by armed force units) were arrested. Within weeks, with the economy faltering and the republics breaking away from the central government, and with leaders fighting among themselves, disorder and complaints escalated. Supporters of the coup still held onto their positions.

Even in the United States, there are people who fear such free expression of ideas. But our political system generally prevents such individuals from restricting public discussion. The CIS systems, historically, do not; people have been left to support the government without reservation, to ignore it, or to reject it, without a middle course of even discussing how to modify it or remove it through elections.

The swing between absolute authority and anarchy is a basic theme in Russian political culture. It is hard for most people within this system—which did not experience the Reformation, Renaissance, or Enlightenment—to conceive of having security and limited freedom to resist the system at the same time.[10] They can conceive of complete anarchy—life without any law or supreme power—and may even find the idea titillating. But they like security, and fear that many of the freedoms commonly enjoyed in the West will threaten it. "It's bad for the country to say so many things have gone wrong. . . . It hurts our prestige. . . . I fear terrible troubles, something awful could happen," said one journalist; his sentiment is widely echoed. Many talk about being on the verge of complete social breakdown. Even the outspoken populist, Boris Yeltsin, president of the Russian republic, cautioned those who would be critical:[11]

What does it mean? Does it mean he can publish, write anything that comes to mind? That is not freedom; that is anarchy. There will be no limitations on talented workers, but there will be limitations on rubbish. Rubbish will be forbidden for publication; nobody needs rubbish.

After enduring heckling at the 1990 May Day parade, Gorbachev sponsored a new law that made insulting him punishable by six years in prison, but the criticism continued, and the law was not enforced. Boris Yeltsin's criticisms of Gorbachev were not reported on television, however, until his supporters gained control of television at the republic and municipal levels in 1990. Later that year, when Gorbachev declared his intent to use the KGB and emergency powers to crack down on the black market and dissent, he had support from both radical and conservative political leaders. The Congress of People's Deputies gave him the power, whenever and wherever he deemed an emergency to exist, to dismiss any public official, ban strikes, impose curfews, take complete control of the media, cut off telephone service, forbid demonstrations, control the movement of citizens, and suspend political parties.

In August 1991, crowds assembled in front of the Russian parliament building to help foil the coup attempt by protecting Boris Yeltsin. One reason they were not attacked was that Yeltsin's own secret police organization had infiltrated the KGB.[12] Within weeks after the attempt, Yeltsin was under attack in his own republic's legislature for ruling by decree without consulting parliament and appointing local leaders and ministers responsible solely to him; a few weeks after that, legislators gave him the power to rule by decree so as to initiate reforms. He took personal control over the prime ministership, the ministry of the interior which controls the secret police, and the armed forces, and he threatened to abolish newspapers critical of him. The KGB, which had over six hundred thousand agents in every institution and an even greater number of informers in private life, was reduced to a staff of under forty thousand. Those agents retain their connections, and the republics have created their own intelligence agencies. Many have connections with growing organized crime networks.

One of Yeltsin's first moves after Russia became fully independent was to consolidate the ministry of the interior police with the remainder of the KGB and place them under his control—without consulting the legislature or even his chief legal advisor. When the legislature voted to overturn this action, he agreed to revise the details of his decree, but still created the new superministry for internal security, called the Agency for Federal Security. The size of this agency was soon on the rise. When members of the former Congress of People's Deputies sought to meet and discuss the possibility of restoring the Soviet Union, Yeltsin and his legislature sent the agency police to prevent the gathering.

So while there is considerable participation in the new public debate, there is also support for censorship. In the past, those arrested for political crimes were not entitled to see defense attorneys and could be locked away without trial; now some are being released after an initial investigation shows no crime was committed, and defense attorneys are seeking the right to represent clients from the moment of detention. Many express fear these new rights for "criminals" while murders, burglaries, and assaults are rapidly increasing, will reduce the certainty of punishment.[13] They fear that publishing reports about faults in their society, natural disasters, and other previously unpublished bad news will put society at risk.[14] In fact, people who complain about the government too often are still subject to incarceration as mental patients; the fact that they complain "proves" they are mentally ill.[15] Groups supporting a return to the tsar[16] and advocating the rights of Slavic people demonstrate regularly, despite being disrupted by police.

Traditions limiting the authority of public officials are not established in the post-Soviet republics. When the populace does not feel government should or can be limited by law, it is hard to create laws to limit government. Leaders must now answer questions posed by the media. Yet new laws (continued by the CIS) provide that only legally constituted and registered "social organizations" can publish regularly and that the media is forbidden from trying to "undermine the social system." Violations could bring criminal charges, or at least a mysterious disappearance of available paper for printing. Even under glasnost, news of space and nuclear accidents, assassination attempts on Gorbachev, and some civil disturbances were delayed, kept to short press releases, or totally suppressed.

The Communist Party was outlawed in 1991 after the coup attempt. Just as it closed down political parties and seized assets in 1917, its rights were taken and assets seized without legal recourse. This was done with little public objection or discussion. But no clear plans were presented for actually carrying this out. Many assets stayed in the same hands, meetings continued as usual, and many *apparatchiki* retained their dachas. The party, and party members, are believed to have transferred over $14 billion in stolen assets into foreign bank accounts, much of it moved within weeks before the aborted coup attempt in 1991. Many assets, including state industries and businesses, were sold cheaply to party members before the party was outlawed.

At the same time as the government announced plans for privatizing the economy and fired sixty thousand bureaucrats from central planning ministries, thirty-six thousand of them were immediately hired by Russia's central ministries. The Russian republic considered wiping out the autonomous republics occupying half its territory and replacing them with "lands" whose boundaries, through gerrymandering or otherwise, would divide the nationalities contained in them. They also considered making mayors unremovable except through impeachment by a two-thirds vote of their councils.[17] Later, many autonomous republics and regions threatened to secede from Russia.

In this changeover, strong leaders were replacing strong leaders. The first had failed to solve the country's problems, but had not knocked out the idea that strong leaders are what it takes to solve those problems;[18] and the second group of strong leaders have not wiped out the large bureaucratic apparatus that prevents anyone else from becoming strong.

On the fringes are many whose views could bring upheaval to the Russian nation-state. Anti-Semitic rhetoric is prevalent among many intellectuals, as are calls for dominance by Great Russians. Attacks on Lenin often include attacks on his Jewish heritage. In 1990, a leader of the anti-Semitic Russian nationalist group Pamyat was sentenced to two years at hard labor for shouting insults at Jews during a writers' conference, but Pamyat continues to demonstrate with Nazi swastikas in the streets and intimidate Jews without the law's interference. One woman writes that although she speaks no Yiddish and has absorbed only Russian culture, she fears being Jewish

because handsome young men from Pamyat have promised to destroy us like insects, and because a woman next door tells us all to 'go to your Israel.' They're saying again there will be pogroms on 19 August [1990]. Jews get leaflets printed in real printing shops with four-letter words, and some doors have been marked with crosses. There are police in the streets, but they can't put one outside the door of every Jewish family. Once I was walking home and was stopped by people who said: 'Show us your shopping bags, you yid. This is who is eating all the

meat.' (Finally they've found somebody to blame for the meat shortage.) . . . I am afraid of you. Congratulations: you've won a great victory.[19]

All this is reminiscent of activities leading up to Adolph Hitler's Kristalnacht and concentration camps, a fear which has impelled massive Jewish emigration to Israel and the United States. While Pamyat itself has made little headway in elections, it is growing; many citizens express support for their own nationality and distrust of their neighbors from other ethnic groups. Civil violence is a real and constant threat. Movements supporting nationalities and resistance to authority are growing rapidly, even forming their own private armies. Complete freedom to organize could allow the organization of groups dedicated to tearing society apart and severely repressing ethnic minorities. Leaders of the newly freed Baltic states are under intense pressure to outlaw the Russian language and jail or execute former communists. Ethnic parties in all republics push for the repression and exclusion of ethnic groups they do not trust. This threat will not subside until the cultures are socialized to have broader concern about one another.

Young ex-Soviets are fascinated with American music, cinema,[20] bodybuilding, and much else; they like escaping into personal fantasies. Gorbachev, by endorsing rock music, encouraged that. Young Muscovites parade the streets dressed in heavy metal gear or as punkers. Young working class gangs roam the street to beat the punkers up. Pornography and prostitution are openly sold on street corners, male homosexuals (defying harsh penalties in Section 121 of the penal code) hold hands and seek sex in public places, and plays and television shows feature nudity. Many veterans of the Afghanistan war returned disillusioned with both the old and new societies; large numbers of ordinary citizens have joined them in private actions defying the system.

Though these individuals are rebellious, they may not be willing to trade the security of their system for the uncertainties accompanying the introduction of free press and assembly, the right to organize alternative political parties (many resist joining or supporting any party), marked increases in prices of basic goods and services, or freedom of employers to fire lazy workers. It is comfortable to toe the line in the daytime in exchange for private pleasures during or after work. A self-destructive form of anarchism in the CIS is alcoholism; one study found that 40 percent of the populace was chronically drunk at work.[21] People in the post-Soviet republics support government when it gives them enough leeway to pursue private passions. Many may, in fact, support government when it attempts to assure that such private passions do not become part of the public domain, that they do not interfere with security by fostering social breakdown. Citizens of these republics do not have a tradition of publicly supporting individuals who stand up to the authorities.

Young Americans also pursue private passions; they use music, cinema, and other activities to escape into personal fantasies. But the public will support responsible attempts to resist authority, and even individual expression of diverse viewpoints that might arouse some controversy. People do not feel their security is threatened by such expressions.

The leaders of the republics would find it difficult to return to the prior level of repression. Even in the countryside, people have now tasted the freedom to publicly criticize the government. Voting in elections for legislators who may now engage in open debate is an additional freedom which may be difficult to remove. Learning to form independent parties and interest groups, and to allow others to form them, may take much more time. Many still long for a return to the security they thought they had under the old regime.

FREEDOM IN THE UNITED KINGDOM AND GERMANY

Very few citizens of the United Kingdom or Germany have produce to sell from private plots of land; those who do are free to sell it. The great majority in both countries are salaried laborers who must work for established businesses. It is hard to switch from wage or salaried labor to start a business of one's own.[22] Established businesses are incorporated or nationalized and must generate profits.

The East German government confiscated land, housing, and businesses when it first came to power. In all of East Germany, there were only 10,000 licenses for private businesses—establishments like hotels, bars, bakeries, butcher shops, and small restaurants. Since reunification, the former assets were placed on sale to investors or claimed by former owners, who largely come from West Germany. Although West Germany and the United Kingdom have many small retail establishments owned by middle-class investors, these investors represent a small percentage of the populace. Most people work for others, often for large businesses.

British unions may strike, and the government can arbitrate settlements; East German workers could not strike or join nongovernment unions. West German unions seldom strike. East Germany forced unions to abide by government decisions; the government forbade strikes. In the United Kingdom, the common law has evolved a notion that courts and every other government agency should stay clear of industrial disputes as much as possible, except to assist impartially in arbitration. This means workers have a right to strike, and employers can lock out workers. The Thatcher Government gave police protection to lockouts but did not go so far as to ban strikes. Parliament has a right to pass legislation changing these rules. But, by tradition, it would not do so without setting up commissions of inquiry and having such commissions' reports debated in the press and on the floor of Parliament. As it happens, several commissions have been set up on this subject, bringing about heated but indecisive debate. So Parliament has been careful about restricting these freedoms.

Private businesses in the United Kingdom and West Germany can generate high profits. Obtaining capital, telephones, licenses and permits, and other permissions required for starting and operating a business can be more difficult than in the United States. Businesspeople in private British and West German firms can invest their after-tax profits in plant improvements, research and development, worker benefits, or interest-bearing accounts or bonds, or distribute them to stockholders. Government, banks, and unions own considerable stock in West German companies; they tend not, in the style of American takeover bids, to buy and sell other companies simply for quick profit. Instead, profits are usually a sign that the company is producing goods that the free market demands.

After-tax profits of East German firms could also be invested in plant improvements, worker benefits, research and development, or interest-bearing accounts or bonds. If the output of a plant exceeded planned levels, the size of the fund going toward workers' benefits increased. That did not mean the plant was generating a profit, or even selling its output. Because most of the recordkeeping was highly informal, one could not verify that the plant had actually exceeded planned levels. Government subsidized plants losing money. Consumers and other socialist firms had little choice of retailers or suppliers. So there was no need to create products that would satisfy customers. This limited the freedom of consumers to buy what they liked, but it assured them of jobs and goods.

The choice of consumer goods is greater in West Germany and the United Kingdom than in East Germany. Travel is not restricted. British and West German citizens can own shares of stock and maintain foreign bank accounts; both have a faster economic pace and lower degree of family and community solidarity than did East Germany. To replace the extensive war damage and make way for highways and modern buildings in West Germany, older housing has been destroyed. Thus, fewer people can live in their old neighborhoods and carry on old traditions. East Germany suffered less war damage. Towns not destroyed by the war were restored and maintained—sometimes in clean, trim, painted condition, but often left drab and sooty. This restoration, and the hiring practices of factories, allowed many people to stay where their families had lived for generations, encouraging community solidarity. Since East Germans seldom move, extended families often keep close contact.

Under German law, citizenship depends on ancestry rather than residence or place of birth, so Germany includes few non-Germans among its citizens, even if (like many Turks) they have resided there for decades. East Germans were under pressure to learn the Russian language, visit Russian war memorials, and accede to Russian demands. They quietly resisted. And they were able to govern in their own language and with their own cultural traditions. The lack of a free press limited discussion about cultural issues. East Germany's only regionally tied ethnic minority is the few Sorbians living in the southeast. No Sorbs have high positions, and no Sorbian nationalist writers could get published; in fact, only one anthology of Sorbian writing was ever published prior to reunification. In contrast, West Germany's federal system allows state governments to control education and to fight to preserve regional differences (though these are not ethnic differences, and the boundaries of the states were only drawn after World War II).

Fewer than a thousand practicing Jews remain in East Germany, and their numbers are declining. The government had poor relations with Israel but helped this small group maintain synagogues and cemeteries. They received the 600-mark-per-month pension for which all survivors of Nazism were eligible. School children were taught about the holocaust, but they learned more about its effects on communists and the Soviet Union than upon Jews. Twice as many Nazi war criminals (thirteen thousand) were tried and convicted in East Germany than in the West. West Germany contains some thirty-two thousand Jews; about half those who married during the 1970s married Gentiles. West German textbooks are starting to discuss the Hitler era and explain its darker side.

In 1984, some neo-Nazis were jailed for attacking some Jews. They were released in 1988, and on the day of monetary reunification in 1990, they formed the German Alternative. The German People's Union (DVU), the Red Army Factions, and other neo-Nazi organizations together have only a few thousand active members. But their strength is greater than their numbers might seem to indicate. They hold rallies that attract skinheads and unemployed youth (including former members of the communist youth organization, who now feel betrayed by reunification) and call for the ouster of non-Germans and the return of Polish territories.

Since unification, hundreds of thousands (1.3 million between 1989 and 1991) of Romanians, Yugoslavs, Vietnamese, Indians, Pakistanis, Bulgarians, and Germans from other parts of Eastern Europe[23] have sought political asylum in Germany under Article 16 of the Constitution, which requires it to take in any victim of persecution who sets foot on German soil. But the 6.4 million foreigners residing in Germany remain non-citizens. The neo-Nazi radicals and skinheads beat up immigrants in railway stations, burn hostels where immigrants are staying, and harass them in the streets. Police put up weak resistance,[24] and demonstrations to protest these actions attract few marchers. A survey among East German school children found a fourth of them consider "action against foreigners" justified.[25] Tens of thousands of immigrants have been removed from towns and placed in fortified "collection centers" surrounded by barbed wire, with onlookers applauding as the vans take them away; some were returned to Romania.[26] Some towns brag that they contain no "foreigners" or Jews, and (though thousands of Germans have organized neighborhood committees to stage protective watches at the collection centers) little resistance arose to this removal policy among the major political parties until radicals began killing some Turks in 1992 and 1993; for the first time, Chancellor Kohl began to speak against the killings and banned German Alternative, and the parties started to seek solutions on immigration policy, though all with great caution. Since 1991, Turks with long residence in Germany can become citizens if they give up Turkish citizenship. And in 1993, Germany began turning back immigrants at the borders under a new law.

The Nazis came to power as the result of a disastrous depression. With economic prosperity high, it is unlikely they will regain power; but recent events do not bode well for the future of race relations in Germany. In some 1992 and 1993 West German state elections, right-wing parties made their best showing since immediately after World War II.[27]

The United Kingdom has serious cultural problems. In 1920, she gave southern Ireland independent status, but kept Northern Ireland tied to England with much the same powers as a state under a federal system. Northern Ireland has power over the economy, taxation, education, and other specified subjects but sends representatives to Parliament in London, which retains control over security and other matters. Its inhabitants include a Catholic minority, most of whom work at more menial tasks. A strong minority of them vote for Sinn Fein, which advocates separating completely from the United Kingdom and joining Ireland and which gives support in street demonstrations to the terrorist Irish Republican Army, which has assassinated over two thousand people in recent years.[28] The economy of Northern Ireland is closely linked to Britain. The majority of protestants, who benefit from those links, do not wish to sever them; nearly all vote for the Ulster Unionists, whose leaders do not wish to share power with Catholics, and who talk openly about killing Catholic nationalists as an ultimate solution. If the British withdrew, southern Ireland could join more resolutely with the Catholic minority in Northern Ireland to weaken the position of the protestants there. As it is, severe cultural conflict manifests itself in continuous violence.[29]

Scotland, too, has a history separate from England. Many Scots resent English influence over their schools, religious institutions, and economy. Millions of acres in the highlands are still controlled by English "lairds" whose ancestors pushed the Scots out over two centuries ago.[30] A half million acres belong to British institutions, and three hundred thousand have been purchased by Arabs and other foreigners. Foreign workers drill the offshore wells for North Sea oil off Aberdeen, and the profits flow through London. In Wales there is also much resentment of the English. Twenty percent of the populace still speaks only Welsh. Most mines and industries are owned by the English; many are closed or operating at low capacity. In both Scotland and Wales, nationalist political parties calling for separation have made little headway in recent years.

Most Scots and Welsh seem to realize going it alone would be difficult. Recession would inevitably follow separation, with outside capital hard to attract. In 1979, the Labour Government offered the two regions a chance to vote on devolution—a proposal which would give their regions assemblies on federal terms somewhat similar to Northern Ireland before 1972.[31] Opponents argued that minority nationalists would use this as a first step in breaking away, that the plan would increase the size of the bureaucracy, that the Labour Party would use it to increase its grip, and that it would drive away business. Some Labour Members of Parliament from Wales actively campaigned against the proposal. It carried by a small margin in Scotland, but not by enough votes to be adopted, and it was resoundingly defeated in Wales. Cultural grievances remain, but these regions will find other ways to air them. After the Conservative Thatcher Government was re-elected in 1987, leaving nearly all constituencies of Scotland and Wales in the hands of Labour Members of Parliament because of the general economic downturn in those regions, sentiment in this direction was again expressed, without receiving great attention.[32] But the Labour Party still proposes the creation of a Scottish parliament, complete with proportional representation in its legislative districts.

The Anglican Church is the established Church in England; government gives it some financial support. British people may belong to whatever religion they like. Nine out of ten West Germans are registered as members of protestant or Catholic churches (about half in each). The government takes 10 percent of their taxes and passes these funds along to the church each taxpayer is registered with. Some clergy are active in supporting the Christian Democratic Union. Some 6 million of East Germany's 17 million people declare themselves protestant, and 6 million Catholic; its government also collected this tithe and passed it along to the churches. A few church people were active in the small Christian Democratic Union (East); most considered this party too pro-government and stayed away from it.

Churches published some thirty newspapers and periodicals, and one of every eight books printed in East Germany (subject to censoring by the censor board). Churches in eastern Germany own half a million acres of agricultural land, making them the largest private landowners prior to reunification. East German government radio broadcast a religious service each Sunday. It also made large grants to churches for maintaining hospitals, nursing homes, homes for the mentally impaired, and other services the state preferred not to perform itself. West German churches also contributed to the charitable activities of East German churches. The government recognized conscientious objection on religious grounds.[33] Anyone who wanted university admission, or a leadership position in the party, government, business, the military, or a profession, could not attend church. In certain regions, local party leaders tried to prevent church attendance. Bishops criticized government policy and were appointed without interference from the government. Local church pastors often had close relations with local party officials. And even party members used church hospitals and kindergartens, which were superior to their state-run counterparts. Church leaders helped persuade government leaders to back down in the face of the final demonstrations calling for an end to communist party domination.

All three systems (the United Kingdom and both parts of Germany) suffer from crimes such as theft, assault, rape, and homicide, though the homicide rates are far lower than in the United States.[34] All three try some sentencing methods which do not involve prison, though there is popular pressure to go back to traditional sentencing and imprisonment.

The three take very different approaches to freedom of thought. The United Kingdom is one of the freer nation-states in the world in this regard, and East Germany was one of the more restricted. West Germany stands in subtle contrast to both. Germany's history has been less friendly to free speech. During the nineteenth century, one could be jailed or lose one's job for expressing political opinions. The repressions of the Hitler era reinforced this type of danger. It is not as easy for the government to censor the press now; public opinion has become more supportive of protecting press freedom.

This paint, sprayed on a sidewalk near the Reichstag in West Berlin (the site of the unified legislature for the new Federal Republic), reads ''Osties Get Out—West Berlin Is Our City!''

© *Gordon Seyffert*

West German newspapers do not need to toe the national party lines. Before his death, Axel Springer, a staunchly anticommunist nationalist who liked to attack the major political parties and advocated reunification, printed more than half of West Germany's daily newspapers and supplied editorial staff for many of the small local newspapers. Newspaper ownership retains this centralized but independent pattern. State governments operate radio and television. Hence, neither the major parties nor smaller, less popular causes (other than regional ones) have steady access to the media. That makes it difficult to conduct national debates on issues. In contrast, major British newspapers tend to support the Labour, Conservative, or Liberal parties. Both the national-government-operated British Broadcasting Corporation and the private Independent Television network give constant access to opposing points of view.

East Germany's period of transition will prove a test of the degree to which free speech will be protected in the unified system. The police organization Stasi was closed, and eighty-five thousand full-time officers lost their jobs. Until the demise of the KGB, many may have continued to work for it. Their links with the Red Army Faction terrorists, Libya, and other groups leading demonstrations and instigating violence may endure. Every agent was required to recruit twenty-five new informants or initiate twenty-five new investigations every year,[35] and citizens had to work with the agency to receive assistance from bureaucracy; hence, many people were involved in some way with the organization. Many files are still missing from the headquarters building. It will be difficult to stop all these operatives from blackmailing citizens who informed in the past. Meanwhile, East Germans continue to read newspapers printed in the East. After years of repression, they have little experience at exercising freedom responsibly. Many feel that they are second-class citizens in the new union, without a chance to achieve political or economic parity with the West:

> Our people don't trust either democracy or the legal system, only the Deutschmark, and that's let them down. They feel doubly betrayed.[36]

On the first anniversary of reunification, millions of West Germans stayed home from the sparsely attended official celebrations around the country.[37]

FREEDOM IN CHINA AND INDIA

Theoretically, Indian workers and peasants have great freedom to buy and sell; in practice, many of them may have less ability to do so than their Chinese counterparts. Wealthy Indians experience fewer restrictions than any Chinese. And India far surpasses China in extending freedom to carry on cultural traditions and express thought; that freedom is sometimes carried to excess.

As we have seen, most Chinese have access to land for cultivation or are employed by a manufacturing unit which provides them with a job and various benefits. Furthermore, these peasant plots and manufacturing units have enough funds, raw materials, and markets to give their employees gradually increasing incomes. Those who have their own plots of land, or work in one of the nineteen million rural cooperatives, can augment their earnings by doing extra work. Stores in all towns and cities are stocked with a wide assortment of consumer goods with brand names familiar throughout the world and are selling clothes, electronics, appliances, and household goods at a brisk pace. Scarcer goods can be obtained on the black market, or by bribing.

Most Indians have none of these benefits. Even those with some land often incur debt to obtain seed, water, and fertilizer, leaving them with high interest payments and little income. The largest village landowners often supply these loans and use them as leverage to control local politics and commerce. Small craftspeople usually work for these landowners, or their associates from the city, at very low piece rates. Villagers and most city workers can buy few manufactured goods.

Wealthier Indians own large firms that buy and sell on a free market. They need frequent government permits, often requiring expensive bribes and fees. Workers in these firms, and in middle ranks of government service, are better paid than their Chinese counterparts and can choose from a wide array of consumer goods. Such workers in China are supplementing their incomes with extra jobs and trading, giving them similar consumer choice. Top-ranking Chinese officials live comparably well.

Chinese must carry identification cards and, until recently, could not move about without permission; now they can get one-year residency permits in other cities. Indians experience no formal restrictions in this regard. However, most villagers are not served by paved roads and cannot afford the bus or train fare out. Those who migrate often end up in squatter colonies sleeping on streets or in makeshift shelters. Millions of Indians live in such colonies; 70 million rural migrants to the newly-industrializing coastal cities of China are competing with locals for scarce jobs, and increasing numbers of migrants are without jobs or adequate housing. Passports for foreign travel are easy to obtain in India; China issues them very selectively (though much more freely than they were issued to citizens of the Soviet Union or Eastern Europe before glasnost).

Indians are free to join unions and interest groups of many kinds. They frequently have street processions celebrating religious holidays or expressing political sentiments. Outdoor meetings addressed by political figures can attract huge crowds, with banners and placards expressing a variety of sentiments. The rhetoric is often critical of government and its policies. Many cultures mingle in cities, with differing languages, eating and bathing rituals, holidays, saints, heroes, dress, living habits, and much else. Many members of these cultures have few relationships with individuals outside their own group and little exposure to the ideas of other groups. When this diversity is combined with free speech and assembly, it sometimes leads to violent clashes the police must break up. When Britain granted the subcontinent independence in 1947, clashes became so violent that Pakistan broke away from India to form its own separate Muslim nation-state. As we have seen, militant Sikhs, Nagas, Kishmiris, and others promote further separation by acts of violence, and militant Hindus (including graduates without jobs) support violence against Muslims. In their rage over living conditions, peasant gangs kill landlords.[38] Especially in areas with armed insurgency, torture and killing in jail may be common, and police are often accused of killing minority demonstrators. Amnesty International reports that over a hundred people die of torture in Indian jails each year.

China's cultural minorities generally live inland. Even there, Chinese live in neighborhoods separate from those of other cultures. Those cultures have the right to practice their cultural rituals and habits, but they may not organize politically. The government has met attempts to form interest groups and demonstrations among Tibetans and inhabitants of far western provinces with stern impositions of martial law. Han regions vary subtly in language and eating habits as well as in other ways. They may not form separate cultural organizations or any other kind of independent interest group. Any street procession or demonstration must be approved by the government, or it is subject to crackdown. People may now attend places of worship, but officials often frown at this. Leaders of religious groups are expected to work closely with Beijing authorities. They are

In May and June of 1989, I taught at two coastal Chinese universities. The students came to my classes fresh from street demonstrations—the events throughout China which were to result in the crackdown at Tiananmen Square. The students complained that their dormitory rooms were hot, dirty, and crowded. Many could afford no more than rice and soup at the school cafeterias. Classrooms and campus grounds were stark. Students had no money to spend on themselves. New graduates were assigned lifelong jobs in government agencies and enterprises which paid little and offered tedious work.

In May and June of 1993, I returned to those universities. Dormitory rooms had been painted and were less dirty and less crowded. Students were piling their metal dishes high with food at the cafeterias. New trees, fountains, flowers, and gardens adorned the campus grounds, along with new buildings. Classrooms had been painted, and some had new furniture. Students were wearing trendy clothes and eating out at the Western-style fast-food restaurants multiplying along shopping streets. Now recruiters interviewed new graduates and gave them choices between jobs. Up to a fifth were finding jobs with joint ventures paying over a hundred U.S. dollars a month; while most found jobs that paid less, they could

hope to switch to a better job later, and they were earning extra money from small business deals on the side. Intense construction was shortening the wait for apartments. Young married professional couples often owned color TVs, tape players, washing machines, refrigerators, and VCRs, and many eyed CD players, microwave ovens, and older couples installing air conditioners in their flats. Though people expressed concern that the prosperity might not reach their home towns and villages rapidly enough, the word "hope" was heard in many conversations; rebellion was far from their minds.

Meanwhile, in the interior province of Sichuan, peasants, complaining that their income was stagnant while the coast was booming, rioted. Their complaints were aimed at local officials who raised taxes to build a road and paid them for crops with IOUs while diverting the cash into land speculation and economic development zones. Thousands of peasants threw rocks at the police called in to quell the disturbance. Hundreds of other villages staged similar protests. The central government responded by reasserting its ban on IOUs and sending the third-ranking member of the Politburo to spend the summer examining the problems of peasants.

expected not to seek converts and are restricted in distributing sacred texts and other literature. In keeping with traditions many centuries old, Roman Catholics may not declare allegiance to Rome; the authorities fear any religion whose top leadership resides outside China.[39] Under martial law, some Tibetan monks have been jailed and their numbers restricted.

People concerned about ordinary public policy issues—corruption, living costs, overcrowding on transportation, pollution, poor social services—are not free to discuss them publicly. Because expressions of criticism can be dangerous, they are usually revealed only to family or close friends. For a brief period during the 1980s, the Chinese press began to write about some issues, and students discussed them informally. Some within the Politburo encouraged this. But when dissent cascaded into street demon-

strations in 1987 and 1989, the authorities firmly forbade all such activity. Unknown numbers of dissidents were—and still are—jailed or executed. From 3 to 20 million people occupy over a thousand labor camps; they are often sent there without trial for unspecified crimes, and forced to manufacture products for export to the United States, Japan, and Europe. Many are executed at a moment's notice, and torture is common. At least one hundred thousand Chinese citizens are thought to be political prisoners.[40] Papers now occasionally dare to run articles about corruption, inefficiency, a controversial film, or accidents the government does not want reported.

China's Confucian traditions vested power in the emperor and the literati, who held authority to make and enforce all laws. Groups were not permitted to organize for petitioning these authorities; that had to be done on an individual basis in connection with one's own personal problems. When the emperor and literati issued orders, they were obeyed without question. Even young people, who increasingly seek free expression of their own individuality, still retain these habits. In Confucian style, the government is less prone to publicly execute intellectuals than common workers or peasants; once it declares public demonstrations or expressions to be treasonous, it does not hesitate to jail perpetrators in sparse conditions without trial, and to put on public show trials of those purported to be leading instigators. Suicides and deaths from illness and maltreatment often result. Free speech and judicial restraint are difficult to introduce. They can come only if top leaders support them.

China's citizens move underground to exert their freedom. During the Cultural Revolution, many neighborhood committees formed to keep their peers under control quietly ignored the return of sons and daughters assigned to work in the countryside. After the crackdown at Tiananmen Square in 1989, many local leaders claimed that no one in the neighborhood had engaged in activities supporting the demonstrations. Operation "Yellow Bird" was organized by Hong Kong Triad Societies—criminal organizations who regularly use paid operatives, both within and outside government, to smuggle goods into and out of China. These organizations smuggled over $2 billion worth of goods in 1990 alone; they operate illegal drug, gaming, and vice activities throughout the world. During Operation Yellow Bird, over 130 dissident students and intellectuals were given false papers, makeup, hotel rooms, train tickets, and dramatic rides on smugglers' armor-plated power boats, sometimes exchanging fire with coast guard patrols. Along the way, they found active cooperation from neighborhood leaders. One senior police officer traveled in a car with an escaping student to get him through a roadblock. A man recognizing dissident Wuer Kaixi on a train looked him in the face and said quietly:

It is a great honor to see our leaders here. But don't worry, all of the people in this wagon will help you. But face out! Face out so the guards don't see your face![41]

India was divided into many separate political entities with differing cultures. Each caste was organized at the village level; the leaders cooperated in governing the village. That provides more basis for free speech and freely organized interest groups. However, until independence, India never before had a central court system seeking to enforce uniform laws throughout the land and restrain the power of national leaders. This sometimes means that courts restrain rather than protect cultural traditions, and it leaves them without a broad popular mandate to restrain chief executives when they restrict cultural traditions. However, since national leaders and judges themselves come from a variety of cultural traditions, they have a strong incentive to assure that freedom of the press continues. Any incursion on the press of another cultural group threatens their own.

FREEDOM IN PERU AND NIGERIA

Like their Indian counterparts, many Peruvians live and work outside the formal economy. However, Peru's land reforms have eliminated most large landowning families. Recipients of land under the reforms are often unable to obtain seed, water, and fertilizer to plant fields. But many villagers and peasants graze some animals. Peruvian peasants, and town and urban dwellers, have been able to develop an informal economy producing many goods and services.

The formal sector of the economy provides a free market. Wealthier Peruvians have a high standard of living. As in India, they must obtain many permits from an extensive bureaucracy and spend many months of waiting; bribes are a normal part of life.

Many mountain villages are remote and isolated. The main roads and railroads have allowed many people to migrate into urban squatter colonies. There are no political restrictions on movement.

People are free to join unions, and political parties frequently form and disband. The press is under few restrictions, and campaign oratory involves vigorous criticism of government. Newspapers may be cautious about reporting on scandals that involve those they need permits from. Though Peru is largely a Catholic country, fundamentalist protestantism has gained a strong foothold. The various categories of Spanish and Quechua culture involve social ranking, but not sharp racial or religious differences causing the sort of bloodshed found in India.

The principal bloodshed has come from **Sendero Luminoso** (Shining Path), whose underground terrorist activities have killed over 30,000 people.[42] Operating entirely in secret without issuing any formal decrees, it has attracted many people whose desires to be socially mobile have been frustrated, including highlanders from poorer families who enter universities but face limited job prospects because of their low social standing and offspring of chola market women. **Tupac Amaru**,[43] similarly secret but less violent, attracts young members from more urban and middle-class backgrounds. In the coca-growing regions of the Upper Huallaga Valley, and the Apurimac and Ene Valleys near Ayacucho (the town from which philosophy professor Manuel Abimael Guzman Reinoso launched the Shining Path movement in 1980), it has been common for these groups to control all courts, schools, and health facilities, redistributing cattle and assets to poorer members of the communities. Local peasants are forced to cultivate coca. In towns and villages not under their control, these groups frequently assassinate leaders or military personnel who resist them; for that reason, a fourth of district councils are not in place. Because of their threats, voter turnout is low in areas where they are active. Sendero may make 30 million U.S. dollars a year taxing flights of coca from clandestine airfields;[44] this region is the source of some 65 percent of cocaine consumed in the United States.[45] Peasants living in these areas receive some services but live under constant harassment and fear of death. By dynamiting factories, banks, power lines, and other facilities in thousands of terrorist attacks, these groups have caused over $22 billion damage to property; fighting them may have cost the state an additional $10 billion.

Persons arrested for murder, drug trafficking, and terrorism are often placed in jails for long periods without trial. They must often pay bribes to jailers, lawyers, and judges to receive any food, a mattress, or a trial. In 1986, inmates were forced to lie on the floor and shot after a prison mutiny. Over eighteen thousand people occupy Peru's prisons. It is common to find military men on street corners with their hands on the triggers of loaded semiautomatic weapons; on other corners, muggings have become commonplace. The government has armed peasants to patrol villages and fight the terrorists. A ''60 Minutes''-type television news program revealed a secret directive to army commando squads stating that the ''best subversive is a dead subversive''; the program was taken off the air under pressure from the military.[46] A journalist videotaped a medical student, passing a raid on a Sendero Luminoso safehouse, who was stuffed into the trunk of a police car and turned up dead with five bullets in his head. The videotape, unlike the news program, was allowed to air.[47] A newspaper reporter wrote about repeated killings of village children under age five by army security forces; the army arrested the reporter for alleged terrorism.[48] In response, President Fujimori issued a decree allowing the army to seize all property and institutions in regions where terrorist attacks might occur, interrogate anyone, and arrest those publishing secret documents. In 1992, police captured Guzman and many top Sendero and Tupac Amaru leaders; incidents of violence have declined, though sporadic terrorist attacks continue. Meanwhile, one of Peru's top generals fled the country, accusing two of President Fujimori's closest aides of leading death squads which killed a professor, students, and other civilians suspected of sympathizing with Sendero. When some Congresspeople called for an investigation, the aides ordered thirty tanks onto the streets.

High percentages of Nigerian families have access to land on which they can raise some food. Traditional village social structures remain intact enough to help them build and maintain houses, roads, wells, and other essential village structures on an informal basis. They can sell to one another in informal markets and engage in traditional cultural activities. Males, or whole families, may migrate to cities seeking work and then return to their villages during economic downturn; most simply stay in their villages. The villages are often very poor, providing bare subsistence.

Wealthier Nigerians may start their own businesses and build expensive homes. Since this involves manipulating government regulations on imports, taxation, access to capital and resources, and other matters, those most successful in this regard tend to be those who are well-connected politically, within political parties which have largely grown on a regional basis. Most urban and rural Nigerians can afford few consumer goods but are free to worship as they please.

Most of Nigeria's twenty-three daily and thirty-eight weekly newspapers are owned by national, municipal, or state governments. Their reporters have considerable freedom to discuss scandals (sometimes with weak evidence) and express opinions; they must be careful not to offend the political leaders who control the papers, or they can lose their jobs. The Nigerian press is often called the freest in Africa. Individual regimes have attempted to diminish this freedom. The civilian government in 1964 had journalists arrested and flogged for publishing information that embarrassed the government. Though President Shagari strongly supported a free press, some journalists were taken to court during the early 1980s, and public meetings were banned after the Muslim rioting in 1980. In his attempts to clean up corruption, Major-General Buhari detained hundreds of politicians, including Shagari and many state governors and ministers. His regime also arrested many journalists. After Major-General Babangida overthrew Buhari in 1985, many of these people were released, and the detention centers were opened to the public. The government reduced sentences for officials convicted of corruption and chose opinionated civilians to head ministries. It encouraged debate on how to deal with the serious economic problems Nigeria faced.

But the economy worsened; oil income dropped from $24 billion in 1980 to $7 billion in 1985; between 1986 and 1987, oil prices fell from $28 to $18 a barrel, and the government introduced new austerity measures that raised prices of other goods.[49] When workers and students protested, the government seized the unions and universities. The editor of the country's most outspoken independent newspaper, *Newswatch,* was murdered under circumstances that implicated some top officials. The editors of *This Week* and *New Breed,* and other journalists, were briefly jailed[50] for publishing offensive articles. Leaders of human rights groups that accused the government of political repression lost passports and high-level jobs; a *Financial Times* reporter who accused the government of wasting oil revenues was deported.[51] Babangida closed more newspapers than any previous regime. Critics charge his police with torturing and killing arbitrarily detained citizens, and assassinating local officials critical of the regime.

Press freedom has benefitted from Nigeria's connection with the United Kingdom. Many Nigerians live in England or have studied there; some print Nigerian journals there, away from censorship and the threat that newsprint will be withheld. The fact that there are three dominant ethnic groups to balance one another also helps; each wants voice and print to present their views.

Rioting is an established form of political expression in Nigeria. In recent years, thousands have died in riots in the north protesting actions of the central government, which they felt interfered with their religious freedom by reducing the political clout of their religious leaders. When a presidential election was finally held in 1993—a contest between two of Babangida's personal friends, whom he himself had chosen to run for the post—General Babangida declared it null and void. He cited unspecified irregularities (though international observers called the election clean and fair) and would not let the results be announced. Social Democratic party nominee chief Moshood Abiola, a Yoruba millionaire newspaper publisher who won by a landslide, protested. In Lagos, tens of thousands of protesters built flaming barricades and looted shops; police fatally shot a number of them. Babangida declared an interim government of soldiers and civilians led by one of his close associates. Some opponents of the move were arrested and charged with treason, and newspapers opposing nullification of the election (including Abiola's) were closed by security forces; Abiola was excluded from the interim government, and barred from running in future elections. That triggered weeks of general strikes in Lagos and other Yoruba regions. As an expression of freedom, the ballot is not strong enough to stand on its own.

CONCLUSION

As we discussed previously, diverse segments of the populace gain influence if the government and high percentages of the populace rely on the same economic institutions within their own nation-state for jobs, goods, and services; if the legislature, executive, judiciary, and bureaucracy recruit diverse segments of the populace; and if people are socialized to believe in civic culture values of national unity, equal legal protection for all groups and individuals, and limits on the authority of public officials. Gaining influence might, in turn, help improve people's living conditions.

All of these conditions exist in the United States, the United Kingdom, and West Germany. In China, East Germany, and the Soviet Union, the first situation exists, and, to some extent, the second. India, Peru, and Nigeria recruit lower castes, regional villagers, and diverse tribes into the military and lower levels of the bureaucracy; otherwise, these conditions are not in place.

In the last two chapters, we learned that equality in the distribution of goods and services, and rewards on the basis of efforts and skills, are more firmly established in the United States, Germany, the United Kingdom, the CIS republics, and China than in India, Peru, and Nigeria. In this chapter, we found that many of the same people who fare poorly in the distribution of goods, services, and jobs also

encounter restrictions on their freedom to buy and sell, carry out cultural activities, and express ideas.

Not everyone who experiences dissatisfaction is deprived in all these regards, and not everyone who is deprived in these regards is dissatisfied. Many people with relatively low standards of living may be quite content, while many others with relatively high standards of living are unhappy—and vice versa. In like manner, one cannot conclude that just because someone has little freedom to buy and sell, carry out cultural activities, and express ideas, one is therefore unhappy or frustrated. As we have just seen, most people in the United States, the CIS republics, the United Kingdom, West Germany, and China are experiencing freedom—or lack of it—in much the same manner as their ancestors did; there is no immediate reason to conclude they are uncomfortable about this.

People are likely to miss freedom in buying and selling, engaging in cultural activities, and freely expressing ideas most when they have been deprived of traditional freedoms—when they had and lost them. Many Catholics in northern Ireland experienced such deprivations when Scotch and English settlers took over their land in earlier centuries. Before that, Scotland and Wales reacted with frustration to English domination. So did Native Americans, Quechua, and slaves and indentured servants brought to the Americas as outsiders formed the United States and Peru. Most groups the Soviet Union and China placed cultural restrictions on have experienced this ever since falling under Great Russian and Han hegemony long ago.

One might expect such deprivations to disturb people even more when they have occurred within living memory; after many generations, they may recede into history. Tibetans, Estonians, Latvians, and Lithuanians were independent earlier this century. Chinese land and business owners experienced a radical change in their freedoms with the revolution; those former land- and business-owning families, however, are probably among the most successful at operating new responsibility-system plots, cooperative enterprises, and joint ventures. All Chinese experienced radical shifts in freedom again during the Great Leap Forward and the Cultural Revolution. So did business and landowners after the Russian Revolution and the forced creation of East Germany. Earlier in this century, all East Germans experienced greater freedom to buy and sell, engage in cultural activities, and express themselves than they did under communism. In addition, in all these nation-states, there are people who, for any number of reasons, are not as well off in one or another of these regards as they used to be in the past, or as they aspire to be.

Clearly, people deprived of freedoms would be helped by restrictions on the authority of governmental leaders. The lack of such restrictions in the CIS, East Germany, China, Peru, and Nigeria, and the weak extent to which they have been established in India, allows government to deprive citizens without restraint. Russia and China have never placed such restrictions on their leaders. In Peru, Nigeria, and more recently in East Germany, former restrictions were set aside by outside conquerors.

Many who dislike restrictions on their freedom, yet are doing well in regard to the aspects of equality we discussed, are, at least, integrated into the economy and have been recruited into the political systems of their nation-states. As a result, they have some basis for influence. They do not always have enough influence to achieve their goals, but at least they can attempt to do so. In the United States, the United Kingdom, Germany, and India, such people have the further advantage of being protected by limitations on the authority of governmental leaders. But those who are deprived in *both* the realms of equality and of freedom tend to have none of these bases for influence, and hence have little chance to better their lives.

Large portions of the populace in India, Peru, and Nigeria have no regular source of food. They have uncertain access to land and livelihood, little assistance in obtaining health care, and their community life is disrupted. Their children have little chance to gain educations. Their shelter is minimal, and they own few possessions. And they lack the political influence to change any of this.

Lack of freedom in buying and selling, carrying on cultural activities, and expressing thought especially weakens a person's influence when accompanied by a lack of opportunity to obtain even a minimal education, job, food, and housing; one has little and can do nothing about it. This is a problem faced by some minorities in the CIS and China, and by much greater percentages of Peruvians and Nigerians. The high portion of Indian villagers with little or no education are hampered in exercising the free speech that exists there. All these groups have little help in overcoming their lack of opportunity.

In systems where influence is widespread, many groups hold political office, and people are socialized to believe in limits on the authority of officials, a great variety of interests must compromise to implement policy. While many may derive benefits from these compromises, those benefits are often not what they originally visualized when they first heard the policy suggested; compromise melds their vision with a variety of others. Reformulating techniques and institutional procedures may have subtle effects on that process. Any attempts to implement policy without compromising with influential groups are likely to be quickly overturned.

Those who are impatient with compromise might consider the alternative. When influence is not widespread, few groups hold political office, and people are not socialized to believe in limits on the authority of officials, policy can often be implemented more quickly. But it is likely to benefit only a few.

SUMMARY

Those with the best access to goods and services often have influence. Those with limited access to goods and services often have limited freedom as well as influence. Those with the most freedom often live in systems offering wide portions of the populace the opportunity to exert influence. Those with the greatest dissatisfaction are often those who have been deprived of influence, goods, and liberties they formerly had.

NOTES

1. Chapter 31 discusses the recent moves toward privatization.

2. *Department of State Bulletin* 85 (September 1985): 73. In the Soviet Union, black market goods were often manufactured after hours in regular government factories using factory supplies, with the connivance of party officials and managers, and then sold in alleys. In retail shops, employees diverted other goods and sold them out the back door to the highest bidder. As we saw in chapter 25, some Soviets became millionaires in this manner. On a smaller scale, some customers at the head of the line bought more than they needed in a shop and then sold the surplus at elevated prices to buyers waiting in the long lines outside.

3. Many Jewish people seeking to emigrate from the Soviet Union found their paths blocked. More exit visas were approved under Gorbachev. Some two million ethnic Germans live within the Soviet Union. They, too, were denied permission to emigrate, but—like the Jews—found emigration restrictions easing during 1988. Jonathan Steele, "Gorbachev Rules Out Reunification," *Manchester Guardian Weekly,* October 30, 1988.

4. The CIS republic cities, already short of living accommodations and food, fear a large influx of residents. In 1991, the first auction was held to sell Moscow residence permits (which simply allow one to move into Moscow, without guaranteeing them any place to live). The auctioneer began bidding on the first permit at 1.5 million rubles, or $840,000; it was purchased at that price. "Inflation Hits Moscow Residence Permits," *Kansas City Star,* July 28, 1991.

5. Before World War II, Stalin sent priests to labor camps and closed Russian Orthodox seminaries and monasteries. During World War II, in an effort to revive patriotism, he reopened their seminaries and churches. Khrushchev reclosed more than half the churches and most of the seminaries and threw many church leaders into prison. In 1988, Gorbachev reopened dialogue by holding the first reception for top church leaders since Stalin. Monasteries and churches have now been returned to the churches' control, and many people are attending. Many Orthodox intellectuals consider Orthodox Christianity to be the "mother" of Russian culture and the Russian state; some 40 to 80 million Russians are estimated to consider themselves believers. The Ukrainian Catholic Church (in the western Ukraine), which was in communion with Rome, was suppressed by Stalin and subsumed into the Russian Orthodox Church (which predominates in the eastern part of the Ukraine). It did not begin to gain full independence until after the Ukraine became independent.

In 1993, the Russian Orthodox Church backed a law passed by the Russian parliament which bans foreign religious groups from organizing or recruiting converts without government accreditation. The Russian Orthodox patriarch had been criticizing Roman-Catholic-affiliated Uniates, Billy Graham, protestant fundamentalists, and Hare Krishnas. "We are just trying to put a stop to all this anarchy that is reigning in our country, when swindlers, criminals, adventurists, and fanatics come here and do what they want, and the state does not interfere," said the Orthodox priest chairing the parliament's Committee on Freedom of Conscience. Daniel Sneider, "Russian Law Imposes Restrictions on Foreign Missionary Activity," *Christian Science Monitor,* July 21, 1993.

6. In 1976, 13 percent of Jewish adults were Communist Party members. Archie Brown and Michael Chaser, eds., *Soviet Policy in the 1980s* (Bloomington: Indiana University Press, 1982), p. 317.

7. Idem., p. 171. In 1970, the Moscow correspondent of The *Times* was told by the chief lama of Buryatiya that " 'practically every village in Buryatiya has its own lama.' He was almost certainly not referring to registered ones, for the popular revival has been considerable and Soviet sources admit this in even more pointed language: 'Pilgrims constantly come to the datsan (monastery) at Ivolginsk, arriving on horseback, in cars and by aeroplane; active religious propaganda in postwar years has succeeded in attracting a considerable number of young people into the religious communities.' " In 1987, the Tajikistan party paper wrote that Islam was on the rise in Central Asia, with enormous crowds gathering at mosques on religious holidays. Jonathan Steele, "Moscow Chastizes Its Record of Religious Intolerance," *The Guardian,* August 19, 1987.

8. The Censorship Decree was issued three days after the communist regime took power in 1917. It read in part: "It is common knowledge that the bourgeois press is one of the most powerful weapons in the hands of the bourgeoisie. Especially at this critical moment, when the new government of workers and peasants is consolidating its power . . . we have taken these temporary and extraordinary measures. . . ." Martin Dewhirst and Robert Farrell, eds., *The Soviet Censorship* (Metuchen, N.J.: Scarecrow Press, 1973), p. 6.

   Party officials and others who could buy at the special stores with higher-grade goods could purchase VCRs. It became fashionable to have friends smuggle in rock records and videos of Hollywood soft-core movies and Westerns. Censored books obtained in a similar manner could be passed around apartment buildings; this was sometimes done in the manner of a closed reserve book in a library, with six-hour lending privileges.

9. In 1988, the state printed 11.5 billion rubles; in 1991, 150 billion. By then goods in stores were regularly doubling and tripling in price. David Remnick, "For Gorbachev, It's Back to the Old Intractable Problems," *Washington Post,* August 11, 1991.

10. At the 1980 Moscow Book Fair, the editor of Random House held a luncheon for all authors in Moscow who had published with the firm. For whatever reason, only dissident authors showed up. During conversation, the editor asked what these authors would do about censorship if they were to come to power. The remarks which followed had a common tone. The authors observed that violence, disasters, pornography, and other such subjects are not morally or culturally uplifting and hence are rightly censored.

   "Even if personally interested in greater political/individual freedom and intrigued by the American system, many [privileged Soviets] hold the elitist view that while they and their peers could cope, widespread freedoms would lead to chaos in society and perhaps undermine their own positions. Thus, while privileged Soviets may desire personal freedoms for themselves, their fear of introducing Western values into Soviet society helps moderate their fascination with the outside world." Gregory Guroff, "Soviet Perceptions of the U.S.: Results of a Surrogate Interview Project," Research Memorandum, International Communication Agency of the United States of America, Office of Research, Washington, D.C. (June 27, 1980): 16.

11. Interview with Judy Woodruff, "Seven Days in May," CBS News Special, June 24, 1987. Ironically, Yeltsin was fired as Moscow party chief and demoted from the Politburo a few months later for being too critical.

12. David Remnick, "Liquidating the Fearsome KGB," *Washington Post National Weekly Edition,* September 2–8, 1991.

13. The first widely publicized public opinion poll, by French and Soviet researchers, found support among Moscow residents for many government policies. Seventy-three percent approved of giving exit visas to those who wanted to leave. But only 27 percent approved of the government's policy of releasing dissidents from prison, while 42 percent disapproved; it was the only question on which so many disagreed with actions taken by the leadership. *Kansas City Star,* November 1, 1987.

14. A foreigner asked some people on a Moscow street what they thought about glasnost: " 'Why, it's excellent,' said one babushka [grandmother]. 'It helps the youth and it's good for our country. It helps promote the cause of peace.' The other murmured agreement, but a man begged to differ. 'If it is so good for our country, then why didn't we publish the picture of that plane that landed in the Red Square [successfully piloted past Russian defenses by a young West German] right away?' he said with some heat. 'Why weren't we told the details? What good is glasnost?' Another eavesdropper . . . couldn't restrain himself: 'Why publish that?' he asked. 'It was our shame. Such things shouldn't be published.' 'He's right,' one of the women chimed in. 'Why do we need such photographs? We already have so many dirty things in the paper.' " *Kansas City Star,* June 25, 1987.

   In a letter to *Pravda,* four readers attacked the new articles exposing Stalin's excesses: "To depict this period as nothing but mistakes and errors is to make the whole party, the whole population, look ridiculous. Who needs this?" *The Independent* (London), August 22, 1987.

15. Marina Pristavka tried to be precise in her assembly line work, and hence did not meet quantity norms.

When the cleaning woman was sloppy, Pristavka finished the work herself, and quarreled with fellow employees whom she deemed to be "getting money for doing nothing." Management had her sent to a psychiatric unit for treatment. Reported in *Komsomolskaya Pravda,* newspaper of the communist youth organization; *Kansas City Star,* February 7, 1988. In the United States, such a person might be sent to a psychiatrist, counselor, or motivational seminar for nondirective counseling to teach "teamwork" and cooperative attitudes.

Komsomolskaya Pravda, and articles from *Moscow News* and *Izvestia* reported in the same article in the *Kansas City Star,* tell of complainers being formally registered by the psychiatric community as "litigious psychopaths" and "litigiously active"; when they complain, word is sent that they are mentally ill and should be ignored.

16. A 1991 poll in twenty regions of Russia found only 8 percent wanted to return to a tsar. When the current heir to the throne visited St. Petersburg late in 1991, few gathered on the streets to see him. Justin Burke, "Russian Czarists See Hope in Economic Woes," *Christian Science Monitor,* November 13, 1991.

17. Jonathan Steele, "Decolonizing the Complex Soviet Mind," *Manchester Guardian Weekly,* October 20, 1991.

18. Early in 1991, people were increasingly endorsing "democracy" and "market reforms" in public opinion polls; as the food shortages turned worse later in the year, "order" and "assured food supplies" were ranked higher.

19. Reprinted from *Ogonyok.* William Millinship, "One Woman Cries Out as Hate Fuels Exodus," *The Observer,* May 13, 1990.

20. By 1991, over half the films playing in Moscow were American.

21. A Soviet professor from the Ministry of Internal Affairs wrote in 1982 that 37 percent of the male work force was chronically drunk at work. Another Soviet study showed that on Mondays 30 to 40 percent of the populace is too drunk to put in a solid day's work. A 1984 poll shows that half the population thought drunkenness was the number one social problem in the Soviet Union. *Kansas City Times,* January 1, 1982. *Department of State Bulletin*

85 (September 1985): 74. One reason people can drink at work is that they cannot be fired; they might not like a system that gives employers the freedom to fire them.

Other countries, of course, are not immune from this problem: "Washington. A Congressional panel says new evidence of alcohol and drug abuse at nuclear plants is just the tip of an industrywide problem. . . . The Nuclear Regulatory Commission and the industry . . . rarely investigate allegations of drug and alcohol abuse at plants. The subcommittee urged the NRC to issue regulations requiring utilities to prevent on-site drug and alcohol use, stop workers from entering plants under the influence, and institute a 'fitness for duty' program." *Kansas City Times,* July 13, 1987.

22. Many smaller businesses in England are owned by Indians, Pakistanis, and Arabs. Very wealthy families often start these businesses, then let poorer families who live in their communities operate them.

Margaret Thatcher's Government created development corporations in some areas, one of whose functions was to help obtain tax breaks, loans, and other incentives for new businesses to open. Many of the firms that moved into these areas were, in fact, large. Many smaller businesses that did open did not survive the recession at the beginning of the 1990s.

23. Over 2 million Germans live in the former Soviet Union. The 1 million in Kazakhstan (moved by Stalin to labor camps there) tried unsuccessfully to return to their former farms along the Volga River; Russian president Boris Yeltsin then offered them eight thousand square kilometers of a former missile test site to create a German Autonomous Republic. Though some have lived in Central Asia for 250 years, many prefer to return to Germany.

24. The Nazi "sieg heil" salute is illegal, with a penalty of a $700 fine and imprisonment. Police often stand by during rallies in which hundreds of people give these salutes. They often are not present when crowds of neo-Nazis gather to burn centers containing foreigners.

25. Leipzig Central Institute for Youth Research administered this survey. David Gow, "Ghettoes With Overtones of the Old Germany," *Manchester Guardian Weekly,* October 27, 1991. Another survey found that 15 percent of youths consider Hitler a

"great man." Prime Time Live, ABC News, January 2, 1992. About two hundred thousand marched in the largest nationwide anti-Nazi rally to date, following the killing of three Turks in 1992.

26. Francine S. Kiefer, "Germans Move to Curb Young Extremists," *Christian Science Monitor,* September 27, 1991. After six weeks, the collection centers either reject the immigrants or release them to find homes.

27. In 1991 and 1992, running on anti-asylum platforms, small, right-wing extremist parties increased their number of seats on the Bremen, Baden-Würtenberg, and Schleswig-Holstein parliaments with 6 to 10 percent of the vote. That forced both the Social Democratic and Christian Democratic parties to reconsider their opposition to changing Article 16 of the Constitution so as to restrict further immigration. After three Turks were killed by firebombs in 1992, pollsters found the number of people rejecting the rightist slogan "Foreigners out!" rose from 43 to 69 percent. Frances S. Kiefer, "Germans Adopt Hard-Fought Compromise Compromise on Asylum." *Christian Science Monitor,* December 8, 1992. German Alternative was banned at that time, along with three other groups; a Nazi leader was imprisoned for making a speech suggesting that Jews be killed; and police raided neo-Nazi homes and offices. But an anti-foreigner party won 8 percent of the vote in a March 1993 state election in Hesse. After neo-Nazis killed five Turkish women in May 1993, Chancellor Kohl (who had spoken forcefully after the 1992 killings) did not attend the funeral. Germany (with four-hundred- to five-hundred-thousand a year) has had more immigrants than other European countries, and it must absorb East Germany as well.

28. The Scottish National Party, founded in 1934 to rally for Scottish independence, is the principal competitor in Scotland. It received the second largest number of Scottish votes and several seats in the 1974 election but has declined since. Plaid Cymru, founded in 1925, supports Welsh independence and its language and traditions and holds about two seats in each successive parliament. The divisions between protestants and Catholics in Northern Ireland are reflected in highly divided splinter parties there, which receive high percentages of the vote. The Ulster Unionist party has been the principal organ of the protestants for many decades, together with the more militant Democratic Unionist party. The Catholics are divided among the Nationalist party (which helped bring Irish independence), the Alliance party (which seeks peace with protestants), and the more militant Social Democratic and Labour Party and Sinn Fein (the political arm of the Irish Republican Army).

29. In November 1985, the prime ministers of the United Kingdom and Ireland signed an agreement which created an Intergovernmental Council through which Ministers from the United Kingdom and Ireland consult on matters pertaining to Northern Ireland. The agreement includes a provision that if a majority of voters in Northern Ireland should desire to separate from the United Kingdom, or unite with Ireland, both Governments would give it the freedom to do so and use the Council to work out an approach. In local elections called in January 1986, the Ulster Unionists won all but two of their former seats (indicating rejection of the agreement by Northern Irish voters), but Sinn Fein (which had about 10 percent of the vote the prior spring) lost votes to the moderate Alliance party which helped write the agreement.

30. Of 41,879,000 acres in Great Britain, 18 million acres (mostly in Scotland) belonged to some two hundred titled families. "The trend on the big estates is for more and more land to go out of productive use." Diamond Commission Report (Royal Commission on the Distribution of Income and Wealth, Background Paper, 1978).

31. Northern Ireland had its own legislature, suspended because of the violence.

32. One counter move from the Thatcher Government consisted of giving Scottish school boards power to veto head teacher appointments, to be represented on senior staff appointment committees, and eventually take on total responsibility for spending school operating budgets. Each school with over 100 pupils has a board, which is elected by mailing ballots to all parents with children in the school. Under 1986 reforms, parents are allowed to send the same number of representatives to school governing bodies as local education authorities do, with teachers and local councils also represented.

   After the election of 1987, in which Thatcher won reelection but fifty of seventy-two Scottish seats went to Labour, the Labour Party introduced a bill into Parliament (in an unprecedented move, using its debate time to introduce a bill) calling for a Scottish assembly with broad powers to raise revenue and regulate education, health, housing, fishing, forestry, and other matters. Fifteen Labour Members of Parliament were talking of forming a breakaway Scottish Labour Party. Philip Webster, "Labour Plans Bill to Create Powerful Scottish Assembly," *The Times,* August 11, 1987.

33. Conscientious objectors could serve in building (rather than combat) units but had to wear uniforms during service. There were about five thousand members in the unofficial peace movement. A July 10, 1983 Lutheran rally in Dresden was attended by over one hundred thousand people. Church leaders addressing the crowd supported conscientious objection and called for rejection of the Leninist distinction between just and unjust wars. Some peace campaigners were arrested. Martin McCauley, "East-West German Relations: A Turning Point?" *Conflict Studies,* 155: 15.

34. In East Germany in 1973, some 5,267 citizens' disputes commissions handled some thirty thousand cases brought by fellow citizens involving neighborhood noise at night, unruly children, and the like.

35. Failure to cooperate in becoming an informant could lead to an investigation. Steven Emerson, "Where Have All His Spies Gone?" *New York Times Magazine,* August 12, 1990.

36. Sandra Dassler, a reporter for an East German newspaper. David Gow and Anna Tomforde, "German Racist Attacks," *Manchester Guardian Weekly,* October 13, 1991. In a 1992 poll 80 percent of West Germans, but only 32 percent of East Germans, called democracy the best form of government.

37. Idem.

38. Bernard Weinraub, "India Peers at Its Future with a Sense of Gloom," *New York Times,* July 14, 1991.

39. A Catholic Patriotic Association works with the government and creates bishops. But experts say half the bishops, 70 percent of the priests, and three-fourths of the 7 million Catholics are loyal to the pope and meet clandestinely in an "underground church." A bishop and some priests associated with it have disappeared or been jailed. Kenneth L. Woodward and Frank Girney, Jr., "Public Enemy Number One," *Newsweek,* August 26, 1991.

40. Some estimate a million, while China's police say four thousand. Catherine Sampsin, "China Holds 4,000 Political Prisoners," *The Statesman* (India), November 20, 1992. "The Last Gulag; 'I Still Have Nightmares'," Harry Wu, "A Prisoner's Journey," *Newsweek,* September 23, 1991. "China Strikes Back at Critics with Document on Human Rights," *Kansas City Star,* November 2, 1991. Tang Bogiao, *Anthems of Defeat* (Asian Watch, 1992). Raymond Whitaker, "Amnesty Says Torture Has Become Endemic in China," *The Independent,* December 9, 1992.

41. Gavin Hewitt, "The Great Escape from China," *Washington Post,* June 2, 1991.

42. Communist Party of Peru by the Shining Path of José Carlos Mariátegui (the founding father of the Peruvian left). This terrorist organization has on several occasions knocked out the power supply of Lima, killed numerous local officials and political activists, and brought considerable concern to political leaders. Two of the most complete discussions of this movement appear in Rogger Mercado Ulloa, *El Partido Comunista del Peru: Sendero Luminoso,* 4th ed. (Lima: Fondo de Cultura, 1987); Carlos Ivan Degregori, *Sendero Luminoso,* Documentos de Trabajo no. 4 & 6, 4th ed., (Lima: Instituto de Estudios Peruanos, 1986).

43. Che Guevarist Revolutionary Tupac Amaru Movement (MRTA). Tupac Amaru is named after Jose Gabriel Condorcanqui, a Spanish-educated Quechua descended from an Inca ruler named Tupac Amaru. Condorcanqui took on the name of his ancestor to lead a rebellion among villagers and mine and textile workers.

44. David Scott Palmer, "Peru's Persistent Problem," *Current History* 89, 543 (January 1990): 32. The drug cartels also pay the army protection money—five thousand dollars a flight. "The Newest War," *Newsweek,* January 6, 1992.

45. Robin Kirk, "Oh! What a Lovely Drug War in Peru," *The Nation* 253, 10 (September 30, 1991).

46. Nicole Bonnet, "Japanese Unmoved by Peru's Plight," *Le Monde,* July 28, 1991.

47. By one estimate, 2.5 million people were stopped and searched by the police and military over a three-year period, and 9,000 were detained; in 1990, 302 of them were reported missing. Police make $30 a month. Nathaniel C. Nash, "Military versus Guerillas:

Ten Die a Day, or Disappear, and Peru Goes Numb," *New York Times,* July 14, 1991.

48. Tina Rosenberg, "Peru's War Against Magno Sosa: The Army versus a Reporter on the World's Most Dangerous Beat," *Washington Post,* September 1, 1991.

49. Larry Diamond, "Nigeria Between Dictatorship and Democracy," *Current History* 86, 520 (May 1987).

50. One journalist was jailed for hinting that the wife of a chief-of-staff vice-admiral consulted a diviner. Ndaeyo Uko, "Press Ups and Downs," *West Africa,* August 27–September 2, 1990.

51. *The Economist,* August 17–23, 1991. He said that $3 billion of the $5.2 billion windfall from added oil sales during the Gulf War was not accounted for.

EXERCISES

Think about the book thus far:

1. How do the conclusions in chapter 17 relate to this chapter?

2. Identify people in each of the nine systems who might find it hard to decide whether they are pan-nationalists or whether they believe in a civic culture.

3. How might the presence of those individuals affect each of the nine systems?

4. In which of the nine is freedom and stability more affected by their presence?

5. How did the leadership of the Soviet Union attempt to control pan-nationalism? Were they successful?

KEY WORDS AND PHRASES
Define the following terms:

Sendero Luminoso   Tupac Amaru

THINKING IT THROUGH

1. Pick a country from each of these groupings:

   The United States, the United Kingdom, or West Germany
   East Germany, the CIS, or China
   India, Peru, or Nigeria

   Compare the three with regard to the *right* and *ability* of their citizens to

   a. produce and sell their own goods
   b. buy land, buildings, and goods
   c. organize and join groups
   d. worship and practice cultural customs freely
   e. live wherever one likes
   f. criticize the government, and/or
   g. obtain justice under the law.

2. Now think about the perspective of individuals who are among the poorest fifth in their nation-state, as discussed in chapters 9 and 25. If you were such an individual, in which of the three countries would you rather live? Why?

chapter 28

THE ENVIRONMENT

In the prior three chapters, we saw that when a political system disperses influence widely among its citizens, it may be better able to distribute goods equitably and offer its citizens freedom. In this chapter, we will learn why such a system may also be in a better position to protect the environment.

A political system is the regular pattern of human relationships by which people resolve competition over various values. Equality and freedom are two of those values; resolving them involves the living humans who compete over them.

These individuals also have conflicting values regarding their aspirations for their physical environment; for instance, some may wish a patch of land to contain trees, while others wish it to contain buildings or a lumber operation. But decisions about the environment may have a more long-term physical effect on surroundings than decisions which simply involve freedom and equality. Future (along with present) generations of humans must live with the consequences of their decisions about the planet's physical environment, as must future generations of plants and animals. The Industrial Revolution brought with it massive capabilities to change and pollute the planet and added urgency to make such decisions intelligently.

As we learned, the degree of equality and freedom in a nation-state is largely an outgrowth of the political system (that is, of the pattern of relationships by which competition over values is resolved). In the case of the environment, humans operating within their political systems have less control. Nature can produce storms, tides, floods, erosion, earthquakes, fires, volcanos, and other forces which alter the environment profoundly. And neighboring nation-states can unleash warfare and pollution and do considerable damage.

Our immediate and remote physical surroundings are potentially a source of pleasure and relaxation, livelihood, income, living space, food, fibers, wood, and energy and mineral resources. Use of any portion of the environment for one purpose destroys it for at least one of these other purposes and may also produce unwanted by-products like pollution. Hence, policies pertaining to the environment inevitably produce political conflict. All decisions about the environment affect someone's freedom to do something, and many may affect people's access to goods and services.

Not all decisions about freedom and equality involve the physical environment. But some do. In our attempts to improve distribution of goods and services, equal access to jobs, or freedom to buy and sell, we sometimes forget the consequences to the physical environment, which later disturb the comfort level within our personal environments. **Political systems which disperse influence more widely may be better able to take the physical environment into account; however, they may not always do so.**

At the start of the Industrial Revolution, few people thought about the damage that would accrue from cutting forests, plowing land, digging mines, dumping wastes, and burning carbon through smokestacks, not to mention from radioactivity or nuclear disasters. In fact, such matters did not begin to extensively reach national political agendas until the 1960s. By 1992, chief executives from around the globe attended an Earth Summit in Rio de Janeiro to sign a treaty targeting environmental goals; the European Economic Community, United Nations, and other international forums increasingly grapple with environmental problems caused by pollution, deforestation, energy depletion, and other by-products of growth.

"INDUSTRIALIZED" COUNTRIES

One Soviet biologist says that 20 percent of the former Soviet populace live in an ecological disaster zone, and an additional 30 to 40 percent live in "unfavorable areas."[1] Managers and labor leaders are rewarded for keeping costs down and production up, but not for preserving the countryside. They have allowed soil to wash away, creating great dust bowls. A 1990 report estimates that 25 to 40 percent of the fertile black soil was lost during the prior decade. Water diverted from rivers and evaporated through irrigation seems destined to dry up the Aral Sea and seriously threaten the Azov and Caspian Seas,[2] destroying the fishing industry and creating salt-sand dust storms that ruin the best irrigated croplands of Uzbekistan, endanger the health of inhabitants, and lower rainfall all the way into India.[3] The very land the dams irrigate, they also destroy. Much of the profit from the fruit and cotton raised on this land ended in the pockets of corrupt politicians,[4] who had little concern for the long-term consequences; runoff water, which they did not pay for, was allowed to evaporate in a huge manmade salt lake where the Aral Sea used to be. The Aral, once the world's fourth largest lake, has lost 65 percent of its water in the past thirty years; its level has fallen forty-seven feet and its area has dropped from 25,800 to 15,500 square miles. A region south of the Aral has a mortality rate of 60 deaths per 1,000 births, the highest in the country; this region uses heavy amounts of pesticides on the cotton crop.

Raw sewage and industrial waste are dumped into rivers and streams; only 30 percent of human and industrial sewage is adequately treated.[5] Three-fourths of surface water is polluted. Limestone quarries and clear-cutting lumber operations have eaten away some of the most scenic resort areas on the Black Sea and in Siberia. Large stretches have been strip mined, without efforts to reclaim the land afterwards.

At Kyshtym in the Ural Mountains, due to a 1957 explosion of nuclear waste stored in a large concrete tank, some thirty villages were abandoned, all vegetation ceased, and nearly 400 square miles of land were rendered radioactive.[6] In 1992, officials disclosed that between 1949 and 1967, the Mayak military facility in the southern Urals released more radiation than the much-publicized major nuclear accident at Chernobyl in 1986. That accident may have dire consequences it will take years to assess; over two million people still live in the area contaminated by the radiation released, and there are growing signs of illness among children in the region.[7] Plant operators had not installed safety backup equipment scientists recommended for the antiquated plant or repaired defective instruments before inexperienced workers conducted the experiment that triggered the accident. The top officials of Kombinat, the organization created to clean up the disaster, were accused of hiring unqualified relatives for engineering jobs.[8] The last testament of a leading nuclear scientist who committed suicide after the event discusses transcripts he placed in his safe; these transcripts from the night before the accident, recorded during the experiment they were conducting, relate that the manual on emergency procedures had several passages crossed out. When the disaster happened and the worker on duty called for advice, the other worker "thinks for a minute and then replies 'Do what is crossed out.' "[9]

When the Soviet government passed laws to correct this and other problems, compliance was often slow, hesitant, and inefficient; by 1990, the concrete sarcophagus built to seal off the defective reactor was collapsing. In 1991, the Soviet prosecutor general charged that officials failed to evacuate people quickly, buried the contaminated wastes haphazardly, and then built resettlements atop them. Some estimate that the costs of removing everyone from the area and dealing with the contamination will eventually top $350 billion. Fifteen Chernobyl-type reactors are still operating, with low operator morale and few spare parts.

A 1990 explosion in a nuclear fuel plant released a toxic cloud of beryllium across Kazakhstan; it was not acknowledged for four days, and the level of contamination was not announced. In 1993, the Tomsk-7 plant for processing nuclear fuels also released a cloud. The Chukotka peninsula just across from Alaska was a nuclear testing site, and residents there suffer severe health problems; the Soviets have also dumped considerable nuclear waste in the oceans off this coast.[10] During the 1950s, atomic bomb factories pumped waste water into Lake Karachay until its radiation level was two and a half times higher than the region surrounding Chernobyl; an hour's exposure to the shoreline is fatal. Leaks in two Siberian nuclear reactors have contaminated hundreds of kilometers of land with radiation levels as high as Chernobyl. A 1991 study found that 16 percent of the former Soviet Union's land was "unfavorable for human habitation." Even so, popular demonstrations to close unsafe nuclear plants have been resisted by plant managers and workers who would be thrown out of work. The CIS republics have 70 nuclear reactors, and alternative sources of power are not available. Moreover, former Soviet factories are now negotiating to sell nuclear reactors and atomic weapons to any country that will pay for them.

Air in major post-Soviet cities has been choked with industrial fumes.[11] The 1988 national environmental report listed 103 cities, with a combined population of over 50 million people, whose pollution levels exceeded clean air standards by ten times; 16 towns periodically exceeded the standards by 50 times.[12] In Moscow, many plants were moved from the city, smoke-control devices were installed on many stacks, and other plants were encouraged to burn higher grades of fuel. This improved air quality. Such efforts in cities away from the capital have been less successful. Many municipalities would rather pay small fines than eliminate the problem. Local residents, like those protesting the new dam at Lake Baikal, can cause delays and design changes to meet their criticisms, but they seldom succeed in halting projects. The post-Soviet republics produce 13.6 percent of the world's "greenhouse" gas emissions (including methane, chloroflourocarbons, and carbon dioxide).

Lake Baikal is the world's oldest, deepest, and largest fresh-water lake. It contains a fifth of the world's fresh water. Surrounded by forests and a climate tempered by the lake's heat retention, the lake was so clear that divers could see 150 feet down into the water; the air around it was clean. Over 1,500 animal species have been found there, including 708 peculiar to Lake Baikal alone—among them, 30,000 of the world's only fresh-water seals.

By the 1950s, fifty factories were discharging into the lake's main tributary river; only nine of them treated their waste. The city of Ulan Ude, where most of the factories were located, 75 miles from the lake, discharged its sewage without treatment. Then, in 1957, plans were drawn for paper and pulp mills which would discharge directly into the lake. Scientists wrote books warning of the environmental implications. The Society for the Protection of Nature, with over 25 million members ranging from school children to professional people, pitted itself against the Ministry of Timber, Paper, and Woodworking. The press entered the fray, along with the East Siberian and Soviet Academies of Sciences, the Geological Society of the USSR, and various commissions. Naturalists, officials from state environmental protection agencies, state conservation groups, and academicians contributed to the reports and discussion. In fact, many of these environmental groups later broadened into the democratic groups which brought an early challenge to Stalinism, and later, communism.[13]

Laws regulating the construction and discharge of waste facilities were passed—and broken. It became clear after the paper plant was built that it could have been built elsewhere. The expensive purification equipment was poorly designed, and it malfunctioned. Huge islands of slime appeared on the lake, and the wildlife population declined rapidly.

The forest cover was rapidly disappearing. The Council of Ministers and, later, the Central Committee of the Communist Party intervened with new regulations for cutting trees and treating water. The plant remains; local citizens, fearing job losses, resist closing it. A hundred industrial plants discharge into the lake.

The coalition supporting Lake Baikal conservation did set new environmental legislation in motion. In 1972, the Ministry of Reclamation was given the main enforcement power over water control. In 1973, the annual investment for water pollution control rose from 300 to 1,500 million rubles; in 1976, it was decided to invest 11 billion rubles in water control as part of the next five-year plan. A special Division of Environmental Protection was created within Gosplan, and environmental protection was made a formal part of five-year planning. In 1987, a number of projects were announced to clean Lake Baikal; while twenty-six were completed by the end of 1989, two-thirds had not yet started.[14] In more recent years, the country's fifteen thousand environmental groups have used popular television naturalist programs and the lobbying efforts of local collective farm leaders to prevent hydroelectric projects,[15] and oil and gas development, from springing up around the spectacular geyser fields of Siberia's Kamchatka peninsula.

There were reasons why managers and bureaucrats could agree on the general value of conservation. Only a fourth of the industrial waste water flowing into the Volga River was treated, and cholera had broken out in several basins from untreated sewage. Fish catches were down. Silting was causing problems, and oil, gas, coal, and grain producers were finding valuable farm land and resources drowned by the reservoirs behind the big dams.

Yet no one wanted their own operation to be affected. The Division of Environmental Protection was given the power to solicit and collate proposals from Volga Basin inspectorates to reduce pollution there, but the branch divisions for industrial ministries (the primary polluters) actually allocated the funds for such projects. The wing of the Ministry of

Reclamation which is responsible for building dams was much larger and had far more resources than the water quality wing. Enforcement of the pollution laws is still handled through state- (now republic-) level ministries of reclamation; they pay the inspectors and scientists poorly and, hence, do not attract the best staff. The worst threats they can make are to fine a factory 500 rubles every three months, deprive the manager of his or her bonus, or shut down the plant as a last resort. The occasional closings that have occurred have always been directed at minor industries and last only two or three days; however, reclamation ministries have imposed many fines and cancelled many bonuses.

There are still no construction organizations specializing in pollution control, and contractors (backed by their industrial ministries) often turn down such projects in favor of constructing more straightforward buildings or dams. New equipment suffers from poor design, construction delays, and negligent operation. Yet municipalities have built many new primary, secondary, and tertiary sewage treatment plants. Especially around Moscow, many factories have installed new pollution control devices. Environmentalists won their case to halt reservoir projects on the lower Volga and Pechara Rivers and induced design changes in others; under Gorbachev, many of these projects were scrapped anyway because of the deemphasis on grandiose engineering schemes to improve agriculture. Feasibility studies continue for diverting the Ob and Irtysh Rivers in Siberia to return water to the desiccated Aral Sea; this has brought intense opposition from Russians, who object to diverting their water to Uzbekistan. A series of decrees have protected the Lake Baikal Basin against further development. An economic reform called *khozraschot* would force factories and farms to pay for inputs like electricity and water; water metering could eliminate waste.

Using large amounts of nitrates as fertilizer causes potatoes to rot, taste bad, and pose a health hazard, but does provide a quick way for collectives to increase production. Pressures to increase production remain. Neglect and abuse of the soil continue. Erosion, acidity, loss of humus, and other types of degradation continue to lower yields on three-fourths of farm land.

Glasnost allowed even freer discussion of environmental disasters. Yet the economic turmoil accompanying it provided little funding to deal with the serious degradation caused by years of abuse. Extensive new Japanese logging operations, and a foreign-backed scheme to dam the Amur, one of the world's ten longest rivers, threaten vast wilderness areas of the east.

In the United States, prairie land was plowed in the late nineteenth and early twentieth centuries and converted into dust bowls. Other prime growing land was stripped to uncover thin layers of coal. Little attention was given to emissions of chemical and nuclear wastes into the air and water. Chains of dams have been built on some of the largest rivers, resulting in erosion, evaporation, and lowered water tables. Destruction of wetlands has increased river flooding and harmed coastal marine life. Entire forests have been destroyed, leaving behind eroding hillsides of stubble and destroying animal species; other forests are falling victim to acid rain.

Thomas Jefferson, Ralph Waldo Emerson, Henry David Thoreau, George Perkins Marsh, and other American intellectuals wrote about environmental preservation long before it became a popular view. But environmental organizations did not organize in the United States until late in the nineteenth century, when John Muir founded the Sierra Club. The creation of Yellowstone National Park in 1872 and Devil's Tower and Grand Canyon National Monuments in 1906, to be preserved from habitation or commercial exploitation in perpetuity, paved the way for many other such preserves in the United States and around the world. Vast tracts in the west became national forests, reserved only for regulated commercial exploitation and recreational usage. Commissioner and city manager reforms, beginning early this century, began to regulate city sanitation, building, and other urban environmental problems. Meanwhile, continued westward settlement and mammoth engineering projects began wiping out natural habitats and spreading pollution. During the 1950s and 1960s, conservation groups began gathering enough public support to stop some dam projects. Under growing public pressure, the government created the Environmental Protection Agency in 1970 and began passing legislation to regulate air and water pollution, protect endangered species, regulate pesticides and toxic wastes, and assess environmental impacts of engineering projects. There are now some ten thousand conservation groups, locally and nationally, fighting to protect various aspects of the environment.

The Environmental Protection Agency created a Superfund from taxes on industry and set standards on water and air pollution levels to be enforced by itself and the states. Funds and staff enable the EPA to tackle only a fraction of reported cases. It has tried to remove lead, mercury, asbestos, and beryllium from older buildings. It requires that strip mines be covered after the coal is removed. The 1,200 dioxin sites it has targeted for cleanup are difficult to manage; attempts to burn the chemical release it into the air, and 104 paper plants dump it directly into rivers.[16] Because congressional members from oil-producing states have influence on committees creating the Superfund, oil refineries have been exempted from such cleanups. Many industries, incinerators, and power plants have installed scrubbers to cut down on air emissions, though standards still allow various pollutants to escape. Many power plants still burn high sulfur coal with little emission control. Automobiles are required to have catalytic converters and burn unleaded gasoline, but they still release extensive hydrocarbons into the air.[17] The United States is the world's largest emitter of greenhouse gasses, creating 17.8 percent of the world's total.

Most cities now have secondary, but not always tertiary, sewage treatment plants. Rural septic tanks are not always regulated, and some small towns lack treatment facilities. Some industrial plants treat their effluents, while others still dump raw chemical wastes directly into streams, rivers, and bays.[18] Fishing and oyster industries have declined with the pollution of offshore waters.

After the 1979 Three Mile Island nuclear melt-down at a nuclear power plant in Pennsylvania (America's worst nuclear accident to date), plant operators admitted they had "systematically destroyed, discarded, and failed to maintain records" of radiation leaks and had concealed data from the Nuclear Regulatory Commission.[19] With 112 reactors in place, new reactors are not under development in the United States, and research on ways to burn coal cleanly has intensified. The Department of Energy has begun massive cleanups of nuclear waste sites on its fifteen facilities in fifteen states, with over 4,000 solid waste sites;[20] its proposed salt mine dump lies directly over aquifers, so questions remain as to where those radioactive wastes will go. Some 54,300 sites in America are contaminated with radiation.

City garbage dumps grow larger, and materials that will not decompose build up despite public programs in 500 cities for recycling paper, cans, and disposable diapers. Los Angeles produces 1 percent of its electricity supply from methane piped from its principal garbage dump. Since Native American Reservations are exempt from environmental laws, some off-reservation cities and firms have contracted with them to dump garbage and toxic waste. Many tons of waste batteries, radiator oil, and toxic chemicals are exported to China, which accepts them officially, and to Mexico, which does not. Japan, in contrast, separates various categories of garbage in its major urban areas. Those emitting dangerous fumes are recycled or dumped separately; the rest are incinerated.[21] About 40 percent of Japan's solid waste is recycled.

Extensive U.S. logging of old timber continues at a rapid pace, stripping entire mountainsides in the Pacific Northwest and elsewhere, even in national forests. During the 1980s, oil drilling, mining, and other commercial activities increased offshore and on protected lands; serious oil spills occurred with greater frequency and virulence. Years of pumping for irrigation from the country's largest aquifers, the Ogallala and Sandhills, have lowered water tables so extensively that large portions of Nebraska, South Dakota, Kansas, Colorado, and Wyoming are turning from grasslands to desert. Underground pumping and river diversions are affecting northern New Mexico, the lands below Yosemite National Park, and other portions of the west in a similar manner. The United States uses far more energy per capita than the United Kingdom or Germany and has done little to discourage energy consumption.[22]

All these issues receive extensive publicity and debate in Congress. They involve the activities of large institutions with much money at stake. While lumber and mining companies receive tax breaks and subsidies, firms engaged in recycling do not.

Treaties between the former Soviet Union and the United States to destroy chemical and germ weapons create new problems. Over 70,000 tons of such weapons are stockpiled. Minute quantities can instantly kill large numbers of people. No one knows how to defuse them. The United Kingdom has disposed of such weapons by sinking them to the bottom of the North and Baltic Seas in barrels. Scientists explore this problem at Yapayak in Russia and at Utah's Toele Army Depot.

Efforts to legislate pollution regulation in the United Kingdom extend at least as far back as the smoke abatement provisions of the Town Improvement Act of 1847. The common law has long allowed people to file lawsuits against nuisances, negligence, and trespass, which provided a remedy especially against minor polluters. Rapid postwar industrialization on the edges of cities, combined with the growth of new towns (suburbs), heightened awareness of the pollution problem and promoted new legislation, especially after a deadly heat inversion hit London during the summer of 1952. But intense interest in environmental legislation did not grow until the 1970s. By 1974, the United Kingdom had 605 environmental interest groups, only 15 percent of which were created before 1958, and 37 percent of which were founded between 1970 and 1974. Since that time, the laws have gradually toughened. Industrial polluters may be fined (400 pounds the first day and 50 pounds each subsequent day) and are liable to two-year jail terms. Those discharging pollutants into sewers and watercourses are charged a fee for doing so, and the money is used to run the regulatory system.

The laws are still far from tough enough. For instance, in England and Wales, water management is in the hands of 79 municipal water undertakings, 106 water boards, 30 river authorities and 21 joint sewage boards. Those boards have considerable discretion in determining acceptable pollution levels. They cannot charge fees to those discharging pollutants directly into rivers and estuaries (and eventually out to sea)—only to those discharging into sewers and watercourses, seeping directly into the water table. They do not have large staffs, and it is hard for them to take polluters to court. Often the authorities monitoring pollution produce serious pollution themselves through their own municipal sewage plants; they do not always install adequate equipment in these plants. Edinburgh, for instance, discharged all its sewage untreated into the Firth of Forth until late in the 1970s, and many towns still do.

In politically conspicuous rivers—for example, the Thames, which runs right past the windows of Parliament—authorities have been able to clean up the water with the cooperation of civic groups concerned with the environment, tourism, and preserving the atmosphere around corporate headquarters. Not all rivers have been so fortunate. A 1970 study by the Institute of Water Engineers found a fourth of the public water supply deriving from polluted sources; numerous studies since have warned about the problem. Between 1972 and 1975, many rivers showed deterioration. The highland Scottish coast suffers pollution from nuclear wastes. A series of acts in the mid-1970s placed limits on public and parliamentary inquiries which might slow down energy development. Economic slowdown reduced the number of water effluent plants under construction.

The newly created Department of Environment finds itself competing with a still newer Department of Energy. The Inspectorate of Pollution has been unable to hire adequate numbers of qualified inspectors; inspections for air pollution declined from eleven thousand in 1985 to less than six thousand in 1989, and efforts to regulate nuclear sites were abandoned, while emissions grew even worse. Four top Inspectorate officials resigned between 1988 and 1990, and its director committed suicide.[23] Laws requiring catalytic converters and unleaded gasoline for cars were not passed until the late 1980s, when the United Kingdom responded to pressures from the European Economic Community to become active in advocating the reduction of sulfur dioxide, fluorides, vehicular, and nitrogen emissions into the air.[24] The full story of radiation leakage at the Windscale nuclear reactor in 1957 was not disclosed until 1988; the graphite fire which caused it was not announced until Dutch scientists detected fallout three days after the accident.[25]

In West Germany, states are in charge of pollution regulation. Clean air and water standards are set by local associations composed of abstractors and the dischargers themselves. Fees charged for pollutants discharged into rivers go to build both public and private pollution control plants. To be licensed, new plants must alter processes to reduce pollution. By the late 1970s, West Germany was spending about 2 percent of its Gross National Product on pollution control—slightly more than the United States. In addition to facing pressure from citizen groups, these regulatory associations are under pressure from the European Economic Community, which has created draft legislation and guidelines on pollution which it encourages its members to apply. French firms located on the banks of the Rhine discharge considerable pollution before the river reaches Germany. Much of West Germany's heaviest industry is located along the Rhine, and these factories pollute it further before it reaches the Netherlands, which derives 60 percent of its water supply from the Rhine. So these nation-states pressure one another not to pollute. The penalty for industrial pollution in West Germany is up to 100,000 Deutschmark, plus prison; at least a thousand suits are always pending, though it is often difficult for the state authorities bringing suit to clearly establish legal blame. The national government has no authority to interfere with the states in these matters. And it is difficult for other nation-states to pressure these state-level authorities.

In 1991, Germany instituted a law requiring all companies to recycle material used for shipping and packaging. The companies themselves started a private firm to collect the material. They pay this company a penny or more per package for the right to place a green "recyclable" dot on their packaging. The company and its subsidiaries pay for people to re-sort green-dot garbage not already sorted by consumers at neighborhood recycling centers or (in cities with the service) at curbside.

Unfortunately, the company now has more material that it knows what to do with; little of the material is actually recycled. Companies have been slow to use recycled material, and new products have not been developed fast enough. The recycling companies ship a fifth of the hazardous waste abroad—ten times the volume the United States ships abroad*—and export a lot of plastic and paper abroad as well. The German public has been reticent about developing plants to reprocess recycled materials in their own neighborhoods. About a third of firms cheat by placing dots on their packaging without paying the fee, so the recycling company is now asking for large government subsidies. And other European countries, deluged with German waste, are encouraging European Economic Community guidelines which would require such waste to be reused, recycled, composted, or incinerated. Legislative proposals to respond by raising the fees on packaging, mandate the use of more recycled material in packaging, ban certain materials in packaging, give preference to reusable containers, and let consumers return packaging directly to retailers are meeting stiff resistance from manufacturers and retailers.†

*"Going Abroad," The Economist, May 29, 1993.
†"Green Behind the Ears," The Economist, July 3, 1993.

East Germany's river system was shared only with Poland and West Germany, who had no organized way to pressure it on environmental matters; Poland, too, is an intense polluter. The areas of greatest pollution or environmental disruption are not heavily populated. For instance, much of East Germany's heaviest-polluting industries, involving chemicals, cellulose, mining, fertilizers, and petroleum refining, were located in Frankfurt-on-Oder, Cottbus, Halle, and Leipzig Counties in towns with fewer than 50,000 people. Between them, these counties contain over a third of East Germany's inhabitants, but their only two cities of any size, Leipzig (575,000) and Halle (260,000), do not contain many heavy industrial plants. City dwellers suffered from terrible air pollution, but could not easily see the stacks from which it was emanating. East Germany did little to regulate water and air pollution issuing from such inefficient, energy-wasting plants, whose high sulfur lignite emissions[26] created such intense quantities of pollution that the countryside everywhere was clouded. Today, buildings are black, forests dying, and rivers choked with uncontrolled runoffs of chemicals and other noxious industrial pollutants. A seventy-mile area around Wismut's uranium mines are heavily contaminated with radium 226.[27] Political discussion of pollution was stifled. West Germany estimates that East Germany's pollution created $18 billion in damage each year (about the same as the annual cost of air pollution for the entire United States); the French estimate that it will cost 200 to 250 billion dollars to bring East Germany's environment up to West German standards.[28]

In contrast, much of West Germany's heaviest industry is located in North Rhine-Westphalia. With over 17 million people, this is West Germany's most populous state; it contains cities such as Cologne (850,000), Dusseldorf (665,000), Essen (695,000), Dortmund (640,000), Wuppertal (420,000), Gelsenkirchen (350,000), Munster (200,000), and Bielefeld (170,000). The Rhine River passes through this state before it flows into the English Channel. Because local citizens and nearby countries focus on this region, much of West Germany's pollution control expenditure is concentrated here. Pesticide emissions into the Rhine meet World Health Organization standards, but not the standards of the Dutch downstream, who depend on the water for drinking and irrigation. In addition to industry, the region contains most of West Germany's lignite reserves, all within a 1,000-square-mile area. By the end of 1977, 67 square miles of this land had been strip mined, and two-thirds of the strip mines had been replaced with lakes and ponds, forest, and farmland.

Most of East Germany's lignite reserves are in Cottbus County. Here, too, the area is reforested after strip mining. Though the population is small, the mining itself requires much water; water is scarce, and the reforestation can prevent excess run-off. This provided strong economic inducement to undertake the expense of reforestation, even in the absence of the sort of popular pressure West Germany experiences. Now that Germany has reunified, many of the chemical plants have been closed, and new plants producing other goods are being built using cleaner and more energy-efficient equipment, burning fuels other than lignite.

Great Britain, because it is an island with no tall mountains, depends directly on rainfall for its water supply, rather than on rivers; its rivers drain water, but they do not supply it. Local authorities seem more diligent about preventing improper dumping on land (which could affect the ground-water for centuries) than they are about protecting water which has already reached the rivers and will then run into the sea without further affecting the groundwater—unless these rivers run near large cities. This example illustrates a general trend: The diligence with which authorities pursue environmental protection in the industrialized nation-states seems to depend on the pressure exerted by the population, and on the economic value authorities believe they can derive from such policies.[29]

"LESS-INDUSTRIALIZED" COUNTRIES

China and India contain the floodplains of the Himalaya Mountains and their adjoining ranges. For millennia, China's bureaucracy has harnessed those waters for irrigation and flood control. Many trees were chopped down to make way for crop lands. During the Great Leap Forward, Mao ordered local officials to fill additional portions of lowland swamps and raze mountain forest land for agriculture. Land area the size of Italy (130,000 square miles) was stripped of trees; much has eroded into

desert and become incapable of holding back floods. The forests in Sichuan, Yunnan, and Guizhou provinces, which contain the upper reaches of the Yangtze River and once held China's second largest forest reserve, were reduced by half (from 28 percent of land area in the early 1950s to 13 percent in the 1980s). The amount of silt carried by the Yangtze River increased by 30 percent during a six-year period during the 1980s, according to measurements taken at the Yichang hydrometric station; the river washes away 1.8 billion tons of topsoil each year, filling lakes and depositing soil behind dams along the way (thus reducing their capacity to absorb devastating floods) and eventually spilling a third of the soil into the ocean.[30]

To recoup the loss, China has undertaken to reforest 17,000 square miles of land a year. Yet peasants gathering firewood and opening new land reduce that benefit. The Longyang hydroelectric dam on the Yellow River has lowered temperatures, creating winds that erode nearby grasslands. Some 80 percent of China's farmland was classified as low- or medium-yield in 1991, vs. 66 percent in 1989.[31] Yet, to deal with floods[32] and demand for electricity, China's People's Congress has approved building an even larger dam along the Yangtze at Three Gorges. Leading members of the People's Consultative Conference published a book entitled *Yangtze! Yangtze!,* whose editor was arrested for instigating the 1989 student unrest. Principal concerns are creation of a wall of mud behind the dam, flooding upstream, and loss of fish, which might be reduced if smaller dams were instead constructed on tributaries. The project will displace millions of people and cost as much as $100 billion (in U.S. dollars). But downstream areas, and agencies operating ships there, support the project.[33] The government has allowed no detailed press reports on criticism of the dam.

Human and animal effluent is used as fertilizer on Chinese fields; factories and people dump trash of all kinds into waterways and rivers. Factories large and small, throughout the land, burn high sulfur coal and lignite without pollution controls—a billion tons a year, mostly burned raw, growing to

1.5 billion by the year 2000.[34] China's emissions of greenhouse gases are the fourth largest in the world; if its growth continues, its emissions could triple those of the United States by the year 2025. China's energy consumption per dollar of GNP is 5.3 to 15 times that of Japan, 2.3 to 4 times that of Germany or the United States, 1.7 times that of the CIS, and twice that of India.[35] Farmers spray pesticides from tanks on their backs. Unleaded gasoline is not available. Local officials accept contracts from foreign countries to dump toxic waste on large land sites. These environmental factors may be responsible for the marked increase in deaths from cancer and lung and heart disease.[36]

The Chinese government is building a giant nuclear reactor near Hong Kong. An international inspection team found that workers building the plant skipped procedures, leaving metal bars out of concrete and ignoring safety measures. A million Hong Kong citizens signed a petition calling for scrapping the plant, but no citizens of China have raised complaints.[37] One nuclear plant is already operating in China and several more are planned, including a joint project with Russia. The government has few programs to protect people from any problems related to pollution. It has set aside land for national parks.

In 1989, recognizing the seriousness of its environmental problems, The Chinese government incorporated a resolve to spend 0.7 percent of its GNP on environmental protection into its seventh five-year plan.[38] It signed the international protocol to limit chlorofluorocarbons, on condition that it receive international aid and technology to replace them. It has instituted fines on polluters, and new plants must receive approval from environmental protection boards; they are, however, controlled by local and provincial leaders who may sometimes be in collusion with polluters. Rural enterprises are among the heaviest polluters.

India, too, has set up numerous small national parks and wildlife refuges. However, encroachment of India's formerly extensive forests began during the eighteenth century, and grew rapidly during the nineteenth, when the British cut trees for bridges, railroad ties, housing, and engineering projects to make way for commercial agriculture. British irrigation projects started leaving salt deposits on the land and lowering the water table. The first investigation of salination in 1891 found 5,000 square miles seriously affected. Today, a third of India's million square miles of agricultural land, including a fifth of its irrigated land, has been turned into wasteland by salinity and erosion.[39] Another third is classed as partly degraded. Much of this is the land occupied by poorer peasants. The average peasant now has only a fourth of the land available at the time of India's independence. Meanwhile the Green Revolution farms use extensive irrigation, chemical fertilizers, and pesticides. During the 1980s, the water table dropped an additional thirty yards; many wells supplying poor peasants have dried up.

The trees, which once provided fruit, fodder, fuel, and protection from India's monsoon flooding, now cover less than 10 percent of the land; every twenty-four hours, 10 million trees are felled by peasants seeking firewood and by industries, while replanting of seedlings barely matches the sixty thousand square miles of timber cut each year by industry (often illegally, with bribes going to corrupt officials). During the 1980s, the amount of land affected by flooding rose from 75,000 to 150,000 square miles despite extensive reclamation projects. Many environmental groups call attention to these concerns. India's emerging middle class is heavily dependent for its wealth on the Green Revolution agriculture, which is at the heart of the problem. Thus, many turn a deaf ear.

In some areas, strip mining and toxic ash from industries and power stations have damaged India's air, land, and water so badly that entire villages must be abandoned. Villagers in these areas often have no jobs, water, or fuel. In other areas, self-help movements (such as "hug the trees") have helped

A month after the troops shot down demonstrators in Tiananmen Square in 1989, my wife and I witnessed another kind of tragedy. We were in the first carload of foreign visitors entering Wolong wildlife reserve after the Tiananmen shootings. High in the mountains of Sichuan province, Wolong is China's largest and most famous reserve for pandas.

Our first stop was the world's most sophisticated research laboratory, nursery, and holding station, built by the World Wildlife Fund to attempt panda breeding in captivity. While—after years of failure—China's zoos captive-bred eleven surviving baby pandas in 1992, pandas have proven hard to breed in captivity. Males only go into heat once a year. Females lose receptivity when caged. Infants are highly vulnerable to disease, and pandas will eat only fresh leaves of a certain type of bamboo.

The gate to the compound was opened for us by a young minority tribal girl holding a baby; she proved to be the only person in attendance of the entire compound. The laboratories were closed and showed no sign of recent use. The pandas sat indoors in their own filth, which coated their fur; though it was hot, the doors to their outdoor play areas were all closed. I left the back gate of the compound open; it was still in the same position when we passed two days later.

The next day, we drove a number of miles further into the park to take a hike and "look for pandas"; peasant houses nestled in valleys and hills along the way. The steep trail, filled with minority tribal workers hurriedly clearing stones fallen since the last round of tourists had come by, offered some spectacular scenery. At the top we visited a peasant's house for tea, and I took pictures of his pigs. The guide told my wife afterwards that he had only seen a live wild panda two times in his life.

Hong Kong and Taiwan businesspeople will pay forty-thousand dollars for a panda pelt and paws (considered a delicacy that induces strength); the fine for poaching is only three hundred seventy dollars. That gives locals a high incentive to assist poachers rather than catch them. The government has provided little staff to patrol the park's 785 square miles; the staff we saw largely hung around headquarters the day we were there. There are no funds for planting bamboo corridors to link areas of panda habitation and end inbreeding. But the Chinese government has received considerable money from conservation groups for panda preservation.*

During the nineteenth century, Bengal tigers roamed India's forests in great herds. A 1972 census found 1,827 remaining; a 1989 census, 4,334. Directors of Project Tiger credit their program with the increase and ask for more funding; critics (including the man, now retired, who founded the project after foreign conservationists expressed concerns about the 1972 census) say the tiger population is declining, not increasing. The large number of peasants surrounding the national parks with tiger habitat, which are seldom much more than ten miles by ten miles in size (and are often smaller than that), illegally collect firewood, fell trees, and graze cattle within park boundaries. Naturalists advocating "ecodevelopment" want to help peasants improve their cattle breeding and veterinary service to give them comparable milk and income with smaller herds, provide them with liquid propane and alternative pastures to reduce their need for wood and in-park grazing land, and improve their educational and medical facilities. The test project has already spent millions of rupees over more than three years and attracted new peasants to the area without producing any of these services.† Meanwhile, wealthy collectors still pay poachers and staff more for a tiger pelt than they could earn in a decade as a peasant or bureaucrat. Pills containing tiger bone sell for over four hundred dollars *each* in Taiwan.

*Others share our impressions. See George Schaller, The Last Panda (Chicago: University of Chicago Press, 1993); Sharon Begley, "Killed by Kindness," Newsweek, April 12, 1993; James L. Tyson, "Pandas Have Their Backs to a Chinese Wall," Christian Science Monitor, September 18, 1990; Julion Baum and Carl Goldstein, "Wildlife: Asia's Untamed Business," Far Eastern Economic Review, August 10, 1993.
†Cameron Barr, "Parks vs. People Dilemma in India," Christian Science Monitor, June 4, 1992.

villagers start craft industries, find employment for their children in nearby cities, and plant trees rather than cut them for fuel or funeral pyres. Government programs to regulate large polluters are largely lacking. The accidental release of deadly chemicals from the Union Carbide plant at Bhopal, which killed twenty-five hundred people in 1984 and injured the health of hundreds of thousands, was partly the result of loose industry regulation.[40] India is the world's fifth largest producer of greenhouse effect gasses. The air in major cities is heavily polluted and getting markedly worse as trucks and cars multiplied from 5 to 15 million between 1981 and 1992.[41] There is no plan to switch to unleaded fuel. Millions of squatters, urban dwellers, and factories dump raw sewage directly into rivers. The Ganges and Jamuna Rivers have been declared biologically dead, and the program begun in 1986 to clean them is moving slowly; a confidential report found that three-fourths of India's water supply is polluted.[42]

India has seven nuclear power plants in operation and another seven under construction. Despite billions of dollars invested, its seven operating plants, plagued by technical problems, operated at only 40 percent of capacity in 1992 and provided only 2 percent of India's electricity.*

On the Narmada, the only large river not formed in the Himalayas, the Sardar Sarovar dam (already a third finished) will raise the water level 450 feet, backed by 30 large, 135 medium, and 3,000 small dams. Millions of acres of farm and forest land will be flooded; tribal peoples refusing to leave their homes will be forcibly evicted. Citing the problems of Soviet megadams to the north, environmentalists question the soundness of the project. World Bank funding was withdrawn in 1993 amid concerns about finances.

*"*India, China Squandering Energy, Says Study,*" Indian Express, *November 27, 1992.*

Peru's native llama and vicuna herds were largely wiped out by the Spanish introduction of sheep and cows in quantities too large for the land to absorb; these animals are not selective in their grazing and can destroy all plant life if left on the same lands too long. At the same time, the elaborate terracing built by the Quechua fell into disuse, causing erosion. More recently, large dam projects have led to siltation. The government has outlawed the sale of vicuna fur and created breeding areas for llama; the numbers of these animals have been rising. The government has few programs to stop erosion or restore plant life to regions affected by overgrazing.

Over 700,000 acres of Amazon rain forest (a land area larger than Rhode Island) is razed each year. In Peru's Upper Huallaga Valley, the trees have been replaced by 375,000 acres of coca to supply the international drug trade. Erosion, along with the herbicides used in government intervention programs, have reduced the quality of this land; if the plants die, the peasants simply raze additional forest. Other Amazon land is being razed and damaged by mercury from gold mining. To the west of the Andes, Peru's many silver, gold, and copper smelters spew fumes harmful to agriculture; there has been virtually no regulation of these emissions. President Fujimori invited American oil companies to drill for oil inside national park areas; under pressure from American environmental groups (and aware that previous drilling in the area had met with little success), they declined.

Peru's urban squatter neighborhoods, or *barrios,* have few facilities for water or sewage. The average *barrio* resident obtains half a gallon of water a day—brought in by truck—to use for drinking, eating, and bathing. The effluents from seven million Lima residents are drained untreated into the Pacific Ocean, contributing to Peru's cholera epidemic. One suburb of Lima has created ponds in which algae and photosynthesis from sunlight clean sewage water, which is then used for irrigation in the surrounding valley—a rare experiment. As in India and Nigeria, garbage dumps are carefully foraged by people looking for anything that might be resold; these dumps retain less bulk than those in industrialized nation-states. Unregulated emissions from factory chimneys pollute the air. Many diseases flourish in the filth and effluents.

Public water tap in Azpitia, Peru, with buckets lined up to collect water for drinking, cooking, and washing. The one-room house in the background is typical of those along this street.

© *Kip May*

Nigeria's squatter neighborhoods, too, lack piped water and sewage treatment. Corruption among officials makes it difficult to enforce environmental standards. Italy has used Nigeria to dump polychloride biphenyls, paying off officials and private individuals.[43] In the Sahel to the north, excessive plowing and grazing have allowed much soil to blow away, and large irrigation projects lower water tables. Intercropping to enhance soil fertility has largely been abandoned. Some tree windbreaks are being planted to fight erosion, and ladybugs are being used to eat aphids. Wild animals are selective in the grasses they eat and hence do not strip land of all vegetation, unlike cows, which eat all forms of grass. Wild animals can also yield six times as much meat per acre as cows.[44] Yet land formerly used by wild animals continues to be converted to cattle grazing, often at densities beyond what the land can support. This is accompanied by the use of pesticides to kill tsetse flies. Renewed emphasis on large export agricultural projects during the late 1980s resulted in the salination and depletion of water tables needed by small farmers who rely on wells. Combined with similar projects throughout central Africa, these projects are contributing to a change in wind patterns which reduces rainfall and spreads the boundaries of the Sahara desert. Logging is expected to remove all of Nigeria's forest by the year 2000.

WHOSE CHOICE?

The United States, the United Kingdom, East and West Germany, and the former Soviet Union have all established programs to deal with environmental pollution and degradation. Those in the United States, West Germany, and the United Kingdom are most successful, at least in tackling problems visible in regions with heavy populations. China, India, Peru, and Nigeria have made little progress in creating such programs; pollution is becoming especially severe in the most populous and industrialized cities.

Citizens of the United States, the United Kingdom, and the Federal Republic of Germany also consume more natural resources and have the capacity to affect more of the globe with environmentally damaging technology. Because of the kinds of products we consume, each American causes nine times as much greenhouse gas emission as a Chinese citizen. In fact, Americans consume more energy per capita than any other nation-state (see figure 28.1).

People often use influence to tackle equality and freedom issues before they address issues relating to the environment. Environmental issues tend to arise only after political systems have matured. They can be more successful when interest group activity and communications are free and unrestricted.

People use influence to keep environmental problems away from the neighborhoods where they live and from scenic areas they deem valuable. In nation-states where few citizens have influence, that

Figure 28.1   Energy and electricity consumption per capita.

1988 kilograms of oil equivalent from World Development Report, Poverty, World Development Indicators 1990. *1989 per capita electricity consumption from CIA,* The World Factbook, 1990.

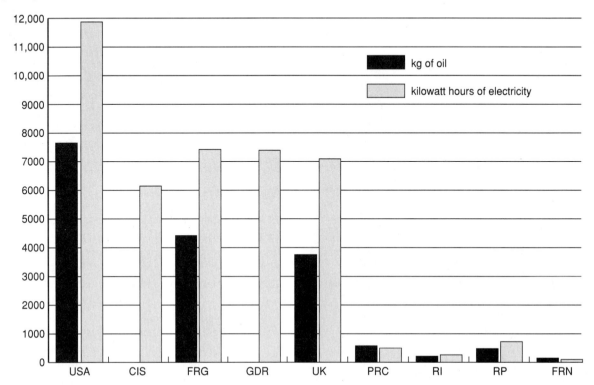

means only a few areas are protected. In nation-states where influence is more widespread, both socially and geographically, more areas come under the umbrella. People may, of course, simply use their collective influence to push environmental problems not only out of their communities but across national boundaries, where they seek scarce natural resources, sites for factories that produce pollution, and places to dump waste.[45]

All these nation-states experience conflict concerning the environment. It is a source of energy and minerals, and it is a source of food, living space, and beauty. The resolution of these conflicts often depends partially on whose livelihood will be affected. People who want their own neighborhoods to be clean may also want gasoline, wood, and perfect fruits and vegetables, and may want to pay as little as possible for them. They want the busi-

nesses where they work to retain as many profits, and to gain as much capital for salaries and wages, as possible. Thus, they are hesitant to see the economic institutions which produce these goods and sources of livelihood faced with high costs to preserve the environment.

This creates a peculiar irony. In nation-states where few have influence, it is difficult to create interest groups that have much impact on preserving the environment. Yet for influence to become more widespread, it is often necessary for many people to be integrated into the national economy; only as industry and the economy develop can influential interest groups arise. So the very people who can exert influence are torn by a conflict: they want to protect a clean environment, but they also want to protect their economic interests. And they often do not want to pay for a clean environment. At least they can make that choice with respect to their own personal environments; if in so doing they degrade the physical environment, they remove those choices from future generations.

SUMMARY

People are more willing to pollute someone else's backyard than their own. If more people have influence, more backyards are protected, partly because more information can be disseminated about how polluting someone else's backyard can harm or help your own. But the same forces which make it possible to obtain and spread this information also increase the potential and inclination to pollute other places for your own advantage. Environmental protection expands when influential people come to realize that degradation of someone else's backyard may harm their own well-being.

NOTES

1. Alexei Yablokov, as quoted by Paul Craig Roberts, "An Ecological Disaster Zone," *Kansas City Times,* June 23, 1989; Roy D. Laird, "An Ecological Ruin is Emerging," *Kansas City Star,* August 9, 1992. Each year one hundred thousand "heredity-sick children" are born due to metal poisoning of their mothers. In some regions of the Ukraine, only a fourth of school-age children can be considered healthy. The number of children with blood diseases and cancer tripled in the past three years.

2. Seventeen billion gallons of untreated toxic petro-chemicals are dumped into the Caspian Sea each year. This sea is the source of the sturgeon which produce caviar; they are dying out. Roberts, "Disaster Zone."

3. Resulting dust storms blow 50 million tons of salt-sand into the air, dropping half a ton per hectare onto Uzbek crop land. Martin Walker, "Sea Turning Into Desert," *Manchester Guardian Weekly,* April 24, 1988.

4. Yuri Churbanov was a mechanic who became a police officer and married former party chief Leonid Brezhnev's daughter. Placed in charge of the interior ministry's political department by his father-in-law, Churbanov offered corrupt officials protection if they cut him in on profits. In Uzbekistan, they overestimated the cotton crop and simply kept the extra money the state officials (also corrupt) paid them for it. When they were placed on trial in 1988 for stealing four billion rubles in this fashion, several shot themselves. The Prime Minister of Uzbekistan and the Deputy Chairman of Presidium of the Uzbek Supreme Soviet were among those who stood trial. Jonathan Steele, "Trial of the Soviet Union's Number One Son-in-Law," *Manchester Guardian Weekly,* September 11, 1988.

5. According to the Soviet government's 1988 environmental report. They classified 30 percent of sewage as improperly treated and 20 percent as raw. Kaunas, Lithuania and Riga, Latvia both have populations of over a half million people but no sewage treatment plants. Hilary F. French, "Environmental Problems and Policies in the Soviet Union," *Current History* 90, 558 (October 1991): 334.

6. Dissident Soviet scientists claimed that such a blast occurred during the winter of 1957–58. A team from Los Alamos National Laboratory in the United States challenged this, maintaining that the desolation occurred as a result of acid rain from emissions of a plutonium-enrichment plant and of discharging polluted water from nuclear reactors. In 1989, Soviet authorities confirmed that the blast occurred in a plutonium processing plant there, but would not confirm the extent of radiation damage. The area has been resettled. Munitions have been produced in this region since the days of the tsars. *Kansas City Star,* April 11, 1982; Bill Keller, "Americans See Secret Soviet Nuclear City," *Kansas City Times,* July 10, 1989.

   The March 1993 issue of the *Proceedings of the National Academy of Sciences* disclosed secret autopsies indicating that a cloud of deadly anthrax spores was released from a germ warfare plant over the million people living in the city of Sverdlorsk; at least forty-two died.

7. Ukrainian doctors regularly diagnose a radiation-induced immune deficiency they have dubbed "Chernobyl AIDS." Every village contains large numbers of deformed babies. In 1990, the computer disks containing medical records on 67,000

radiation exposures were reported stolen. Daniel Sneider, "Byelorussia Backs Gorbachev Plan," *Christian Science Monitor,* March 14, 1991; Andre Carothers, "Children of Chernobyl," *Greenpeace Magazine,* January/February 1991, pp. 10, 12. A secret directive in 1987 forbade doctors from connecting any illness to radiation.

8. *New York Times,* April 25, 1988.

9. This scientist wrote of confusion and lack of responsibility stemming from the large number of departmental and interdepartmental committees managing reactor design and operation. He said that scientists knew the safeguard procedures were defective, but did not want to do the extra work to correct them. Prior to the accident, one Chernobyl director claimed the reactor "is like a samovar and much simpler than a thermoelectric power station. We have experienced personnel and nothing ever happens." Valery Alekseevich Legasov, "The Disaster Just Waiting to Happen," *Manchester Guardian Weekly,* June 19, 1988. Reprinted from *Pravda.*

10. The *Moscow News* reported that Academy of Science documents show the average life expectancy of residents of the Chukotka peninsula to be 45. Ten percent of full-term babies are stillborn. *Kansas City Times,* August 17, 1989. Environmentalists claim that large amounts of nuclear waste and reactors from fifteen decommissioned submarines were also dumped in the Arctic Ocean north of Archangel. Around Archangel, 10 percent of children are born in a weakened condition—higher than in 1946, at the end of World War II.

11. While American industries emit 2.7 billion pounds of toxic chemicals into the air each year, Soviet industries emit 22 billion pounds. Roberts, "Disaster Zone." A 1989 report says it is theoretically impossible to live in every seventh Russian city. One city has 598 times the acceptable amount of benzopyrene in its air.

12. French, "Environmental Problems," p. 333.

13. See D. R. Kelley, "Environmental Policy Making in the USSR: the Role of Industrial and Environmental Interest Groups," *Soviet Studies* 28, 4 (October 1976): 570–79; R. B. Remnek, *Social Scientists and Policy Making in the Soviet Union* (New York: Praeger, 1977); P. Kneen, "Why Natural Scientists Are a Problem in the CPSU," *British Journal of Political*

Science 8, 2 (1978): 177–98; T. H. Friedgut, "Interests and Groups in Soviet Policy Making in the USSR: The MTS Reforms," *Soviet Studies* 28, 4 (October 1976):524–47; W. Taubman, *Governing Soviet Cities* (New York: Praeger, 1973); R. Tokes, *Dissent in the USSR* (Baltimore: Johns Hopkins Press, 1975); P. Reddaway, "The Development of Dissent and Opposition," in A. Brown and M. Kaser, eds., *The Soviet Union Since the Fall of Khrushchev,* 2d ed. (London: Macmillan, 1978), pp. 121–50; Thane Gustafson, *Reform in Soviet Politics* (New York: Cambridge University Press, 1981); and Murray Feshbach and Alfred Friendly, Jr., *Ecocide in the USSR: Health and Nature Under Siege* (New York: Basic Books, 1992).

14. John Massey Stewart, "The Great Lake is in Great Peril," *New Scientist,* June 30, 1990.

15. One crew sent in 1989 to build a hydroelectric dam along the completely wild Kamchatka River was greeted by leaders of a local fishing collective. During their chat, members of the collective stole all the motors from equipment and flew away with them by helicopter; this gained the group enough time to send a delegation to Leningrad, which talked the ministers into abandoning the project because it would destroy fishing. 1991–92 PBS series *Adventure,* "Yankee in Kamchatka."

16. Mark Mayfield, "States Clash Over Dioxin-Laced River," *USA Today,* August 9, 1989. Of 7,592 hazardous waste sites identified, only 150 have been fully cleaned up under the Superfund! Brad Knickerbocker, "Environmentalism Extends Its Reach," *Christian Science Monitor,* January 12, 1993.

17. California has developed far tougher standards for auto and industrial emissions and has stronger regulations and tax incentives to encourage energy conservation, than most of the rest of the country. Over one hundred cities violate federal clean air standards. Knickerbocker, "Environmentalism." The United States spends $100 billion a year on pollution controls.

18. The one thousand largest American corporations spend four times more on legal bills for environmental matters than on tax disputes. "Business This Week," *The Economist,* August 17, 1991.

19. Carothers, "Children of Chernobyl," p. 12.

20. At Hanford, Washington, 1,377 radioactive and chemical waste sites are large enough to bury a football field 700 feet deep, and billions of gallons of liquid waste have seeped into a 200-square-mile area along the Columbia River. Cleaning this one region alone could take $3 billion a year for thirty years. Brad Knickerbocker, "Huge Cleanup Awaits Arms Plants," *Christian Science Monitor*, March 15, 1991. In addition to land sites like this, nuclear waste was also dumped in the ocean off San Francisco and elsewhere.

21. Japan has 1,899 garbage-burning plants, versus 155 in the entire United States. Even though the Japanese plants carefully sort garbage, they still emit some toxic fumes. Garbage dumps are covered with golf courses and other recreation areas. "Teeing Off on Japan's Garbage," *Newsweek*, November 27, 1989.

22. In 1987, the United States used up the equivalent of 9,542 kilograms of coal per person, while the United Kingdom used 5,107 and Germany 5,624. *Statistical Abstract of the United States 1990*, pp. 842–53. In 1990, gasoline taxes were $.25 a gallon in the United States, $1.66 (in U.S. dollars) in the United Kingdom, and $1.80 (in U.S. dollars) in Germany. *New York Times*, September 24, 1990.

23. Geoffrey Lean, "Crisis For Pollution Watchdog Casts Doubt Over the Green Bill," *The Observer*, May 13, 1990.

24. Richard Elliot Benedick, *Ozone Diplomacy: New Directions in Safeguarding the Planet* (Cambridge; Mass.: Harvard University Press, 1991).

25. Carothers, "Children of Chernobyl," p. 11.

26. Lignite supplies 60 percent of East Germany's energy. East German power stations use about 10 percent more lignite than do West German stations for the same amount of output. Authorities wished to replace inefficient lignite-fueled locomotives with electric ones. But eighty percent of East German-produced electric locomotives were exported to the Soviet Union, and it could not afford to curtail these exports. Martin McCauley, "Power and Authority in East Germany: The Socialist Unity Party (SED)," *Conflict Studies* 132 (July 1981): 16.

27. Some say the Wismut contamination level is surpassed only by Chernobyl. Thousands of miners died from exposure, and thousands of acres of mine shafts, soil, and lakes are contaminated. Girard C. Steichen, "Soviets Leave Germans a Radiation Disaster," *Christian Science Monitor*, June 21, 1991.

28. *Kansas City Star*, November 18, 1990.

29. See *This Common Inheritance: Britain's Environmental Strategy* (London: HMSO, 1990); Friends of the Earth, *How Green Is Britain?* (London: Hutchinson Radius, 1990); Chris Rose, *The Dirty Man of Europe: The Great British Pollution Scandal* (London: Simon & Schuster, 1990); Timothy O'Riordan and Albert Weale, "Administrative Reorganization and Policy Change: The Case of Her Majesty's Inspectorate of Pollution," *Public Administration* 67 (Autumn, 1989): 277–94; and David Vogel, *National Styles of Regulation: Environmental Policy in Great Britain and the United States* (Ithaca; N.Y.: Cornell University Press, 1986).

30. Chinese Academy of Science study, 1988.

31. Robert Nadelson, "The Ruined Earth," *Far Eastern Economic Review*, September 19, 1991.

32. The 1991 floods cost provincial and national governments $13 billion and left the national government $4 billion in debt even during a year of record growth. Ann Scott Tyson, "China's Floods Strain 'Boom-Bust' Economy," *Christian Science Monitor*, September 23, 1991. Also see Lyshui-hung and Joseph Whitney, *Megaproject: A Case Study of China's Three Gorges Project* (Armonk, N.Y.: M.E. Sharpe, 1991).

33. Kenneth Lieberthal and Michel Oksenberg, *Policy Making in China: Leaders, Structures, and Processes* (Princeton, N.J.: Princeton University Press, 1988), pp. 269–338, discuss the interplay of bureaucracies in planning this dam.

34. This supplies 76 percent of China's energy. Nadelson, "Ruined Earth." In 1991, 10,000 workers died in coal-mining accidents, mostly in the smaller of 230,000 mines employing 7 million people. These accidents are rarely reported in the press. Current plans to modernize and close mines would leave 400,000 people without jobs, so government is cautious about proceeding with them. Sheila Tefft, "Chinese Enterprises Neglect Safety Issues," *Christian Science Monitor*, August 9, 1993.

35. The smaller figures are from Ann Scott Tyson, "China Seeks Aid to Curb Pollution," *Christian Science Monitor*, October 30, 1990, and the larger (1989) figures from the Overseas Development Council in Mark Trumbull, "Battles in the Greenhouse: Economy vs. Environment," *Christian*

Science Monitor, June 4, 1982. Its emissions of carbon dioxide from fossil fuels per dollar of GNP (1987) are 12 times that of Japan, 10 times that of Germany, 6 times that of the United States, 4 times that of the CIS, and 3 times that of India. But its per capita carbon-dioxide emissions (1989) are one-eleventh that of the United States, one-seventh that of the CIS, one-sixth that of Germany or Britain, but three times that of India. "Towards Agreement," *The Economist,* May 30, 1992.

36. See chapter 25.

37. Ann Scott Tyson, "China's Nuclear Plan: On the Line," *Christian Science Monitor,* December 25, 1990.

38. The $2 billion (in U.S. dollars) this would encompass over five years is a fraction of the estimated $30 to $100 billion cost of building the proposed Three Gorges Dam complex on the Yangtze. For an overview, see Vaclav Smil, *China's Environment: An Inquiry into the Limits of National Development* (Armonk, N.Y.: M. E. Sharpe, 1991).

39. Walter Schwarz, "The Menace of Development," *Manchester Guardian Weekly,* July 3, 1988.

40. See Sanjoy Hazarika, *Bhopal: The Lessons of a Tragedy* (London: Penguin 1987); V. L. Iyengar, "The Price of Life," *The Times of India,* December 6, 1992.

41. Only Seoul, Karachi, Cairo, and Beijing have worse air than Bombay, Calcutta, and New Delhi—which have double the World Health Organization limits. "WHO Blacklists Bombay, Calcutta, and Delhi," *Indian Express,* December 5, 1992.

42. Barbara Crossette, "India's Descent," *New York Times Magazine,* May 19, 1991, p. 57.

43. *Macleans* 101, 32 (August 1, 1988).

44. Geoffrey Lean, *Rich World, Poor World* (London: G. Unwin, 1978), p. 35.

45. Hawaii has attempted to tap geothermal power from the active volcanic area of its big island to produce electricity without using oil or coal. Building these facilities necessitates destroying 300 of 60,000 acres of tropical forest on that island. This brought objections from environmental groups and neighbors of the project. The same people have not objected to building a substitute power plant which will use coal from beneath thousands of acres of tropical forest in Indonesia.

EXERCISES

Think about the book thus far:

How does this chapter relate to chapters 18 (on assimilation) and 24 (on law and public policy)?

Discuss the following questions:

1. What are some policies by which the governments of the United States, the United Kingdom, the Federal Republic of Germany, the CIS republics, China, and India attempt to improve the environment?

2. Who has been influential in implementing such policies? Who do they help? Who do they harm?

3. Why do these policies sometimes fail to protect the environment?

4. Why is it difficult to initiate environmental protections in India, Peru, and Nigeria?

THINKING IT THROUGH

Which endangers the environment more: a country whose populace is poor and uninfluential, and whose technology is outdated, or a country whose populace consumes heavily and has influence, and whose technology is state-of-the-art?

chapter 29

PUBLIC ORDER

Systems which excel at distributing goods, offering citizens freedom, and protecting the environment may be in a good position to preserve order as well. But so may systems which do not. Change can disturb order; whether it will do so depends in the long run on whether those with influence remain satisfied.

SATISFACTION

Keeping order brings to mind police and armies. **Stable order,** however, **rests on satisfied citizens**. Politics, once again, is the conflicting demands people make on one another. A political system may resolve those demands. When it does not succeed in doing so, conflict persists—leaving disharmony, discord, disorder. When the system finds satisfactory solutions to the demands, it reduces conflict and creates harmony and order.

Order, like freedom, is inherently involved with the political system. A political system is the pattern of relationships through which competition over various values is conducted and resolved. Conflict, and the policies adopted to resolve it, affect the freedom of various groups and the overall order of the nation-state. All nation-states impose some restrictions on freedom, and all experience a degree of disorder. Physical coercion and violence, however, represent degrees of order and disorder most people prefer to avoid. People who are manacled and physically forced off to jail know they have tested the limits of freedom. Systems experiencing violence know order has been breached. Stable public order requires that competition be conducted and, if possible, resolved without violence and with minimal coercion.

At its best, order means all members of a nation-state are so satisfied with the way competition is oc-

curring and being resolved that they feel no need to resort to violence. Unfortunately, the absence of violence in a system does not mean this test is being met. Order may derive when people know and fear the consequences if they revolt, or when they believe that God wants them to quietly bear pain. Fear, not satisfaction with one's personal conditions, may account for a system's peacefulness. Order based largely on fear may end with dramatic suddenness if events remove the source of that fear. Factors that can endanger public order include the following:

1. Shortages of food, clothing, and shelter. People deprived of basic necessities may resort to any means to obtain them.

2. Restrictions on freedom. Groups may resist restrictions placed on their freedom.

3. An end to restrictions on freedom. People who have lived under tight political controls may use their freedom recklessly if those controls are removed.

4. Economic downturn. Citizens may accept the violence of groups attacking immigrants, or warfare against other countries, if they blame the immigrants or other countries for poor economic conditions.

Order, then, depends on what people ask for and accept from others. Giving them what they ask for does not always increase order. If Peru's or the

CIS's underground economy ended, their customers would be deprived of necessities the legitimate economy might never produce; yet those underground economies divert resources away from the legitimate economies. A government budget cannot accommodate unlimited demands for goods and services; ultimately, someone must be taxed to pay for the expenditures. Giving in to demands from a group or another nation-state may simply cause them to make additional demands. In deciding when to say "yes" or "no" in such situations, a government inevitably rewards some people and harms or disappoints others.

Increasing equality and freedom does not always improve order. If some groups gain greater freedom and equality, other groups may fear this and retaliate with civil disobedience or even violence. The changes may disrupt the families and communities of those being assisted, inducing disgruntled citizens to cause disorder. Well-intentioned efforts to help other groups may prove harmful. A dramatic example of this was the nearly two million people murdered in communal rioting during the first month after Britain granted independence to India and Pakistan, intent on providing both Hindus and Muslims self-governing homelands. Distrust was so great that people used their newfound freedom to kill people with differing religious beliefs. In a similar vein, as freedom has increased in the post-Soviet republics, so has ethnic conflict and urban crime. Paramilitary units have formed, and demands on the governments constantly escalate. Economic reforms in China, too, have brought demands for political freedoms or a share in the new prosperity that led to violence. India has increased poor peasants' chances to achieve high school educations, but university enrollments lag behind; high school graduates with high marks cannot enter university and become frustrated and bitter and more willing to engage in riots. Peru's Sendero Luminoso finds recruits among the rapidly growing ranks of children from poor families who receive university diplomas but cannot find jobs. Too much freedom to rebel can even lead to total destruction of government, as in Somalia in the early 1990s.

Conversely, denying equality and freedom to groups actively seeking it may also break down order. The Irish Republican Army, Sikh militants in India, and Peru's Sendero Luminoso and Tupac Amaru have become permanent fomenters of disorder. The latter two movements have vague and unarticulated demands for bettering the lives of the poor; the demands of the former two are unacceptable to their governments. As long as their demands are denied, they fight. Extending the availability of food, clothing, and shelter to discontented groups while at the same time limiting their freedom of expression can also backfire. The particular reforms the government orders may not be those they want, and they will resist them. Terrorism continues in Northern Ireland and Peru despite numerous reform initiatives meant to lower discontent. Those initiatives may have simply stiffened the resistance of those who feel the attempts at reform are inadequate.

Allowing regions to split away so their groups can be autonomous is also a risky approach to creating order. If Tibet and Xinjiang in China, or the Punjab in India, achieved total independence, they would become isolated from the larger economies they were a part of. They could run their own affairs, but the groups the locals were fighting with would still remain inside, or just across, the new borders. Their new armed forces would have to patrol those borders, which many would not recognize as legitimate. Regional economic decline could further stir tensions, especially if adjoining nation-states were experiencing greater or less prosperity. Those are the dangers that confront the fifteen post-Soviet republics as they seek to become fully autonomous nation-states.

If regions or nation-states with common cultures or interests merge into one larger nation-state, formerly weak cultural groups may emerge stronger. Some Catholics in Northern Ireland want to merge with Ireland; instead of being a minority, they would be part of the majority there. But protestants living in the north would find their condition radically changed as a small minority in the new nation-state. Sometimes, the emergence of such a large new political unit could threaten the security of other, smaller adjoining nation-states with differing cultures. And the new nation-state might suppress its own minorities, rather than trying to develop a civic culture with tolerance for them.

Separating regions from larger nation-states composed of many cultures and merging them into a political unit composed primarily of one cultural group (as happened with the breakup of the Soviet Union) can also reduce the possibility of developing a civic culture that encourages different groups to cooperate. That in itself can increase the possibilities of conflict. However, when two cultures who do not trust one another can form separate, economically viable nation-states, that can sometimes reduce conflict.

Thus, efforts to lower discontent by extending greater equality and freedom can boomerang and lead to conflict. Suppressing expression of discontent can also increase conflict. This makes it hard to fashion and implement policy aimed at promoting order. Policies that are unrelated to building arms and armies, police forces, or riot control may still have a strong effect on keeping order.

Even policies specifically designed to promote order can cause disorder. The United States[1] and the former Soviet Union[2] have spent high percentages of their national budgets on arms and defense; on a smaller scale, so have Peru and Nigeria.[3] These expenditures can lead to fiscal instability and neglect of social and economic inequities which cause imbalances in people's lives. Sophisticated weapons are of little use if an underfunded education system cannot teach students enough language, mathematics, and science to use these weapons after they are recruited into the armed forces, and if the populace does not understand how to keep the economy strong. Innovation and investment may spur economic growth, increasing a nation-state's responsibilities and inducing it to expand its military; this diversion of resources, talent, and energy can then weaken the economy and allow other nation-states to surpass the nation-state economically.[4] West Germany has kept its defense expenditures low and the growth of its consumer economy high. The Soviet Union fell apart partly because of excessive expenditures for weapons and troops, which could now be used for warfare between the separate republics which left it.

Imposing martial law or security restrictions to create order may interfere with the discussion needed to innovate for market competition, or to adapt political processes to changing circumstances; that, in turn, can actually lead to disorder. For example, the continuing presence of British troops in Northern Ireland provides a focus for demonstrations and violence, as does the use of police in India to break up violence among Sikhs, in urban squatter colonies, and among militant Hindus and Muslims. In Peru, Sendero Luminoso focuses its bombing attacks on military headquarters, and troops have sometimes killed innocent civilians in efforts to destroy these terrorists. All of these efforts to promote order instead caused disorder.

The military often plays a role in keeping civic order. In systems like the post-Soviet republics, China, Peru, and Nigeria, where limits on the authority of political leaders are not clearly established, the military periodically intervenes to remove civilian heads of state when it feels there is undue unrest. In the former Soviet Union and China, the military does little more than work with other factions to remove an unwanted leader and help another civilian assume control; the Soviet Union was able to disband because the military agreed to allow that to happen, even though their civilian commander-in-chief (Gorbachev) objected. The military will be instrumental in deciding which subsequent governments will be allowed to continue. In Peru and Nigeria, the military has often seized rule. In most nation-states, the military is sometimes called upon to control rioting or other civil disturbances. In China, since the 1989 activities at Tiananmen Square, troops are stationed at the heart of Beijing and some other cities to be called upon demand. In Peru, it is common for street corners to be patrolled by soldiers with their hands on the triggers of semiautomatic weapons.

The mere presence of a military establishment may deter another nation-state from contemplating invasion. It is often hard to tell whether such an

This demonstration field of beans in Nigeria, sponsored by Christian churches, is part of a center which attempts to show villagers how to improve their living standards.
© *Rodney Wilson*

invasion would occur if troops and weaponry were reduced. A populace may be content to live on a diminished standard of living in order to support such a defense establishment and the sense of safety it brings. People may, in fact, gain jobs and contracts from defense activities and feel that all aspects of life are enhanced by a strong military and defense. On the other hand, the military may not be popular. When many are unsatisfied with their living condi-

tions, and armed forces are extensive, the government may be tempted to invade foreign territory to divert people's attention from their discontent.

The breakdown of the Soviet Union shows the complexity of using weapons as deterrents. The Ukraine wants to become a nuclear-free zone, while Russia seeks to be the sole base for the former union's nuclear weapons; the Ukraine fears having such weapons poised at its borders. Some of the republics want to form their existing troops and weapons into separate armed forces. While this military establishment was originally formed to deter the United States and Europe, under these circumstances, its component parts threaten to pit one republic against another. If combined with economic disintegration and ethnic conflict, the presence of such heavy concentrations of weaponry could result in regional conflicts with devastating consequences.

Dealing with disorder, then, does not simply involve using force. It may entail removing or alleviating causes for discomfort in people's lives that make them challenge government or other groups—or persuading them to be satisfied with what they have and to stop challenging government or harming other groups. In international relations, this may be accomplished through diplomacy; domestically, it may require television appeals and personal appearances by leaders, and public policies dealing with all or parts of problems.

Order involves trade-offs. What makes one group's lives more comfortable may make another's less comfortable, so they resist. People may be willing to give up some material comfort to guard against others they feel are threatening them.

We have seen that equality, freedom, and the physical environment have an effect on people's values. So does the ability of the political system to promote compromises on divisive issues. Such compromises are necessary not only if people are to live in harmony with one another, but also to help them reconcile their values with the realities of the way they live. This reduces their impulse to engage in political conflict. When people are satisfied with the way they live, there is more chance for order.

ORDER AND CHANGE

Thus far in part 4, we have found that equality of opportunity, freedom, and environmental protection are probably greater in the United States, the United Kingdom, and West Germany than in China, East Germany, and the CIS republics, which—in turn—probably surpass India, Nigeria, and Peru in those regards. A similar descending order may characterize these systems in regard to the percentage of the populace satisfied with the way they live. If that is so, satisfaction is higher, and violent conflict lower, in the nation-states where political influence is most widespread (figure 29.1).

Dissatisfaction among people without political influence need not disrupt order. As we have seen, high percentages of people in India, Nigeria, Peru, and the CIS republics have reason to be dissatisfied with many aspects of their lives. Many of these individuals have little influence. Because they cannot organize, or sustain resistance, such individuals may be restrained by arrest or intimidation when they cause disorder. Ironically, in the United States—where lower percentages of the populace may have reason for discontent, yet people are freer to purchase guns and other weapons—the murder rate is twice that of Northern Ireland, nine times that of England, and higher than that of any Third World country.[5]

Ultimately, order depends upon whether those who are influential are satisfied. When most of the people with influence want order, it is hard for those promoting violence to succeed. Political activists who promote disorder need at least passive support from a portion of those with influence, or massive support in street demonstrations from those ordinarily without influence, or they can be arrested or diverted. So long as influential people are comfortable with their conditions, they are unlikely to give support to promoters of violence.

In the short run, order may exist largely because people have become used to the way they are living, and because those with the greatest influence are satisfied with their situation. Dissatisfied people

Figure 29.1 One conception of relative degrees of opportunity, freedom, environmental protection, and satisfaction in third-world, industrialized, and advanced industrialized nations.

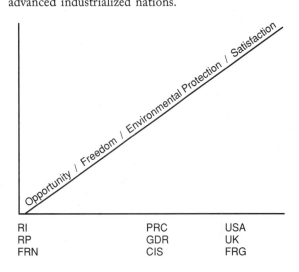

RI	PRC	USA
RP	GDR	UK
FRN	CIS	FRG

may not make the effort to cause disorder, or they may be so impoverished that they lack the energy to do so. So order, in the sense of little violence, does not always mean that people are satisfied. In fact, new initiatives to promote equality or freedom may frighten those who like their conditions and awaken from apathy those who do not, promoting conflict and disorder.

Part 5 examines some potential future threats to order. We shall see that seeming disorder at one phase of life, or in one phase of a political system, may signal the birthpangs of a new phase of order. Such transitions may occur when politically influential people become dissatisfied and start supporting changes that shift benefits and widen satisfaction. Ultimately, the greatest threat to order in such a situation stems from those with the least influence, whose lives may be disturbed by these changes but who have little to gain from them. In the short run, such groups may be kept down by force. Those with influence can often find nonviolent ways to hold onto their privileges when threatened by change.

Rajiv Gandhi's Government in India, Margaret Thatcher's in the United Kingdom, Ronald Reagan's and Bill Clinton's in the United States, Mikhail Gorbachev's in the Soviet Union, Deng Xiaoping's in China, Alan Garcia's and Alberto Fujimori's in Peru, and the governments of each successive military regime in Nigeria all brought into political prominence new groups of business and professional people, and other groups as well; in so doing, each of these governments challenged politically prominent people and aroused people with little influence. In the United States and the United Kingdom, where more people have a basis for satisfaction, such shifts are less threatening to order than in systems where those with low influence are numerous and dissatisfaction is intense. All such transitions are accompanied by incidents of violence.

Such governments might change rules and structures to help their constituencies assert influence. Gandhi attempted to weaken the bureaucracy that regulates smaller businesses. Thatcher rigidly resisted strikes, reduced agency activities to enforce environmental and other laws which interfered with her policies, assisted innovative entrepreneurs, and reduced the authority of local governments (which were opposition strongholds). Reagan brought new social groups and entrepreneurs into prominence, weakened the ability of the labor movement to strike, and strengthened the service and defense sectors of the economy. Gorbachev shifted sovereignty from the Communist Party, introduced competitive elections, and weakened centralized control over the economy and political activities. Deng sought similar economic, but not political, changes. Garcia sought to promote young university graduates and to broaden the political involvement of non-Spanish speakers, while Fujimori increased opportunities for foreign business investment. Each successive military coup in Nigeria exiles political elites and replaces them with people who formerly held lower positions. All these leaders brought along to power younger professionals who challenged those in established circles.

These changes benefited many groups, and caused some who had not previously done so to exert influence. They harmed other groups, which used their influence to resist. Groups without influence were also sometimes harmed by these policies. During Gandhi's rule, millions of Indians joined the ranks of the middle class; even more millions of peasants suffered setbacks from inflation, loss of land, and other incursions. In the United Kingdom, unemployment rose markedly; cities like Liverpool, Glasgow, Manchester, and Leeds suffered rapid physical deterioration, with 30 to 40 percent of the male populace unemployed as heavy industry moved out. Violence at sporting matches, and violent street demonstrations, erupt periodically. But the percentage of middle-class voters rose from 33 to 40 percent; with three parties running in elections, Thatcher never gained more than 44 percent of the vote. In the United States, the percentage of middle-class voters increased as well, though voting declined to less than half of adults. As we have seen, the number of American millionaires rose by one-hundred thousand each year during the 1980s. Old industrial cities, many rural communities, and inner cities have deteriorated, and unemployment has risen among blacks and other segments of the poor. Inner cities suffer from frequent shootings, drug wars, and incidents of racial and social violence.

In the Soviet Union, Gorbachev brought the new generation of university graduates created by Brezhnev's expansion of education to positions of prominence and opened opportunities for existing nomenklatura to make money. Meanwhile, rural communities, industrial cities, and outlying republics watched their economies continue to decline. Incidents of civil violence grew commonplace. The nation-state broke into fifteen separate republics, some with much more power and many more assets than others. Deng's reforms in China raised the incomes of peasants and workers, but not always uniformly; those tied to work units cannot easily break away to compete with those outside. Urban incomes rise faster than rural, but urban housing is cramped and scarce. Unemployment is growing. In Peru, runaway inflation and a declining economy left few people better off after Garcia's reforms, but he did bring a new generation into politics; under Fujimori, even greater numbers suffered a decline in income, but the number of Sendero Luminoso attacks on political leaders, power stations, and the militia declined and inflation was brought under control. The changes all these leaders instituted helped some and harmed others.

PLEASING THOSE WITH INFLUENCE

People with influence, and comfortable lives, have a strong incentive to keep order. Because it involves the continuous redistribution of values, politics constantly affects people's lives. When political change improves lives, it doesn't threaten order unless expectations for additional improvement leap ahead of actual advances. When change harms them a little, those with influence are unlikely to step outside the normal bounds of political action to resist; the disorder that might occur often frightens them more than the setback they have experienced. When people without attributes needed for influence are harmed radically, they may react violently; the government is likely to respond forcefully to restore order because those with influence will generally support that action. So change is not inherently a threat to order.

Such change becomes a serious challenge to order if it makes influential people suffer a decline in comfort and power so severe that they no longer mind disturbing the peace. Those challenged may rally to stop the changes or shift them in new directions. At that point it becomes important whether (1) there are effective limits on public authority, and (2) citizens are widely involved in the economy and government.

In nation-states with neither of these attributes beyond a weak integration of various groups into lower levels of government, such as Peru, Nigeria, and India, such challenges can cause Governments to fall and make policy hard to implement; the government can count on little support in its efforts to keep peace or force legal solutions. If the government is bold about reforms that help uninfluential segments of the populace at the expense of groups

with influence—as under General Velasco's regime in Peru—that Government may soon be toppled from power. Otherwise, it must seek to please all influential groups and be very cautious about disturbing them; that means it must not attempt to divert the resources of influential people to help others, but may need to divert the land, skills, and other resources of those without influence to help these influential groups. For most people, changes can be violent and unpredictable and provide little chance to improve their lives. Meanwhile, groups with influence may alternate in positions of power, always being careful to share part of the rewards with influentials out of power.

In nation-states like the United States and the United Kingdom, with limits on public authority and widespread involvement in the economy and government, it is easier to challenge other influential people within established political processes and ultimately prevail. Government leaders can create policies that harm influential people and then insist that any resistance they mount take place within legal channels. With general support for its authority, government can pass laws and issue directives with some assurance they will be obeyed even when they disturb influential people. In the British system of parliamentary government, such changes can take place more quickly and decisively than under the American presidential system, though the British Government must not harm the influential so much that it precipitates a vote of no confidence and a new election at a moment of low popularity. Under a presidential system, a leader can forcefully promote widely unpopular policies for brief periods, knowing elections are some years away; but he or she can still be checked from implementing those policies by uncooperative legislatures or courts. Life can change favorably, or unfavorably, for wide portions of the populace because they are involved in interlocking economic transactions. Those who disagree can help elect a new Government that will turn the policies around—without violence.

In the CIS republics, most of the populace is integrated into the national economy, and many groups are represented within political parties and government, but there are no effective limits on authority. The centralized economies contain many agencies; most of the work force is directly employed by these agencies. To involve more people directly in ownership or decision making about productive enterprises, this complex of agencies must relinquish power over allocating raw materials, setting production quotas, prices, and wages, and making distribution decisions to its workers, who must even be free to leave the agencies' employ. They resist giving up all these powers and all this control over workers. At the same time, political reforms threaten to set aside the power of the military high command. Since there are no clear rules for how changes are to take place, every change must occur within a vast variety of agencies partly composed of reformers and partly composed of opponents of reform. Obviously, change is not easy to carry out. Changes could affect large segments of the populace because they are involved in centrally controlled production and consumption; but the effects will be slow and uncertain. The *nomenklatura* will see to it that any changes benefit them.

In China, too, most of the populace is integrated into the national economy, and many groups are represented within the party and government. But most laborers are not directly employed by large government agencies. Much of the populace is engaged in agriculture, which has never been highly mechanized on large plots of land. Giving people more control over the land and crops they already tilled did not radically shift power away from bureaucrats, who still control output quotas. Cooperatives often produce parts for assembly in the large government factories the bureaucracy runs. The new incentives, along with joint ventures, have increased production in these government firms as well. Since the economic reforms are not accompanied by political reforms, they do not immediately threaten the positions of party bureaucrats. So it is easier to arrive at a consensus on trying the new economic reforms. Since all parts of this economic structure are related, everyone can benefit. However, when groups within society complain about conditions or

policies, the government is not prepared to respond. Interest groups have not traditionally directed complaints to government, so the government often mistakes resistance to policies as an effort to overthrow the government itself, and suppress that resistance.

Because they so directly control productive processes, Chinese workers and peasants have an edge over workers in the CIS republics, who merely provide labor to antiquated, but highly mechanized, agricultural and industrial concerns. Government can benefit by giving Chinese peasants and cooperative workers added incentives to produce, while still leaving bureaucrats in control of most marketing and heavy production; the peasants and cooperatives will produce, even if the bureaucrats are sidetracked by other matters. Because high percentages of the populace in India, Nigeria, and Peru are not needed by their governments for production, government derives little benefit from rewarding them. Ultimately, citizens who have access to government posts, and who can insist on regular, traditional rules of behavior from government—as in the United States, the United Kingdom, and the Federal Republic of Germany—have a more stable basis to ensure that changes benefit them.

When people have enough influence to foment changes which benefit them, or to resist those which hurt them, they need not resort to violent solutions. Excluding the most economically disadvantaged from political participation can reduce conflict within and among government institutions. But it may ultimately lead the disadvantaged to reject or defy government. Those with the attributes, discussed in part 2, to gain some influence may ultimately benefit from the changes such confrontations might bring. Those without attributes of influence are unlikely to benefit. First they need education, information, and access to principal economic and political institutions; paradoxically, to obtain these, they may need influence. This presents them with a chicken-or-egg dilemma. When high percentages of a populace have potential to exert influence, change can spread benefits to many citizens. When low percentages have such potential, similar change may benefit few people. Those latter systems have little potential to achieve order based on widespread satisfaction.

SUMMARY

In nation-states with limits on public authority and widespread involvement in the economy and government, it is easier to challenge other influential people within established political processes and prevail. Government leaders can create policies harming influential people and then insist that resistance take place within legal channels. When much of the populace is integrated into the economy but there are no effective limits on authority, such influentials—though their numbers are large—must challenge each other outside legal channels, making change uncertain and potentially more violent. In either case, change may ultimately broaden satisfaction and thus strengthen order. When few are integrated into the economy or government, it is easier to create policies satisfying those with influence; they are likely to be few in number. For everyone else in such systems, order is often the result of coercion rather than satisfaction.

NOTES

1. The $300 billion 1989 military budget represented 6 percent of Gross National Product. By 1991, the United States was spending more to service the interest on its debt (much of which resulted from defense spending) than on defense. *Kansas City Star,* May 30, 1989. In 1989, Germany spent 2.8 percent of its GDP on defense; in 1990, the United Kingdom spent 3.9 percent. NATO Press Service, *Financial and Economic Data Relating to NATO Defence* (Brussels: NATO, December 6, 1990), p. 4.

   John Lehman, former U.S. Secretary of the Navy, estimates that twenty thousand companies have more than $10 million apiece in contracts with the Pentagon. McNeil-Lehrer News Hour, PBS, June 25, 1990.

2. Mikhail Gorbachev revealed in 1989 that the Soviet Union was spending $118 billion (in U.S. dollars) a year on defense, or about 9 percent of the Gross National Product. *Kansas City Star,* May 30, 1989. Later, Soviet economists estimated that military spending consumed 25 percent of the country's output. *Kansas City Star,* April 24, 1990. Still as late as 1991, 80 percent of machine-building was arms related. David Remnick, "For Gorbachev, It's Back to the Old Intractable Problems," *Manchester Guardian Weekly,* August 11, 1991. Most plants presumably being converted to civilian production were producing a few consumer goods while continuing to produce weapons.

3. According to a World Bank report, by the late 1980s, high-income countries were spending $860 billion a year on defense, while developing countries were spending $170 billion. "$1 Trillion Spent on Militaries," *Kansas City Star,* July 8, 1991.

4. Paul Kennedy's *The Rise and Fall of the Great Powers* (New York: Random House, 1987) examines five centuries of North Atlantic history in terms of that thesis.

5. United States Senate report based on FBI and Justice Department statistics. Rates on rape and robbery are also far higher than in France, England, Italy, and Japan and above those in any other country for which statistics are available. *Kansas City Star,* March 13, 1991.

EXERCISES

Think about the book thus far:

1. Relate chapter 6 to this chapter.
2. Relate the "protest" and "impotence" sections of chapter 18 (on assimilation) to this chapter.
3. Relate the discussion about dissatisfaction in chapter 26 (on equality of opportunity) to this chapter.

Answer each of the following questions in one sentence:

1. Why may dissatisfaction contribute to disorder?
2. What are examples of the types of dissatisfaction that may contribute to disorder?
3. How do values, realities, and compromise relate to order?
4. Why is it easier for Chinese bureaucrats to accept economic reforms than bureaucrats in the CIS republics?
5. Why do most Chinese rural dwellers have more chance to receive government benefits than most rural dwellers in India, Peru, and Nigeria?
6. Does nationalism contribute to order when it counters pan-nationalism? Why or why not?

THINKING IT THROUGH

1. How may giving people what they want create disorder?
2. How may policies totally unrelated to building arms and armies, police forces, or riot control affect order?
3. How can policies designed to promote order cause disorder?
4. Why is it hard for initiatives that promote freedom and equality to aid those who lack influence?
5. Why may systems which place limits on authority have more potential than those without such limits to harm influential people?
6. Why is it hard for those without influence to disturb order?

part 5

SYSTEMS, INFLUENCE, AND CHANGE

We have looked at these systems now and in the past and examined some factors that affect change. Now we will explore the future. Consciously or unconsciously, human beings view the future in terms of values. They ask what will happen to factors they value, and what will threaten those factors or cause them to flourish. We have been exploring factors people value—home, food, clothing and shelter, health care, jobs and education, and agreeable cultural surroundings. How can we expect these valued resources to be distributed in the future? How satisfied will people be with that distribution? How will the dispersion of influence affect this?

What about political systems themselves? Which nation-states will retain sovereignty? How will sovereignty be organized and guided in the future?

To examine all this, we shall begin by creating some social science models to describe these systems and explore how they evolved into their present forms. Then we shall simply extend the present to peer into the future.

chapter 30

INFLUENCING CHANGE

A DEVELOPMENT MODEL[1]

A political system giving high and rising percentages of its citizens satisfying personal environments may be viewed as experiencing political development. If the government and most families rely on the same economic institutions for jobs, goods, and services; if diverse segments of the populace are recruited into political institutions; and if people are socialized to believe in placing limits on the authority of public officials, it is easier for political development to occur. **Interfamily and corporate-consumer systems have all three of these traits, and state-consumer systems have at least the first, while patron-client systems have none of them. When productivity is lower than current levels[2] of technological innovation will sustain, smaller economies and their supporting political institutions can be destroyed by larger ones.** *Interfamily and patron-client systems usually cannot achieve such productivity; state-consumer systems come closer.* **If an interfamily system becomes a raw materials supplier to** *interdependent corporations or* **a corporate-consumer system,** *or if productivity slows in a state-consumer system,* **it may transform into a patron-client system.** *If productivity slows in a corporate-consumer system, it may be pushed to the edges of corporate-interdependence, reducing limits on authority and recruitment into relevant political institutions, and hence the ability to sustain satisfying personal environments. But patron-client systems disengaging from corporate interdependence may move toward interfamily and corporate-consumer relationships; with limits placed on the authority of public officials, state-consumer systems may become corporate-consumer systems. That can improve their ability to support satisfying personal environments.*

POLITICAL DEVELOPMENT AND PERSONAL ENVIRONMENTS

Influence is the capacity to change or reinforce the attitudes and behaviors of others. Over time, the percentage and social composition of those with this capacity may shift. So may the values of those exerting influence; if they are successful, the political system (the regular pattern of human relationships through which competition over goods and services and conflicts over cultural traditions, ideas, and other values are conducted and may be resolved) may itself support values—a political culture—which it previously ignored or rejected.

Some people may approve of these changes; others may frown on them. Those who approve may think of the changes as development. We may define **political development** as change in the operation of a political system in the direction of a specified goal or state of being. This is an open-ended definition; it leaves it up to you or me to specify exactly what constitutes political development, or the goal we want the political system to move toward. I may desire one goal, and you another. That goal may be relatively specific, such as increased communication leading to better living standards. Or it may mean a whole series of dramatic changes to transform the current political system into a new type of one. To decide whether development is occurring, one must first specify the state of being one considers the goal of development.

At this point, we could just as well be discussing "political stability,"[3] "equality,"[4] "material progress or widespread participation in politics,"[5] "prosperity or widespread education or modern technology or competence or low death rates or national power,"[6] "fair distribution of goods and services,"[7] "government responsiveness to citizen demands,"[8] "transforming imbalances,"[9] or a variety of other goals or states of being. All of these terms are goals or states of being toward which a political system might move. These are words and phrases various political scientists use to define the goals of political development.

Throughout this book, we have been examining a state of being that is closely related to all those words and phrases—adequate food, health care, and housing; agreeable neighbors and cultural opportunities; and a satisfactory education and job for oneself and one's children. Before we try to draw conclusions about whether or not these systems are moving toward or away from this goal for their citizens (that is, whether these systems are experiencing political development as we have defined it), we should pause to refine our definition of this goal.[10]

We have learned that political demands are resolved when parties to a conflict change their attitudes or behavior. That simple fact has a profound effect on the ability of diverse people to live in an orderly state. Some people may have many material goods while others have very few; but if the latter are socialized to be satisfied with what they have, they may not be tempted to produce conflict by making demands. Their satisfaction with the way they live has to do with much more than equality or abundance in the distribution of material goods; it involves a variety of related factors impacting the way each of us live, and our attitude toward those factors. For the discussion in this chapter and the rest of part 5, we call that combination a satisfying personal environment.

To be **satisfied** simply means to be content, at ease with one's situation. Some poor people are at ease with their situations, while some rich people are not. The same holds true of old and young, educated and uneducated, those with modern gadgets and those without. One finds it hard to imagine someone on the edge of starvation, or untreated for a serious disease (note the derivation of that word) being "at ease" with his or her situation. Beyond those basics, there is tremendous variation in what makes people feel at ease. What makes you very comfortable may make me very uncomfortable.

Therefore, it is not possible to list specific states of being, or results of government policy, that would make everyone satisfied with their immediate personal environment. It is also a very personal decision whether one would, for example, prefer an equal distribution of goods, or political stability achieved without distributing goods equally; there is no objective standard by which to measure any government policy. If government policy guaranteed everyone a big house, some people would complain that this policy is unfair; some people might not like big houses, or might not be able to afford to maintain their big house. Others might complain about current inadequate housing and welcome the new policy. Although housing, along with food, bodily health, cultural setting, job, and education, is an essential part of everyone's personal environment, there is no one type of housing that would suit everyone. As important to an individual, perhaps, as how his or her housing compares with that of others, is how his or her housing fits other personal aspects and needs in life. When an individual has enough food to eat; access to health care; housing that is affordable and satisfying to live in; neighbors and cultural opportunities members of the household feel comfortable with; a job that pays adequately, and is satisfying and secure; and the education one desires for oneself and one's children, that individual has a **satisfying personal environment.**

Again, a combination of these aspects that satisfied me might not satisfy you; you might hate the food I eat, the house I live in, my neighbors, my social activities, my job, and many other aspects of my life which I find thoroughly pleasurable. But there is a relationship among these various aspects of one's life; most of us want them to be in some sort of balance. Improving one aspect of one's physical surroundings and resources, such as income or housing, would create an imbalance if it detracted from other aspects, such as education or cultural setting. If I moved into a much more elegant house, which I could not afford in a neighborhood I did not like, with bad schools, a long way from my work place, it would not necessarily make my personal environment more satisfying, even if both you and I thought it a wonderful house. It might also mean moving out of a neighborhood where we have friends, and pulling the children out of a school where they are doing well and placing them into a new one where they cannot adjust.

Thus, improvements in equality of treatment, freedom, order, and physical surroundings—especially if they occur in the wrong sequences or regions—can actually harm the balance between values and environment necessary to a satisfying personal environment. The availability of frivolous consumer goods such as television sets and videocassette recorders, for example, can tempt people to spend money they need for food, clothing, and shelter; and they may plant images and ideas that cause dissatisfaction with present conditions. Likewise, nation-states have long traditions with regard to the freedoms their citizens do or do not experience. Rapid changes, even in the direction of greater freedom, can bring discomfort to citizens' personal environments. Freed from restraints, people may be tempted to take actions which break up their families or cause them grief, and then regret these actions afterward. Or some groups may use the new freedom to harm other groups and disrupt order. Sometimes people have satisfying environments even when their equality of treatment, freedom, order, and physical surroundings do not seem favorable from our perspective (or even theirs); they are satisfied with life as it is. Improving one or more of those conditions too fast, or in the wrong order, can serve to decrease, rather than increase, a person's satisfaction with his or her personal environment.

Everyone has unique personal values. Most of us share a desire to eat enough to stay alive, and to be healthy; beyond that, what suits me may not suit you. We tend to compare ourselves with others; what satisfies us may depend upon whom we are comparing ourselves with. And what suits a person at one stage of life might not suit them at another; physical surroundings (including the values of those who surround us) and resources must adjust to changing values if one's personal environment is to remain satisfying. All of us have moments of dissatisfaction with our lives. But we have our own perceptions of what constitutes a satisfying personal environment for ourselves at any given point in our life, and our own perceptions of whether we have that environment. Are you basically satisfied with how you are living at this point in your life? What might cause that to change?

When people compete for goods and services and try to change or preserve cultural traditions, ideas, and other values (that is, participate in a political system), they are attempting to bring their physical surroundings and resources into conformity with their values—to change their physical surroundings so that their own personal environments will be more satisfying. Or they may be trying to halt a change that they feel would cause them dissatisfaction in their personal environments. They may make mistakes and end up creating unexpected, undesired results. They may push for changes in one aspect of their environment which ends up harming another aspect of it.

Sometimes, too, political competition involves changing people's values so they feel more satisfied with the personal environments they already have. One can achieve a satisfying personal environment by changing one's physical surroundings, or one's values—or both—until one is satisfied with one's food, health, housing, cultural setting, job, and education.

Obviously, no nation-state could ever provide all its citizens a satisfying personal environment. Some people (at least for certain periods of their lives) even seem to like misery; they do not try to be satisfied, even if means are available, and may even put effort into keeping themselves dissatisfied. But, because it affects both physical surroundings and values, the political system of a nation-state also affects personal environments.

In this chapter and the rest of part 5, we will discuss political development as a change in the operation of a political system in the direction of helping greater percentages of citizens to achieve more satisfying personal environments.

It is very common to hear comparisons of life in various countries: The Gross National Product or per capita income are higher here than there. More people own their homes in that country than in the other one. That country has more cars and roads. Another has more pubs and restaurants. That country's infant mortality rate is double this one's. Does that mean life is better in one place than the other? What do all these statistics signify?

Thinking in terms of satisfying personal environments helps answer those questions. I am not a Briton or a Russian or a Peruvian, and they are not Americans. The question is not whether their lives and countries are the way I would like them to be. What matters is whether their lives and countries are the way *they* like them. To assess that, one must first get a feel for how they want their lives to be, and then judge whether their lives are indeed that way. It means putting oneself in the place of peo-

ple living elsewhere and deciding whether the basic elements of their lives fall into place for them. Then the statistics can be analyzed in terms of whether they seem to help or hinder those elements, and the statistics are no longer just random numbers. Perhaps the citizens of a nation-state have far more of something than they did at an earlier time, and are therefore content with the rate of advancement; so the statistics help measure their satisfaction. Perhaps they do not place the same value on that factor as we do and do not care whether they have more or less of it; the statistics about the factor are then irrelevent to (or might even indirectly contribute to undermining) their satisfaction.

What people like, of course, is partly determined by what they are taught to like. If they were taught differently, they might like something else. One can go round and round with such exercises. The starting point must still be what they actually do like, and whether they are getting it.

Most people have food, shelter, health care, jobs, and education. What is harder to judge is whether these blend together to produce a life that is satisfying to them. Whether housing is affordable, or whether a job can produce a balanced budget, can be objectively measured. To know whether housing, neighbors, cultural facilities, and jobs and education are *satisfying,* we must know something about the person's values. That is why we tried to keep people's values in mind throughout the discussion in part 4.

In part 4, we noticed a correspondence between the percentage of a populace which might have reason to be satisfied with their situations, and the portion of citizens with influence derived from (1) relying on the same economic institutions as government, (2) being recruited into political institutions and (3) being socialized to believe in placing limits on the authority of public officials. One must be careful not to jump to the conclusion that influence automatically results in satisfaction. To explore such causation, one would need to look at more examples and use polling and other devices more uniformly to measure satisfaction. Nevertheless, we can safely say that influence and satisfying personal environments often coincide. In the United States, the United Kingdom, and West Germany, all three of the factors which can enhance influence are in place. In China, East Germany, and the CIS republics, the first applies, and to some extent, the second. The second and third factors apply to some degree in India. The military and lower bureaucracy of Nigeria and Peru recruit from many levels of society; otherwise, none of these factors are in place in these two nation-states. Greater portions of the populace in the United States, the United Kingdom, and West Germany might also be expected to have satisfying personal environments than in India, Nigeria, and Peru.

Can we conclude from this that the development of the nation-state and of satisfying personal environments proceed simultaneously? Do satisfying personal environments depend on healthy nation-states? Just what is a healthy nation-state?

PERSONAL ENVIRONMENTS AND THE NATION-STATE

Nation-states have not always held sovereignty, and may not in the future. Yet people were able to experience satisfying personal environments before nation-states arrived on the scene, and could afterward, if the systems that replaced them allowed influence to be widely dispersed. Systems in which influence is not so widely dispersed may be more vulnerable in the face of change.

When societies were organized so as to supply most of their needs within villages, families relied on one another. Villagers grew most of the food they consumed. Materials for housing and clothing were largely of local origin. Family members, and families, cooperated with one another to produce.

Villagers chose their own leaders. Those leaders made most of the decisions affecting the production and distribution of resources. Villagers participated in a number of formal institutions in the village and voiced opinions on many issues directly to their leaders.

Figure 30.1   Interfamily cooperation.

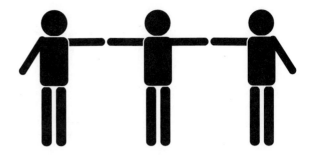

Kings and empires relied on villages for food to maintain their capital towns. The capital towns, too, were organized around extended families. Families of kings, nobles, merchants, bureaucrats, and military leaders relied upon and bargained with one another. The kings were often called upon to settle disputes.

Most disputes that arose within villages, though, were handled by the village. The main village issues the king handled were those pertaining to collection of the king's taxes or to crimes that extended beyond villages. Villagers were also expected to serve in the king's armed forces.

This system allowed for widespread participation in production, consumption, and decision making. Decision makers stayed in close proximity to those they were making decisions for. Most decisions pertaining to production, distribution, and justice were left up to individual families themselves. Hence, they could decide on their own personal environments and had considerable influence to protect those environments. High portions of the populace relied on the same economic institutions as government, were recruited into the political institutions that most affected their lives, and were socialized to believe in placing limits on the authority of public officials. Because they had little contact with outside cultures, they had little conception of alternative personal environments. For purposes of this discussion, we shall refer to this type of arrangement as an **interfamily system,** in which politics and production center around families (figure 30.1).

Figure 30.2   Interfamily systems' historical existence in various cultures.

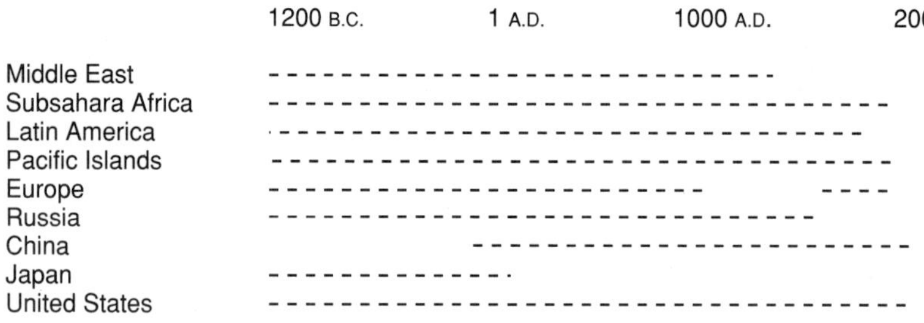

	1200 B.C.	1 A.D.	1000 A.D.	2000 A.D.
Middle East	- -			
Subsahara Africa	- -			
Latin America	· -			
Pacific Islands	- -			
Europe	- - - - -			
Russia	- -			
China	- -			
Japan	- - - - - - - - - - - - ·			
United States	- -			

Interfamily systems prevailed in much of what we now call the Third World (South and Southeast Asia, the Middle East, Africa, Latin America, and the Pacific Islands) well into the sixteenth and even nineteenth centuries, though Muslim areas of northern Africa, the Middle East, and central Asia shifted away from them as early as the eleventh century (figure 30.2). Such systems also prevailed in premedieval northern Europe and around the Mediterranean Sea before the ninth century; they returned after the fourteenth century. They had probably disappeared in Japan by the time Christ was born, and in Russia by the sixteenth century, but prevailed continuously in China, with lapses only from about 1,200–200 B.C., until the mid-nineteenth century. The United States (both before the arrival of Europeans and after) was characterized by many of the features of interfamily systems until late in the nineteenth century.

When they are confronted with superior technology, villagers can easily lose control over their lives. They have no bureaucracy or advanced technology to compete with. Europeans used sea-going ships and advanced weaponry to divert agricultural land in Asia, Africa, and Latin America into large estates producing goods for export with fewer workers than the land had supported in villages. That lends itself to **patron-clientism** (figure 30.3), a set of relationships in which one person, who becomes the patron, receives deference and substantial (often illegal) favors from another person, who becomes his or her client. The client obeys the patron, even when custom, laws, and formal leaders forbid it, because he or she has superior wealth and status, gives favors to the client, and has the power to dismiss subordinates without reason and without fear, because the client is unable to retaliate.[11] First the patron outsiders buy raw materials from local individuals, giving them a separate income and hence independence from their traditional villages, but making them dependent on the new purchasers. The economic institutions exporting these goods create new government institutions, which supercede the old. They create their own laws, determine who is recruited into government, and take direct control of the land. Those who lose both land and jobs have no skills needed by the government or these economic institutions. They can be left out of production, consumption, and decision making.

One variation on this arrangement is a **manorial patron-client system.** Patron families acquire control of land and villages and turn everyone working that land into clients. The patrons live in a large house, a manor, which sits on a largely self-sufficient piece of land, producing nearly everything needed by both patrons and clients, and sometimes furnishing troops to the patron or his or her monarch as well. Patron families are able to do this because they (or their political allies) control metals that give them superior weaponry, and they can see that food from the manor is transported and stored for the troops and their families. Under this system, nearly everyone produces, and everyone consumes. While most people are not recruited into political institutions, they

Figure 30.3   Patron–clientism.

Manorial patron-client systems existed in feudal Europe from the ninth to fifteenth centuries, and in parts of the southern United States before the Civil War (figure 30.4). They also existed in China from 1,200–200 B.C.; in Japan from the time of the Roman Empire until the twentieth century; in Russia from the sixteenth through the nineteenth centuries; and in Latin America, the Philippines, and some parts of the Mediterranean, during recent centuries.

can expect patrons to fulfil obligations to provide them with food, clothing, and shelter. They have little contact with other ways of living. The patrons need some of them to produce crops and provide troops. If the patron is kind, those skills enhance their chance to experience satisfying personal environments. If the patron is not kind, they are subject to his or her whims.

The development of towns creates a geographic separation between those who rely on one another for support. Towns affect the countryside, whether it is dominated by an interfamily or manorial system, when they help convert agriculture into production for trade rather than production for local consumption. This physically separates producers and consumers. In Asia, Africa, and Latin America, the first crops grown or hunted for export to Europe were luxuries such as spices, sugar, tea, coffee, pecans, dates, coconuts, and ivory. The towns also gathered work forces to mine gold and silver. Later,

the Industrial Revolution required and made it possible to transport large quantities of rubber, tin, iron, tungsten, chromium, zinc, phosphates, manganese, antimony, nickel, aluminum, petroleum, wheat, cotton, and bananas. When a town and its countryside rely heavily on trade with foreign nation-states, which in turn control the terms of trade (for example, what is to be traded and the price to be paid), decisions about production and consumption are made far away from producers. As a result, those conducting the trade may become patrons to those in the cities and towns who control production; the town tradespeople in turn become the patrons of those doing the producing; and a system evolves— patron-clientism beyond manors. This is called **nonmanorial patron-clientism** (figure 30.5).

Town merchants try to convert as much land as possible into production for their trade. If many people are needed for production, and the prior system was interfamily in nature, distribution may still remain fairly broad and patron-client relationships may not develop. If, because of the nature of the crops or advanced technology, fewer people are needed, large numbers may be left out of the distribution process—and also displaced from their land, now needed for market farming or commercial plantations. Most of the best resources tend to be consumed or sold by the top patron (located either in a town, a city, or in another nation-state) who controls the markets.

Those trying to perpetuate interfamily systems while nonmanorial patron-client relationships are developing usually find their position weakening.

Figure 30.4 Manorial patron-client systems' historical existence in various cultures.

	1200 B.C.	1 A.D.	1000 A.D.	2000 A.D.
Europe			- - - - - - - - ·	
Japan		- -	
Russia			- - - - -	
Latin America			- - - - - -	
Philippines			- - - - - - -	
United States			- - - - - -	
China	- - - - - -			

Figure 30.5 Nonmanorial patron-clientism can leave many out of production, consumption, and decision making.

Those who choose to produce for the market no longer depend on their village ties, and increasingly rely on the patrons for selling commodities. This also means they can ignore the village leaders.

Governments, too, come to rely on the nonmanorial patrons to supply their revenues. This greatly enhances the political influence of these patrons and reduces the need for government to concern itself with providing its citizens satisfying personal environments.

Nonmanorial patron-client systems may be found today throughout South and Southeast Asia (including India), the Middle East, Africa (including Nigeria), Latin America (including Peru), and the Pacific Islands (figure 30.6). Late in the nineteenth century Russia and China were converting into such systems, but they ended in the twentieth century with the advent of communism.

Early technological advance helps *create* patrons and clients; in turn, more advanced technology can serve to *reduce* the influence of patrons within the nation-state that controls the technology. The rise of technology brought with it the rise of the modern nation-state, with various cultures inside common boundaries ruled by parliamentary, presidential, or military leaders. If a nation-state achieves military and naval superiority, it can force others to give it trade preference. With inexpensive resources from abroad, it can put its own people to work manufacturing products to sell at home and abroad. People thus occupied come to rely on larger economic institutions for jobs and goods. This gradually

Figure 30.6 Patron-client systems: historical existence of manorial and nonmanorial patron-client systems in various cultures.

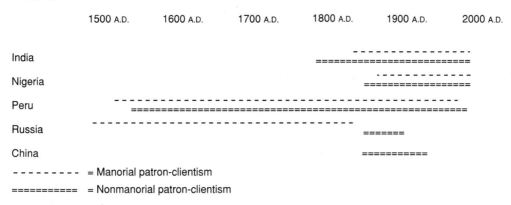

= Manorial patron-clientism

= Nonmanorial patron-clientism

reduces their reliance on families, royalty, and patrons for the goods they consume and ties them into a national economy. With many jobs created at home, the nation-state is in a position to export more than it imports and to accumulate capital at home for investment around the world. Government and industry seek to find jobs for all families; everyone can then purchase the goods produced by the new farms and industries. When the businesses are independent of government, and free to set their own prices, hire their own workers, and acquire their own raw materials and markets, a **corporate-consumer system** has developed. When the state runs the businesses and makes these policies, a **state-consumer system** is in effect. Both these systems try to promote full employment at home, to sell consumer goods to all these employees, and to develop a national income by exporting more than they import (figure 30.7). But to promote the free markets needed to sustain their businesses, corporate-consumer systems seek to recruit diverse portions of the populace into bureaucracy and government, and they also try to place legal and political limits on government officeholders. State-consumer systems, needing to keep control in the hands of bureaucracy and officeholders, are more reluctant to do so.

Figure 30.7 State- and corporate-consumer systems: The state tries to distribute its services uniformly, and to create full employment.

Since the **Industrial Revolution,** the rapid conversion of production to factories and mechanized farms which began in the eighteenth century,[12] corporate-consumer and state-consumer systems have prospered along with the nation-state.

Figure 30.8   History of corporate- and state-consumer systems in different nation-states.

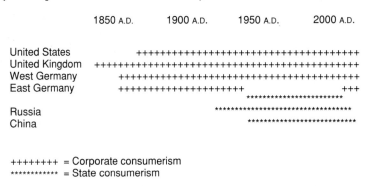

During the nineteenth century, corporate-consumer systems rose in Britain, Germany, and the United States, and in much of the rest of Europe (figure 30.8). Japan joined this fold after World War II. The revolutions in Russia in 1917, and in China and Eastern Europe after World War II, established state-consumer systems in those nation-states.[13]

Governments have influence over economic institutions in both corporate-consumer and state-consumer systems. Companies need government to protect world markets, build roads and other **infrastructure** (physical facilities needed to move about the nation-state, dispose of waste, and provide water and other public amenities), supply an educated work force, and keep money in circulation for consumers to spend. Governments of corporate-consumer systems tax businesses, fix interest rates, and regulate money supplies. And, in response to appeals from influential workers and consumers, they place restrictions on business activities. In state-consumer systems, governments regulate all aspects of company policy.

In corporate-consumer systems, corporate entities move assets, supplies, and markets freely from one nation-state to another. Corporate employees often purchase housing, appliances, clothing, and other goods from similar realtors and discount houses, in similar styles. Some people choose their neighborhood, house, clothing, reading matter, leisure activities, children's schools and curricula, party affiliation, point of view, and other important aspects of their lives with reference to their corporate careers. Corporations that buy and sell to individuals and one another, and influence people's values across national boundaries, gain some independence from nation-states.

The new European Economic Community places trade restrictions beyond Europe but will increasingly tie together the economies of its members. This may reduce the role of individual nation-states in regulating their economies or strengthen the roles of the stronger ones. Germany is extending its businesses into the CIS republics and Eastern Europe; the government is a major stockholder in those businesses. Farms demand continuing heavy subsidies. But the emerging consumerism moves across national boundaries and creates corporate interrelationships in which corporate economic entities deal with one another directly over the heads of governmental authorities. These relationships may be harder to control from within countries that are not the home base of one of the industries involved; when corporations form such relationships, it is known as **corporate interdependence.**

Corporate interdependence brings with it better products, widely distributed. It does not always create the right balance of these products, at the right prices, to give those affected by it satisfying per-

Old church building being demolished to make way for downtown development in Denver, Colorado.
© *Mike Gamer*

sonal environments. Especially in systems where many people are assimilated into interacting economic and political institutions, corporate interdependence can serve to augment satisfying personal environments. Those environments may be increasingly uniform as people absorb common values; some call this "McDonaldization."[14] That can ultimately deaden the sort of personal initiative which is part of a sense of efficacy. On the other hand, by fostering education and cross-cultural contacts, corporate interdependence can promote civic culture values and responsibility. When new schools, roads, and other programs are needed that the economic institutions do not desire or provide, people may be faced with a choice: supporting their companies or their countries. As we have seen, European companies have traditionally supported their workers with more social benefits than many American companies do. Those not employed by such institutions will be forced to turn directly to the state for assistance, which European governments have also traditionally provided. With weakened tax bases and support for social spending, that may be harder to provide in the future.

Technology and the state have helped one another. But their interests do not always converge. Nation-states whose corporations cannot compete, or register themselves on Caribbean islands away from state regulation, may find their citizens largely buying goods from foreign corporations, giving the nation-state a reduced tax base, fewer jobs, and more imports than exports. In this situation, the nation-state would need goods from the outside, but have less money to pay for them; its ability to regulate commerce would be reduced. Important decisions about the production and distribution of goods and services would be made elsewhere, widening the political system and reducing the participation of their citizens in those decisions.

Since corporate profits depend on growing markets, corporations are likely to foster an expanding economy. That market may, however, largely depend on selling additional goods to the same range of people who could afford them in the past. In fact, those with the highest-paying jobs on assembly lines, in offices, and in management would be in the best position to gain the attention of corporate management. The influence of others could decline along with the influence of the nation-state. The nation-states which might benefit, and whose citizens might most benefit, from corporate interdependence are those most closely tied to the particular corporations which prosper. Elsewhere, corporations might even prefer working with governments that suppress participation, civil rights, and equality of rewards but keep markets open to foreign trade. So, while corporate interdependence can promote civic culture, it may also reinforce parochial, inward-looking dominance of some ethnic groups over others.

Nation-states in which high percentages of the populace are assimilated into the national economy can keep control over that economy by letting political party and government leaders run factories and businesses in a state-consumer system. The price they pay for this, in a system where limits on authority are weak, is the continuance of patron-clientism. The economic institutions need not make a profit, since government will bail them out. Government and much of the populace depend on these institutions for all their major needs. The individuals monopolizing both economic and political control of the nation-state can divert many consumer goods to the black market; they can keep great rewards for themselves and special clients who do them favors before sharing the residue with everyone else. They cannot be politically controlled. Under this type of system, the government often finds itself spending more than it is taking in. That was the problem in East Germany before its absorption into West Germany. It remains a serious problem in the CIS republics as they grapple to create political controls on the power of such individuals. Their continuing grip on power makes it hard for modern private businesses to establish themselves; a market which must receive bureaucratic clearance on virtually every business decision is not free. There are no incentives to support technological innovation, and it is tempting to divert money earned into the hands of patrons and clients, who may also direct their energies toward fighting regional ethnic battles.

China's state-consumer economy, too, is guided by such patrons. Their notions of *guanxi* help them resist any directive from the top which would force

them to stop being patrons. They depend heavily on the peasants for food. Those peasants must give them special favors to obtain fertilizer, seed, access to water, and other needs; but they retain interfamily economic, social, and political relationships which help counterbalance this patron-clientism. Producing their own, and much of China's, food makes them partially independent of the patron-client system. New cooperatives and businesses must constantly pay bribes to the bureaucracy, making it hard to implement technological changes. As educated urban people discover the outside world, they want more; this can make them dissatisfied with their personal environments.

China and the Soviet Union held together their multicultural empires largely by force. Therefore their leaders fear(ed) moves toward placing popular limits on authority through multiparty elections, an independent judiciary, or free speech and assembly. Yet without these supports, a free market cannot easily succeed. The very limits which held different cultures in subservience also isolated them from one another and the outside world, preventing them from developing a civic culture. Their unwillingness to cooperate with other cultural groups, and their desire to break away,[15] not only limits the nation-state; it also limits the ability of modern technological institutions to change society. Yet that in itself can give the countryside some stability and prove welcome to outside investors looking only for inexpensive labor in border regions.[16]

Large portions of the populace in India, Nigeria, and Peru are not assimilated into the national economy. Even though modern technology increasingly appears in the cities, the economies of these systems remain much as they were in early periods of patron-clientism. With the nation-state largely controlled by patrons, it is hard for other members of the populace to increase their influence enough to tax and regulate the larger economic institutions, as the United States, the United Kingdom, and Germany do. Citizens of the CIS, most of whom are already assimilated into the larger economic institutions, may be able to improve their personal environments if they can create limited government in

Figure 30.9 Possible futures of different systems.

	Possible Futures
Corporate-Consumer Systems	Corporate consumerism
	Corporate interdependence
State-Consumer Systems	State consumerism
	Corporate consumerism
	Patron clientism
Patron-Client Systems	Patron clientism
	Corporate consumerism
	Interfamily

their new nation-states, but the obstacles are great. Citizens of India, Peru, and Nigeria face a much more formidable task in this regard. Figure 30.9 shows possible futures for each type of system.

None of these systems are completely without patron-clientism. *Guanxi,* savings and loan scandals, favors to large political contributors, and stock market manipulations bear witness to the power of special patron-client relationships. However, in the United States, the United Kingdom, and Germany, widespread assimilation into economic institutions, combined with broad recruitment into political institutions and established limits on political authority, counterbalances that influence. When modern economic institutions operate in systems which have not established such limits, patron-clientism tends to divert resources away from serving the needs of a wide spectrum of the populace, and personal environments suffer.

Nation-states, modern business enterprises, and personal environments depend on one another. Modern economic enterprise needs a powerful nation-state to provide a legal framework and order for its business dealings. As long as a nation-state has limited authority and an economy that encompasses most of its citizens, modern business enterprises can benefit the personal environments of broad segments of the populace. When such bases for widespread influence are lacking, a nation-state is easily captured by patrons, and business enterprises cannot benefit the personal environments of many people—or thrive themselves. Simply introducing democratic institutions would not in itself change these conditions.

SUMMARY

Existing political systems can be classified as patron-client, corporate-consumer, or state-consumer systems. Interfamily systems once existed, and corporate interdependence may alter existing systems. In the next three chapters, we shall discuss whether current systems are likely to remain intact and whether they will be able to provide their citizens with satisfying personal environments.

NOTES

1. "A model is an abstraction of reality that is developed for presenting systematically the most important relationships in the situation that is being described." George J. Graham, Jr., *Methodological Foundations for Political Analysis* (Waltham, Mass.: Xerox College Publishing, 1971), p. 112. "[A] good model . . . suggest[s] further questions, taking us beyond the phenomenon from which we began, and tempts us to formulate hypotheses which turn out to be experimentally fertile . . . The acceptance of the model is justified in the first place by the way in which it helps us to explain, represent, and predict the phenomenon under investigation." Stephen Toulmin, *The Philosophy of Science: An Introduction* (New York: Harper & Row, 1960), pp. 37–38. Abraham Kaplan, *The Conduct of Inquiry: Methodology for Behavioral Science* (San Francisco: Chandler, 1964), pp. 260–64, says that models should be in postulational or formal style. This one is postulational: The foundation is a set of propositions whose "truth is dependent on matters of fact."

2. "State-of-the-art."

3. Samuel P. Huntington relates political development to whether the system experiences stability, revolution, instability, or stagnation. That involves the

relationships among culture, political institutions, leadership, policies, and groups. Change in each of these components will affect the course of the others. Samuel P. Huntington, "The Change to Change: Modernization, Development, and Politics," *Comparative Politics* 3, 3 (April 1971). In his earlier "Political Development and Political Decay," *World Politics* 17 (April 1965), Huntington suggested that the two key variables in political development were mass mobilization and governmental institutionalization. See Robert E. Gamer, "Can China Modernize Without a Fight for Democracy? Samuel P. Huntington and the 'Neo-Authoritarian' Debate," *Crossroads* 35 (1994).

4. Robert A. Dahl believes that as systems move from hegemony to polyarchy (pluralist democracy), they improve their ability to balance equality and consent. Robert A. Dahl, *A Preface to Democratic Theory* (Chicago: University of Chicago Press, 1956); idem., *Who Governs* (New Haven, Conn.: Yale University Press, 1961); idem., *Modern Political Analysis,* 4th ed. (Englewood Cliffs, N.J.: Prentice-Hall, 1984); idem., *After the Revolution* (New Haven, Conn.: Yale University Press, 1970); idem., *Polyarchy: Participation and Opposition* (New Haven, Conn.: Yale University Press, 1971); idem., "On Removing Certain Impediments to Democracy in the United States," *Political Science Quarterly* 92 (1977): 1–20; idem., *Democracy in the United States,* 4th ed. (Boston: Houghton Mifflin, 1981); idem., *Dilemmas of Pluralist Democracy: Autonomy vs. Control* (New Haven, Conn.: Yale University Press, 1982); and idem., *Democracy and Its Critics* (New Haven, Conn.: Yale University Press, 1990).

5. John H. Kautsky sees political development deriving from the ascendancy of "modernizers . . . people who value material progress, equality, and widespread participation in politics." *The Political Consequences of Modernization* (New York: John Wiley, 1972).

6. Karl W. Deutsch, *Politics and Government: How People Decide Their Fate,* 3d ed. (Boston: Houghton Mifflin, 1980), p. 558. He sees such development as deriving from social mobilization (that is, a rise in per capita income, literacy, or circulation of newspapers, for example) and assimilation into modern social groupings (versus more traditional family and tribal groupings). See also Karl W. Deutsch, *The Nerves of Government,* 2d ed. (New York: The Free Press, 1966); idem., *Nationalism and Social Communication,* rev. ed. (Cambridge, Mass.: MIT Press, 1966).

7. Leonard Binder, "The Crises of Political Development," in *Crises and Sequences in Political Development,* ed. Leonard Binder et. al. (Princeton, N.J.: Princeton University Press, 1971), pp. 3–72, argues that political development entails passing through "five crises"—the creation of national identity, legitimacy for the leadership, broad participation by citizens, fair distribution of goods and services, and penetration of the nation-state into all its regions.

8. Gabriel Almond sees systems divided into input functions—including articulation and aggregation (the expression of demands and their gathering together), communication, political culture (which affects the way demands are made), recruitment of people into politics, and support for government—and output functions, including making, applying and adjudicating rules, and extracting, regulating, and distributing resources and services. He suggests that development involves the extent to which government output is responsive to the input demands made upon it. Gabriel A. Almond, Taylor Cole, and Roy C. Macridis, "A Suggested Research Strategy in Western European Government and Politics," *American Political Science Review* 49 (December 1955): 1042–49; Gabriel A. Almond and G. Bingham Powell, Jr., *Comparative Politics: A Developmental Approach* (Boston: Little, Brown, 1966); Gabriel A. Almond, Scott C. Flanagan, and Robert J. Mundt, eds., *Crisis, Choice, and Change: Historical Studies of Political Development* (Boston: Little Brown, 1973).

9. Manfred Halpern sees political development as the development of the government's will and capacity to transform the imbalances that exist among the systems of society in the direction of an intrinsic capacity to generate and absorb continuing transformation. Manfred Halpern, *The Politics of Social Change in the Middle East and North Africa* (Princeton, N.J.: Rand, 1963); idem., "The Revolution of Modernization in National and International Society," in Carl J. Friedrich, ed., *Revolution-Nomos VIII* (New York: Atherton, 1966); idem., "The Rate and Costs of Political Development," *The Annals* 358 (March 1965): 20–28; idem., "A Redefinition of the Revolutionary

Situation," *Journal of International Affairs* 22 (1969): 54–75; and idem., "Egypt and the New Middle Class: Reaffirmations and New Explorations," *Comparative Studies in Society and History* 11, 1 (January 1969): 97–108.

10. See Robert E. Gamer, *The Politics of Urban Development in Singapore* (Ithaca, N.Y.: Cornell University Press, 1972), pp. 191–93; idem., *The Developing Nations: A Comparative Perspective*, 2d ed. (New York: Allyn & Bacon, 1982), pp. 8–9, for an earlier discussion of this concept. Chapter 6 of the latter book gives an overview of a number of theories of development.

11. For more on this definition see Gamer, *Developing Nations,* pp. 101–8, 120–22.

12. See David S. Landes, *The Unbound Prometheus: Technological Change and Industrial Development in Western Europe from 1750 to the Present* (Cambridge: Cambridge University Press, 1969).

13. Czechoslovakia, eastern Germany, and Hungary were already corporate-consumer systems before communist takeover; some other parts of Eastern Europe were more interfamily.

14. McDonaldization is ". . . the onrush of economic and ecological forces that demand integration and uniformity and that mesmerize the world with fast music, fast computers, and fast food—with MTV, Macintosh, and McDonalds, pressing nations into one commercially homogeneous global network: one McWorld tied together by technology, ecology, communications, and commerce." Benjamin R. Barber, "Jihad vs. McWorld," *The Atlantic,* 269, 3 (March 1992): 53. Russian writer Yevgeny Yevtushenko quotes Octavio Paz's fears about the " 'faceless, soulless, and directionless economic process of the market' " which " 'knows prices, but nothing about values.' . . . I call it 'the McDonaldization of European Culture' . . . an autistic trance of psycho-boredom, consigning national cultures and artistic risk to the margins." "Russia Needs Real Sustenance—Not Big Macs," *Kansas City Star,* March 17, 1992.

15. ". . . culture is pitted against culture, people against people, tribe against tribe—a Jihad [holy war] in the name of a hundred narrowly conceived faiths against every kind of artificial social cooperation and civil mutuality." Barber, "Jihad vs. McWorld."

16. See Gamer, "Can China Modernize without a Fight for Democracy?"

EXERCISES

Think about the book thus far:

1. Relate part 4 (on influence and people) to personal environments.

2. Reread the conclusions of chapters 18 and 29. How do these ideas relate to political development?

3. Consider this statement: Improving equality of treatment, freedom, order, and physical surroundings too fast, or in the wrong order, can decrease, rather than increase, satisfaction with one's personal environment. How does this relate to chapter 21 (on consensual parties and change), and to the conclusions of chapters 26 and 27?

KEY WORDS AND PHRASES

Define the following terms:

political development	patron-clientism	state-consumer system
satisfied	manorial patron-client system	Industrial Revolution
satisfying personal environment	nonmanorial patron-clientism	infrastructure
interfamily system	corporate-consumer system	corporate interdependence

THINKING IT THROUGH

Answer each of the following questions in one sentence:

1. Must one be wealthy to have a satisfying personal environment? Why or why not?
2. As people acquire more consumer goods, will their personal environments automatically become more satisfying? Why or why not?
3. Can we talk about political development without discussing satisfying personal environments? What are some other goals we could discuss instead?
4. How might an interfamily system help create satisfying personal environments?
5. How might an interfamily system harm personal environments?
6. What might cause an interfamily system to become a patron-client system?
7. Why is patron-clientism difficult to control without placing limits on authority?
8. How does a corporate-consumer system differ from a patron-client system?
9. How may state-consumerism and patron-clientism coexist?
10. How may peasants affect that coexistence?
11. How may corporate interdependence dampen personal initiative?
12. How may corporate interdependence affect the nation-state?

Now, ask yourself:

1. Can you objectively determine whether my personal environment is satisfying? Explain.
2. How might a shift from manorial to nonmanorial patron-clientism affect personal environments?
3. How may expansion of modern economic enterprises help diffuse influence to a wider portion of the populace and promote change?
4. How may patron-clientism impede change in a state-consumer system?
5. Why is it hard for patron-client systems to change?

chapter 31

CORPORATE- AND
STATE-CONSUMER SYSTEMS

A DEVELOPMENT MODEL

A political system giving high and rising percentages of its citizens satisfying personal environments may be viewed as experiencing political development. If the government and most families rely on the same economic institutions for jobs, goods, and services; if diverse segments of the populace are recruited into political institutions; and if people are socialized to believe in placing limits on the authority of public officials, it is easier for political development to occur. **Interfamily and corporate-consumer systems have all three of these traits, and state-consumer systems have at least the first,** *while patron-client systems have none of them. When productivity is lower than current levels of technological innovation will sustain, smaller economies and their supporting political institutions can be destroyed by larger ones.* **Interfamily and patron-client systems usually cannot achieve such productivity; state-consumer systems come closer.** *If an interfamily system becomes a raw materials supplier to interdependent corporations or a corporate-consumer system, or if productivity slows in a state-consumer system, it may transform into a patron-client system. If productivity slows in a corporate-consumer system, it may be pushed to the edges of corporate-interdependence, reducing limits on authority and recruitment into relevant political institutions, and hence the ability to sustain satisfying personal environments. But patron-client systems disengaging from corporate interdependence may move toward interfamily and corporate-consumer relationships; with limits placed on the authority of public officials, state-consumer systems may become corporate-consumer systems. That can improve their ability to support satisfying personal environments.*

During the twentieth century, technology has improved the lives of many people. It has developed more rapidly and spread benefits to more people in some systems than others. In this chapter, we examine some of those more successful systems. Three of them are corporate-consumer systems, and three are state-consumer systems (figure 31.1). One of the state-consumer systems has been more successful than the other two at adapting new technology and spreading its benefits to the citizenry. None of them

has been as successful at doing so as the corporate-consumer systems. They, too, vary in their ability to do so.

Entrepreneurs assume the risks and management of business. Even interfamily villages contain people with the temperament and skills to be entrepreneurs. But the village environment seldom allows people to develop the skills to handle the latest developments in metallurgy, mathematics, and other matters associated with higher technology. **Innovation** is the

Figure 31.1   State- and corporate-consumer systems.

act of introducing a new or creative idea. Some cultures have been friendlier than others to the advancement of science and the introduction of technological innovation. When both entrepreneurship and scientific advance are lacking, the state may try to advance them. That is seldom as effective as when they emerge spontaneously from within the culture.

USA AND CIS

President John F. Kennedy said that everything rises with the tide. Today the tide that moves nation-states upward is technology. A nation-state that grants new freedoms, but fails to take advantage of new advances in synthetics, robotics, photovoltaics, superconductivity, computers, ceramics, semiconductors, fiber-optics, genetics, and other new technologies may be missing the chance to rapidly expand the standard of living of its citizens. Ultimately, spreading opportunities evenly involves making optimal use of technology.

The reasons nation-states do not always make optimal use of technology vary. A nation-state may have problems equitably distributing goods and services and making use of skills and efforts partly because it is short of resources. It may have the resources, but be unable to use them for the common good because it has not learned to utilize technology adequately. Or it may achieve technological progress, but spread the benefits to only a few.

The United States (a corporate-consumer system) and the CIS (a state-consumer system attempting to transform itself) diverge sharply in this regard. Both are blessed with vast resources to serve a low-density population. But the United States has been much more effective than the Soviet Union in utilizing technology to develop those resources. This has raised the general prosperity level in the United States much higher than in the Soviet Union and the CIS republics.

When Peter the Great opened state-operated iron works, mines, sailmaking and saltpeter plants, glass factories, cotton and wool mills, and armaments factories late in the 1600s, peasants were in a period when they had some flexibility to work in towns or in their huts, at least part-time. After 1723, these plants were transferred to the ownership of merchants and nobles who acquired or owned their own work forces. During this period, as Western Europe was beginning the Industrial Revolution, Russian serfs[1] were tied ever more tightly to their place of work in a manorial patron-client system, so they could not constitute a free work force. The state and nobility kept tight control over capital and marketing[2] and were conservative about adopting new technology. Russia's many inventors were largely ignored. The new cloth-making and iron-smelting machinery of the 1800s was imported. Emancipation allowed former serfs to hire out their labor more freely, aiding the growth of larger industries. But a high percentage of both worker and peasant income was spent on basic necessities, and many of the manufactures went to railroads, steamships, the military, and out for export.

The British also regulated technological innovation in the American colonies. Yet from the beginning, Americans (other than slaves, indentured servants, prisoners in penal colonies, and—ironically—the original inhabitants, Native American Indians) were free to work wherever they liked. Those settling virgin land sought new inventions to help them. After the Declaration of Independence was written, inventors were free to produce machinery, protect their inventions by patents, and sell them where they liked. Because American farmers had access to new lands and could also sell their goods on the open market, they were ready and willing to buy many of these goods. The American Civil War created a great need for manufactured iron goods and quickly expanded the market for such goods through government purchases; afterwards, there was a readily available civilian consumer market for such goods, so the Industrial Revolution could take off.

Between 1850 (when there were 1,333 manufacturing firms) and 1925 (when there were 303), the value of agricultural implements manufactured in the United States grew from $150 million to $2.7 billion. The American land tenure system avoided the fragmented landholdings, feudal rights and obligations restricting labor and markets, and lack of capital which impeded similar industry development in Russia.

Investors in Russia had assured foreign markets for their goods. They had long-established trade monopolies with certain European nation-states on certain goods. They did not need to innovate to sell these goods. They were close to Europe and could ship their goods without long sea voyages. America, by contrast, was isolated from the lucrative European trade. It made sense for American investors to seek markets at home; unlike Russians, American consumers had considerable money to spend. Aside from farmers, the next best market was urban workers. Often paid more than subsistence wages for their labor, they could purchase more than just subsistence goods. Manufacturers also promoted high tariffs to assure that wages were not spent on foreign goods. Efforts by William Jennings Bryan and President Woodrow Wilson to reduce these tariffs were strongly and successfully resisted.[3] So the home market remained strong for American manufacturers.

American labor was free to turn to industrial jobs before Russian labor was. American inventors were rewarded, while Russian inventors were not.[4] Americans could invest in enterprises, while Russian industry tended to remain a state monopoly. Russian methods of agriculture were, for the most part, not compatible with industrialization until the 1920s. Russia had markets abroad, while America had to create them internally. And Russia was barraged by a series of bloody wars, from the early nineteenth-century invasion of Napoleon to the stalemate of World War I, which affected America much less directly. America's short (but very bloody) Civil War spurred the North into heavy industrialization. All of these facts—which clearly relate to political culture but not necessarily to differences in forms of government—help explain America's superior utilization of technology in producing consumer goods. Had Great Britain not established patents and let them extend to her colonies, our technology might have developed more slowly. If the tsars had done so, Russian technology might have expanded more rapidly. Had Russia experienced a different system of land tenure, America adopted the southern plantation system across the whole nation-state, or America had fewer immigrants and more markets abroad, the situation might have been reversed.

This is not to say that America always experiences free competition and the Soviet Union never did. In fact, many areas of American commerce are closed to all but a few established competitors. Some areas of Soviet commerce had many competitors. For instance, as we saw in chapter 23, in the Soviet Union, materials-moving equipment was made by 380 factories; in the United States, far fewer companies make such equipment. Many giant firms produce little except weapons they have exclusive U.S. government contracts for. But in America, sizable fortunes can be accumulated by people who develop new products or production equipment that meet a demand, or by selling familiar products, such as hamburgers, in popular ways. In the Soviet Union, no such fortune could be made.

In the Soviet Union, innovation did not pay. Because prices were fixed by ministries, foreign goods were kept out, managers were rewarded simply on the basis of how many units they produced, and factories that could not sell their goods received monetary subsidies, there was little incentive to innovate.[5] With no patents or rewards, individual incentives to innovate were also low.[6] And workers had little incentive to innovate.[7] *Pravda* told a story about workers who were paid one ruble, sixteen kopecks for every ton of dried milk they carried. The workers tried to carry more sacks to increase their pay; since they soon were exceeding wage-earning norms, their pay was lowered to one ruble, eight kopecks.[8]

For short periods of time—under Lenin's New Economic Policy during the 1920s, and under Khrushchev and Kosygin—top Soviet leaders tried some decentralization and privatization of the Soviet economy to spur innovation. Gorbachev revived this initiative. Industries freely contracted with other firms for equipment, deciding on at least part of what they would produce, designing their own products, and retaining part of their own profits to reinvest. They could fire some inefficient workers or deprive them of bonuses; in 1991, a system of government unemployment compensation was established. Mandatory quotas from centralized agencies were replaced with suggested guidelines. Firms were permitted to go bankrupt and to set their own prices. Private businesses could develop joint ventures with government firms or with foreigners. A stock market was proposed which would allow people to buy shares in government-owned businesses. Pressure was placed on bureaucrats and factories to emphasize quality along with quantity in planning decisions; a new agency was empowered to reject goods that failed to meet standards. In 1991, the Supreme Soviet approved a plan to sell two-thirds of the country's industry to private investors by 1996, retaining about half of the energy and defense industries in state hands.

But the economy continued to stall. Managers borrowed money from banks, keeping it and income from enterprises for themselves by diverting goods to the black market. That reduced government income even more, at a time when it was increasing subsidies and welfare spending; it simply printed more rubles to make up the deficit, fueling massive inflation. Heavy government taxation discouraged exports.

In 1992, freed of central government controls, Russia launched a radical reform to open a free market. The ruble was made convertible on international markets and prices were allowed to rise. State businesses were converted into worker-owned joint-stock companies, and small shops were auctioned off. Many closed and left their workers jobless. Small private "collective" businesses, begun in 1987, were expanded.[9] Yet prices of many essential goods remained under state control, and privatized businesses were forced to continue producing and selling these goods. Presidential decrees by Russian President Boris Yeltsin called for 70 percent of state industrial production, and 35 percent of state mining production, and 80 percent of earnings from exports to go to the state—higher proportions than under the old system. Nonetheless, essential state enterprises losing money continue to be subsidized by the state, which prints money and thus encourages inflation. Most of the over thirty-five thousand employees in the dissolved central ministries received jobs in comparable Russian ministries. Former party officials often "sell" the state businesses to themselves. Production continues to decline.

Gorbachev allowed collective farms to sell some crops directly to stores (at prices set by administrators) after assigned quotas were sold to the state. Farmers began neglecting the harvesting on state and collective farms to bring in their own harvests. To prevent this, in 1991, farmers were offered imported consumer goods in exchange for any grain they harvested for the state. The wages of state farm workers, doctors, and others were raised, and bonuses were paid for expanded output. Families or groups of workers within collectives contracted to produce meat, milk, fruit, or vegetables on collective land for personal profit; these "family brigades" rented land and machinery from the state in a variation on China's responsibility system.[10] Over a million city dwellers rented or bought nearby plots of land to grow crops, and a few were allowed to buy a plot of land for building a home.[11] Profits from innovations that increased agricultural productivity could be shared equally between farms and researchers.[12] In 1992, members of state and collective farms in Russia were allowed to lease land for longer terms and then market crops through their farms. No private individual can yet buy farm land.

This still leaves allocation of farm land, marketing, loans for developing land, and procurement of supplies in the hands of the same bureaucracy, which is also in charge of determining how high "deregulated" prices can rise and which items will not be allowed to rise in price. This leaves lessees uncertain as to whether they can make enough from what they grow to support their families; the bureaucrats and former bureaucrats who sell the crops in the cities may make far more than the individual growers. During 1992, agricultural production dropped significantly. Most young people prefer to leave the countryside if they have a chance, and those over forty are reluctant to try farming on their own.

Reductions in military spending begun in 1991 were meant to free up capital, labor, plants, and raw materials to produce consumer goods. However, many plants continue to produce arms.

These moves toward decentralization are very radical departures from the history of Rus, Russia, and the Soviet Union. The centralized bureaucracy which has controlled economic transactions for centuries will not relinquish power easily and has little experience in modern management techniques. To revert to the old systems, all they need do is continue their inefficiency and corruption and allow discontent to grow over the reforms. Any reforms that do not eliminate the black market let them create artificial shortages by diverting goods to the black market, where they can sell goods for high prices and keep the profits without paying taxes. Black market "mafia" also charge legitimate businesses 15 percent "blackmail" or "protection" money to stay in business. The public applauds reform, but is also uneasy about reduced job security, higher prices, lower pay, and other disruptions market reforms entail.[13] They also dislike displays of conspicuous wealth and are suspicious of private entrepreneurs, whom many regard as greedy.[14] Few people have any experience with such endeavors. Polls show that they are reluctant to end state control of heavy industries and basic public services.[15] In the first major test of a joint venture between a large capitalist firm and a republic, bureaucrats leaked documents to the independent Moscow News, which called it a "dirty deal," that took the nation's resources and "plundered and sold [them] for a mere song."[16] When the Russian government issued vouchers giving citizens "ownership" of state enterprises in 1992, few showed up at the distribution centers to claim them (in sharp contrast to neighboring China, where 5 million applications were sold out on the first day of a share offering at the new Shenzhen stock exchange). Pyotr Filopov, a liberal member of parliament, says, "The majority are for private property and a market, but they are against free prices and competition. People aren't used to risk, and they don't want to risk. They feel they deserve to be paid just for showing up to work."[17]

The immediate results of reforms were longer queues and decreasing supplies of goods in the shops,[18] lowered harvests because volunteers engaged in other pursuits, much higher prices, the replacement of low-cost goods with more expensive goods with greater profit margins, bankruptcies of firms which lost subsidies that had artificially propped them up, layoffs, and increasing demands made on workers. Many of the quarter million new private cooperatives simply specialize in selling scarce stolen goods.[19] Hundreds of auction centers have been established where groups and individuals barter goods and services without exchanging cash. Innovation does not come easily in this system.[20] In attempting to turn profit into a driving force, leaders must continue to guarantee people employment, basic goods at low prices, housing, and an overall sense of security. And to do so they must upset the job security and privileges of many entrenched party leaders and bureaucrats and reduce the power of the military. That is hard to do; such privileges extend far back in history. Since those bureaucrats control most natural resources and factories, they are able to keep new investors from obtaining the materials, land, buildings, and tools they need to set up competing firms.

Furthermore, trade and capitalism have their own dynamic. Each republic specializes in certain products. All depend on others for many types of manufactured goods and to market their own goods. Regions such as Siberia, northern Russia, the Ukraine, Armenia, Kazakhstan, Uzbekistan, Tajikistan, Kyrgyzstan, and Turkmenistan, which have produced primarily heavy industry, agriculture, and raw materials, must get nearly all their consumer goods from outside.[21] A single plant may produce over 90 percent of one part needed by every power plant in the CIS; other single plants produce over 90 percent of its polyester, die-casting machines, trolleys, locomotives, sewing machines, printing ink, oil rigs, or corn harvesters. Thousands of products are manufactured at only one site.[22] All the republics except Russia depend on trade with the other republics for at least a third of their Gross National Product.[23] Manufactured goods are generally below world standards of quality, so they will not sell in other countries; if they cannot sell in the other republics, these factories will close. The smaller republics have small populations with little personal savings for purchasing goods, so it is hard to attract private investors to produce goods. If they simply use raw materials to trade for them, their economies will not modernize rapidly. Outside investors may be tempted to bring in labor-intensive factories producing luxuries or export goods for the outside world; that will not keep citizens of the republics supplied with jobs or goods, and leaves the republics just as dependent on one another for food, clothing, and shelter. The ruble was traded at the commercial rate of 1.8 rubles to the dollar; when it was moved into free competition on international currency markets, where one could suddenly obtain 650 rubles to the dollar, the revenue from goods sold abroad plummeted. All this makes it hard to raise living standards in the republics.

The old communist *nomenklatura* are well-positioned to retain authority in the new republics.

When economies flounder under reformers, the experienced bureaucrats and politicians of the communist era will point out that ethnic tensions were fewer and economic stability greater under their rule. In 1991, the head of ideology for the Ukraine's former Communist Party, converted into a "reformer" but still making use of the entire structure of *apparatchiki* (who retain their former positions), became president in a free election.[24] The noncommunist opposition was divided between RUKH and the more radical nationalist Republicans, who frightened non-Ukraine citizens with their language and ethnic policies.

The "reformed" former communist leader in Azerbaijan pursued a similar strategy against his noncommunist opponents. He was ousted in 1992 by the reformist Popular Front, but was soon back in power after Azerbaijan became mired in fighting Armenian troops. Noncommunist reformer leaders of other republics face similar pressures from "former" communist candidates as economies falter and ethnic tensions mount. Turkmenistan, which Russia and the Ukraine depend on for natural gas, has not even legalized opposition parties or instituted economic reforms. Uzbekistan's former communist leader has strongly suppressed opposition activities, and Tajikistan's overthrown communist leader returned to power in bloody civil war; Russian troops have increasingly come to his aid.

In Georgia, a noncommunist dissident poet won a landslide victory early in 1991; he failed to implement reforms, showed little willingness to listen to the legislature, and continued to suppress the rights of ethnic minorities. This split his Popular Front. The president had a strong political base with clans in rural western Georgia, while the National Democratic Party (whose leaders he promptly jailed, and who then led a coup which overthrew him) had its greatest support among the middle class and intellectuals around the capital of Tbilisi. Another group, the League of Georgia Citizens, called for restricting citizenship to those whose families had lived in Georgia before it became part of the Soviet Union in 1921. Former Soviet Foreign Minister Eduard

Shevardnadze took power in Tbilisi, but failed to gain military control of western Georgia, or rebel-held areas of Ossetia and Abkhazia.

In Russia, some former communists combine with Russian nationalists to invoke the Russian Orthodox Church, Russian ethnic solidarity, the need for a strong leader, and fear of the West, in calling for a return to a centralized economy run by Russians. Everywhere, clan groups dominate local and regional politics; the communists had years of experience incorporating this patron-clientism into a larger political organization. This uncertainty and division among ranks of reformers provides a risky, unwelcome investment climate, makes it hard to transform the state-consumer system into a corporate-consumer system, and offers potential for a counterrevolution to end the reforms.

In the United States, new innovations are often more accessible to the rich than the poor. Their homes, neighborhoods, hospitals, and offices have the newest and most advanced technology. Factories which automate or move abroad can, in fact, displace workers. Much technological innovation goes into refining frivolous products already used by those with high living standards, rather than devising basic goods for those with low standards of living. Some are designed to wear out quickly so they must be replaced. But many new products do add to health, safety, and general welfare. The production and distribution of new technology and the raw materials it requires involve many people. Many inventive people came from immigrant groups without a major role in landholding, business, or professional life. They have developed superior products to drill for oil, mine coal, move earth, store data, broadcast pictures, radiate cancers, strain out pollution, probe outer space, and generate power. Businesses and industries are free to start up and innovate independently and to provide economic incentives to their owners and employees. Widespread education makes it possible for people from all walks of life to work for those businesses. These firms benefit by selling to Americans, and hence try to create products and retailing techniques which will appeal to them. Patents allow people to derive profits from inventions. American firms are aggressive about developing sources of inexpensive raw materials at home and abroad. With mass production, many goods have become widely available for the homes of Americans of all incomes. This has been the basis of much of America's economic and political strength. That is why it is a corporate-consumer system.

In the CIS, too, innovation is more accessible to the rich than to the poor. The innovation itself is halting and far from optimal; much of the factory equipment, and many of the roads and products themselves, predate World War I. At least in urban areas, education is available to all classes of people. But the right to innovate has long been the monopoly of a few. Markets, too, have been monopolized. Prior to the revolution, those who held these monopolies had great wealth, which they used to buy estates and lavish ornamental furnishings, while most people lived close to subsistence level. The communists seized that wealth and sought to redistribute it to the rest of the populace via a state-consumer system. But they did not end the monopoly on innovation; instead, they solidified it within the layers of bureaucracy all decisions about production must pass through. The public had only one legitimate source for goods, and factories were rewarded for quotas produced even if they were not sold, so there was little incentive to innovate. The CIS has vast natural resources, but still uses labor-intensive methods to tap them. Hence, each worker produces less, and pay is low. People have been guaranteed jobs that provide few rewards for extra effort.[25] Much of the domestic production which does take place is for ordinary people. But they must spend long hours waiting in line to obtain the products, which are not of very good quality. This has helped to even out living standards. But now that they are level, it does not help to raise them. Black marketeers and their political and bureaucratic allies, who used the state factories after hours for their production facilities, became millionaires with large country houses and cars. They prospered without innovating. Now they are still in the best position to prosper by taking legitimate control of the factories.

Without our form of government, which allows open political competition and the removal of leaders who interfere with the citizenry in ways the citizens do not like, our approach to innovation would be impossible. Our ability to innovate, however, is also rooted in our culture. We have people who like to profit from invention, we have a tradition of doing so, and our populace accepts both the advantages and disadvantages that derive from this. As Gorbachev tried to open the Soviet form of government to allow for greater innovation, he faced a populace not only with little experience at, but also great fear of the consequences of, innovating for profit. He ordered soldiers, bureaucrats, and workers to work hard and assist in economic development or disaster relief,[26] and he ordered them to open the path for creative entrepreneurs; but he could not make them do any of this.

The Soviet Union created a state-consumer system to spur technology in a system with little experience at innovation; it created internal consumption, but added new impediments to innovation. The United States was able to create a corporate-consumer system because it had a history of innovation and of support for preventing government limits on it.

THE UNITED KINGDOM AND GERMANY

The Industrial Revolution began in Britain during the eighteenth century; the second area to experience extensive industrialization was western Germany in the 1840s.[27] Both had active merchant classes eager for investment opportunities. Their cities had been freed from the nobility's control. Their peasants had been released from bondage to feudal estates, so they could migrate to the cities. Universities and science had taken firm root and rulers permitted them to expand. Both systems had protestant religious movements emphasizing hard work, acquisition, and learning. Both had coal and iron, together with experience in mining.[28] They were active in commerce by sea, and they both contained many skilled artisans. Their governments permitted poor families

to accumulate capital and protect inventions with patents. Germany had gained access to the best markets in Europe, and Britain to those of the rest of the world. They were ideally suited for developing new technology.

The Hitler era, especially, helped industry spread throughout Germany, into the east. During World War II, much of the older West German industry was flattened to the ground by Allied bombing, but this was replaced by new plants and technology during and after the war. With new plants, an influx of the best technical minds after World War II, and labor movement involvement in improving productivity, West Germany efficiently produces high-quality goods attractive to consumers on world markets. It consistently exports more than it imports, producing more steel, chemicals, cars and trucks, plastics, electrical and electronics equipment, and textiles than the United Kingdom.

East Germany produced extensive manufactured goods, many of which it exported to the Soviet Union and the West. It had, until the 1980s, one of the world's fastest growth rates in Gross National Product. As of 1939, per capita industrial output was 16 percent higher in eastern Germany than in western Germany—especially in chemicals, textiles, machine tools, synthetic rubber, and consumer goods. By 1944, despite war bombings and with the aid of constant new building, total German output—and eastern Germany's percentage of it—rose even higher. But most of the coal and iron ore was located to the west, and the Soviets were more aggressive than the other Allies in dismantling production facilities after the war; moreover, they did not compensate with anything like Marshall Plan aid. Still, East Germany became one of the world's top producers of electric power, artificial gas, chemical fibers, fertilizer, plastics, synthetic rubber, railroad rolling stock, radios and television sets, household appliances, industrial machinery, machine tools, and optics. In the period after World War II, it built fifteen iron and steel mills, ten electrical combines, twelve machine tool factories, seven electrotechnical and optical plants, eight cement works, and four shipyards—all very large in size, but with very basic technology.

East Germany invested heavily in agriculture. In 1949, each farm worker produced enough food for nine people; by 1975, enough for thirty. Farms were highly mechanized. By 1965, East German farms yielded 3.67 tons per hectare of wheat, versus 3.26 in the Soviet Union.[29] East Germany used 1,600 pounds of fertilizer per acre, mechanized 96 percent of its potato production, irrigated about 20 percent of its farmland, and used large numbers of tractors (149,000 in 1970), harvesters, and trucks. It steadily increased its production of milk per cow and eggs per hen.

West Germany, the Soviet Union, and the rest of the Eastern Bloc absorbed most of East Germany's output. East Germany had special marketing arrangements with all of them which prevented it from having to face much competition from foreign products. But East Germany was more technologically innovative than the Soviet Union, and in some realms as innovative as the United Kingdom. Many of its best products were for competitive foreign trade, earning hard currency, rather than for the domestic market or the Eastern Bloc. Its optics, precision tools, chemicals, flower seeds, computers, and fishing trawlers competed on markets all over the world. A third of Robotron's computer components were sold outside the Communist Bloc; before reunification, Robotron had seventy-thousand employees. Germany exported a third of its pharmaceuticals to the West. But East Germany was not able to keep up with advances in microchips and computer technology, synthetics, fiber-optics, and many other fields connected with its manufactures. With each passing year, its ability to compete declined. After reunification, it was hard to find buyers for its antiquated plants.

The United Kingdom, meanwhile, still uses many of her original nineteenth-century plants. Its strong labor movement gained high wage increases and excessive numbers of laborers in plants, without incurring responsibility for improving productivity. A study of identical Ford and General Motors car doors manufactured in almost identical Belgian and British plants found the British plants producing only 55 percent as many doors per hour with 80 per-

cent more workers. Another study found it took an average of 4.1 workers to build a Ford Escort in a West German plant, while it took 9.5 workers to build the same car in a plant in Liverpool, England. Despite having 50 to 70 percent more maintenance workers than the West German plant, the British plant lost twice as many production hours from mechanical breakdowns.[30] The United Kingdom has lagged behind West Germany in technical education, plant modernization, research and development, and quality control.

East Germany offered awards (prizes up to 300,000 marks for workers or writers with suggestions leading to new inventions) and special contracts (up to 20,000 marks a month for workers with desired talents)[31] as incentives lacking in the Soviet Union and the United Kingdom. The United Kingdom and the Soviet Union also have had basic raw materials at home and could extract the rest from colonies without having to trade with them; with the Ruhr alternately under French control, Germany has depended more on trading sophisticated manufactures for iron, coal, and other raw materials (though, because the Soviet Union set its trade terms, East Germany paid too much for its fuel).[32] So both East and West Germany learned to adapt to the necessity of innovating to turn a profit.

Because East and West Germany were able to create markets for all the goods they can produce, and because high percentages of their populace have learned to take on useful roles in production, these systems could spread consumer goods to high percentages of their populations. People with skills and capital existed before the Industrial Revolution and were free to open factories, raise more capital, and explore new markets within large, private economic institutions; they continue to do so. Reunification placed West Germans in control of the economy. They chose to close many plants in the East and convert workers to service economy jobs, while building new plants to replace others. Wages are higher (though still only 70 percent of those in the West), so work forces are smaller and asked to produce more. Workers are being retrained; they should be able to adapt to this innovation.

The United Kingdom has accumulated great fortunes by innovating. Its recent prosperity stemmed from an early start on the Industrial Revolution, which came because of (1) its convenient access to coal and iron, (2) freedom to innovate and religious and economic motivation among various dissenting protestants to do so, (3) its naval power and aggressive pursuit of raw materials and markets abroad, (4) capital derived from controlling the exports of colonies, and (5) the freeing up of labor in the countryside. But, unlike the United States and Germany, the United Kingdom became heavily dependent on captive foreign markets to sell manufactured goods. With the fall of its colonies, it lost access to that capital, and to many raw materials and markets. It had to turn to foreign investors less concerned about keeping profits (and thus capital) within Britain. Many of the most educated young British people with innovative inclinations move to other countries. So the United Kingdom has less capital to create jobs for its own citizens, and little experience at designing exports to sell on competitive foreign markets.

The Government of Margaret Thatcher made a major effort to change all this during the 1980s.[33] Thatcher threw the force of Government against strikes and reduced the power of unions.[34] She encouraged unproductive plants to close and offered tax and other incentives for newer high-tech industries to open in their stead. She privatized government-owned industries and encouraged millions of Britons to invest in these industries' stocks. She sold public housing to many of its occupants and made home loans available to many who could not previously afford to buy. She switched many industrial plants, and much home heating, from coal to British North Sea oil. She encouraged Americans to invest in Britain, and British to invest in America. She (not entirely enthusiastically) strengthened ties with the European Common Market, allowing imports of products from other parts of Europe in exchange for exporting British goods. All this was designed to spur innovation and create new markets. At the same time, it created inflation in housing prices, lowered the incomes of many working people, left entire re-

gions without an economic base of support, reduced the government's assets, and caused the United Kingdom to import far more than it exported—raising questions about the long-term success of the new plan. It may yet succeed only if the British people use these opportunities to create goods that can be competitive on international markets, rather than simply making quick profits from selling stocks and shares, creating shopping malls, and providing other services which do not expand capital and markets.

Innovation has been a spur to equality of opportunity in both these nation-states. Germany's Industrial Revolution was begun by an alliance of merchants along the Rhine valley and landowning nobility to the east. Martin Luther's Reformation had allowed established leaders in both these regions to become protestants, with a strong interest in making money and consolidating the fragmented territories so as to promote both trade and national power. The Junker monarchs used the growth of industry along the Rhine to enhance their military power and build the wealth of their formerly poor region. The industry allowed workers in Rhine valley cities and estate workers on the Junker estates of eastern Germany to advance themselves.

Britain's Industrial Revolution was not begun by its nobility. They had already consolidated control of their territories and benefitted from long control over trade on the high seas; they preferred investing their money in country estates rather than new industry. Quakers, Presbyterians, Methodists, and other dissenters from the established Anglican Church (excluded from Oxford and Cambridge, and from top posts in local and national government) started the industries in northern England, Scotland, and Wales. Skilled artisans were incorporated into many manufacturing pursuits, along with unskilled laborers who could work at high wage scales.

Today in the United Kingdom, there is an added twist. The Anglican educational establishment, centered around Oxford and Cambridge, has long frowned on seeing its graduates participate in manufacturing pursuits;[35] these graduates, who dominate Parliament, have allowed the aging manufacturing plants of the dissenters to close and have failed to follow through with competitive innovation since World War II. Much of the new thrust for investment in service businesses has come from around London. Anglicans are involved, along with immigrants from the Middle East and elsewhere. It remains to be seen whether this new mix will produce results that allow the United Kingdom to compete on world markets again. But as the dissenters are shoved more to the background in innovation, Scotland, Wales, and northern England—the strongholds of Presbyterians, Quakers, Methodists, and other dissenters—are receding to the background in terms of economic prosperity. Instead, the Thatcher Government attempted to kindle interest in innovation within more established educational channels.[36] Meanwhile, in Germany, many students in the best universities are shifting from the industrial interests of their grandparent alumni, preferring to pursue other fields.[37]

The Industrial Revolution, which brought the continuing sweep of technological advance, began in Britain and Germany. Both allowed cities and trade to develop early as free merchants accumulated large amounts of capital. They had freed portions of their rural populace to come to the cities and work. Religious traditions that emphasized hard work, acquisition, and learning were widespread. They were pioneers in developing educational institutions at all levels. The universities were free to pursue scientific investigation. They had raw materials and were early to develop transportation. Both had banks which began lending capital to new ventures and pioneered cooperation between governments and trading firms to encourage foreign trade. Britain, especially, had a strong navy plying all the seas. Germany created joint stock companies to allow government and individuals to pool their capital within large enterprises. All these factors are ideal for developing technology.

Because it had established colonies abroad, Britain was able to start out with captive sources of raw materials and markets for its goods. Tariff barriers kept out foreign manufactures, and colonies were not permitted to create competing plants. As we shall see in the next chapter, Britain could also de-

rive large amounts of capital purely from conquest. As its industrial base was laid, it had little incentive to expand it. Those acquiring large fortunes were tempted to spend them on country estates, emulating those of the old nobility, rather than on more advanced technology or on higher wages to create a large middle class. The newly educated could serve abroad in the colonies in jobs more bureaucratic than entrepreneurial. The old nobility and more established social elite was slow to engage or invest in the new commercial pursuits.

Not so in Germany. Its early cooperative ventures between government, the old nobility, bankers, and entrepreneurs from the cities aggressively invested profits in new technology. They created large, monopolistic, powerful firms. Once Germany had built its railroads, ships, and plants, much of its market had to come from competing on the world market. Universities were quick to research and develop innovations useful to industry. All this stimulated many jobs in the modern sector, in contrast to Britain. In addition, the destruction of old plants in Germany as a result of World War II encouraged the introduction of plants with new technology after the war; Britain continued to use its old plants. This commitment to new technology has helped Germany expand middle-class prosperity.

As we have seen, after World War II, West Germany adopted a form of government with features found in other Western European democracies; East Germany adopted a form of government more akin to that in the Soviet Union. Yet East Germany was more like West Germany than the Soviet Union in its ability to innovate technologically. Their common cultural attributes help explain that. However, East Germany was forced to devote a lesser portion of its output to consumer goods than West Germany, and to sell to the Soviet Union on unfavorable terms, leaving less to spread down to the overall populace. And its economy fell under the control of bureaucrats slow to relinquish their power as the two economies now integrate.

The United Kingdom and Germany created early and advanced corporate-consumer systems; Germany was forced to compete more aggressively with technological innovation. East Germany created a state-consumer system in a country which had been a pioneer in entrepreneurship and technological innovation; the innovation continued, but at a slowed pace.

CHINA

We have examined the CIS, a group of nation-states whose culture discourages technological innovation, and Germany, a nation-state whose culture strongly encourages it. Britain is torn between two cultures, one of which encourages innovation more than the other. We have seen that the cultures which encourage entrepreneurship and innovation disseminate technological advances more widely to their people than those that do not encourage these qualities. Where does China fit into this picture? China's culture traditionally encouraged entrepreneurship and some technological innovation. But it has never encouraged the dissemination of technological advances to its people.

China, with a fourth of the world's population, is capable of great technical achievement. It has vast deposits of coal and large quantities of petroleum and other minerals. For over two millennia, China had no feudal restrictions preventing labor from moving to cities, or preventing individuals from freely engaging in cottage industry and commerce. Especially to the south of China, traders took to the sea in ships with all manner of commercial goods; canals linked the north and south for internal trade. Merchants created cottage industries producing silk, porcelain, furniture, and many other goods. Though China's emperors gave commercial people little influence in government, they were free to pursue trade and manufacture, as long as the goods sold were traditional and the plants in which they produced the goods remained small.

But China had no cities free to run themselves, as those in Germany and Britain could. Merchants had to finance their own activities by selling more than they bought abroad. The government was not involved in foreign trade and discouraged it during the most recent dynasties, the Ming and Qing. To keep local officials cooperative, merchants routinely bribed them. Confucian ethics gave merchants low status and caused both officials and the public to frown on ostentatious displays of wealth and on excessive profits. To raise their social status, merchants often invested surplus capital in land, rather than in further commercial pursuits. The government benefitted from taxing commerce and consistently kept surpluses in the treasury. Government officials benefitted from bribes. Little capital was left for innovation.

Many important inventions, from gunpowder to printing, came from China. The *literati,* however, regarded such inventions as toys. The technology that commanded their interest surrounded irrigation; one of their principal duties was to keep China's extensive irrigation and canal system operating, so food could be grown and distributed throughout the land. The *literati* purchased irrigation products but did not encourage the development of new ones to raise yields as population grew. The government invested little in other industries. In 1842, China lost to Britain in the Opium War[38] and was forced to allow the opening of treaty ports to Westerners. In 1860, British troops captured Beijing; they then helped the empire organize armies to defeat the Taiping Rebellion, which had captured Nanjing and much of the lower Yangtze River valley. Only after Western armies began to conquer their territory did Chinese political leaders begin to take other kinds of technology seriously; even then, some of them saw this technology as a threat to Chinese cultural values. The government began to take out loans from foreigners to pay for weapons and war indemnities.

Mechanized factories began to multiply in 1895; by 1933, there were 3,167 mechanized plants, with half a million workers,[39] largely located along the coast in the treaty ports. Some were operated by Chinese and others by foreigners. The workers were often poorly paid. Political turmoil and price and currency fluctuations made sales and profits erratic; many firms ended up in the hands of banks or the state after foreclosures. Both workers and owners were harmed by this. Most of the new factories made cotton yarn and cloth, processed food, and produced chemical products. The competition of new factory goods ruined many labor-intensive cottage industries scattered throughout interior regions. Peasants had depended on these for extra income, and their demise resulted in an agricultural decline[40] and a surge of unemployed people to the cities. All of this caused even greater inequalities.

Much of the equipment and many of the raw materials for the new plants, and for railroads and electrification, were imported. The government took out loans from foreign banks to develop the military, railroads, and electricity. Many of the loans to start modern factories came from foreign banks. And wealthier Chinese in the cities developed a taste for imported consumer goods. As a result, for the first time, China ran up a large foreign trade deficit, with the declared value of the imports higher than that of exports.

Lenin's centralized control over industry and commerce in the Soviet Union was a continuation of a long tradition going back to Peter the Great; Mao's introduction of centralized control in China was a radical departure from tradition. After Mao's death, it was far easier to move away from centralization than it has been for the republics that formerly were part of the Soviet Union. Rather than taking the lead in developing and licensing innovation, China's central government under the empire discouraged it; under the early years of the republic (from 1911 until the 1930s), the central government had little control over the economy. Mao had watched with dismay the rising deficit, the decline of agriculture, and the masses of urban unemployed; he also noted that the main gains of national importance, such as electrification and railroads, came with government participation. After the communists took power, they largely returned to the policy of Imperial China, promoting irrigation,[41] roads, and other agrarian projects; but this time the government involved itself in manufacturing pursuits connected with such projects. And the nation-state once again maintained an even trade balance, not allowing imports to exceed exports.

Since China was no longer isolated from the outside world, government restricted commerce in ways which had not applied in the past; government ministries kept all industries subordinate to their control. The industries put the urban population to work producing goods to help rural agriculture mechanize, electrify, and benefit from fertilizer and new seed strains; that, in turn, kept rural people employed in labor-intensive agriculture. Factories were deliberately scattered in many parts of the country to spread their benefits. To avoid extensive imports, these factories produced factory machinery[42] and iron, fuels, and other materials needed in industry; between 1949 and 1973, the percentage of industrial output devoted to such producer goods rose from 28 to 65 percent.[43] Later, factories began to produce greater quantities of consumer goods that could be widely purchased by peasants and urban workers. To a lesser extent, the Chinese have invested in roads, railroads,[44] steamships, and weapons. Investments were largely financed by selling to the domestic market and reinvesting profits. Before 1949, savings represented 5 to 7 percent of Gross Domestic Product; by 1970, they were a third of GDP.[45] But private commerce was far more restricted than in the past.

Peasant communities remain intact, while producing enough food and raw materials to supply both themselves and the cities; the buildup in rural technical capacities laid a base for more individualized agriculture under the responsibility system. As under Imperial rule, this centralized direction of effort, and the strong dependence on human labor to tend fields, maintain dikes and waterways, and manufacture, has restricted technological innovation. The social networks of *guanxi* among local leaders remain intact, strengthened by their ties with new, intermediate levels of bureaucracy, and allowing them to resist efforts which might attempt to remove their grip on workers and markets.[46] Peasant cooperatives even fabricate individual parts for products assembled in factories; this makes it difficult to change and refine their design. Manufacturers have little freedom to innovate and seek new markets. There are more officials than ever to bribe. Rewards are distributed in exchange for compliance with the factory leaders and their friends in bureaucracy and politics.[47] But the investment has contributed to both a growth and an equalization of income.

Thus, the communist state-consumer system has used China's traditional entrepreneurship and technical acumen to produce goods for popular consumption; but the same state control that limited technological innovation in the past continues to do so. Without a tradition of placing limits on government, it is hard to move into corporate-consumerism.

Under earlier systems, landowners could at least raise profits by producing more output from their land. The introduction of communes destroyed that incentive. Under the responsibility system, peasants may once again invest in their own land and benefit from increased yields; many have taken advantage of the new system to amass profits. But peasants are reluctant to invest in new technology, for fear that they may lose their leases in the future if the government demands they "voluntarily" surrender them. Often their fields are so small that they cannot easily use machinery on them. Instead, they use profits to build themselves new houses. New taxes are often wasted on cars, land speculation, and other perquisites for officials rather than used for investment. In a similar vein, inhabitants of Hong Kong await their submergence into China in 1997; though the agreement under which they enter guarantees them free trade, it could be broken at any time. Without clear legal limits on state power, no investment is safe.

Despite these pitfalls, the new joint ventures and cooperatives have taken full advantage of China's entrepreneurial talents and the willingness of its citizens to work, save, and invest. In 1992, China contracted $60 billion in foreign investment—more than in all prior years combined; fixed capital investment rose by 38 percent and industrial output by 21 percent.[48] The great majority was spent on real estate and low-technology factories using many poorly paid workers to make goods for export. Many of the transactions are structured to avoid taxation.[49] Meanwhile, government banks increase their lending 10 percent a year, with loans going both to profitable firms and to losers with good political connections. The central government's budget deficit

grows, and in 1993, years of trade surpluses ended as imports rose and a trade deficit developed.[50] Inflation rose to over 20 percent. Freed from restrictions and facing competition, many government-owned firms improved their efficiency or became joint ventures and laid off excess workers. Most of China's eleven thousand large- and medium-sized government-owned enterprises, which produce more than half its industrial jobs and profits and 60 percent of its industrial taxes, are located outside major cities.[51] That has spread loans, investments, and wage increases, but most of those firms lose money. People throughout China are buying new clothes, electronics, and other luxury consumer goods. When, in 1992 and 1993, local officials withheld crop payments from peasants to divert the money into new investments, the peasants marched in defiance. China's top leader assigned to that problem threatened to "cut off the heads" of officials engaging in that abuse.

The relaxation of centralized controls on industries, which began in 1978, offers people incentives to work and innovate but also poses many problems. The expanding economy calls for more raw materials, energy resources, and pollution controls. The government lacks taxation money to develop those resources or raise the pay of government workers to keep up with inflation. It refuses to borrow abroad and spends only $8 a year per capita on education,[52] hampering literacy and the acquisition of advanced skills. It frequently restricts imports when they rise too fast (as in 1993) so that China will not use up its reserve capital. This cools the economy, slows technological innovation, keeps inefficient state industries alive, and increases unemployment by forcing new businesses to close for lack of resources, capital, and markets.

The principal restraint on technology in China, then, is not price controls, monopolies, lack of incentive for invention, lack of available skilled labor or savings, or limits on competition. Instead, it is a shared intent to keep jobs, goods, and capital circulating within China—from corrupt officials at the top on down to peasants and workers. Export more than you import, don't owe foreigners money, don't let innovations destroy jobs. Chinese commonly express shame over the period from the nineteenth century until 1949 when foreign powers dominated many aspects of their society and economy, and they do not wish to become heavily indebted to outside nation-states or let them have direct intervention in the economy. If China already had extensive capital reserves, that would not present a problem; it does not, partly because this attitude is deeply rooted in its political culture. While this caution about importing assets to help build mines, pipelines, and high-technology factories slows technological innovation, it also helps assure that innovation serves the needs of China's population.

England had a similar attitude it expressed as **mercantilism**—a policy that exports must always exceed imports. However, for reasons we shall see in the next chapter, the United Kingdom was able to maintain that policy and accumulate capital at the same time. That makes a critical difference.

China cannot innovate rapidly. Because of this, peasants are able to stay on the land and be assured of an urban market. Limited freedom to innovate has long helped equalize opportunities in China. Peasants with low incomes could supplement earnings with handicrafts and commerce. Urban dwellers of low status could become prosperous by trading and purchase land to raise their status. But China was not in a position to raise new investment capital by aggressively pursuing new markets abroad; this created inequalities while preserving jobs.

China has a long history of individual entrepreneurs who were free to invest in land, goods, and ships and could buy and sell without centralized governmental control. It has a long history of scientific discovery, unhampered by the sorts of religious restrictions which dampened scientific thought in Europe prior to the Renaissance. It has a skilled and motivated populace. But, except for the decades preceding World War II, Chinese governments have kept merchants from achieving high positions in politics, and they have discouraged imbalanced trade or innovations which would disturb the rigid social structure. That encouraged merchants to bribe officials and try to get around the rules, wasting money

which otherwise might have been used to encourage innovation. Chinese government also has a long history of regulating the water system which serves agriculture; it retains that control of the infrastructure and tries to prevent innovation which would divert heavy resources from current uses. Those exerting such control still remain open to bribes. Much of current water and resource use is for labor-intensive agriculture. This means technology benefits large portions of the populace, whose skills are put to use. But technology changes very slowly. The fastest changes have been in the joint ventures, which produce goods of world-standard quality in factories built by Taiwanese, Japanese, Hong Kong, Singaporean, European, and American partners. All this helps China maintain a state-consumer system. The lack of limits on state sovereignty discourages the introduction of a corporate-consumer system.[53]

China's traditional method of limiting the power of public officials has consisted of rare popular mass movements rising against the executive and bureaucracy, or peasants marching outside their homes in a show of defiance against the misdeeds of officials. The recent Cultural Revolution used this approach to temporarily switch authority from one group of public officials to another. Short of that kind of activity, however, chief executives desiring to divert resources from *guanxi* networks are subject to swift removal if their fellow decision makers disagree. Zhao Ziyang used mass demonstrations at Tiananmen Square in 1989 to counter such threats of removal; he failed. Yet, when officials at all levels see resource sharing or other policies as to their advantage, Chinese traditionally defer to rapid policy changes made by emperors and other top leaders—a tradition of deference useful for promoting change. That is how the 1978 reforms began, and why they continue. Once fertile, watered, land was made available by the responsibility system, and small business enterprises made available by the cooperatives, Chinese workers and peasants returned to their long-standing entrepreneurial proclivities. But other segments of the populace who might want to move beyond the limits rulers set can easily be squelched, especially if jobs are at stake.

In 1988, the statue of Mao Zedong on the campus of Beijing University is dismantled to make way for a flower bed and greater economic reform.

© (a) Peggy Mitchell; (b) (c) (d) © Roy Gridley

(a)

(b)

(c)

(d)

The United States, the United Kingdom, and West Germany have developed corporate-consumer systems. The Soviet Union, East Germany, and China developed state-consumer systems. A corporate-consumer system's ability to survive, and a state-consumer system's ability to adapt into a corporate-consumer system, depends on their citizens' ability to become entrepreneurs, innovate, and place limits on government.

SUMMARY

Nation-states with traditions of entrepreneurship and technological innovation have more chance to offer their citizens satisfying personal environments than those without these traditions; to become corporate-consumer systems, they also need to support placing limits on government. Nation-states without traditions of entrepreneurship and technological innovation can be state-consumer systems, but they cannot easily spur entrepreneurship or technological innovation. Nation-states with traditions of both entrepreneurship and technological innovation which become state-consumer systems may find their innovation reduced. And nation-states with traditions of entrepreneurship but not of technological innovation may become state-consumer systems and spur a limited amount of technological innovation.

NOTES

1. Serfdom only began in 1581, when the tsar passed a law preventing the free movement of peasants on the land of *pomiestchiks,* new nobility created to compete with the boyars, who had become too independent to suit the tsars. The peasants, however, retained their civil rights. A 1648 law tied most peasants to the soil of their landlords. Peter the Great strengthened this law to make them the property of their owners, without civil rights. Catherine the Great, who ruled late in the eighteenth century when the Industrial Revolution was beginning in the West, allowed the nobility exceptional freedom to control their serfs.

2. "Progress of every sort is only made by the use of authority . . . and progress in agriculture more than anything else—the potato, for instance, that was

introduced among us by force." Leo Tolstoy, *Anna Kerenina* (New York: Norton 1970).

3. This helped spur innovation to appeal to customers on the home market who could choose among various domestic manufacturers. However, as the number of manufacturers declined, so did the competition. The experience with tariffs did not prepare American manufacturers to compete on world markets.

4. Russian inventors have far lower status than American inventors. Kulubin, who invented an automatic bicycle, a projected arch bridge, and a semaphoric telegraph, spent his time building ornamental clocks for the court of Catherine II. In 1763, Polzunov invented a steam engine, but he could stir no interest in it and died in poverty. Their inventions were simply not useful to their societies. Yablochokov's electric light did find a limited market to light the homes of wealthy urbanites until it was overshadowed by Edison's better invention. A society which lacks a large internal market, or which lags behind in basic technology, is likely to have use for few inventions.

5. Abel Aganbegyan, an economist at the Soviet Academy of Sciences, says there are more manual workers in the Soviet Union than there were thirty years ago. Trevor Fishlock, "Tale of a Tipsy Russian Takes on Deep Economic Meaning," *Daily Telegraph* (London), July 31, 1987. In 1990, government subsidies to industries surpassed $133 billion at the commercial exchange rate. Justin Burke, "Prices Take Hike in Soviet Capital," *Christian Science Monitor,* April 3, 1991.

6. *Pravda* reported that the Volga Pipe Mill invented a way to make high-quality, thin-walled steel pipe weighing half as much as its current pipe, using half as much steel and costing less to produce. When it began producing the pipe, output stayed the same, but its value dropped because it sold for less. Since plant wages depended on the value of output, wages dropped 15 percent; construction companies did not want to buy the pipe, because this would lower the value of their output—and thus their wages—as well. Robert Gillette, "Creaking Economy Needs More Than a Little Repair," *Kansas City Times,* November 26, 1987.

7. See Joseph S. Berliner, *The Innovation Decision in Soviet Industry* (Cambridge, Mass.: MIT Press, 1976); Peter Kneen, *Soviet Scientists and the State: An*

Examination of the Social and Political Aspects of Science in the USSR (Albany: State University of New York Press, 1984); Robert F. Miller, "The Role of the Communist Party in Soviet Research and Development," *Soviet Studies* 37, 1 (January 1985).

8. "So working hard is unprofitable," a worker told *Pravda*. "It is depressing to think this, especially now when the *perestroika* (Gorbachev's reconstruction) is underway," Steve Goldstein, "Gorbachev Efforts Stymied by Excess of Red Tape, Shortage of Incentives," *Kansas City Times,* January 26, 1987.

9. Lydia Petrovna, who made 100 rubles ($160) a month at a textile factory, joined nineteen other women in her factory to form a factory-sponsored cooperative. Using an imported Japanese knitting machine at home, she made seventy pairs of cold-weather pantyhose a month, for which the cooperative paid her 4.5 rubles each; they sold in the farmers' market for 25 rubles each, boosting her income to 280 rubles ($448) a month after taxes. She considered buying the machines and opening her own made-to-order business. Robert Gillette, "Creaking Economy." At the time of this article, three-thousand small cooperatives and several thousand family-owned shops had been established in the Soviet Union, from cafes to automobile repair shops to hair styling businesses. These establishments often give better service, but they charge as much as ten times more than state shops, so many people could not afford to use them. Within a year, their number had grown to nine-thousand, with ninety-thousand employees, most of them part-time. New laws passed in 1988 allowed the cooperatives to hire full-time employees laid off by state firms, and even permitted people to quit their jobs at state firms to start cooperatives. There were still limits, removed in 1992, on the amount of equipment such firms could own.

10. Mary Dejevsky, "Gorbachev Opens Door to Renting of Farmland," *The Times,* August 7, 1987. Some land in Siberia could be rented with lifetime leases. " 'But the Chinese still have their traditional society,' one man said. 'We destroyed our peasantry. We don't have farmers who care about the land anymore. They are employees. We have *unlearned* them how to work.' " Flora Lewis, "Important Crossroads in Soviet History," *Kansas City Star,* September 13, 1988.

Collective and state farms were urged to extend leases. Short-term leases and rules that supplies must be obtained through and produce sold to the collective or state farm lowered incentive to add improvements (for which no loans were available anyway) and reduced profits. However, the chairman of a model state farm shown frequently to visitors commented, regarding one of his model lessees: " 'Gusenkov doesn't go absent. He doesn't drink. If a man is drunk all day, he won't feed the cows.' Gusenkov's cows produce 60 percent more than those on the state farm, and his milk is cleaner. But cooling facilities are inadequate, and his milk gets dumped into large containers with the less sanitary milk from the state farm for transport to the city." Jonathan Steele, "The Lease Worst Option Down on the State Farm," *Manchester Guardian Weekly,* November 13, 1988.

11. At Pavlodar, a team set up in 1983 to produce beef cattle, costs declined markedly, production rose, and bonuses boosted wages to $850 (in U.S. dollars) a month. Under a scheme approved in 1987, city dwellers could rent or buy nearby plots of land to produce goods partly for collectives and partly to sell in the markets; there were already an estimated eight-hundred thousand such plots in 1987. Rupert Cornwell, "Gorbachev Sows Seeds of a Revolution in Agriculture," *The Independent* (London), August 11, 1987.

12. Mary Dejevsky, "Soviet Plan to Improve Harvests," *The Times,* August 14, 1987.

13. Boris Yeltsin, in support of policies to reconstruct the Soviet economy by eliminating waste and inefficiency, stated: "There are some people who don't support reconstruction—the ones who have been forced to work harder. The reconstruction may have chased them from their cozy, comfortable chairs, forced them to think faster, more creatively. If the guy is idle, if the guy is a bum, he's not going to be for reconstruction." "Seven Days in May," CBS News Special, June 24, 1987.

14. Members of the new cooperatives, like workers in state industries, paid a flat income tax rate of 13 percent. Local authorities can still tax at a flat rate, which they play a role in setting. But they can also introduce progressive income taxes, in which rates rise along with income; many local leaders face popular pressure to make rates progressive. Progressive tax rates which are too steep, of course, will discourage people from entering these businesses and increase the prices they charge consumers. Many local officials shut down cooperatives which become too successful. During the last year the Soviet Union existed (1991),

one-hundred twenty thousand entrepreneurs were arrested; many have still not been exonerated.

15. A 1991 poll found that 76 percent of respondents in Russia and 86 percent in the Ukraine favored continued state control of heavy industries, and majorities favored state control of banks, schools, utilities, health care, railroads, buses, and radio and television, though a bare majority favored the introduction of a free market economy. "Soviets Leery About Free Market, Poll Shows," *Kansas City Star,* July 28, 1991. Robert Shiller, Maxim Boycko, and Vladimir Korobov, "Popular Attitudes Toward Free Markets: The Soviet Union and the United States Compared," *American Economic Review,* 81, 3 (June 1991): 385–400, found that Moscow's citizens are as tolerant of income inequalities as Americans but are less likely than Americans to have friends who are businesspeople.

16. The 25-year, multibillion dollar joint venture negotiated between the central government and Chevron, with Kazakhstan's government entering, would develop the Tengiz oil fields near the Caspian Sea. The profits on the field, which could reach $100 billion, would be split fifty-fifty between Chevron and Kazakhstan's government. A related consortium of Chevron, RJR Nabisco, Eastman Kodak, Johnson & Johnson, Archer-Daniels-Midland, and a New York merchant base would open medical- and food-processing plants. Former Foreign Minister Eduard Shevardnadze, responding to the series of articles in the *Moscow News,* wrote that 2 billion rubles already invested wasted resources and the environment and had not made a profit, but "it has been dinned into our heads since childhood that capitalists do nothing but rob other states by buying up their wealth for peanuts . . . Should we continue to 'develop' natural resources in the same barbaric way, or should we turn for help to knowledgeable and skilled people equipped with advanced technology and experience in running business and making a profit?" Francis X. Clines, "Fears of Capitalist Exploitation Slow Soviet-Chevron Oil Venture," *New York Times,* August 16, 1991.

17. Justin Burke, "Soviet Mindset Seen as a Cause of Current Trials," *Christian Science Monitor,* March 24, 1993.

18. The annual 1988 CIA-Defense Intelligence Agency Report to the Joint Economic Committee of the United States Congress stated that the growth rate of the Soviet economy in 1987 had leveled off to zero,

as before Gorbachev took office. Sales of clothing and vegetables declined, while military spending increased 3 percent. *Kansas City Times*, April 25, 1988. That trend continues.

19. Trains are regularly robbed, with the assistance of rail employees. The government estimates that 2 billion rubles in bribes were paid in 1990, 1.2 billion to responsible officials, in connection with diverting state-made goods to stores selling stolen goods. Privileges once reserved for the party elite—cars, vacations, quality medical care, or imported luxury goods—are now sold to the highest bidder. Serge Schemann, "As Soviets Wait Tremulously, Ailing Economy Struggles On," *New York Times*, July 14, 1991.

20. " 'Of course we are skeptical,' said a fifty-year-old school teacher. 'Every twenty years there is a new policy. People will go along, herded like sheep. But these people'—the woman was standing on the sidewalk on Kalininsky Prospect, where scores of people were lined up to buy tins of crushed pineapple from a street vendor—'these people have lost their initiative. They've lost their dignity. They've had seventy years of this. They do not know anything else. They are not interested in *perestroika*. They want their pineapple.' " Charles T. Powers, "Most of Moscow Seems to be Falling Apart," *Kansas City Star*, May 22, 1988.

In a poll conducted by the *Moscow News* on the Trans-Siberian Express, 64 percent of respondents said *perestroika* had not affected their daily lives. Only 16 percent expressed enthusiasm for it, 13 percent opposed it, and 71 percent said they would wait and see. Only 26 percent endorsed the law providing cost-accounting and self-financing for Soviet factories, compared to 33 percent opposed and 41 percent expressing no opinion. An army officer attacked the reductions in military personnel. A woman complained: "I do not know what will become of me. Staff reductions have started at the Moldovan *Agroprom* where I work. The smart and well-connected will most probably retain their jobs. But I am just a bookkeeper: a single mother with a teenage daughter. Who will take care of me?" Christopher Walker, "Moscow Poll Shows Cool Public View of Reforms," *The Times*, January, 4, 1988.

In Leo Tolstoy's novel *Anna Karenina*, the wealthy nobleman Konstantin Dmitrievitch Levin decided to involve the peasants on his large estate in making decisions and sharing in profits. He discovered that his peasants did not wish to give up their security to take advantage of a plan designed to move them beyond the level of subsistence.

21. Amy Kaslow, "Republics Ill-Prepared for Solo Economies," *Christian Science Monitor*, September 5, 1991. Soviet industries were divided into 7,664 "product groups"; 77 percent of those groups were produced by a single plant. "Success Dressed as Failure," *The Economist*, December 5, 1992.

22. Tim Snyder, "Antitrust for USSR," *Christian Science Monitor*, October 2, 1991.

23. The amount of GNP dependent on trade ranges from 32 percent in the Ukraine and Kazakhstan to 76 percent in Turkmenistan (1988 figures). Jonathan Steele, "Fear and Folly in Moscow," *Manchester Guardian Weekly*, March 1, 1992. Oil-rich Turkmenistan has continued to sell its oil to Europe and the other republics in exchange for basic consumer goods, which are then sold in its state-run stores at low, heavily subsidized prices. It has allowed almost no economic or political reform, and its authoritarian government has kept social peace while neighboring republics engage in civil war.

24. He (Leonid Kravchuk) won 62 percent of the vote. RUKH's candidate, Vyacheslav Cernovil, received less than 25 percent in a six-candidate race. Eighty-three point seven percent of Ukrainians, 76.4 percent in the portions with the heaviest Russian population, voted for independence. Daniel Sneider, "Independent Ukraine May Seal Soviet Fate," *Christian Science Monitor*, December 3, 1991. In 1993, with polls showing 80 percent of Ukranians below the poverty line, Kravchuk was forced to make unpopular concessions to Russia to raise money. But his opponents were still in disarray.

25. Preparing for U.S. President Ronald Reagan's visit, a team of eight laborers was sent to the children's playground in the foreign compound. "At almost any time of day, a casual glance at the worksite reveals six of the workers sitting down or standing idle watching the two others work." A worker spent all day installing new linoleum on the floor of an elevator, reusing the old broken molding to tack it in place. "The Soviet Union is a land where shoddy workmanship and grudging service are the norm . . . Offering incentives, such as higher pay for better

work, is among the innovations being tried, but skeptics also must be persuaded that there will be something for them to purchase with their increased incomes. And even a desire to do the job right doesn't help much when parts and materials are ordered by central planners who don't necessarily send them when and where they are needed." Michael Putzel. "Glasnost Alone Won't Bring Soviet Reforms," *Kansas City Star,* May 25, 1988.

26. *Pravda* reported that during the relief operation for the 1988 Armenian earthquake, trained dogs, electronic listening devices, and specialists in using both were available to search for survivors under the rubble. However, they were in three separate departments, which did not arrange to coordinate their efforts. *Pravda* noted that a French team set up operations within minutes after its arrival. In contrast: "For every one of our workers, there are ten observers, 'who offer advice rather than clear the ruins.' " Paul Quinn-Judge, "Soviet Quake Intensifies Political Tremors," *Christian Science Monitor,* December 13, 1988.

27. The Industrial Revolution began in France in the 1820s and in Germany in the 1840s, but took off at a far more intense pace in the latter.

28. Unlike Britain, Germany's coal and iron ore resources were not accessible to one another or to urban centers by water. Germany had to develop railroads before it could begin to tap those resources.

29. The spread between these figures would be closer if a limited region of the Soviet Union with comparable growing conditions were compared.

30. The West German plant, with 7,165 workers and a capacity to produce 1,080 vehicles a day, produced to capacity; the Liverpool plant, with 10,476 workers and a capacity to produce 1,365 vehicles a day, produced fewer than 1,000 a day. In 1977, the West German plant was never closed; the Liverpool plant lost 2.5 million labor hours and 61,254 vehicles in 208 labor disputes. Stephen Fay, "Britain's Poverty: The Role of Union Power," *The Sunday Times,* March 3, 1978. During breaks, Belgian workers would tend to machines needing maintenance. During their breaks, Britons had tea; when machinery broke down, the entire assembly line closed while it was being fixed.

Investment per employee in West Germany in 1971 was roughly double that in Britain. Part of this

is due to discrepancies in exchange rates. But part comes from the sorts of facts discussed in the last paragraph. The high rate of unemployment, combined with new laws concerning such matters as union elections, has caused many British unions to agree to a reduction in such featherbedding practices.

31. Certain scientists and artists (a hundred or so) with talents the government did not wish to see go to the West were awarded special contracts paying them salaries up to 20,000 marks a month at a time when most workers earned less than that in a year.

32. The Soviet Union controlled East Germany's trade terms. A fourth of the USSR's imports of machinery and equipment came from East Germany. More than 50 percent of East Germany's hard coal, 35 to 50 percent of its coke, 60 percent of its wheat, 75 percent of its oil, and nearly all its natural gas came from the Soviet Union. Once free to do so, East Germany could acquire some of this cheaper elsewhere.

33. See Alan Walters, *Britain's Economic Renaissance: Margaret Thatcher's Reforms, 1979–1984* (Oxford: Oxford University Press, 1986); Allan Cochrane and James Anderson, eds., *Restructuring Britain: Politics in Transition* (London: Sage, 1989); Joel Krieger, *Reagan, Thatcher, and the Politics of Decline* (New York: Oxford University Press, 1986); William Keegan, *Mrs. Thatcher's Economic Experiment* (London: Allen Lane, 1984); Peter Jenkins, *Mrs. Thatcher's Revolution: The Ending of the Socialist Era* (London: Pan, 1987); and Peter Riddell, *The Thatcher Decade* (Oxford: Basil Blackwell, 1989).

34. At times, she settled strikes by laying off workers in unproductive plants and giving them generous severance pay.

35. In 1974, out of fifty-two thousand university graduates, only 15.7 percent went into industry. Even among the 4,000 who graduated in science-based subjects outside the university, only 40 percent went into industry. A 1974 report by the British Institute of Management on Business Graduates in Industry found that though 17 percent of business graduates were employed in production before going to business school, only 6 percent returned to production.

In another study, 1 percent of top industrial management in Britain came from Oxford and Cambridge; 60 percent of top management in the United States came from the Ivy League.

The polytechnics had seven thousand five hundred empty places in science, technology, and engineering. Anthony Bambridge, "Why Britain Can't Manage," *The Times*, November 30, 1975.

36. The Engineering and Technology Programme established in 1985 added five thousand new places for British students in advanced engineering and information-technology curricula. Twenty-five polytechnics and colleges created conversion courses for secondary school graduates without sufficient background for university engineering courses. The Education Act of 1986 provided employer representatives on the governing boards of some schools. The Industry Year campaign of 1986 placed Schools-Industry Liaison Officers in seven out of ten local education authorities in England and Wales. Proposals called for a national curriculum (later adopted to some extent) with emphasis on mathematics and science. Kenneth Baker, "The Challenge That Britain Can Meet," *The Times*, August 6, 1987. Mr. Baker, Secretary of State for Education and Science, referred to "the anti-industry culture which says that 'industry does you harm.' "

37. A 1990 survey of German university students reported that only 3 percent indicated an interest in manufacturing. Joel Kotkin, "They Order These Things Worse in Europe," *Manchester Guardian Weekly*, October 13, 1991.

38. Britain was trying to force the Chinese to allow the importation of opium it was raising in India.

39. Gilbert Rozman, ed., *The Modernization of China* (Macmillan Free Press: New York, 1981), p. 322.

40. Before 1920, income distribution in China was equalized by several factors. Tenants had quasi-rights to land; distribution of land was relatively equal in some places; and peasants could supplement their incomes with handicrafts or commerce. During the 1930s, peasants began losing land and handicrafts, and income grew unequal. Charles Robert Roll, Jr., *The Distribution of Rural Income in China: A Comparison of the 1930s and the 1950s* (New York: Garland, 1980).

41. Eighty percent of China's water consumption is for irrigation. In some northern watersheds, two-thirds of the runoff is already tapped, creating water shortages. Inefficient machinery uses large amounts of fuel as well.

42. China came to lead the world in the number of machine tools manufactured. Rozman, *Modernization of China,* p. 327.

43. Idem., p. 328. China generated 108 billion kilowatts of electricity in 1974, versus 7 billion in 1952; 35 billion cubic meters of natural gas, versus 0; and 63 million metric tons of petroleum, versus 0.4 million.

44. During the 1960s, China built a spectacular railroad link between Chengdu and Kunming, a third of which runs inside tunnels. During the 1980s, China extended rail service to link with the Soviet Union and other areas.

45. Idem., p. 327.

46. See Vivienne Shue, *The Reach of the State: Sketches of the Body Politic* (Stanford, Calif.: Stanford University Press, 1988).

47. See Andrew G. Walder, *Communist Neo-Traditionalism: Work and Authority in Chinese Industry* (Berkeley: University of California Press, 1986).

48. "Yuan a Debased Currency?" *The Economist,* April 24, 1993.

49. See "Keynesian Communism," *Financial World,* April 27, 1993.

50. In the first quarter of 1992, China had a trade surplus of $1.2 billion; in the first quarter of 1993, a deficit of $1.2 billion. "Yuan?" *The Economist,* April 24, 1993.

51. Sheila Telft, "State Firms Play Catch-Up in Rural China," *Christian Science Monitor,* December 1, 1992.

52. Kenneth Lieberthal. Public speech, University of Missouri-Kansas City, September 25, 1990.

53. See Robert E. Gamer, "Helping History Find Its Way: Liberalization in China," *Crossroads* (Jerusalem), 32 (Fall 1991): 54–67.

EXERCISES

Think about the book thus far:

1. Relate the discussion of capitalism, communism, and socialism in chapter 8 to this chapter.
2. Relate the discussion of the responsibility system in chapter 9 and of realignments in China in chapter 21 to this chapter.

KEY WORDS AND PHRASES

Define the following terms:

entrepreneur
innovation
mercantilism

THINKING IT THROUGH

Discuss the following questions:

1. What conditions are needed for a country to encourage technological innovations and share them with large portions of the populace?
2. Why is the United States more innovative than the CIS, and how does that help produce a higher standard of living?
3. What may make it difficult for the CIS to improve on innovation in the future?
4. How do East and West Germany, and the United Kingdom, compare on incentives to innovate?
5. What has held innovation back in the United Kingdom? Can it compete better now?
6. What holds innovation back in China?

chapter 32

PATRON-CLIENT SYSTEMS

A DEVELOPMENT MODEL

A political system giving high and rising percentages of its citizens satisfying personal environments may be viewed as experiencing political development. If the government and most families rely on the same economic institutions for jobs, goods, and services; if diverse segments of the populace are recruited into political institutions; and if people are socialized to believe in placing limits on the authority of public officials, it is easier for political development to occur. Interfamily and corporate-consumer systems have all three of these traits, and state-consumer systems have at least the first, while **patron-client systems have none of them. When productivity is lower than current levels of technological innovation will sustain, smaller economies and their supporting political institutions can be destroyed by larger ones. Interfamily and patron-client systems usually cannot achieve such productivity;** *state-consumer systems come closer.* **If an inter-family system becomes a raw materials supplier to** *interdependent corporations or* **a corporate-consumer system,** *or if productivity slows in a state-consumer system,* **it may transform into a patron-client system.** *If productivity slows in a corporate-consumer system, it may be pushed to the edges of corporate-interdependence, reducing limits on authority and recruitment into relevant political institutions, and hence the ability to sustain satisfying personal environments. But patron-client systems disengaging from corporate interdependence may move toward interfamily and corporate-consumer relationships; with limits placed on the authority of public officials, state-consumer systems may become corporate-consumer systems. That can improve their ability to support satisfying personal environments.*

We have looked at three corporate-consumer systems and three state-consumer systems. Now we will look at three patron-client systems. They have not been able to develop innovative technology or spread benefits widely to their citizens. Why not?

One of these systems—India—has some elements of a state-consumer system, since a high portion of its industrial output comes from government-run firms. As we just saw, state-consumer systems contain elements of patron-clientism as well. But India's economy has never been run entirely by the state, as were the economies in China and the Soviet Union. And, as we will see here, India's prin-

cipal patrons—who have extensive control over the economy—function outside the state as well (figure 32.1). They prevent India from acquiring another principal element of a state-consumer system: full employment at home and sale of consumer goods to all these employees.

INDIA

India has a history of both culture and government encouraging technological innovation. Sikhs, Marwaris, Parsis, Jains, Gujarati Vaisyas, Maratha, and other groups contain individuals who are highly at-

F*igure 32.1* Nonmanorial patron-clientism can leave many out of production, consumption, and decision making.

About 1500, Indian merchants entered the lucrative European textile trade. They commissioned village artisans to weave locally grown cotton and silk into fabrics in exchange for modest cash payments. The merchants then sold these fabrics to Europe, via Britain's East India Company, for large profits. They shared part of their profits with princes and invested part of their earnings by making loans to village Brahmins at high rates of interest to help them purchase seeds and other necessities.

During the same period, Spain started mining great quantities of gold and silver in Mexico and Peru. The British began supplying them slaves from West Africa (many left through the port at Lagos) to use in America. The Spanish paid the British in gold and silver. This gave the East India Company considerable bullion to use for purchasing Indian textiles. Since India imported very little, most merchants' profits remained in India. The East India Company, in turn, made high profits selling the cloth in Europe, and returned large quantities of unspent gold and silver to England. Under the policy of mercantilism, once this bullion reached England, it did not leave.

In 1757, the military forces of the East India Company defeated those of the Nawab of Bengal in the Battle of Plassey, and the Company took control of Bengal and revenue collection there. The export of textiles continued. But now the East India Company arbitrarily set the price that both artisans and merchants would receive—as little as a fifth of what it had been. Thus, the Company was obtaining the goods far more cheaply than before. And the artisans and Indian merchants were receiving less for their work.

That was only the beginning of England's capital accumulation. The East India Company also developed four new concepts so lucrative they would change the entire course of both India's and the United Kingdom's history and profoundly affect the ability of India's technology to benefit people's living standards: (1) the Company's "investment"; (2) India's "debt"; (3) tax farming; and (4) managing agencies.

tracted to technological innovation. India has the fifteenth largest industrial economy in the world and has the third largest number of technical and professional personnel. Yet it is considerably less successful than the systems we have discussed thus far at adapting technology to widely benefit living standards. Historically, the reasons for this have less to do with India's culture than with the cultures of several of the other nation-states we are examining.

India's traditional social system let people leave the village but gave them strong incentive to stay since they would be involved in grain distribution and other benefits. At the same time, it left little surplus money in the hands of either peasants or village leaders. Hence there was no internal market to stimulate technological advances.

1. The Company's Investment

From 1766 to 1768, India exported 6.3 million pounds sterling of merchandise, and imported 624,000 pounds sterling, giving the nation-state a very favorable balance of trade. Before the Battle of Plassey, those exports would have been valued two to four times higher, since merchants would not have sold them so cheaply.[1] Now they had a much smaller income and could keep none of it. The East India Company claimed that the difference between the value of exports and imports constituted its "investment." So, as chief revenue collector, the Company took enough gold and silver from Bengal banks and tax collections to make up the difference. From 1766 to 1768, that amounted to:

India's total exports	£6,311,250
India's total imports	–£ 624,375
The Company's "investment"	£5,686,875

This money, which would normally have enriched India's merchants and given them money to invest, was taken out of India and wiped out their current income. Since it drained gold and silver from India's banks, it heavily taxed their *past* earnings as well. Britain, wanting to maintain mercantilism at home, was concerned that its imports from India exceeded its exports to India; it solved this problem simply by taking enough money from Indian banks to make up the difference. The more Indians exported to Britain without, in turn, importing British goods, the more their savings would be taxed and sent to Britain.

India still had little internal market. Now its merchants—the class of people who would soon trigger Britain's Industrial Revolution—had no investment capital either.

2. India's Debt

The Company also claimed India owed it money for operating expenses, so it charged for supporting the British army. India paid for the conquest of Bengal and the rest of India, the wars to subdue Afghanistan, the Chinese War (to secure a Chinese market for Indian opium), the battle to subdue northeast Africa (which, ironically, resulted in Egyptian cotton competing with that of India), and another army composed of Indians.

3. The New Tax Farming System in the Countryside

The *zamindars* were formerly the Moghul emperors' official tax collectors. They simply collected a percentage of the crop from the villages, kept some for themselves, and passed the rest along to the emperor. Now they were asked to collect *cash*. To raise the money, villages had to switch from food crops to cash crops. If they could not pay, *zamindars* were permitted to seize land and keep it for themselves. Later, in southern India, the cash payment was expected to come directly from the peasant, or *ryotwari*; if he could not pay, he had to sell his land.

Thus, land ownership shifted from villages to individual owners. The owners had to switch to cash crops for export such as indigo, jute, opium, cotton, sugar cane, and tobacco, and later, rubber and tea, and (after the repeal of England's Corn Laws, opening up agricultural imports there) wheat and rice. The British heavily taxed the farmers' profits.

4. Managing Agencies

Employees of the East India Company became the exclusive agents to sell Indian commodities and loan capital to other businesses, which were now desperately short of it. They received lucrative fees for this. Indian merchants trying to function without the services of a managing agency found themselves without capital, commodities, or markets. They had to go to managing agencies to stay in business. So these agencies assured that all business was under control of the East India Company, which could pay low prices to producers.

Meanwhile, the Industrial Revolution was taking off in Britain—aided considerably by the capital obtained from India. The first two thrusts of that Revolution centered around building railroads and the Lancashire textile industry. Indian textiles were cheaper and of higher quality than those made in

Lancashire. In 1813, Lancashire mill owners persuaded Parliament to pass a high tariff effectively excluding Indian fabrics from the British market. Because Indian artisans were being paid less for their product than before, many no longer produced. Merchants were reaping profits from agriculture, and the Indian textile weavers largely went out of business. The Lancashire mill owners, whose Parliamentary representation was now strong enough to compete with the East India Company, pushed for the sale of English cloth on the Indian market. Soon India became a principal market for Lancashire textiles. Technological development within India fell even farther behind.[2]

England's railroad industry also looked to India as a market, with the cooperation of the East India Company, which exported British rails, locomotives, and rolling stock to India. Indian steel, cement, and chemical plants, and iron and coal mines, were created to help with railroad construction. Soon railroads criss-crossed the country, picking up agricultural products for the East India Company to export.

Now Indian technological innovation resumed. While India continued to export more than it imported, the gap between the two was closed, meaning less bullion flowed out.[3] India had switched from exporting manufactured goods to exporting agricultural products, many of which still went through British firms. Nevertheless, some modern industries were created with the aid of companies other than the East India Company. The managing agencies were deriving capital from many sources. After British armies defeated a rebellion called the Bengal Mutiny, these varying interests persuaded the Crown to take control of India from the East India Company.

At this point, then, technological advance had disrupted organized villages and removed many from the land. Weaving had declined, sending many people to cities without jobs. No new industries had appeared to hire them. And the new landowners were heavily taxed by the British.

Britain sought to increase productivity in export crops and expand India's imports from Britain by enlarging the internal market there. British public works projects developed irrigation and some mechanization of agriculture. The British government and private investors set up a few Indian industries to sell machinery to local farmers. This improved export agriculture and gave income to those who could purchase British machinery.

The British also let a few Indian merchants create managing agencies to invest in mechanized textile weaving to sell to the Indian market. The largest of these agencies, Tata and Birla, contributed heavily to the Congress party at its inception, pushing for the right to open more such industries. At first they were unsuccessful. But as the power of the Congress party grew, they received permission to invest even in firms that competed with local British firms. The opening of the Tata steel mill in 1907 was a major breakthrough. Indians were once again able to accumulate some capital.

When India won its independence in 1949, the colonial Government owned 557 firms, British managing agencies controlled 1,008 British and American firms, and Indian managing agencies controlled nearly 12,000 firms (9,000 of which were under the managing agencies of Tata, Dalmia Jain, and Birla) with three times the assets of the British firms.[4]

The new Congress party Government (calling on its socialist ideology) sought to move technological innovation away from export products and focus it on improving Indian living standards by creating government firms to supply basic commodities. It also sought to insure that foreigners could not dominate India's economy. As of the 1980s, public sector firms supplied nearly all of India's fuel, three-fourths of its steel, most of its nonferrous metals, and nearly half its fertilizer.[5] This is intended to let the government direct the economy toward socially useful projects. As the last three paragraphs of chapter 25 indicate, "luxury" consumer goods are not abundant in India. Thanks to these government policies, most of these goods purchased by Indians are produced in India by Indian-owned firms. Only 6 percent of investment comes from abroad. But these policies leave most capital in a few private hands. Occasionally, as in 1951 and 1971, the government tried to reduce the concentration of wealth in the hands of the managing agencies by limiting the number of firms they could control or outlawing them altogether. But the agencies found ways to circumvent these laws. The government has largely had to exert control over them through licensing, import and export restrictions, devaluing currency, price controls, tax incentives, and credit policies. These controls have not been effective for several reasons:

1. Bureaucrats managing public sector industries feel little need to perform since they need not make a profit. The government cannot easily close inefficient operations because their output is needed. Workers frequently strike for higher pay; because they are politically active in the Congress party, it is difficult to ignore this.

2. The government has experimented with licensing many kinds of industries, applying certain criteria to them in exchange for a license. These criteria often raise costs and reduce profits. Licensing both small and large industries created enormous bureaucratic complexity (including greater potential that officials would be bribed to ignore the regulations); when the government switched to licensing only large industries, managing agencies began investing in smaller industries. When the government licenses certain categories of industry, investments switch into other business categories. It is easy to get around regulations by hiding records and selling through the black market. By 1970, the licensing approach had largely been abandoned. Bribes can also be used to get around export and import restrictions.

3. The government tried devaluing the rupee, to make Indian products less expensive and hence more tempting to foreign buyers. The result was shortages of goods at home. Price controls have the same effect; producers stop making the goods that are subject to controlled prices. Tax breaks to businesses which invest profits in certain less profitable industries are often not enough to compensate for the resulting loss of profit.

4. While most banking remains in private hands, the government has a number of lending agencies, together with the fourteen banks which Prime Minister Indira Gandhi nationalized in 1969. They, too, are ineffective at directing the economy toward socially useful projects. They have little money to lend, since resources are strained by defense spending, grain price supports, and repaying international debts accrued while building government-sponsored industries. Government loans to agriculture are handled by *panchayat* leaders, who are almost universally large landowners.[6] And most loans to industry go to the largest managing agencies, which can juggle their assets to create their own priorities. The managing agencies control the capital; if they cannot make a lucrative investment within India, they prefer to invest abroad. Investments to produce goods sold to the poor are generally not lucrative.

5. Prime Minister P. V. Narasimha Rao, who came to power in the 1991 election, introduced a new round of radically different reforms. These reforms, which the International Monetary Fund suggested, were designed to encourage imports and investments by foreigners and thus provide competition and new capital. Except for in a few industries, Rao moved to abandon government licensing, cut defense spending, end many government subsidies to business, devalue the rupee and let it fluctuate on the international currency market, and let foreign investors control Indian businesses and invest in Indian pension funds. His Congress (I) party ruled with a minority in Parliament. He faced opposition from bureaucrats, military officers, subsidized businesses, big landowners, government factory workers, consumers confronted with higher prices on food[7] and imported consumer goods,

and labor unions at affected businesses—the principal constituents of the Congress and opposition parties. His reforms, too, are likely to attract investment only in the areas which assure substantial profit.

Government in India can do little to redistribute capital or assure that a wider range of people obtain jobs and consumer goods. On the surface, the "Green Revolution" seems the exception to that. Since 1970, India's principal planning focus has been on the Green Revolution, introducing new strains of hybrid wheat and rice to improve agricultural productivity. In 1954, India had practically no modernized small industries. By 1974, one-hundred twenty thousand of them turned out tube wells, irrigation equipment, diesel pumps, small farm implements, and other products needed to grow the new, high-yielding seeds. Each year more land is irrigated to supply the water these seeds need. Large private plants produce fertilizer and pesticides from petrochemicals. With no price controls, all these activities are very profitable. The industries hire new workers. The farmers, now more mechanized, can dispense with much of their hired labor and retain more profits. There is more money for discretionary spending. With high tariffs to protect them, new industries appeared to make shoes, textiles, tobacco products, and packaged foods. This, in turn, created more jobs.

The government gives these businesses many tax incentives. It also provides them with inexpensive iron and steel, railroad equipment, heavy machinery, electricity, chemicals, petroleum, and other minerals from government-operated mines, wells, and plants (low-priced goods which they neither want to produce themselves nor do without) and from subsidized imports; Prime Minister Rao vowed to cut many of those subsidies, but he found it hard to do so.[8] The government has borrowed from foreign and international lending agencies to pay for these expensive plants. Yet with inefficiencies and low selling prices, they produce little revenue. The tax incentives and widespread poverty leave the tax base weak. The government now owes more to foreign banks and agencies than it has in reserve, and the budget deficit grows larger each year. To repay these loans, the government must encourage an increase in exports. High production costs make it hard for the steel industry to compete with importers of foreign steel now that tariffs are lowering. Many other industries face this problem, too. And lowered tariffs have caused imports to rise, further increasing the trade deficit.[9]

By directly devaluing the rupee by 20 percent, and later making it convertible on international currency exchanges, Rao lowered its value for foreign purchases. The plants constructed with foreign loans and by multinational corporations welcomed by the new reforms must agree to use much foreign equipment.[10] Devaluation raises the cost of that equipment and necessitates further borrowing. It also diverts private capital from supplying the domestic market (which is the purpose of the program) into exports,[11] and shortages reappear. Export of crops reduces the domestic food supply.

The main goal of the Green Revolution is to feed India's people. The program has succeeded in markedly increasing India's grain production. But the costs (paying the growers and all these supporting industries) of the new grain are high; its wholesale price is too expensive for the average Indian peasant to purchase. Furthermore, few of India's forty-two thousand rice mills, or the wheat mills, are licensed by the government. This means they can charge whatever they can get. If grain is to be made affordable, its distribution must somehow be government-controlled. Government control is not popular with the Green Revolution farmers or industrialists who form the backbone of the Congress and opposition parties. In 1992, large farmers resorted to hoarding grain when the government tried to force them to sell a portion at below-market prices to create emergency food granaries; they supported a plan in which government purchases grain for more than market price and then sells it below market prices. This would cost the government a great deal and make it impossible to distribute much grain. The Green Revolution farmers also resist the government's attempts to end their subsidies. A few days

Jaipur, India. Delivering kerosene from the national oil company.

Bob Gamer

before the destruction of the Ayodhya mosque in 1992, half a million farmers marched on New Delhi to protest proposed cuts in fertilizer subsidies.

Smaller peasants cannot afford the costly irrigation equipment, water, hybrid seeds, fertilizers, pesticides, and other equipment the Green Revolution entails. They lack access to the low-interest loans and subsidies. They face inflation on other goods they must purchase.[12] And they are increasingly shut off from the part-time work once available on the now-mechanized larger farms. Many must sell their land to the larger landowners.

The larger landowners tend to purchase goods made by the modern industries. Landless peasants and artisans have largely relied on barter for their survival. There are, for example, still some 10 million handloom weavers in India. Their products cost more and are of poorer quality than those produced in factories. They must rely on bartering with people who cannot buy with money but do have grain; as small landowners sell out, their customer base is declining. These people faced 50 percent inflation of grain prices between 1965 and 1970, 350 percent between 1971 and 1974, and additional fluctuations since. With decontrol, and with the government importing some grain in 1992, concerns about prices rose again in the early 1990s.

Much of India's land and industry is in the hands of a small percentage of the populace. Since most Indians earn too little to purchase factory-made products, and those who can often prefer to buy imported consumer goods, the greatest profits can be obtained by producing for export or by producing grain (and the products needed to grow it) for the middle-class market. The biggest beneficiaries of Rao's reforms have been multinational companies such as Phillips, ITC, and Unilever, who have introduced their products to India's middle class. Newly eased restrictions allow them to take profits abroad.

Aside from producing agricultural equipment, India's industry finds it hard to innovate. In nineteenth-century Europe, during the Industrial Revolution, people left the land and found jobs in the cities. In India, there is little for them to do in the countryside. But there is little for them to do in the city, either.

The government cannot keep imports from exceeding exports. This makes it hard to accumulate investment capital for production, which would induce greater equality. Nor do India's products compete well enough abroad to raise extensive revenues. So growth cannot be easily sustained and spread to wider portions of the populace.

India has a long tradition of scientific inquiry and technological innovation. It contains many ethnic groups who are highly motivated to trade, save, develop sophisticated skills, and pursue entrepreneurial pursuits. Its lands are fertile, and it has many natural resources. Some estimate its land could yield three times as much food as it does.[13] Government leaders encourage the use of technology to improve living standards and devote considerable resources to that end. India has a free labor market and allows private investment in all types of economic activities. But investment capital flows out of the country and diverts land and income from poorer Indians, who constitute the majority of the populace. Most live at subsistence level. The minority who produce for the market are clients of larger patrons. The patrons resist investing in technological innovation or allowing money and production to spread.

PERU

Like India, Peru has a history of both culture and government encouraging technological innovation. It, too, is considerably less successful than the nation-states we have discussed thus far at adapting technology to benefit people's living standards.

Before the Spanish conquest, Chimu, Quechua, and Aymara civilizations developed advanced technology. The earliest communities grew along the mouths of streams running from the Andes Mountains to the Pacific Ocean. Families supported themselves with fishing and agriculture. Gradually they developed sophisticated irrigation far more extensive than today's networks. They built giant pyramids—initially of small clay bricks, but later of stones weighing many tons, requiring pulleys or other devices to move them, and cut so precisely they still withstand frequent earthquakes. Surplus crops stored by priests supported large cities. Nobles with retinues of soldiers, administrators, and miners fought bloody wars to consolidate large territories. Approximately forty years before the arrival of the Spanish, the Incas in Cuzco conquered the powerful Chimu Empire to the north and other territories to create the Inca Empire.

The villages organized around family leaders. They distributed fields to all villagers and kept grazing lands for community use. Villagers pooled their labor to help one another clear land, plant, and harvest, and also to build roads, bridges, and religious structures. They set aside land, which all able-bodied inhabitants worked, to support the aged, orphans, the sick, and the lame, and to maintain a granary for emergencies. The aged and those with disabilities, in turn, helped supervise irrigation water allotted to the community. Major irrigation works were kept up by urban workers.

The Incas required all villagers to work a certain number of days each year on fields set aside for the region's nobility or for the Inca. Food from these fields fed soldiers and townspeople. Able-bodied fathers with sons who could maintain fields at home were expected to serve in the army for a period of time. Administrators provided villages with improved metal plows to increase agricultural output. Corps of engineers linked roads and bridges maintained by villagers into a transportation network.[14] One highway ran two-thousand miles from Quito to what is now northern Argentina; portions of it are still in use. Another ran one-thousand five hundred miles along the coast from what is now northern Peru to northern Chile; during the 1920s it was incorporated into the Pan American Highway. Mountain mines, operated by full-time miners, produced gold and copper for temple gods, plows, jewelry, and weapons.

The cities contained plazas, water sources, parks, and elaborately embellished public buildings. Craftspeople produced gold ornaments and jewelry, while household goods of many kinds were mass produced for bartering in large markets. City dwellers sometimes may have helped rural relatives, such as soldiers returning from their tours of duty, move to the city. The positions of the ruling classes were hereditary, but merchants, artisans, soldiers, architects, engineers, administrators, and politicians, who constituted the bulk of the urban population, were socially mobile.

After the conquest, the Spanish destroyed these cities and looted them of gold objects. They built new towns on top of some of them and left others abandoned. Irrigation systems[15] and much of the road system fell into disuse. Mercury poisoning decimated the ranks of highland peasants forced to work the larger new gold mines. The rest were required to work the lands of the *encomiendas* for long hours, and later moved into the *reducciones*.[16] Village agriculture declined.

Encomendados and Church leaders dominated the new Spanish towns. They were almost completely isolated from outside commerce. The *encomiendas* produced much of what they used. The wealthiest homes were elaborate and largely finished by local artisans, who often built them atop preconquest foundations.[17] Lima, center of gold export, became one of the world's most elegant cities, with magnificent public buildings and homes for the wealthiest traders. Gold, not productive agriculture or manufacturing, paid for this prosperity.

Lima's nineteenth-century development affected provincial life in two important ways. Some *latifundia* brought large herds of sheep to the highlands to compete with peasant herds and graze on the only valley lands well-suited for growing food crops. So food production in the highlands declined even more. Along the coast, great wealth was made from guano, coastal plantations, and investments in Lima—but not from food production. Food imports grew. Inland, the *encomendados* were unable to adapt to the modern economy.

Development of the road system during the 1920s brought many highland peasants into Lima and immigrant merchants and factory goods out to towns. Many of those that moved into Lima remain on the fringes of the economy, without the supporting social structure of the village. The towns provide limited social mobility to some highland peasants and great wealth to some merchants; most town dwellers live at a level of bare subsistence.

The towns with the greatest wealth are those which developed mining, tourism, wool, coffee, and other export items. But even the wealthy families who stay in the towns invest their earnings outside Peru and spend personal income on trips to and goods from Lima and abroad. So the money does not produce technological innovation and a corresponding increase in consumer goods for more than a small percentage of the populace.

During the early 1980s, a drought decimated sugar and cotton output. Then, when these crops began to recover, the international market price of these commodities and of metals shot downward. Oil production, and its export price, were and are still uncertain. The export sector has changed little since the 1960s, with mining production (oil, copper, iron, and gold) and export agriculture (in sugar and cotton) stagnating. Because it is illegal, the country's primary export, cocaine, adds nothing to the formal balance of payments. Despite Peru's low exports, the urban middle-class demand for foreign foods and consumer goods creates steady pressure to import. High imports without correspondingly high exports put the balance of payments out of line and have used up Peru's capital reserves.

To reduce imports, the government increases import tariffs, which raises the prices of food and other goods. Government subsidies, and printing new currency to help consumers buy goods, raise prices even more. To encourage exports, the government devalues currency—raising the cost of imports still higher. This has become a perpetual cycle. Prices stay high, often doubling or tripling in the course of a year; in 1990, inflation reached 7,650 percent. Local investors convert their money into more stable U.S. dollars and invest abroad. Foreign investors seldom invest in domestic production of consumer goods to sell in this constantly inflating and uncertain market. They import their own equipment when investing in export ventures such as gold, copper, oil, sugar, or cotton. Uncertain weather and land ownership have made mining investments more popular than those in agriculture. To help with these ventures, the government took out extensive loans to build dams, roads, and other supporting facilities. These loans, too, stipulated that machinery and equipment be imported, further eroding the balance of payments. Due to inflation and mismanagement, the projects were often abandoned before completion, leaving them useless. Unstable exports and prices reduce government revenues and make it hard to repay these loans, which now consume over 40 percent of export earnings for debt service. Thus, more loans must be extended just to help repay the initial ones. This leaves Peru with little capital or skilled labor and few raw materials for improving the domestic economy.

People with extensive personal assets or involved with the most essential exports and imports can survive this. So can those who function largely outside the monetary economy. Others find themselves in a precarious situation. Innovation has done little to improve living standards.

The current emphasis is on oil drilling and opening jungle areas east of the mountains. The government is helping finance new roads, dams, and hydroelectric projects to accomplish this. These infrastructure expenses require the importation of equipment and products to build and maintain factories and plants; they also require borrowed international capital. Two of the greatest sources of wealth in these areas are panning for gold and operating agricultural plantations worked by hired highland peasant laborers. Some of the recovered gold will undoubtedly be smuggled out of the country. The government will need to recover extensive tax revenues to repay its costs. Food production and employment are unlikely to benefit from these industries; nor are new consumer goods.

Since 1532, Peru has not used technological advances to exploit resources for a home market. Even the new businesses in Lima at the turn of this century, which produced goods for the home market, relied (except for the modern textile factories) primarily on artisan labor, rather than on new technologies.[18]

Peru attracted few investors. Investors were rewarded, but the most lucrative investments involved supplying a foreign market. Those exports were not innovative manufactures; they were commodities and raw materials. Mechanized agriculture was only introduced to raise export crops. Technology was later imported to produce some consumer goods for domestic consumption; few machines and tools for industry are produced. Peru increasingly exports its extensive supply of raw materials, rather than using them for internal consumption.

Peru's political system provides little control over this process. Since 1532, government leaders have been strongly interested in exports. Military and civilian governments alike consistently promoted the export of gold, guano, sugar, cotton, wool, copper, and oil. This focus on exports has been possible because of Peru's long history of weak constitutional guarantees and its social and economic domination by small numbers of newly arrived *criollos,* long-established *mestizos,* and nineteenth-century immigrants from other parts of Europe, all of whom benefit from exports. Lima's long political and economic domination, and the exclusion of highland peasants from politics, add to the problem. In colonial Peru, the departments were allowed some autonomy over their own affairs as long as the gold flowed out; there was no question that the regions might interrupt, or benefit substantially, from that outflow. This is still the case.

Many in rural areas are left with insufficient land to support themselves. Innovators and investors in the cities create few jobs and consumer goods because it is not profitable to use their raw materials and capital to do so, and they are free to do what they like with their money and energy. This leaves large numbers of urban people without sufficient jobs or income. As a result, much of the population does not benefit from innovation.

To sum up, then, Peru has innovators who are free to pursue various projects, especially if they pertain to the export sector. But only small percentages of the populace can afford to buy more than occasionally from the modern sector. The government cannot keep imports from exceeding exports. It is hard to accumulate enough investment capital for production—through taxes, incentives to private investors, or even by redistributing land in land reform—to benefit wide portions of the populace. Nor do Peru's products compete well enough abroad to raise extensive revenues. Profits from gold and cocaine are hard to tax. So growth cannot be easily sustained and spread to wider segments of Peru's populace.

Peru, like India, has not been able to make optimal use of technological innovation or to improve living standards beyond a limited circle of people. Peru has less of a sustained tradition of scientific inquiry and technological innovation than India. It does contain immigrant groups highly motivated to trade, save, develop sophisticated skills, and pursue entrepreneurial pursuits. Its lands are fertile, and it has abundant natural resources. Many of its government leaders are committed to improved living standards, a free labor market, and allowing private investment in all types of economic activities. However, much of that investment leaves the country. Investment that enters seldom involves much labor or production for domestic consumption. Peru has tried reforms to broaden land ownership; as we saw in part 3, that goal was not achieved. Some families in Lima, and in each region, have accumulated wealth; they wield great influence in commerce, bureaucracy, and politics.

NIGERIA

With some notable exceptions (such as the advanced skills of bronze casting in the city of Benin), western Africa did not experience innovation in its earlier history to the extent of either India or Peru. Villagers did support themselves, and administrators, warriors, nobility, and merchants of capitol cities engaged in prolific agriculture and trade. Muslim scholars, traders, and administrators introduced commerce and learning from the Arab world. Artisans of all kinds produced fine cloth, household utensils, alcoholic beverages, buildings, and other goods and necessities. Most communities distributed communal lands to villagers. As a result of warfare, some became slaves.

Unlike the Spanish in Peru, the British did not immediately destroy these villages, cities, and social relationships in West Africa. Instead, they worked with existing elites to develop new forms of trade beneficial to Britain. As we saw earlier in the chapter, indigo and slaves from West Africa were part of Britain's East India Company textile trade in India. After Britain annexed Lagos in 1861, it gained control of all the firms (British and French) trading on the Niger River and gave the trade and administration of the region to the Royal Niger Company. In 1900, the British Government revoked that company's charter and took charge of administration and government (using local elites whenever possible to carry out its commands). They built roads and bridges and promoted the export of palm oil, cocoa, cotton, and peanuts. Marketing boards, which controlled the exportation of all these commodities, allowed urban elites and foreign investors to keep the large difference between the price paid the farmer and the amount received when the goods were sold to foreign firms. The Unilever Company sent its own ships to pick up palm oil for its margarine business. It filled the ships on the journey to Nigeria with Unilever products and soon became the country's largest importer. Then it began setting up its own plants in Nigeria. By the late 1960s, it was producing or assembling beer, trucks, bicycles, earthmoving equipment, civil engineering machinery, air conditioning, other electrical goods and office equipment, printed textiles, cotton yarn, sugar, cement, vehicle batteries, cigarettes, fiberboard packaging, foam rubber, radios, reconstituted milk, beds and mattresses, ice cream, meat products, sewing thread, plastic products, timber, plywood, and furniture. As with many other foreign investments, local partners allow these companies to call themselves Nigerian-owned. That allows a few politically well-connected Nigerians to reap rewards from imported technology.

In 1971, Nigeria passed its first patent law, presumably intended to encourage Nigerian invention. Between 1971 and 1984, 6,170 patents were issued; only 1.1 percent of these were owned by Nigerians, while 85 percent were owned (nearly all by corporations) in advanced industrial nations.[19] Seventy percent of these patents were for products not being produced in Nigeria, and many had already been patented elsewhere; the patents were taken out to prevent Nigerians from producing the products. Licensing agreements permitting Nigerian firms to use or produce equipment patented by foreign firms almost invariably restrict the products the Nigerian firms may export and import and restrict these firms' right to conduct research and development of new products. Nigeria's Federal Institute of Industrial Research, and numerous university laboratories, are limited to doing research on raw materials. They have no way to commercialize their inventions. This places a tight and effective lid on innovation.

Nigerians have the ability to produce technology. During the Civil War, when Ibos broke away to form Biafra, they were blockaded and the multinationals went home. Biafran entrepreneurs began to produce gin and brandy, soap, pharmaceuticals, and salt. They devised a cassava-processing technology still used in large-scale production. Using large water tanks, they distilled crude oil into usable fuels, machine-tooled replacement parts for equipment, and created armored vehicles, guns, land mines, aerial bombs, rockets, grenades, and even a tree-mounted shrapnel device capable of destroying a company of soldiers.

In recent years, Japanese entrepreneurs copied a Nigerian cassava-pounding machine and sold it back to Nigerians, putting a Nigerian manufacturer out of business.[20] Most current development centers around oil production, using technology entirely produced abroad. Investment in other sectors, many of which are state-owned enterprises, has lagged or has been diverted for personal spending by corrupt politicians. The state enterprises utilize a small percentage of their productive capacity; some influential people get free or ridiculously cheap fertilizer, cement, paper, gasoline, and plane tickets from them, while others experience water tap and power cutoffs, delays in garbage pickups and airline and railroad schedules, and dead telephone lines. While Nigeria clearly has the capacity to innovate, its ability to do so on its own is severely restricted. Permission is needed from abroad to do research and use patents. Much of the money from oil has been diverted into the hands of politically influential people who use it for their families' lavish consumption or for investment abroad. Nigeria relies on investments foreign firms are willing to make. Those investments often result in products consumed outside Nigeria or by only a small portion of the Nigerian populace.

Except for fine new highways between major coastal and Hausa cities, Nigeria's road network is primitive. Agricultural regions share little in modernization or prosperity. During the late 1970s and early 1980s, agricultural export production declined markedly (except for palm nuts, which grow on trees that need little tending). Unlike Peru's peasants, who migrate to cities to stay, Nigerian villagers who move to cities tend to retain social ties to their own villages and may return there. They seldom prosper in the city, or return with wealth; they go back when economic downturn leaves them unemployed and homeless.

Some town dwellers and smaller farmers produce surplus food and products for export. Most do not. Urban elites, mostly profiting from the oil production developed by foreign drillers in association with Nigerian politicians and administrators, demand foreign imports. Frequent shifts in world oil prices keep the balance of payments highly unstable.

To correct these problems, Nigeria has been under constant pressure from the International Monetary Fund to reduce government spending, devalue its currency, and cut imports. When it did so in 1986, many industries failed. Because of still-unpaid debts, the country could not obtain trade credits. An end of government subsidies raised the price of gasoline. Many businesses relied on foreign technology and parts, now markedly more expensive. Dismissals of many government workers, and inflation (at 50 percent in 1989), hampered people's ability to purchase. New rules allowing foreign investors 100 percent ownership of firms in many sectors of the economy did bring new capital to oil and oil-related industries. But in twenty years, known reserves will be gone; and little oil income stays in the country for development or debt repayment. Outside those sectors, political and economic uncertainty keep investors and capital away.

The 1987 dismantling of the corrupt marketing boards considerably raised the prices that producers, who now can sell directly to foreign customers, receive and spurred production of rubber and cocoa. Inflation and lowered world cocoa prices, however, reduced some of the value of this new income, which largely goes to big producers.

As in Peru, people in Nigeria who have extensive personal assets or government connections can survive these difficulties, along with those who function outside the monetary economy. Others find their living standards deteriorating. Innovation has spurred some export sectors but has done little to improve living standards at home. Political and military leaders are a part of the process which inhibits technological development that would benefit the home market, and keeps imports exceeding exports. More Nigerians than Peruvians have land to support themselves; but beyond providing minimal caloric intake, that support is often meager. The economy remains in the hands of a few patrons who hire small portions of the populace to help them with their investments. Others largely function outside politics and the formal economy.

CONCLUSION

The United Nations Development Program estimates that the world's billion richest people have one hundred fifty times the income of the billion poorest.[21]

There is considerable variation among the nine systems in the extent to which citizens benefit from improved living standards brought about through technological progress. In the United States, the CIS, the United Kingdom, East and West Germany, and China, living standards have improved for most segments of the population. The middle classes in India, Peru, and Nigeria have also experienced improvements; other segments of the population, to the contrary, often have found their standard of living stagnating or even deteriorating.

Historically rooted differences in innovation, availability of capital, industrial organization, and control over labor and marketing help account for some of this variation. Nation-states which cannot use capital to create jobs for those displaced from more traditional occupations experience economic deterioration. Early stages of technological development often replace labor-intensive production techniques. Especially if capital is limited or controlled from abroad, industries may be tempted to expand production by producing goods for the few newly enriched by the earlier spurt of innovation, or by selling to markets abroad. The United States, the United Kingdom, and West Germany were able to move beyond this because they (for differing reasons) had access to large amounts of investment capital, were quickly able to include high percentages of the populace in modern production (creating a home market with income to spend), and provided government assistance to build the roads, canals, railway networks, and other infrastructure needed to support new ventures. In contrast, India, Peru, and Nigeria had little capital or control over the capital that was available, could involve few people in modern production, and had few tax revenues to create infrastructure.

Communist systems have tried to harness technological innovation to improve living standards by giving the government control over both investment capital and production. That may help stimulate or protect some jobs but also slows the technological innovation which can improve living standards. Government control of capital and production let the Soviet Union, East Germany, and China draw many people into modern production and create investment capital. At the same time, it inhibited innovation and gave great opportunity for official corruption. This was a particularly debilitating problem in the Soviet Union, where innovation had always been restricted. In all three systems, it meant living standards could improve for high percentages of people, but that improvement would seldom benefit from the latest technology.

The Indian government has sought to control extensive capital and production while doing little to restrict private use of either capital or influence. Since neither capital nor influence is widespread, this has not helped widen benefits from technological advance.

India, Peru, and Nigeria place few restrictions on private use of capital. Much of that capital falls into a few hands, which do not use it to develop modern technology or an internal market in their countries. Community life, land ownership, and access to political institutions decline. For most Indians, Peruvians, and Nigerians, living standards have not risen as technology improves. Among the nine systems we have studied, the most successful in spreading the benefits of technology widely among the populace are those with both a free market and high percentages of citizens with access to both political and economic institutions.

SUMMARY

Patron-client systems may have more entrenched traditions of entrepreneurship and technological innovation than some state-consumer systems. However, even systems with a tradition of entrepreneurship and technological innovation may become patron-client systems if they heavily export raw materials or manufactured goods, under the control of investors who take capital abroad, before they become industrialized. It is hard to pry loose the grip these patrons have on capital and innovation; that grip makes it hard for wide portions of the populace to develop satisfying personal environments.

NOTES

1. So the exports would have been worth 12 to 24 million pounds. Anupam Sen, *The State, Industrialization, and Class Formations in India* (London: Routledge & Kegan Paul, 1982), p. 52.

2. During the prior century, these kinds of pressures on American producers provided part of the impetus for the American Revolution.

3. Under normal trade circumstances, a country could accumulate more gold and silver bullion if the value of its exports exceeded that of its imports. But the Company's "investment" concept, just discussed, reverses this logic; less bullion leaves the country if imports increase and exports decline.

4. Sen, *The State*. The British and American firms, which were generally larger, produced about 25 percent of total output. Half of this was made up of export items such as jute, tea, mica, manganese, and textiles. The Indian firms, too, predominantly specialized in exports.

5. Lincoln Kaye, "India's Dinosaur Legacy," *Far Eastern Economic Review* 139, 2 (January 14, 1988): 56.

6. Some targeted loans from the short-lived programs of that era did produce beneficial results for the poor. One study of thirty-four of those programs found that improvements made through loans and other assistance they rendered raised incomes of beneficiary families by over $100 (in U.S. dollars) a year. Lloyd I. Rudolph and Susanne Hoeber Rudolph, *In Pursuit of Lakshmi: The Political Economy of the Indian State* (Chicago: University of Chicago Press, 1987), p. 328.

7. The price of fertilizer was up 40 percent. Sheila Tefft, "India's Premier Launches Radical Economic Reforms," *Christian Science Monitor,* August 1, 1991. Lowered subsidies will raise the costs of other aspects of production.

8. Rao sought to "rehabilitate" or close the 58 (out of 253, 131 of which are profitable) government enterprises designated as "sick" by using additional government subsidies. Trade unions proved reluctant to negotiate about privatizing (or, more politically correct, to "disinvest" in) plants. Little has been done to restructure bad loans from state-owned commercial banks to state-owned industries. The first sale of public firms was limited to 10 percent of the equity in thirty-one profitable firms, and sales were made only to mutual funds held in government-owned banks.

9. Petroleum, fertilizer, defense equipment, drugs, and raw materials are among the more expensive imports, which are rising each year. The 1992 trade deficit was over $3 billion—more than twice that of 1991. R. Krishnan, "How Long to Wait for the Reform Gains," *The Hindu,* November 29, 1992. The 1992 federal budget deficit was $1.7 billion.

10. To further encourage these imports, import tariffs on capital goods were placed at a maximum of 35 percent of their cost and on general merchandise at 85 percent—down from previous tariff maximums of 55 and 110 percent.

11. Rao's program began during the collapse of one of India's chief customers, the Soviet Union. Grain production (partly due to poor rainfall), industrial production, and gross domestic product also declined. That reduced exports.

12. Inflation rose from 6 percent a year in 1989 to 14 percent in 1991, but declined to 8 percent in 1992. Lower import tariffs reduced prices, but devaluation of the rupee made imported goods almost as expensive as before.

13. Kevin Rafferty, "Economic Survey," *The Far East and Australasia 1980–81* (London: Europa Publications, 1980), p. 429.

14. These roads were unpaved and lined with stone along the sides. They were about sixteen feet wide in the mountains and twenty-four feet wide along the coast. Local villagers collected tolls for the portions of the roads they maintained.

15. The irrigation system was revived along the coast during the nineteenth century, but to support sugar, cotton, and other export crops.

16. This method of moving villages into a new, controllable location had been used by Inca, Chimu, and previous empires to deal with rebellious villages, but never in this wholesale manner.

17. Many Peruvian town buildings even today have lower walls built before the Spanish conquest. They are characterized by very straight cuts and tight fits which have survived the many earthquakes endemic to the region. In contrast, the more recent stonework is more crudely hewn.

18. New immigrants set up factories to manufacture hats, cottonseed oil, soap, cigarettes, matches, shoes, lumber, spaghetti, leather, furniture, soft drinks, wine, liquor, beer, and other items. See Rosemary Thorp and Geoffrey Bertram, *Peru 1890–1977: Growth and Policy in an Open Economy* (London: Macmillan, 1978).

19. Owen T. Adikibi, "The Multinational Corporation and Monopoly Patents in Nigeria," *World Development* 16 (April 1988): 513.

20. Scott Tiffin, "Technological Innovation and Technical Entrepreneurship for the Development of a Nigerian Agricultural Machinery Industry," *World Development* 15, 3 (March 1987).

21. *United Nations Human Development Report*, 1992.

EXERCISES

Think about the book thus far:

Relate the discussion of India, Nigeria, and Peru in chapter 21 to this chapter.

Discuss the following questions:

India

1. Explain how each of the following entities and events took capital out of India.
   a. the Company's "investment"
   b. India's debt
   c. the new tax farming system
   d. managing agencies
   e. Lancashire mills
   f. English steel mills and railways

2. Why have each of the following policies failed to reduce the concentration of wealth or to spur production in India?
   a. licensing
   b. devaluing currency
   c. price controls
   d. tax incentives
   e. credit policies
   f. free trade

3. Why have the following events spurred production but failed to substantially reduce the concentration of wealth in India?
   a. the Green Revolution
   b. government subsidies to business

Peru

4. Why do each of the following fail to spur technological innovation or more widespread consumption in Peru?

   a. *encomiendas*
   b. mining
   c. sheep
   d. coffee or cotton
   e. cocaine
   f. import tariffs
   g. foreign investment
   h. government loans for roads and dams

5. Why is Peru unsuccessful at maintaining a policy of mercantilism?

Nigeria

6. Why do each of the following fail to reduce the concentration of wealth or to spur innovation in Nigeria?

   a. marketing boards
   b. dismantling of marketing boards
   c. patent laws
   d. petroleum
   e. state-owned enterprises

7. In Nigeria, foreigners own many businesses; in India, they do not. Does that make a difference in the ability of government to distribute benefits widely?

THINKING IT THROUGH

Briefly relate the **boldface** statements in "A Development Model" at the beginning of this chapter to the following words and phrases. How does patron-clientism affect each of them?

labor   internal markets
capital   free competition
patents

Now, ask yourself:

1. How might exports and imports hamper development? How might they assist it?

2. Why is India short on capital for generating technological innovation?

3. Why have higher percentages of Chinese than of Indians benefitted from innovation?

4. Why do India, Peru, and Nigeria lag behind the others in benefitting their citizens through technological innovation?

chapter 33

TRANSFORMING SYSTEMS

A DEVELOPMENT MODEL

A political system giving high and rising percentages of its citizens satisfying personal environments may be viewed as experiencing political development. If the government and most families rely on the same economic institutions for jobs, goods, and services; if diverse segments of the populace are recruited into political institutions; and if people are socialized to believe in placing limits on the authority of public officials, it is easier for political development to occur. Interfamily and corporate-consumer systems have all three of these traits, and state-consumer systems have at least the first, while patron-client systems have none of them. **When productivity is lower than current levels of technological innovation will sustain, smaller economies and their supporting political institutions can be destroyed by larger ones.** *Interfamily and patron-client systems usually cannot achieve such productivity; state-consumer systems come closer. If an interfamily system becomes a raw materials supplier to interdependent corporations or a corporate-consumer system, or* **if productivity slows in a state-consumer system, it may transform into a patron-client system. If productivity slows in a corporate-consumer system, it may be pushed to the edges of corporate-interdependence, reducing limits on authority and recruitment into relevant political institutions, and hence the ability to sustain satisfying personal environments. But patron-client systems disengaging from corporate interdependence may move toward interfamily and corporate-consumer relationships; with limits placed on the authority of public officials, state-consumer systems may become corporate-consumer systems. That can improve their ability to support satisfying personal environments.**

Ultimately, in any system, providing a satisfying personal environment for increasing percentages of the populace involves maintaining high productivity, jobs, and consumption. If these are not maintained, the system is vulnerable to transformation.

PRODUCTIVITY, JOBS, AND CONSUMPTION

Productivity is the extent to which a producer (a person who fosters and prepares animals, vegetables, or minerals for human consumption) satisfies the wants and needs of consumers (those who use the goods produced). Sometimes the term *producers* is applied to people who deliver services unrelated to the cultivation of agricultural products and the manufacture of goods—services such as cleaning house or waiting on retail customers. Here, we are talking only about producing agricultural products, other raw materials, and manufactured articles when we speak of producers or productivity.

Nation-states with corporate-consumer systems are prosperous only when both their production and consumption are high. When goods are imported rather than produced, less money remains to circulate within the nation-state; it must be sent abroad to pay (directly or indirectly)[1] those who produced the goods. For a time, people can live well by importing and consuming goods. But unless goods are also produced for export, the nation-state will soon be spending more abroad than it is taking in—the balance of payments will be unfavorable—and the nation-state will eventually have to either borrow heavily from abroad or reduce its imports. The money borrowed from abroad must be paid back with interest, and it can be withdrawn at will.

Internal consumption can remain high only if many people are employed at high-paying jobs. When many citizens earn good livings, they can buy goods or provide tax revenues to government so it can buy goods; the money to pay these workers must derive from producing goods. People need basic goods; they cannot survive on a strictly service economy. Government can survive for a time by deficit spending, or spending money it has not yet received. Eventually it must raise that money by increasing taxes or by promoting productivity at home so as to widen the tax base. Otherwise, it will cease to be a corporate-consumer system with high employment and consumption.

At the same time, corporate-consumer systems increasingly shift jobs to patron-client systems to keep labor costs down. They try to replace the lost jobs at home with jobs which do not produce goods, but help package, distribute, and sell them. The result is lowered productivity. Or workers produce goods such as housing, offices, or weapons, which will never be consumed or paid for.

Because they are subject to constant recession and inflation, and banks during the 1970s were seeking places to invest oil money, many patron-client systems borrowed extensively from banks and international lending agencies. Their low and fluctuating productivity, and the limited taxing abilities of their governments, make it difficult for them to pay this money back.

Some North Atlantic systems, facing trade imbalances as they transform into service economies, have had to seek money from outside investors. These investors have generally been patrons from patron-client systems, banks operating in smaller nation-states, and individuals from one nation-state

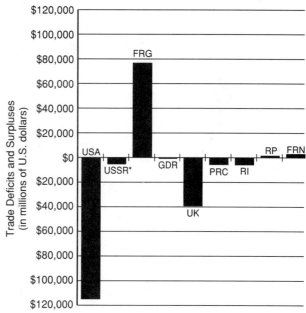

Figure 33.1 Trade deficits and surpluses in millions of United States dollars, not including services.

These figures are the U.S. dollar value of the annual exports of each country, minus the U.S. dollar value of their imports. 1989 figures. Europa World Yearbook 1991.

*Based on .58 rubles to the dollar.

with an advanced economy (such as Japan or West Germany) investing in another. Figure 33.1 shows trade balances for the nine nation-states.

As governments of both corporate-consumer and patron-client systems borrow, they further reduce their ability to control the export of jobs and capital while raising productivity. Furthermore, to do this they depend on a healthy system of international banking. As banks lend more money to insolvent patron-client systems to help them pay back former loans—pushing them further into insolvency—the economic pressure on the governments of the corporate-consumer systems becomes even greater; the banks ask the technologically advanced economies for money to prevent the patron-client systems from defaulting on the loans. Yet the depositors they protect are patrons in the patron-client systems.

F*igure 33.2* Government indebtedness to foreign leading institutions, in billions of United States dollars.

These figures are the amount of money the government of each country owes to individuals, institutions, and other governments, in U.S. dollars. 1989 figures. Europa World Yearbook 1990; *UK, GDR, PRC, RI, FRN from* CIA, The World Factbook 1990.

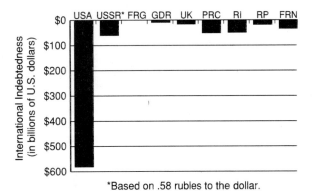

*Based on .58 rubles to the dollar.

By 1987, the international debt (see figure 33.2) of the sixty-two developing countries had risen to over a trillion dollars; yet their incomes were decreasing because their governments are not in a position to adequately tax patrons, commodity prices set from abroad are low, and imports constantly exceed exports. The international development banks, in response, increased their lending by 50 percent and committed commercial banks to making $20 billion in loans over three years. The debt kept climbing. In the meantime, the total public debt of the United States government (to all individuals and institutions) approached $3 trillion; its trade deficit also widened. Between 1981 and 1983, United States exports to Latin America dropped from $41.9 billion to $25.3 billion as the debt crisis forced Latin-American countries to cut back on imports.

In 1985, incoming Peruvian president Alan Garcia introduced a major challenge to the system when he announced that Peru would not pay more than 10 percent of its total income to lending institutions. That is considerably less than it owes each year on its $21 billion in loans; at the time Garcia was elected, Peru was already $425 million behind on

interest payments and its annual interest and principal ($3.7 billion) exceeded its annual export earnings ($3.1 billion). The government owed this money for many uncompleted projects—dams and nuclear plants that do not produce electricity, hospitals that cannot operate because they do not have electricity, refineries that are not functioning. The income from those that do function often never reaches the hands of government.

Soon after, Bolivia announced it would not repay its loans. Brazil suspended interest payments on half its $112 billion debt and only agreed to resume payments after receiving $3.4 billion (in U.S. dollars) refinancing. Nigeria (with $20 billion in loans, growing to $35 billion by 1993) followed suit. In 1987, Citicorp of New York, the largest bank in the United States, set another precedent by setting aside $3 billion to cover anticipated defaults on its $14.7 billion loans to Third World nation-states. About half of its deposits belonged to Latin Americans. Chase Manhattan, BankAmerica, and other banks soon followed this lead.

By 1986, deposits made in U.S. banks by Latin American individuals totalled $120 billion, and loans made to Latin American countries amounted to $83 billion. So the banks owed their Latin American depositors more than the Latin American governments owed them. Ironically, much of this deposit money was acquired by patrons who diverted it from loans made to their governments and then deposited it in America to escape taxes to the very governments which must repay those loans. The banks made a good profit on the transactions, but only so long as the depositors kept their money in the bank and the countries paid back the loans. The prosperity of the banks, and the depositors, depended heavily on Latin Americans.

The same banks made loans for real estate speculation and buyouts of American firms subsequently seeking bankruptcy; this resulted in substantial losses. The United States government borrows extensively to give additional loans to foreign governments to repay the banks and to itself repay depositors in American savings institutions. But little of this money is producing goods for consumption. High employment and consumption requires investment to produce goods for consumption; productivity requires capital and markets. These loan activities divert money away from investment and consumption.

PRODUCTIVITY, CAPITAL, AND SYSTEM SURVIVAL

If you follow a highway under construction in China over many miles, you may see thousands of workers carefully laying a stone base between gutterlike edgings; in the same stretch, you may see little heavy equipment. The stone is crushed and tossed into the bed by hand; banks and walls are carefully cut and laid in piece-by-piece.

If you watch a highway under construction in the United Kingdom, you will find, as in the United States, almost as many pieces of heavy equipment as there are workers. Increasing amounts of the machinery is imported as domestic factories close. Wages, for those who work, are much higher than in China. If these road workers' productivity is also high, and if the state has enough income to pay them and pay for the heavy equipment, the British government can build the road without borrowing. The workers' high wages help them buy expensive goods and services; if those goods are domestically produced, their purchases will create jobs for their fellow citizens. That allows the corporate-consumer system to continue. But if the heavy use of imported machines puts fellow citizens out of work and causes the U.K. to owe money abroad, it jeopardizes the continuance of a corporate-consumer system.

The Chinese state-consumer system may work its laborers harder and pay them less; if it can keep high percentages of the populace producing and consuming, it can continue as a state-consumer system. Both state-consumer and corporate-consumer systems must provide employment for much of their population if they are to continue. If employment reverts back to subsistence agriculture, they will be transformed into an interfamily system. If the economy returns to supplying raw materials for export, using few laborers, they may become a patron-client system. If, through corporate interdependence, the state loses control over major economic decisions,

the best jobs may move to other countries, reducing the satisfaction of personal environments and the sovereignty of state institutions.

Chinese political culture includes, we have seen, a belief that periodically public authorities may be deposed from power by popular means; in between the changeovers, however, limits on authority are weak. The recruitment of peasants and workers into top levels of the party and government has been minimal. So those two factors may reduce the likelihood that China will improve its people's personal environments. But the economic institutions providing basic goods and services for both government and masses of the public depend on the skills of high percentages of the populace. These segments of the populace also control much of the land and tools required; that may be their most solid basis for influence. It guarantees them jobs. If their control of land and tools were removed by consolidating the land into mechanized agribusinesses and by replacing other skilled workers with machinery, the effects could be more than massive unemployment. It could mean removing the basis for the influence these peasants and workers enjoy. The same would hold true if the state tried to switch to simply exporting raw materials requiring little labor. The peasants and workers have an incentive to retain both their base of influence and their means of livelihood and thus to keep the system intact.

In 1978, China made a fundamental change in the way government and nearly all the populace acquired grain, vegetables, meat, milk, fruits, clothing, furniture, and other basic goods. The new policies of the responsibility system gave incentives to producers of these goods by letting them retain more income as production increased on farms and in cooperative industries. Because high percentages of the populace worked in or were able to work in such cooperatives, and acquired these basic goods from them, this benefited many people in China. Furthermore, decisions about what to produce, prices, and where to sell have been rapidly shifted to the peasant, cooperatives, four-hundred forty thousand individual state enterprises, and the new joint-venture industries. The success of the program

Figure 33.3   Per capita Gross National Product (in U.S. dollars).

These figures are the U.S. dollar value of the annual economic output of each country (from the Europa World Yearbook *1990), divided by the number of its inhabitants. By that method of accounting, China's 1991 per capita GDP was $370, and India's $330 (giving them the world's tenth and eleventh largest GDP's).*

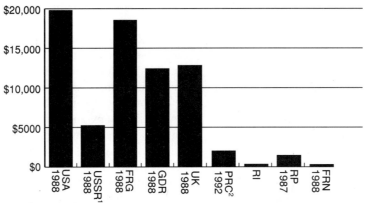

[1]Based on .58 rubles to the dollar. At a 1990 conference, Soviet economists estimated that the Soviet Gross National Product was 14 to 28 percent of that of the United States. If they were correct, the figure for the Soviet Union may be half this high. *Kansas City Star*, April 24,1990.
[2]A moderate estimate based on purchasing power parities, which takes into account what money actually buys in the country. ("The Titan Stirs." *The Economist*, November 28, 1992.) In a May 28, 1993 appendix to its *World Economic Outlook*, the International Monetary Fund rated India's 1991 per capita GDP at $1,150 and China's at $1,450. By this method, it ranked USA's total GDP first in the world (with 22.5 percent of world output), China's third (with 6 percent of world output), Germany's fourth (with 4.3 percent), India's sixth, and Britain's eighth.

thus depends on the great majority of people working to keep the new individual land plots and cooperative industries producing; peasants and workers can influence the direction and success of the program simply by contributing or not contributing to it. They have, in fact, contributed. Industrial output growth was 14 percent in 1984 and 18 percent in 1985—two and a half times the government's target; it continues at over 20 percent, with the growth rate 40 to 75 percent in some "special economic zones" along the coast.[2] The government's share of capital construction investment was only 25 percent by 1985; the rest comes from private investment.[3]

But a seventh of the government's budget goes to subsidize the 70 percent of government firms that lose money, often because their directors, taking advantage of new freedoms, have stolen their profits.[4] Inflation, raw material shortages, unemployment, and other problems common in a corporate-consumer system began to arise. Peasants and

workers have often profited more than intellectuals (though those with technical skills businesses need are now profiting immensely). Over 100 million people became a floating population without jobs, and an additional 100 million may appear during the 1990s. Still, though coastal regions have benefited more than those inland, personal environments of large portions of the populace have been enhanced as the economy grows (see figure 33.3).

By 1994, China's economy was four times larger than it was in 1978, and it is likely to be eight times larger by 2002. It is the world's third or fourth biggest economy, behind only the United States, Japan, and perhaps Germany. The article used to calculate the per capita GNP for China that appears in figure 33.3 estimates that in 1992, China's economic output was 25 to 60 percent that of the United States, depending on the method of calculation used. (Per capita GNP represents GNP divided by the number of inhabitants. Since China has four times the population of the United States, you must multiply its per capita GNP by about four to compare its total GNP with that of the United States.)

Lack of limits on authority, and recruitment of peasants and workers into government, harms productivity and personal environments. The new system lends itself to corruption; party cadres are often corrupt. For example, many peasants have purchased diesel pumps for their fields. Diesel fuel is rationed with ration cards; this allows corrupt officials to divert fuel to their friends and withhold it from those who will not give them special considerations. Cadres can divert profits from the new joint ventures controlled by municipalities, from the grain quotas handled by bureaucrats, from raw materials acquired by factories, or from imports of consumer goods to selected individuals or to top cadres; one high official estimated that the amount of money diverted in this fashion amounts to twice the national budget, and over 10 percent of revenues from exports end in illegal private bank accounts abroad.[5]

Still, peasants have enough influence to resist government and bureaucratic initiatives. Some villages have used the lack of limits on authority to their advantage. They have been building recreation centers and temples with land, capital, and materials they are supposed to be using for production. Peasants have found they can successfully resist the government's one-child policy, having more children to help in the fields. Since this policy is enforced locally, local officials may be influenced to look the other way by family ties, bribes, their unfamiliarity with migrants, unwillingness to deal with the problem of caring for the old (who used to stay with their children and earn their keep by looking after grandchildren), and the desire to increase production in their areas.[6] However, economic growth has far surpassed the 2 percent population growth.

In the nineteenth century, clans may have owned a third of the land in southern China; in interfamily style, the family elders controlled entire villages and decided how land would be distributed, who would receive loans, and who could marry.[7] Sometimes they warred with clans from neighboring

villages.[8] Mao forced families to condemn wealthy kin and give up kin rituals (though many production teams were composed of extended family);[9] with this relaxation in control, many kin leaders have reasserted themselves in helping peasants ignore family planning policies, find jobs, borrow money, and trade goods.

Peasants have also discovered they can make more money by raising vegetables and selling them individually in the market than by raising wheat or rice or cotton, or even pigs, and selling them through government boards. As a result, supplies of these basic goods have diminished, and the market price has risen.[10] This widens the gap between the higher price paid the peasant and the still-low price paid by the consumer; government subsidies make up that difference, and the cost of these subsidies has risen markedly. Government has also moved to distribute greater amounts of water, fertilizer, and improved seed strains. To pay for this, it has charged compensation from factories which occupy land once used for growing grain and is forcing individuals to buy bonds and pay taxes.

China is becoming increasingly dependent on paid bureaucrats to manage factories, marketing, irrigation, housing, and many other vital functions. These individuals are hard to control, especially as the party's bureaucracy is reducing its supervision. China does not have regularized means for distributing many materials, and leaders of factories and bureaucratic units often barter with one another— directly trading goods, services, land, and other valuable assets. Some Shanghai tea houses are haunts for such trading. Hundreds of thousands of leaders descend on Shanghai to make deals, entirely outside the supervision of any public authorities.

Furthermore, the government hoped its huge spurt in production and exports would expand reserves and give it the opportunity to import advanced production technology. Instead, the public, often by illegal means, imported television sets, automobiles, VCRs, washing machines, refrigerators, watches, radios, bicycles, air conditioners, electric heaters, and other consumer goods in such quantities that the resulting trade deficit wiped out all of

China's foreign exchange reserves.[11] These products also strained China's available electricity, creating a need for additional capital investment in electrical generation and transmission. The government attempted to crack down, but discovered that the decentralization of economic decision making had made it extremely difficult to do so. It could neither control the imports, nor fulfill planned quotas of exports. After the crackdown at Tiananmen Square in 1989, these imports declined sharply, while exports rose (from $10 billion in 1978 to $90 billion in 1992),[12] ending that problem for a few years; in 1992, China had a $10 billion trade surplus with the United States, but by 1993, its overall trade surplus turned once again into a deficit as imports soared. That money does not all go for investment. Local party officials help foreign companies avoid paying the stamp and value-added taxes. They use income to invest in real estate speculation in Hong Kong. The biggest plants locate near the border, where they can avoid taxes and hire cheap labor. Most of the growth is in small, low-technology factories.

Despite problems, China's state-consumer system, which combines elements of corporate-consumer, patron-client, and interfamily systems, continues to enjoy high production, employment, and consumption. Because of this, and its access to low-cost skilled labor, it continues to attract capital; by 1991, less than half of China's industrial output came from state factories. Foreign joint ventures doubled in 1990 alone and continue to burgeon.[13] Actual productivity of individual workers has not increased, but more workers have been set to work at new economic activities. However, lack of limits on authority creates uncertainty about order, and the dispersion of power and revenues to provincial and municipal leaders weakens central control.

Chinese leaders could *try* to increase the use of synthetic fertilizers and extensively mechanize farms, irrigation, and factories to reduce the need for labor, destroying the interfamily aspects of production. Workers and peasants would fiercely resist because that would put many people out of work and eliminate their ability to buy the goods—which could instead be sold abroad. Bureaucrats and party

Parked bicycles in Souzhou, China. The bicycle remains China's principal means of transportation. Each bicycle has parts from many different cooperative companies.
Bob Gamer

officials, who would no longer need the peasants for production or for a market, could then largely ignore them. They would be permanently removed from productive employment in the national economy. With few limits on authority, the patron-client aspect of the system would come to the fore. Without such radical technological conversion, the system has the potential to remain a state-consumer system. Conversion could transform it into a patron-client system distributing goods to only a portion of the populace, or into a corporate-consumer system.[14]

India experienced radical technological conversion during the eighteenth and nineteenth centuries. We saw in chapter 32 how land was converted from labor-intensive interfamily communities, capable of feeding and clothing themselves and the urban populace, into capital-intensive, patron-client farms producing for export and importing what they need for themselves. Independence widened land ownership, but at least half of all rural families cannot fully support themselves on the land they have, and only a small percentage of holdings provide food for those living outside villages. Mechanization of agriculture continues at a fast pace and makes India largely self-sufficient in providing its people with food, although many do not have enough to eat. When new technology lets national leaders produce the goods and services they need without the participation of much of the populace, government can ignore the wishes of those people. Most rural Indians can find work as agricultural laborers at least part of the year; they need nearly all their income for food. India remains a patron-client system, with a high trade deficit and $71 billion in foreign debt with inadequate current funds to repay.[15]

India is self-sufficient in providing consumer goods for that portion of the populace which can afford to buy them. But increased mechanization of production decreases the number of high-paying jobs. They may be replaced with service jobs or with new high-tech industries already busy devising ways to further reduce the number of employees they need. Production of high-technology products such as computer components and software, consumer electronics, and communication and broadcasting equipment, which amounted to $1 billion in 1982, reached $9 billion by 1990. This expansion provides work for the 33,800 engineers graduated each year from India's 150 engineering colleges and for some skilled workers. Prime Minister Rao's decision to permit foreign firms to own Indian businesses will further expand such job openings. When a Bombay computer programmer makes $240 (in U.S. dollars) a month, his or her pay is low by international standards.[16] When it is sold domestically, this equipment will eventually decrease jobs in other fields, such as the clerks who keep bank ledgers by hand. As those workers move out into other service-sector jobs, or into unemployment, it becomes increasingly difficult for them to organize trade unions. And it becomes easier to ignore their needs because their skills are no longer used by government or the economic institutions that produce basic goods and services. That amounts to a decline of influence within the political system which they will resist. As a patron-client system, India can provide few of its citizens with jobs or the ability to

purchase consumer goods. High percentages of the populace are integrated neither into political institutions, nor into major economic institutions providing jobs, goods, and services.

Peru and Nigeria, too, are patron-client systems. Nigeria's agriculture is largely in decline. Income comes principally from oil; it goes into the hands of a small group of people. Unlike in India, smaller industries operating within the national economy have made little progress in recent years. During the 1970s, with the emphasis on oil production, Nigeria's agricultural production declined from 63 percent to 22 percent of GDP; palm oil and peanuts, once major exports, were being imported. Manufacturing stayed at 5 percent of a greatly increased GDP. But imports grew over 20 percent a year.[17] Small businesses without enough influence to acquire import licenses could not obtain the raw materials and spare parts they needed.

When General Babangida massively devalued currency in 1986 to cut down on imports, many industries (already harmed by import restrictions imposed by his predecessor) failed, but oil industries and agriculture—especially farms exporting rubber, cocoa, and palm oil, or producing large amounts of grain—were encouraged. Only the oil industries responded strongly. Top officials who could share in oil income were building themselves expensive houses.[18] New money was being spent on education, but 61 percent was going to universities attended by the top strata of society. These universities, like businesses and industries, were suffering from a lack of equipment, books, and other basics. A senior professor who earned the equivalent of $30,000 in naira in 1985 was bringing home the equivalent of $4,000 in 1989, so even those with the highest incomes could no longer afford a car, foreign education for their children, or travel abroad.[19] Meanwhile, per capita income dropped from $1,000 in 1980 to $360 in 1991,[20] cardboard shacks multiplied in city slums, 1993 inflation exceeded 100 percent a year,[21] and layoffs of civil servants increased. Nigeria (though it is one of the world's ten leading oil exporters) ranks as the world's fifteenth poorest country.[22]

Peru's agriculture and industry are also in decline. Exports of copper and other metals, and of cotton and wool, have fallen. Its largest source of outside capital is the drug trade. Some seventy thousand peasant families have moved into the Huallaga Valley and perhaps one-hundred thousand more into adjoining areas to grow coca, which brings in billions of dollars from illegal trade. Millions of U.S. dollars are flown to Lima each day (in bales) from illegal airstrips and sold on the streets by money changers or through foreign branches of the Banco de Credito.[23] The Central Reserve Bank (by simply printing intis, the Peruvian currency) buys as much as 13 million of these dollars each day, and since 1990 has used them to make regular payments on Peru's international debt.[24] During the end of military rule, Peru abolished exchange controls to make such currency transfers easier. Most of the income goes to those who make the final sales to the Colombian dealers and handle the "laundering" of dollars through the flights and banking; they strongly resist interruption of this income.[25]

Since 1985 to 1987, when President Garcia used up the government's reserves to subsidize low food prices and raise wages,[26] prices have steadily risen and real wages dipped. By 1990, inflation had reached 7,650 percent a year! When President Fujimori, after vague rhetoric in his 1990 campaign, announced an austerity program immediately upon being elected, slum dwellers rioted. The prices of rice, bread, and cooking gas rose up to four times (though soup kitchens were to be opened),[27] and the price of gasoline rose to sixty times its previous price. By 1992, inflation had declined to 57 percent; unprofitable state-owned businesses were for sale (and, with the decline of Sendero Luminoso, beginning to find buyers). Government was collecting taxes from businesses (which were again hiding earnings); the government had ended subsidies to pay workers; wages of government workers were frozen; the government was seeking outside investment; and the government was asking for renewed loans to continue the projects which had created the international debt. During 1992, $400 million in new investment entered the country to purchase government-owned businesses. Sendero Luminoso and army killings declined, but the military budget (and powers) kept growing.[28] Fixed incomes (a luxury reserved for a minority) fell so low that few had enough to buy food; the situation was even worse for those outside the formal economy. The only thing keeping millions of people in Lima's *barrios* alive are the soup kitchens organized by members of the informal economy using food furnished by churches and relief agencies. After falling 25 percent, gross domestic output, spurred by the outside investment, began to rise 1 to 4 percent a year. With Peru's internal market shattered, and with calmer places with stable work forces beckoning for investment, private long-term investment will be hard to attract. President Fujimori is counting on doing so by keeping a firm hand on the Congress and the courts, now filled with many of his followers. Corruption in the military and the courts lets the drug trade continue.[29] The new investments in mining, export agriculture, telecommunications, and electricity will help keep the patron-client system alive.

The United Kingdom, in contrast, is a corporate-consumer system. To remain one, it needs the capital to provide high percentages of its citizens with jobs and consumer goods. Margaret Thatcher's reforms radically changed the positions of people in Liverpool, Leeds, Manchester, Glasgow, and other cities of the industrialized north. She broke the power of labor unions, turned nationalized industries into private corporations, lowered income taxes, and increased the island's dependence on imported goods from the Common Market, Japan, and elsewhere. The National Union of Mineworkers, which in 1980 had two-hundred fifty thousand members, was down to ninety thousand by 1987.[30] Similar reductions took place in other unions,[31] as the government threw its weight to break strikes, close old industries, and modernize production.

In 1981, the United Kingdom exported 26 percent more than it imported; by 1986, the United Kingdom imported $19.2 billion more than it exported.[32] That deficit grows larger. For the first time in a decade, more than half of all cars purchased in the United Kingdom were assembled there, but they were largely put together from parts made in other countries. In 1985, the trade deficit on importing automobiles was 2.7 billion pounds; in 1986, 3.9 billion. The 1987 figures turned that around, but still left the vast majority of new car owners driving automobiles entirely or partially imported.[33]

Many heavy industries closed, and their owners turned to other investments,[34] leaving entire neighborhoods unemployed and entire regions with unemployment levels above 30 percent. Between 1979 and 1987, the United Kingdom lost two million manufacturing jobs. While skilled manual workers comprised 47 percent of the populace in 1964, they accounted for just 31 percent in 1987.[35] Coal mines were supplanted by North Sea oil, which in turn experienced a downturn as oil prices fell. A 1987 study compared ten economic indexes such as unemployment, housing prices, population movements, and proportion of the work force employed in high-technology industry and services such as banking and industry. The study found that the top-performing thirty-five areas all lay to the southeast. Yorkshire and Humberside, to the north, had 72 percent more people living below half the average income than did the southeast. The poorest areas were generally industrial and located in Wales, western Scotland, and northern England.[36]

Many people lost the influence that comes from employment in economic institutions. With a firmly implanted system of limited government, those individuals harmed in this way at least continue to have a chance to vote opposition parties into office. Many continue to elect Labour city councils. But limits have been placed on the tax rates these councils can charge, and their tax base is weakened by the number of people on state assistance. So they have little power to deal with these problems on the local level.[37] With labor unions weakening and the middle class growing, the Labour Party has turned away from its commitment to policies to aid the poor. Tight budgets make it hard for government to provide jobs for people whose skills are no longer needed to produce basic goods and services; this means it is hard for these people to regain satisfying personal environments. Two of the bargaining points

this group of workers had in the past—their needed skills, and the market they provide for finished goods—are gone. Many speak with remote local accents, have little education, and have never been more than a few miles from home; it is difficult for them to move elsewhere in search of new jobs.

Meanwhile, in the south, the country experienced economic renewal. Sale of stocks in the newly privatized businesses brought a boom to the stock market and sparked demand for retail firms to supply consumer goods and services. Tourism expanded. From 1982 to 1987, retail sales grew an average of 5 percent a year.[38] New motorways linked other cities to London's prosperity. Professional salaries rose. The government lowered subsidies to the poor, students, and other groups, and passed along savings to the taxpayers. It offered new subsidies to small high-tech and service firms. This helped expand the size of the middle class and raise the living standards of many in upper reaches of society.

The accompanying rise in imports, inflation, trade imbalances, and deficit spending, combined with unemployment, threaten to undo some of these gains. Because the United Kingdom is producing fewer tangible goods, it has less to export, and hence cannot count on that source of revenue. For every 1 percent increase in Gross National Product, there has been a 1.5 percent increase in imports.[39] Between 1982 and 1986, inflation hovered below 5 percent a year. In 1987, it began to rise, and continues to rise at around 5 percent while the economy grows less than 2 percent a year after several years of shrinking.[40] Thatcher's reforms were aided by revenue from North Sea oil. She also sold other government assets such as publicly owned industries and utilities and public housing; when these were gone, budgets became harder to balance.[41] So, while Thatcher's plan moved rapidly to make initial gains, it has not kept up the momentum. The United Kingdom approaches the European Economic Community, which lowers trade barriers, poorly placed to compete on selling manufactures. If it cannot recoup its old mercantilism, with exports exceeding imports, and balance its budgets, its corporate-consumer system—with high productivity, employment, and consumption—may be hard to maintain.

Figure 33.4   American's GNP as a Percentage of world output.

OECD, The World Economy in the Twentieth Century (1989). *The May 28, 1993 appendix to the International Money Fund's* World Economic Outlook *estimated that, based on purchasing power parity the United States produced 22.5 percent of the world economic output in 1990.*

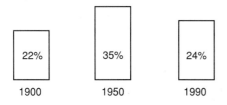

The United States is moving in a similar direction: in recent years, we are importing our basic goods and services, exporting industrial plants, mechanizing the plants that remain, and expanding service industries that require basic labor rather than specific skills. Every 1 percent increase in Gross National Product is accompanied by a 1.4 percent increase in imports.[42] Since we have not always been good at studying foreign markets and adapting our products to them, many of our goods do not compete well. In 1963, our share of world trade in manufactured goods was 21 percent; by 1974, this figure had dropped to 17 percent, and it continues to decline.[43] Figure 33.4 shows America's GNP as a percentage of world output.

Over a fourth of our Gross National Product consists of imports and exports.[44] In 1980, the United States exported $12 billion more manufactured goods than it imported; in 1986, it imported $166 billion more than it exported.[45] By 1992, we imported $15 billion more from China (where many American firms are moving) than we exported to it.[46] Foreign firms have set up plants in the United States, often assembling parts that are mostly produced abroad. Farmers are being replaced by more mechanized agribusinesses. In 1986, there were 2 million fewer jobs in manufacturing than in 1979. In 1968, 35 percent of employment in the United States was in manufacturing; in 1992, 16 percent.[47] Neither the government nor consumers need these displaced factory workers to produce wheat, steel, automobiles, television sets, computer chips, processed fish, or much else. Their ability to influence the political system on the basis of its need for their skills is thereby diminished. It is further reduced because many of the new jobs replacing these require only generic labor, with generic capabilities, rather than specific skills that take a long time to acquire, so people become more interchangeable and expendable, and wages decline.

To further worsen the outlook, much of our investment capital is being used to simply purchase existing businesses in corporate takeovers; the government is increasing its indebtedness at a rapid rate; and Americans save little for investment. The first year the United States had a current account deficit (including all trade, foreign aid, and investments) was 1985; by 1991, our current account deficit of $382 billion was the highest in the world.[48] The national debt (the amount the government owes creditors) may reach $5 trillion dollars by 1995; that places it in the middle range of industrialized countries as a percentage of GNP, but it is a large amount to repay and pay interest on.[49] The $500 billion or more it will cost to pay for the savings and loan bailout, caused by speculators who put money into unproductive loans, will equal West Germany's expense in rebuilding East Germany's infrastructure and industries, which will then be highly productive as a result. We are floating new loans to pay off the savings and loan debts—debts the government will never be paid back for.

Part of the secret of our historically high employment has been government contracts to defense-related industries (now in decline) and investments in infrastructure, and social subsidies like social security, payments to businesses and farmers, and veteran's benefits. Another has been high agricultural production and low energy taxes, keeping living costs down. Americans spend 96 cents of every dollar they earn, versus 78 cents for Japanese and 65 cents for Chinese workers; that raises our consumption, but lowers savings.[50] This has created the need for us to borrow from abroad; half of our $4 trillion debt is owed to foreigners.[51]

High percentages of our citizens are still needed as employees and consumers, still place limits on government authority, and still have access to political institutions. If the United States reaches the point when it can no longer borrow money abroad[52] to pay for this living standard, it will be very difficult to maintain a high level of employment and consumption. Government leaders may listen in time to popular pressure to reverse that decline. (Unemployment reached 7.8 percent in 1992, including many from the middle class.) If government response includes heavy tariffs on imports, productivity will have to rise at home, or living standards will fall. If it entails joining the European Economic Community, a North American free trade zone, or an Asia-Pacific trade zone, and our productivity fails to rise, our living standards will fall as more jobs leave the country, destined for places like China. Either strategy would lead us further toward corporate interdependence; whether our sovereignty and personal environments are weakened or strengthened by that shift depends on our ability to accumulate capital and produce.

America's middle class is shrinking. Scores on mathematics and verbal scholastic aptitude tests decline. Rather than desiring to start their own businesses and produce their own inventions, many Americans wish to work for organizations run by others. Those organizations often do not know how to compete on world markets; they divert production to foreign factories, and fail to incorporate the latest technology into their production facilities. Americans accumulate many high-technology gadgets; they often lack curiosity as to how they are made or lack the ambition to improve on them.

The post-Soviet republics already face the disintegration of their state-consumer system. Whether they will become corporate-consumer or patron-client systems depends largely on their citizens' ability to create limits on government authority and develop entrepreneurial skills. When Gorbachev took power in 1985, the Soviet Union had been experiencing a decade of economic decline. Even by notoriously bloated official figures, 1985 economic growth was 2 percent, versus 4 percent in 1975.

Food production was barely keeping apace with the 1 percent rate of population increase.[53] Thirteen percent of industrial enterprises and 30 percent of farms officially lost money. The gold and oil it could extract by primitive (and environmentally damaging) methods, which accounted for half its hard currency earnings, were running out.[54] Government efforts to improve production by importing more sophisticated equipment, and the decline of world oil prices and of the U.S. dollar (to which it pegged the prices of its oil exports) moved the Soviet Union from a 1984 trade surplus of $2 billion to $534 million in 1985.[55]

The government's response was to borrow money (up to $67 billion by 1991)[56] to pay for annual deficit spending surpassing $100 billion, and to slow imports, using up nearly all its extensive gold reserves; the accumulated national deficit grew from $265 billion in 1985 to $962 billion in 1990.[57] This was complicated by the fact that two-thirds of hard currency earnings were needed to import food.[58] The reforms removed pressures on farms and factories to produce and distribute goods, and output dropped markedly. By late 1991, prices were rising 4 percent a week, for an annual inflation rate of 450 percent. When the ruble was made convertible on international markets in 1992, its value in world trade declined from 1.8 rubles to the dollar to 650 rubles to the dollar, making importation nearly impossible, but tempting new businesses to produce exports rather than goods for internal consumption. Much of the CIS republics' production still emanates from outmoded state factories, which all the republics continue to subsidize.

Since firms need not make profits under this system, workers cannot exert pressure by withholding labor and consumption. With no traditions limiting the authority of government institutions, it is hard to organize public pressure to change them. Various social classes and regions are poorly represented in political institutions. That frees bureaucrats to continue policies which weaken the state-consumer system's ability to keep its public employed and consuming, and thus to continue as a state-consumer system. Bureaucratic behavior also makes foreign investors wary of making capital investments. At the same time, these *nomenklatura* use their positions and connections to start their own businesses; they run the state economies with one hand and their own private monopolies with the other. They are likely to use the wealth they acquire to strengthen their grip on the bureaucracy, politics, and the state enterprises. Strong public support for a free market, and for the limits on government which must accompany one, must arise if the reforms are to usher in corporate-consumerism rather than merely strengthen the patron-client aspects of the system.

In sharp contrast to all these nation-states is Germany. It is fully maintaining its status as a corporate-consumer system. The emerging question is whether it will help others create or maintain a similar status, or whether its productivity may hasten the decline of other systems. The 1980 to 1983 recession raised West Germany's unemployment past 2 million and slowed its output, but that setback was temporary. In 1989, its trade surplus was $85 billion. Industrial output rose 3.6 percent, and Gross National Product 4 percent. A third of the four-hundred thirty thousand new jobs it created that year were in industry. While unemployment stayed above a million, the nation-state experienced a shortage of skilled labor. A third of its labor force was employed by industry. Its Gross Domestic Product was third in the world, ranking behind only the far more populous and resource-rich Japan and the United States. Germany's workers were among the highest paid in the world.[59] Its $265 billion in assets made it the world's second richest creditor nation-state, after Japan.[60] It made $75 billion in investments abroad. Rebuilding East Germany has necessitated higher taxes, a round of trade deficits, government debts that could exceed $2.8 trillion by the year 2000 (51 percent of GNP, below the current average 60 percent GNP-debt ratio in other leading European community members), and a fall in economic output (though output is now rising again in the East, nearly 10 percent a year). Germany began its task with a sound economic base.[61]

Three-quarters of the 6 percent of GNP spent on the East goes for welfare, health care, and pensions to keep "Ossies" capable of being consumers in a corporate-consumer system. The remaining quarter invested in rebuilding East Germany goes to West German firms, creating jobs (already paying, on average, more than U.S. workers earn) that boost future output and taxpayer revenue. Around six thousand state enterprises have been converted to private businesses, and two hundred thousand small private firms have been created. Giant new plants are being constructed, along with highways and every kind of public infrastructure and amenities. Grand new buildings are sprouting up everywhere.

West Germany has 60 percent of East Germany's market; France, its nearest competitor, has 5 percent. In 1989, West Germany controlled a third of the Eastern European market; its nearest competitor, Italy, had 7 percent. Germany accounted for a fifth of all exports to Eastern Europe by industrialized countries and 42 percent of the contracts made by European Community joint ventures in the Soviet Union. Over a third of Sweden's, Finland's, Austria's, Switzerland's, and Norway's imports come from West Germany.[62] Czechoslovakia's Skoda automobile plant chose Volkswagen as its partner. General Motors bypassed Britain for its new automobile plant to build in Cologne instead.

So, despite economic and social stresses caused by absorbing the East, Germany has high potential to retain jobs, consumption, and capital. This is because it is highly productive and there is a high demand for its products. Furthermore, its investments are unlikely to be diverted to foreign banks, corporate raiders, or foreign owners. The Deutsche Bank oversees many of the annual mergers, buying many shares. Banks control 25 percent of shares in the thirty-three leading companies. Government and unions also own stock. Social customs dictate that people be hired for life and be guaranteed many benefits. Siemens, with plants in thirty-five countries, makes sure two-thirds of its three hundred seventy-three thousand employees are German. Unlike British and American firms, which face constant pressure from individual stockholders or threats of corporate buyouts to produce short-term profits, German businesses can plan for the long term—making investments that do not produce immediate profits but eventually result in controlling the markets.

Nation-states who wish to compete must produce products that will sell better than those of Germany and Japan.[63] Otherwise their jobs, capital, and consumption may erode. That, in turn, could harm both the influence and personal environments of their citizens and the ability of corporate-consumer states to support their populations with jobs that allow them to consume.

There are signs both that other nation-states are improving their ability to compete, and that jobs, capital, and consumption may erode. Germany's average increase in labor productivity is rising more slowly than in Britain, the United States, and other European countries, while its labor costs are rising more quickly. In 1982, Germany's worker productivity was 51 percent higher than Britain's; in 1992, only 19 percent higher (though Britain's real output per employee in manufacturing is still half to three-quarters that of other leading European Economic Community members, and it has a rate of return on capital invested less than half that in Germany or the United States).[64] Germany's labor is the highest paid in Europe,[65] causing many businesses to think about relocating abroad. Much of Germany's industry centers around engineering, chemicals, and automobiles; it is meeting tough competition from Japan and elsewhere, where design and quality are improving while costs rise more slowly. Germany's industry receives the heaviest government subsidies in Europe, stretching government revenues. Faced with stiff foreign competition and a decline in auto production, its steel industry is cutting back forty thousand jobs.[66] Germany's auto industry is also laying off up to three hundred thousand workers; its new models do not compete well with those produced by the Japanese and the French.[67] Germany has done little to enter the new high-technology industries. It still spends 2.8 percent of its GDP on research and development (versus 3.5 percent in Japan whose own economy has suffered from the worldwide re-

cession), but it cannot increase this spending because of the cost of rebuilding East Germany. The United States also spends 2.8 percent of its GDP on research and development. While 60 percent of U.S. government spending on R&D has been on defense, a small portion of that spending is now shifting into fields such as advanced materials processing, biotechnology, computing, and manufacturing research (though spending on other fields like mathematics and physics is declining).[68] Britain is radically reducing its spending on research and development.[69] So these countries are both improving and making mistakes as they try to compete. That levels the playing field a bit; but the game each of these nation-states must play if they are to remain viable corporate-consumer systems depends on ever-increasing productivity—creating products for their citizens to use, and jobs to keep consumption high.

Production for use cannot be induced simply by applying economic stimuli. Releasing investment capital into a patron-client system is likely to create new products for export—not for domestic use by the nation-state's citizens. Capital investment in a corporate-consumer system is often used to transfer jobs abroad. Neither strategy directly helps feed, clothe, shelter, fuel, or defend the members of the nation-state.

The high productivity needed to support a corporate-consumer system with satisfying personal environments is hard to maintain. Nation-states with multi-party systems, strong limits on authority, broad participation in politics, and no nationalization of production are potentially the most productive. But even under these ideal conditions, productivity cannot be taken for granted. Ultimately, a nation-state must stimulate its own productivity through the right mixture of policy initiatives; it must limit the export of jobs and capital and encourage greater production at home. Those initiatives can be endangered by forces beyond the nation-state's control. And they must occur in unison; raising the cost of labor, for example, without simultaneously raising productivity, is a sure formula for exporting capital and jobs. Such initiatives are unlikely to occur within a patron-client system, or a state-consumer system without limits on the authority of leaders or economic incentives for industries to produce.

Either improved productivity in corporate-consumer systems or the decline of such systems can change the nature of patron-client systems. West Germany and Japan have been able to increase their productivity without assuming direct political control of any outside regions. They, along with other corporate-consumer systems, have helped prop up patron-client systems by buying their raw materials inexpensively and selling them expensive foods and finished products. However, should political instability, unrepaid debts, or other phenomena make it less profitable or politically desirable to continue such relations, they could dispense with such dealings; their economies are strong enough to sustain themselves by other means.[70] Other corporate-consumer systems, overburdened by debt and trade imbalances, might be forced to sharply reduce such trade.

Without markets in corporate-consumer systems, patrons in patron-client systems might find it difficult to export sufficient crops or minerals to maintain their wealth. No longer able to profit by growing export crops on land, they could lose interest in controlling it. Individuals or communities might use this land to produce food items for sale in their own regions and nearby cities. Those owners would have little investment capital to pay for machinery, but much inexpensive labor to draw on. That could give large numbers of people local control over land, power to cooperate in solving agricultural problems, and incentives to produce. No longer dependent on distant patrons, they might be able to restore some political control to villages themselves and recreate elements of an interfamily system. Jobs, control over food the other portions of their nation-state's populace need, and involvement in local political institutions could give them greater influence than they have today.

A downturn in exports would harm people in cities such as Singapore who depend heavily upon manufacturing goods consumed in corporate-consumer systems. But if that downturn is accompanied by more jobs and food in the countryside, the capacity for consumption within the nation-state may grow and the need for imported food decline. That could

set the stage for more corporate-consumerism in those cities and regional towns, as they produce products for consumption by rural inhabitants.

The multicultural nature of most patron-client systems, and the fragility of limits they place on leaders' authority, make them unlikely candidates to become complete corporate-consumer systems, even under the circumstances just discussed. A return to interfamily relations in rural areas may be a more secure and culturally satisfying basis for gaining influence and satisfying personal environments. As in China, it might be difficult to introduce truly independent judiciaries or multiparty competition in these settings; they might find other ways to place some limits on authority. Without changes in the demand for their goods and raw materials within corporate-consumer systems, however, they are likely to simply remain patron-client systems.

Access to food, clothing, shelter, energy, and defense, and protection of the environment and human freedoms, are all affected by the nature of the political system in a nation-state. A patron-client system provides inadequate access for most people to food, clothing, shelter, and fuel; little protection for the environment; and a defense system that can easily be turned against the freedoms of the people. An interfamily system may offer wider access to food, clothing, shelter, and fuel; uncertain protection for the environment, as technology contributes new polluting agents; and free cultural and religious expression, at least for dominant groups. Consumption is likely to stay at a basic level. State-consumer systems find it hard to maintain full employment and consumption, or protection of the environment and minority cultures, because they are easily infiltrated by patron-clientism.

It is difficult for other systems to defend themselves against corporate-consumer systems. Corporate-consumer systems offer wide access to food, clothing, shelter, and fuel; they vary in the degree to which they protect the environment, and the degree of cultural and religious expression they allow. They can only remain corporate-consumer systems if they maintain enough productivity to constantly replenish capital for jobs and consumption.

Systems can change, and the influence and personal environments of their citizens fluctuate with those changes. Presidential and parliamentary systems of government with open party competition can help maintain entrepreneurship and innovation if they are accompanied by a political culture that encourages innovation; if the culture doesn't encourage it, innovation is unlikely to occur. State-consumer and corporate-consumer systems can remain productive if their citizens stay productive. That requires more of citizens than working a forty-hour week for someone else and returning to spend their weekends in a leisurely manner; it requires more than exposing consumers to modern communication and technology. It means that those with the most influence must study hard, save, and use their knowledge and capital to produce goods which can improve the living standards of fellow citizens.

It also means that people with influence must resist the efforts of fellow citizens or foreign countries to use their nation-state's capital, land, and manufacturing capacities for pursuits that reduce production for consumption by the country's own populace. These efforts could easily diminish the portion of the populace experiencing a satisfying personal environment. When that happens in a system which once enjoyed productivity, freedom and prosperity are hard to sustain, even if democratic institutions thrive. And exporting democratic institutions to a system whose citizens do not practice thrift, hard work, and innovation is unlikely to encourage productivity; it may even reduce the number of individuals with these traits and harm productivity in the end.

SUMMARY

A corporate-consumer system which cannot sustain high productivity, and which steadily imports more than it exports, may find its standard of living declining and its sovereignty giving way to corporate interdependence. A state-consumer system which can sustain growing productivity may remain intact, but it is likely to have trouble absorbing radical technological conversion. A state-consumer system whose productivity starts to decline is in danger of becoming a patron-client system unless it places limits on government authority and develops entrepreneurial skills to move it toward corporate-consumerism. As long as patrons can prosper, patron-client systems are likely to remain intact; they need not achieve high levels of productivity, innovation, or employment to survive. But if shifts in world trade patterns cut off patrons' income, these systems could move toward a mixture of interfamily and corporate-consumer traits.

It is hard for any system to extend satisfying personal environments to increasing numbers of its citizens unless it sustains high productivity. Corporate-consumer and state-consumer systems are capable of that; patron-client systems are not. Patron-client systems cannot create satisfying personal environments for much of their populace unless the productivity of their system *declines*. This weakens the patrons and frees others to reactivate interfamily systems or to develop corporate-consumer political and economic relationships.

NOTES

1. The money pays the grower, the patron of the grower, the army which protects the patron, and so on.
2. "A Great Leap Forward," *The Economist,* October 5, 1991. *The Straits Times,* June 11, 1993.
3. The state had targeted investment growth of 10 percent in 1984 and 8.8 percent in 1985, and industrial output growth of 5 percent and 8 percent, respectively, in those two years. The money supply was also growing much faster than planned. Prices of steel and other raw materials rose quickly. Enterprises often expanded without considering how much goods would cost and whether they would be marketable. The government began to tax excessive employee

bonuses, raised interest rates, tightened bank credit-approval policies, and tried to reduce the money supply. Robert Delfs, "Collective Efforts are Overwhelming State Enterprise," *Far Eastern Economic Review* 131, 12 (March 20, 1986): 77. The rapid growth of 1992 and 1993 triggered similar responses.

4. At least 40 percent of state-owned companies operate at a loss. They cost the government $17 billion in subsidies. The general manager of Hainan's Overseas Chinese Remittance Corporation left the company with $21 million in debt and only $14 million in assets after taking hundreds of thousands of dollars in kickbacks for himself and fellow members of his clan. In a precedent-setting move, the courts considered allowing the firm to declare bankruptcy. The three-hundred seventy thousand party-directed workers' congresses have also been reactivated to oversee factory managers—a move which may merely broaden corruption and weaken those state factories which are improving output and profits. Ann Scott Tyson, "China Grapples with Failing State Sector," *Christian Science Monitor,* July 11, 1991. James L. Tyson, "Chinese Conservatives Reverse Factory Reforms," *Christian Science Monitor,* November 20, 1991. "Cleaning Up the Chinese State," *The Economist,* November 14, 1992.

5. Kenneth Lieberthal was given this estimate during the summer of 1990. Public lecture, University of Missouri-Kansas City, September 25, 1990.

6. China's birthrate jumped from 17.8 per 1,000 in 1985 to 20.77 per 1,000 in 1986. About half of the increase can be attributed to peasants in rural areas having more than one child.

   To the peasant, having more sons is attractive; there is room to add on to houses, and the extra help allows more income from growing and marketing food. For China as a nation-state, population growth is not attractive. In 1958, its birth rate stood at 43.4 per 1,000; the reduction has helped limit an already growing unemployment problem. Increases in the birth rate will cause that problem to grow. Ellen Salem, "Procreating for Profit," *Far Eastern Economic Review,* 136, 26 (June 25, 1987): 56–57.

7. The Chinese motion pictures "Red Sorghum" and "Jou Dou" depict the role of family elders in controlling life earlier in this century.

8. Ann Scott Tyson, "Clan Rivalries Take Hold in China," *Christian Science Monitor,* April 23, 1991, reports on a bloody ongoing feud between the Wu and Wang clans in Guangdong Province. They disrupt one another's festivals and tombs.

9. Jean C. Oi, *State and Peasant in Contemporary China: The Political Economy of Village Government* (Berkeley: University of California Press, 1989) discusses Mao's success and lack of it.

10. Agricultural production does not seem to rise, but may be underreported due to diversions of crops into private market sales.

11. Louise do Rosario, "The Cars-and-TVs Nightmare that Dented Reserves," *Far Eastern Economic Review,* 131, 12 (March 20, 1986): 91–93. These products also strained China's available electricity, creating a need for additional capital investment in electrical generation and transmission. Between 1986 and 1990 alone, electrical output grew by 57 percent but still lagged far behind demand. Carl Goldstein, "China's Generation Gap," *Far Eastern Economic Review,* June 11, 1992.

12. Since the yuan rose from 1.7 to the dollar in 1978 to 5.5 in 1992, the growth is actually greater; at the 1978 rate of exchange, 1992 exports would be worth about $300 billion.

13. Daniel Southerland, "How China's Economy Left Its Comrade Behind," *Washington Post Weekly Edition,* September 2–8, 1991. By 1991, there were two hundred thousand joint ventures, with their numbers and investment rising rapidly. By 1990, $22 million had been invested; in 1991, $3.5 billion, and in 1992, $11 billion more. But state enterprises still produce about half of industrial output and furnish 60 percent of industrial employment (with the 19 million workers in rural cooperatives contributing another 25 percent), only a third make a profit. "Down on the Farm," *The Economist,* November 28, 1992.

14. For more on this, see Robert E. Gamer, "From Zig-Zag to Confrontation at Tiananmen: Tradition and Politics in China," *UFSI Field Staff Reports* 10 (1989–90); idem., "Helping History Find Its Way," *Crossroads* 32 (Fall 1990); idem., "Can China Modernize Without a Fight for Democracy? Samuel P. Huntington and the 'Neo-Authoritarian' Debate," *Crossroads* 35 (1994).

15. Sheila Tefft, "India's Premier Launches Radical Economic Reforms," *Christian Science Monitor,* August 1, 1991. India's 1990–91 trade deficit was $6 billion. In 1991 and 1992, it brought its foreign

exchange reserves up from almost nothing to $6 billion, largely by granting a one-time amnesty to Indians who wanted to return illegal funds from abroad. But debt repayment and rising costs of oil imports already reduced those reserves below $5 billion by the end of 1992. R. Krishman, "How Long to Wait for the Reform Gains?" *The Hindu,* November 29, 1992.

16. *Kansas City Star,* January 24, 1988.

17. Jon Kraus, "Nigeria Under Shagari," *Current History* 81, 473 (March 1982): 106. By 1992, real GDP growth was at 3.6 percent a year.

18. A beachfront slum with fifteen thousand homes, nine schools, ancestral shrines, churches, and mosques was razed to the ground by bulldozers in 1990, forcing the residents to build shanties elsewhere, amid speculation that the land "is going to be developed into luxury villas." Robert M. Press, "Nigerians Set to Vote in Primaries in Step toward Civilian Rule," *Christian Science Monitor,* October 18, 1991.

19. Larry Diamond, "Nigeria's Third Quest For Democracy," *Current History* 90, 556 (May 1991): 202.

20. World Bank figures, adjusted to 1991 census figures.

21. A tin of milk which cost 10k (Nigerian cents) in 1985 cost 4 naira (Nigerian dollars) in 1990. *Nigerian Abroad* 1, 20 (November 1–15, 1990): 9.

22. Diamond, "Nigeria's Third Quest." Nigerians have U.S. $25 to 50 billion in foreign bank accounts. "Breaking the Cycle," *The Economist,* August 21, 1993.

23. Peter Andreas, "Peru's Addiction to Coca Dollars," *Nation* 250, 15 (April 16, 1990).

24. Robin Kirk, "Oh! What a Lovely Drug War in Peru," *Nation* 253, 10 (1991): 376. "Suddenly the Money Goes Home to Peru," *The Economist,* June 22, 1991. Nathaniel C. Nash, "Fujimori Talks Tough But the Coca Thrives," *New York Times,* April 26, 1992. The head of Peru's intelligence agency under Fujimori has ties to drug cartels. General Rodolfo Robles, former third in command in Peru's armed forces, who sought refuge in the U.S. Embassy, accuses the head of Peru's armed forces and this intelligence head of supporting the drug trade. "Puppetry in Peru," *Kansas City Star,* May 15, 1993.

25. Twenty-four developers and other interest groups signed a 1991 letter to the Congress objecting to the treaty with the United States for eradicating coca and substituting other crops. The People's Defense Front

for San Martin (where the Huallaga Valley is located) opposes the treaty, as do many military officers who object to the presence of U.S. military on their soil. Sally Bowen, "Leading Peruvians Spurn Antidrug Pact with United States," *Christian Science Monitor,* April 15, 1991. Cocaine production remains steady.

26. In 1987, Garcia moved to nationalize banks and insurance companies so more money might be available for rural and small business development projects instead of leaving the country. This angered the business community. The army gave initial approval, signalling that the move would not precipitate a coup. But the courts disapproved, and Garcia agreed to abide by their decision until the bill went through the legislature. The leading bank announced it lost a third of its credit lines abroad; the move actually shrunk development funds and private investment.

27. With over 12 million living in poverty, the soup kitchen program was feeding only 300,000 a day in 1991. Sally Bowen, "Peru's Fujimori Weighs In on Behalf of Street Sellers," *Christian Science Monitor,* March 4, 1991.

28. In addition to funding the "drug war" and increasing the regular budgeting, Fujimori allocated $200 million to "patrol" forty-eight miles of border with Ecuador where that government was reneging on a 1942 treaty. Ecuador had been fumigating the border and cleaning a rubbish-filled canal which divides the two countries to keep Peru's cholera epidemic out. Meanwhile, the 1992 budget allotted $30 million to poverty relief.

29. Sally Bowen, "Fujimori Claims Successes: Critics See Long-Term Rule," *Christian Science Monitor,* April 5, 1993. In 1992, the program assisted by the U.S. Drug Enforcement Administration captured 1 percent of Peru's 600 million metric tons of cocaine production; a foreign legal expert says Fujimori's judicial appointees are as corrupt as the judges he removed from office.

30. Tim Jones, "British Coal to Talk with Miners on Discipline," *The Times,* August 4, 1987.

31. Between 1979 and 1989, total union membership declined from 12 million to 9 million. Alexander MacLeod, "British Labor Seeks Common Voice," *Christian Science Monitor,* September 7, 1989. In 1991, Britain's export-import ratio on manufactured goods was .94 and that of the United States .83.

West Germany's was 1.22, showing (unlike the British and U.S. situations) more goods exported than imported.

32. *Kansas City Star,* June 7, 1987. "Too Good a Job," *The Economist,* October 24, 1992.

33. Daniel Ward, "British-Built Cars Are Back with 50 Percent of Home Market," *The Times,* August 8, 1987.

34. By 1991, manufacturing investment was 10 to 15 percent below 1979 levels, and output had not risen since 1974. "A Way Out of Britain's Recession," *Manchester Guardian Weekly,* August 11, 1991.

35. Michael Meacher, "Why Labour Must Expand Its Class Appeal," *The Guardian,* June 25, 1987. By 1992, overall unemployment reached 10.5 percent. In 1979, manufacturing accounted for 27 percent of GDP; in 1993, 20 percent. "Too Good a Job," *The Economist.*

36. *Financial Times,* January 6, 1988. See Jim Lewis and Alan Townsend, eds., *The North-South Divide: Regional Change in Britain in the 1980s* (London: Paul Chapman, 1989).

37. The national government abolished metropolitan authorities, which had formerly dealt with such problems on a regional level, and set up sixteen inner-city task forces and four urban development corporations run at the national level with little involvement from local councils, businesses, or citizens. The old metropolitan authorities could at least force some dialogue between people in wealthier neighborhoods and planners for poorer neighborhoods; these national bureaucrats have little contact with any of those groups. The largest of the new national groups, the London Docklands Development Corporation, developed eight and a half square miles on the south end of London by acquiring buildings occupied by low-income people and allowing developers to replace them with modern offices, expensive apartments, and factories. Though some council flats were sold to their tenants, and the Whitbread brewing company and other businesses set up a school for retraining people, and although forty thousand new jobs were created for skilled laborers, little was done for those who remain unskilled and have lost their homes in the process. In Liverpool, the national government's Merseyside Development Corporation trains about forty-five hundred people each year and still cannot find enough skilled workers for the high-technology jobs it has created; it has no

programs to help those without skills or jobs. And the London Docklands Development Corporation (which has received more government funding than all other development corporations combined) received £249 million in government grants in 1992, versus £25 million for Merseyside. Under this system, the Labour Party would need to regain control at the national level before it could have much impact.

38. Ralph Atkins, "Richer Britain on a Buying Spree," *Financial Times,* August 10, 1987.

39. This compares to 1.4 percent in the United States and 1.1 percent in the Federal Republic of Germany. Ralph Atkins, "Richer Britain."

40. "Grrowth in Store," *The Economist,* May 1, 1993. Germany's inflation has not surpassed 4 percent. "See Who Salutes It," *The Economist,* May 24, 1992.

41. Her Government tried to keep government borrowing below 3 percent of GNP; that rose. In 1993, the budget deficit approached 9 percent of GDP.

42. Atkins, "Richer Britain."

43. Anthony Bambridge, "Why Britain Can't Manage," *The Times,* November 30, 1975. In 1992, the World Economic Forum ranked the United States fifth among twenty-two industrialized nations (behind Japan, Germany, Switzerland, and Denmark) in international competitiveness. We ranked near the bottom in a number of its 283 criteria.

44. Twenty-four percent in 1985 versus 9 percent in 1950 and 13 percent in 1965. UAW, "The Trade Gap," (Detroit: UAW, February, 1987). Many of our exports are agricultural products, timber, and other harvested commodities. Between 1985 and 1990, our exports grew more rapidly (from $213 billion to $363 billion) than our imports (from $345 billion to $495 billion).

45. U.S. exports barely changed during this period, while our imports soared. In 1980, we exported $26.7 billion more high-technology goods than we imported; in 1986, we imported $2 billion more than we exported. In 1985, we imported 50 percent of the apparel, 34.9 percent of the machine tools, 25.6 percent of the automobiles, and 25.2 percent of the steel we purchased. In 1986, Japan had a trade surplus of $82.7 billion, and the Federal Republic of Germany a surplus of $52.2 billion. Idem., pp. 4, 6, 9. *Kansas City Star,* June 7, 1987.

In 1986, Third World nations cut back on their international borrowing when lending agencies began pressuring them toward fiscal austerity; this made it harder for them to purchase agricultural and other products from the United States. At the same time, new loans to Brazil to stave off default on their massive debt made them more competitive against American soybeans. And subsidies to agriculture from the European Economic Community made European agricultural products more competitive on the international market.

Lester Thurow estimates that if U.S. international trading deficits amount to 3 percent of GNP during a given year, we must sell .75 to 1 percent of our assets; if the situation continues for forty years, that would amount to 30 percent of our assets. "Will America Change Course?" *Kansas City Star*, February 18, 1990.

46. The figures for previous years show the steady increase: $10.4 billion more in 1990 and $12.7 billion more in 1991.

47. Jack Ward, "Will Clinton Plan Bolster U.S. Economy?" *Kansas City Star*, April 25, 1993. A study by the William T. Grant Foundation found that between 1979 and 1985, 1.7 million manufacturing jobs disappeared, forcing many of their occupants into "unsteady, part-time, low-paying jobs". In 1973, 60 percent of men aged twenty to twenty-four earned enough to support a family of three above the poverty line; in 1985, only 44 percent did. By 1986, high school graduates in the same age group were earning 28 percent less in constant dollars than their counterparts in 1973. The report concluded: "This nation may face a future divided not along lines of race or geography, but rather of education." *Kansas City Times*, January 21, 1988. The trend continues: 440,000 manufacturing jobs disappeared during 1991.

48. In 1986, the United States' deficit was $220 billion; Brazil's was second highest, with $108 billion (U.S. dollars). In 1986, for the first time since 1914, foreigners owned more investments in the United States than Americans owned abroad. *Kansas City Star*, March 17, 1987. That trend continues: By 1991, foreign investment in the United States totaled $2.49 trillion, while U.S. investment abroad totalled $2.11 trillion.

49. The debt reached 3 trillion by 1992. The Congressional Budget Office estimated a record $362 billion shortfall in 1992 (after paying $216 billion in interest payments on the debt and $115 billion for the savings and loan cleanup). R. A. Zaldivar, "Deficits to Top $150 Billion for Several Years," *Kansas City Star*,

August 16, 1991. Robert Pear, "Leap in U.S. Deficit is Seen Next Year Despite 1990 Law," *New York Times*, August 16,1991.

50. David Satterfield, "Buying American: Japan Pays Cash," *Kansas City Star*, January 18, 1987. In 1992, personal savings in China stood at 40 percent of GNP. "Still the Middle Kingdom," *The Economist*, December 12, 1992.

Lester Thurow, "Will America Change Course?" estimates that if our consumption declined one percentage point less rapidly than our GNP rose for ten years, our savings would reach the level of the Germans and we could correct our balance of payments problems.

51. The limit on the government's debt rose from one trillion dollars in 1980 to 2.5 trillion dollars in 1987. Half this debt is being acquired by foreigners, mostly Japanese. Satterfield, "Buying America."

From 1953–71, for every dollar we invested in manufacturing, we produced only 60 percent as much output as Japan did for a dollar. Anthony Bambridge, "Why Britain Can't Manage," *The Times*, November 30, 1975.

52. In 1989, net inflow of direct foreign investment in the United States came to $72.3 billion; in 1990, that reversed into a net outflow of $22 billion. *Kansas City Star*, October 8, 1990.

53. Robert Gillette, "Creaking Economy Needs More than a Little Repair," *Kansas City Times*, November 26, 1987.

54. Between 1970 and 1985, the Soviet Union made $200 billion exporting oil; this was in real ("hard currency") U.S. dollars, instead of rubles, which were worthless abroad. The USSR also had over 2,000 tons of gold reserves in 1985, which fell to 240 tons by 1991. Michael Dobbs, "Gorbachev," *Kansas City Star*, December 25, 1991.

55. Clyde Farnsworth, "Kremlin's Debt to the West is Put at Over $20 Billion," *Kansas City Times*, December 3, 1987. *PlanEcon Report* 2, 7 (February 17, 1986): 3–4, 13; *PlanEcon Report* 2, 14 (April 7, 1986): 2. Norwegian contracts to supply natural gas to Western Europe will further slow exports. In 1980, the Soviet Union's trade surplus was around $4 billion (in U.S. dollars).

56. A third of the borrowed funds were owed to German institutions. Western banks, government, and private creditors lent the USSR $21.5 billion during 1985 and 1986, giving them a gross debt of $38.2 billion.

This was counterbalanced by $15 billion deposited in banks abroad, leaving a net debt of about $23 billion. Those were CIA estimates. Clyde Farnsworth, "Kremlin's Debt." David Hoffman and Steven Mufson, "Who Will Write the Check, And Who Should Receive It?", *Washington Post National Weekly Edition,* October 21–27, 1991.

57. Fred Coleman, "Last Minute in Moscow," *Newsweek,* October 1, 1990. By 1991, the combined budget deficits of the fifteen republics amounted to about 25 percent of GNP. *The Economist,* September 28, 1991.

58. D. Gale Johnson, "Agricultural Productivity in the Soviet Union." *Current History* (October 1985): 342. On top of this, the government increased the prices paid to farms for grain by 50 to 100 percent, while keeping the price of bread at the same low price. Similar increases occurred on flax, cotton, tea, milk, wool, livestock, citrus fruits, and grapes, with *oblast* authorities setting the selling prices on some of these goods. *Kansas City Star,* March 30, 1986. Poor harvests in 1985 and 1987, and poor transmission of the harvest to cities in 1990, necessitated especially high imports of grain at a time when oil prices were low. All of this depleted the government treasury.

59. In 1990, German workers made $21.53 an hour (and had six-week vacations, fifteen annual holidays, health care, social insurance, and other fringe benefits). This compares to $14.77 for American, $12.64 for Japanese, and $3.40 for Hong Kong workers. The German work week averages twenty-nine hours. U.S. Labor Department study. *Kansas City Star,* January 4, 1992.

60. "Perestroika Survey," *The Economist,* April 28, 1990; "There She Blows," *The Economist,* May 23, 1992.

61. For more on this, see Robert E. Gamer, "East Europe's Search for Freedom Without Disruption: Avoiding the China Syndrome," *UFSI Field Staff Reports* 3 (1990–91). At the time of unification, East Germans went on a buying spree which strained imports. A survey conducted a year later found that 42 percent of households in the east had a compact disk player, 34 percent a personal computer, and 28 percent drank champagne or whiskey at least once every two weeks. Stephen Kinzer, "East Germans, Nurtured by Bonn, Take Heart and Begin to Prosper," *New York Times,* September 29, 1991.

62. Gamer, "East Europe's Search."

63. David Halberstram addresses these issues in *The Reckoning* (New York: Avon, 1987) and *The Next Century* (New York: Morrow, 1991).

64. "High Performance Hypochondria," *The Economist,* May 23, 1992; "What a Way to Make a Living," *The Economist,* October 24, 1992; "Great Expectations," *The Economist,* October 24, 1992.

65. "Great Expectations," *The Economist.*

66. Francine S. Kiefer, "Recession Batters German Steel," *Christian Science Monitor,* March 22, 1993.

67. Francine S. Kiefer, "As Demand From East Drops, German Carmakers Feel Bite," *Christian Science Monitor,* December 2, 1992.

68. Robert C. Cowen, "U.S. Science Magnifies Its Social Role," *Christian Science Monitor,* February 10, 1993; Francine S. Kiefer, "Joblessness, Weak Economy Hamper German Research," *Christian Science Monitor,* February 10, 1993.

69. "Great Expectations" *The Economist;* Alexander MacLeod, "Britain Looks to Private Sector for Funding," *Christian Science Monitor,* February 10, 1993.

70. For more on this, see Robert E. Gamer, *The Developing Nations: A Comparative Perspective,* 2d ed. (Boston: Allyn & Bacon, 1982), chapter 8.

EXERCISES

Think about the book thus far:

Relate chapters 8 and 9 to this chapter.

KEY WORDS AND PHRASES

Define the following term:

productivity

Answer each of the following questions in one sentence:

1. What threatens production in corporate-consumer systems?
2. Where do U.S. banks obtain money to lend to Latin America?
3. To whom do they lend the money?
4. Where does that money go?
5. What may cause a corporate-consumer system to lose capital?
6. How have recent reforms cost jobs in northern England?
7. How have Chinese peasants developed enough influence to resist government and bureaucratic initiatives?
8. How can government promote productivity?

THINKING IT THROUGH

Discuss the following questions:

1. Why are nation-states with corporate-consumer systems prosperous only when both production and consumption are high?
2. Why do new jobs created in patron-client systems fail to expand employment and consumption?
3. How can deficit financing endanger a corporate-consumer system?
4. Why is China more successful than the Soviet Union was at maintaining a state-consumer system? What endangers China's system?
5. How can Nigeria be one of the world's ten leading oil exporters and still rank as the world's fifteenth poorest nation-state? Do drugs in Peru play a role similar to the role of oil in Nigeria?
6. What makes the United Kingdom's growth more fragile than Germany's?
7. Can the United States remain prosperous and the CIS become so without extensive government spending? How can they achieve balanced budgets?
8. How might improved or declining productivity in corporate-consumer systems affect patron-client systems?
9. How might access to food, clothing, shelter, energy, and defense, and protection of the environment and human freedoms, be affected by the nature of a nation-state's political system?
10. What kind of government action can stimulate production? Can high productivity be maintained without such action?

INDEX

UNITED KINGDOM (UK)

SCOTLAND

NORTHERN IRELAND

IRELAND

WALES

ENGLAND

Population: 57,000,000
Area (Sq. Miles): 94,226

THE WORLD

EAST GERMANY (GDR)

Population: 17,000,000
Area (Sq. Miles): 41,766

WEST GERMANY (FRG)

Population: 61,000,000
Area (Sq. Miles): 95,826